PSYCHOANALYTIC INVESTIGATIONS

Eduardo VAL
2219 central PARK
EVANSTON
869-8586.
November 1974

PSYCHOANALYTIC INVESTIGATIONS:
Selected Papers

THERESE BENEDEK, M.D.
WITH A FOREWORD BY GEORGE H. POLLOCK

QUANDRANGLE/THE NEW YORK TIMES BOOK CO.
10 EAST 53RD STREET, NEW YORK, N.Y. 10022

Library of Congress Catalog Card Number: 70-130377

International Standard Book Number: 0-8129-0347-1

Production supervised by Planned Production.

Acknowledgments

As this volume comes closer to its publication, I am often seized by the awareness of separation from the productive part of my life. But soon the fear of termination is silenced by remembering the friends, colleagues, and patients, all of whom participated in some way in what appears now as my achievement. I owe thanks to many. Where to begin?

Dr. Franz Alexander first comes to mind. He made immigration easy by affording me a professional home with its—at that time—unique interest in psychosomatic research. I owe thanks to Dr. Boris B. Rubenstein who was a reliable and patient collaborator on our common project. Then, of course, I think of the Chicago Institute for Psychoanalysis, a family of professional colleagues who were also my friends; their warm interest and unwavering encouragement always sustained me. In order to avoid making a roster, I mention only a few: Drs. Thomas M. French, Helen V. McLean, Lucia E. Tower, Joan Fleming. Nameless remain here those who were once my students and are now practicing psychoanalysts, researchers and teachers. In the same way, I remember my patients who felt they were being helped while I was learning through them. I think of all with deep appreciation for the manifold stimulation which I received from them.

After silencing the memories of the many to whom I cannot do justice, the gap is filled with gratitude to my husband Tibor whose loving patience made it possible for me to work without feeling guilty.

All this, however, would not have made possible the finished product, the book. First I want to thank Dr. George H. Pollock whose persuasiveness convinced me that my publications merit being made available in one volume. Helen Ross's invaluable contribution is on a different level. Her friendship has been a beam of light since I arrived in this country. When the idea of this volume came up, she not only enthusiastically supported it, but immediately assumed the responsibility of editing. I know how much attention, time and work she devoted to improving the manuscript and making my English readable. Last, but not least, I thank my secretary, Mrs. P. G. Gordon, whose conscientious attention to all details seemed inexhaustible as she typed and retyped the manuscripts.

Therese Benedek, M.D.

Chicago, Illinois
April, 1973

Foreword

It is not often that a former student has the privilege of writing a fore-word to the selected papers of an esteemed teacher. It is with great plea-sure that I exercise that privilege here, to present a few aspects of Therese Benedek that are not widely known. My own warm feelings toward her stem from contact with her as a teacher, advisor, colleague, and friend. The respect she has earned as a scientist is international, and her work stands on its own. But the humanness of her being is less easily discerned from her scientific contributions, although her writings, which are of the highest scientific excellence, are also autobiographical. She discovers something in herself, and this becomes the focus for a creative journey that eventually contributes to our knowledge.

In her Introduction to this volume, Dr. Benedek writes that "Scien-tific production reflects the personality of the scientist." We know the research that the psychoanalyst undertakes is always influenced by his life, past and present. This may be reflected in the very area he chooses to study. The external research process may mirror the intrapsychic process involved in working out areas of unfinished internal business. The scientist, his work processes, and his contributions indicate the imbrication of his creative life with all facets of life.

In her original statement of purpose of this book, Dr. Benedek takes note of the importance of intuition and introspection for the scientist. As a result of his internal struggles, the scientist is able to make conscious what is emerging "from the unknown depths of the unconscious." Freedom "from internal control permits the forgotten to be remembered," but also allows for an ordering, understanding, and conceptualizing of what has entered the mind. The "free association" and the "free-floating attention" of the clinical situation, when employed by the scientist himself, allow for the playback of fantasy and checking in the mind of the scientist, and the scientist "listens" to what his mind is bringing forth; thus, freedom to perceive and freedom to receive are

5

essential to the creative investigator. But this may not be enough. From this crucible of feelings and fantasies, ideas reverberate in the mind: Past experiential reflections are added to the caldron, cognitive understandings appear, and a new idea, closure, or insight is produced. Words may be found to express creatively what has finally been distilled into a logical and understandable premise, while the pleasure of discovery provides the impetus for further searching and testing. In this fashion, the creative process parallels the analytic therapeutic process. Experiencing, observing, and conceptualizing new levels of understanding and discovery are the key steps. "Only by continually retesting abstractions can knowledge grow . . . [however] an interpretation is not yet knowledge, but it is an hypothesis which fits or might fit" one situation. "The formulation of hypotheses is not yet research. Investigation begins with the analyst 'working through' his material."

Dr. Benedek asks in her usual penetrating way, "Where was I in this process? How did I come to this idea?" Exposing herself to these new questions, she arrives at answers which do not always appear in print, but are dramatically present in the ideas that are published. Her "consistent introspection" of the sustained transaction between her ego and her self, her self and her work, her work and her field, reveals new relationships for herself and for our science.

Even when Dr. Benedek discusses the intertwining of psychoanalytic education with research training, we can perceive in her presentation a unique mode of operation. "As the student learns to articulate behavioral data of analysis with explanatory concepts of theories, as he learns to correlate analytic events with the learned concepts of dynamics, economics, and genetics of behavior, he practices distancing himself from experience. This is a primary requisite for research." She again asserts, "Freedom of intrapsychic communication, unhampered by blind spots and other impediments," facilitates this research set. Dr. Benedek further notes, "After the pleasure of discovery comes its confrontation with the known. The uncovering of new relationships among both new and old data, fitting the new idea into old theories, or establishing why and in what respect they do not fit—this is the tedious job of the researcher." Dr. Benedek's researches on the female sexual cycle and on the supervision process are exemplary illustrations of her more general proposition. But as she goes on to say, creativity involves "synthesizing new patterns out of data whose interdependence and mutual reliance have not been seen by others." Can this creative activity be taught? She answers, and I would concur, that it may be developed if it has heretofore been silent or latent.

Here, in this volume, are Dr. Benedek's outlines of the creative research process. They represent a life's work developed on the special foundation of being one of the early European psychoanalysts. Those analysts, including Dr. Benedek, worked in a relative isolation which often served as a mutually productive force for stimulation. From her early days in Leipzig, Dr. Benedek was able to develop and reflect on her work without interference.

What about Therese Benedek, the individual? She was born on November 8, 1892, in Eger, Hungary, a middle-sized town where her father was a successful businessman. When she was six, the family moved to Budapest, where she went to secondary and medical school. She was the third of four children of the Friedmann family. Her oldest sibling, a brother, was killed in the First World War and her youngest, a sister, died in a Nazi concentration camp in the Second World War. Therese and her remaining sister, who was four years older, were the only family members who came to the United States.

While in the "gymnasium," although intending to study Latin and history, she heard Jenö Hárnik give a lecture on psychoanalysis. Stimulated, she determined to study medicine and psychiatry instead. During her first year in medical school, she went to optional lectures by Sandor Ferenczi at the Sociological Society, and this further strengthened her inclination. When asked by fellow students why she chose as she did, she replied, "Because I want to know why I am living"—an early manifestation of the curiosity that has been a hallmark of Dr. Benedek's personality and career. We may also note a freedom to seek answers outside the regular curriculum and on her own initiative. At that time, most Hungarian medical students worked in clinical settings; so in 1914–1915, Dr. Benedek found herself in the foundling hospital, where she studied the reactions of young children and babies separated from their mothers.

Upon finishing medical school in 1916, she interned and was a pediatric resident in Pozsony until 1919. During this time she made her first "psychodynamic" observation. Mothers brought their babies to the clinic because of constipation or diarrhea. Dr. Benedek had the idea of finding out about the mothers' own complaints in this area. Much to her surprise, she found that the babies had the same symptoms as their mothers. We see here the anlage of what was later developed and elaborated in her work on the mother-child unit ("Psychosomatic Implications of the Primary Unit: Mother-Child") and on mothering ("Psychobiological Aspects of Mothering").

She began an analysis with Ferenczi in November of 1918. Although her analysis was short by today's standards, it was a meaningful experience "which carried with it the conviction of knowing something that was unknown and unknowable before. It was the specific experience of one's self against something else that was also oneself, from which new awareness and new knowledge emerged." [1] She married Dr. Tibor Benedek, a dermatologist, in May 1919, and in February 1920

1. Fleming, J., and Benedek, T., *Psychoanalytic Supervision* (New York, Grune & Stratton, 1966), p. 9.

left Hungary for Leipzig, Germany, where her husband obtained a position at the university. She wrote to Ferenczi, who in turn wrote to Karl Abraham in Berlin, and Therese Benedek was welcomed into the ranks of psychoanalysis. Leipzig was two hours from Berlin and Dr. Benedek could commute for consultation on her cases.

When she became the first psychoanalyst in Leipzig, there was a group of medical students who, before they returned from army service, had gone to Vienna to tell Freud that they wanted to become psychoanalysts. Freud gave them a set of the available *Imago*'s with a personal inscription (these are now in the Chicago Institute Library—the gift of Dr. Benedek) and advised them to read and wait until somebody arrived in Leipzig. Abraham later wrote to the students advising them to contact Therese Benedek, which they did; she began to do analyses and organized a study group for psychoanalysis. She traveled by train to Berlin at monthly or bimonthly intervals to receive clinical "supervision" from Karl Abraham and Max Eitingon. Although the Berlin Institute was started in the same year (1920) that Dr. Benedek moved to Germany, she could not attend courses from Leipzig. But she went to meetings of the Berlin Psychoanalytic Society and gave her first paper to this group.

This paper, sociological in nature, was never published but in retrospect was prophetic. Based upon Freud's insight into group psychology, it seemed to forecast a Hitler-type regime. Karl Abraham wrote to Freud about it on November 26, 1923. "Dr. Benedek of Leipzig was elected a member [of the Berlin Psychoanalytic Society] after her paper on Development of the Organization of Society, which was very good indeed." [2] In 1924, she presented her first psychoanalytic paper on erythrophobia. Of this paper, Abraham wrote to Freud on December 3, 1924, "Yesterday we had a meeting . . . and among others heard an excellent short clinical paper by Dr. Benedek from Leipzig on erythrophobia (this has already been accepted for the *Zeitschrift*). She is of great value in her ability to attract young people as well as in her excellent practical work" [3]—an assessment that has repeatedly been proven correct over the years. The paper was published both in German and in English in 1925.

Therese Benedek was in Germany for sixteen years, working partly in Leipzig and partly in Berlin until 1936, when she came to Chicago. Karen Horney had left the Chicago Institute and Franz Alexander, needing an experienced training analyst there, offered her a position, which she accepted. She was reluctant to leave those who were close to her, to change her accustomed way of life and work, to adopt a new

2. Abraham, H. C., and Freud, E. L., eds., *A Psycho-analytic Dialogue— The Letters of Sigmund Freud and Karl Abraham, 1907–1926* (New York, Basic Books, 1965), p. 343.
3. Ibid., p. 376.

language, and to come to a country with new ways and values. But as always, she quickly recognized the inevitable and left Europe, arriving with her husband,and two children in Chicago on May 6, 1936, which happened to be Freud's eightieth birthday.

Therese Benedek met Freud on several occasions. She recently told me about her first contact with him: "I saw Freud the first time in 1922 when the congress was in Berlin. It was the first such meeting I participated in and the last one he attended. After that Freud was operated on. He was very hoarse, but gave the first chapter of *The Ego and the Id*. Eitingon introduced me on the staircase. He said, 'This is Therese Benedek,' and Freud said, 'You are such a little woman? I thought that you would be so big, so strong.' "

Starting with Ferenczi, Dr. Benedek came into intimate contact with many of the pioneers of analysis. Abraham and Eitingon were her teachers and her friends. She also knew Hanns Sachs, Ernst Simmel, Melanie Klein, Sandor Rado, Franz Alexander, Otto Fenichel, Wilhelm Reich, Theodore Reik, and many others in Berlin.

After arriving in New York, where she and her family spent several days, she came to Chicago on May 6, 1936. While in New York, an eminent European analyst who had settled there gave her a few words of warning in an orientation session. Dr. Benedek recounts that he said, "You know psychoanalysis is not the same thing here as in Europe. The Americans are not coming into analysis to fall in love with their immortal souls. People who come into analysis want to be helped and one has to understand this."

In Chicago, she renewed old ties and made new ones with Franz Alexander, Thomas French, Helen McLean, Catherine Bacon, Leon Saul, George Mohr, Helen Ross, and many others who became her lifelong friends and colleagues.

On the day she began work, five analysands started their treatment with her. She also started teaching at the Institute. Active research set the tone there and, in December 1936, Benedek and Rubenstein began their classic investigation of the female sexual cycle represented in this volume with a paper entitled "Correlations Between Ovarian Activity and Psychodynamic Processes: Part I—The Ovulative Phase, and Part II—The Menstrual Phase."

Dr. Benedek wrote the first five papers in this collection while she was in Europe. The first American contribution deals with her research on the female cycle. Although this paper and several others which deal with infertility, the reproduction drive, female sexuality, and the climacterium were written in Chicago, some of their antecedents were present in earlier times. When Dr. Benedek was about sixteen years old, she heard a lecture by a leading woman feminist in Hungary who talked about the slave condition in which women are put by men because they have to bear and care for children. After thinking about it, Therese told her classmates that this could not be true. "I just don't believe women live as slaves. They must have something out of it. They must want to have children; otherwise they would not have them," she now remembers telling them. "When I worked on this," she explained recently, "I thought that experience was latent for so many years. Of course, my two children were born in the meantime, too. I realized that life was certainly influential on my work."

Reference to her published papers shows other instances in which life's experiences affected Dr. Benedek's research. In her published works, in her lectures, and in her teaching, her presentations are characterized by their clarity, their relevance, and their freshness. She is avant garde, looking for the new, challenged by unanswered questions, courageous and ready to venture into unexplored fields. Her warmth, her great capacity for empathy and intuition, blended with her objectivity and her wisdom, make her an excellent clinician.

The meaning of this book can be grasped when one views the papers in it from the perspectives provided by the discussions, all newly written by Dr. Benedek, for each paper in this volume. Seen as a whole, the essays fit like parts of a mosaic. For more than fifty years Therese Benedek has been associated with psychoanalysis. Hers has been a rich professional life. Through the reading of her selected papers, one can become aware of the great changes and progress in psychoanalysis, in psychoanalysts, and in Therese Benedek's thinking over those decades. She is optimistic about the future of psychoanalysis, believing that psychoanalytic science will continue to make important contributions to many other fields of knowledge. She foresees shorter training for analysts and a new rapprochement between them and their colleagues in other disciplines, including the possibility that psychoanalysis may be entirely absorbed by those disciplines.

In her summing up, Dr. Benedek asks in her typical fashion if she has succeeded in her task. With a sensitive balance of humility and pride, she decides that she has. She is an unusual person who recognizes herself, takes the uncertainties along with the accomplishments, and makes them all part of self-discovery. Her essential credo was perhaps best expressed in her own recent words to me: "One changes, and one changes one's outlook and what one chooses to work on, which is all related to one's own personality." This theme has been a consistent one in the work of Therese Benedek.

GEORGE H. POLLOCK, M.D., Ph.D.
The Institute for Psychoanalysis
Chicago, Illinois

December 20, 1971

Contents

Introduction:
On Psychoanalytic Investigation

Scientific production reflects the personality of the scientist. The imaginative, daring scientist creates, seemingly out of nothing, the foundation and the structure of a new, unexpected, and often perplexing architecture to which conventional, cautious scientists add smaller or larger stones throughout generations.

Just as each science has its methodology, derived from the necessities presented by the problems to be solved, the opposite is also true. The method is often the avenue for new discoveries. For example, the optic lens was originally a simple, little instrument, but as it spread the universe before human eyes it opened a horizon of unsolved problems. Psychoanalysis is in some respects comparable to this.

The investigative methods of the natural sciences are clearly defined. The nature of the data and the method of collecting, classifying, and organizing them are prescribed; the logic of arriving at results and evaluating them also is well studied, making all safe and secure for the reliable, conscientious, cautious scientist.

Nevertheless, how a creative scientist arrives at an original discovery is rarely studied. It is often considered an enigma, an almost mystic phenomenon of genius beyond the realm of scientific scrutiny.[1] The word "intuition" has the connotation of being unscientific. Although it is acknowledged as a quality of the creative mind, it still carries a stigma of disrepute. Did great scientists acknowledge their debt to their intuition? Rarely, and only after many years of their greatest achievements.[2]

Freud was the genius whose investigative instrument, like the optic lens, opened up new horizons of the mind and revealed the intrapsychic processes by which learning, knowing, and creativity result. His instrument was the systematic exploration of "free association." He might have revealed the secret of the creative process soon after his unique experiment of self-analysis, but he did not. Besides the mul-

15

tiple significance of self-analysis it gave him an opportunity to exercise his obviously primary inclination for free association and self-observation. It gave him an opportunity to abstract from the exquisitely personal what could be generalized. But he did not reveal the secret of his intuition because he was a scientist who considered it his first obligation to verify what his introspection revealed. He generalized from his internal struggle the resistance of his conscious mind against what was emerging from the unknown depths of his unconscious. He could not fathom then that the method of free association would be the key to a holistic approach to the investigation of the human mind. Indeed, he did not plan a research project which could lead to such evaluation of his simple, human, investigative tool.[3]

In 1920 Freud published a brief paper in which he acknowledged the influence of a forgotten memory on his own discovery of free association.[4] He said that when he was fourteen years old he had been given the works of Ludwig Börne as a present. There, in a story entitled "The Art of Becoming an Original Writer in Three Days," he read: "Take a few sheets of paper and for three days write down without fabrication or hypocrisy everything that comes to your head . . . and when three days have passed, you will be quite out of your senses with astonishment at the new and unheard-of thoughts you have had. This is the art of becoming an original writer." Did Freud's intuition in applying free association in his self-analysis originate in this forgotten memory, remembered probably thirty years after free association had been in use?

Free association, it seems then, was not a unique discovery by Freud.[5] What was Freud's great discovery was the consistent use of free associations with a listener tuned into them; Ludwig Börne did not advise that. Indeed, Freud's style itself, so masterfully concise in expressing in cognitive terms the most difficult ideas, is the best example of the two levels of functioning of the mind: the one, free from intentional control, permits the forgotten to be remembered; the other organizes what enters the mind. One person may make of it a story, whereas another, a genius, may make it into a science.

Freud rarely conveyed in his scientific writings that freedom of mind which comes with the naturalness of free association. But he taught his students and prescribed for his patients the technique of free association. He explained to students of psychoanalysis the function of the "free-floating attention" of the listener. For this function of the nonverbal communication between the free-associating subject and the listening analyst is the narrow path from the conscious, cognitive mind to the unknown but knowable spheres of the psyche. Having given to his students this key to the unconscious layers of the mind, Freud assumed they would achieve the freedom and the knowledge necessary for psychoanalytic investigation.

The free associations of the patient, his dreams, his responses to events in his early life, including the analysis itself, are the input to which the analyst listens with free-floating attention, which, like radar, receives information along with what is verbalized. The analyst also hears what is not told—feelings and forgotten reactions of his analysand. As all this reverberates in his mind, it picks up reflections from his own experiences. In the analytic situation, what is primarily important is what the analyst has learned, the cognitive experiences of his own analysis and the explanatory concepts of psychoanalytic theories. All this comes to a sudden closure and forms a new gestalt, an insight.

Who can account for the innumerable primary processes which have gone on in the analyst while listening with his "third ear" to his patient? Who can record how his preconscious picks up the symbolic representations which would fit what is going on in the patient's mind at one particular moment? Whatever these symbols represent, they are just bubbles thrown up by the unconscious sources of primary processes. Nothing can do this but that marvelous computer, the human brain. While the analyst finds the words to convey to the patient the meaning of their mutual experience as it relates to the patient, he formulates a creative interpretation—based on insight, not just on the logical application of what is already known.

However illuminating such insight may be, however convincing the hypotheses derived from it might appear to the psychoanalyst, or however certain he feels that he has arrived at it entirely from the associations of the patient, this is only rarely and at best partially so.

The relief of the "ah-ha" experience is the pleasure of discovery. To speak in terms of metapsychology, a sense of relief comes from the discharge of the cathexes that were bound in the various components of the closure. Now, in the closure, they converge to cathect the discovery with all the analyst's integrating narcissistic energy. This explains why hypotheses arrived at by empathic understanding and introspection are difficult to correct, whether the patient or the analyst arrived at them in the live analytic process or whether the analytic investigator formulated them as he studied his material in the framework of the general theory of psychoanalysis.

We turn our attention now from the more or less acute "ah-ha" experience of the analyst to its derivative, the psychoanalytic interpretation. Interpretation is the second level of communication between the analyst and the analysand. It is also the first test of the analyst's empathic understanding; the patient's response to the tone and wording of the interpretation (explanation) will show its validity, its usefulness in the analytic process.

Interpretation is the result of a cognitive overview of what was going on in the patient—or better, what was perceived by the analyst. Even if it appears that the interpretation is the analyst's effort to objectify what he has received, the interpretation is the result of communication between two participants involving the personality of each according to his individual role in the process. The analyst making an interpretation acts in his role as analyst. Whatever self-analytic associations enter his mind while listening to his patient, they are withheld in the service of the analytic process. The analyst's mind scans the field of the multi-level communication for cues which indicate the patient's readiness to approach cognitively what went on in the free associative communications within himself. In directing this process with subtle interventions, the analyst aims to help the patient to arrive at a closure, at the experience of insight. The patient's closure will probably not be as complex as the analyst's, but it often leads the patient to a formulation of a new understanding of himself. Whether this confirms the analyst's insight or corrects his formulation, it will be meaningful for the patient as an experience which bridges past and present. The patient's insight connects the unconscious spheres of his mind with his conscious ego, so that he recognizes it as a constituent part of himself. Thus the patient is making a discovery in the same way as the analyst made his discovery.

Freud and the pioneers of psychoanalysis were not the only ones who had these experiences. Psychoanalysts of later generations learned the concept of the unconscious by discovering it in themselves. Through such discoveries they learned the technique and the theory of psychoanalysis. Whether one learned it as a person being analyzed or as an analyst from his patients, the learning itself was experienced as a discovery. This seems to justify the still echoing assumption that psychoanalysis is always research—a false assumption, however rooted in the experience of the analytic process. Truth is a taskmaster difficult to satisfy; experience itself is not research.

Interpretation is the analyst's attempt to integrate what he has gleaned intuitively with what he knows cognitively and to put this in the language of the patient's experience. "As the patient's individual, personal experience is brought into the analyst's field of cognitive scrutiny, he correlates the analytic event with his learned concepts of dynamics, economics and genetics of behavior."[6] The secondary processes which lead to knowledge by abstractions and through reductions have to be tested again. Only by continual retesting of abstractions can knowledge grow. How logically correct is the deduction arrived at from interpretations of the ongoing analytic process? An interpretation is not yet knowledge, but it is an hypothesis. It should not be forgotten that an interpretation is burdened by inherent faults of subjective experiences.

There are few investigations of the processes through which knowledge is derived from the noncognitive experience of analysis;[7] the first such report was published by Freud in his letters to Fliess.[8] This succinct description of the process has not been followed by self-observations of later psychoanalysts. There are few investigations of self-analysis or of analysis of the factors which by abstraction and generalization influence the analyst's interpretation. Too often they are subsumed under the catchword "countertransference."

The significance of countertransference was discovered early, and its hampering effect on the analytic process has been evaluated from many viewpoints. Here I want to extend the meaning of the term to include all communications of the psychoanalyst with his patient, since all carry the stamp of his personality and thus the influence of the unconscious motivations of his behavior. Countertransference is not a good term; it is often taken as referring to the process which characterizes transference-countertransference proper. However, countertransference is useful until a better term is found to signify that the personality of the analyst has an influence on the analytic process independent of and beyond transference-countertransference interactions.[9]

It is tacitly assumed that through his personal analysis each analyst has free access to the motivations of his own psychic processes, that he is aware of them and can even evaluate them in action. However, this is far from being so. Closer to the truth is the assumption that each psychoanalytic case and each research problem may mobilize reactions in the analyst-investigator which influence his attitude toward his material. I am reminded here of the well-known fact of the investigator's investment in his project. While this investment is a necessary prerequisite for the work, its drawback is that the wish to succeed, the fear of failure, or other emotions may influence his attitude and distort his objectivity. Since this is generally true for all investigators in our hard-striving, competitive civilization, the situation is much more difficult for the psychoanalytic investigator whose discipline ". . . employs the mind of the explorer as its only scientific instrument, a tool which in the eyes of the critics sadly lacks objectivity."[10]

The science of psychoanalysis is unique. The origin of our data is in the multi-level communication of the analytic process which cannot be repeated; they afford the nucleus of our hypotheses. But the formulation of hypotheses is not yet research. Investigation begins with the analyst "working through" his material. (Freud used the term "working over.") Thus psychoanalytic data are secondary; they imply organization of psychic processes which cannot be completely registered, cannot be counted, tabulated, or tested experimentally. The first check is the investigator-analyst's retrospective inquiry regarding his own function. Removed from the pressure of the actual interpersonal communication he can ask, "Where was I in this process? How did I come to this idea?" Exposing himself to new questions, he may arrive

at unexpected answers. Skeptics may say that an investigator's evalua-
tions of factors which influence his interpretations, i.e., his secondary
data, are not more valid than primary data, since these too are the
result of another attempt at consistent introspection. They may be
right. In this sense of objective science they are not scientific data but
they have meaning from within.

In psychoanalysis the concepts of multiple motivation and multiple
function are well established, but the concept of multiple meanings is
not. One could probably formulate a hierarchy of meanings if one could
find isolated meanings. However, meaning is never per se, but always
expresses a relationship; it is always the meaning of something for
something else. The sense (meaning) of a communication from a father
to his child changes with the tone of voice in which it is given. The
meaning of a flow of free associations of a patient may be partially
motivated by the analyst's waiting for a cue which gives the whole chain
a particular significance. Does it mean the same to the patient? Does
the analyst's interest in the material invest it with meaning?

Psychoanalysis is a system of deterministic theories. Ascribing
causal relations to intrapsychic processes has been one of the achievements of psychoanalysis. To Freud, so it seems, causality encompassed
the meaning of psychic events. Certainly causality cannot be imposed
from the outside and therefore it might scientifically be better definable, more of a proof. But a concept or a theory, old or new, may be
invested with a meaning that is not in accord with or relevant to the
patient's problem. In the live analytic process, the patient offers—
sometimes deliberately, sometimes preconsciously—checks and balances
to the analyst's interpretations of hypotheses. In group studies, the
opinions of others afford control of hypotheses derived from the analytic
process. But when the psychoanalytic investigator follows Grete Bibring's
counsel[11]—that he works alone, using analysis as a research tool—only he
is his judge, only he can become aware of the motivations which influence the meanings he attributes to the material.

It is the investigator's obligation to observe and analyze his function in collecting his secondary data for further study. Every instance in
psychoanalytic material has several meanings. While the investigator is
usually unaware of attributing meaning to the material, he is the one
who selects from multiple meanings the one that relates to the subject
matter he is most interested in at that time. So I come to the crux of all
research: the investment, the countertransference, of the investigator to
his patient, or to his material, or to both.

The "difficulties in the path of psychoanalysis" (referring to Anna
Freud's publication which includes her father's concern about the future
of psychoanalysis) originate not only in the eagerness of the younger
generation to adopt academic methods of research but also in the con-

sequences of psychoanalytic education, which, conveying cognitive knowledge, inhibits and consequently underrates the scientific value of hypotheses which originate in experience.[12] (Indeed, they do not come about so easily now as in early times. I have been puzzled about the dialectic of psychoanalytic education.)

Psychoanalytic education, in three interrelated phases, represents a unique educational system, planned with the implicit vision of developing psychoanalysts who can also be scientists of psychoanalysis. In 1920 when the first psychoanalytic institute was established in Berlin, or even in 1936 when Eitingon, in his "Report to the International Training Commission," described the intrinsic struggles of the system,[13] he did not formulate explicitly the aim of psychoanalytic education— the development of scientists of the mind, researchers of a holistic science.

The study of the mind cannot be dichotomized; its experiential source cannot be completely separated from the abstractions derived from it. Yet experience itself, even if it could be completely described, is not research, certainly not yet science. All by itself, without organization, experience would be chaos. The introspections of a Buddha, Kierkegaard, Buber, or any great poet are organized to express a higher level of insight that can be generalized but not separated from its experiential origin. Their insights become experiencable for others.

Ordering experiences in some relationships is the beginning of cognition, without which human beings could not survive. To illustrate: whether time is the primary organizing principle which teaches the infant that satiation follows hunger, the concrete experience becomes part of the infant's relationships which orient him toward the complex world in which he is to survive. Hence abstracting is seen not as a luxury of a highly developed intellect but as an organizing principle of mental processes. Abstracting and reducing the multiplicity of factors in any phenomenon become the habit of the human mind, as is manifest when a child begins to talk. Our concepts and theories are also arrived at by reductions and abstractions from the multiple aspects of our experience. Often the abstractions appear isolated from their experiential origin.

Freud moved easily between these two areas of the mind, the experiential and the reductionist. But he was concerned. He worried, in various contexts, that the known is written on another level of the mind, meaning that it becomes empty if deprived of that richness of experience which he attributed primarily to the unconscious. To Freud, reductionist theoretician, the avenue to the empirical reservoir of his theories was always accessible; his science was holistic. But he felt early that it might not always be so for those who were instructed in psychoanalysis, although "instructional analysis," to use Eitingon's term for the personal analysis, was not conceived as an instruction but as an experience.

Thus we have arrived at one of the dilemmas of psychoanalytic education. The personal analysis is a prerequisite for developing that quality of introspection which makes insightful experience possible for the newcomer; it trains him to examine his own experience and so refines his instrument for his function as a psychoanalyst. But is the nature of the analytic experience of the student of psychoanalysis the same now as it was fifty, forty, or even thirty years ago? The student analyst today, in contrast to previous generations, learns many of the concepts and understands cognitively some aspects of psychoanalytic theory before he gets to his personal analysis.[14] Even if his analysis is carried out in the most classical manner, his "ah-ha" experience might be the reversal of that described before. Arriving at a meaningful memory, he may say, "Ah-ha, here comes what I expected, what I know."

Yet every psychoanalyst, having been analyzed, has experienced some significant phenomena of his developmental past and worked through some of his conflicts in the transference. One might add that the student of psychoanalysis during his own analysis has learned to apply some aspects of the established theory to himself. Important as that may be, it is even more important that through his analysis he learns the tools of his craft—he observes and so learns how he learns. This is not to be understood as secondary gain, but to emphasize the importance of the analyst's observing ego, which should be trained to perceive parallel and different processes in himself and in his patient.

Speaking here of the intertwining phases of psychoanalytic education, our aim is to show that psychoanalytic education is (or can be) training for research. As the student learns to articulate behavioral data of analysis with explanatory theories, as he learns to correlate analytic events with the learned concepts of dynamics, economics, and genetics of behavior, he practices distancing himself from experience. This is a primary requisite for research.

Psychoanalytic theory is complex; its teaching depends not only on those who prepare the curriculum but also on the teachers and on the student. If it is true that everyone can be taught only what he is capable of learning, this is especially true for psychoanalysis. If there is a great difference between the student of psychoanalysis in earlier times and today, that difference lies in the depth of insightful experiences during the first training analysis. Students of today learn the complex theories easily, but this knowing may be written in on another level of the mind, and if this be so, then their capacity for perceiving and formulating problems becomes limited.

The third phase of psychoanalytic education, the supervisory teaching, can be viewed from this perspective. Supervisory teaching is a clinical teaching devised by Eitingon in the face of considerable resistance. Analysis under supervision was planned to help the student in understanding his case and in conducting the analysis as his supervisor would. Since those early times (which began as late as 1925) supervisors have learned a great deal. It was almost twenty-five years later that Isakower formulated the aim of supervisory teaching as clarification of the "psychoanalytic instrument."[15] By this he meant that the aim of supervision is beyond the clinical problems of the individual patient: it is the development of the student analyst's mind as the instrument of the psychoanalytic process, a tool of psychoanalytic investigation.

Though this is not the place to go into detail about the techniques and problems of this complex and individualized teaching method, its fundamental principle is the same as that of the psychoanalytic process. "The two kinds of learning, experiential and cognitive, continue to confront both students and teacher."[16] The teacher, listening to the student analyst, simultaneously relates his performance to the need of the current analytic situation and to the young analyst's experience and ability to go beyond what the supervisor wants to communicate to him.

The supervisor's choice is broad, although it derives directly from the material presented by the student. If the student is inexperienced, he cannot easily and spontaneously apply what he has learned preconsciously in his personal analysis. He may need technical advice and help in understanding the patient and the supervisor. In the supervisory session the student is tuned in less to the patient and more to his supervisor. If the student is more experienced, more sure of his understanding and handling of the analytic situation, he listens more to himself as he reexperiences the psychoanalytic interactions in reporting them. Thus he might go beyond the material and have ideas and associations which he did not have when he was with his patient or when he read his material in preparing for the supervisory session. With his questioning, the student may then go beyond the information of his material and may formulate a question, a problem. This gives the supervisor an opportunity for "surplus teaching," as Joan Fleming has termed the function that follows. The question will not be answered with a theory, although related literature might be referred to. Before this, however, the student's question is responded to with questions that underscore the original problem implicit in the material. Then in a give-and-take discussion the supervisor-teacher helps the younger colleague to develop his idea as a problem for psychoanalytic investigation. Thus supervisory teaching becomes more than clinical teaching. It is another level of experience by which the student learns to structure knowledge from empathic understanding, his own and his supervisor's. Using the technique and theory of psychoanalysis, supervision helps the student to integrate two kinds of knowledge, empathic and cognitive, while he is sharpening his investigative tool.

A question often raised by academic teachers is, can creativity be taught? The answer is yes, if there is a potential for creativity. For such teaching, psychoanalytic supervision is a good model. Its fundamental theory was formulated seventy years ago when Freud, in the famous seventh chapter of his *Interpretation of Dreams,*[17] first conceived of the communication between the topographic layers (systems) of the mental apparatus—between conscious, preconscious, and unconscious. Probably all the other theoretical formulations of Freud are easier to grasp than the assumption that the conscious mind is just an organ of perception of the input which it continuously receives from within and without, even during sleep. But we are caught in our conscious mind, since our security depends on our cognitive processes. Even we psychoanalysts who understand "dreamwork"—the function of the preconscious mind, the processes by which day residues, memories, and impulses become woven into a dream for the conscious self to look at or turn away from in terror—also have difficulty in accepting the function of the preconscious mind.

Freud described the preconscious as a reservoir of symbolic representations of instinctual processes, a depository of all word symbols, of all memories accessible to consciousness. In spite of this, it took many years for philosophers, psychologists, and even psychoanalysts to become able to deal with the role of the preconscious in our everyday mental functioning, in learning, knowing, teaching, in creative processes in general. The incessant interplay between the three layers of the mind is taken for granted; the dynamics of those communications are assumed to be known. But only in the last decade or so has the abundant evidence been emphasized that among ". . . these three layers the more pervasive, continuous and dynamic is neither conscious nor unconscious but preconscious."[18]

To help the student of psychoanalysis acquire such freedom of intrapsychic communication, unhampered by blind spots and other impediments, is the goal of psychoanalytic education. But freedom of preconscious processes in itself is not creativity. Although the first level of testing insight through interpretation is a cognitive effort, its success depends to a high degree on the freedom of preconscious communications; they account for the choice of what and how to put into the language of experience what the student analyst may know from theory; *ceteris paribus,* the supervisor's intuition is revealed in the depth and ease of his communication with his student.

How, then, does the creativity of the psychoanalyst manifest itself when, while investigating his material, he realizes that he has experienced something new to him? "The creative scientific act comes before the operations which lead to the establishment of truth."[19] This is a frequent experience of psychoanalysts. Whether the new insight emerges independent of work with a patient or is activated by external factors, after the pleasure of discovery comes its confrontation with the known. The uncovering of new relationships among both new and old data, fitting the new theory into old theories, or establishing why and in what respect they do not fit—this is the tedious job of the researcher. Investigating the established theories in the light of new facts and adding the results of such inquiries have modified and clarified much of psychoanalysis.

Since every psychoanalyst discovers some facet of psychoanalysis within himself and rediscovers the same with modifications in his patients, psychoanalysis always appears to be research. Creativity implies more than working in the subjective manner of the psychoanalytic process; it requires courage to work with the unknown objectively. This implies synthesizing new patterns out of data whose interdependence and mutual relevance have not yet been seen by others. In such abstract terms, creativity appears far from the experiential knowledge and empirical theory of psychoanalysis. But psychoanalysis would not be a useful science if it did not reach beyond its boundaries and thus humanize other scientific endeavors to understand man.

After this lengthy elaboration of psychoanalysis as a research method, I feel I must write "in defense" of my papers about psychoanalytic research as it was in the years 1925–1940. I have chosen the work of those years to illustrate the fact that I am speaking about myself, about my own research. I assume, on the one hand, that there were many others who worked with better preparation and greater thoroughness and, on the other, that there must have been many others who did not do better, since my papers were accepted for publication without question or objection. It was in 1925 that my first psychoanalytic paper was published.[20] The first paper based on material from the psychoanalyses of my patients in Chicago was written in 1937.[21]

Psychoanalysts working in that era were imbued with the conviction that psychoanalysis is always research. The method of research was exclusively psychoanalytic. Anything else would have been unthinkable. I believe that no psychoanalyst, in formulating interpretations, thought of separating the process which led to insight from the more or less cognitive processes. What could be expressed in interpretation and was confirmed by the analysis of the patient was more than psychoanalytic data; it was closer to a fact. The experience of insight, however, was deeply ingrained in the analyst's mind. Accumulation of other similar or dissimilar events happened in the same way as the primary insight occurred and led to an *Einfall,* the German word for free association, which fits this psychic event better.[22]

The structure of the psychoanalytic theory, based mainly on the first instinct theory, was the system which organized and controlled the hypothesizing predilections of analysts. Incorporated partly by the experience of personal analysis and partly by thorough study of the literature, the psychoanalytic investigator felt himself on safe ground when, on the basis of his own psychoanalytic investigation, he had ideas which seemed to confirm already existing theories; he enlarged upon these with slightly differing observations. Psychoanalysts of the second generation or even of the third, having learned what seemed to be the facts in psychoanalysis, presented their ideas with greater self-assurance than do younger generations of analysts today, who feel that their hypotheses need to be checked by elaborate research projects. In writing this I do not want to praise the old at the expense of the new methods of research. I say it because I have read my early papers with genuine surprise and wondered at some naiveté in them, but at the same time I have been astonished by the scope of my ideas.

It is not easy to realize the productive stimulation of that relative isolation in which early psychoanalysts worked, especially if one compares it with the almost compulsory collectivism of groups of psychoanalysts doing research today. Crowded by ever-intruding thoughts from innumerable papers, by communications which clarify concepts and observations from so many viewpoints, the researcher seems to lose sight of his own guideposts.

Psychoanalytic investigations will always have their pitfalls—a fact well known to workers who have struggled for clarity within themselves and with the concepts formulated by Freud. Only by sharing this awareness will the reader find these papers useful to himself and to other psychoanalysts, researchers, and practitioners today.

NOTES

1. Caws, P., "The Structure of Discovery," *Science,* December 1969, pp. 1375–1380.
2. Intuition operates unconsciously, and after his hypothesis is formulated, the first intention of the scientist is to collect evidence which confirms or negates his hypothesis. Einstein, the foremost physicist of our epoch, acknowledged the role of intuition in his formulation of the hypothesis that changed our concepts of the universe. The physician-historian Gerald Holton, combing the Einstein archives at Princeton, found several letters in which Einstein referred to experiments often credited with being the harbingers of the Special Theory of Relativity. In the letters Einstein described the influence of these experiments on the formulation of his theory as "negligible," "rather indirect," or "not decisive." Holton quotes Einstein: "There is no logical way to the discovery of these elementary laws. There is only the way of intuition." ("The Origin of Relativity," *Time,* January 26, 1970.)

3. Or did the Project include such a plan? Freud, S., "Project for a Scientific Psychology" (1895), *Standard Edition of the Complete Works of Sigmund Freud* (London, Hogarth Press, 1955), hereafter cited as *Std. Ed.*, I, 295–343.

4. Freud, S., "Zur Vorgeschichte der Analytischen Technik," *Int. J. Psycho-Anal.*, VI (1920), 79. "A Note on the Prehistory of the Technique of Analysis" (1920), *Std. Ed.*, XVIII, 263–265.

5. Trosman, H., "The Cryptomnesic Fragment in the Discovery of Free Association," *J. Am. Psychoanalytic Assn.*, XVII (April 1969), 489–510.

6. Fleming, J., and Benedek, T., *Psychoanalytic Supervision* (New York, Grune & Stratton, 1966), p. 26.

7. Using the relatively constant environment of the analytic office and couch in order to eliminate external variables, psychoanalysts consider this arrangement comparable to experiment. Kubie, L. S., "The Fostering of Creative Scientific Productivity," *Daedalus* (Spring 1962), 294–309.

8. Freud, S., *The Origins of Psychoanalysis: Letters to Wilhelm Fliess, 1887–1902*, Letters 72 and 74 (New York, Basic Books, 1954), pp. 225, 228.

9. The concept of countertransference, as used in the context of this essay, does not refer to the analyst's responses to the patient's neurotic motivations but to that level of communication which normally transpires in the analyst's personality and, being perceived by the patient, influences his attitude and behavior in the analytic situation.

10. Freud, A., *Difficulties in the Path of Psychoanalysis*, 18th Freud Anniversary Lecture (New York, International Universities Press, 1969), p. 19.

11. Bibring, G. L., "Research in Psychoanalysis," Panel Discussion reported by A. Z. Pfeiffer, *J. Am. Psychoanalytic Assn.*, IX (1961), 567.

12. Glover, E., "Research Methods in Psychoanalysis," *Int. J. Psycho-Anal.*, XXXIII (1952), 403–409.

13. Eitingon, M. A., "Report of the General Meeting of the International Training Commission," *Int. J. Psycho-Anal.*, XVIII (1937), 346–348.

14. Fleming, J., and Benedek, T., *Psychoanalytic Supervision*, p. 26. One might interject that it was so even before the second generation of analysts began to study analysis, stirred up by their first, often accidental meeting with it. This is true, but then the first response to analysis carried with it an awareness of the unconscious so intense that the need to know more remained as a permanent motivation.

15. Isakower, O., "Problems of Supervision," Report to the Curriculum Committee of the New York Psychoanalytic Institute, unpublished.

16. Fleming, J., and Benedek, T., *Psychoanalytic Supervision*, p. 32.

17. Freud, S., "The Interpretation of Dreams" (1900), *Std. Ed.*, V, 509–622.

18. Kubie, L. S., "Unsolved Problems of Scientific Education," *Daedalus*, XCIV, no. 3 (Summer 1965), 564.

19. Maslow, A., *The Psychology of Science: A Reconnaissance* (New York, Harper & Row, 1966), p. 132.

20. Benedek, T., "Notes from the Analysis of a Case of Erythrophobia" (paper read before the Berlin Psychoanalytic Society, December 2, 1924), *Int. J. Psycho-Anal.*, VI (1925), 430–439.

21. Benedek, T., "Defense Mechanism and the Structure of the Total Personality," *Psychoanalytic Quart.*, VI (1937), 96–118.

22. *Einfall*—comes into one's mind—better expresses that almost disconnected freedom of the association. This is the way I remember how the hypothesis, the topic of the first paper in this series, occurred to me.

1. Death Instinct and Anxiety

INTRODUCTION

To those who are interested in the history of psychoanalysis and psychosomatic medicine, or in the scientific development of early generations of psychoanalysts, I owe an explanation for my decision to start this book with a discussion of the relationship between death instinct and anxiety.[1] When I began rework on these early publications, I was surprised by their inherent unity. The idea that anxiety is the awareness of the death instinct entered my mind by analyzing acutely anxious and phobic patients and remained with me many years after the publication of this paper, but it never challenged me enough to investigate this concept again. Reading theoretical studies dealing with the problem of anxiety, I felt that my concept was just for private use. Therefore, it was astonishing to realize that my later investigations—for example, the "Depressive Constellation"—were rooted in the same theory, the second instinct theory of Freud. Thus, it seems logical to use this paper as the first in this book.

Psychoanalytic investigations, past and present, are overburdened with theorizing. The reasons for this are manifold. Psychoanalysis as an ongoing process cannot be communicated. Psychoanalytic data derived from the process, as well as how one arrived at them, are difficult to describe even approximately. This explains the scarcity of our phenomenologic material and the necessity to explain the findings with the help of relevant investigations and theoretical formulations arrived at by others. On rereading this paper, I realized that I omitted my clinical material, though it was so vivid that I can still recall it. Apparently I assumed that the mention of "phobic patients" would recall to every psychoanalyst what he knew from experience—not only the psychodynamics of phobia as a defense against anxiety but the struggle of the patient to establish such defense. I have never forgotten the intensity of anxiety in those patients whose phobic defenses spread like fire from one symptom to another, since none was sufficient to mitigate the affect. These observations were responsible for the *Einfall,* the idea that spontaneously came to me: anxiety is the psychic representation of the death instinct.

I began my psychoanalytic career in 1920, the year in which "Beyond the Pleasure Principle" was published.[2] Although I had been a careful student of the psychoanalytic literature, I did not really grasp the significance of this work, so different from everything else in psychoanalytic theory up to that point. Freud seemed to be warning us against his hypothesis. He considered it merely a philosophical speculation and, as such, beyond the boundaries of psychologic, psychoanalytic investigations, although he did support his thesis by assumptions derived from biology, from Fechner's principle of the "tendency towards stability," on which he based the dynamic concepts of psychoanalysis. Freud himself and many of his followers doubted the heuristic value of his new hypothesis which served to uphold the fundamental assumption of psychoanalysis—the theory anchored in the dialectic of opposing psychic forces that originate in the physiologic processes of the organism.

Although the significance of that work escaped me, I did notice that the new hypothesis was received with resistance, with disinclination to apply Freud's new concept to fresh observations. This was an unusual attitude among psychoanalysts. My idea, however, appeared as a confirmation of the death instinct. I searched for material in biology and physiology, since this new level of the instinct theory is rooted more deeply in biology than in the libido theory. The investigations cited in my paper encouraged the publication of my hypothesis. Ehrenberg found in the physiologic processes of "structure building" and decomposition the way to organic, natural death.[3] Abderhalden's physiologic "defense mechanisms" (*Abwehr* mechanisms), the organism's physiologic defense against illness, deferred death.[4]

Abderhalden's concept of physiologic defenses made me realize that there were reasons for mistrust of the term "instinct." Instincts are organizing principles that bring about behavioral patterns in the service of survival of the individual and, beyond this, of the species. Can the opposite of survival, death, be safeguarded by instinct?

In 1923 Freud wrote two articles for encyclopedias in which he summarized his new views:

> On the ground of a far-reaching consideration of the processes which go to make up life and which lead to death, it becomes probable that we should recognize the existence of two classes of instincts, corresponding to the contrary processes of construction and dissolution in the organism. On

this view, the one set of instincts which work *essentially in silence* [italics added] would be those which follow the aim of leading the living creature to death and therefore deserve to be called the "death instincts"; these would be directed outwards as the result of the combination of numbers of unicellular elementary organisms, and would manifest themselves as *destructive* or *aggressive* impulses. The other set of instincts would be those which are better known to us in analysis—the libidinal, sexual or life instincts, which are best comprised under the name of *Eros;* their purpose would be to form living substance into ever greater unities so that life may be prolonged and brought to higher development. The erotic instincts and the death instincts would be present in living beings in regular mixtures or fusions; but defusions would also be liable to occur.[5]

The thesis of psychic energy aiming at construction of greater unities, contrasted with energy the goal of which is destruction, was easily accepted by psychoanalysts. The hypothesis of fusion and defusion of psychic energy was employed to explain clinical phenomena and elaborate further theoretical problems. Love against hate is a concept rooted in human experience. But the term "death instinct" remained alien and sounded wrong. Yet Ehrenberg's theoretical biology asserted the same intertwining parallels between processes of construction and dissolution, leading finally to death, as did Freud's theory. Freud emphasized the "essential silence" of the death instinct in the normal processes of living. However, if under increased pressure defusion occurs and, according to Freud, aggression as a manifestation of the death instinct is set free, I assumed that the primary perception of the defusion would be a sensation of anxiety.

Anxiety, whether as a signal or as a flagrantly acute experience, is in the service of life; in man and in animals anxiety serves to assist the survival of the individual. My concept of anxiety is derived from the phenomenon of free-floating anxiety with its driving intensity and its propensity for mobilizing intrapsychic defenses, thus to be bound or discharged via the motor apparatus. Yet anxiety is not a drive; it is an affect. It seems necessary to separate the concept of instinct from the concept of anxiety.

The concepts of fusion and defusion of opposing psychic forces opened new avenues to clinical research but left psychoanalysis in the throes of unsolved theoretical dilemmas.[6] In translating Freud's *Hemmung, Symptom und Angst,* the translator felt justified in titling the book *The Problem of Anxiety*.[7] In this work Freud gave up his previous theory of anxiety, thus flustering many of his followers. James Strachey, in the introduction to his later translation of the work, reviews Freud's opposing concepts of anxiety, a central problem in Freud's thinking. He comments that Freud first regarded anxiety as a result of ". . . a purely physical process without any psychological determinants." But Strachey goes on to say:

> . . . In 1920, Freud added in a footnote to the fourth edition of the Three Essays: "One of the most important results of psychoanalytic research is this discovery that neurotic anxiety arises out of libido, that it is a transformation of it, and that it is thus related to it in the same kind of way as vinegar is to wine." (Standard Edition 7, 224) It is curious to note, however, that at quite an early stage Freud seems to have been assailed by doubts on the subject. In a letter to Fliess of November 14, 1897 (Freud, 1950a, Letter 75),[8] he remarks, without any apparent connection with the rest of what he has been writing about: "I have decided, then, henceforth to regard as separate factors what causes libido and what causes anxiety." No further evidence is anywhere to be found of this isolated recantation.[9]

It appears that the structural theory developed in "The Ego and the Id" (1923) distracted Freud's attention from the death instinct.[10] The psychic representation of the superego—conscience that punishes aggressive impulses, hostile wishes, and behavior—sufficed to explain anxiety as a reaction to intrapsychic danger. Both concepts, that of the punitive superego and the anxiety activated by aggressive impulses via the superego, could be assumed to originate in the ambivalence of primary object relationships. Six years after the publication of the theory of the death instinct when Freud returned to the problem of anxiety, ". . . he no longer regarded anxiety as transformed libido but as a reaction on a particular model to situations of danger."[11]

Freud's exclusion of the problem of anxiety from his instinct theories did not deter me. He gave me the key to the conceptualization of my hypothesis. If, under increasing psychic tension, a defusion of psychic energies occurs, then the psychic apparatus, perceiving the unbound (unneutralized) death instinct, can respond to it as to intrapsychic danger, i.e., with anxiety. This would make anxiety, whether an unconscious signal anxiety or vigilant anticipation of danger or acute anxiety, a reaction to a situation of danger, albeit one which would integrate the further reactions in the service of survival. Thus anxiety would act as an instinct in the service of survival. It would probably also qualify as a *drive*. In any case, anxiety would not act as a psychic representation of the death instinct, of aggression, but as a warning against it. I have to add here that at the time I wrote the paper and courageously presented its daring abstractions, I was not aware of its inherent problems. The vividness of my observations carried more weight than logic. It is also true that at the time "Inhibitions, Symptoms and Anxiety" was first studied, no one confronted its beautiful deductions with the instinctual nature of anxiety. Only in Strachey's remark (cited above) does one hear the echo of regret.

The theory of the death instinct remained in limbo. How easy it would have been for Freud to find the key to a unified theory of anxiety if he had had available even some of the information about the physiology of anxiety that was developed in the 1930s and after.

I can only trust that my groping attempt to integrate psychoanalytic concepts with data of physiologic investigations will be viewed historically.

NOTES

1. Chronologically, this is my third paper. The first was presented to the Berlin Psychoanalytic Society in 1923 and received a friendly reception, as Abraham's letter to Freud indicates. [*The Letters of Sigmund Freud and Karl Abraham,* Hilda C. Abraham and Ernst L. Freud, eds. (New York, Basic Books, 1965), p. 343.] I did not feel, however, that it merited publication. My first published paper was of a clinical nature, and since it was the usual demonstration of a young analyst's ability to find the accepted theory in the motivations of the particular symptoms of a patient, I assume it would offer nothing valuable to readers today. ["Notes on the Analysis of a Case of Erythrophobia," *Int. J. Psycho-Anal.,* VI (1925), 430–439.]

2. Freud, S., "Beyond the Pleasure Principle" (1920), *Std. Ed.,* XVIII, pp. 7–64.

3. Ehrenberg, R., "Biologie und Psychoanalyse (Biology and Psychoanalysis)," in *Auswirkungen der Psychoanalyse in Wissenschaft und Leben,* H. Prinzhorn, ed. (Leipzig, Die Neue Geist Verlag, 1928), pp. 247–262.

4. Abderhalden, E., *Die Abderhaldensche Reaktion* (Berlin, Verlag Springer, 1922).

5. Freud, S., "Two Encyclopedia Articles" (1923), *Std. Ed.,* XVIII, pp. 258–259.

6. Schur, M., "The Ego in Anxiety," in *Drives, Affects and Behavior,* Vol. I, R. M. Lowenstein, ed. (New York, International Universities Press, 1953), pp. 67–103.

7. Freud, S., *The Problem of Anxiety,* trans. H. A. Bunker (New York, W. W. Norton, 1936).

8. Freud, S., "Extracts from the Fliess Papers, Letter 75, November 14, 1897," *Std. Ed.,* I, p. 271.

9. Strachey, J., "Editor's Introduction" to "Inhibitions, Symptoms and Anxiety" (1959), *Std. Ed.,* XX, pp. 78–79.

10. Freud, S., "The Ego and the Id," (1923), *Std. Ed.,* XIX, pp. 3–66.

11. Strachey, J., "Editor's Introduction," to "Inhibitions, Symptoms and Anxiety" (1959), *Std. Ed.,* XX, p. 79.

DEATH INSTINCT AND ANXIETY[1]
(1931)

I am aware that we stand on uncertain ground when we consider the hypothesis of the death instinct at the present time. How certain we feel, in contrast, when we speak of the sexual instinct and of the partial instincts. We are accustomed to assume that an instinct is a "borderline concept between the psychic and the somatic" and that by instinct we are to understand "the psychic representation of a stimulus originating in somatic sources."[2] We know something about the origins, the course, and the fate of these instincts.

It is quite a different matter with the death instinct. Immediately the question arises—where do we find its source? If we want to contrast the death instinct with the general concept of the life instinct, then we can find the biological source for the life instinct in the life span of the cell. Whether there is a fundamental drive for living, one cannot decide psychologically. Such a drive, however, appears to us intuitively as inevitable. Life is so full of tensions, so pressing, its direction toward the organization of ever larger units is so thoroughgoing that we have to attribute an instinctual quality to life.

It was not only Freud who, as a result of his dynamic orientation, asked the question whether the manifestations of life which appear to us so urgent—as he put it, so "noisy"—follow from the course of a single instinct, or whether they result from the workings of two opposing forces. Ehrenberg has expressed this as ". . . the duality, the actual operation of which leads to unity (oneness)."[3] Physiological and biological studies lead to very similar problems and also to similar philosophical solutions. Among the various opinions which physiologists and biologists have expressed about life and death, the concepts of Ehrenberg are of particular interest to us. This scientist arrived at concepts similar to Freud's from biological considerations. His book, *Theoretical Biology from the Viewpoint of the Irreversibility of Elementary Life Processes,* is also extensively quoted in a paper by Westerman Holstijn entitled "Tendency of Death, Death Instinct and Instincts of Killing."[4]

I present a brief abstract. The life processes of even the simplest unicellular organism, an unstructured droplet of protoplasm, are complicated; they consist of several enzymatic and fermentative processes. These processes not only serve the intake of foodstuffs, digestion, and assimilation, but at the same time they also lead to the precipitation of materials which were in solution. These precipitates form the first primitive structure in the cell and as such are irreversible. The function of protoplasm is the building up of structures in the widest sense. Structure consists of any substance which is transformed—without any radical operation and in an irreversible manner—from a fluid and dissolved state into a solid and insoluble one. What assimilates is living matter and what arises through assimilation is an alteration within the cell. This alteration which we recognize as a higher structuralization and as a manifestation of life processes is no longer life, but death. However, the alteration continues to be operative as a structure which influences the further course of life processes. We conceive of structure as living, although we know that the structuralized substance is inimical to life. Ehrenberg recognizes a source of energy which operates from the beginning of life and directs the life processes that are manifest in all the activities of the cell and of higher cell organizations. The evidence he gives in support of this idea is physiological and chemical; therefore it is not of further value to us. What is significant is the insight that these problems belong most intimately to the domain of physiology and biology, and that with the methods of these sciences a solution can be approached.

Abderhalden's discovery of *Abwehrfermente* seems pertinent to our problem. He described in fermentation the production of defense ferments (antihormones) that worked against the indigenous hormones of the organism.[5] Abderhalden originally called defense ferments those specific enzymes which arise in the living organism as a reaction to the parenteral administration of foreign proteins; these enzymes (antibodies) appear shortly after the introduction of foreign protein and have as their function the destruction of foreign materials.[6] Later it was found that the organism produces defense ferments not only against substances from without but also against substances produced by its own cells. This fact was first discovered in cases of pregnancy and of malignancy, in which cases, however, the products of pregnancy and of the tumor were regarded as foreign to the body proper. Following this, the problem of whether the body's own endocrine products are destroyed in such a manner was investigated.

At first, Abderhalden assumed that the organism's own hormones are destroyed only when a dysfunction of the respective endocrine organs occurs. But it was found that the organism always produces defense ferments against its own hormones, even in healthy, undisturbed conditions.

Zimmer, Länder, and Fehlow examined normal individuals and on the basis of their results established a so-called standard curve (*Normalkurve*).[7] With great caution they demonstrated in the blood serum of normal individuals the presence of specific defense ferments, directed against the cells and cell products of their own organs and present in definite, relative amounts. From their data, obtained from this standard curve, it may also be noted that different individuals yield different values for the same defense ferments, but when an individual is healthy, the relationship between the various defense ferments is constant. Similarly, the same individual, examined on different occasions, will yield different values, but the curve will still have the same form because the relative proportions of the enzymes do not change. In the normal state there exists a certain typical correlation among the endocrine organs, five of which stand in a particular type of "exchange relationship" with the genital apparatus.[8] However, this correlation is immediately altered in pathological conditions.

What is the origin of the defense ferments? This question has not been answered, but ". . . there is much evidence that would indicate," says Abderhalden, "that the enzymes which are found in the blood are, in general, not (and perhaps never) newly formed, but most likely originate in the same cells from which come the hormones and together with them they pass into the blood."[9]

Whatever the mechanism by which defense ferments against the hormones are produced, one thing is clear—the hormones produced by the organism are also destroyed by the organism.[10]

The above should serve to illustrate that in the organism there are substances other than those which mediate libidinal, i.e., integrating, impulses; these other substances are opposed in their action to those which mediate libido, and what we perceive is always the result of the fusion and interaction of both types of substances.

Psychoanalysis has investigated and demonstrated the manifestations of dammed-up libido (*Libidostauung*). If we wish to pursue a biological study of the phenomena of drives (instincts), we must ask ourselves, what is it that takes place within the organism when we speak of a state of libidinal tension (*Libidostauung*)? Is it really an accumulation of substances which mediate libido, or do the antihormones (*Abbaustoffe*) predominate? Or are both kinds of substances equally responsible? Is this state based perhaps on a disturbance of the correlation between various substances and, if so, of what substances?

These and similar questions stimulated me to make repeated hormone determinations in some patients and to study their hormonal fluctuations during psychoanalytic therapy. Among those studied were cases of severe hypochondriasis, acute anxiety states, and paranoia. This is not the time or place to discuss these cases in detail, since at the present time the studies are few in number and inconclusive in results. I expect, however, that these observations suggest that a strong damming-up of the libido in various clinical syndromes is accompanied by varying degrees of hormone destruction; also, in the correlation of changes, certain deviations seem clear-cut; the latter phenomenon is particularly clear in relation to bisexuality which is apparently most clear-cut in acute anxiety states. We do not know whether it is the chemical substances which stimulate libido, or the defense ferments against these, or, more likely, a mixture of the two, or perhaps an alteration in their relative proportions which brings about the state which we call damming-up of the libido.

It is at this point that the two different approaches in research—the physiological and the psychoanalytic—meet again.

The state which arises as a result of the effects of various hormones and their antibodies stimulates the organism to the elimination of certain cell masses which possess the quality of reproduction, i.e., the power to build up new structures. Should the possibility of this elimination and its accompanying satisfaction be disturbed, there arises in the organism a state of tension (due to need) which manifests itself as conscious anxiety and simultaneously stimulates the organism from within to form psychic structures such as defenses and symptoms.

With the advent of the impressive concept of the death instinct, it appeared to me that the problem of anxiety was intimately related to that instinct.

Ever since the beginning of psychoanalytic research, the question has been asked, does anxiety stand as the motive power behind all symptoms? Freud discussed the problem of anxiety in "Inhibitions, Symptoms and Anxiety." According to this work, anxiety is defined phenomenologically as "a special state of unpleasure accompanied by motor discharge along definite pathways."[11] The organism discharges the anxiety from within. This function is performed by the motor apparatus, even if skeletal muscles are transiently paralyzed or if they regress to an earlier phase of function by becoming withdrawn from voluntary control so that they discharge anxiety by finer or grosser movements. We then say that the stimulus barrier (the protection against overexcitation), which is an essential function of the ego, has been overcome. The organism is inundated—but with what? The organism seems to defend itself against some sort of attack, and one of its defensive measures is discharged through motor activity. But the discharge of anxiety is not identical with the anxiety affect proper. Similarly, pain and sorrow influence the functioning of the lachrymal glands and may be discharged by crying; crying, however, is by no means identical with these affects. In the same way, the discharge of anxiety cannot be equated with the affect of anxiety. Thus the question, What is the source of anxiety? is still to be answered.

According to Freud's latest concept, *anxiety is a danger signal of the ego.* Among the dangers which are perceived by the ego, we are interested in those arising from the id. "These are the processes initiated in the id, which give the ego occasion to develop anxiety,"[12] and Freud defines anxiety as an affect which arises whenever there is a tension due to a need in the id (*Bedürfniss-spannung im Es*). The need, the emergence of which is anticipated, may vary according to its specific content; the tension (due to need) may have a different libidinal-dynamic content according to each phase of the individual's development (fear of loss of object, anxiety of anal and genital damming-up of libido, castration anxiety, fear of the superego, etc.). In adults, according to the varying genetic significance of these developmental factors, anxiety results also from regression.

The state of tension itself, however, does not explain the genesis of the anxiety affect; it is only a prerequisite of the latter. Freud himself says that there are many tensions due to need which are perceived in other ways, such as pain and sorrow; or the same tensions may, in various people and under various circumstances, lead to different degrees of anxiety. Thus the statement that minimal anxiety is a danger signal of the ego tells us only something about its function. Anxiety protects the ego. For the ego, preparing itself with anxiety for the traumatic situation, experiences the oncoming threatening event in small doses and thus saves the ego from a sudden breakdown of the *protective barrier*. This is its "gain through illness." This consideration, though an economic one, is not an explanation for the dynamics of the anxiety affect.

To this question we can find a complete answer from Freud only when we consider the instinct theories which he first introduced in "Beyond the Pleasure Principle"[13] and which were examined by him in their clinical implications in "The Ego and the Id."[14] In these works Freud emphasized that the two instincts, Eros and Thanatos, never occur in the organism singly or independently of each other, but always in a mixed, mutually allied manner. If one understands him and Ehrenberg correctly, one may assume that this fusion of the two instincts brings about a "labile equilibrium" which may be disturbed under certain circumstances. "As a hurried generalization, we may assume," says Freud, "that the existence of a libidinal regression, e.g., from a genital to an anal-sadistic phase, depends upon a defusion of instincts."[15] This process we may picture as follows: There arises a tension (due to need) which, in turn, disturbs the existing labile equilibrium; under this pressure, a regression occurs, instinct defusion takes place, and as a result the death instinct, which is always present in the organism, becomes transiently free. The danger situation which thus arises consists of a liberation of quantities of death instinct, which is first perceived as anxiety affect. The anxiety is thus not a fear of death, but *it is the perception of liberated death instinct (primary masochism) within the organism.*

Freud held the same view to some extent in his "Inhibitions, Symptoms and Anxiety." In a footnote he writes, "It may quite often happen that although a danger-situation is correctly estimated in itself, a certain amount of instinctual anxiety is added to the realistic anxiety. In that case the instinctual demand before whose satisfaction the ego recoils is a masochistic one: the instinct of destruction directed against the subject himself."[16] *I propose to extend this concept to all anxiety which arises out of inner instinctual needs.*[17]

This conclusion may sound perhaps too hurried and strange. It is, therefore, necessary to attempt to prove it again and also to ask whether such a conclusion is justifiable. If it seems likely that a state of damming-up of the libido in the organism comes about as a result of various hormonal processes—and we hope that with improvement in physiological research methods this will be subject to experimental proof within the near future—it would then be easily understandable that hormonal processes may directly influence the vegetative system and thus bring about the excitation which is perceived as anxiety.[18] If this appears so simple physiologically, then we must ask further whether it is justifiable to add the difficult concept of instinct defusion to the explanation.

I hold the concept of instinct defusion, as stated by Freud in "The Ego and the Id," indispensable for two reasons.[19] First, without such a concept it would be difficult for us to find an explanation for the fact that anxiety not only may be discharged physiologically, but also that there is a road from the physiological to the psychological and that under certain circumstances anxiety may again be bound psychically, as for example in cases of obsessional neurosis. Second, I believe this view becomes necessary as soon as we attempt to account for the varying degrees of preparedness for anxiety and the various modes of mastering anxiety which exist from earliest childhood on among different individuals.

Freud introduced the concept of the death instinct along with that of the repetition compulsion and he illustrated this with the beautiful example of the one-and-a-half-year-old child who plays "being away" in order to master the tension or anxiety which occurs when his mother leaves. It occurred to me, in considering this instructive example, that not all children are capable of reacting in this way; not all children are able to counterpose enough activity against the passive suffering of a loss and so to re-create the anxiety-producing situation. The child described by Freud internalized the trauma and through his anxiety presented the self-created situation to the suffering, passive part of his personality as if at the same time saying, "Look here, it is not really so bad; I can do this myself and I can bear it." The child was able to bear the inner tension, an ability that made it possible for him to prepare psychologically for a real loss and thus diminish the expected anxiety by working it through in anticipation. In this way he saved himself from the shock and moreover, he did this by a performance which at the same time enhanced and gratified his ego. This play—the primordial form of sublimation—is not always produced under similar circumstances. Many children cannot reproduce in fantasy the idea of the mother's going away because the idea causes them so much displeasure (*Unlust*) that they must react to it with anxiety. For this reason, they do not deal with the unpleasant experience actively; they divert themselves from what they fear. With each repetition they suffer a new shock. They scream and kick on each occasion or, if they are more passive, they withdraw each time and become depressed (*unlustig*). These children cannot spare themselves the anxiety because they cannot tolerate the partial tension which would have to arise by the repetition of the fantasy.

Such a labile equilibrium is found not only in suckling infants and small children. We see this in our patients of any age. There are many people who cannot tolerate any increase in excitation because increased tension liberates mobile energy which must immediately be transformed. These are the individuals who can never wait for gratification but who immediately produce anxiety or aggression; since they can bind anxiety only temporarily and with difficulty, they go from one symptom to another. These are the severe neurotics, par excellence, in whom—after we have analyzed their innumerable phobic, obsessional, perverse, and organ-neurotic symptoms—passivity and primary masochism finally emerge to the foreground. We encounter our greatest difficulties in analyzing this latter condition.

From Freud's example of the playing child, as well as from many cases seen in analytic practice, we see that the *primary lability of the equilibrium, the primary predisposition for anxiety, depends upon the unbound, unused part of the destructive instincts; aggression which, turned toward the self, is defined as primary masochism.* Freud made a contribution to our knowledge of constitution by his discovery of primary masochism; the full meaning of this contribution and its value will be determined only by further research.[20]

Let us return to the problem of anxiety. We know that anxiety must be discharged or bound. The question of exactly how this occurs was the original and still not completely conquered domain of psychoanalysis. In summary, it should be noted that through the binding of anxiety new structures arise. In the above-mentioned case of the playing child, we can see the preliminary steps of sublimation; we also know that liberated anxiety becomes bound in symptoms which, with the passage of time, are built into the ego as insoluble or hardly soluble constituents. It is similarly through complicated bindings and identifications that the superego, the most recent structure phylogenetically and ontogenetically, develops by mutual interaction of the life and death instincts and, because it is the most recently formed, it is most readily the object of our scientific scrutiny.

In this paper I have pointed out only a small part of the general problem of anxiety to which the assumption of a death instinct furnishes new and important viewpoints. I have touched upon the problem of aggression, which is closely connected with the concept of the death instinct, only in passing when I mentioned that anxiety, which is liberated death instinct, immediately cathects the motor apparatus. It appears more difficult to discuss the problem of ambivalence and/or identification from the point of view of a primary destructive instinct.

Through the structure-forming processes of decomposition of organisms (*Abbau*-processes), be they unicellular or highly complicated, we recognize the original dualism. The decomposition processes which relate to the substances that form libido may contribute to the stimulus increase which, mastered by the nervous system, contributes to the formation of psychic structures.

If we follow the dualism to its ultimate conclusion, then the organization of the human psyche falls into its natural place as the highest and most recent formation of psychic structure. If we do not want to do this, if we want to utilize the dualistic instinct theory only in the sense of the older concepts of instincts, then a hiatus appears. In this case the question of why there have developed in man institutions (such as the superego) which work against the sexual instinct remains unanswered. In this way the human psyche would be given an exceptional place among the events of nature. At this point we may refer again to certain biological facts: the long period of helplessness of the human infant and the biphasic nature of sexual development. In a small brochure by Professor Bolk, the biological and anatomical findings presented indicate the importance and correctness of the view first introduced by Freud in the study of human psychology: the phasic nature of sexual development and its accompanying hormonal influences.[21] Thus we come again to the domain of physiology which should provide us with further solutions.

Freud himself regarded the assumption of a death instinct as "speculative"; I believe, however, that biological research and study of the dynamics of instincts may substantiate his speculations.

NOTES

1. Originally presented in a discussion of the death instinct at a meeting of the German Psychoanalytic Society, March 21, 1931. Published in *International Zeitschrift für Psychoanalyse*, Vol. XVII (1931), pp. 333–343. Revised for this volume.

2. Freud, S., "Instincts and Their Vicissitudes" (1915), *Std. Ed.*, XIV, pp. 121–122.

3. Ehrenberg, R., "Biologie und Psychoanalyse (Biology and Psychoanalysis)," in *Auswirkungen der Psychoanalyse in Wissenschaft und Leben*, H. Prinzhorn, ed. (Leipzig, Die Neue Geist Verlag, 1928), pp. 247–262; *Theoretical Biology from the Viewpoint of the Irreversibility of Elementary Life Processes* (Berlin, Springer, 1923).

4. Holstijn, A. J. W., "Tendency of Death, Death Instinct and Instincts of Killing," *Imago*, XVI (1930), 207–231.

5. Abderhalden, E., *Die Abderhaldensche Reaktion* (Berlin, Springer, 1922).

6. Emil Abderhalden (1877–1950) was one of the leading biochemists of the first half of this century. He worked at first on protein synthesis with Emil Fischer, then surpassed him by first synthesizing a protein containing nineteen amino acids. His main work was on protective ferments (1909–1912) and the synthesis of the cell (*Bausteine*). In his study of the protective ferments in the animal body, Abderhalden evolved a biochemical test for pregnancy and other conditions by ferment (enzyme) reactions (1912). [From F. H. Garrison, *The History of Medicine* (Philadelphia, W. B. Saunders Co., 1929), p. 698.] It is appropriate to call attention to the fact that the *Abwehrferment* could be translated "defense ferment." The term *Abwehrferment, Abbaustoffe,* recalls the analogous term "defense mechanism" in psychoanalysis.

7. Zimmer, Länder, Fehlow, *Fermentforschuung*, Vol. X (1928).

8. The following are in close correlation with the testes and ovaries: pituitary, pineal, thymus, thyroid, and adrenals.

9. Abderhalden, E., *Die Abderhaldensche Reaktion* [Author's note, 1970: Whether modern concepts and laboratory techniques of defenses against foreign proteins represent the further development of Abderhalden's significant contributions, I cannot substantiate since I did not follow up the development of that research. Reports on the organism's reaction to surgical implantation of kidneys, heart, etc., would indicate that Abderhalden's original conclusions were correct.]

10. Similar thoughts are expressed by Federn in his article entitled "The Reality of the Death Instinct," *Almanach der Psychoanalyse* (1932). Psychoanalytic Review 19 (1932), pp. 129–136.

11. Freud, S., "Inhibitions, Symptoms and Anxiety" (1926), *Std. Ed.,* XX, pp. 77–156.

12. Ibid., p. 140.

13. Freud, S., "Beyond the Pleasure Principle" (1920), *Std. Ed.,* XVIII, pp. 7–64.

14. Freud, S., "The Ego and the Id" (1923), *Std. Ed.,* XIX, pp. 3–66.

15. Ibid., p. 42.

16. Freud, S., "Supplementary Remarks on Anxiety," Addenda B to "Inhibitions, Symptoms and Anxiety," *Std. Ed.,* XX, p. 168.

17. All anxiety by definition arises from inner instinctual needs. Other fear reactions are motivated by external stimuli or the interaction of external and internal stimuli.

18. Wilhelm Reich, in his book *The Function of the Orgasm* (New York, Orgone Institute Press, 1942), pp. 110–112, suggests that free-floating anxiety is an accompanying manifestation of a certain vegetative irritation of cardiac anxiety. Similarly, Reich finds that whenever the sexual instinct is not satisfied, the destructive instinct becomes liberated and expressed. Reich is correct, with certain limitations, when he states that the intensity of the destructive instinct depends upon somatic damming-up (somatic tensions) and that the destructive instinct increases if the libido is not gratified.

19. Freud, S., "The Ego and the Id" (1923), *Std. Ed.,* XIX, pp. 3–66.

20. Freud, S., "The Economic Problem of Masochism" (1924), *Std. Ed.*, XIX, pp. 157–172.

21. Bolk, P., *Das Problem der Menschenwerdung* (Jena, Fischer, 1926).

DISCUSSION

"The theory of instincts is our mythology," said Freud in his paper "Anxiety and Instinctual Life."[1] When I. Arthur Mirsky, a psycho-analytically trained biochemist and physician, presented a lecture in which he condensed the biochemical, neurophysiologic, endocrine, and psychologic processes which interact in anxiety, he introduced it with the following statement: "Nothing can induce as much anxiety as the attempt to define the concept and the phenomena of anxiety."[2] Indeed, I grappled with a problem the size of which I could not then appreciate. Now when I can distance myself and see the interactions between the physiologic and psychologic processes, I am aware that the problems of anxiety can be solved only by multidisciplinary efforts. Mirsky's presentation, condensed as it was, represents such an effort. He conceives of anxiety as the last link of the physiologic processes which arouse a warning signal so that the danger can be perceived.

Freud assumed that anxiety originates in physiologic processes without psychologic motivation (1894–1896).[3] How right he was! It took physiology many years to substantiate his vision. Now psychoanalysts have to fill the gap in the theory by integrating what we can learn from physiology. Psychoanalysts have not been unaware of the physiologic symptoms that accompany anxiety and have thought in a vague, nonconcrete manner about the hormonal and neurophysiologic processes which interact in bringing about the sensation of anxiety. Nevertheless there has been no attempt at confrontation. Their attempts to arrive at a unified theory of anxiety did not consider that physiology had to be a part of such unified theory.

What is anxiety? Is it an instinct, a drive, an affect? What is its relation to libido and to aggression? When Freud said, "We shall no longer maintain that it is the libido itself that is turned into anxiety,"[4] he did not elaborate his alternatives. Did he assume that other instinctual forces such as aggression might cause an increase in psychic tension that would be perceived as anxiety? If so, that would confirm my assumption, but he did not say this. Kubie, on the basis of his extensive neurophysiologic investigation, assumes that ". . . libidinal tension inevitably builds up states of central excitations which lead in turn to the danger of diffuse irradiation of excitation. . . . Libido as such is not transformed but frustrated; but frustrated libido brings about the accumulation of excitation from which the rest follows automatically."[5]

This, however, is not a review but a discussion of the problems raised by my paper. Freud differentiated anxiety from fear. According to him, anxiety is an affect arising as a warning signal against a danger from within, against a danger arising from instinctual sources; fear is a warning against real danger from without. This pragmatic differentiation served us well through many years of clinical observation, but so far as we can assume now, it does not hold true on the level of physiology. The physiologic processes which activate fear are the same as those which activate anxiety.

It is probably our highly complex mental apparatus which induces physiologic response to nonrealistic perceptions and then modifies that response *in statu nascendi* in a variety of ways which we can then recognize as anxiety, whether in the present, in the past, or in anticipating the future. Since anxiety is a reaction of the highly differentiated human nervous system, intuitively experienced and further elaborated by the creative mind, it at one time appeared accessible only to psychologic, intuitive methods of investigation. Yet in recent decades physiologic investigations have yielded results which elucidate the problems of anxiety from the perspective of physiology. Therefore I shall point out those findings which appear most pertinent to this discussion. I am relying on the information obtained from Mirsky's succinct presentation cited above.

Cannon was the first to prove by experiment that physiologic processes give rise to affective behavior. His classical observation led to the concept of homeostasis and also to the formulation of fear as a warning of homeostatic imbalance, comprised in the phrase "flight or fight."[6] Neurophysiologic investigation indicates the relation between homeostasis and the physiology of the brain. In viewing anxiety as a warning signal, Mirsky called attention to the function of the reticular system, the activating arousal or alerting system.[7] "The integrity of this system determines sleep and wakefulness, relaxation and tension. It is the alerting action of this system that appears to be responsible for the excitation that is subjectively perceived as mounting tension."[8] Cannon's observation provided the first definitive data on the mechanisms which involve physiologic factors in producing anxiety and anger.

On the basis of their clinical observations, psychoanalysts recognized the interrelation of these two phenomenologically different effects, but they remained uninformed of the fact that Cannon's investigations substantiated the connection between fear and anger on physiologic grounds. Cannon demonstrated that the physiologic responses which prepare the organism for flight or fight, such as vascular, respiratory, metabolic, and muscular changes, are reflexive in nature; they are due to activation of the orthosympathetic outflow from the hypothalamus and the release of epinephrine from the adrenal medulla. Since not all his findings could be explained on the basis of epinephrine alone, Cannon postulated the existence of two other sympathomimetic substances, sympathin E and sympathin I. Sympathin E is now identified as norepinephrine, which differs from epinephrine only in the absence of the N-methyl group. Epinephrine induces the physiologic changes that characterize the emergency response (flight or fight) caused by fear. The major effect of nor-epinephrine is a general vasoconstriction.[9]

It seems as if psychoanalysts could not have missed associating the nonexternalized vasoconstricting effect of nor-epinephrine with withdrawal and/or introversion and contrasting it with the externalizing effects of epinephrine. More sophisticated experiments appear to substantiate other psychoanalytic assumptions such as "anger turned toward the self." Mirsky cites the investigation of Funkenstein et al:[10]

> . . . [He] and his colleagues proposed that subjects who respond to a particular situation with anger which is directed outward, i.e., with the "fight" reaction (aggression), activate the excessive secretion of nor-epinephrine and exhibit relatively minimal physiological reactions. In contrast, individuals who respond to the same situation with anger directed toward themselves or with severe anxiety generated by hostile impulses, i.e., the "flight" reaction (submission), activate the excessive secretion of epinephrine and exhibit the generalized reactions described by Cannon.[11]

Thus with the finesse of more recent investigation Cannon's original conclusion stands: aggression is related to the secretion of nor-epinephrine, and anxiety and fear to the secretion of epinephrine. These investigations demonstrate the physiologic correlates to such human reactions as "aggression turned toward the self." It appears to be a reaction similar to that described by ethologists who have observed that wild animals, fighting with superior adversaries, in defeat expose the jugular vein as a sign of complete surrender.

The biochemical response to a perception is not immediately an affect. It may be the first link in the chain of neurophysiologic processes of perception which will qualify the stimulus as arising within or without the body, signaling danger. All levels of the central nervous system play a role in it before the cortex, functioning in man as ego, deals with the anxiety affect. Again, quoting Mirsky:

> . . . It is the primitive cortex, the archipallium, and particularly in the limbic lobe, that the earliest patterns of affective experiences are elaborated and stored. As MacLean[12] has emphasized . . . the frontotemporal portion of the limbic

system is largely concerned with mechanisms involved with functions subsumed as "self-preservation" while parts of the septum, hippocampus and cingulate gyrus are concerned with functions essential for the preservation of the species.[13]

Although these significant discoveries do not seem relevant to the problem of anxiety as we conceived it forty years ago or even more recently, they are significant road signs for the development of research. They remind us that the earliest affective experiences are elaborated and stored in the oldest portion of the brain; thus they give us safer footing for discussion of such hypotheses as the trauma of birth, infantile separation anxiety, and memory traces originating in the infant's instinctual experience of being fed. Such investigation has confirmed Freud's concept of instinct "on the frontier between the mental and somatic." The reference to the function of the limbic lobe as the common physiologic denominator of emotional and viscerosomatic function could be interpreted as an indication that the earliest infantile experience is imbedded in the physiology of the warning system itself.

Irrespective of the mechanism involved, exposure to threatening events results in the release of hypothalamic neurohormones, adrenocorticotropin, epinephrine, corticosteroids and a variety of other agents. Not only do these agents exert peripheral changes, but they also influence the activity of the central nervous system and thereby enhance the activities of physiological processes associated with anxiety.[14]

What is anxiety? As the biochemistry of the warning signal shows, anxiety is the moment on the border between physiology and the psychic response to it. But in a broader sense, anxiety is the manifestation of the universal instinct of self-preservation that is expressed in every living organism. The coordinated organic and psychosomatic responses to anxiety which cause the flight or fight reaction would qualify anxiety as a drive. In man anxiety is an affect originating in the id and experienced by the ego. Differentiated as "signal anxiety," however, it motivates the evolution of psychic structures; beyond this, transformations of anxiety play a role in all forms of man's higher creativity.

Aggression as the manifestation of the death instinct was a touchy subject for psychoanalytic theoreticians until Hartmann, Kris, and Loewenstein discussed the modification of the instinct theory and drew a line of demarcation between the philosophical speculation and the heuristic value of the new instinct theory.[15] These authors refer to Ehrenberg's biological parallel to Freud's concept of the death instinct, but they emphasize their independence from further biologic speculations by stating that they consider psychic energy only that which originates in instincts and can be recognized in the manifestations of instinctual drives.[16] These authors define aggression as psychic representation of energy originating in the instinctual drive; they conceptualize aggression not as a drive that motivates behavior but as psychic energy, thus a counterpart of libido. Their investigation was the first to describe aggression systematically: its characteristics as instinct, its genetic development, and its vicissitudes. The antagonists, libido and aggression, are in a state of fusion or dynamic equilibrium and as such are neutralized. In response to stimuli from within and without, transient defusions occur which motivate response to stimulus. Although this is repetitious, it recalls the biochemical closeness between epinephrine and nor-epinephrine, between anxiety and aggression, and the possibility that one affect will overcome another in the reality of a situation. This might account for the vicissitudes of aggression as instinct. Rising psychic tension, whether caused by libido or by aggression, was viewed as signal anxiety; the rising tension might break down the barrier and activate acute anxiety. As Freud stated, anxiety ". . . is being created anew out of the economic conditions of the situation."[17] In a similar way one can say that anger, aggression, is created anew from the psychophysiologic state of frustration. This concept was accepted as a substitute for the concept of the death instinct and it stimulated fresh investigations of the problems of anxiety.

Investigating Freud's concepts regarding anxiety forty years later, Waelder suggests that ". . . there may be a biological warning system necessary for survival, of which the sensation of anxiety may be merely the organism's awareness of it."[18] In his article he discusses the teleological concept of anxiety implied in the function of the danger signal, which, besides the massive reactions to danger (panic, flight, or fight), induces adaptation processes. Signal anxiety, however, means something more than, and different from, anticipation of smaller or larger traumata. The origin of signal anxiety is in the phylogenetic history of man; it has equipped the human species with a kind of awareness of anxiety that comes to function as signal anxiety. Indeed, the defense mechanisms of the ego are primary psychic structures which evolved in man from vigilance (from a physiologic response to danger); they evolved in "silence," they represent the fusion (or the labile balance) of the contrasting psychic energies, aggression and libido. Signal anxiety does not originate in manifest imbalance as anxiety does; it does not cause tension states or affective emotions as long as it remains unconscious. I have always understood signal anxiety as an unconscious measuring rod of intrapsychic balances, probably a phylogenetically deferred aftereffect of the massive physiologic processes which activate acute anxiety, a guardian of the dynamic stability of the mental apparatus. I agree with Waelder that signal anxiety is unconscious and participates in the smooth evolution of adaptational processes. In his review, Waelder emphasized the ego's struggles with libido, but aggression, the antipode of libido, is not mentioned as relevant to the problems of anxiety.

Psychoanalysts shy away from the dilemmas posed by the theory of the death instinct. The tendency to die by natural causes built into every organism is not an instinct but a consequence of the physiology of living, a genetic characteristic of each organism. Metabolism itself, regulated by the homeostatic instinct, has its orderly way of dissolution. One could assume (if one wants to philosophize) that by deferring death, life, with all its instinctual safeguards for survival, is in the service of orderly decomposition or dissolution of the living. This would imply that natural death can occur only after the germ plasm has accomplished its function. "A 'death instinct' in individuals, if it really exists, may well be in the service of the species."[19] As we learn about the interactions of physiologic and psychologic processes in the anxiety affect, Lewin reminds us that "Anxiety, though a signal, is not merely a signal. It has a content and it is a sort of 'memory.' "[20] Since he has so sensitively observed anxiety in the analysis of men and women, it is good to know that it is not a fantasy.

Whether there is a death instinct or just a fear of death as an external power, there must be psychic representations of the power of death. The ever-threatening apperception of death as reality is experienced as fear of death. This is programmed in the mind and expressed by separation anxiety, through mourning rituals and religious beliefs, all of which serve the purpose of alleviating the fear of death. In spite of the innumerable investigations dealing with individual and collective manifestations of the psychologic elaborations of the fear of death, psychoanalysts have avoided the problem of the death instinct.

Among many investigators, Rangell is the only one (as far as I know) who has tackled the problem with great circumspection. In three thorough investigations in which he evaluated all the relevant publications on the problems of anxiety (except mine of 1931), he arrived at the concept which I formulated crudely about forty years ago.[21]

In the first of these three papers, Rangell declares his intention to formulate a unitary theory of anxiety. The second and third papers deal with the nature and theory of intrapsychic conflict. These two closely interrelated papers reflect the thoroughness of the investigation. Yet he gives his conclusion with timid tentativeness at the end of the second paper:

> One thought keeps presenting itself to me . . . a thought which I fear may speak against the most basic point which I have made. That is, it may be, following Freud, that the basic and irreducible conflict is between life and death instincts. . . . But perhaps . . . if this is so . . . these two relentless

forces are, in relation to each other, partners rather than in conflict![22]

Indeed, Rangell's argument underscores Freud's hypothesis that fusion and defusion occur together in every living organism. Life and death represent phenomenologically and experientially extreme opposites. Biologically, as Freud's broad and nonspecific concept of fusion and defusion indicates, they are partners, and most of the time the death instinct works in silence.

In his third paper, Rangell defines anxiety as a psychophysical organismic response to a traumatic situation. Both the traumatic state and the resultant anxiety have a combination of physiologic and psychologic components, each of which feeds back into its complex network. Since a unified theory of anxiety, therefore, involves the knowledge of the interactions of these interrelated networks, they will have to be investigated with different methods and instruments. Biologists and physiologists know more of those processes which lead to aging and the causes of death than do psychoanalysts. Although the death instinct probably cannot be isolated in pure chemical form, since it is a part of living, as a philosophical concept it represents Freud's vision into the secret of life. Ehrenberg, in his theoretical biology, confirmed Freud's concept in the lawfulness of biology.

NOTES

1. Freud, S., "Anxiety and Instinctual Life," in "New Introductory Lectures on Psychoanalysis" (1933), *Std. Ed.*, XXII, pp. 81–111.

2. Mirsky, I. A., "Psycho-Physiological Basis of Anxiety," *Psychosomatics,* I, no. 1 (1960), 29–36.

3. Freud, S., "Extracts from the Fliess Papers, Letter 75, November 14, 1897," *Std. Ed.*, I, p. 271.

4. Freud, S., "Anxiety and Instinctual Life," *Std. Ed.*, XXII, p. 271.

5. Kubie, L. S., "A Physiological Approach to the Concept of Anxiety," *Psychosomatic Med.*, III (1941), 272.

6. Cannon, W. B., *Bodily Changes in Pain, Hunger, Fear and Rage: An Account of Recent Researches in the Function of Emotional Excitement* (Boston, Branford, 1953). Cannon's first major work was published in the same year in which Freud's "Instincts and Their Vicissitudes" appeared, but this first physiology of the theory of anxiety remained unknown to Freud even in its later editions.

7. Magoun, H. W., *The Waking Brain* (Springfield, Ill., Charles C. Thomas, 1958).

8. Mirsky, I. A., "Psycho-Physiological Basis of Anxiety," p. 30.

9. Ibid., p. 30.

10. Funkenstein, D. H., King, S. H., and Drollette, M. E., *The Mastery of Stress* (Cambridge, Harvard University Press, 1957).

11. Mirsky, I. A., "Psycho-Physiological Basis of Anxiety," p. 31.

12. MacLean, P. D., "The Limbic System with Respect to Self-Preservation," *J. Nervous & Mental Diseases,* CXXVII (1958), 1–11.

13. Mirsky, I. A., "Psycho-Physiological Basis of Anxiety," p. 30.

14. Ibid., p. 33.

15. Hartmann, H., Kris, E., and Loewenstein, R. M., "Notes on the Theory of Aggression," *Psychoanalytic Study of the Child,* IV, pp. 9–36.

16. Of course, the processes of decomposition cannot be recognized as such. Aggression, however, being biochemically very closely related to anxiety, qualifies as instinct, i.e., as instinctual drive.

17. Freud, S., "Inhibitions, Symptoms and Anxiety" (1926), *Std. Ed.,* XX, p. 130.

18. Waelder, R., "Inhibitions, Symptoms and Anxiety, Forty Years Later," *Psychoanalytic Quart.,* XXXVI (1967), 1–36; XVI (1968), 399.

19. Bakan, D., *Disease, Pain and Sacrifice* (Chicago, University of Chicago Press, 1968), p. 22.

20. Lewin, B. D., "Phobic Symptoms and Dream Interpretation," *Psychoanalytic Quart.,* XXI (1952), 311.

21. Rangell, L., "On the Psychoanalytic Theory of Anxiety: A Statement of a Unitary Theory," *J. Am. Psychoanalytic Assn.,* III (1955), 389–414; "The Scope of Intrapsychic Conflict" and "Structural Problems in Intrapsychic Conflict," *Psychoanalytic Study of the Child,* XVIII (1963), 75–138; "A Further Attempt to Resolve the Problem of Anxiety," *J. Am. Psychoanalytic Assn.,* XVI (1968), 371–404.

22. Rangell, L., "Structural Problems in Intrapsychic Conflict," p. 137.

2. Mental Processes in Thyrotoxic States

INTRODUCTION

At the time I wrote these papers, psychoanalysts did not think in terms of psychosomatic medicine. The idea of an interrelation between psyche and bodily changes is probably older than Hippocrates. It was not doubted by modern doctors as medicine developed during the nineteenth century. Freud's "Studies on Hysteria"[1] was a striking demonstration of unconscious motivation symptoms. Although psychosomatic processes were not central in Freud's theories, his instinct theories opened the scientific approach to the psychogenesis of somatic illness; the instinct theories demonstrate that "psychic and somatic phenomena take place in the same biological system and are two aspects of the same process."[2]

Freud suggested in 1894[3] and many times thereafter that the effort the ego makes to defend itself against instinctual demands is the nucleus of neurosis. It is a long way from that formulation to the modern concepts in psychoanalysis and psychosomatic medicine. It is not our task to point out the landmarks on the way, but I should emphasize that these papers, based on the analyses of patients treated in the early 1930s, explaining the disease processes in terms of Freud's second instinct theory, lead directly to the modern concepts of psychosomatic medicine. Whether the defenses are necessitated by libidinal conflicts or by anxiety and aggression, the conflict tension activates the process that causes symptoms. In the case of a preexisting vulnerability of an organ or organ system, the psychogenic process causes a somatic illness.

It took many years for the etiology of organic diseases to be freed from the confining doctrine of specific etiology for each disease, even for each symptom. Cannon's investigation of the relation of emotions to bodily changes set the stage for later clinical and experimental research.

Endocrinological investigation led Selye to the formulation of a new concept of pathology which is a close parallel to Freud's concept of neurosis. Selye states that although there are illnesses caused by the direct influence of disease-producing agents such as microbes, viruses, poisons, and physical injuries, many more illnesses result from the body's own response to some unusual situation. "It is not always immediately obvious that in the final analysis our diseases are so often due to our own responses."[4] Sometimes the body's reactions are excessive and quite out of proportion to a seemingly innocuous irritation. For example, a splinter under the skin may cause inflammation that is experienced as a symptom. Yet the inflammation is a defensive reaction against the irritant. Selye asked, could it be that an adaptive endocrine response can become so intense that the resulting hormone excess would damage organs in distant parts of the body? He investigated many organs and organ systems and found that this was true. On the basis of this finding he formulated the concept of "general adaptation syndrome" and the consequent "diseases of adaptation."[5]

The analogy and convergence between the theories of Freud and Selye do not need further explanation for psychoanalysts. Both theories are based on observations of primary reactions to homeostatic disturbances, to use the same term for both physiologic and psychologic imbalance, which normally activate appropriate built-in defenses. However, these defenses in the course and consequence of their own dynamics may lead to illness and even to death.

So far as pathology is concerned, the psychodynamic processes of neuroses and their interaction with environmental and intrapsychic conditions qualify them as diseases of adaptation.[6] Selye demonstrated the dynamics of stress and the spiral of its interactions with environmental and organismic factors.[7] The philosopher Bakan asked, why are organisms so constructed that what serves as defense can lead to further illness or death?[8] This would indicate that not only individual-survival–positive mechanisms function in the organism, but also individual-survival–negative mechanisms as well.

A few decades ago such a hypothesis would have been unheard of. Darwin demonstrated the value of the individual-survival–positive mechanism for the survival of the individual and of the species. Natural scientists not only accepted Darwin's theory but the theory of the survival of the fittest was so persuasive that it was taken for granted.[9] Haldane questioned the Darwinian assumptions which seemed to show that natural selection worked in favor of individual adaptation, thus quite automatically favoring reproductive success.[10]

This was not before Freud's time, but it was two decades before Selye's discovery which can be restated in Bakan's formula that ". . . defense is a key notion for unlocking . . . the mystery of disease process."[11] Through a thorough investigation of Freud's theory formation,

Bakan arrived at the conclusion that individual-survival–negative mechanisms account for what Freud meant by death instinct. In a state of threatening defusion, the death instinct activates the warning signals which are perceived as anxiety. The anxiety then mobilizes defenses which alleviate anxiety. If the ego's defenses break down and anxiety overflows, conditions arise such as those which brought into psychotherapy the two patients who are the subject of the following study.

Their acute anxiety was labeled as a symptom of a thyrotoxic state. The dynamic described is general and would fit any acute anxiety state. Why deal with it as if caused by a pathologic function of the thyroid gland? Strictly speaking, this would indicate that it was a somatopsychic and not a psychosomatic condition. This was my conception of my patients' condition. Today the first question would be, what caused the imbalance in the function of the thyroid glands? The answer would call attention to the life histories of the patients which would reveal that the stress or load did not begin with the thyrotoxic syndrome but was the result of chronic stress which would be the primary finding of a present-day psychosomatic investigator. But can one be sure what the primary process is? One can be certain only that there was a spiral of interactions between physiologic and emotional processes which led to the disease condition.

There is an extensive literature on the correlation between the psychologic and endocrine factors in the causation and process of thyrotoxic states. However, at the time I wrote the paper, I relied only on what was classical since I was a medical student. Graves' disease focused attention on the secretory overactivity of thyroid glands and emotional reactions. He connected the condition to hysteria.[12] As his title reveals, Graves' paper (1835) was not the first on the subject. During the ensuing years there have been repeated discussions pro and con on the role of emotional factors in the etiology of thyrotoxicosis. In 1897 Raymond Crawford in defense of Graves stated, ". . . that sudden emotion or prolonged worry commonly sets in motion symptoms of Graves' disease will be so universally conceded as not to demand extensive illustration."[13]

As a psychoanalyst I could gain evidence for my orientation only from my patients. Studying these cases again, I find some problems which may be of interest to psychoanalysts of the present generation.

NOTES

1. Freud, S., "Studies on Hysteria" (1893–1895), *Std. Ed.*, II, pp. 1–310.
2. Pollock, G., "Psychosomatic Illness," *International Encyclopedia of the Social Sciences* (New York, Macmillan Co. & Free Press, 1968), p. 135.

3. Freud, S., "The Neuro-Psychoses of Defense" (1894), *Std. Ed.*, III, pp. 43–61.

4. Bakan, D., *Disease, Pain and Sacrifice* (Chicago, University of Chicago Press, 1968), p. 22.

5. Selye, H., *The Physiology and Pathology of Exposure to Stress* (Montreal, Acta, 1950).

6. Freud described the intrapsychic processes of adaptation to symptoms in "Inhibitions, Symptoms and Anxiety" (1926) (*Std. Ed.*, XX, pp. 87–175) although he did not designate the process with the same term.

7. Selye, H., *The Stress of Life* (New York, McGraw-Hill, 1956), pp. 128–129.

8. Bakan, D., *Disease, Pain and Sacrifice*.

9. Peller, L. E., "Biological Foundations of Psychology; Freud vs. Darwin," *Bul. Philadelphia Psychoanalytic Assn.*, XV (1965), 79–96.

10. Haldane, J. B. S., *The Causes of Evolution* (London, Longermans, 1932).

11. Bakan, D., *Disease, Pain and Sacrifice*, p. 22.

12. Graves, R., "New Observed Affection of the Thyroid Glands in Females," *Med. & Surg.*, VII (1835), 516.

13. Crawford, R., "Graves' Disease: An Emotional Disorder," *King's Coll. Hosp. Reprint*, III (1897), 45.

MENTAL PROCESSES IN THYROTOXIC STATES[1] (1934)

In spite of the great amount of literature dealing with thyrotoxicosis, information concerning the attendant mental states is usually limited to generalities. It is said that states due to an excessive function of the thyroid gland—hyperthyroid states—are accompanied by various nervous and psychic alterations: mental unrest, exaggerated reaction to mental stimuli, accelerated mental tempo, flight of ideas, and a tendency to sudden shifts of mood from unmotivated euphoria to depression. Besides these, there are true psychotic states of which a large proportion resemble manic-depressive conditions. According to Parhon, fifty-seven of eighty-six hyperthyroid psychoses which he observed were manic-depressive disorders.[2] To what extent or even whether one should regard hyperthyroidism as a causal factor is not our concern here. It is known that psychotics have greatly improved with treatment of the thyroid condition, and similarly that psychoses have been precipitated by the administration of thyroid preparations; yet in most cases it is impossible to exclude concomitant psychogenic factors. It is equally well known that strong mental excitement can produce Graves' disease abruptly and acutely. Admitting the obscurity of the causal relationships between Graves' disease, hyperthyroid states, and psychoses, Ewald states that "the frequency with which the particular combination of manic-depressive and Basedow's disease is found depends on more than a coincidence."[3]

My contribution to this problem consists chiefly in the presentation of two cases in which the mental features were anxiety, depression, and phobic and compulsive reactions. I thereby hope to show why manic-depressive clinical states occur so frequently in hyperthyroid disorders.

CASE 1

In the first case the initial symptom of the depression was morbid fear. The patient, a woman of thirty-three, as a sequel to a mental shock had developed a typical Graves' disease with classical symptoms and an accelerated basal metabolism, for which she was under medical treatment. She was referred to me because of manifold phobias accompanied by intense anxiety; she did not dare enter her kitchen because she was afraid of the door that led to the balcony. When I first saw the patient she was agitated, she wept, and spoke reluctantly and in a confused manner. When asked about her children, she answered that she had three. She then vaguely reproached herself for the death of her only son and said that the life of her oldest daughter, then seriously ill in the hospital, was on her conscience. But this topic did not hold her attention; she was predominantly anxious, afraid "of the door to the balcony."

Superficially, the story of the balcony door is as follows. In the same building, a Mrs. B. lived alone; she was ill and depressed and sought the patient's company and friendship. A few months before the patient became ill, Mrs. B. made her first suicidal attempt. The patient had taken her to a neurological hospital, but Mrs. B. was discharged prematurely and shortly thereafter hanged herself from the door in her kitchen that led to the balcony. Greatly shocked, the patient attempted to avoid all further thought of this event; she refused to speak to the widower or look at the motherless children. She began to feel oppressed; she could not rightly say why, but would repeat to her husband, "If I only had never known Mrs. B.!" To avoid hearing about Mrs. B. she kept away from persons who had known the dead woman, yet she persistently followed the newspaper accounts of suicides. Her unrest and anxiety were finally focused: she became afraid to enter her kitchen for fear of the door to the balcony. She moved away from her house, first staying in another city, where a physician was suspicious of a hyperthyroid development. But on her return she moved to a new house where her gradually increasing suffering forced her to seek treatment.

Our first impression here was surely that a mental shock precipitated a Graves' syndrome. The patient's history indicated some possible earlier dysfunction of the thyroid gland. She was frigid; she at one time had a small, inactive goiter; her menses were scanty and of brief duration.

The patient was the youngest of ten children in a lower middle class household. Her mother was hysterical and often threatened to commit suicide. The patient was affectionately devoted to her mother and had been a jovial, merry girl who had made a conscious effort to escape from this milieu into the security of a good marriage. Married at nineteen, she was a happy, active wife with few worries. She enjoyed spending money, liked her own comfort, and did not take her household responsibilities too seriously. However, one thing could disturb this equanimity profoundly—she could not endure seeing anyone ill or in pain. When her oldest child had a heart attack, the patient had to run from the room. When her husband or someone else became ill, she was so tormented by fear that she had to leave. One could say that the patient reacted to others' illness by identifying herself with them. However, up to the time of Mrs. B.'s suicide, she had never been considered ill.

It is not difficult to see that her ensuing fear of the door expressed the idea, "I shall hang myself like Mrs. B.," an idea which, arising from her identification, was excluded from consciousness. Indeed, when the analyst gave the patient this interpretation of her door-phobia, she was amazed and much excited.

The patient had gone blithely through life until she was rudely checked by the tragic event. Her identification with her friend expressed itself as an alteration of the relation between her ego and superego. She suddenly began to feel severe guilt for things which she had earlier regarded lightly, her suffering and self-accusation accumulated. She defended herself against this sense of guilt by keeping apart in consciousness the guilt and the fear, refusing to perceive their causal relationship. For her, the door was isolated; her desperate self-reproach did not seem to her a reason for suicide. Repression of suicidal thoughts and isolation of the sense of guilt became the defensive mechanism to combat her aggression.

CASE 2

The second case is that of a thirty-four-year-old woman. When first seen, she was a thin, quite obviously excited woman, with rather wide-open eyes, but without the typical signs of hyperthyroidism. According to her statement, she had been ill for five and a half months. Her illness was easy to date because it coincided with her moving into a new apartment. During the moving she had been extremely restless, and became increasingly so in the new home. She became possessed with the thought that the occupancy of the new apartment was illegal, that she had one room more than was allowable under the housing regulations. The knowledge that she had in fact been granted this apartment with all due consideration by the official housing bureau did not serve to allay her fear and uneasiness. She went to the bureau and denounced herself. Even when the official there reassured her, her sense of guilt and anxiety persisted. It was thought that she might be helped by a vacation trip to another city, but actually this journey only increased her anxiety. She stopped worrying over the legality of her apartment but suddenly began to wonder whether she was not to blame for the murder of a young girl whose body had been found in the mountains. The assailant had not been apprehended. She could not free herself of the accusation, "You are the murderess! You killed that young girl!" In despair she would marshal arguments to prove that she could not have committed the crime.

It should be noted that these ideas were not hallucinations or true delusions, but struggles between her ego and superego. "I must defend myself before the judge," she would say, but her proofs of innocence quieted her only for a short time. The anxiety and accusing rumination constantly recurred. Thus she would demolish her own defensive arguments by presenting the idea that she might have murdered while in a twilight state. She kept her obsessions secret, not because she was afraid of being arrested, but because she realized that she might be considered insane. She did not take even her husband into her confidence. She understood then the nature of her anxiety, but she had a frantic need for reasons, for rationalizations that might explain it to herself.

But she could not hide her anxiety indefinitely and she finally sought the aid of a magnetic healer. When this proved unsuccessful, she revealed her secret to her husband and was sent to me for treatment. She stated that her symptoms were not always of the same intensity but bore a striking relation to her menstrual cycle. Her periods were very regular, occurring every twenty-three days (which is "male periodicity" according to Fliess[4]), but the flow was scanty, the blood pale in color and serous, and the duration only one and a half to two days. Although her obsessions were constant, her anxiety began to increase appreciably only ten days to two weeks before the onset of menses, becoming most intense just before bleeding began. After the flow ended, her anxiety was relieved and for a week or so she would be free of anxiety and depression, after which a new series of anxious days would begin.

The patient had been frigid for years, but her conflict concerning sexuality did not resemble the usual frigid woman's; she did not refuse to have intercourse or submit with indifference (she thought or rationalized that this might drive her husband to other women), but she worried during the act as to whether she would have orgasm. She would "try hard" to have orgasm and did not want to have intercourse unless she could. Thus one aspect of her frigidity was her anxiety during the act and her rumination "Will I have orgasm?" accompanied by an introspective attention comparable to the narcissistic interest of a hypochondriac. The other aspect was a fear of becoming pregnant. This latter fear, she admitted, had no rational grounds since her husband was careful and efficient and, in addition, she really loved the one child she had and could well have supported a second. This frigidity and anxiety during coitus had been present for five years before the patient came for treatment, but she had not thought of them as symptoms; only her new symptoms were a source of inquietude. She added that she had always been much interested in murder, had read murder news and attended murder trials, declaring, "They excited me!" But this proud declaration could not be used by the analyst to show the patient what was troubling her since an increase of awareness of her aggression would have heightened her sense of guilt and increased the danger of a suicide.

In the patient's personal history, it was revealed that she came of a lower middle class family in which the father was subject to depression and drank to excess; the mother was suspicious, strict, stubborn, not only with her daughters (of whom the patient was the youngest), but with her husband also. Indeed, she actually punished her husband so that the daughters often pitied him; her severe punishment of her daughters evoked in them an attitude of submissive love and reverence. The patient, overly good, developed an obsessional character; she became orderly, overconscientious in her studies and timid about playing pranks with other children, for which she suffered mentally even when she was not caught. Yet she yielded to her husband before marriage despite the strict parental background. Her first act of intercourse was followed by pain in the urethra, a condition that was treated for years as a cystitis with hundreds of irrigations. After about ten years these pains suddenly disappeared for good; their disappearance coincided with the onset of the anxiety states that five and a half months later brought her under my care.

Nevertheless, the first years of her married life had been happy. Though not easy to gratify sexually, she was not frigid vaginally. In the fifth year of her marriage while she was pregnant, she discovered her husband playing sexually with a young girl of fourteen in the household. Although jealous and indignant, her dominant emotion was a sense of guilt, for she felt that she was responsible for the girl. Not wishing to become embroiled with her husband because of her pregnancy and not wishing to hate him, she consciously fought to control her feelings of hostility. She delivered at term a daughter whom she loved intensely from the beginning and toward whom she felt no conflict and no aggression. She breast-fed the child for seven months. After her child was born, she became frigid and obsessive about orgasm. She lost her appetite, became stubbornly constipated, suffered from headaches, and lost weight. But the symptoms did not immediately suggest a hyperthyroid condition.

When I first saw the patient her intense agitation precluded immediate initiation of analytic therapy. At the same time, I wished her to try endocrine therapy because her acute anxiety states and depression bore a definite relationship to her menstrual cycle. Hence, an interferometric hormone examination, according to Hirsch's method, was carried out by Professor Hirsch himself.[5] The blood was drawn seven days before the onset of the menses at a time when the patient was agitated and anxious. The interferometric examination showed markedly increased lysis of the thyroid and ovaries. The lysis of testes was almost as great as that of the ovaries, and lysis of the pancreas was exceptionally elevated (22.40). Here I point out the endocrinological proof of bisexuality, not an exceptional finding.[6]

I shall now describe the stages of this treatment and the sequence of the mental processes. I first attempted to influence the action of the ovaries. The endocrine therapy (begun November 27, 1930) was also designed to affect the antagonist of the ovaries, the thyroid gland. The patient was given one to two Horpan tablets (anterior lobe plus ovarian hormone) and one Ostranin tablet daily. She reacted immediately; her sexual interest increased and with this her mood became cheerful. At first this mood was by no means constant; symptom-free states alternated rapidly with states of anxious excitement.

Besides the endocrine therapy, the patient was treated by psychotherapy (not formal psychoanalysis). The first important change occurred in the seventh week of treatment when the patient told me that for several days she had been hating her husband intensely. This was the first occasion on which this guilt-ridden woman had been conscious of any feeling of hatred. It was not difficult to explain to her that it was her husband whom she accused of assault and murder because of his misbehavior during her pregnancy.

This resulted in the first good psychotherapeutic effect. The depressive self-accusation was really an accusation of someone else, her faithless husband. This hatred, repressed for years, had originally referred to him, but was then loosed against herself. In fact, the patient had been a devoted and grateful wife who had few difficulties in her everyday life with her husband. But the repressed hatred had shown itself during coitus; her restless, jealous, narcissistic attitude during coitus meant, "He thinks only of his own pleasure; he is a murderer; he is poisoning me; he is giving me a child."

From this recognition of her hostility, we may date the second phase of her treatment. Her depressed agitation altered—coming after instead of before her periods—and her sexual appetite increased. She took greater pleasure in sexual activity and soon found that she no longer feared becoming pregnant during coitus. The latter fear was the first symptom to disappear and did not recur. The increased sexual interest was expressed also in dreams and fantasies. Previously able to think of her guilt only, she was now fantasying about sexual relations with strange men.

The hormone therapy served to increase the ovarian substances and in this way appears to have stimulated her heterosexual libido. Her ego too had been sufficiently fortified to enable her to recognize her hostility toward her husband; this may have diminished her unconscious hatred and sense of guilt.

The next depressive phase, which appeared about her menstrual period (October 2, 1931), was ushered in with the idea that though she was not a murderess, she might be reported as one by the magnetic practitioner who had treated her. Her anxiety was now just as intense and her despair as great as when she was tormented by the idea of having murdered someone while in a twilight state. There was, however, a new structure evident in this idea—the superego was replaced by the former transference object. Whereas previously she had been tormented by her own superego, now her superego was projected outward, the former love-object became an objectified portion of the superego. Here we see a nascent paranoid idea. It is a successor of the depressive idea, after the identification was replaced by an object relationship. This represented a "reparative attempt" in Freud's sense. Whereas in her depression, aggression had been too strong and libidinal tension too weak, now her repressed hostility was released and the fear of heterosexual activity disappeared. The physiologically increased anxiety met with a fortified ego which, more firmly attached to objects, defended itself by an object relationship, that is to say, a projection. The paranoid idea protected her from her own forbidden wishes, so that she could repudiate her love for the practitioner: "I cannot love him for he is persecuting me."

As time went on, the strength of her forbidden heterosexual wishes increased; not only was she afraid of being reported by the magnetist, but she began to fear that she might become involved because of a certain Mr. R., or because of neighbors who might have heard her discuss her illness with her husband. Her positive transference to me kept her from bringing me into these fantasies. The paranoid ideas related only to men.

Except for a brief relapse after having the grippe, the patient continued to improve during the succeeding weeks. She became freer from anxiety and depression. In the fifth month of treatment she became freer of paranoid preoccupations so that she only thought, "The neighbors may have heard something, but I am innocent." However, the delusion of being a murderess and the ideas of persecution recurred from time to time. She would write all the proofs of her innocence on pieces of paper and when she began to accuse herself would read these over. The paranoid system thus became an obsessional one. As time went on and her anxiety diminished, the mere thought of the paper would dispel her worry. She could finally say, "These ideas are merely worries."

Her condition then appeared stable. Feeling that ovarian therapy had done all it could, I administered another antagonist of the thyroid function in the form of small doses of insulin (five to ten units) three times weekly. This inaugurated the third phase of her treatment.

The paranoid ideas faded away, but a trace persisted in the obsession that people, knowing she had so much fear, would say she must have a bad conscience and others hearing this would not realize it was due to her illness. But this notion was not accompanied by any intense anxiety or despair. She was pained by the thought that people might talk, but knew they would not think her a murderess or do her any harm—a markedly less aggressive phenomenon than her previous ideas. She knew furthermore that she was projecting her own conscience onto her neighbors.

Her improvement now became more firmly grounded. Though she was not entirely free of self-reproach, she projected her guilt less and reproached herself for having made herself ill. In this we still see traces of her original delusion, but much attenuated. She said, "I cannot forgive myself for becoming ill," but her illness in its original form was overcome. She was able to read the newspapers, including the court news and the police reports, without anxiety, no longer identifying herself with the murderers. Her superego was in harmony with her previous obsessional character and with the strictness that had forbidden all pampering of herself. Occasionally a vague unrest arose within her and she had to say, "But you have a clear conscience."

An obsessional-neurotic symptom appeared at this stage. The patient dreaded making an error while writing, therefore she had a compulsion to keep every letter or card for several days before mailing in order to reread it several times for possible errors. As we see, the sense of guilt appeared again but was not expressed in the identification of being a murderess; instead the ego-superego realtionship appeared as a doubt. The uncertainty—Is my superego stronger than my ego? Am I a murderess or not?—was no longer projected, and object relationships were untouched by it. It was displaced to an unimportant matter—the writing which might betray her. This symptom lasted only two or three days, then disappeared to recur at intervals for a short while.

It may well be asked why this story of a nonpsychoanalytic therapeutic procedure should be reported in such detail. Its justification lies in the mental changes that took place. Essentially they were similar in both cases. In the first case, where there was a hysterical character, the illness developed more acutely. The depressive idea, formed by identification with a friend who had committed suicide, was immediately relieved through a projection. During the treatment for hyperthyroidism, her anxiety and guilt feelings diminished, and her phobia disappeared.

The second, more complex case consisted of chronically progressive hyperthyroidism in a woman with an obsessional character. The sense of guilt, originally expressed in a minor matter, found expression in the acute worry over the housing situation. But this attempted rationalization was not suited to the intensity of the aggression, corresponding to which there arose the delusion (a) I am a murderess, altered during treatment so that it became in the second phase (b) I am not a murderess; they think I am, a projection which occurred when the libido was increased and the ego structure correspondingly changed. With the diminution of her physiologically determined anxiety, the delusion and the projection waned, so that in the third phase there appeared (c) I am not a murderess, but people might ask why I have a bad conscience, and later (d) I am angry because I have tortured myself with such unnecessary thoughts.

Here her sense of guilt was referred back to her own superego which, now grown less severe, no longer reproached her with murder but with having caused her illness. Hence in rapid succession we may observe in this patient three different mechanisms of defense:

      1. Identification—the depressive idea.
      2. Projection—the paranoid idea.
      3. Displacement—the obsessive doubt.

The changing defense mechanism expressed the varying intensity of ego cathexes necessary to protect the ego against anxiety provoked by the id impulse. The greater the anxiety and the aggression, the weaker was the ego so that it was overwhelmed in the identification; the ego, more libidinally cathected, could defend itself by means of projection, maintaining a better relationship with the environment and objects. Finally, the still more strongly cathected ego fought the conflict with its superego in an obsessional neurosis.

In the beginning of treatment, because her aggressive tendencies had been repressed, anxiety prevented her from talking about anything except superficial events, conscious material. While under insulin therapy, the patient was able to perceive the origin of her aggression and hatred in her early relationship to her mother. She reported the following dream:

> Mother did something bad. They wanted to arrest her and she was frightened and hid. She heard steps and said, "Now they are coming." I noticed that it was the waitress and reas-

sured her saying, "I'll keep them away." Then my mother's
father appeared and I said to him with joy, "I am quite free
from guilt. I always have the best possible conscience. Only
Mother hasn't." Afterward I dreamed I was pregnant; the doctor came and I went through labor and had a boy.

Even the patient recognized in this dream what she had previously not
been able to admit, that she was blaming her mother.[7]

Reconstructing the development of the patient's illness, we find
that she originally felt that her mother hated her; then she repressed
her reactive aggression, "I do not hate Mother, but she hates me; I
love her," and "I must love her although I have reason enough to hate
her." The patient's obsessional character developed on the basis of
this ambivalence conflict.[8]

The prevalent symptom in the clinical picture is determined by
the type of defense mechanism which the ego employs against the destructive forces of the superego. This patient was keenly aware of her
conflict and very precise in her formulations; she would often declare,
"My ego is weak today and cannot protect itself." Freed from the need
to accuse herself of murder, she recognized the unburdening and
strengthening of her ego.

In the most severe stage of her illness, when the aggression was
most intense and directed against her ego, the anxiety attached to the
fear of conception and the narcissistic, anxious self-observation represented aggression directed outward. When heterosexual libido became
available, it was employed to neutralize the aggression and the anxiety.
Therapy fortified the ego in two ways: it diminished the aggression and
anxiety and increased the ego's libidinal cathexis. Therefore, the fate
of the aggression and the outcome of the attempt to overcome anxiety
depends not only on the intensity of the aggression but also on the available libido.

It was found that heterosexual libido, even with the possibility for
normal gratification, did not bind all the anxiety. In the latter part of
the treatment when anxiety recurred, it seemed to represent the inwardly
turned hostility. Whence, then, arose this anxiety?

Freud assumed that anxiety was a direct transformation of libido,
although he later came to believe that anxiety develops in the ego as a
reaction to disturbance in the instinctual life. Yet, ignorant as we are
of what constitutes "libido stasis," some believe that it has a different
endocrine basis in different cases. In our second case, a specific form
of libido stasis was demonstrated more precisely than in the first case.
In these cases an increased thyroid secretion through irritation of the
vegetative nervous system, particularly the sympathetic, produced anxiety and nervous symptoms. In other cases it has been demonstrated

that Graves' disease represents a disorder of several glands, indicating the interdependence of the endocrine system.[9]

In these cases the inhibition of ovarian function so altered the hormonal status as to disturb the bisexual equilibrium and made the male hormonal action more conspicuous, although uncertainty attaches to their seat of origin in the female, and there is reason to doubt whether they are specifically the ones that produce stasis. Psychoanalytically, it is known that certain symptoms are directly due to stasis based on bisexuality and that a certain increase of aggression and anxiety has the same source.

Accustomed to linking maleness with activity and femaleness with passivity, we could assume that an increased production of male hormone would result in an increase of aggression. However, it is conceivable that this would be true only if in addition to the bisexuality there is, for any cause, a defusion of instincts.

A third case may be of interest. A young woman had been in analysis for a long period of time because of an obsession that she might strangle a man, any man, possibly the one who might have become her future husband. As a result of treatment, she married and had a child but remained frigid during intercourse. After the birth of the child she went through a severe organic illness and, as a result of her physical exhaustion, her mental illness recurred in a severe form. She developed hostile impulses against her husband and child, reacted with marked anxiety, feared her own ability to cope with her impulses, and was stricken with a strong sense of guilt. As in the previous cases, the Hirsch test was performed and showed a greater lytic value for testes than for ovaries. Therapy was based on an attempt to improve the ovarian function.

During the treatment much psychoanalytically interesting material came to light. With the increase in libido there was no relief; instead, the aggressive tendencies were intensified. Observation revealed that the patient became anxious whenever the libidinal pressure was frustrated or disturbed by aggressive impulses. The impression was that an increase in the quantity of tension immediately brought about a defusion of instincts and that the liberated aggression was transformed into aggressive impulses and anxiety.

The question whether anxiety or aggression is primary arises. Both seemed to appear at the same time. Consistent with Freud's theory that anxiety is a danger signal informing the ego of increasing instinctual tension, of threatening disequilibrium, it might be assumed that anxiety is primary. It we assume that due to disequilibrium in the endocrine system and/or the irritability of the autonomic nervous system, a defusion of instincts occurs with the liberation of aggression and the consequent danger signal, anxiety, then aggression might be primary. It seems that it depends on the developmental organization of the personality whether anxiety or aggression will be the dominant factor in the formation of a particular symptom.

In view of the small doses of endocrine preparation that brought about psychological reactions, it might well be asked whether there are correlations between the course of the disease process and the particular hormones. In the *New Introductory Lectures on Psychoanalysis,* Freud expresses the hope that our advancing knowledge of endocrine action will furnish us with the means of dealing with the quantitative factors in disease.[10] The cases here reported may exemplify this statement. Mindful of Freud's feeling that endocrinology, our biological neighbor, will someday overtake us, we may say from our observations that our good relations with this neighbor are just beginning; but it will be the psychoanalytically schooled observer, capable of distinguishing the fine points of mental life, who will be best equipped to observe the effect of hormonal action.

SUMMARY

The psychoanalytic study of two cases of hyperthyroid psychosis demonstrates that somatically motivated anxiety appears as a symptom involving the destructive instinct. In these cases it is impossible to say whether anxiety or aggression is the primary state, since they appear together. An increase in heterosexual libido in both cases bound the aggression and anxiety so that libido appeared as an antagonist of the aggression. It seems to be a new point that the anxiety and aggression produced by thyrotoxicosis are elaborated by the psychic apparatus to increase the severity of the superego and give rise to a clinical picture of depression.

NOTES

1. Benedek, T., "Mental Processes in Thyrotoxic States," *Psychoanalytic Quart.,* III (1934), 153–172. Translated by William J. Spring (originally written in German in Leipzig). Presented before the German Psycho-Analytic Society, November 26, 1932. Revised for this volume.

2. Parhon, C., "Uber das Vorkommen von Verworrener Manie bei einer Kranken von Schilddrusenhypertrophie," *Wien med. Wchnschr.,* Bd., LXV (1925), 18.

3. Ewald, G., "Psychosen bei Endokrinen und Stoffwechselerkrankungen," *Bumke's Handb. d. Geisteskrankhesten,* Bd. VII sprz. Teil 3 (Berlin, Springer, 1930).

4. Fliess, W., *Zur Perioden-Lehre* (Jena, E. Diederichs, 1925).

5. Translator's note: The Hirsch reaction is a modification of the Abderhalden reaction. The serum is tested for the presence of proteolytic antibodies against grandular substances by being exposed to small quantities

of dried gland. The products of proteolysis alter the retractive index of the serum. This change is measured quantitatively with an interferometer against a standard consisting of the same serum not exposed to dried gland. See Paul Hirsch, *Klin. Wchschr.,* IV (1925), 1365–1412.

6. In the discussion of this paper at the meeting of the German Psycho-Analytic Society it was said that my arguments seemed to be based solely on the Hirsch test and were consequently insecure since the validity of this method in determining the products of hormonal lysis is still debatable; some investigators, among them Hermann and Witzleben, contend that the method is scientifically interesting but diagnostically useless, though others, after careful study, believe that their technique will reveal findings characteristic of the individual phases of the disease process. (See notes 11–13.)

W. Patterson conceives of bisexuality as a "two force system," male-female. He based his therapeutic experiments on this concept, and used Hirsch's method to furnish endocrinological proof of bisexuality. The lysis of male and female hormones seems to substantiate the existence of bisex-uality. Only a disturbance in the relative proportion between these two is to be regarded as pathological. Psychoanalysis has always recognized that bisexuality in general is a motive for the formation of symptoms. (See note 14.)

7. In his essay on the sexuality of women (*Psychoanalytic Quart.,* I, 191) Freud writes, ". . . this early dependence on the mother has in it the germ from which a woman may later develop paranoia. This germ referred to is apparently the surprising but typical fear of being killed, devoured by the mother."

8. Author's note, 1970: Since aggression was not analyzed in the transference, analysts today might wonder, what caused the patient's hostility and guilt to diminish? In this psychotherapeutic process, the analyst was the good mother, and the patient's ability to relate to her as "good mother" enabled her to feel accepted and acceptable; she formed the introject, good mother = good self. I assume that this accounts for the thera-peutic result. The permanent effect of the therapy depends on the effective-ness of the introject and on the realities of her life situation which may expose her to experiences which would upset her emotional balance.

9. The physiological antagonism between thyroid and ovaries is mani-fested in cases of hyperthyroidism, either as sexual inhibition and frigidity, sexual excitability, or dysmenorrhea.

10. Freud, S., *New Introductory Lectures on Psychoanalysis* (New York, Norton, 1933).

11. Hermann, F., and Witzleben, H. D. von, "Zum diagnostischen Wert der interferometrie in der Psychiatrie," *Klin. Wchschr.,* Bd. VII (1928), 494.

12. Zimmer, A., Lendel, L., and Perlow, W., "Zur Kritick der inter-ferometrischen Methode der Abderhaldenschen Reaktion II: Untersuchung bei der Basedowschen Krankheit," *Fermentfschg.,* Bd. XI (1930), 557.

13. Petterson, W., "Endokrine Behandlung mit andersgeschlechtlicher Keimdrusensubstanz," *Arch. f. Frauenkunde u. Konstitutionsfschg.,* Bd. XVIII (1932), 184.

14. Petterson, W., "Feminismus und Geist," *Arch. f. Frauenkunde u. Konstitutionsfschg.,* Bd. XVII (1931–1932), 222.

DISCUSSION

If I had been treating the patients in later years, my report of the clinical investigation would, of course, be very different. I would not have been so blatant in presenting those endocrinological tests and my therapeutic experimentation; I would have been more aware of my older, more experienced colleagues in Berlin who probably followed Freud's advice to use none but psychoanalytic methods for the investigation of a psychoanalytic problem. I recall that after the discussion of this paper at the German Psychoanalytic Society, Eitingon said to me in a kind of congratulatory tone, "You are a very courageous woman." At that time I thought he was referring to the potential danger of suicide in these cases. Studying the paper recently, I assume that he may have considered me courageous because I interpreted the dynamic of the pathology in terms of Freud's second instinct theory. Use of the death instinct to explain a clinical condition was then not common among psychoanalysts. He could have warned me against my tendency to form hypotheses since, in this paper, I dealt with bisexuality as if it were a laboratory finding. Even if those tests had been valid, they would hardly permit such far-reaching conclusions. However, neither he nor the others discouraged me.

Reviewing the two therapeutic agents—psychotherapy and hormones—one should raise the question, Which was the main factor in the therapeutic process and which was the adjuvant? Although I considered even those small doses of hormone (they were natural, not synthetic hormones) effective in changing the hormonal balance, now I would assume that they were adjuvants. Whether they were effective pharmacologically or not, they were certainly adjuvants in the psychotherapeutic process.

In Leipzig at that time, psychoanalysis was not commonly known. These patients were housewives, not well-educated but intelligent in a practical sense. In their acute anxiety and in the torment of obsessional doubt, they could hardly have accepted psychotherapy, especially since it did not promise a certain or quick therapeutic result. Getting a medicine was a reassurance; it increased their confidence in the therapist. Their satisfaction in understanding themselves, understanding their anxiety and doubts as a result of a sequence of events, gave them the reassurance that instead of becoming "crazy," they were becoming more discerning individuals. This is commonplace knowledge, yet it is worth emphasizing since nobody is free from a therapeutic bias. Favoring one's own therapeutic method, it is easy to neglect those adjuvant factors which support the therapeutic process by increasing the patient's confidence in himself and in the therapist.

This material was not published for the sake of illustrating the therapeutic process, but primarily to discuss specific psychodynamic processes referable to the imbalance of the thyroid function. But the two cases are not quite comparable. The first was an acute emergency reaction connected with marked symptoms of Graves' disease in a personality which had a hysterical character structure. The other patient had a compulsive-obsessional neurosis; her anxiety was chronic and was motivated (rationalized) by guilt. Since it was not typical of Graves' disease, that aspect of the diagnosis probably was not correct. Yet the two cases illustrate the thesis that chronic conflict tension may create imbalance in the endocrine system and produce thyrotoxicosis. The acute, phobic defense is characteristic of hysterical individuals. Guilt-laden, paranoid defense is characteristic of the compulsion-neurotic personality. This indicates that the structure of the personality may play a role in the course and control of the endocrine balance.

After World War II when Alexander and his coworkers conducted psychoanalytic investigations in several thyrotoxic cases, they found that a fear of death is the typical psychologic stress precipitating thyrotoxicosis.[1] In the cases studied, the infantile conflict and the spiral of the defenses against conflict were established and formulated. Lidz in his various studies has shown that the stress of combat or other stresses made this illness frequent during and after the war. Hyperthyroidism appears to be a condition which resists categories. Lidz mentions that "the disease was considered a neurosis by many before Mobius focused attention on the secretory overactivity of the thyroid gland."[2] This implies that from then on thyrotoxicosis was considered an organic illness. Lidz also states that hyperthyroidism ". . . is not a matter of a single cause but rather of multiple factors upsetting the ability of the organism to maintain or regain equilibrium."[3]

In the large-scale investigation which by now is known as "psychosomatic specificity," thyrotoxicosis was one of the seven diseases studied by Alexander and his coworkers. In his historical introduction of the research, George Pollock characterizes thyrotoxicosis as follows:

> The central dynamic issue in thyrotoxicosis is a constant struggle against fear concerning the physical integrity of the body and, more specifically, fear of biological death. Even more characteristic is the attempt to master fear by denying it and counterphobically seeking dangerous situations and coping with them alone.[4]

Indeed, the first case fits verbatim the definition of thyrotoxicosis; the second shows the compulsive coping alone with provoking environmental situations which aggravate the chronic stress of the emotional condition.

Even more interesting is the mutual confirmation afforded by the two sets of investigation, far apart in time and in methodology. Alexander's basic hypothesis was that each psychodynamic illness investigated in this group corresponds to a psychodynamic constellation which originates in an instinctual conflict, characteristically significant in that individual's development. One of the illnesses does not fit such a psychodynamic constellation. The instinctual conflict which motivates thyrotoxicosis originates in the urgency of survival in the face of the fear of death. The thyroid gland is a significant regulator of the concert of endocrine glands.

Before the "crystallized fright" of acute thyrotoxicosis develops, there is the chronic, continuous influence of a signal anxiety which, by forming defense reactions, predisposes the personality to anxiety reactions since the defenses may exhaust the libido reservoir. This is observable in the first woman, who was the youngest of ten children, probably pampered in some sense yet she thought she was superfluous, and unwanted, and was therefore burdened by conflicts. When she became a mother, her children became an unbearable burden. She talked about them as if they were "things." Their closeness reminded her that she had to worry about them, fearing that they might die. The vicious circle between her concern for the children and her guilt because her anxiety motivated death wishes against them finally mounted to panic, to fear that only suicide would free her from anxiety. At the time this patient was in treatment, analysts did not conclude, only on the basis of the patient's history, that the process originated with the patient's identification with and fear of her mother, who, with her threats of suicide, implanted the fear of suicide in the girl.

In talking about the dynamics of mounting anxiety, we tend to overlook the lifelong reactions to anxiety, the interactions, not only between psychic conflict and psychic defense, but also between psychic defense and somatic interactions. Signal anxiety itself may account for incipient states of hormonal imbalance; the continual excitation of fluctuating emotional tensions has to be balanced by the chain of endocrine processes which provoke hyperfunction of the thyroid gland and thus might lead to the psychosomatic condition of thyrotoxicosis.

Much more could be said about the step-by-step development of the anxiety state in the second case, since we know that she was an overly conscientious, good child, worrying about her mother, whom she feared and hated with the repressed intensity of primary ambivalence. The mother who is feared and hated is also needed and therefore loved even more. Indeed, the wish to get and have more than her share and the resultant guilt was the first symptom that indicated that her compulsively defended emotional balance could not be maintained. The chronic, compulsive, neurotic defenses created such an intrapsychic stress that the energy necessary to maintain the defenses exhausted the integrative capacity of the ego and defusion occurred. The feedback circle between aggression-anxiety-defense "devoured her ego," as the patient expressed it. She could have ended in a psychotic depression or in suicide. In any case, the thyroid gland seems to be secondary in the process of her illness.

In discussing the disease processes in these two cases, the dynamics of one would fit the diagnosis of anxiety hysteria; the other would have the diagnostic label acute anxiety in a compulsive, neurotic personality with paranoid defenses. In this respect, is there a difference between "stress" and "intrapsychic tension" caused by the conflict? The only difference is that the terms belong to two different disciplines—stress to physiology, conflict and its cathexis to psychoanalysis. The term "stress" implies its origin in environmental factors which mobilize organic defenses which in turn motivate psychologic reactions. Psychoanalysis traces the inception of stress to a signal anxiety which originates in the primary needs and conflicts of infancy. These considerations show the close affinity between psychoanalytic theory and the concepts of modern physiology. In psychosomatic medicine the two disciplines meet as Freud once hopefully imagined.

NOTES

1. Ham, C. G., Alexander, F., Carmichael, H. T., "A Psychosomatic Theory of Thyrotoxicosis," *Psychosomatic Med.,* XIII (1951), 18–35.
2. Lidz, T., "Emotional Factors in the Etiology of Hyperthyroidism," *Psychosomatic Med.,* XI (1949), 2.
3. Ibid., p. 7.
4. Pollock, G. H., "History," in *Psychosomatic Specificity,* vol. I, Alexander, F., French, T. M., and Pollock, G. H., eds. (Chicago, University of Chicago Press, 1968), p. 15.

3. Dominant Ideas and Their Relation to Morbid Cravings

INTRODUCTION

Studying these early papers was an interesting experience. Rereading them, I was reminded of the warning I often give to my younger colleagues. They frequently try too hard to explain everything from many points of view and consequently they submerge their own propositions in extraneous arguments. I realized how true this was for me. But on the second or third reading, I was pleasantly surprised that I had intuitively introduced a viewpoint that was not a part of psychoanalytic theory at that time. What may appear superfluous or repetitious to a reader today may have been a new theory then and may now throw light upon accepted propositions from an historical perspective.

Indeed, I did not think of theory or even of diagnosis when I saw an emaciated, alcoholic girl who spoke with feverish brightness and gave the impression that she could be helped, wanted to be helped. Her alcoholism was the first focus of the therapy. That alcoholism is a disguise for depression was known and was assumed in this case. I actually never saw her drunk. This might have been a short-lived effect of her positive transference which could be paraphrased as her attempt to be a "good child to a new, good mother." This effort may have activated the outbreak of her ambivalent transference which caused her acting-out and made the therapy impossible. Her behavior, however, called my attention to a psychiatric concept formulated by Wernicke as *die Überwertige Idee,* meaning the dominant idea.[1]

The analysis of this symptom, its multiple motivations, its structure, and its function in the psychic economy of addiction, which in alcoholism alternates with bulimia and starvation, is discussed in the following paper. According to the developmental history of the two patients described, one could easily have assumed that both of them starved themselves as a defense against oedipal tendencies; but this

71

concept appears meek considering the defense mobilized against it, i.e., destroying one's own femaleness and one's body by refusing foods = mother. To inflict such chronic suffering upon oneself, the aggression has to fight the primary instinct, the need for nutrition. In these cases the dominant idea, "I don't want to have a woman's body," was the motor that supplied the aggressive energy to maintain the pathologic process.

In the early 1930s, psychoanalysts were interested in applying the structural concept to character trends and symptom formation beyond the psychic apparatus as a whole. Franz Alexander in his study (1933) described structure formation in specific manifestations such as the sense of inferiority, exhibitionism, and others.[2] In my investigation, I described the relation of structural and instinctual conflicts as a changing process, motivating the symptoms of a chronic psychosomatic disease. The dominant idea in interaction with conflicting normal and pathological instinctual needs led me to the formulation that instinctual conflicts present themselves within the structures that they have had a part in forming. This, however, can be true only if there is continuous feedback between instinctual conflicts and structural conflicts, between instincts and structure. From psychic event to psychic event, day after day, year after year, new instinctual conflicts occur and are in transaction with available structures. As they fall back on structures created previously, they develop a new structure or reinforce an earlier one that will serve tomorrow. This is a recent conceptualization of those processes which were described in this paper about forty years ago.

How far away from the original instinctual conflicts do the psychopathologic processes lead in the cases discussed here? In what dimension could we measure such a distance? One of the thyrotoxic cases broke down relatively suddenly after a latent stress condition which probably began when her first child was born. The other patient had the chronic stress of her guilt-laden, compulsive, neurotic personality which maintained an oscillating control during her thyrotoxic state. It seems as if the distance could be measured by years. In these cases the nature of the defense did not change. It is different in cases of a dominant idea. This is a defense structure which seems to take hold of the psychic apparatus suddenly and will not let go. This condition usually begins in adolescence when sexuality appears to be a grave threat. Then there is a period when the ego struggles against the "unacceptable defense," but after a time, or because of an additional trauma, the ego submits to the self-destruction and the anorexia nervosa follows.

Anorexia nervosa has puzzled observers since antiquity.[3] Its symptomatology has been unmistakably described. Whether termed "nervous consumption" or "anorexia hysterica," the behavioral manifestations of the condition indicate that it was recognized. More attention was given to the illness after World War I when Simmonds' disease was discovered and it was necessary to differentiate between the two illnesses, between the primary hypophyseal insufficiency and the psychosomatic condition.

The following study originally aimed at describing the structure and function of a dominant idea; that it is a contribution to the psychopathology of anorexia nervosa is a secondary gain.

NOTES

1. Wernicke, C., "Über Fixe Ideen," *Deutsche medizinische Wochenschrift* (1892).
2. Alexander, F., "The Relation of Structural and Instinctual Conflicts, *Psychoanalytic Quart.*, III (1933), 181–207.
3. For a brief medical history of anorexia nervosa see: Bliss, E. L., and Branch, C. H. H., *Anorexia Nervosa, Its History, Psychology and Biology* (New York, Paul B. Hoeber, Inc., 1960), pp. 1–22.

DOMINANT IDEAS AND THEIR RELATION TO MORBID CRAVINGS[1] (1934)

In a recent paper Rado has presented a schematic basis for the process of morbid cravings.[2] He has given us such a broad foundation of clinical experience and analytical knowledge that we may now assume that we have grasped the laws governing their course. His investigations begin at the point when unaided psychical means no longer suffice to master the preliminary depression and the patient takes recourse to medicinal remedies. However, we have still to inquire whether the preliminary depression presents a uniform clinical picture; if not, what is the nature of the processes that furnish a compelling motive for the "pharmacothymic discharge" of the tension produced by conflict?

The problem pertaining to the libidinal structure has been clarified to a great extent. Since the earliest relevant work of Abraham[3] and Rado,[4] a large number of analysts have brought forward substantial confirmation that an oral fixation and the associated disposition to states of depression provide the libidinal conditions for morbid cravings. Nevertheless, questions arose as to the nature of such cravings, or more correctly, as to the specific morbid process by which the oral fixation leads to addiction. On this point there is as yet no unanimity. Simmel[5] is of the opinion that addiction represents an obsessional-neurotic mechanism of defense; Glover[6] raises the question whether there are cases of addiction which develop from a deep regression, in the sense of a paranoia which is succeeded by a second phase of illness—the restoration of relations with the environment in which the addiction functions as a quasi-curative process.

In this connection, the following case is especially instructive. The structure of the depression leading to the addiction is convincingly revealed as a primary pathological condition. It was possible to obtain an unusually clear view of the addiction as a secondary illness, a defense against the initial depression.

CASE I

An unmarried woman of twenty-six, emaciated to the bone, was brought to me because she was addicted to alcohol. Anamnesis showed that she suffered from a very complicated form of addiction which had been expressed in various ways at different periods of her life. When she entered treatment she was taking every kind of alcoholic drink, mild and strong, to intoxicate herself. Since it was not always easy to get alcohol, she took recourse to Hoffmann's drops—a mixture of ether and alcohol—by which means she was able to become intoxicated quickly and cheaply. Besides alcohol and ether, the patient took vast quantities of aperients, thyroid preparations, and various salts, as well as homeopathic preparations. Narcotics excepted, one might say she took everything. She was afraid of narcotics.

During periods in which she felt better, she was able to renounce alcohol; the addiction itself was then succeeded by an obsessional-neurotic system. She associated herself with a dietary movement and lived on uncooked foods, or became a vegetarian, and for a time took her nourishment in accordance with these systems, exerting every ounce of strength in her personality until she once more lost control and the craving broke through afresh.[7] The driving force behind this complicated addiction was the idea, which for the patient was conscious, that *she did not want to have a woman's body*. This idea suddenly emerged with overwhelming force when the patient was fifteen and a half years old.

The patient came from a well-to-do, lower middle class family. Her father was a man of athletic build and robust appearance for whom eating and drinking were very important, though he never became an "addict." He had died some years before from a neurological illness, probably of postluetic origin. Her mother was a frail woman, lovable and indulgent, efficient, modest, and unassuming, though able to meet the claims made on her by her husband and daughter.

The patient was an only child, born by means of forceps after a normal pregnancy. According to the mother, the child took the breast well and was breast-fed for nine months. The mother could not remember that weaning and changing to solid food caused any difficulty. As a child, the patient had eaten well and, like her father, ate a great deal of meat. Until she reached her fifteenth year, she was a healthy, talented child, rather frightened and shy with her father, but lively and clever at school. She was stout and was often teased on that account. She was greatly upset when a male teacher teased her in front of the whole class in a manner which was far too friendly to be misunderstood, taking hold of her and fondling her. Both the patient and her mother brought forward this incident as the reason for the hate which she began to feel for her body and for her desire to become thin at all costs.

It is not unusual for an adolescent girl to wish to be slender, but in this case the slimming cure was carried out with such relentless destructive rage that we may justifiably suppose it covered a mental process of serious import.

Some years later the patient suddenly managed to give up eating almost completely and in a few months she lost sixty pounds. From then on she was ill-tempered, defiant, impatient, and insatiable in her demands. The alteration in her behavior went so far that she destroyed and burned food, even throwing it into the toilet and occasionally, in an excess of rage, she tore her clothing and linen, or burned it in the stove. Her whole existence was one long struggle against getting fat and this became harder as her pleasure in eating went beyond normal limits to a veritable gluttony. At first she was able to work and from time to time, when something provided the necessary spur, she would make up her mind to take some nourishing food. But when she ate, she thought that her figure altered and increased in size and that her breasts got larger; then she could not keep her good intentions. She would have liked to destroy her body and tear off her breasts; she raged against herself in the full sense of the word. This struggle had been going on for years, interrupted only by intervals passed in various sanatoria, before she took recourse to alcohol.

Her condition was essentially a struggle against polyphagia. If it were ever legitimate to speak of intoxication with reference to food, then it certainly would be in this case. I had opportunity to observe the different modes and forms assumed by her attacks of polyphagia. When the patient had taken alcohol, all her inhibitions vanished and she ate enormous quantities without restraint. She consumed the most impossible things, the most highly seasoned foods, without making her stomach rebel. One had the impression that she stupefied herself with alcohol in order to be able to permit this release of impulse. But this was only a rationalization of her craving for alcohol, because after a period of abstinence she could consume very large quantities of food without having to intoxicate herself. Instead of the "alimentary orgasm," remorse invariably appeared.[8] The fact that she had eaten made her profoundly unhappy; she would have liked to destroy her body and get the food out and away from her again. Remarkably enough, she never tried to force regurgitation. The oral way was always reserved for pleasure; she was content to take aperients in huge quantities and if her remorse was too great to be borne, she became intoxicated.

Her craving for alcohol reached the point where it presented all the features of a severe addiction. The patient could not walk along the street without stopping at every tavern; she procured alcohol however she could, either on credit or by borrowing or stealing money from her mother. Other drug substances were of secondary importance and could be classified as (1) substances used for thinning purposes—thyroid preparations, aperients; (2) substances designed to alleviate hunger—food substitutes or those which reduce appetite; and (3) various food substances conforming to the prescriptions of certain dietetic schools. This would enable her to live in accordance with her ego ideal.[9]

The following material is from the analytical anamnesis. The patient was a much spoiled, only child who had experienced bitter disappointment with her father. In her earliest years, her father could not do enough to spoil her. He courted her, fed her, played with her, and bought her new toys every day, especially dolls of every sort and design, wearing an endless variety of clothes. Then her father's behavior underwent a sudden change. He became churlish and mean to her and would not buy her even the barest necessities. He now hated her and ordered her to work. He required her to fetch chicken food from restaurants and carry it through the streets in pails. As in the fairy tale, he had turned a princess into a servant girl. It sounds as if this were a "screen memory"—a fantasy of the patient—but this was not the case. The alteration in the father's character had started years before his meta-syphilitic illness was diagnosed. His disease shook the patient to the depths of her being.

The patient became awkward and timid with her father and now hated him. She loathed his love of eating and his coarse muscular figure. Later she came to hate most in herself those things which resembled her father. Her conscious ego ideal was the antithesis of her father and all her energy was directed to the destruction of this resemblance. She tried to bring the conflict to an end by finding a new way of life, not enslaved by the claims of materialism and the passions.

At puberty, the patient experienced a profound shock, occasioned by the sensual advances and caresses of her teacher, a father substitute. She reacted to this incident with deep regression and repudiated the feminine role. But this repudiation was not confined to the repression of vaginal sexuality with which we are familiar in cases of hysteria. The regression proceeded further and comprised the whole body. She rejected the *female body in its entirety,* together with all its visibly feminine attributes, on the ground that *all this served the man as a sexual object.* That was her rationalization, but the driving force behind this urge to annihilate her femininity was the need to ward off not only sexual impulses toward her father but also the repressed ambivalence toward her mother.

It is characteristic of the course taken by the morbid process that the patient, who as an adult suffered many other disappointments at the hands of men, continued to seek refuge with men and was filled with a pathological mistrust and hatred toward women. In spite of all her real experiences of disappointment with men, it was clear from the very beginning of the treatment that her hatred of women was deeper and more relentless than her ambivalent relations with men. It was, in fact, psychotic. This paranoid hatred of women which inspired her rage against her own body was also revealed in the transference, with a psychotic freedom of expression.

Her hatred of her mother was expressed in various direct and indirect destructive tendencies and even in crude forms of abuse and acts of violence. At the beginning of the treatment, she made an attempt to play off the two mothers, one against the other, and to injure both of them. This was most clearly revealed when the transference was functioning with ambivalence at its height. At that time she had the following dream:

> There is a quite small baby on my arm. Usually I hate babies, but I pressed this child to me. The child belonged to you. I wanted to fondle the child and was "nasty" with it, i.e., I kissed the child as one doesn't kiss children, eagerly and erotically, licking and devouring it.

It soon became clear to her that it was not a child but the breast which she embraced and kissed and would have liked to devour.

Following this dream, she became very excited in spite of the insight which appeared to have been gained, or perhaps because of it. She had the need to express, even demonstrate, her urge to destroy mother = breast = food. That afternoon she ordered a large meal. When the food she requested had been collected, it was noticed that she had already "stolen" and consumed quantities of dairy products. I went to see her. The trays were lying empty outside her door. It was impossible for her to have eaten such quantities in that time. She had asked for and taken the food, not that she might eat it, but to hide and destroy it, as she admitted in tones of scorn and triumph over me.

This acting out in the transference had the significance of oral aggression aimed at her mother's breast and was lived out with the full ambivalence appropriate to the oral stage. The gratification of the wish to incorporate the desired object would have furthered her femininity; it would make her identification with the hated mother manifest. In the symbolic action of destroying the food, she destroyed not only her mother and her mother's breast, but also her own feminine body and breasts, mortifying herself by refusing food. We see here unfolding in the transference the same process of discharging aggressive impulses that she constantly repeated from the beginning of her illness.

The suffering caused by her conflict was immeasurable. Eating was indispensable and was pathologically intensified in the attacks of polyphagia. The remorse liberated by the eruption of impulse always lent fresh strength to her tendency to self-destruction.

The genetic process of this condition can be outlined as follows. The indulgence of the father and the little girl's love for him may have stimulated a premature development of her oedipal phase. The developing pathology of the father, his turning against the child, must have been even more traumatic because of her idealization of him. The disappointed child withdrew from him and began consciously to hate him. At the same time she maintained a normally dependent relationship to her mother that covered the deep-seated, ambivalent conflict which came to the surface during adolescence when the teasingly humiliating approach of the male teacher repeated her experience with her father and hurt her deeply. Humiliated in her self-concept as a woman and now disappointed by men in general, she made her choice—she did not want to be a woman. (It may be surprising that I refer to a choice in describing the outcome of a regression, the dynamics of unconscious conflict. However, this appears to be appropriate because of the ego's involvement in the course of her illness.) Since eating made her plump and attractive as the teacher had demonstrated, not eating was her way of not becoming a woman. The instinctual need for food and the denial of that need, just as it represented her sexual conflict on the oral level, protected her against men, against her sexuality. The alternation between hunger strike and polyphagia released again and again her destructive tendency; yet by revealing her weakness it did not activate her anxiety.

The spiral of the instinctual conflicts was (1) oral (need for food and the denial of that need), (2) narcissistic (repression of her feminine narcissism turned the aggression toward herself), and by this activated (3) the primary ambivalence toward mother = food (to devour or be devoured). The dynamics of the instinctual conflicts explain the several aspects of her frustration and the intensification of aggression, but they do not explain why her aggression did not cause manifest anxiety. This turns our attention to the ego's role in the disease process that should be elucidated after we examine Case II, whose dominant idea did not lead to addiction, at least not during the period of my observation.[10] The personality structure of the patients and the disease process in each showed extensive similarities.

CASE II

The second patient was a girl of twenty-one years, slender and boyish in physique and like her father. She was the younger of two sisters. The elder sister and her mother, unlike the patient, were pyknic in type. The patient, so far as she could remember, had always stood in conscious opposition to her mother, who preferred her first child, "her daughter." This girl had been easy to bring up, lovable, and extravert; whereas our patient was timid and inhibited in her school work, felt herself unequal to competition with her talented sister, and so became increasingly introverted. It was of no avail that she was regarded as "her father's daughter" and was spoiled by him, because at the same time the father stood by her mother and often punished the wayward, inhibited girl. As was revealed in the analysis, the embittered child had suffered markedly from depression between the ages of eleven and twelve, and was perhaps in actual danger of suicide. Until her fifteenth year there was nothing significant to be noted regarding her eating habits. After puberty she began to avoid meat; later she reached a point when she avoided all cooked foods and still later this extended to all nourishment that was really nutritious, so that she mechanically ate only apples and tomatoes. To be sure, she ate them by the pound in order to escape feelings of hunger and to be certain that she did not get fat. At times when her impulses broke through, as they did eventually, she consumed large quantities of biscuits, only to want to tear herself to pieces from remorse afterwards and to storm in rage at her mother and sister for enticing her into taking food and becoming fat.

Very striking was her attitude of paranoid mistrust toward her mother and sister. Whereas other paranoiacs have fears of being poisoned or given bad food, our patient was in perpetual fear that her mother or sister might succeed in tempting her to eat. In her eyes, all food which might have caused her to put on an ounce was the same as poison and her reaction of avoidance was correspondingly strong. But she herself persecuted her mother and sister with the very thing which she feared at their hands; she controlled their eating and tried to prevail upon them to do all those things which she so strictly avoided for herself. She chose gymnastics as a vocation, went in for sports a great deal, and walked long distances so as to be sure of losing weight. In the same way, she kept watch over her mother and sister to see that they were always driven in a car. The aggression expressed in this behavior is evident. The patient was dominated by the idea that she must not eat in order not to have the body of a woman, *not to become like her mother,* whom she hated and killed in her own body.[11]

In this case the prohibition against food is derived from the idea

"I do not want to have the body of a woman." This idea is the result
of an instinctual conflict arising from oral anxiety and oral hatred toward the mother and, by way of identification, rages against her own
body, evoking a paranoid illness with a reversal of aggression against
the self.

In both these cases we see that the primary pathogenic process—
repression followed by regression—leads to repudiation by the subject
of her female body. This repudiation is kept in force by means of an
imperative which manifests itself in the system Pcs = cs and runs:
"You are not to eat and have the body of a woman." Our interest is
aroused by the question where the idea finds its intrinsic energy and
what means it employs to dominate the personality and bring about its
ruin with such merciless and unyielding persistence.

If we regard this idea as a symptom, it will strike us that from the
very first it was felt as an essential part of the ego. In the transference
neurosis, there is a struggle between the ego and the symptom. This
struggle is enacted on more than one stage and employs manifold resources. In the course of time the symptom often is incorporated by
the ego.[12] But the symptom described here shows that "time and heavy
labor" were not required to effect this; it appeared from the very first
moment as an irremovable part of the ego. This is a peculiarity of symptoms which are released by psychotic processes. Whereas fantasies,
compulsive ideas, and neurotic symptoms remain outside the ego, the
ego playing the part almost of a spectator in relation to them or else
struggling against them, every *delusion* occupies a central position in the
structure of the ego. If an idea or presentation acquires the quality of
reality, the ego alteration which then takes place exerts a decisive influence on every subsequent testing of reality.

How is an ego alteration of this kind achieved?* Freud's investigations into the psychoses led him to assume that at the beginning of every
psychotic disorder "the world comes to an end," meaning that a deep
regression takes place and a withdrawal of all object cathexes occurs.[14]
When the world comes to an end, the individual is at the moment of the
psychotic experience—for however brief a moment—*wholly id*. This
psychotic regression is, as Freud assumes to be the case with every
psychotic regression, accompanied by a defusion of instincts so that
aggression is set free.

* Author's note, 1969: What I refer to as an ego alteration can be considered
one form of "ego distortion" described by Gitelson[13] and by others as
characteristic of borderline cases. Since any conflict might bring about
adaptive or maladaptive consequences in the ego, each ego distortion has to
be analyzed as to the dynamic of the symptom that causes the distortion and
its function in the future course of the disease process. The ego distortion
caused by the encapsulated psychotic core of the dominant idea was elucidated from these aspects in this paper.

After regression has reached its deepest point, the process of recovery sets in. It is this attempt at cure that we see unfolded in the clinical picture of psychosis. But this process of recovery does not constitute merely a fresh attempt to invest libido into objects (the aspect on which observers have so far laid most emphasis), but comes about by means of a fresh investment of the aggression which has been liberated. Accordingly, the symptom represents a fresh instinctual fusion; its structure will not depend simply on the fate and amount of *libido* involved, but also on the fate of the primary instinctual *aggression* set free by the regressive process. It can be bound and warded off in various ways. Closer examination of these methods will provide us with an opportunity to discover finer shades of difference in the structure of the psychoses.

In these particular cases, the aggression was bound by the formation of a symptom which brought about an alteration in the ego. The aggression liberated by the regressive process accrues to the system Pcs = cs where it cathects the representation of the instinctual conflict, i.e., the idea of not wanting to have the body of a woman. So cathected, the idea becomes an essential constituent part of the ego. I prefer not to say the superego, because the criterion of the superego, according to "The Ego and the Id,"[15] is that it belongs to the system Ucs. This idea, which we have depicted as a circumscribed but irremovable part of the ego, is always conscious and hence belongs topographically to the ego. But inherent in it is a *severity appropriate to the superego*. The ego is delivered over to the idea; if the ego throws off its yoke, anxiety and remorse arise. The tension of conscience, the punishment inflicted on the ego, is as great as that which we know generally to characterize superego conflicts. Accordingly, *the dynamic and economic function of this idea corresponds to the function of the superego; topographically, however, it belongs to the ego*.

I call to mind an old psychiatric concept which has received no attention from psychoanalysis—that of a *dominant idea*. It originated with Wernicke, who was unable to define clearly the boundaries separating it from obsessive and delusional presentations.[16] The concept was challenged over and over again and the question of its admissibility gave rise to a controversy in psychiatric literature. Many authors embrace all presentations invested with affect, including obsessive ideas, in the concept of the dominant idea and look for its distinctive feature in a persistent feeling tone. Bleuler, however, understands by the term "dominant idea" one which is constantly obtruding, but differs from an autochthonous idea since it is not regarded as foreign to the personality and differs from an obsessive idea since it is not perceived as false.[17] In this way Bleuler endeavors to distinguish a dominant idea phenomenologically from both an obsessive idea and from a delusion.

From our reflections on the structure presented by our two cases, we do not find it difficult to subscribe to Bleuler's definition and to express it with greater precision from the standpoint of psychoanalysis. Regarding the relation between dominant and obsessive ideas, we are liable to be misled by the function of the dominant idea and its conformity with the superego. Regarded metapsychologically, however, there exist considerable differences between the two groups of ideas. Both obsessional-neurotic symptoms and obsessive ideas arise from a regression to the anal-sadistic phase. The aggression then set free by the regressive process effects a general strengthening of the superego, but does not give rise to an alteration in the ego. In contradistinction, the dominant idea corresponds to a more profound regression which effects a transitory annulment of all transitory object and ego cathexes and therefore is considered the result of *psychotic regression*. Thus we regard a dominant idea as a *monosymptomatic psychosis*. We have still to examine the question whether it admits more exact demarcation in its relation to delusions.

The delusion ". . . is found like a patch on the spot where originally there was a rent in the relation between ego and outer world."[18] "Two steps, moreover, are discernible in a psychosis, the first of which tears the ego away from reality, while the second tries to make good the damage done."[19] It is this second phase which is responsible for the formation of fresh relations to objects and to reality. Where true delusional ideas are present, this result is achieved by means of projection. The affects liberated by the regressive process, and this includes both aggressive and libidinal ones, are in a sense intermingled afresh and are bound by new attachments to objects. This is what distinguishes them from a dominant idea. The latter does not involve projection. The affects liberated by the process, both libidinal and aggressive, are worked over and bound without passing beyond the institutions which compose the mental apparatus. Similarly, no alteration is perceived in the environment; simply an ego alteration occurs which is operative as a new structure within the personality.

Putting it as briefly as possible, the dominant idea is distinguishable from its obsessional-neurotic counterpart in that it answers to a more profound regression, one which has brought about an alteration in the ego. This alteration in the ego owes its origin to a psychotic regression as is also the case with delusions, but differs from paranoia in that the affects which have been liberated in the course of regression are bound within the institutions which compose the mental apparatus and are not projected onto the environment. This results not in the perception of an alteration in the environment, but in the ego.

When we consider narcissism as a component of the conflict that motivated the dominant idea with the aim of annihilation of the body by oral frustration, it is relevant to mention that the great majority of such cases, especially of anorexia nervosa, are women. Narcissism in women, in contrast to that in men, is a "retreat from the genitals,"[20] and cathects the body as a whole, whether it annihilates or affirms it. In men narcissism is concentrated far more on the genitals, especially on the penis; because of this, narcissistic delusional ideas relate mainly to the penis or to a substitute for it. In this context it is also illuminating to find that the mechanism of a dominant idea often emerges with hypochondriacal delusions as its content. But there are also dominant ideas independent of somatic components. For example, there are those which impose tasks upon the personality such as the obligation to reform mankind. Such cases do not perceive an alteration of the world according to their wishes in the sense of a true paranoid idea, but they attempt to effect a change in the environment according to their dominant idea. It may be assumed that in these cases the symptom contains a greater admixture of narcissistic libido than we attribute to the psychopathology of the cases discussed in this paper.

It may be asked whether the introduction of the concept of dominant idea represents a gain for the general theory of the neuroses. It seems that the dominant idea is a striking example of the "synthetic function of the ego." The ego binds aggression with the available libido and the new structure thus created is stable. At this point the struggle to ward off the primary instinctual conflict is brought to a conclusion. But the equilibrium of the mental apparatus is not thereby increased; on the contrary, it is upset permanently in one direction. Because of its aggressively severe nature, the dominant idea releases further conflict tensions. The resolution of these tensions can no longer be accomplished entirely by endopsychic means. The symptom which originally rejected oral gratification, at another stage enforces it, thus releasing the addiction in the second phase of the pathological process.

In discussing the relation of the instinctual conflict—oral regression—to the structure of preliminary depression, it was mentioned that the preliminary depression may have different structures leading to addiction. In these two cases the driving force behind the anorexia nervosa is the dominant idea, a monosymptomatic psychosis. This in turn, by commanding starvation, heightens the oral instinctual tension and consequently leads to addiction. The psychodynamics of addiction in these cases is a variant of the process which is considered typical of alcoholism.

NOTES

1. Read at the Thirteenth International Psycho-Analytical Congress, Lucerne, August, 1934; published in *Int. J. Psycho-Anal.*, XVII, part 1 (1936), 1–17. Revised for this volume.

2. Rado, S., "Psychoanalyse der Pharmakothymie," *Internationale Zeitschrift für Psychoanalyse*, Bd. XX (1934), 16–32.

3. Abraham, K., "The Psychological Relations between Sexuality and Alcoholism," *Selected Papers* (London, Hogarth Press, 1927), pp. 80–89; also "A Short Study of the Development of the Libido," *Selected Papers,* pp. 418–421.

4. Rado, S., "The Psychical Effects of Intoxicants," *Int. J. Psycho-Anal.,* VII (1926), 396–413.

5. Simmel, E., "Zum Problem von Zwang und Sucht," *Bericht über den V. Allgemeinen Artzlichen Kongress für Psychotherapie* (Baden-Baden, 1930).

6. Glover, E., "The Etiology of Drug Addiction," *Int. J. Psycho-Anal.,* XIII (1932), 298–328.

7. Glover calls attention to similar cases: the changeover from a true addiction to an obsessional-neurotic condition. Eating, ceremonial in itself, points to the part played by the superego in morbid cravings.

8. Rado, S., "Psychoanalyse der Pharmakothymie," pp. 16–32.

9. Wulff, M. ("Uber einen interessanten oralen Symptomenkomplex und seine Beziehung zur Sucht," *Internationale Zeitschrift fur Psychoanalyse,* Bd. XVIII [1932], 281–302) reports similar cases including one of a patient who was polyphagous and ultimately became an addict.

10. The treatment was interrupted by the family emigration to Switzerland where it was continued according to plan.

11. I refer in this connection to Freud's concept of the development of paranoia in women. (Freud, S., "Female Sexuality," *Std. Ed.,* XXI, pp. 225–243.) Freud holds that the fear of being eaten by the mother represents in women the fixation point of paranoia.

12. Freud, S., "Inhibitions, Symptoms and Anxiety" (1926), *Std. Ed.,* XX, pp. 87–174.

13. Gitelson, M., "On Ego Distortion," *Int. J. Psycho-Anal.,* XXXIX, (1958), 245–257.

14. Freud, S., "The Loss of Reality and Psychosis" (1924), *Std. Ed.,* XIX, pp. 183–187.

15. Freud, S., "The Ego and the Id" (1923), *Std. Ed.,* XIX, pp. 12–66.

16. Wernicke, C., "Uber fixe Ideen," *Deutsche medizinische Wochenschrift* (1892).

17. Bleuler, E., *Affectivity, Suggestibility, Paranoia* (1906–1926), (Utica, New York, State Hospitals Press, 1912).

18. Freud, S., "Neurosis and Psychosis" (1924), *Std. Ed.,* XIX, pp. 149–153; quote from *Collected Papers,* II, p. 252.

19. Freud, S., "The Loss of Reality and Psychosis," *Collected Papers,* II, p. 278.

20. Harnik, E., "The Various Developments Undergone by Narcissism in Men and in Women," *Int. J. Psycho-Anal.,* V (1924), 66–83.

DISCUSSION

This investigation set out to illustrate that addiction is a consequence of oral fixation and serves as substitute and disguise (equivalent) for depression. The investigation revealed another structure and motivation for addiction in the form of the dominant idea which led in these two cases to the syndrome of anorexia nervosa. The dominant idea was the core structure of the ego distortion which destroyed the personality organization of one of these patients and might have done the same to the other if the process had not been reversed. In both of these cases the disease process became manifest with the idea "I should not have a woman's body."

In her investigation of a large group of cases with severe eating disturbances, Hilde Bruch found the first outstanding symptom of anorexia nervosa to be ". . . a disturbance in the body image and body concept of delusional proportions." Anorexia patients may gain weight under some circumstances, but ". . . without corrective change in the body image, improvement is apt to be only a temporary remission. The second outstanding characteristic is a disturbance in the accuracy of perception or cognitive interpretation . . . of enteroceptive signals indicating nutritional need."[1] Physiologic alterations, such as overactivity and the denial of fatigue, are manifestations of the overriding power of the self-destructive wish to change the body.

Although anorexia nervosa is not caused by hormonal imbalance, it may lead to such a condition if consistently pursued by the patient. The differential diagnosis between anorexia nervosa and Simmonds' disease is often difficult. If protracted, anorexia nervosa may cease to be a struggle against appetite and the wish to eat, for its organic consequence might be actual loss of appetite which may lead to cathexia and even to death.[2] The differential diagnosis of refusal to eat in connection with other types of psychiatric conditions is easy to establish on the basis of the symptoms of the primary illness. Neurotic conflict might also motivate a refusal to eat, but the symptom is not as persistent as in anorexia nervosa.

In what category of psychosomatic conditions does anorexia nervosa belong? It is a condition which usually begins in adolescence and is much more frequent in girls than in boys. In many instances it begins with mourning after an object loss. But at first sight it does not fit Engel's categories.[3] Indeed it would be difficult to describe these cases either as manifestly depressed or as overly "energy conserving" in that phase of the illness in which they fight against the normal sensation of hunger. These cases are also described as not having anxiety states, or even anxiety affects. Where is the anxiety affect in these patients? Is it possible to maintain such regressive ego states without signals of intra-organismic danger?

One may hypothesize that there was a moment, a dream, a fantasy, or a flash of a recurring memory of a primal scene which activated anxiety because being a woman appeared as annihilation; or maybe the woman appeared to be a monster, threatening as death itself, and as a monster, has to be annihilated. Such a conjecture could not be verified in the treatment of my cases. Since these cases were not analyzable, their infantile fantasies could not be verified unless one had been able to observe and analyze the psychotic outbreak which preceded anorexia nervosa. But we can fit the fantasy into the hypothesis of the dominant idea and support this with the concept derived from the developmental process of the primary object relationship.

If we assume that such a fatal event is involved in the onset of every psychotic process,[4] then we may conclude that in this case the intrapsychic event did not split the ego as in schizophrenia but split the vital energy and set free the aggression which turned toward self = mother. This identification, which implied female sexuality and child-bearing, had to be annihilated when the patients reached adolescence and feminine sexuality became a threatening reality. The choice of alimentation as the means of self-destruction paradoxically retains a remnant of infantile impotence. Not only do such patients reject their feeding mothers, but they also hold on to the willful attempt to starve themselves. As the "bad self" refuses food = good mother, their bad-ness—their self-directed aggression—is more powerful than the good objects. It is, indeed, aggression triumphant in this chronic process of suicide.

We thus may assume that massive anxiety was mobilized and bound in the primary psychic event which brought about the dominant idea. After anorexia nervosa develops, these patients get upset, prob-ably anxious, and remorseful only after they are enticed to eat nourish-ing food. Not in vain did we speculate about the superego function of the dominant idea. The dominant idea is a symptom and, at the same time, the driving force of the pathologic process. It maintains the in-teractions between instinctual impulses of oral intake and the relentless punishment of a pathogenic conflict embedded in the structure of the dominant idea.

What is the genetic background of a self-concept which is charged with such fear of one's sexual self that after puberty this part of the self has to be destroyed at the cost of the total self? The answer is not sim-ple because it cannot be all-inclusive. There are too many variables and many of the variables are unknown.

Since Freud described introjection and identification as the process of personality development, we have learned a great deal about re-ciprocal interactions between the processes by which object relation-ships and self-concepts are established. Yet the word "established" appears inappropriate. It seems to attribute to self-concept a stability which this structure does not have. The self as an experiential concept expresses the unity, the wholeness, of the organism delineated against its surroundings. But awareness of the self oscillates throughout life; it depends on a general feeling of well-being and registers every nuance of it. Although the usual normal fluctuations of physical and emotional well-being pass like ripples on a large body of water, the self-concept may change in every critical phase, with every trauma.

This recalls the theories and assumptions which indicate that the self-concept is the consequence of the earliest experiences of alimentation. The infant introjects the image of the smiling, feeding, good mother as equal to the well-fed, lovable self. The self-concept of the two patients discussed appeared extremely vulnerable in relation to self-destructive aggression. What external (environmental) factors during early infancy interfere with the normal development of anorexia patients? How does the family transmit to the child such vulnerable self-concepts?

Bruch states with precision, ". . . behavior from birth on needs to be differentiated into two forms, namely, that *initiated* in the individual and that *in response* to external stimuli." Consequently, ". . . For normal development it appears essential that appropriate responses to the clues originating in the child and stimulation coming from outside be well balanced." From this it follows that ". . . the sum of parental interactions with the child forms his self concept, his self image, his personality."[5]

Indeed this concept is deeply interwoven in the psychoanalytic theory of personality, in its development and attainment, as well as in its pathology. But the concept as it stands needs qualification and amendment. There are many normal adults who lacked the "averagely expectable environment" during their infancy and even later in their development.[6] We can account for traumata, for critical situations, but if unknown factors of predisposition work in a fortunate direction, we have no need and even less opportunity to investigate. In cases of severe pathology and characterologic aberrations, what we know is not enough and what we do know raises new questions. We can, of course, always fall back on the unknown predisposing factors, be they genetically given, intrauterinely transmitted, or imbedded in the primary instinctual processes—in their gratifications as well as in their frustrations. The fact that we cannot change those factors does not release scientists from the obligation to raise questions and search for answers.

The first question may arise in reference to the influence of constitutional bisexuality as it motivates aggression against the feminine body, against the feminine self. Is such a constitutional factor behind the hatred toward the mother = feeding self? Or is it when the hormonal processes activate femaleness at puberty that they awake in the girl not only the repressed memory of the ambivalence toward the mother, but also the dejected femaleness of the girl who wished and at the same time feared the tendency to yield sexually to the father, to the superior man? When the intensity of the frustration brings about defusion of instinctual energies and turns the aggression toward the self, does the aggression cathect a self which is psychologically set against

its genetically given sexual function because of the strength of the bisexual potentiality of her organism?

We know that androgens and estrogens are secreted by the ovaries
and adrenal glands. Their relation to each other is quantitatively
changeable but normally in balance. Thus the question raised above
creates another insoluble problem, or can it be approached by further
psychoanalytic investigation? The only dream recorded in my report
was a transference dream of the first patient: on the manifest level it
showed motherliness, but the intense emotional charge had complex
instinctual motivation; it was an erotic wish to be close to the child =
breast and at the same time it was charged with the wish to devour and
so annihilate the breast = child = mother. The dream does not indicate
any bisexual motivation or any heterosexual motivation. It reflects only
the intensely charged oral impulse to be mother and feed the child
and/or incorporate and devour the child. It seems that the problem of
bisexual motivation cannot be investigated in these cases since orality
completely dominates their emotional life.

The next problem is, where does the ego receive the aggressive
energy necessary to deny the vital needs of the body? The psychodynamic
function of the dominant idea in the disease process answers the question from the point of view of psychology. We may add what we have
learned from physiology: nor-epinephrine is the biochemical substratum
of the aggressive affect.[7] We can hope that correlations between hormonal findings and psychologic processes can be established. This may
sound naively optimistic, but it is not impossible. Aggression turned
toward the self is an old concept in psychoanalysis. But it is relatively
new that physiologic experiments can demonstrate stress situations in
which aggression is turned toward the self.[8]

We know more about the allotments of libido within the psychic
apparatus than about those of aggression. We know about primary and
secondary narcissism, the latter referring to the libido in relation to the
self. But we do not know about secondary aggression. Is all aggression
bound in defense mechanisms neutralized?[9] What furnishes ego strength?
Is it normal will power or pathologic strength of the ego?

Freud answered this last question in terms of the first instinct
theory. He identified the self-preservative instincts with "ego drives,"
and the cathexes proceeding from them he termed "interests" in contradistinction to libido, which he attributed to sexual drives.[10] Such tendencies, aims, and interests center around the self. Our anorexia nervosa
cases demonstrate that aggression may motivate "interests" which are
not in the interest of survival of the organism. In the anorexia nervosa
patients, the warning signal of anxiety is suspended to permit the aggression to act against the self.

In a study of ego functions Hartmann investigated the psychodynamics of irrational action and emphasized the intensity of the energy

with which such interests are pursued.[11] Our puzzling anorexia cases may supply an answer. The dominant idea is a symptom; it represents a new fusion of libido and aggression, but aggression is overweening; this pathologic fusion gives the ego strength to ward off hunger and anxiety, to accept the hostile, aggressive self as reasonable, even justified. The self-protective, narcissistic energy borrows strength from aggression and maintains the idea's separateness and its power. The changes in the behavior and symptom formations which served as adjuvants to maintain the effectiveness of the dominant idea—such as large quantities of unnourishing foods, alcohol, or physical exercise—point toward the movements of cathectic energies within the psychic apparatus. It is a complex way of pathology by which the ego's "interest"—self-destructive and not self-preservative—is maintained.

Considering the psychopathology of anorexia nervosa, the interpretation offered by the second instinct theory is simpler. Since death instinct means that not only survival-positive but also survival-negative mechanisms operate in every organism, the question is, what causes the survival-negative mechanism to prevail and what determines the choice of its means? The course of the anorexia nervosa indicates that the primary motivation is the (existential) basic anxiety activated by the awareness of gender identity: a complete rejection of the female body. The regression which turns the aggression against the self appears to operate on the level of ambivalent oral symbiosis with the mother.

Anorexia nervosa is a truly psychosomatic illness; although the intrapsychic conflicts operate from infancy on, only after puberty is the reality of being a woman experienced as a threat. But anorexia nervosa is not a disease belonging to the flight or fight pattern. The fear of womanhood creates a structure which operates on aggression and directs the aggression toward the self. The emotional equivalent of anorexia is depression. Anorexia leads finally to such an exhaustion of the metabolic system that the withdrawal-conservation pattern evolves, and it may lead to death.[12]

NOTES

1. Bruch, H., "Anorexia Nervosa and Its Differential Diagnosis," *J. Nervous and Mental Diseases,* CXLI, no. 5 (1965), 560.

2. Person, P. B., and McDermott, W., *Textbook of Medicine* (Philadelphia and London, W. B. Saunders & Co., 1963).

3. Engel, G., *Psychological Development in Health and Disease* (Philadelphia, W. B. Saunders & Co., 1962). See pages 319–320, this volume.

4. Freud, S., "Neurosis and Psychosis" (1924), *Std. Ed.,* XIX, pp. 149–156.

5. Bruch, H., "Anorexia Nervosa and Its Differential Diagnosis," p. 564.

6. Hartmann, H., *Ego Psychology and the Problems of Adaptation* (New York, International Universities Press, 1961), p. 23.

7. Benedek, T., "Death Instinct and Anxiety," Chapter 1 Discussion, this volume.

8. Funkenstein, D. H., Sking, S. H., and Drollette, M. E., *The Mastery of Stress* (Cambridge, Harvard University Press, 1957).

9. Hartmann, H., Kris, E., and Loewenstein, R. M., "Notes on the Theory of Aggression," *Psychoanalytic Study of the Child III & IV* (1949), 9–36.

10. Hartmann, H., "Comments on the Psychoanalytic Theory of the Ego," *Psychoanalytic Study of the Child V* (1950), 90–91.

11. Hartmann, H., "On Rational and Irrational Action," *Psychoanalysis and the Social Sciences,* vol. I, G. Roheim, ed. (New York, International Universities Press, 1947), pp. 359–392.

12. Bruch, H., "Death in Anorexia Nervosa," *Psychosomatic Med.,* XXXIII, no. 2 (1971), 135–144.

4. Some Factors Determining Fixation at the "Deutero-Phallic Phase"

INTRODUCTION

The following investigation deals with the development of a compulsion-neurotic individual and the motivations of his homosexuality. It was stimulated by Jones's thorough investigation of the preoedipal phallic phase which he termed "deutero-phallic" (deutero meaning secondary). The term implies that this is not a normal developmental phase but one which, if caused by overcathexis of the genital zone, motivates neurotic symptoms which have individually differing significance. I retained the term coined by Jones to signify my agreement with his concept. Freud considered a phallic phase to be normal in both sexes leading to genital primacy through the oedipal phase.

This recalls a long forgotten controversy between Freud and Jones regarding the early development of female sexuality, not yet settled in psychoanalytic theory. In 1923 Freud expressed his concept of the phallic phase as "an interpolation into the theory of sexuality" (of "The Infantile Genital Organization of Libido") by stating that the infantile genital organization differs from adult genital organization ". . . in the fact that for both sexes only one genital, namely, the male one, comes into account. What is present, therefore, is not a primacy of the genitals, but a primacy of the *phallus*."[1] This became the established theory. Jones's investigations, however, led to other conclusions. His first paper on this subject dealt with the early development of female sexuality. In 1927 he read a paper before the Tenth International Congress of Psycho-Analysis at Innsbruck in which he put forward the hypothesis that ". . . the phallic phase in the development of female sexuality represents a secondary solution of a psychical conflict of a defensive nature, rather than a simple and direct developmental process."[2]

Freud did not accept Jones's argument. Indeed in 1933 Jones introduced his paper, "The Phallic Phase," with the statement: "Last year Professor Freud declared this suggestion to be quite untenable."[3] In a somewhat emotionally charged argument, Jones reiterated and paraphrased Freud's concept as presented in 1923.

> [Freud assumes that there are] . . . two distinct stages in the phallic phase. . . . The first of the two—let us call it the *proto-phallic* phase—would be marked by innocence or ignorance—at least in consciousness—where there is no conflict over the matter in question, it being confidently assumed by the child that the rest of the world is built like itself and has a satisfactory male organ—penis or clitoris, as the case may be. . . . In Freud's description[4] of the phallic phase the essential feature common to both sexes was the belief that only one kind of genital organ exists in the world—a male one. . . . The reason for this belief is simply that the female organ has at this age not yet been discovered by either sex.[5]

The later stage of the phallic phase, the deutero-phallic phase, is characterized by "a dawning suspicion," according to Jones,

> . . . that human beings are . . . divided into two classes: not male and female in the proper sense, but penis-possessing and castrated. . . . The deutero-phallic phase would appear to be more neurotic than the proto-phallic. . . . For it is associated with anxiety, conflict, striving against accepting what is felt to be reality—i.e., castration—and over-compensatory emphasis on the narcissistic value of the penis on the boy's side with a mingled hope and despair on the girl's.
>
> It is plain that the difference between the two phases is marked by the idea of castration, which according to Freud is bound up in both sexes with actual observation of the anatomical sex differences.[6]

After discussing various aspects of the problem, Jones finished his thesis by pointing to the battle of the sexes. "Both sexes strive against accepting the belief in the second class, and both for the same reason—namely, from a wish to disbelieve in the supposed reality of castration."[7] He closed his essay with the all-inclusive reference, "In the beginning . . . male and female created He them."[8] Jones's almost embittered argument led to the conclusion that both sexes reach maturity by overcoming the fear of the other sex.[9] Horney was the first who was consistent in developing the idea that penis envy is a cultural phenomenon, not rooted directly in biology.[10] Jones discussed her findings in the light of Freud's hypothesis. In a later paper Horney says, "The 'undiscovered' vagina is a denied vagina."[11] Jones expresses the same idea stating, "In the feminine wishes of the boy must lie the secret of the whole problem. . . ."[12]

We know a great deal about the manifestations of the "fear of the other sex," but we always look for the reason outside of the individual who is afraid, in the other sex. Yet one can generalize that this fear originates in one's bisexuality, in the other sex in oneself. We know very little about the biology of bisexuality, but we do know that it is a dispositional quality; there is no psychic structure which under certain conditions would not show the influence of the bisexual anlage.

At the time the paper "The Phallic Phase" was published, I was analyzing a patient whose homosexual perversion illustrated Jones's emphasis on the deutero-phallic phase. The detailed discussion of the instinctual conflicts in relation to the development of psychic structures may appear cumbersome to psychoanalysts today when everything moves rapidly, when the complexity of our knowledge brings observations and theories quickly, probably too quickly, to closure, sometimes excluding details that belong not to the surface but to the depth of the picture.

NOTES

1. Freud, S., "The Infantile Genital Organization of Libido: An Interpolation into the Theory of Sexuality" (1923), *Std. Ed.*, XIX, 141–145.

2. Jones, E., "The Early Development of Female Sexuality" (1927), in *Papers on Psycho-Analysis* (Baltimore, Williams & Wilkins Co., 1948), pp. 438–451.

3. Jones, E., "The Phallic Phase" (1933), in *Papers on Psycho-Analysis* (Baltimore, 1948), p. 452.

4. Freud, S., "The Infantile Genital Organization of Libido: An Interpolation into the Theory of Sexuality" (1923), *Std. Ed.*, XIX, p. 142.

5. Jones, E., "The Phallic Phase," p. 453.

6. Ibid., pp. 453–454.

7. Ibid., p. 453.

8. Ibid., p. 484.

9. This was also the assumption of Karl Abraham. Abraham, K., "A Short Study of the Development of Libido, Viewed in the Light of Mental Disorders—Part II. Origins and Growth of Object Love" (1924), in his *Selected Papers* (London, Hogarth Press, 1942), pp. 480–501.

10. Horney, K., "The Flight from Womanhood," *Int. J. Psycho-Anal.*, VII (1926), 324–339.

11. Horney, K., "The Dread of Women," *Int. J. Psycho-Anal.*, XIII (1932), 358.

12. Jones, E., "The Phallic Phase," p. 462.

SOME FACTORS DETERMINING FIXATION AT THE "DEUTERO-PHALLIC PHASE"[1] (1933)

In a recent work Jones discusses problems connected with the phallic phase.[2] He distinguishes as the deutero-phallic phase the highly exaggerated and narcissistically cathected phallic phase. This phase he holds to be a neurotic compromise. If it plays a leading part in the subject's later sexual development, it amounts to a perversion in Sachs's sense of the term and often results in homosexuality.[3]

The case I shall discuss is particularly instructive in this connection. Not only does it corroborate Jones's hypothesis, but its structure throws light on certain factors which may lead to fixation at the phallic phase.

In the accounts of manifest male homosexuality contained in psychoanalytic literature, two main types have hitherto been described. In the one, the subject's mother identification with its narcissistic cathexis causes him to seek for love objects resembling himself; he desires to love them as he himself wished to have been loved by his mother. In the second, the object choice again follows the lines of mother identification but, owing to a greater passivity and a firmer anal fixation, the subject aims at passive surrender to his father. He desires to be loved by his father as his mother was loved. Freud has described yet a third form of manifest homosexuality, and this is deeply colored by the subject's masculine identifications. In these cases rivalry which has been overcome and aggressive impulses which have become repressed are often combined with the typical conditions known to us.[4] In this third type the masculine identifications play a greater part. The following case belongs to this category.

The patient, a man of twenty-eight, was in a state of acute anxiety when he came to me. He was deeply depressed and greatly agitated by the idea that a man whom he had recently met in the street might know that he was a homosexual. Moreover, he was afraid that the man might say this to him in public or even in his mother's presence and expose his secret. He found this paranoid anxiety intolerable; it intensified the wish, which he already had, to be free of homosexuality to such a degree that he determined to undergo treatment.

In appearance and figure the patient had something slightly feminine about him, but neither in his bearing nor in his dress could one detect anything characteristic of the homosexual; on the contrary, his inconspicuous clothes and demeanor and his way of speaking struck one as masculine. His character appeared to be of the obsessional type —pedantic, correct, and self-controlled.

His anamnesis was as follows. He was an only child. His parents' marriage was outwardly happy, but he recollected that his father insisted that in their married life his will was law. Nevertheless, as the patient remembered, he had given all his love to his father. He described this feeling by saying, "In his presence I was at peace, blissful, good; I always felt safe." He remembered how urgent was the affection that drew him to his father. He imitated him in every trivial detail. His father did not eat chocolates or cakes and this was reason enough for the patient to refuse to touch them throughout his childhood—a notable achievement for a child. So long as his father lived, no other man made any impression on the boy; his schoolmasters left him indifferent. To him his father was the ideal man.

When the boy was ten years old, his father fell ill (of metasyphilis) and died a year later. After that, except for a few terms when he was a student, the patient lived with his mother. As a child he was often ill and used to suffer from chills and swollen glands. Although he was nursed and cared for by his mother, he seemed to have no recollection of any exchange of tenderness between them. She struck him as severe, cold, and distant, although he realized that his own shyness with her might be responsible for their very correct but strained relationship. Even at the time of treatment, his mother treated him in many respects like a child; he still deferred to her will and was very dependent on her.

At the age of eleven, the patient was initiated by his swimming master into the practice of mutual masturbation. A second man to play the part of seducer in his life was a middle-aged workman, "a man in corduroys." The patient believed that many of the conditions which were now essential for his love life had their origin in his relationship with this man. When he was seventeen, he fell in love during dancing lessons (which he detested) with a young girl, but this came to nothing. At eighteen he fell in love with a school friend. This was an enthusiastic calf love, but the youth in question was already in love with another boy and after this disappointment the patient withdrew into himself. From that time on he realized that he was definitely homosexual. He was in despair about it; he went to church constantly and wrestled with this tendency in himself.

It seemed to him that as a child, after his father's death, he was always looking for someone on whom he could lean and who would give him protection and security from his anxiety and disquiet. This was why he constantly sought men who impressed him as masculine. "If I throw myself into the suit which such a man has worn, I have a great accentuation of libido and feel much more masculine." But it was not indispensable that there be such a suit. As time went on he grew more and more masculine and rejected everything suggestive of femininity in himself and in his sexual partners.

With the exception of his first and single love, he had loved no-

body, man or woman. During his analysis he came to realize the nature
of his relations with men. He described them as follows:

> I certainly don't *love* the other man; what I feel is envy and
> jealousy. I feel like that because he is normal and capable of
> love for women; I attribute to him all the qualities which I
> lack but which seem to me enviable. I envy and hate him and
> I do not know when this hatred and pugnacity change into
> love or how and why they give rise to sexual feeling. I never
> feel as if I were a woman nor do I surrender myself like a
> woman. I hate passivity; a passive man is not a man at all.
> He is repulsive to me and sexually he does not excite me in
> the least, and I am not passive either. If I could do as I liked,
> I should always start the sexual act with a fight, not from
> sadistic or masochistic impulses, but because I want to try my
> strength. I picture the man whom I love as strong, powerful,
> good, protective, and sexually potent, and at the same time I
> hate him because he is superior to me. I don't want to get the
> better of him from a sadistic motive, but I want to *grow*
> through my relationship with him; by mastering him I hope to
> become more than I was. I know that one cannot add to
> one's own stature nor lift oneself above one's level; one can-
> not become more than one actually is, and yet every time I
> perform the sexual act, I have the feeling that I want, as it
> were, to take the man, the masculine, into myself. It hardly
> ever happens that I find the kind of sexual object that I look
> for or that the act quite comes up to my desires, but when-
> ever it has been so, I have had the feeling that it strengthened
> me and my usual depression has left me.

Generally, however, the patient's sexual partners were not as
masculine as he hoped. He then would try to supply what was lacking
in them by his imagination, and he described how sometimes, when he
was greatly stimulated, he succeeded in playing both parts—that of the
masculine father and that of the child. The act then signified: "A child
is loved by his father who confirms him in his masculinity and makes
him a man like himself," or "An elder brother is fought with and
incorporated in order that the younger one may become his equal."
"When I am greatly excited, I am both at once—the child and the adult
—and all I need to borrow from my sexual partner is his erotogenic
zone." The "erotogenic zone" was always the penis.

The only thing which interested him in his partner was the penis
or, possibly, the upper part of the body. The buttocks and thighs, which
play a part with other homosexuals, had no significance for him. In
every case the sexual act was performed from the front and he main-

tained a constant observation of his partner. What interested him the most was the whole process of excitation in himself. His libido was invariably confined to the act itself; he could feel no tenderness. He felt obliged to isolate himself and withdraw at once after the act. His sexual relations were always quite transitory. His desiderata in love were so infinitely complicated that they could never be fulfilled. His fixation caused him to long for his father; what he desired was the complete heterosexual man, not in order to be loved by him but that, through him, he might become truly masculine. Thus his sexuality remained fixated on this narcissistic-phallic gratification; the love object itself was a matter of indifference. His search was an endless one. The same man had not the power to stimulate him on a second occasion because there was no longer the exciting question which of the two was the stronger. If the other showed a tendency to cling to him and endeavored to keep up their relationship, he felt that such dependence was feminine and so lost interest in him. One weaker than himself could never be his sexual object, for his choice was determined by his narcissistic identification with a stronger man. This narcissistic identification was wholly concentrated on the penis, which meant his father's penis. He repeated with each sexual partner his rivalry; the goal of the act was to overcome his rival and, by incorporating his penis, become a man through him.

In the patient's mind women were altogether free from sexuality. He did not, like many homosexuals, consciously regard them as lower creatures on account of their lack of a penis; on the contrary, his own sexuality caused him so much moral suffering that he regarded the lack of a penis as a moral asset. It made women impregnable and elevated them to a higher, better world from which he himself was excluded. He believed, on one hand, that sexuality in every form was repugnant to women and that their attitude to the sexual activities of men was merely critical. On the other hand, he thought that women loved only those men who were manlier than himself, men of the kind that he desired for his masculine love objects. From this attitude, we see at once that his mother played a great part in his superego and in his ego ideal.

In this case, dread of the vagina and denial of the female genitals with its suggestion of castration formed the nucleus of the perversion. Repression of the idea of the female genitals was accompanied by an unusually strong inhibition of the scoptophilic and exhibitionistic tendency and we devoted special attention to this at the beginning of the analysis. The patient revealed a great deal of sublimated scoptophilia. He was keenly interested in painting; observation of nature and of art was one of his chief outlets. It was therefore remarkable that he professed scarcely even to see women in the street. His scoptophilia was inhibited in that direction; his exhibitionism was inhibited chiefly in relation to women; he could not endure to be looked at by them. Even at a cinema he was uncomfortable if there was a scene in which a woman undressed. He disliked everything that suggested nudity; he felt an aversion to women's clothes, especially their underclothes. On the other hand, he took a decided interest in men's clothing. At the age of ten he put on some of his father's underwear when masturbating. As time went on, men's underwear assumed an increasingly important place in his sexual life. The more masculine and coarse the garments, the better. At first, he put this down to the influence of his relationship to the man who seduced him, "the man in corduroys." But the analytic material showed quite plainly that his interest in the masculine appearance of his sexual objects and in coarse underwear served the purpose of an escape from the thought of women. However, he did not develop a genuine fetishism. In spite of the pleasurable tone and the erotic effect of the underwear, it was not a substitute for the woman's missing penis; rather it was a defense against the anxiety called up when he was forced to think of women.

The patient's scoptophilia had not always been so strongly inhibited as he insisted at the beginning of his analysis. Once his severe castration experience was analyzed, the scoptophilia of his earliest years came to light. He remembered that his father laughingly used to call him a rascal because, at home or elsewhere, he would press against girls or women and try to peek under their skirts. This first blissful period of childhood lasted until he was between three and a half and four, when he underwent an especially intense castration trauma. He suffered from phimosis which from infancy had given him a great deal of trouble. He still remembered how every time he urinated there had to be great preparations and how his penis had to have special treatment—bathing with warm water, using ointment, and so forth. We may suppose that this care and attention aroused in him early a strong penile erotism. His infantile sexuality was thus characterized by a relatively uninhibited preoccupation with his penis and by a scoptophilic interest in the female genitals.

When the patient was three and a half, he had his first operation for phimosis. The operation was unsuccessful and after a period of painful treatment it had to be repeated. Only then was he relieved from his trouble. The operation had a profound effect on his development. There was an immediate change in his character and in his relationship to his parents. He recollected that after the operation he would no longer get into bed with his mother but only with his father. The earlier, more normal relationship between mother and son was disturbed and inhibited; he turned away from her and devoted himself exclusively to his father. We can date the repression of his scoptophilic urge from this period.

His development in the opposite direction was very striking. He remembered that when he was five or six, he took great interest in all the men who came to the house; he wanted to know if they were married and had any children. He was interested in the penis of these men, but he no longer wanted to think about the sexuality of women. In talking of his emotional life at that period, he represented himself as having been "dependent upon men." He sought protection and love in a man stronger than himself—one who had not been castrated. This enabled him to forget his own castration. The result of such a situation is generally a purely passive attitude toward the father, but in this case not only was the mother identification repudiated consciously, but even in the unconscious its acceptance did not involve a definitely passive attitude toward the father. It is true that he chose his father as a superior and protective love object, but the choice was based on narcissistic identification with him: "You and I, who both have a penis, belong together." His father, the man with the penis intact, became at the same time his ego ideal and his love object. This identification came to occupy a central place in his psychic economy. First, the exaggerated emphasis on his comradeship with his father and the exclusion of the mother from their intimacy represented a defense against castration anxiety and a denial of his own femininity. The more intense the castration anxiety, the stronger became the narcissistic cathexis of his own penis and that of his father. At the same time, the narcissistic importance of his father's penis, its significance as his ego ideal, produced a sense of inferiority. The result was a narcissistic instinctual tension; the patient aimed at becoming his father's equal through incorporation of his father's penis. The sexual act served to relieve this tension and to complete the imperfect identification.

After the final operation for phimosis (when the patient was five or six years old) he began to masturbate to the accompaniment of fantasies. In these he imagined that he had older brothers who loved and protected him. The fantasies corresponded exactly to the mechanisms postulated by Freud for certain forms of homosexual perversion.[5] Freud says that the conflict due to ambivalence toward older brothers finds its solution in identification; once this has taken place, the brother can be loved. In his masturbation fantasies the patient substituted for his father brothers who were what he wished to be, what he perhaps might have been but for the surgery on his penis. But the wish indicated in these fantasies, to love an older and protective brother, was never translated into reality, for in actual life substitutes for older brothers merely intensified the conflict due to his ambivalence and sense of guilt. To escape this the narcissistic cathexis of the ego was increased and the patient withdrew from real love relations. However, in fantasy his identification with an older brother, i.e., with his father, was successful and in this way the conflict was resolved in fantasy. The fantasy performed two functions: it relieved the tension of the conflict and it completed the imperfect identification. Later, in the fully developed perversion, the patient was once more ceaselessly striving to complete identification, and thus the fantasy accomplished more than did the actual perversion.

Analysis revealed that in early childhood and even for a time after the surgery the patient took an interest in women. During the treatment we saw reenacted the way in which women affected the development of his homosexuality. For example, rather late in the analysis, when he was already having intercourse regularly with women and was less troubled by the perversion, a visit from a cousin caused him to relapse. She had played a part in his childhood; he often spent his holidays with relatives and this elder cousin had looked after him, really taking the place of a nurse. He had been very fond of her and was "going to marry her." He had forgotten all this, but meeting her again was enough to bring about a relapse. His cousin was a mother imago; when he was in her company his sense of impotence, his dread of women, and the dread of his own femininity increased and he took refuge in homosexuality. Thus before our very eyes, the mechanism that had produced the inversion was recapitulated.[6]

In another way the central importance of the mother in this perversion repeatedly manifested itself. While analysis was going on, it often happened that the patient would have a sudden increase of anxiety and disquiet and his anxiety would be projected into the idea that a man might attack him in his mother's presence so that she would discover his perversion. From this paranoid idea it is obvious that his anxiety really had reference to his mother and was merely displaced to the man to whom he was otherwise sexually indifferent. When this sense of guilt because of homosexuality made the dread of his mother unbearable, it discharged itself in the paranoid symptom. The acuteness of the anxiety and the structure of the symptom were evidence of his superego anxiety toward his mother.

The patient's character was colored by his dependence on women. A man's unfavorable judgment never cast him down; he did not particularly care what men thought of him and so did not suffer from inhibitions or anxiety in his work. His only dread was the criticism of women because that would bring his weakness home to him. It was not simply dread of impotence or narcissistic anxiety at the thought of ridicule;[7] it was superego anxiety. He always saw himself with the mercilessly critical eyes of the women for whose love he was not good enough, but whose love he must win. Love, therefore, assumed for him the guise of a task. His homosexual activities were a struggle to gain self-confidence, a fight for equality with the ego ideal, and a straining toward the unconscious goal of being worthy of women. He dared not actually fight to win them, for he believed that his very survival depended on non-physical victory.

It seems almost superfluous to describe these ideas in such detail, but I wish to convey my vivid impression that the severity of the patient's superego came from his relationship to his mother. The anxiety originally mobilized by her lack of a penis became more severe when it became fear of his superego, for then it was always with him. This superego fear of his mother was transferred to all other women who came to represent the superego and for this reason women could not serve as sexual objects.[8]

Since the publication of Freud's "Drei Abhandlungen zur Sexualtheorie" ("Three Essays on the Theory of Sexuality") it has been recognized that the homosexual perversion tends to occur in persons who have grown up without a father. In such cases it is the mother alone who inflicts upon the subject all those frustrations which vitally affect his development. She is the sole authority to impose commands upon him. In the light of what we know today we should express the situation thus: in this patient's case, as in others where the structure of the perversion is similar, the mother becomes the nucleus of the superego.

Now how does this type of superego develop? How does fixation take place at this level of superego development? At the age of ten the patient lost his father and thereafter was brought up by his mother alone. But his development had taken this turn before his father's death and the superego is already formed by that age.

After the phimosis operation, the four-year-old boy turned away from his mother as a love object. It is remarkable that, although he was twice operated on by men, the boy did not relate the shock of castration to his father but to his mother. We conclude from this that the same individual may react differently to the perception of the female genitals at different phases of his development. The nature of the reaction is determined by various factors.

Apart from a patient's biological (dispositional) bisexuality which affects the facility of identification with the mother and the strength of that identification, it further depends on the phase of libidinal development he has attained whether his perception of the female genitals has a crippling effect and results in a definitive identification with the mother or whether he tries to overcome his anxiety with all the libidinal energy at his disposal. From the analysis, it was quite certain that before his operation the child had known of the existence of female genitals and had taken a lively, erotic interest in them and that he finally turned away from them only when large quantities of anxiety had been mobilized by the trauma. He then projected his castration anxiety onto his mother who, as he supposed, already had been deprived of a penis.

Psychoanalytic literature contains many descriptions of the way in which perception of the female genitals brings home to boys the possibility of castration. Much less attention is paid to the manifestations of the child's scoptophilic instinct. When a child takes every opportunity to touch and look at the genitals of girls and women it is very often regarded as a perverse kind of play for which he is scolded. Why are not all children content with a single discovery of the existence of female genitals? As a rule this behavior on the child's part is interpreted as an urgent desire to prove that a woman, after all, does have a penis. But that explains only the causal aspect of this form of infantile sexual curiosity; from the economic standpoint, scoptophilia is a form of sexual activity that helps to master the shock of castration. Just as the economic function of play is to master situations and tension produced by anxiety, so scoptophilic activity has the economic function of overcoming the dread of female genitals.

As a child the patient manifested his scoptophilic interest in the plainest fashion and we may assume that his sexual curiosity—the playful wish engendered by these impulses to peek at and try to embarrass women—was also an attempt to get over the shock of castration. It was while he was in this phase that he underwent the surgery which so enormously intensified the castration anxiety. Now it seemed he was castrated; he was like his mother and he rebelled against this identity. In order not to be reminded of it he inhibited his scoptophilic instinct, denied the existence of the vagina, ceased to notice women at all, and devoted all of his love to his father with whom he tried to identify.

In this case the consequence of the castration trauma was precisely the opposite of that which we are accustomed to regard as the normal termination of the oedipal phase. Normally when a child renounces the oedipus complex because of his fear of castration, he introjects the father who then forms the nucleus of the superego, "which takes its severity from the father."[9] "Variations in the sequence and the linking up of these processes must be very significant in the development of the individual."[10] In this special case it appears there were factors that modified the formation of the superego because the patient's oedipus complex never reached its full development. It seems as if the classical termination of the oedipus complex is determined by particular factors in the subject's penile sexuality, especially during the deutero-phallic phase.

The development of penile erotism has been little discussed in psychoanalytic literature. The penis is the leading zone which exercises genital primacy at puberty and discharges the greater part of the libido. Analytic observation of adults and direct observation of children suggest that in earliest childhood the penis is largely a passive pleasure organ, that the early infantile evolution of penile sexuality passes through various phases before the phallus can become the vehicle of the "oedipus wish." This sounds like a strange assumption; it seems to endow the oedipal male child at age four to six with a penetrating, thrusting penis. This is impossible. The oedipus complex is a fantasy representation of a biological potentiality and is therefore unconscious. Only if we assume that the oedipal phase, through all its vicissitudes, continues after puberty can we follow the shifts in changing object relationship until its resolution is prompted by physiologic processes[11] when the subject can attain the active, thrusting phase in which his aim is to penetrate the vagina. And *only* this final development will bring about the classical termination of the oedipus complex. Perhaps the biological basis of the father identification is the active, thrusting penis whose aim is identical with that of the father's penis. The oedipus wish itself thereby acquires psychic reality and, accordingly, the rivalry with the father becomes more intense because more psychically real. It is only now that the oedipus wish becomes an offense against the father so that it is possible to project onto him the subject's castration anxiety. The penis must now be protected from the father because it is from him that punishment is anticipated. It is the anxiety felt for the penis in this phase that breaks up the oedipus complex. Identification with the father, which follows a biological pattern, prepares the way for his final introjection when he becomes the nucleus of the superego. He is now the representative of moral law and as such can no longer be a sexual object. On the other hand, the anxiety cathexis of the mother diminishes and, in the next phase of penile activity, she may become a sexual object.

We now have to consider whether the occurrence of the castration trauma at a particular period is sufficient to account for the severity of the maternal superego and the dread of the mother, or whether there are even earlier phases of superego formation which have had a decisive influence. Melanie Klein[12] and Ernest Jones[13] take the view that it is the original oral aggression against the mother which determines the dread of the mother once and for all, that this is the reason for her significance in the superego. In view of the markedly ambivalent attitude of this patient toward his mother, it was quite natural that he should have aggressive fantasies relating to her. But the analysis did not go deep enough for us to decide whether these fantasies originated in the oral-sadistic phase. The history of this patient suggests that his aggressive impulses toward his mother arose only as a reaction to his dread of her —they sprang from a transformation of inhibited, sexual aggression. Analysis showed that up to the time of the castration trauma, his relation to his mother was normal but that afterwards he was altogether too good, a child suffering from inhibitions. Nevertheless, even in childhood there were marked oral traits in his character. An important point in the development of his oral libido was his renunciation of chocolate and cake. He gave them up in order to emphasize his identification with his father. But this oral frustration cannot have been simply an imitation of his father; the ascetic energy fulfilled an important economic function. He refused to incorporate sweets, the symbols of the breast and the penis. His perfectly conscious emphasis on this renunciation had the same economic value as that of a screen memory. It implied, "I am not a woman; I have no passive oral erotism and also I am not in any way guilty for I have no active, aggressive oral erotism." This renunciation of sweets was equivalent to a symptom. It gave the patient the gratification of identifying himself with his father while it represented the denial of the oral-sadistic phase necessary for such identification.

However, we are interested not only in the patient's oral sadism but in the fate of his aggressive instinct in general and its particular manifestations. First, let us examine his aggression from the point of view of the instincts motivating the perversion itself. The patient's type of homosexuality has been characterized by Freud as an overcompensation for hate. The patient himself has described the degree of conscious hatred and envy with which he entered his sexual activities. In the cases mentioned by Freud, the subjects had passed through conflicts due to ambivalence toward real brothers and had resolved them by means of identification. Our patient, however, had no real masculine object for his ambivalence except his father. His childhood, after the castration trauma, was deeply filled with love for his father and his anxiety and aggression were from that time on projected onto his mother. We may well ask, what was the source of the marked ambivalence when he performed the sexual act? The conflict thus expressed in his sexuality was the repetition of his infantile ambivalence toward his father that had been repressed by reason of the dread of castration at the time when the child took refuge with his father in order to escape the same dread. We are therefore concerned with an early infantile oral and anal aggressiveness which is linked with narcissism. The greater the narcissistic cathexis of the penis, the greater the desire to possess a powerful genital organ so as to conquer women with it. Thus his ambivalence increased as a result of the compulsive effort to reach a level which in childhood he could not attain. This was the meaning and the mechanism of the aggression which found its outlet in the perversion itself.

Not only is the strength of the patient's aggressive instinct noticeable in the sexual act itself, but it makes itself felt also in the severity of his superego. Freud has demonstrated the origin of such severity and has showed that the formation of the superego is preceded by regression.[14] He shows further that regression itself is a process involving the defusion of instincts. The aggressive impulses liberated by the defusion of the patient's instincts were distributed between the superego and the ego. We have already considered the resulting severity of the former. In this case we can observe clearly that the aggression is located within the ego.

According to the theory of perversion, its economic function, like that of screen memories, is to retain repressed instinctual impulses in the unconscious.[15] Part of the subject's infantile sexuality is fixated and appropriates a large quantity of the available libido; this overemphasis of the conscious instinctual wish enables the ego to repress another part of infantile sexuality. Jones, in "The Phallic Phase," adopts this hypothesis and shows that we must attribute the same significance to the narcissistically cathected, deutero-phallic phase as Sachs attributed to the perversions in general and Fenichel to screen memories.[16] The case of homosexual perversion discussed in this paper is a good illustration of this proposition. We have seen that the deutero-phallic phase persisted because the castration trauma led to an early formation of the superego and checked the further evolution of the oedipus complex and hence the development of the normal superego.

We must now consider whence the ego derives the energy necessary for the maintenance of the anticathexis. According to the psychoanalytic psychology of the ego, the energic cathexis of the ego has its source in desexualized libido.[17] This desexualization occurs in various phases. The first is through regression, accompanied by defusion of instincts. The aggression thus liberated remains partly in consciousness, ready to be mobilized in the form of free aggression, and partly allies itself with the superego in the unconscious. This is the second phase, but that is not all. A third part—and this is the point to which I particularly want to draw attention—is diverted from its original aim and is introduced into the structure of the ego. Just as those instinctual representatives which are kept at bay by various defense mechanisms lose their libidinal cathexis, so the aggressive instincts may be diverted from their original aim and subsequently cathect the perceptual plane or serve as the source of the energy required for anticathexis.[18] The more of this aim-deflected aggression the ego has at its disposal the greater is its capacity for anticathexis and the more intact the personality remains.

Such a utilization of aggression, which is typical of the obsessional character, appears to be one of the conditions determining the continued existence of the deutero-phallic phase. If, following Jones, we regard the latter as being cognate to a screen memory, it can only persist when the subject possesses an ego that is in keeping with the obsessional character and is susceptible to anticathexis.

To summarize, we first traced our patient's libidinal development and its abnormalities. We then considered the importance of his aggressiveness and showed that aggression liberated through the defusion of instincts is a decisive element in the structure of personality.

In addition to these points—the development of the libido and the superego, and the utilization of aggression in the personality—there is yet a third important factor in the genesis of perversion, the subject's *dispositional bisexuality*. The strength of biological bisexuality determines the meaning (significance) of the incorporated female identifications in the castration complex of men.[19] The quantitative differences in the bisexual balance are responsible for the variations in the mode of reaction. Hence it is probable that those individuals who, after a castration shock, regress to a passive feminine phase which persists throughout life have biologically a stronger passive feminine disposition than those who surmount such a shock or take their stand in intermediate phases as a means of defense.

CONCLUSIONS

We have considered the problem of our patient from three separate angles. The question of dispositional bisexuality has been only briefly touched on, but the vicissitudes of his libido and his aggression have been dealt with more fully.

Let me briefly recapitulate. This extreme case of fixation at the narcissistic-phallic phase confirms Jones's hypothesis that homosexual perversion is its result. Furthermore, the fixation would appear to depend on the following factors:

(1) The particular phase of libidinal development reached when the castration trauma occurs.

(2) The intensity of the trauma determines whether or not it inhibits the further development of penile sexuality. If it does, it hinders also the further development of the superego and prevents it from reaching its final form. If these inhibitions produce a superego whose nucleus is the mother, the subject's capacity for heterosexual love will be restricted and the narcissistic-phallic phase will persist.

(3) There is yet another point. When the perversion occurs, the subject's aggression is utilized within the ego as follows: the oral and anal aggressive impulses, liberated through regression, are diverted from their original aims and so to speak are sublimated, i.e., they are employed in the ego in such a way that a continuous anticathexis can be produced. The result is an ego which can combat its feminine identification by maintaining a narcissistic-phallic phase, i.e., by adopting a pseudo-masculinity.

NOTES

1. Read before the German Psycho-Analytical Society, November 18, 1933. Published in *Int. J. Psycho-Anal.*, XV (1937), 440–458. Revised for this volume.

2. Jones, E., "The Phallic Phase," *Int. J. Psycho-Anal.*, XIV (1933), 1–33.

3. Sachs, H., "Zur Genese der Perversion," *International Zeitschrift fur Psychoanalyse*, Bd. IX (1932), 172–182.

4. Freud, S., "Some Neurotic Mechanisms in Jealousy, Paranoia and Homosexuality" (1922), *Std. Ed.*, XVIII, pp. 223–232.

5. Ibid.

6. Freud, S., "Three Essays on the Theory of Sexuality" (1905), *Std. Ed.,* VII, pp. 123–243.

7. Horney, K., "The Flight from Womanhood," *Int. J. Psycho-Anal.,* VII (1926), 324–339.

8. Klein, M., *The Psycho-Analysis of Children* (London, Psycho-Analytical Library, 1932).

9. Freud, S., "The Dissolution of the Oedipus Complex" (1924), *Std. Ed.,* XIX, p. 176.

10. Ibid., p. 179.

11. In "The Dissolution of the Oedipus Complex," Freud described the process, the shifts of cathexes by which the primary father image becomes a structure of the superego.

12. Klein, M., *The Psycho-Analysis of Children.*

13. Jones, E., "The Phallic Phase."

14. Freud, S., "The Ego and the Id" (1923), *Std. Ed.,* XIX, pp. 13–47; "Inhibitions, Symptoms and Anxiety" (1926), *Std. Ed.,* XX, pp. 87–156.

15. Sachs, H., "Zur Genese der Perversion."

16. Fenichel, O., "Zur Okonomischen Funktion der Deckerinnerungen," *Int. Zeitschrift fur Psychoanalyse,* Bd. XIII (1927), 58–60.

17. Freud, S., "The Ego and the Id."

18. Nunberg, H., *Allgemeine Neurosenlehre auf Psychoanalytischer Grundlage* (Berlin, H. Huber, 1932).

19. While this article was in press I received a number of the *Psychoanalytic Quarterly,* II (1933), 181–207, containing a paper by Franz Alexander entitled, "The Relation of Structural and Instinctual Conflicts." In it Alexander takes a very similar view regarding innate bisexuality as one of the bases of instinctual conflict.

DISCUSSION

What impresses me now and might impress the younger generation of psychoanalysts are the changes in presentation of clinical investigations that have occurred since the thirties. A detailed description of a case history and the discussion of its transparent dynamics appear almost superfluous today. As the paper reflects the struggle of psychoanalysts in the 1930s to incorporate the structural model in their working equipment, it also shows how new viewpoints slowly found their way and became conceptualized in the general theory of psychoanalysis. It was not enough to assume that the mother plays a role in the formation of a precursory superego, as Melanie Klein began to emphasize at that time; it was necessary to investigate the shifts of cathexes between and within the psychic representations of primary objects, the father and the mother. The wish to support observations which could not be repeated prompted psychoanalysts to describe the dynamic factors from as many viewpoints as appeared meaningful to clarify the intrapsychic situation.

In such microscopic investigation the psychoanalytic process seemed to be neglected.

Psychoanalytic publications of that period differed from the more recent ones in that the former concentrated on metapsychological problems without paying attention to variations in the analytic process itself. About the analytic process itself, we knew little beyond the dynamics of the transference which, taken for granted as the background of theoretical formulations, was rarely discussed in publications. Variations or complications of the analytic process, supposed to be caused by countertransference reactions of the analysts, were considered a private, confidential part of the analysis. This report clarifies the dynamic interaction between instinctual conflicts and the structure of personality.

Looking at the same material with the eye of an analyst today, I ask myself, why did I not write about the transference in this case? It was specific enough to deserve attention. I trust that the case material presented makes the nature of the transference transparent. The patient took great pains to be honest and correct in describing his feelings as he knew them. To me he was always polite and respectful. He concentrated on the problem of his therapy. Hating women as he protested he did, I asked myself, why did he come to me for treatment? Why did he not go to a male therapist? I felt that I was not a person to him, neither a woman nor a man, but the representation of an institution, psychoanalysis, in which he put his hope for cure. He came for treatment when his anxiety became intolerable. Originating in his castration fear, his anxiety now represented the fear of total collapse of his self-esteem if his mother were to know of his homosexuality. Did he come to me, a woman, to relieve his anxiety by exposing to me what he had to hide from his mother? This might have been the unconscious motivation.

I understood the message. His compulsive reaction formations barely protected him from a psychotic break. I was aware of his inability to know more of the origin of his conflict than he was able to tell me. If I had given him the slightest inkling that I had more insight into his problem than he revealed, he either would have interrupted treatment immediately, or would have had an attack of panic, or both. My therapeutic position was simply to support his defense transference. The non–object-directed transference may be interpreted as a relationship to the psychoanalytic situation that represents the universal mother of the symbiotic phase of infancy,[1] such as might lead to an intensely dependent transference to the analyst. This reaction was easily avoided since his hostility toward women as well as his narcissistic character operated against such a course.

Since the transference process was suspended, a transference neurosis did not develop. The analysis thus did not yield data on the basis of repetition of the repressed in the transference. Indeed his natural tendency to analyze his emotions and his capacity for intellectual insight enabled him to learn more about himself and his neurosis under the protective shield of the analytic situation. The analyst, aware of the therapeutic alliance on the patient's terms, had an opportunity to study the case and achieve symptomatic improvement through a psychotherapeutic process which revealed the reciprocal processes between instinctual conflicts and formation of psychic structures.

This paper, characteristic of psychoanalytic publications of its time, shows the freedom of the analyst to apply his therapeutic technique according to the attainable goal of the psychoanalytic situation. (Here I differentiate the psychoanalytic process from the psychotherapeutic aim within the controlled psychoanalytic situation.) Since the therapeutic problem was not the topic of the paper, the psychodynamic factors which impeded the psychoanalytic process and restricted the goal of the therapy and the factors which made possible its limited and easily reversible success were not discussed in the paper.

From our current point of view, what new questions could be raised to illuminate the personality problems of this patient? Two come to my mind spontaneously, but many more are possible. One question relates to the disposition of narcissistic, self-directed libido in the symptom formation and personality organization of the patient; the other refers to the fact that his father died when he was eleven years old.

In regard to the first problem, the answer would have many aspects. The cathexes that protect the endangered penis are a manifestation of self-directed libido which Freud described as a motivation for hypochondriasis.[2] It is assumed that the urgency of self-preservation increases the flow of libido to the penis and maintains the overcathexis of its psychic representation after the operation when the organ was healthy. Although the penis in any case is a highly cathected organ, there seems to be a difference between normal development and that which the patient experienced. In the course of normal development from infancy to genital maturity, the libido which cathects the organ serves as defense against signal anxieties arising from psychic tensions. However, in this case actual pain and long preoccupation with the care of the organ caused an intrapsychic struggle. From boyhood on, the patient labored unconsciously to establish and maintain in his self-image the integrity of his penis. This internal struggle between the wish for perfection of the penis and the anxiety that it was inferior created a narcissistic conflict that caused shifts of his object relationships and led to the homosexual neurosis, i.e., perversion.

Let us consider the second question—Did the death of his father when he was eleven years old have an influence upon his development? At the time the case was studied, this problem was not considered. Investigations during the last decade have led to an assumption that individuals who lose a parent through death (or with whom communication has been completely and permanently interrupted) are arrested at that level of development which they had attained at the time the parent loss occurred.[3] How does this case fit the hypothesis? His psychosexual development was fixated much earlier. When puberty aroused his sexual impulses, his sexuality expressed itself in active homosexuality which he consciously experienced as an attempt to grow in virility by incorporating the penis of another male. He was eleven years old, in prepuberty when his father died; the deutero-phallic fixation evolved when he was four or five years old, during his oedipal phase. The death of his father just recathected or reinforced the earlier fixation to the identification with an idealized father image.

This raises the question—Is there a split between the idealized father and his sexual objects? The idealized father was a cherished memory, an unattainable goal of his self-image. His sexual objects, in some respects depreciated individuals, served the illusory aim of self-completion through the homosexual act. One may speculate whether the death of his father liberated him from the bondage of his idealizing passivity and activated other aspects of his personality, probably at the cost of his compulsion neurosis. The main symptom of this false solution was expressed in his active attitude in incorporating the virility of his sexual partner. In this way he relentlessly searched for the unattainable completeness within himself.

Completeness in this case did not mean the tendency "to be both sexes."[4] He did not fantasize that his male sexual object was a substitute for a woman, at least, not as far as the analysis followed his fantasies. His character structure and behavior did not reveal signs of feminine identification. A desexualized mother image was represented in his superego and in his everyday life with his mother. I could find only one area of empathic understanding for his mother and this expressed itself in his mortifying shame lest his mother would find out about his homosexuality. His rationalization of his shame was, "I cannot live up to her expectations." This really appears to be like the knowledge of the oedipal child regarding both parents—on the boy's side, the wish to be a man and satisfy the mother in fantasy as a child and in reality gratify another woman as an adult. Because of the surgery his sexual development became fixated. The patient's growth after the father's death appears to be more of a development defined and motivated by that phallic fixation than an arrest.[5]

The symptoms of this patient have several surprising features. One is that in spite of his history he did not show the fear of the other sex in genital or erotic content. This man never doubted his sexual potency, never had dreams or fantasies about vagina dentata or other dangers to the penis in the sexual act with a woman. However, heterosexual intercourse interested him only as a badge of normalcy, just as the homosexual act served the purpose of growing up to that illusionary normalcy which his father image represented.

Since I set out to demonstrate Jones's thesis regarding the deutero-phallic phase and its relation to bisexuality, I shall attempt to locate the manifestations of bisexuality in this patient. It was an actual trauma that concentrated narcissistic cathexis on the penis. Would the surgery have necessitated such intense and continual counter-cathexis if there had not been an underlying bisexual anlage? Our assumption is that bisexuality is the prerequisite of any form of homosexuality. But homosexuality is not a necessary consequence of phimosis surgery, in spite of the universal (but individually different) bisexual potential, even if the operation occurs in the critical oedipal phase. Other psychodynamic factors account for the outcome. Pain and anxiety require continuous cathexis of the penis. This increases the narcissistic significance of the organ which at the same time is considered inferior. The "fear for the penis" which was hurt by surgical instruments increases the anxiety originating in the ubiquitous fear of the vagina; this is a representation of the fear of the other sex within oneself.

Bisexuality as a fundamental concept of the psychoanalytic theory of personality development is considered a factor in any symptom formation. It is of interest to show the different manifestations of the bisexual tendencies in the case histories studied in the two papers, "Dominant Ideas and Their Relation to Morbid Cravings," and the one being discussed. The anorexia cases reaching the oedipal phase abhorred femaleness and destroyed it in their own bodies because of the dread which the female sexual function aroused in them. The psychotic regression caused by this anxiety set free the aggression which motivated the disease process. In the homosexual patient the male sex with all its properties had to be guarded, overcathected, so that its perfection or completion remained an aggressively pursued goal, in some sense comparable to the goal of self-destruction in the anorexia patients. Both of these investigations, undertaken with no assumption of their relevance to each other, show that the defense system, which in interaction with the instinctual conflicts maintains the disease process, is charged with aggression. The organization of the aggression in the various structures depends on the depth of the regression which induces the disease process. The depth of the regression and the strength of the ego determine the distance of the symptom from the instinctual conflict.

What then is the significance of bisexuality in these very different disease processes? The fear of surrendering to the male (father) caused the destructive hostility against the own body in the first case; in the second case, the fear of being rejected by the father brought about a similar result. In the male patient the trauma of losing the penis activated the bisexual potential against which the counter-cathexis of the deutero-phallic phase had to be maintained with all its consequences.

Bisexuality is a genetic characteristic but it indicates no sex at all. Just as psychic energy assumes its quality as libido and/or aggression according to the motivations of the systems and structures necessary for its discharge, so bisexuality remains neutral as long as the growing psychosexual organism is in balance. As Jones assumed, the proto-phallic phase has no sexual differentiation since the child is not yet aware of the meaning of the difference. The phallic phase which Freud assumed to be interpolated in the development of both sexes has no behavioral manifestations, and does not cause anxiety except in conditions which cause concern with the other sex and consequently problems about the own sex. Then the bisexuality emerges from its neutrality and attaches itself to the developmental processes which establish the sexual identity and the self-concept.

NOTES

1. Stone, L., *The Psychoanalytic Situation* (New York, International Universities Press, 1961), p. 105.

2. Freud, S., "On Narcissism; An Introduction" (1914), *Std. Ed.*, XIV, pp. 67–102.

3. Fleming, J., "The Evolution of a Research Project," in *Counterpoint*, H. S. Gaskill, ed. (New York, International Universities Press, 1963), pp. 75–105.

4. Kubie, L., "The Drive to Become Both Sexes," unpublished. Read before the Annual Meeting of the American Psychoanalytic Association, May, 1954.

5. Fleming, J., and Altschul, S., "Activation of Mourning and Growth by Psychoanalysis," *Int. J. Psycho-Anal.*, XLIV (1963), 419–431.

5. Adaptation to Reality in Early Infancy

INTRODUCTION

This paper is the last of those which I consider my early papers. It represents a transitional period in my personal and professional life. It was written in Europe during 1935 and translated for presentation at a meeting of the American Psychoanalytic Association in Washington, D.C., in 1937.

The paper was based on two sets of observations. The earlier observations belong to the year 1916 when I was working in the Hospital for Foundlings in Budapest, and the later belong to 1918 when I worked in the Department of Pediatrics of the University Medical School of Pozsony (now Bratislava). Thus I was able to compare the infants I saw in the outpatient clinic with those physically and emotionally abandoned children in the Hospital for Foundlings. The emaciated condition of the latter and their lack of interest in the tangible world was then given the diagnostic label "marasmus."[1]

These observations were in contrast to what I saw in my own children. Their growth and development led me to the insight that development has to be studied, not only in terms of libido, but also in terms of ego development. I realized then that libido development, although it evolves in the sequence of the biologic laws of maturation, is a construction.[2] The child's ego, however, evolves before the mother's eyes, perceivable with her senses and responded to with her own feelings and emotions. Through experience with my own children I realized what the abandoned infants missed, in spite of the care of their hygienic hospital environment and the regularity of their feeding schedules.

Vivid as the impact of that experience was, its conceptualization took a long time to ripen before it could be formulated. At that time there was little direct observation of infants available in psychoanalytic literature. The term "adaptation" in the title of this paper has no refer-

113

ence to Hartmann's concept which had not yet been published. There was only one paper in the literature, written also by an analyst-mother, which dealt with the same problem and came to similar conclusions.[3]

When this paper was in preparation, my aim was to describe and explain the difference in the modes of learning between healthy infants and those suffering from hospitalization. Extensive literature in the early thirties by psychologists on the effects of emotional deprivation confirmed my observations of 1916–19. The routine, impersonal manner of infant care in hospitals and foundling homes resulted in a kind of retardation. Conditioning as an educational method led to pathology. Yet conditioning is also applied by loving parents, and its advantages in habit training are very much approved. Indeed the fact that infants need some kind of routine does not contradict the fact that they have a greater need for love and affectionate stimulation in order to develop normally. While the institutionalized children were impeded in their mental development because of conditioning, the children who were well-loved learned by internalization. Their learning implied the development of their personalities; it could be defined as a process of "individuation."[4]

Through observation of the feeding behavior of infants, I arrived at a formulation of the psychodynamics of these two primary modes of learning. Learning by conditioning limits the adaptive capacity of the ego since for the deprived child any variation in routine represents a threat. The ego of the emotionally gratified child develops through internalization of the need-gratifying object. The processes pertaining to the gratification of needs promote the development in the child of a faculty for adaptation within the normally acceptable environment. This way he grows freely. The healthy infants thus develop an all-important mental faculty, confidence.

NOTES

1. "Marasmus," according to Webster's Dictionary, Second Edition (1944), is "a state of progressive emaciation, especially in infants because of malnutrition and enfeebled constitution." The term "hospitalism" described by Bühler, Durfee, and others in the early 1930s was introduced to psychoanalysis by me in this paper, and by René Spitz in his paper "Hospitalism; An Inquiry into the Genesis of Psychiatric Conditions in Early Childhood," in *The Psychoanalytic Study of the Child*, Vol. I (New York, International Universities Press, 1945), pp. 53–74.

2. Abraham, K., "A Short Study of the Development of the Libido Viewed in the Light of Mental Disorders" (1924), in *Selected Papers* (London, Hogarth Press, 1927), pp. 418–501.

3. Balint, A., "Die Entwicklung der Liebesfähigkeit und der Realitätsinn," *Leleklemzesi tanulmänyok* (Budapest, 1933).

4. Mahler, M. S., "Thoughts about Development and Individuation," in *The Psychoanalytic Study of the Child*, Vol. XVIII (New York, International Universities Press, 1962), pp. 307–324.

ADAPTATION TO REALITY IN EARLY INFANCY[1]

The psychology and the physiology of the newborn child cannot be separated. The psychoanalytic theory of the instinctual reactions of the newborn is based upon the fact that the infant upon leaving the womb, which offers comparatively few stimuli, enters into an environment which presents a superabundance of them. Because no protective barrier (*Reizschutz*) against these stimuli has been developed, the infant is overwhelmed with excitation. This concept does not conflict with the generally accepted assumption that the nervous system of the newborn is not mature. This immaturity, not yet fully understood in all its physiological details, is responsible for the fact that the motor excitability of the infant is much greater than that of later life and that inhibitions are not yet fully developed.

In recent years observations of early reactions have led to the generally accepted opinion that the newborn reacts to every form of stimulus with an undifferentiated, general motor discharge. Numerous choreoathetoid movements, too vague to be described, do not cease completely even during sleep. These movements, under the influence of strong stimuli from without or stimuli from within (instinctual needs), increase to a veritable "storm of excitation."[2] The storm of excitation invades the whole motor system, including the visceral. The crying fit is only one special form of the storm of excitation; in this sense it is not a teleological action in that though it has a goal, it presents merely a motor discharge of excitation; it is unable to gratify the instinctual need. Therefore motor excitation becomes increasingly intensified until gratification of the instinctual need is achieved. Should gratification fail to ensue, the motor discharge continues as long as the physiological forces permit. It is characteristic of the healthy newborn that no substitute and no delay of gratification exist without the motor discharge of the excitement caused by the instinctual need.

The original psychoanalytic theory concerning the psychic condition of the newly born infant was based on the assumption of primary narcissism. According to this hypothesis the sleeping infant finds himself in a condition very similar to that of his intrauterine life. This condition is disturbed by instinctual needs. An instinctual need releases crying, a signal which brings the mother, who for the newborn is not yet perceived as a part of the environment but only as a part of the process of instinctual gratification. This concept of primary narcissism postulates a condition in which the instinctual need releases a reaction in the infant's own body which in turn makes possible a release of tension and permits the child to go to sleep again. According to this theory the course of gratification of instinctual needs during the first 4 weeks following birth occurs in the following sequence: instinctual need, crying, gratification. The next possible step in the course of the process would be: instinctual need, hallucinated gratification which is insufficient, crying which brings on real gratification so that the child can then sleep again.[3]

The succeeding step in maturation is that, after the real satisfaction, the child does not fall asleep immediately, but after the physiological satisfaction of the need a libidinal satisfaction follows. The child may suck playfully on the breast and play with his hands. The libidinal satisfaction keeps the child awake so that he perceives the environment beyond the immediate satisfaction of the need.

Although the reactions of the newborn to all stimuli are undifferentiated motor discharges, if the stimuli are not so strong as to produce a crying fit, it is possible to observe isolated reactions at a very early age.[4] Several observations show that within the first month of life reactions appear which are specific as to stimuli and as to effect. The majority of the reactions take place around the mouth and are usually sucking or grasping movements.[5] The first specific affective reaction is considered to be the turning of the head toward the breast of the mother. Ripin and Hetzer[6] emphasize that such reactions appear when the infant is in a situation of *expectation*.[7] This situation of expectation can be produced experimentally. For instance, the infant when put in the feeding position begins to search for the breast with sucking movements of the mouth.

Although the data as to age given by various authors differ, we can observe the state of expectation in a healthy infant as a normal reaction as early as the third month of life. The time of the appearance of these reactions depends on constitutional factors, on the condition of the infant's health, and on the technique of feeding. A child fed on the bottle begins to show the reaction of expectation in the fourth month of life and after this age will show disappointment whenever the bottle fails to be offered or whenever it is taken away. The corresponding reactions in a breast-fed child develop earlier. Before the fifth month intense hunger and the subsequent crying fit inhibit specific reactions; but in the fifth month or after, the feeling of hunger directly evokes specific reactions. At this time the infant does not show his hunger with an immediate cry but follows with concentrated gaze the preparations for feeding. Thus the child has learned to wait.

As a reaction to an instinctual need, waiting is the opposite of direct development of excitation. The infant in this fourth to fifth month of life has developed from the stage of immediate demand to a stage in which he is able to keep his need, at least for a time, in suspense. This arrested tension turns the attention of the infant to the environment, from which he expects the gratification. The ego, which forms itself by these acts of perception, establishes its relationship to the environment; this relationship is based on confidence that the instinctual need will be pleasurably satisfied.

From many observations of the facial expressions of infants, I want to emphasize the following: the infant recognizes the face of the mother or of the nurse at an earlier age than he recognizes the bottle; his gestures are directed toward the person and not toward the object of gratification. I consider this fact, mentioned especially by Bühler and her school,[8] a landmark in the development to the stage of object relationship. In the state of primary narcissism there is no separation between ego and external world. The mother belongs to the ego. Further elaboration of this theory is the assumption that the first recognition of the mother as a part of the outer world is induced by the certainty that the mother=breast will return to the ego, that the mother will be within reach for gratification of the instinctual need. This confidence is a stage of object relationship which precedes the positive object love. It has, on one hand, connection with the primary narcissism; on the other hand, it already reaches out for the object. This step levels the way from the stage of primitive omnipotence to the reality of the object world. It is rooted in the experience of the infant that the gratification of needs will be attained before the instinctual need has increased to a painful sensation which has to be discharged in a crying fit. The amount of the confidence could perhaps be measured by the behavior of the infant during this period of expectation. The smiling and cooing are directed toward the mother. Confidence enables the child to wait and leads his attention to the mother and thus also directs the libido. In expectation the child turns to the outer world, whereas during the crying fit the infant turns away from the outer world. This can be directly observed: the infant, who has turned all his expectant facial expressions toward the mother, becomes angry when satisfaction does not follow. We observe that for a time he expresses anger without crying, but when he cannot wait any longer, he turns his head away and starts to cry. From this moment on he is not to be comforted by words or gestures—only real satisfaction of the need can calm him. Thus, in this stage we can recognize the regression of the still very labile ego.

Searl[9] in her excellent paper on the psychology of screaming made a clear distinction between the cry of dissatisfaction and the crying which brings on the satisfaction which can therefore be called, in the terminology of Ferenczi, a cry of omnipotence. She explains the psychological meaning of the screaming fit for the development of the ego in terms of the well-known theoretical assumptions of the English school. Although analysts have different opinions about the psychological and instinctual processes which take place during the screaming fit, all agree that it influences the child deeply. It causes disagreeable visceral sensations, perhaps even pain, and it can end with exhaustion. Even if it does not last that long, it can be traumatic for the infant. During the screaming fit the infant is not responsive to any attempts to quiet him. Very often the crying infant, half exhausted at the peak of his crying, receives the nipple in his mouth but has to undergo a series of disagreeable sensations during which he repeatedly loses the nipple until he achieves the rhythm of sucking. It is easy to understand that the tension of the instinctual need, which itself would be enough to produce anxiety as Freud assumes, is now complicated by screaming and painful sensations during feeding. The satisfaction of the feeding is mixed with anxiety.[10] This anxiety interferes fundamentally with the development of the infant. The development of the ego is impaired because the primary object relationship, the confidence or trust in the mother, could not develop.

Dr. Max Seham describes the suckling's reaction to the feeding process as follows: fed day after day in a certain place at a certain time, the suckling will refuse to accept the same food if the circumstances under which he has been accustomed to being fed are suddenly changed.[11] Even though he is fed in the same bed but in a different position, he may refuse to take the bottle. The smile at the sight of a parent, the opening of the mouth at the sight of a spoon and hundreds of similar examples can be taken from the daily life of a child. And just as these stimuli may have a favorable effect on the child's mental and physical health, so also may they have an unfavorable effect and produce many and various disturbances.

This observation is thoroughly recognized in hospitals, institutions for infants, foundling homes, and orphanages, and is called "hospitalism." Hildegard Durfee and Kathe Wolff, in an extensive study of hospitalism in infants during the first year of life, state that those children in institutions, exposed to the so-called best hygienic conditions, are markedly different from the children raised in homes.[12] The typical reaction of the infants raised in institutions is fear, which constitutes the only reaction to all kinds of stimuli. The group of children studied by Durfee and Wolff in the second half-year of life showed a marked asocial attitude due to general reactions of fear. Though the conditions of the control children raised in homes were not as hygienic as those in the institutions, the reaction of this group to objects, their social behavior, and their motility showed higher development. The object world, even though offered to the child, remains strange, distant, and incomprehensible without proper emotional relationship to a human being who helps the child to master the object world.

The undisturbed relationship of a normal infant to the outer world is based on the relationship to a person; the eyes of the infant follow the movements of the nursing person and not the bottle. Therefore there is no great difference in the sequence in which the manipulation is brought about. Those infants whose relationship to the mother is not disturbed will take the bottle or other routine things of nursing from the right or left or from whatever direction they come. However, sometimes we can observe a sign of surprise or astonishment on the face of the child if something unexpected or something especially new occurs in this sequence. The child turns his head and eyes toward the mother and is reassured—he has developed the emotional relationship of *confidence*.

By introducing this term, "confidence," into psychoanalytic literature, I am conscious that I am describing a state in libido development which is closely similar to the phenomenon which Balint designates with the abstraction "primary object love," which is based on the dual unit of mother and child.[13] Balint interprets the psychological content of primary object love as: "I should be loved and satisfied, but without the least return of love on my part." I agree with Balint on the concept of the dual unit of mother and child as the basis of the further development of libidinal relationship, but I cannot follow his interpretation of the psychological content of this state, especially the second part of it: ". . . without the least return of love on my part." Here we see the projection of the psychology of the adult into the psyche of the infant. Observations show undoubtedly that an infant, as soon as the relationship with the environment develops, instinctively returns as much love as lies within his physiological maturity.

The term "passive object love," or the "state of tenderness" as Ferenczi calls it,[14] describes a later stage of development than we are primarily concerned with in this paper. It refers to a condition in which the infant has a conscious need of love and tenderness; he is able to fantasy. I believe the more satisfactory the development of confidence has been the less loud and demanding is the need for tenderness or passive object love, which is found so often persisting in oral-demanding characters.

It is questionable whether it is useful to introduce this descriptive psychological term "confidence" instead of the metapsychological term "primary object love." However, I believe that we can better understand the condition in which the infant finds himself in relation to the object world when we extend our terminology by using terms with more detailed psychological shading. I shall try to define metapsychologically and phenomenologically this confidence which is the basis for the development of a positive object relationship between mother and child.

As to the metapsychological significance, I have explained that confidence corresponds to a state of libido development in which narcissistic libido is turning into object libido. It corresponds to a state of ego development in which the borders between "I" and "you" are not yet marked as definitely as in later life and thus can be easily suspended —the "you" becoming part of the self again. Assuming that confidence is a wavering exchange between the id of the infant and the mother, we can ask whether it is justifiable to extend our terminology or whether it would be better to classify confidence as a manifestation of identification. The observations on which these explanations are based show clearly that the libidinal process which has developed from the infant's early experience of satisfaction enables the child to wait. Waiting is a condition in which libido is directed toward the outer world and constitutes the opposite of incorporation or identification. It leaves the mother as a part of the outer world and prepares the object love, step-by-step, and thus functions as the forerunner of the development of object love.

These conclusions are in conflict with the theories of Melanie Klein who assumes that the development of the object relationship between mother and child is based on the process of identification and projection.[15] I believe that the observations on which this paper is based can be helpful in clarifying this point. Neither the bad nor the good mother is projected into the outer world, but the libido, turned to the outer world, finds there the satisfactory, good mother or the frustrating, bad mother. In the former case, the object-libidinal relationship develops with all the protective consequences. In the latter case, the libido will be withdrawn and we can observe in the child the effects of the lack of libidinal relationship. At first this is expressed by the crying fit due to frustration of instinctual need. The repetition of frustration, however, leads to withdrawal and depression.

It is difficult to describe the phenomenological content of the positive emotional state of the infant since this, by its essential meaning, does not amount to an emotional tension. Confidence, especially in childhood, does not develop into a conscious emotion. Lack of confidence causes discomfort and tension which can grow into anxiety. Confidence, as we understand it now, is a disposition which protects the emotional life from oscillations; it protects the ego from the fear of object loss. Thus it saves one from pain. Confidence plays an important role in the economy of the psychic apparatus. It helps to preserve the mother-child unit, it helps to decrease the intensity of outer stimuli and helps to avert anxiety. It is a part of the defense apparatus of the psyche which has its origin in the development of object libido from the narcissistic libido reservoir. On this basis, it seems to me that confidence can be metapsychologically differentiated from the other defense mechanisms of the ego. Indeed confidence is not a defense mechanism of the ego in the terms of Anna Freud. These represent counter-cathexes of the ego against anxiety caused by internal or external danger. In contrast, confidence originates in the gratifications of primary instinctual needs and the ensuing primary object relationship. It is a primary mental structure, the result of the interaction of physiologic and object-related processes.

The development of this emotional shelter, confidence, in its importance to the libido economy is responsible for the marked distinction between the children we ordinarily call normal and the children described by Seham.[16]

Seham emphasizes that every change in the routine of nursing releases fear which can cause functional disorders. The paper of Durfee and Wolff and other studies about hospitalism state that the reactions of the infants subjected to hospital routine are characterized by fear.[17] Sucklings, doomed by nursing routine or by physical sickness to repeated and long screaming fits, are conditioned on a lower than age-adequate, maturational level. Thus every unexpected movement seems to remind the infant of the danger with which he is always surrounded. Every new situation increases the tension, releases the shock and with the shock the screaming fit, which causes the disagreeable sensation of anxiety. Thus is created a vicious circle which has to be avoided. In this process of self-protection the infant is deprived of his powerful ally, the mother, to whom the child capable of waiting can turn with the conviction that help and satisfaction will come from her. The infant who cannot entrust himself to the mother is left alone; he does not turn attention libidinally to the mother; at best, he turns to inanimate objects surrounding him.

He is abandoned by the mother and therefore concentrates his weak ego on things, in an attempt to save himself from any new situation which is frightening. The infant becomes dependent on the sequence of the procedure of nursing, on the manipulations of the nursing persons, and on the articles used. This kind of conditioning must be differentiated from the learning process which we described in connection with the development of the attitude of confidence in the mother.

In the latter process the ego is assured, enhanced by a reliable ally, the mother, who regulates the things of the outer world and saves the child from anxiety. The ego, strengthened on one hand by the libidinal relationship to the mother and, on the other, by the absence of anxiety, has a greater capacity to perceive the objects of the outer world. The ego is able to accept new and unexpected situations, always in a degree which corresponds to the developmental level of the child, and masters them by trust in the mother. In the adaptation to reality he has a greater span and greater versatility.

Quite different from this development is the adaptation to reality in those children whom we describe as affected by hospitalism, by lack of love, or by too much routine. These children cannot establish confidence as the precursor of the primary object relationship. Therefore they develop a greater amount of anxiety with which they have to contend.

Their anxiety has several sources. One of them is the body itself which causes the infant pain by sensations of unsatisfied instinctual needs. The other source of anxiety is the real danger in which the weak ego finds itself in the object world. Perhaps we could assume as a third source at a later age the instinctual tension which develops as a result of the disturbance of the object relationship to the mother.

Whatever the source of the anxiety, it is clear that it is a heavy burden for the young ego to deal with. The ego, beset with anxiety, turns only a small part to the object world, cannot select and learn, but reacts with rigid adaptation.

Such reflex adaptation saves the child from an increase of tension and is helpful in the avoidance of anxiety; but every new situation, in contradiction to the old ingrained reflex, will be experienced again by the weak ego as a danger to which it cannot adjust itself immediately, but to which it reacts with crying, the discharge of fear reaction. There is another reaction which is also possible—avoidance of fear by refusal to accept a new situation. Both of these reactions, crying and rejection of the new situation, restrict the ego's capacity to adapt itself to changes in reality.

The profound effect of early disappointments during the feeding process on later development has been studied often by psychoanalysts. Melanie Klein emphasizes that a disturbance in the relationship to the mother causes an early and strict development of the superego which determines the development of the individual.[18] Rado[19] assumes, and Fenichel[20] has in a recent work again explained, that the first regulator of self-regard is the emotional satisfaction which accompanies feeding, and he concludes that the later disturbances of self-esteem and inferiority feelings are to be connected with early disappointments during the feeding process and with the feeling of being helplessly abandoned to the object world.

I wish to emphasize in this paper that the ego's capacity to learn to master the object world goes hand-in-hand with the development of its object-libidinal relationship. When the object-libidinal relationship is disturbed the ego's learning capacity is inhibited and narrowed by anxiety. The psychic economy of such children is concentrated on the avoidance of anxiety. This avoidance can be achieved if the child remains at the level of conditioned reflexes. I want to stress again the great importance this may have for the mechanism of fixation.

The conditioned reflex also forms the pattern of coping with anxiety in later life. The early mechanization of mastering anxiety is the same as fixation to a special form of solution of a conflict. It is easy to understand that every anxiety will subject the individual to the old feeling of inadequacy and weakness that was present at an early age when the good relationship to the mother, the development of confidence, was thwarted.

What disturbs the relationship between the mother and child so early? When Ferenczi conceived the idea of infants in their primary narcissistic omnipotence and Abraham described oral libidinal satisfaction as the most important factor in early life, they were not mistaken in their concepts, though they differed greatly from the newer conceptions in psychoanalytic literature based on frustration, on unsatisfied needs, and on the crying of infants. These newer conceptions are justified by experience in the analysis of adults and in observations of children. Why do we find so many rejected children and so many adults with the psychology of the rejected child?

Bernfeld in his *The Psychology of the Infant* devotes a chapter to the problem of the history and sociology of nursing and he shows that nursing techniques in all cultures are determined by several social and psychological factors.[21] They have changed a great deal in our civilization during the last thirty years. The fact of overfeeding led Czerny to introduce strict regulations. The fear of spoiling the child, perhaps the fear of the child's demands, caused these rules to be observed with religious rigidity. Balint quotes many pediatricians who state that if their directions regarding the feeding regime and prohibition of lifting up the child are not strictly followed from the first day of life, they cannot hold themselves responsible for the development of the infant because the regularity of body functions, disturbed the first day, cannot be established later.[22]

Fortunately, there are also many pediatricians who are beginning to realize that our children cry too much.[23] Infants born in this hygienic age are raised by a strict ritual which is dictated from the first moment of life by what seems to be the most important element in our civilization—time. The child has to be adapted to the time regulations of the hospital or the home, as the doctor prescribes. It is also true, and pediatricians describe this often observed phenomenon, that mothers awake from sleep when the infant awakes, even though they have not heard the child or before they could hear him. The so-called nursing rapport of the mother with the child illustrates the conception which was evaluated from the psychoanalytic viewpoint by Alice Balint, *namely, that the mother-child unit exists not only within the child but has also its biological representation in the mother, at least during the period of nursing.*[24] This unit is broken if and when the infant is to be molded to the customs of our civilization.

The general rule for the normal infant is a feeding every four hours starting, for instance, in the morning at six o'clock and ending at ten at night. There is no deviation from the rule, no change in the time schedule, even when a very orally inclined baby cannot tolerate the gap from ten P.M. until six A.M. So it happens that the majority of infants cry hours and hours in the first days of life.

It would be worthwhile to study in detail the question of why in this century of children, mothers so readily accept the rigid type of hygiene as the highest precept in their relationship to their infants; why they relinquish so easily their emotional relationship to the child and very often reject it with the rationalization that they are doing only what has been prescribed and is therefore best. I think that it would not be very difficult to prove that this century of children is in reality the century of women. It is the emancipation of women that elevated nursery hygiene to its present height and with the help of narcissistic satisfaction intellectualized the mother's relationship to the child.

The technique of feeding as it is practiced directly contradicts all our leading principles of education. We endeavor to find a way to satisfy the needs of the child which guarantees the best development of the personality. All modern studies of education are aimed toward finding methods to save the child from inferiority feelings and from the under-mining of the ego. But it seems that we start with a system which in reality does not take into consideration the child's own rhythm of in-stinctual needs and we condition the child to factors which are really not in harmony with his physiological rhythm. I am not in favor of overfeeding; moreover, pediatricians state that overfeeding does not easily occur. I want to come back to the modern pediatrician's state-ment that a well-satisfied infant has nothing to cry about. I also wish to call attention to the observation that it is possible to satisfy the child's needs and regulate the feeding regime in accordance with the child's own rhythm. It is possible to offer the child an adequate quantity of food without under- or overfeeding and not more frequently than neces-sary, and yet have the feeding schedule determined by the factors to be found within the child rather than within the mother or the outside world.

I am aware that following this suggestion will not prevent all developmental disturbance in later life, but I think what little we do know about the factors operating in early infancy justifies our attempt to achieve better conditions for the development of the infant. We know that psychological development cannot be separated from physiological development. Therefore we ought to bring our knowledge into harmony with the physiological maturation of the child. The first nursing and feeding regimes are of primary importance in the complicated interre-lationships between individual, environment, and society. The influences to which the newly born child is exposed are individual and personal in relation to the family and are especially determined by the mother's personality and her relationship to the child. These very important factors are not included in this study. I want only to point out that the child's environment is determined by an interdependence of a number of factors which operate through the panacea of hygiene. These factors should be analyzed, divested of their magic power, and subordinated to the task of providing our infants with the best environmental condi-tions for growth.

NOTES

1. Read before the American Psychoanalytic Association, Washington, D.C., December 28, 1937. Published in the *Psychoanalytic Quart.,* VII (1938), 200–214. Revised for this volume.

2. Galant, J. S., "Uber die Rudimentären Neuropsychischen Funktionen der Säuglinge," *Jahrbuch f. Kinderheilkunde,* CXXXIII (1931), 104–108.

3. We can observe an intense rhythmical sucking in the infant shortly before he awakens. These sucking movements during sleep represent the primary biological form of dreams because they seem to have the same economic function which Freud ascribes to dreaming. It preserves sleep, utilizing the reflex coordination of sucking which exists also in intrauterine life. This primary dream—hallucinatory satisfaction—proceeds on the level of biological processes and does not justify our assuming any dream content.

4. Model, M., "Besonderheiten des Sensorapparates des Neugeborenen," *Zenteralblatt für die Gesammelte Kinderheilkunde,* XXVII (1931), 129.

5. Ripin, R., "A Study of the Infant's Feeding Reactions During the First Six Months of Life," *Archives of Psychology,* CXVI (1930), 1–44.

6. Ripin, R., and Hetzer, H., "Frühestes Lernen des Säuglings in der Ernährungssituation," *Zeitschrift für Psychologie,* CXVIII (1930), *82* ff.

7. The term "anticipation" would better fit the developmental level of the child. *Expectation* implies a more mature ego that makes use of the memory traces of the experience, the repetition of which he expects. *Anticipation,* on the other hand, is closer to id processes, to the instinctual demand. Instinctual tension stimulates anticipation which directs attention and registers change in the level of tension.

8. Bühler, C., "Die Reaktionen des Säuglings zu dem menschlichen Gesicht," *Zeitschrift für Psychologie,* CXXXII, 1 ff; Ripin, R., and Hetzer, H., "Frühestes Lernen des Säuglings in der Ernährungssituation," *Zeitschrift für Psychologie,* CXVIII (1939), 82 ff.

9. Searl, M. N., "The Psychology of Screaming," *Int. J. Psycho-Anal.,* XIV (1933), 193–205.

10. From the analytic material of adults, Weiss (Weiss, E., "Die Psychoanalyse eines Falles von Nervösen Asthma," *Int. Z. Psychoanalyse,* VIII, 440 ff.) concluded that the coincidence of crying, sobbing, and swallowing may be pathogenic for later development of asthma. Harnik (Harnik, J., "Uber eine Komponente der Frühkindlichen Todesangst," *Int. Z. Psychoanalyse,* XVI [1930], 242 ff.) found in adult cases that anxiety was caused by forced feeding. These findings in the psychoanalysis of adults are in accordance with Peiper's (Peiper, A., "Die Entwicklung des Mienenspiels," *Monatschr. f. Kinderheilkunde* [1935], 35 ff.) observations and experimental studies about the sucking function of the infant: during sucking the infant sucks, swallows, and inhales simultaneously.

11. Seham, M., "The 'Conditioned Reflex' in Relation to Functional Disorders in Children," *Am. J. Diseases of Children,* XLIII (January, 1932), 163–186.

12. Durfee, H., and Wolff, K., "Anstaltspflege und Entwicklung im I. Lebensjahr," *Z. f. Kinderforschung,* XLII (1934), no. 3.

13. Balint, M., "Frühe Entwicklungsstadien des Ichs. Primäre Objekt-liebe," *Imago*, XXIII (1937), 270–288.
14. Ferenczi, S., "Sprachverwirrung zwischen den Erwachsenen und dem Kind," *Int. Z. Psychoanal*, XIX (1933), 5–15.
15. Klein, M., *The Psycho-Analysis of Children* (New York, W. W. Norton, 1932).
16. Seham, M., "The 'Conditioned Reflex' in Relation to Functional Disorders in Children."
17. Durfee, H., and Wolff, K., "Anstaltspflege und Entwicklung im I. Lebensjahr."
18. Klein, M., *The Psycho-Analysis of Children*.
19. Rado, S., "The Psychical Effects of Intoxication," *Int. J. Psycho-Anal.*, IX (1928), 301–317.
20. Fenichel, O., "Frühe Entwicklungsstadien des Ichs," *Imago*, XXIII (1937), 243–269.
21. Bernfeld, S., *The Psychology of the Infant* (London, Kegan Paul, French, Trubner & Co., 1929).
22. Balint, M., "Frühe Entwicklungsstadien des Ichs. Primäre Objektliebe," *Imago*, XXIII (1937), 270–288.
23. Zahorsky, J., "The Discard of the Cradle," *Journal of Pediatrics*, IV (1934), 660 ff.
24. Balint, A., "Die Entwicklung der Liebesfähigkeit und der Realitats-sinn" (Budapest, Lelekelemzési Tanulmanyok, 1933).

DISCUSSION

Since this paper was published, the direct observation of children has been developed both as a source for psychoanalytic hypotheses and as a field for confirmation of hypotheses through planned research. It is gratifying that the hypotheses presented in this paper have been confirmed by innumerable psychoanalytic investigators. The effects of emotional deprivation have been well studied in relation to personality development and its pathologic deviation, but not directly to elucidate the modes of learning in early childhood. Learning in this context means adaptation. One could say that learning through conditioning leads to fixation, rigidity of adaptive processes. Learning through confidence leads to freedom in relationship to the object world and to its mastery.

The concept *confidence* found an identical twin much later. Erik Erikson independently developed the concept of *trust*.[1] He attributes the development of trust to the same primary processes between mother and infant; he considers the function of this intrapsychic construct to be the facilitation of object relationships as I have described.

I chose the word confidence because this word for me implies reciprocity, mutuality, con-fideo. Erikson feels that he chose the word trust because it implies "complete reliance" vested in the trusted person.

As I related this little semantic dispute, it suddenly became meaningful to me. Thinking in terms of Erikson's paper on womanhood,[2] trust would be a man's word—reliance on the self, trusting because he is trusted; confidence is the woman's word—it relates always to another person who shares the trust.

The concept "emotional symbiosis" was not introduced in this paper. Indeed my emotional and cognitive conviction at the time I wrote the paper was that of a one-sided relationship—the mother, the absolute giver; the infant, the absolute receiver. The content of the paper had been fixated that way in my memory. On rereading the paper for this publication, I was very much surprised by a purely literary dispute with Michael Balint,[3] who interpreted primary object love of the infant with the words, "I should be loved and satisfied, but without the least return of love on my part," to which I responded in this paper, "Observations show undoubtedly that an infant, as soon as the relationship with the environment develops, instinctively returns as much love as lies within its physiologic maturity."[4] No doubt, only an unconscious reliance on the mutuality of the love, i.e., upon the emotional symbiosis, could dictate my retort. Now I realize what my blind spot was—that love is in the eye of the beholder. Only the mother who perceives the baby's smile or touch as love can feel that it is love. When I wrote this paper, it was a projection of things past. (The same blind spot indicates probably why it took so many years for me to arrive at an experimental, non-theoretical concept of the origin of ambivalence. See "Toward the Biology of the Depressive Constellation," this volume.)

However, writing this now I realize what a good illustration this is for the process about which so many questions are raised nowadays. How did psychoanalysts make their discoveries in those early times? How did the mind of the psychoanalyst work? Here is an example in which not even psychoanalytic insight into dreams or the processes experienced by analyzing patients led to formulation of a concept that has been confirmed.

Where should one begin? Where are the origins of one's perceptual faculties and interests? No doubt, unconscious motivations participate in the choice of profession; external events and deeply rooted, instinctual motivations interact in preparing the soil. My brief psychoanalytic experience occurred after my pediatric training. Meaningful as this analysis was, it did not deal with problems of motherhood. It taught me to listen to my patients and to my own responses; it mobilized the desire to *know* what was going on during psychoanalytic sessions. Thus, learning from experience and studying the experience of learning were inseparable. It became a mental habit.

I intended to answer the question of how early psychoanalysts conducted their investigations and I have talked about the attitude of the mind that oscillates from the patient's associations to one's own and works through one's own experiences while helping the patient to understand his. But these experiences might have remained on the primary process level if I and other psychoanalysts of that period had not been lucky. I was entrusted very early in my career with the teaching of psychoanalysis to students; this required objectivation of my intrapsychic experiences.

This was also true even with my own children. I learned from and through them. Teaching others what I had learned was a working-through process. In this way, I might say, insights were formulated, but insights are not "formulated," rather they suddenly appear in one's mind as a valid explanation of things felt, known, forgotten, perceived again, and remembered in other contexts and strengthened by new observations.

All this sounds diffuse, tentative, incoherent in time and aim. Yet it was just that way. Was it an investigation? It was not undertaken to make a point or to write a paper. It developed like something alive. An emotionally charged experience had to be understood. For that purpose, observations had to be collated in the light of the experience; differences in the behavior of infants had to be observed in the light of the mothering the infants received. Thus my own ideas solidified. Then came the second, the goal-directed part of the research—searching in the observations of others for assurance that I was on the right track, that my conclusion was not based only on one set of data. Many other investigators may have come to the same conclusion. The difference was in the hypothesis which, at the beginning, was unconscious but became conscious as the result of investigation. It seems to me that such an investigation can be compared with psychic development. Just as in mental development the remnants and derivatives of the experiences of an earlier phase survive in the next, so the blind spots in this paper forecast the next research that became ready for publication a decade or more later.

NOTES

1. Erikson, E., *Childhood and Society* (New York, W. W. Norton, 1950).

2. Erikson, E., "Inner and Outer Space: Reflections on Womanhood," *Daedalus* (1964), 582–606.

3. Balint, M., "Frühe Entwicklungsstadien des Ichs. Primäre Objektliebe," *Imago,* XXIII (1937), 270–288.

4. Benedek, T., "Adaptation to Reality in Early Infancy," pp. 115–125, this volume.

6. The Correlations Between Ovarian Activity and Psychodynamic Processes

INTRODUCTION

The following two papers were published as preliminary reports on the research that appeared as a monograph under the title "The Sexual Cycle in Women" (1942).[1] Since the monograph is too voluminous to be included here, I hope that these publications, with the added discussion, will serve the purpose of this volume. They call attention to the original investigation and to the conclusions derived from it and they offer an opportunity to demonstrate psychoanalysis as an investigative tool in psychobiologic research. Since they served as the basis for my further theoretical work, they present the appropriate introduction to those papers which deal directly or indirectly with the reproductive function of women.

To publish a pioneering research is a hazardous undertaking. Republishing it forty years later is probably not less so if we consider the development in physiologic research and in the basic behavioral sciences such as psychoanalysis. Ovulation, which once appeared an almost mysterious event, is now a controllable fact; temperature charts are in general use for the purpose of establishing the time of ovulation; the histologic evaluation of vaginal smears has wide diagnostic application. But psychoanalytic theory and practice have not advanced in the clarification of the psychobiology of women. It seems paradoxical that at the time when this investigation began, the techniques of establishing the time of ovulation were new; the interpretive technique of psychoanalysis, in contrast, was considered established and was applied in research of psychosomatic symptoms.

The significance of this investigation depended on the reliability of the methods of the investigators. It was implicitly assumed that the method of the physiologist—evaluation of vaginal smears combined with measurement of the basal body temperatures—provided checks

129

on the prediction of the time of ovulation based on psychoanalytic
interpretations. The application of psychoanalytic interpretations to
assessment of qualitative and quantitative changes in psychodynamic
tendencies was untried and vague. We tacitly assumed that careful
analysis of conflicts, affects, and feelings, as they were conveyed through
recorded psychoanalytic material, was the method that would serve our
purposes.

In preparing these reports for this volume, I recall with compelling
intensity a feeling that I did not have when the material was collected,
but only years later when I discussed problems of psychoanalytic research in various contexts. Then I began to wonder about the naiveté
that prompted me to undertake this investigation without hesitation.
It may be unbelievable to investigators today that I began studying the
case records without reading the rich literature on the gonadal cycle.
(All the relevant literature on hormones appeared after my medical
school years.) Was it confidence in psychoanalysis or was it scientific
rigor that prohibited me from doing this? I approached the analysis of
the recorded material as I would that of an analytic patient. The un-
concerned attitude saved me from the reproach that my knowledge of
physiology influenced my interpretations; I could regard my conclusions with good conscience as my discovery.

Actually the problems we set out to investigate were simpler than
many others that psychoanalysts chose for study. This investigation did
not intend to illuminate the ontogenetic development of female sexuality
or femininity as a biopsychologic characteristic of the female of the
species, or any of those problems which are the crux of psychoanalytic
theories regarding women. Dr. Boris B. Rubenstein came to the Institute (Chicago) with the questions, is there a period of heightened
sexual receptivity in women comparable to estrus in animals? Could
psychoanalysis help in arriving at an answer to this question? To put
it in psychoanalytic terms, could we differentiate from among the multiple motivations of human behavior those which are fundamentally
related to the influence of ovarian hormones? The question seemed as
simple as it was challenging.

To bring my eagerness in undertaking this investigation closer to
the empathic understanding of the reader, I am inserting here excerpts
from a paper presented to the Columbia University Psychoanalytic
Clinic, New York City, March 31, 1962.[2]

> In this research-minded age when methods of investiga-
> tions rank high among your interests, I feel out of place, or
> rather out of date, since I plan to discuss a research which
> began 35 years ago. In order to do this with any hope of suc-
> cess I ask for your willingness to reverse your thinking and to
> imagine psychoanalytic research as it was at that time.

Because mechanical recording appears to be a necessity to many investigators, I shall remind you that until about 40 years ago psychoanalysts adhered to Freud's advice not to take notes during analytic sessions, but to make case records, only after the session was over or at the end of the working day.[3] Alexander was the first to break with this tradition, and he did it on a relatively large scale.[4]

When the Chicago Institute for Psychoanalysis was established in 1932, the role of emotional factors in duodenal ulcers and other gastro-intestinal disturbances was the immediate subject of investigation.[5] It was a group research project. Each psychoanalyst participating in this project undertook the psychoanalytic treatment of one or two cases with the same psychosomatic disturbance. In contrast to the customary practice, each analyst took notes throughout the analytic sessions. The notes were not verbatim, but dreams and associations were recorded carefully and the interventions of the analyst were also jotted down. The notes were typed and bound in loose-leaf folders. The advantage of note-taking was obvious. Not only did it facilitate presentations by each analyst to the group for discussion, but also it made the record available to each member of the group for study, corroboration and criticism. The records made group investigation possible. . . .

I do not know whether I have conveyed to you the mood of the Institute at that time. It was eager, enthusiastically research-oriented, searching for "controls" of psychoanalytic observations to support psychoanalytic hypotheses. I was waiting for a problem that would provide the impetus for independent research. Then one day a young endocrinologist asked Alexander for permission to present his research problem to the Institute Staff. He was Dr. Boris B. Rubenstein, who at that time was associated with Western Reserve University in Cleveland, Ohio. He had been studying the ovarian cycle in monkeys, in lower mammals and in women. He had observed the behavioral manifestations of "heat" which accompany the fertile period in animals and wondered whether women at the time of ovulation show psychologic manifestations paralleling "heat" in animals. . . .

Concomitant methods of observation—the vaginal smear technique and psychoanalysis—seemed promising for a correlational study. With relatively little inconvenience to the patient, the vaginal smear and basal body temperature technique made possible a series of daily observations of ovarian function. Through psychoanalysis, daily observations of psychic manifestations could be made which, according to psychoanalytic theory, are referable to the sexual drive. We were skeptical, but we felt challenged. Would our material and our method prove satisfactory? I was eager to find out.

Just a few weeks before the staff meeting with Rubenstein, I had begun the analysis of a woman whom I considered an excellent subject for what today we would call a pilot study. She was a married woman in her mid-thirties who, during her only pregnancy eight years before, had suffered a psychotic episode from which she recovered after a period of postpartum depression. Since then she had suffered from periodic depressions and from a variety of psychosomatic symptoms. She had a narcissistic, hysterical character structure. She proved to be unusually suitable for this research. . . .

After nine months I began to study the record. In this preliminary phase of the investigation I considered it my task to find out whether the psychoanalytic material reflected the ebb and flow of recurring emotions and whether at any point I would risk a prediction that ovulation had occurred or was about to occur. We set our first date for comparing data when we had completed the preliminary study of ten cycles. In the presence of a secretary who recorded the meeting, I showed my calendar with predicted dates for ovulation and then Rubenstein revealed his data and diagnosis. To our great surprise, we found that our data showed complete coincidence if we disregarded a discrepancy of 24 hours in some cycles. On later investigation of the material, this time difference could be attributed to the difference between the date of the analytic session and the post-ovulative smear. We were incredulous; our colleagues congratulated us. But to the question, "On what did you base your assumptions?" I had to reply, "I don't know yet."

We added other subjects to the project. I studied the records again and in a short time could report that after varying periods of increasing tension, an emotional relaxation occurred during and after which the psychodynamic manifestations were distinctly different from those of the previous day. This finding made it clear that I had diagnosed ovulation by the occurrence of relaxation. This was still a "macroscopic" diagnosis, however, based on conscious emotional manifestations of a very introspective and articulate woman, my patient. A more detailed microscopic analysis of the recorded psychoanalytic material was necessary to obtain (1) evidence of the effect of gonad hormones upon psychologic manifestations and (2) proof by correlation between data attained by a physiologic method of investigation and psychoanalysis that psychoanalysis is a dependable tool of research.[6]

In this context I want to differentiate psychoanalysis as a therapeutic process and procedure, and psychoanalysis as a research method. The psychoanalytic process itself cannot be simultaneously a method of therapy and research. Freud and the early psychoanalysts were convinced that it was justifiable to assume that the therapeutic process of psychoanalysis was an adequate method of research since with a formalized, quasi experimental method—the analytic situation—a process was initiated which led them to discover what had not been known before. But even if everything were equal, I would hesitate to call the psychoanalytic process going on between analyst and patient "research." The ongoing psychoanalytic process itself is so complex that it does not lend itself to the investigation of any particular problem. The process is directed, primarily, although not completely, by the patient's needs and defenses. No doubt, those fifty-minute sessions stimulate in us "primary processes" which we experience as "insights"; from them our ideas and concepts emerge; these, in turn, direct our anticipation and perception so that, through repetition of comparable experience, we formulate our hypotheses which we hope will clarify our concepts. This method of empiric investigation was inspirational 40 or 50 years ago and was not often challenged, even 30 years ago. It is different today. Nevertheless, the same approach still has its primary significance, for the psychoanalytic process is the source of our experience and also of our recorded material. Psychoanalytic research, however, begins with the study of recorded material.

Our material was not mechanically recorded. Our records were not verbatim. They included, however, dreams, fantasies and free associations which reflected the flow of emotions. They were sufficient for investigation by the method of psychoanalytic interpretation. Today, when mechanical recording appears necessary to many investigators, I want to emphasize the advantage of records which were not intended to be complete; they are less confusing; they contain fewer misguiding details. . . . Not only might such recording interfere with the psychoanalytic process, but much of the psychoanalytic material is not recordable, even with the most exacting methods. Thus psychoanalytic records are never truly complete. Since it depends upon and is mediated by the empathy of the observer, psychoanalytic "observation"

and data are deductions from the recorded interaction between analyst and patient, and later, between investigator
and the material (of the analyst and subject). Thus psychoanalytic data are never raw, primary data. These data undergo further selection and organization according to the
problem being investigated. In the research project itself, assumptions and hypotheses act as selectors and organizers of
the material. They help to reduce the mass of material to
selected data which are relevant to the particular investigation. I was not as clear about this then as I am now.

The analysis of recorded psychoanalytic material has to be differentiated from the analytic process. The investigator is not the psychoanalyst, even if the same person functions in both roles. The psychoanalyst analyzing a patient is the object of the patient's transference
needs; accordingly, he has counter-reactions to the patient. In any case,
in all his communication with the patient, the analyst has to consider
the effect of his verbal and even of his nonverbal communications to
the patient. In contrast, the investigator is not a transference object; he
is outside the psychoanalytic process and views the analyst-patient
communication as a distant observer and can therefore be more objective.[7] Nonetheless, as the researcher studies the record, he has some
definite advantages. Without the pressure of the clock and without the
necessity for understanding and responding immediately in the one-to-
one relationship of the analytic or supervisory situation, he learns about
the affective reactions of the patient, about the interpersonal situations
which activated them; he can differentiate multiple intrapsychic motivations and evaluate the ego's defensive operations.

I would like to convey the relatively leisurely scanning of case
records, absorbing the image of the personality of the subject and, at
the same time, perceiving the day-by-day variations of emotions. This
is easy for the empathic and trained analyst. Psychoanalytic interpretation is the usual procedure, whether it concentrates upon the developmental motivations or upon the affective manifestations of the interpersonal relationship. Our research required, however, that we conclude
from the interactions of these two areas of motivations the hormonal
state of the ovarian cycle. The method was not unique. It required,
however, closer analysis of psychoanalytic communications in order to
trace the specific drive impulse to its "source of stimulation."

Since our investigation was directed toward the manifestation of
the sexual drive, we became blatantly aware of the obvious. Sexual
impulses, wishes, drives in adults are normally accessible to consciousness. Even if hidden in fantasies and dreams, they precipitate moods
and feelings which are experienced and for the most part understood
by the person, even if not admitted. Psychoanalysts are so accustomed

to searching for repressed sexual tendencies that we often forget that we arrive at them from currently experienced or experienceable phenomena such as dreams, fantasies and from behavior. Since in adults sexuality, even if suppressed, motivates derivatives—emotional manifestations that are accessible to empathic understanding—why was it so surprising that the first approach to our investigative task was successful, though based only on our empathic perception of the ebb and flow of emotions? Indeed, such communication between the record and the investigator is probably as unavoidable a first step for orientation as is an experienced psychoanalyst's response to reading a case record.

Psychoanalysts reading case reports organize the data almost intuitively into the developmental history of the patient. Long training has developed their perceptivity of the evaluation of the nuances in interfamilial relationships and their effects on the lives of the subjects. As the course of the analytic process deepens the analyst's understanding, the investigator is soon able to formulate the personality organization of the subject in terms of its genetic, adaptive, and structural processes. It is assumed that the organization of the personality is a permanent system, even if this is true only in a limited sense. Changes in the personality occur during and as a consequence of psychoanalytic therapy; they occur under the influence of life experiences that require adaptations. It is the everyday task of the therapist to gauge the adaptive capacity of his patient under the given intrapsychic and environmental conditions. Therapeutic orientation, however, does not necessitate the consistent observation of intrapsychic changes day after day.

The second stage of our investigation implied the necessity to analyze the day-by-day changes in the frame of the organization of the personality. After we "knew" the patient from the longitudinal aspects of her development, we examined in the cross section of daily events the oscillations of the psychic equilibrium. In other words, we analyzed the day-by-day variation of emotions in the light of the development of the integrated personality.

> We considered the manifest content of the record to be our primary observational data. These data were interpreted in terms of the personality organization and also in terms of the daily variation of emotional manifestations. In that way we arrived at our secondary data. Since each interpretation was based upon one or more hypotheses belonging to different theoretical systems of psychoanalysis, in evaluating our secondary data we paid attention to the theoretical concepts used almost automatically in our interpretations. As our research progressed, it became clear to us that the consistent interpretations of dreams and affects provided the most reliable answers to our inquiry. . . .[8]

As we interpreted the fluctuations of the psychic equilibrium, we considered the external motivations, stimulating and inhibiting factors, and after we accounted for them, we considered the intrapsychic factors which motivated the mood, the affect and the individual's defenses against them. Gauging the emotions against the "constant" personality pattern of the individual, we recognized a variation in the individual's basic preparedness for a specific sort of emotional reaction. The capacity for love, the manifestations of sexual desire or motherliness, of active, constructive tendencies or their opposites, hatred and aggression, are motivated by the individual's past experiences. These are often effective as unconscious or preconscious conflicts. In investigating the day-to-day changes in emotional manifestations, we observed that the patient's unconscious conflicts carried different amounts of charge at different times, thereby producing a variation in the intensity of emotional expression and symptomatic manifestations. Sometimes the conflicts seemed remote from consciousness, while at other times they were near the surface, striving for discharge. We found that knowing the individual's basic reaction patterns and making allowances for actual current environmental influences, we could identify an ebb and flow of emotional intensity which reflected the physiologic stimulation attributable to gonadal hormones. . . .[9]

Details of our use of dream interpretation and the consistent approach to interpreting the dynamics of affects were discussed in the preliminary reports and illustrated in more detail in the monograph. Even so, I have always felt that problems and techniques of psychoanalytic investigations have been shortchanged in our publications, though for good reasons. Psychoanalytic records cannot be published because of their confidentiality and because of their prohibitive volume. The psychoanalytic material in the preliminary reports and also in the monograph had to be abstracted; the interpretations were tabulated. Therefore, in discussing the interpretive method as applied in this investigation, I am aware of how much my intuition might have played a role in arriving at the predictions and at the correlations, and I realize how much empathic understanding is required of the reader to follow them. I hope that the "content" of the material has been illustrated by the dreams in a manner that is experientially accessible to psychoanalytically trained, intuitive readers and that it conveys the sequential changes in the manifestations of the sexual drive as they occur under the influence of and in correlation with the cyclical changes of the ovarian hormones.

NOTES

1. Benedek, T., and Rubenstein, B. B., *The Sexual Cycle in Women; the Relation between Ovarian Function and Psychodynamic Processes* (Washington, D.C., National Research Council, 1942).

2. Benedek, T., "An Investigation of the Sexual Cycle in Women," *Archives of General Psychiatry,* VIII (1963), 311–314.

3. It is understandable that each analyst remembers what made sense to him, i.e., what fitted his expectations or touched his empathy. Thus the core problem of psychoanalytic research became an inevitable part of the investigative method.

4. Franz Alexander (1891–1964) was the founder and director of the Chicago Institute for Psychoanalysis from 1932 to 1956.

5. Alexander, F., et al., "The Influence of Psychologic Factors upon Gastro-Intestinal Disturbances: A Symposium," *Psychoanalytic Quart.,* III (1934), 501–539.

6. This investigation was not the first that used recorded psychoanalytic material to investigate minute details of periodically recurring psychosomatic constellations. The research on asthma conducted at the Chicago Institute for Psychoanalysis at about the same period used a similar application of psychoanalytic technique.

7. There is only one serious countertransference problem that might distort the investigator's response to his material, i.e., his bias toward his working hypothesis.

8. Benedek, T., "An Investigation of the Sexual Cycle in Women," p. 319.

9. Ibid., p. 318.

THE CORRELATIONS BETWEEN OVARIAN ACTIVITY AND PSYCHODYNAMIC PROCESSES: THE OVULATIVE PHASE[1]

With Boris B. Rubenstein, M.D., Ph.D.

The existence of a relationship between gonadal function and emotional states was inferred before the dawn of history and can be traced in the folklore of nearly all peoples. The emotional changes associated with puberty and menopause in both sexes are well known.

The ebb and flow of emotion in the adult woman has also been associated in a vague way with the cycle of sexual function. Premenstrual nervousness, apathy, and depression have often been described in the clinical literature. Less well known, but recognized, are the sudden changes of mood associated with *Mittelschmerz* and other midperiod symptoms which have recently been related to ovulation.[2] Proof of such correlations has, however, been strikingly absent due to ignorance concerning the precise details of the cycle in women on both the physiological and psychological sides. The recently described day-by-day study of vaginal smears and basal body temperatures offers an approach to the problem on the physiological side.[3] The psychoanalytic method offers a powerful tool for such investigation.

The cycle of sex function in the adult woman centers about ovulation. The process of ovulation is merely the rupture of a mature follicle and expulsion of its ovum. It implies preliminary phases of follicular maturation and subsequent phases of corpus luteum formation. During this entire period, the ovary is the source not only of the ovum but also of hormones which exhibit their characteristics throughout the body, preparing it for pregnancy. If the mature ovum is not fertilized, pregnancy does not occur. The uterine mucosa which hormonal stimulation had prepared for nidation of an ovum breaks down upon cessation of the hormonal stimulus and menstruation occurs. It is usual to think of the cycle from one menstrual period to the next. The present description will follow this scheme.

Usually, by the end of menstrual flow, the ovary shows first evidence of follicle development. Follicle maturation usually continues for about ten days during which time there is an increasing production of estrone (the follicular or female sex hormone) which stimulates proliferation of the uterine mucosa. At about the time of maturity, but before rupture of the follicle, lutein cells appear in its lining (granulosa) and begin production of progesterone which stimulates the secretory activity of the uterus. Normally, follicular rupture (ovulation) occurs a few hours later, but is occasionally delayed for some days. After ovulation the former follicle space is invaded by more lutein cells from its lining and these produce both progesterone and an estrogen which maintain the uterus in a state suitable for reception of the fertilized ovum. Upon atrophy of the corpus luteum, progesterone production having diminished, the uterine mucosa breaks down and menstruation follows.

The existence of a hormonal cycle which is reflected in the vaginal smears and basal body temperatures has been established. It was, therefore, interesting to see whether the psychological material could be correlated with the hormonal cycle. Our first question was whether the phases of the ovarian function are reflected in the psychic processes as observed during the psychoanalytic process. Patients who were under treatment for various neurotic disturbances at the Institute for Psychoanalysis in Chicago were selected for this purpose. They were instructed to make their vaginal smears and take rectal temperatures daily. The smears and temperatures were sent to Dr. Boris B. Rubenstein of Western Reserve University, Cleveland, Ohio, for study. The psychoanalytic records were studied by Dr. Therese Benedek at Chicago. After ten months had elapsed the two investigators met to compare for the first time the data of their independent investigations.

THE NORMAL SEX CYCLE

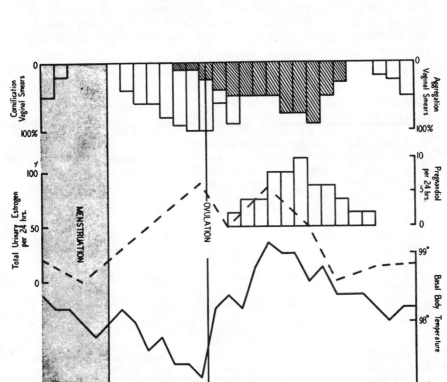

GRAPH I. The normal sex cycle: The solid curve represents the basal body temperatures; the broken curve presents the excretion of estrogenic substances (female sex hormone); the clear blocks in the center are the excretion of pregnanediol sodium glucuronidate (metabolite of progesterone, the corpus luteum hormone); the uppermost set of blocks presents the vaginal smears—the clear blocks indicating cornification, the shaded blocks aggregation. The broken curve is a composite from the data of Gustavson et al., Pedersen-Bjergaard, and Palmer. The pregnanediol excretion is after the data of Venning and Browne. The temperature and smear representation is from my own data.

Both sets of records had been summarized in tabular calendar form.
The calendars were superimposed. We were pleased and surprised to
find an exact correspondence of the ovulative dates as independently
determined by the two methods. The following table represents such a
procedure.

TABLE I

Case I. G. S.	Prediction on the basis of psychoanalytic material		Physiological findings	
Cycle IV Aug. 28–Sept. 23 26 days	Sept. 2:	Heterosexual tension starts	Sept. 2:	Smear full of masculine secretion
	Sept. 4:	Preovulative tension		
			Sept. 3:	Very beginning of cornification
			Sept. 4:	Increasing cornification
	Sept. 7:	Preovulative		
	Sept. 8:	*Postovulative* material	Sept. 8:	*Ovulation*
	Sept. 14:	First premenstrual evidence	Sept. 14:	First premenstrual evidence
	Sept. 23:	Menstrual flow	Sept. 23:	Menstrual flow
Cycle V Sept. 23–Oct. 19 28 days	Oct. 1:	Preovulative tension	Ovulation could occur from Sept. 28–Oct. 7. There is	
	Oct. 3–4:	Ovulation(?)	evidence that it occurred	
	Oct. 4–5:	Ovulation(?)	before the 6th; assume October 3rd.	
	Oct. 9:	First premenstrual evidence	Oct. 10:	First premenstrual evidence
	Oct. 18:	Increased premenstrual tension	Oct. 18:	Cornification
	Oct. 20:	*Menstrual flow*	Oct. 20:	Menstrual flow
Cycle VI Oct. 20–Nov. 14 25 days	Oct. 23:	Heterosexual tension	Oct. 24:	Minimal cornification
	Oct. 27:	Preovulative	Oct. 27:	Increasing cornification
	Oct. 31–Nov. 1:	*Ovulation*	Oct. 31:	Complete cornification Ovulative
			Nov. 1:	Postovulative
	Nov. 5:	First premenstrual evidence	Nov. 5:	First premenstrual evidence
	Nov. 14:	Menstrual flow	Nov. 14:	Menstrual flow

It might be assumed that the psychological structure of the patient whose records we first studied facilitated the location of the ovulative dates. We made the same comparative study of three other cases with various symptoms and different psychodynamic structures, with the same results. In those cycles in which hormonal and psychoanalytic material were available for the ovulative period, the date of ovulation was predicted. We missed complete coincidence only in those cycles in which either the patient failed to take the smears or when there were no psychoanalytic sessions.

After our first encouraging results our task was to find those characteristics of the psychoanalytic material which enabled us to distinguish the various phases of the cycle.

We therefore reviewed the same material day by day. We studied one case during ten cycles, a second case during eight cycles, and the third and fourth cases during five cycles each and found that the psychoanalytic material in the normal cycle showed typical changes which are described briefly in the following paragraphs.

During the follicle ripening phase the psychological material is dominated by heterosexual interest. The libidinous tendencies are concentrated on the male. The heterosexual desire becomes increasingly strong during the ripening phase. With normal sexual adjustment the increasingly strong heterosexual desire finds normal gratification. Without sexual gratification, the heterosexual tension must be dammed up, and increasing hormone production causes increased tension.

In neurotic persons we observe that the increasing estrone production activates psychological conflicts, thus intensifying neurotic symptoms. The heightened psychic tension is suddenly relieved (but only for a short time) when ovulation occurs. The libidinous interest is withdrawn and centered on the woman herself. She is self-satisfied, wants to be loved and taken care of. She is content to be a woman. The period of postovulative relaxation is necessarily of short duration. Hormone production increases rapidly after ovulation. Although both hormones are produced during the luteal phase, progesterone now dominates the hormone picture. The psychological material corresponding to this phase of the cycle shows the tendency to be passive and receptive. The tendency to be impregnated, the tendency to be pregnant, the tendency to care for a child, and the various reactions to all these are reflected in the psychological material. After this phase of the cycle reaches its peak, the corpus luteum gradually regresses and simultaneously the production of progesterone diminishes. After regression of the corpus luteum, many new follicles begin to develop. Ordinarily, none of these follicles is destined to mature. However, they do produce estrone in small quantities. This is immediately reflected in the psychological material by the reappearance of heterosexual interest.

The heterosexual desire of the premenstrual phase is similar to

that of the preovulative phase. In the late premenstrual state this heterosexual tension is complicated by the expectation of menstruation. The
expectation of menstruation is in turn reflected in the psychological
material.

Normally the follicles regress by the end of the cycle. Occasionally,
one of the immature follicles may be luteinized and therefore will complicate the hormone picture by producing minimal amounts of progesterone. This will also complicate the psychological material.

As an example of our day-to-day study and the correspondences
it demonstrated we have presented Table II, one cycle of patient R.E.

TABLE II

CASE R.E.*

Date	Psychoanalytic Material	Prediction	Physiological Findings
Oct. 19–24			Menstrual flow; no smears
Oct. 25	Cheerful; no dream		No smear
Oct. 26	Heterosexual dream content and associations	Starting estrone tension	Beginning cornification. Extreme leukocytic invasion. Definitely preovulative
Oct. 27	Heterosexual desire and feminine exhibitionistic tendencies	Increasing estrone tension	
Oct. 28	Cheerful. Dream material: admiration of brother—associations: fear of brother and of incest	Increasing estrone tension	Increasing cornification
Oct. 29	Castration wishes—heterosexual material—impregnation wish—lutein; Mittelschmerz	Preovulative tension	Lowest point of temperature curve. Minimal folding of completely cornified smear -late preovulative

* The ovulative phase of this cycle, Oct. 30–Nov. 4, is presented in detail in
the text of this paper.

CASE R.E.—*Continued*

Date	Psychoanalytic Material	Prediction	Physiological Findings
Oct. 30	No analytic material		Cornification 75% (slight regression)
Oct. 31	Dream: Strongly heterosexual—fear of impregnation	Preovulative	Cornification 90%. Minimal folding
Nov. 1	Dream: Heterosexual material. 1° Masochistic and identification with brother. 2° identification with mother. Impregnation material	Preovulative	Cornification 100%. Slightly more folding and aggregation
Nov. 2	Dream: Heterosexual wishes and fear of being attacked. During hour fear of pregnancy, increased fear and suffocation	Ovulative	Cornification 100% with more luteal activity—Ovulative
Nov. 3	Cheerful, rushing: Analytic association superficial hypomanic	Postovulative	Leuk influx— clearly postovulative
Nov. 4	No dream; excited, happy, eager, animated. Associations are resistive	Postovulative	Definitely postovulative
Nov. 5	No dream. Feels full and bloated. Associations deal with fear of identification with mother. Fear of pregnancy	Lutein phase	Definitely postovulative
Nov. 6	No analytic hour		Clear lutein state
Nov. 7	No analytic hour		Occasional cornified cell. First premenstrual evidence
Nov. 8	Dream: heterosexual wish and aggression toward brother	Premenstrual	Premenstrual; low estrone level

TABLE II

CASE R. E.—*Continued*

Date	Psychoanalytic Material	Prediction	Physiological Findings
Nov. 9	Fear. Great need for protection. Great dependency		Premenstrual with low estrone
Nov. 10	Craving for sweets. Dream shows castration wish toward a boy. Boy's bleeding—menstruation —castration	Premenstrual	Premenstrual
Nov. 11	Fear of identification with mother on sexual level; fear of insanity	Premenstrual with increased estrone and minimal progesterone	Late premenstrual
Nov. 12	Tension increases. Pain in stomach. Fear of sexual attack. Relaxed during analytic hour	Increased premenstrual estrone	Increased estrone output. Premenstrual
Nov. 13	Aggravation of symptoms, especially fear, diarrhea. Analytic material: Fear of sexual attack	Increased premenstrual estrone material	No smear
Nov. 14	Heterosexual material	No relaxation of estrone tension	Menstrual flow starts. Cornification 90%

On the basis of our preliminary study we set ourselves the following hypotheses:

(1) Increasing heterosexual tendency is correlated with increasing estrone production.

(2) Relaxation and contentment are correlated with ovulation.

(3) The passive and receptive tendencies, the tendencies toward pregnancy and nursing are correlated with progesterone production.

(4) The reappearance of heterosexual tendencies marks the onset of the premenstrual phase which results from new estrone production.

Further studies were carried out in the light of these hypotheses. This report is based on our study of seventy-five cycles of which twenty-three were ovulative. It is of interest to note the frequency of anovulatory cycles in our neurotic patients although the patients were of childbearing age. Even in the anovulatory cycles, there was sufficient fluctuation of hormone production to define the characteristics of the cycle. The psychological material reflected these daily changes and naturally failed to show the psychological relaxation characteristic of ovulation.

METHOD

Physiological. For our evaluation of gonad function, we employed the vaginal smear–basal body temperature technique recently described by one of us with certain modifications.[4] Since the patients were in Chicago and the laboratory work was done in Cleveland, slides of the vaginal smears had to be shipped and therefore dried. To compensate for loss in cytological detail consequent on drying, we advised the patients to take the smears with a stiff wire loop inserted into the posterior fornix of the vagina; we thus obtained comparable smears from day to day. The smears were stained according to the method of Papanicolaou[5] and evaluated without reference to either the temperature or the psychological data. In general, they were adequate for a decision concerning the phases of the cycle represented. It should be noted that since much of the material was damaged, we followed a scheme for evaluation of slides as follows.

Slides were examined and a rough quantitative estimate made of the proportions of various squamous epithelial cell types as follows:

(1) Normal cells with vesicular nuclei.
(2) Cells with granular cytoplasm and pyknotic nuclei.
(3) Cells with keratinized cytoplasm and pyknotic nuclei.
(4) Cells with keratinized cytoplasm and fragmented nuclei.
(5) Cells with "moth-eaten" edges, folded over.
(6) Cells folded and aggregated into masses.

The presence of marked desquamation of epithelial cells in the absence of sperm and red blood cells was given careful consideration. The presence or absence of leukocytes, red blood cells, thick tenacious mucus and of spermatozoa was noted.

Under the influence of estrone, whether produced by the maturing follicle or injected, all mucous membranes,[6] particularly the vaginal mucous membrane, proliferate.[7] The superficial cells grow away from their blood supply and begin to undergo the degenerative processes called cornification (types 2 to 3 to 4). We assume, therefore, that in an untreated woman the progressive change in smears from type 1 through to type 4 is indicative of a progressively maturing follicle. Luteal cells appear in the granulosa of the follicle just before ovulation and frequently even when the follicle is doomed to atrophy.[8]

Minimal evidence of progesterone activity associated with a high estrone level is therefore the criterion of the ovulative phase. In the vaginal smear it is recognized by either increased desquamation of type 4 cells or by the appearance of type 5 and 6 cells together with type 4. In the postovulative phase the increasing level of progesterone neutralizes the effect of estrone on the mucosa.[9] There is progressive desquamation and degeneration of the proliferated, cornified epithelium and therefore the preponderance in vaginal smears of type 5 and 6 cells, together with the appearance of occasional cells from deeper layers, i.e., nonsquamous epithelium. Upon atrophy of the corpus luteum, new follicles develop under stimulation by the uninhibited anterior pituitary, even before menstruation. Therefore, there is usually a recurrence of estrone activity, of cornification in the vagina in the premenstrual-menstrual phase. The smear evidence indicates that menstruation occurs despite the presence of a low or even moderate estrone concentration.

Recent studies[10] confirmed by Zuck[11] demonstrate the existence of a temperature curve in the normal adult woman. There is a rise of temperature in the mid-month period correlated with ovulation as determined by smears,[12] electrical disturbance,[13] and by pregnancy due to single coitus.[14] The temperature then falls gradually during the next two to three weeks presumably under the influence of the gradually increasing estrone level which inhibits the pituitary progressively until several hours before ovulation when the temperature reaches its nadir (i.e., maximum estrone, no progesterone production).[15] As soon as luteinization of the mature follicle begins, the temperature again starts to rise signaling impending ovulation. The patients selected for this research were given instructions by a woman physician as to how to take the vaginal smears and the rectal temperatures. They received the necessary material and other instructions regarding the handling of the slides from a laboratory technician, to whom they gave the smears and temperature records every two or four weeks. This whole technical procedure was managed so that the analyst working with the case was not involved.

Psychological. One of the cases was studied for the period of fifteen menstrual cycles, two cases for twelve cycles, one for eleven cycles, and the others for a period of four to six cycles. Seventy-five cycles of nine patients were studied; this means about 2,000 day-by-day diagnoses of their psychodynamics.[16] Besides this, the author (T.B.) studied and made similar diagnostic interpretations of the same cases during those periods of their psychoanalytic treatment when vaginal smear tests were not made. Of these nine cases, two were analyzed by the author (T.B.); seven by other psychoanalysts in connection with the Chicago Institute for Psychoanalysis.

These investigations based on psychodynamic changes occurring every day and related to specific days would not have been possible except on the basis of daily recorded material.

We do not have mechanical records and therefore no verbatim record of any analytic session. In spite of this a "good record" conveys the content of the psychoanalytic session to another psychoanalyst. It contains the patient's recent important experiences, the emotional state, and the various topics of the session in the sequence of the associations. Even when the record is not verbatim, it should cite the patient's own expressions. The patient's verbalization reflects her feelings and enables the person studying the record to perceive intuitively the emotional state which the recorded data reflects.

The most important parts of the records are the dreams. The dream is the most sensitive instrument for the registration of psychic changes. In these investigations the dreams were used as the "objective" material of the psychoanalysis.[17] It is necessary, as far as possible, to record the dreams in the patient's own words and the flow of the associations. If the record does not contain the course of the analytic session, at least partially expressed in the patient's own words, it deprives the (psychoanalytic) investigator of what can be called in this situation "firsthand material" and thus enhances the probability of errors in interpretations. Records which contain mainly the summaries of the hour in psychoanalytic terminology permit only a review of the interpretations of the analyst. No matter how correct the interpretation may have been, psychoanalytic interpretation by another investigator is possible only with great tolerance for error.

Of course, it is impossible to go into detail about the technique of interpretation of the recorded psychoanalytic material. Every kind of psychological material available was utilized. We had to evaluate the conscious emotional and physical condition of the patient, her actions, and her experiences. The symptoms of the patient belong partly to conscious material and partly to unconscious material. Psychogenic symptoms are results of conflicting psychodynamic tendencies and can be analyzed in relation to the hormonal state. The most important materials for this investigation were the dreams, the associations, and the transference.[18] The interpretation of all this material differs from the usual interpretive technique of any experienced analyst in but one respect, i.e., not all the recent determinations and overdeterminations are emphasized as would be necessary in the actual course of a psychoanalysis. The material is reduced to a few underlying determinants—to the instinctual biological tendencies.

The tentative conclusions utilized for the predictions of the hormonal state were also checked in another way. One of us studied the vaginal smears of unanalyzed cases. Those cases gave a day-by-day report of their conscious emotional state and reported their dreams on a questionnaire. The material was submitted for psychological study and it was possible to determine in which phase of the cycle the dream occurred.

The aim of our investigations was to describe the emotional states as they are correlated with the hormonal states. The results show that the emotional states, as expressions of the underlying instinctual tendencies, easily coordinate with the conception of the instinct theory of psychoanalysis.

DATA AND DISCUSSION

Follicle Ripening Phase. Estrone is the hormone produced by the ripening follicle; it makes the animal ready for and desirous of copulation. The conscious and, even more, the unconscious psychological material during the phase of follicle development deals with the heterosexual tendencies of the woman. It is impossible to give a full account of all the ways in which heterosexual tendencies can appear in psychological material. The records of our comparative material show clearly what, in this presentation, gets lost through abstraction and condensation, i.e., the complexity of the motivations of the emotional states of women.

The feeling of incipient estrogenous tension is chiefly one of wellbeing. Patients say that they feel young, alert, that they can work well and think more clearly. For example, Case G.S., 8/9/37:

> "This morning I felt 17 years old so far as my mood was concerned. I met C. I felt sexually attracted to him which I did not feel when I met him last time."

The vaginal smear 8/9/37 shows cornification about the 50% level; moderate leucocytosis and mucus output. The basal body temperature is significant only in relation to the entire temperature curve for the cycle and will therefore be presented in that form in the charts of the summary.

On September 4, the same patient said: "I was energetic and active. I felt quite well."

The dream of September 5 allows the following interpretation: she wants to be a good-looking woman, attractive to men, and able to handle her sexual temptations. This is an obvious expression of heterosexual tension. On the following day, September 6, the patient described her mood at a picnic:

> "I felt very young and carefree. I liked everybody. I climbed on a tree. I sang. I did not have any self-consciousness about my body."

At about the same phase of another cycle, on January 18, the patient had the following dream:

> "Mike came and paid me a lot of attention. I was aware that he was a writer and I was flattered that he had singled me out. He embraced me and fondled me a great deal and I responded."

The vaginal smears 9/6/37 and 1/18/38 showed 50% cornification, moderate leucocytosis and mucus output.

These examples show that the heterosexual tendency appears undisguised on the manifest level of dreams and reveals itself in the patient's mood. The example shows that on September 6, 1937, and four months later, January 18, 1938, the dreams and the emotional states are the same.

The psychic energy corresponding with estrone production can be characterized as follows: it is active, directed from the individual as source of libido toward the object, just as Freud originally described object libido.[19] The active libidinous desires are directed toward sexual objects in the patient's sphere of action. This active libido may be expressed not only as heterosexual tendency but also by increased strength of the ego in maintaining self-regard, object relationship, and by more active defenses of the ego. During this phase of the cycle libido supplies the ego with an active quality. This seems to prove Freud's conception[20] that Eros is the energy which unites the parts to a higher organization. (However, detailed study of the psychodynamics of individual cases in relation to their menstrual cycles must be deferred to a later publication.)

Although the active charge of the ego is productive and agreeable, it can, when no gratification or transformation into satisfactory activities is permitted, be converted into a disagreeable tension—restlessness and irritability which are an expression of the dammed-up, originally libidinous charges. With increasing hormone production the ungratified active charge may achieve psychological expression in the form of aggression directed toward the male. Thus in our material, which is chiefly pathological, there is only a brief period when the initial low hormone content is associated with an agreeable libidinous state. It often develops into a tense emotional state in which the psychological material is characterized by aggressive tendencies or by anxiety. The emotional state may be dominated by fear of being attacked sexually. The following dream of Case L. (9/12/38) demonstrates unmistakably that increased heterosexual tension may be accompanied by fear:

> "Some huge fossil belonging to the reptile family, mounted, standing upright in the museum. Some remark or other brought it to life and it began to crawl over the land. People fled before it in terror. Very slimy and shining ugly green. I think it punctured the tire of an automobile and then proceeded to attack the occupant. The dream woke me up."

The vaginal smear 9/12/38 indicates that this was the peak of estrogenous activity in the cycle.

In this dream, even though the snake symbolism is disguised, it is clearly enough a penis symbol in which even the function of erection is easily recognized when the dream describes how this fossil became alive and then dangerous. The ambivalent attitude of the dreamer toward the penis is very clear; admiration is expressed by exaggeration of its size and power; fear and revulsion are expressed by its becoming ugly and revolting. The tension in the dream increased so much that the dreamer awoke. Patient R.E. on 2/11/38 related the following dream, very typical for her:

> "The thing that I was afraid to think about or to talk about, the thing that stands out clearly is that there was a bed and no one was in the room except my father and myself. He was trying to urge me to have intercourse with him. He was shoving me to the bed and I was moving toward it. I was willing. Then suddenly it occurred to me, 'It is my father.' I was ashamed. It was frightening. He was right after me. I do not want to think of it."

The vaginal smear 2/11/38 shows about 90% cornification and minimal evidence of aggregation and folding. It is probably a smear of the preovulative phase.

Very often increased estrone production leads to aggression which in dream material may appear as penis envy or as an intense wish to castrate the male or to incorporate the penis and become a male. Clear tendencies toward masculine identification and masculine competition are often observed in the preovulative state. How much estrone tension a woman can stand without turning it into aggression depends on various factors which can only be discussed in connection with the psychodynamic structure of each case individually. It is self-evident that actual sex experiences, gratification or disappointment, may influence the psychological reaction. For example, Patient V.M. reported a dream on 12/1/37:

> "A man rolls a cigarette, a large one. Then the cigarette is being sliced off, like plates or drops. I was conscious of its dryness."

The vaginal smear 12/1/37 consists of purely cornified cells with only an occasional red blood cell and indicates extreme estrone production, which usually precedes ovulation.

It needs no deep interpretation of the above dream to sense the hostile, castrative, depreciative attitude toward men. This is emphasized more strongly by the associations. At the same time the patient was seeking gratification by promiscuous sexual relations. It is obviously a preovulative tension.

We now present one patient's preovulative phase from its inception right through ovulation. Patient G.S. on 12/17/37 expressed a heterosexual wish but with a helpless feeling and desire to be helped. The vaginal smear 12/17/37 showed beginning cornification.

On the night of 12/18/37 the patient dreamed:

> "My nose or someone's nose was smashed, or perhaps a skull. Immediately on awakening I thought of a face all swathed in bandages. It was our coal man whom I had seen in a coffin when I was a young child."

The vaginal smear 12/18/37 showed increasing cornification to about the 75% level.

The destructive aggressive tendency is easily recognized as a characteristic of preovulative tension, especially in this patient whose hostility toward her mate and at the same time her low tolerance for frustration motivated her hostility. On December 19 she dreamed:

> ". . . of a head that was cut off or hanging connected with a holiday candle."

The vaginal smear 12/19/37 showed cornification at about the 90% level with abundant mucus and progressive reduction in the number of leucocytes, clearly preovulative.

In this dream the aggressive tendency of the previous dream was repeated. The patient described her emotional condition of 12/20/37 as follows:

> "I feel rotten. I have a dull headache. I was disgusted with you. I was furiously angry."

And on 12/21/37 she reported the following dream:

> "I felt a temper tantrum, breaking things and shaking with
> rage. My *oldest sister* K., my *youngest sister* R. and I were
> together. R. was critical. K. was studying what was the mat-
> ter with me. I yelled to R., 'You are afraid of me. You think
> that I am insane. If I were insane I would not show it to you.'
> I felt weak in the dream. I had the feeling I was dissipating
> my energy in fruitless rage."

The vaginal smear 12/21/37 showed 100% cornification, leucopenia, beginning aggregation, and folding. This is a smear that signals
impending ovulation.

Ovulative State. As we observed in the last few examples, the psychological changes related to the production of estrone develop gradually or in sudden leaps to their highest point, when the ripe follicle
bursts and ovulation occurs. However, before ovulation does occur,
lutein activity begins. The very first evidence of function of the corpus
luteum is a change in direction of metabolic activity and is reflected by
corresponding change in the psychodynamic tendencies. The examples
cited above showed the heterosexual interest with its various emotional
expressions such as love, fear, and hostility. When the function of the
corpus luteum hormone (progesterone) begins, this exclusive interest
in men changes. The heterosexual tendency appears combined with
passive-receptive instinctual tendencies. The psychoanalytic material reflects the libidinous interest in one's own body. The emotional interest
is self-centered. The woman appears more passive and dependent.

Patient V.M. on 3/15/38 had the following dream:

> "I was coming down the steps with Jack carrying a creature
> which I decided was a baby. It was not the proper way to
> carry it. The baby was not properly dressed. I was sure it was
> a girl, but to my surprise it was a boy. I felt badly since I
> wanted a girl. I felt so badly, I considered cutting off its
> penis. I could not accept it as my child, having a penis."

The vaginal smear 3/15/38 showed complete cornification, folding, and aggregation corresponding to ovulation.

This dream expresses a great conflict tension, the solution to
which is castration of her own child. The dream solution shows the
direction of the instinctual conflict, which is here aggression toward the
penis. We distinguish this in the first dream thought, which shows ambivalence toward the child. In the second dream thought the wish to
have a daughter is expressed. (The associations emphasized the wish
to have a daughter more beautiful and more feminine than the patient

herself.) These two dream thoughts show a content which we correlate with the lutein activity. Then the conflict shifts to the aggression toward the boy, toward the penis. The aggression toward the penis is the predominant direction of instinctual tendency in this dream because it offers the dream solution. Therefore the incipient lutein activity and stronger estrone tension were diagnosed—*preovulative tension.*

On 6/24/38 Patient R.G. reported:

"Yesterday evening I had a bad spell of eating and today too. Today I ate a very adequate lunch and slept an hour and awoke hungry. I thought of my brother. I felt I wanted to destroy his genitals. Well, it is a real wish, to pull him out. The thing that bothered me so much is that I still have the wish to do it. I connect it with the fact that my mother used to tell me that she'd cut my thumb off when I used to suck it. It is as if I almost want to feel depressed. This day after the analytic hour was the worst day I ever had. After I finished lunch I had a terrific craving for candy. I got quite depressed."

The vaginal smear 6/24/38 showed 80% cornification with minimal folding and aggregation, indicative of the incipient luteinization, chiefly preovulative.

This example of craving along with the wish to incorporate the penis shows the reaction of this patient to the preovulative state, to the increased estrone and incipient lutein function.

Our observations so far permit the statement that our patients can handle their hormone balance psychologically much better so long as only one of the hormones is active. In the case of a normal woman with normal sex life, increased heterosexual tension is usually relieved by sexual gratification. Thus the preovulative tension will not achieve a level at which symptoms develop. Most of our cases, however, do not find complete sexual gratification, even when they have had heterosexual relationships. The emotional expressions of this state turn into great tenseness or depression, irritability and sensitiveness, weeping spells and rage reactions. An insatiable need for some type of gratification develops. Cravings and incorporative wishes of all kinds appear and lead to sadistic and masochistic tendencies which occur chiefly when both estrone and progesterone are active. When ovulation actually occurs, the tension is suddenly relieved and relaxation takes place. We now present some examples of ovulative change.

Ovulative Change. The psychoanalytic material and corresponding endocrine findings of Case G.S. from 12/17/37 to 12/21/37 were cited above as an example of aggressive tendencies which developed during the period of increasing preovulative tension. The dream of 12/21/37 shows homosexual content also, corresponding to incipient corpus luteum activity; the smear was seen to be preovulative. On 12/22/37 she reported the following dream:

> ". . . young girl. She talked in a very facetious way. She must, must be me. This girl talked with a man who had flaming red hair, curly lashes. He was interested in this girl and made a date with her. I talked to the girl. I told her about a case. Someone was pregnant and the man did not assume responsibility. I told her men don't like to do this. She answered, 'Is that so? Do you mean this, really?' In the same dream somebody said, 'He is *very hurt.*' "

The vaginal smear 12/22/37 showed marked desquamation and leucocytic infiltration typical of the first postovulative day.

In this dream it is obvious that sexual temptation is directly connected with the danger of being impregnated and then abandoned. "He is very hurt" is the expression of her wish for revenge as well as the projection of her own being hurt. The dream shows marked heterosexual wish, expression of estrone activity and fear of pregnancy, expression of lutein activity, and therefore might be interpreted as clearly preovulative. During the analytic hour on 12/22/37 the patient felt relaxed. She started her associations jokingly: "Oh, my dear, it is a hard job to overcome an inertia against talking." During this hour she talked about her admiration for her body, how she used to stand in front of the mirror admiring herself. She talked in a relaxed, receptive mood about her need to be loved. But she brought up bitter associations about men who did not love her as she wanted to be loved. The mood and content of the hour clearly showed the postovulative relaxation and narcissistic gratification. On 12/23/37 the patient said:

> "I functioned well yesterday. I loved myself very well on the basis that if nobody else loves me, I will love myself. Last night I was pleased with my body. My husband made overtures but I felt removed from him. I loved my breasts. I did not want him to touch them. Though my body was burning for love, I withdrew."

This recital of her emotions shows that her libidinous interest was withdrawn from the sexual object and centered on her own self, which is not an individual characteristic of this patient but may be found more or less clearly expressed in all cases after ovulation has occurred. However, the management of this erotization by withdrawal from the heterosexual partner had individual significance, the consequences of which can be seen on the next day. The relaxation and happiness was of short duration for on the night of 12/23/37 she dreamed:

> "Jim's mother was walking with Jimmy. We were on the railroad tracks, Jim and I. Suddenly the child dropped his mother's hand and dashed toward the tracks, threw himself on the rails and rolled about. When my sister on the other side saw the child, she shrieked."

The vaginal smear 12/23/37 was clearly postovulative.

In this dream the patient's aggression toward her own child was evident. The associations during the analytic hour showed that the dreamed suicide attempt of the son is a substitute for her own suicidal wish; she identified herself with her son. The apparent aggression that developed toward her own pregnancy was really an aggression toward herself. The aggression directed toward the man's penis during the previous days (12/19 and 12/20) was now—after incorporation of the penis, i.e., pregnancy—directed toward the son and therefore indirectly toward herself. The introversion of the aggression is indicative. It supports the general observation that the psychic energy which was directed toward the object during the preovulative phase is turned toward the patient's self in the postovulative phase of the cycle.

It is interesting to compare this ovulative state with the following cycle of the same individual. We have already cited the pleasant, erotic sensation associated with minimal estrone activity which persisted from 1/18/38 to 1/20/38 of G.S. On 1/21/38 she had many symptoms including perspiration and irritation of the rectum. In fantasy she identified herself with prostitutes and became extremely angry and hostile toward all authorities.

The vaginal smear 1/21/38 showed complete cornification.

On 1/22/38 she forgot the main part of her dream. The fragment which she remembered had homosexual content. During the analytic session she was excited. Her fantasies were aggressively directed toward the penis which she wanted to pull and incorporate.

The vaginal smear on 1/22/38 was clearly ovulative, showing complete cornification, minimal folding, with leucopenia, similar to the smear on 12/21/37.

After the analytic session the patient had a dream which contained an involved argument with her mother about the feminine role. The dream showed an intense dynamic conflict between the wish to be like her mother (i.e., accept the motherly role), and the overwhelmingly powerful sexual desires which expressed themselves in prostitution fantasies, the opposite of motherliness. The dream permitted the conclusion that although there was an increasing tendency toward accepting the mother role, heterosexual tension was nevertheless maintained; therefore, the diagnosis of preovulative state was made.

On the next day, 1/23/38, she felt weak, ". . . like a baby; my hands look washed out. I ate a great deal, slept a great deal."

The vaginal smear on 1/23/38 was clearly postovulative and showed marked desquamation of cornified cells and leucocytic infiltration.

On 1/24/38 her dream showed identification with her child but not in the suicidal aggressive manner of the preceding month, rather in a positive satisfactory attitude of being proud of the son. The last part of the dream expressed various hostile impulses in connection with pregnancy.

The vaginal smear 1/24/38 showed definite luteal phase with reappearance of a few normal cells and increased mucification of all cells.

Postovulative relaxation on 1/23/38 was accompanied by a regression, being weak like a baby, sleeping and eating like a baby. The oral dependency, the need for love, as well as the awareness of her own genitals were manifest in symptoms and in feelings. They express the need to be close to the mother like a baby, to be protected by love, and gratified by food. The change from the aggressive incorporative, preovulative tension to postovulative relaxation and oral regression (identification with the infant) can be observed in this cycle which shows some psychological improvement as compared to the previous cycle.

These two subsequent ovulative periods of one patient may suffice to demonstrate that the instinctual tendency changed its direction after ovulation took place. While it was active and directed toward the sexual object during the follicle-ripening phase, it became passive and directed toward one's own self after ovulation. Further examples of other patients with quite different personality structures make it evident that the change in direction of the instinctual tendency is not characteristic of an individual case, but is the usual correlate of ovulation.

A patient, R.E., with severe phobia and passive infantile personality, had two dreams in the same night, 11/1/37.

"My husband, my sister and myself were at a show and on the screen two shots were fired. Someone was getting killed or there was a war or something. Anyhow, some shots were fired. I heard somebody in the audience sort of scream in Jewish, 'Oi veh!' as though she couldn't stand the shooting on the screen. The voice was very familiar to me. I turned around, it was my mother standing in the aisle hollering at the top of her voice. I was very embarrassed. I sort of pulled her toward where we were sitting on the aisle. I felt embarrassed and kind of funny about having people know it was my mother screaming that way. I asked where my brother was who stays with her. She pointed to him sitting in a seat all by himself. She said, 'He's sick.' He was holding his forehead and I got scared and went up to him and asked him what was the matter. I don't remember and don't know the end of it."

This dream shows the fearful defense against heterosexuality. The aggressive scene in which the mother is desperately wailing is the typical representation of her early experience of her parents' coitus. In the dream it is partly projected to the screen which decreases her fear of being attacked sexually. The next dream thought considered the brother. (She had experienced a sexual attack by her brother in her childhood.) But now he was sleepy or sick; now he is not dangerous. Thus she could act in a motherly fashion and take a kindly interest in his condition. This last part of the dream showed a motherly attitude. The next dream in the same night showed impregnation symbolism on an infantile, oral level.

"I was in my sister's house eating fried fish and a baked potato. I was on very good terms with her. All of a sudden, I heard a loud noise outside, people hollering and screaming, and I thought it was my mother, so I ran out to see who it was. There were some people on the street fighting, police officers with guns in their hands and clubs. I couldn't find my mother. I thought it was her doing all the screaming. I looked around for her. I came back to my sister-in-law's, but the baked potato was gone. Only the fish was left. But she had eaten the baked potato. I asked her if she had enough fish for supper. She showed me a platter with enough fish for supper and in the dream I wondered why I was speaking to her when I'm supposed to be angry at her. Then I remembered that some woman with whom I played poker said, 'You'll be speaking to her soon.' That thought of what this woman really said came to me in the dream. So that was the end of it."

In its manifest content the dream showed only a slightly disguised childlike conception of impregnation.[21] The first dream expresses the heterosexual tendency and, in addition, some motherliness; the second dream expresses the same tendencies, but the wish to be impregnated is stronger.

The vaginal smear 11/1/37 showed 100% cornification, some folding, and aggregation typical of the *ovulative phase*.

In the analytic hour on 11/1/37, oral regression seemed to dominate. Like a child, the patient came in with a chocolate bar in her hand, eating it and offering some to the analyst. On 11/2/37 the analytic material showed increased fear of being attacked sexually. She recalled a dream fragment in which her husband had protected her against sexual aggression of other men and associated it with the sexual attack on her by her brother when she had been a child and to which she had reacted with the fear of being pregnant. This material is thus an elaboration of the problem expressed on the previous day.

The vaginal smear on 11/2/37 showed 100% cornification plus folding and aggregation as on the previous day, still ovulative phase.

On 11/2/37 the patient could not take a basal metabolism test because she felt she was suffocating. On 11/3/37 she came into the analyst's office, cheerful and relaxed. She recited the happenings of the previous day in a normal way, described her suffocation, her tenseness, and her extreme irritability toward her husband. The entire session was filled with uninterrupted, free-flowing, cheerful, but rather empty talk. When the analytic session was finished, she arose from the couch and asked proudly for praise because she "associated so freely" without being urged.

The vaginal smear 11/3/37 was postovulative and showed leucocytic infiltration of the previously leucopenic vaginal mucosa.

The state of intense preovulative tension persisted from 10/31 to 11/3. The heterosexual tendency of this period was masked by fear, while the progesterone activity was expressed by the wish for impregnation and regression to oral state. In another cycle of the same patient, on 1/18/38, the dream material was interpreted as *fear of impregnation*. During the analytic hour she felt peaceful, quiet, contented, tired, and without fear.

The vaginal smear 1/18/38 showed complete cornification with minimal folding, probably a smear of the ovulative day.

The postovulative relaxation was clearly marked. On the next day, 1/19/38, she reported:

> "I had a dream about playing poker. We were going to play poker in one of the women's houses. My brother's wife was going to watch me. Even in the dream I knew I was afraid to be alone. She took the baby along. She was going to give her some milk for lunch. I asked her, 'Is that all you are going to give her? Why, that isn't enough. It's very hungry.' My brother loved the baby a good deal and if anything happened to the baby, if she didn't get enough to eat, it would be my fault and I'd be blamed by him. So I asked the hostess if she had any eggs and she said they didn't eat eggs in her home. I was sorry that I didn't take one along with me from my mother-in-law's because I knew that she had eggs."

The vaginal smear 1/19/38 shows marked desquamation of cells and a slight regression from the complete cornification of the previous day, clearly postovulative.

The dream has a slight heterosexual content. The patient cannot indulge in sexuality because she is jealously watched, but in the dream her brother's baby is her baby. Here we see the same wish to have a child as we found in the material on 11/1/37 and 11/2/37. Here is repeated again the competitive attitude toward the mother. When she is the mother, she feeds the baby more and better than the real mother does. She also showed the tendency to identify herself with the child whom she feeds as she wants to be fed and taken care of.

The ovulative change of Patient V.M. is presented here. Her dream of 12/1/37 has already been reported above as an example of increased heterosexual tension in the preovulative phase. On 12/2/37 she reported:

"I hate my mother. She likes to talk about intimate things. I don't want her to be that close to me. I have an unpleasant feeling in my vulva when my mother talks of intimate things."

The vaginal smear 12/2/37 was clearly ovulative and showed complete cornification, leucopenia, and an occasional red blood cell.

The change of heterosexual tendencies into a clear awareness of her own body and into conflict with her mother might be characteristic of the ovulative and early postovulative state. This material exposes, however, still too much active hostile feeling toward the mother, and the dream as well as the associations during the analytic session fail to show relaxation. Even though the mother conflict is estimated as corresponding to lutein activity, on the basis of this hostile tension the diagnosis of preovulative tension with increased corpus luteum function was made. On the next day, however, she reported the following dream. (The patient was analyzed by a man.)

"You and I were sitting in an operating room. You said that an operation would take place and that the cost would be fifty dollars. I felt very thankful and thought it was worth any price. I thought that the operation was to be on my throat."

The vaginal smear 12/3/37 showed continued cornification but beginning aggregation indicative of ovulation.

Comparing this dream with that of 12/1/37, the difference in direction of the psychic energy is obvious. On 12/1/37 the patient dreamed that a man's penis was being sliced, while on 12/3/37 she yields to a passive, masochistic, feminine tendency. Gratitude instead of vindictiveness is evidence of relaxation which permits the conclusion that the characteristic postovulative emotional state had developed. The psychoanalytic hour offered further evidence of relaxation. The flow of associations started playfully: "Humpty Dumpty sitting on a wall. Wiener frankfurter my favorite food."

In another cycle V.M. on 10/13/37 felt tense. Her dream expressed a strong defense against the feminine sexual role and an intense wish for masculine identification.

The vaginal smear 10/13/37 was ovulative and showed 100% cornification, with some folding and aggregation.

On the next day, 10/14/37, the patient was depressed and calm. She wanted to be taken care of, to be nursed by her husband. This passive, dependent attitude expresses the regression which we consider characteristic of early postovulative phase.

The vaginal smear 10/14/37 showed increased desquamation and aggregation, clearly postovulative.

This brief selection of psychological material of the ovulative state demonstrates the main correlation. Other cycles investigated show the same correlations, but the underlying psychodynamics assumed a more complicated form. This material has displayed the increasing intensity of conflicting psychodynamic tendencies during the preovulative state, when both estrone and progesterone were diagnosed. It should be emphasized that the basic unconscious conflicts of the individual come closer to consciousness during this period of the cycle. Very often dreams and the conscious emotional attitudes do not adequately discharge the tensions. Symptoms increase in intensity and new symptoms develop. (Again, we must defer the characteristic symptomatology of this period to a later publication.)

Ovulation is characterized by the sudden decrease of estrogenous activity and by the increased activity of corpus luteum. Hence, after ovulation the active heterosexual libido decreases and the passive, libidinous tendencies appear with greater intensity. Emotionally this state is mainly characterized by the relaxation of the preovulative tension which was activated by the conflicting tendencies of estrone and incipient lutein activity.

Our examples have demonstrated the relaxation which follows ovulation. This relaxation has various emotional concomitants. Sometimes the patient becomes talkative or even hypomanic. Preovulative and postovulative talkativeness are distinctly different. While tense, rapid speech, increasing sensitiveness, and the feeling of being compelled or driven to talk are characteristic of the preovulative state, a satisfied, pleasant, and relatively passive free flow of associations distinguishes the postovulative state. The most valid psychological sign of ovulation is a relaxed feeling of well-being which is accompanied by positive, pleasant feelings about the subject's own body; for example, V.M. on 12/7/37 felt well and relaxed. She enjoyed herself passively and said:

> "I saw my breasts; I wanted to be recognized as a woman.
> The sexual feeling I had was going through my breasts. I put
> my arm around myself and I remember the sensation in my
> breasts, the sensation of shame."

On the basis of the narcissistic sensations, the diagnosis of post-ovulative was made.

The vaginal smear 12/7/37 was definitely postovulative and showed marked desquamation and aggregation of cornified cells.

The very similar material of G.S. on 12/22/37 has already been cited as falling in love with her own body. On 10/5/37 she described her emotional state in another postovulative period, "I feel young, alert and unantagonistic."

The vaginal smear 10/5/37 showed increased aggregation and secretion. Very few cornified cells; clearly postovulative.

A gratified warm feeling follows the great tension. In the post-ovulative condition the body is flooded with libidinous feelings. This erotization of the patient's own body may also be conveyed to other persons. A need for closeness, for love in a general sense, is the emotional expression of this hormonal state.

The relaxation may express itself as a sudden regression such as we saw in G.S. on 1/23/38 when she felt her body "weak and passive like a baby," sleepy and hungry, or in V.M. on 10/14/37 who acted out her wishes for dependence and her desire to be nursed and taken care of, or in R.E. on 11/1/37 who acted out the regressive oral condition by coming with a chocolate bar in hand to the analytic session.

The immediately postovulative state is also characterized by an increased libidinous charge of the propagative organs. This charge is frequently strong enough to result in a conscious awareness of her own genitals. It may also be expanded to include the entire body. The reaction to this feeling is normally pleasant. It may give rise to strong feminine exhibitionistic tendencies, to the wish to dance alone, as in V.M. on 3/17/38. The increased sexual charge may result in masturbation or may give rise to defense against being a woman and arouse inferiority feeling.

Lutein Phase. The characteristic progesterone attitude increases during the ovulation phase and thereafter the psychodynamic material is either narcissistic or clearly passive receptive. The passive receptive tendency determines the psychodynamic situation as long as progesterone dominance persists. Progesterone is the hormone chiefly concerned with preparation of the uterus for nidation and with maintaining pregnancy. The physiological preparation of the uterus for nidation implies a task for the psychic apparatus to be dealt with in every cycle, namely, to solve the problem of being a woman. While the activity of the corpus luteum increases, we observe in the psychological material the attempt of the individual to prepare herself for the propagative role of womanhood. During the study of the psychological material related to the menstrual cycle, it was striking to see that under the influence of corpus luteum activity the psychological material shifts to the mother conflict, to the problems of the relationship with the mother. For example, V.M. reported on 2/22/38:

> "A hotel, lots of strange people, I was afraid of them. My mother was with me. Mother and I picked up drawers and took them to the kitchen. A young man then was laughing at my mother. I went to help her. Somebody laughed at me. I decided not to pay any attention. I began to feel affection for her; I began to feel like rubbing myself against her leg. She seemed to be bothered by it. I did it more openly and then decided she was my mother. She became disgusted with me."

Her associations were:

> "My mother in the dream was much younger. Something about the way she treated me caused a peculiar feeling inside. She was afraid other people would see it. I remember her sitting on the floor playing dolls with me when I was six years of age. Her face in the dream was more like then. I have a feeling my mother was very lovely. I never could feel like a woman should feel. I have a very unlovely feeling most of the time. The only time I feel that way [womanly] is in a nightgown that I like. As soon as I look in the mirror, it cancels the feeling I get."

The vaginal smear on 2/22/38 showed marked aggregation and folding with gradual disappearance of cornified cells, typical of lutein phase.

The outstanding feature of the dream is the relationship to the mother. The solution of the dream problem is to separate the mother from her heterosexual interests and possess her entire attention, even in the sense of physical gratification. In this material the longing to have positive, undisturbed feminine feelings toward her own body is also obvious. This tendency is typical of the undisturbed lutein state.

On 2/23/38, the dream showed homosexual content. One part of it was, "I finally said the woman can come and sleep with me."

The vaginal smear on 2/23/38 was typical of the lutein phase; all the signs of lutein function were increased beyond the previous day.

The emotional state corresponding to lutein activity is not always so happy and gratified as this material indicates. Here the patient was able to develop her fantasy of being accepted and loved by her mother. The same patient on 5/23/38 was depressed, cried, and did not know what to do. She felt unwanted and unloved. She complained that the analyst did not love her either. The patient was pleading for the analyst's love and understanding. The mother transference was obvious in this material.

The vaginal smear on 5/23/38 showed aggregation and folding of desquamated, cornified cells, typical of progesterone activity.

On 5/24/38 the patient felt the same disappointment because of lack of love. She comforted herself with the fantasy and associations that her mother kissed her buttocks when she was a baby.

The vaginal smear on 5/24/38 showed increased aggregation—lutein phase.

We have already followed the cycle of G.S. which started on 12/10/37, through the very aggressive preovulative phase, and through ovulation on 12/22/37 which was marked by an intense but short-lived narcissistic relaxation, followed again by tension and depression. On the night of 12/24/37 she had the following dream:

"We were on our way somewhere and had been admitted to a home. We were going through the house and talking in a friendly fashion to the children in the house. One part of the house appeared to be locked against us, but we were able to wander through the other rooms which were light, spacious and somewhat cluttered. It appeared to me that it was necessary for us to go. Suddenly my mother appeared in a bathrobe. She had my son in a bathtub filled with water. She appeared very tense. The other people and I watched with interest what occurred and were surprised. My mother kept pressing the child down in the water. He was completely submerged, struggled for a while and then lay quite still under the water as though lifeless."

The vaginal smear on 12/25/37 showed marked aggregation with only an occasional cornified cell and was typical of the lutein phase.

In these general interpretations of the correlations between emotional state and hormonal state, case histories have been purposely omitted. At this point, however, it is necessary to state that in this case the aggressive impulses toward pregnancy and the infant were, indeed, the central conflict which resulted in depression. In spite of this, in reviewing the dream material of this cycle, we recognize that the conflict of the patient is not apparent in the psychological material of the preovulative phase. The aggressive impulses in the dreams of the preovulative state were directed toward the man (dreams on 12/18/37 and 12/21/37); they increased to rage in the dream on 12/21/37 and then the ovulation occurred, accompanied by emotional relaxation. After the ovulation, the aggression turned toward herself and toward her child in the dream (12/23/37). In this last dream the conflict with the mother is obviously expressed. She was afraid of her mother because she felt rejected by her. In the manifest dream the mother drowned her child in the bathtub. The aggressive impulse is here passively experienced. The passive direction of the instinctual tendency and the repetition of the conflict with the mother and with the child are those contents of the dream which we correlate with the intensified function of the corpus luteum. It is understandable that after this dream the patient felt tense and remarked, "I was aware of all my nerves, even those in my ears." The awareness of her female body burdened by fear of the mother's aggression toward her and by the guilt for her own aggression toward her child charged the problem of mother-child with fear, aggression, and guilt.

The complicated relationship between mother and daughter (from the beginning of life) has been the subject of psychoanalytic investigation of individual development. The conflicts vary in depth and structure in every case and change during the course of psychoanalytic therapy. It is not germane to this paper to describe the different types of conflict or their changes during analysis—tending toward reconciliation with the mother—except for the following point: as long as the unconscious relationship to the mother is hostile, the oral material becomes aggressive and tensions develop which destroy the pleasant, passive-dependent narcissistic feelings which were found to be characteristic of the postovulative state. Thus hostility leads to more or less severe depression during the lutein phase as shown in G.S. 12/25/37 and in V.M. 5/23/38.

The psychological material corresponding to the activity of the corpus luteum would in the usual psychoanalytic terminology be described as belonging to the pregenital, oral level of libido organization. From the cycles we have studied, we may describe the course of instinctual tendency as follows: after maintaining active heterosexual libido directed toward the object on a genital level for a period of time (estrone phase), the libido changes its direction and appears as a passive receptive tendency which, during the preovulative state, may conflict with the heterosexual object libido. The passive receptive tendency becomes stronger after ovulation. The earliest object of the passive receptive libido was the mother who satisfied all needs of dependence, the need to be loved, sheltered and fed. We dare say that passive, oral-receptive tendencies appear in the psychological material of an adult woman only when progesterone is present. Of course, it is possible to observe "oral material" in the follicle-ripening phase of the cycle as well; then the aggressive incorporative tendencies are directed toward the sexual object. The distinction between passive receptive and aggressive incorporative, oral tendencies is important in recognizing the various phases of the cycle. The former belongs to the postovulative, the latter to the preovulative phase.

The passive receptive tendency of the corpus luteum phase has its normal emotional representation on the genital level; this is the wish to be impregnated, the wish to have a child. The tendency toward nursing and feeding appears as a manifestation of the same tendency toward motherhood. Thus the passive receptive, genital desire manifests itself in connection with an active oral, "oral-giving," tendency, i.e., the desire to feed. Both instinctual tendencies unfold as successful identification with the mother. Hence in dreams and in other psychological material they appear together with the wish to be like the mother. Between these extremes—(1) the wish to be a baby, to be nursed, and fed by the mother and (2) the wish to be a woman, to be impregnated, and become a mother—we find all the varieties of female development. The biological preparation for pregnancy is reflected in the psychological material as pregnancy fantasies or dreams and appears sometimes as the early expression of corpus luteum activity, even in the preovulative state. Such early pregnancy material, however, is projected to the mother as shown in R.E. on 11/2/37 and in R.G. on 6/26/38. Such pregnancy material is referred to the mother's pregnancies and may be expressed by birth fantasies or womb fantasies. It may repeat the conflicts and traumata caused by the birth of siblings as, for example, in R.E. on 1/19/38.

The psychological material corresponding to late progesterone activity shifts from the conflict with the mother to the problem of being a mother and to the relationship with the child. Pregnancy material is then concerned with the fears and desires of their own pregnancy (not that of the mother). The wish to nurse, feed, and take care of the child is characteristic of very late corpus luteum activity. This material can rarely be demonstrated apart from other factors which influence the cycle at this time. One such example is provided by G.S. on 1/28/38. (The earlier part of this cycle has already been cited.)

"I seem to have been told that I could get clothes for a small child, but I forgot about it when I saw the child. I made preparations to cut its nails. The person in charge of the clothes came along and told me that I keep forgetting to take care of the clothes. Then we came to a place which looked like a kindergarten."

The vaginal smear on 1/28/38 consisted mostly of normal cells indicating very low hormone content.

Progesterone dominance persists only a few days unless pregnancy occurs. Otherwise, the new follicle starts ripening and reflects its activity in the psychological material. With reappearance of estrogenous activity there is again a period in which tendencies corresponding to both corpus luteum and follicle-ripening function influence the emotional state simultaneously, for example, V.M. on 12/8/37. V.M. reported the following dream (the ovulative state from 12/1 to 12/3/37 has already been presented) to the male analyst:

"I am in your office waiting for you. I wanted you to pay attention to me. I looked in the mirror. My hair was all white. My skin was smooth, my figure slender. I was dressed in a long, velvet cloak. I thought you were punishing me by not looking at me, so I decided to go to the North Side. I went into a store on X Avenue. I felt somebody changed things and I was tired out. I thought I would be late and that I should phone you. I decided to call you up at home. You were not there. Finally I went to your home. You lived in a little frame cottage. A little boy was in the window. I decided to save him and I did."

The vaginal smear on 12/8/37 showed, along with the extreme aggregation typical of the lutein phase, minimal cornification which is evidence of newly ripening follicles—premenstrual state.

In the beginning of the dream, the satisfaction with her own body is expressed. She felt feminine and attractive. This part of the dream expressed the feelings which are associated with progesterone production. It is obvious that she was directing her attractiveness toward her male analyst with normal heterosexual feeling. The heterosexual tendency is also expressed by fear of prostitution tendencies. The dream thought, "When my father does not love me, I am like a lost child, in danger," is another expression of her heterosexual tendency. There was sufficient heterosexuality to diagnose this as a premenstrual state. The heterosexual feeling on the oedipal level appeared to be a defense against the actual positive transference to the analyst.

We have already reported the lutein phase on 5/23/38 to 5/24/38 of V.M., showing conflict with her mother. On 5/25/38, still in a depressed and dependent mood, the patient reported the following dream (male analyst):

"I changed my profession and got into school teaching. I went across the hall and put my hand on a child. I went down the corridor and saw my own son who did not belong here.

Then I was here, telling you about it. I became very angry because you did not give me a chance to express myself. A man and woman came in and you were angry at their coming. I began to cover up so she would not think that anything was going on. Then I decided I did not need to be scared because another man was there too."

The vaginal smear on 5/25/38 showed initial cornification—premenstrual.

The patient in this dream sought a solution for her dependence. The only possible solution was to be a good mother and protective to her son, but the heterosexual wish toward the analyst-father whose attention she wanted for herself interfered with her wish to be a good mother. The dream was therefore concerned with the mother-child relationship (lutein phase) and expressed heterosexual tendencies (newly ripening follicle).

The first evidence of premenstrual change is a consequence of a slight influx of estrone which usually remains at a low level for some days. During this period the heterosexual content of the psychological material does not overshadow the material which is related to nidation. With further atrophy of the corpus luteum and the consequent diminishing progesterone output, there is again a change in the direction of instinctual processes. This is reflected in the psychological material. The psychological complexities of the premenstrual-menstrual phase, except at its very beginning, require more detailed description than can conveniently be included in the present paper. These complexities, however, can be correlated with the simultaneous hormonal complexities of this phase of the cycle as we plan to show in the second part of this publication.

SUMMARY

We have presented and discussed the psychological and the ovarian hormone material of that part of the menstrual cycle which centers about ovulation: the preovulative, ovulative, and postovulative phases. The presentation of material of the premenstrual-menstrual phase will occur in the second part of this publication. See Graph II (p. 168) for a graphic summary of the ovulative phase of the cycle of one of our subjects, G.S., 1/15–1/30 as an example of the cycles in which ovulation occurs.

Careful study of vaginal smears and basal body temperatures and of the psychoanalytic records led us to infer the correlations presented in the following diagrams. In the light of the foregoing material, the diagrams are self-explanatory.

BASAL BODY TEMPERATURES, VAGINAL SMEARS,
AND
INSTINCTUAL TENDENCIES DURING
ONE OVULATIVE PHASE
OF PATIENT G.S.

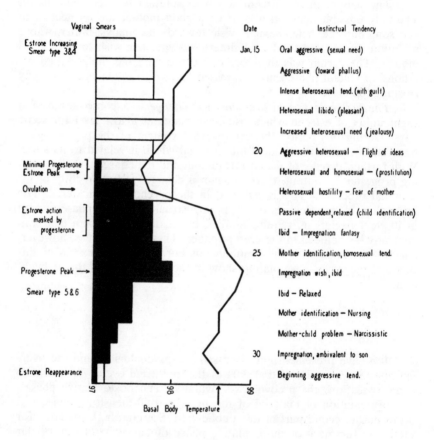

GRAPH II

DIAGRAM I

Hormone	Instinctual Tendency	Neurotic Elaborations of Tendency

Estrone,
 	
Follicular hormone
	Active object libido on genital level: heterosexual desire	1. Aggressive incorporative: penis envy, castration wish
		
		2. Masochistic: masochistic concept of female sexuality
		3. Defense reactions:
		  a) fear of being attacked
		  b) masculine protest

Progesterone dominant
 	
Corpus luteum hormone
	Passive receptive tendency on genital level
	
	desire to be loved: and wish for impregnation:
		Passive receptive tendency on regressive level:
		
		oral receptive and oral dependent wishes, may be directed toward
		  a) mother
		  b) homosexual object
		  c) heterosexual object

DIAGRAM II

Phase of Cycle	Hormone State	Psychological Material
Follicle ripening	Initial estrone function	Heterosexual tendency, usually pleasant, feeling of well-being
Late preovulative	Increasing estrone plus minimal progesterone	Relief by sexual gratification or increasing tension—conflicting tendencies (See Diagram I.)
Ovulative (immediately after ovulation)	Diminishing estrone plus increasing progesterone	Relaxation of conflict tension. Erotization of female body, passive receptive. Pleasant emotional state.
Postovulative, luteal	Progesterone dominance	See Diagram I, especially passive receptive tendencies and object libido toward mother or homosexual object.
Late luteal, early premenstrual	Diminishing progesterone plus resultant reappearance (unmasking) of estrone effects	Recurrence of heterosexual tendency on mostly receptive level, and pregnancy fantasies

The content of these two diagrams may be summarized in the following correlations:

(1) The estrogenous phase of the cycle corresponds to an emotional condition characterized by active heterosexual gratification, but it may turn into aggression toward the man or into a fearful defensive attitude. The psychological material during this phase of the cycle reflects the psychodynamic aspects of the relationship to the male sex or to the other sex.

(2) The function of the corpus luteum corresponds to the erotization of the female body. In this phase of the cycle the libido, which appears more passive and dependent, is turned from the outer world toward the self. The psychological material during the corpus luteum stage reflects the erotization of the female body and the preparation for motherhood.

(3) Ovulation is characterized by sudden decrease of the estrogenous activity and by the influx of the narcissistic erotization according to the greater activity of lutein hormones. Emotionally this state is mainly characterized by the relaxation of the preovulative tension which was caused by the conflicting tendencies between the increased estrone and incipient lutein activity.

CONCLUSIONS

(1) The day-by-day study of vaginal smears and basal body temperatures provided a useful and enlightening method for analysis of gonad function of adult women.

(2) The psychoanalytic method could also be employed for a day-by-day study of the emotional cycle accompanying the (ovarian) hormone cycle.

(3) The simultaneous use of the two methods provided clear correlations between the physiological and psychological processes.

(4) The investigation suggests that in the adult woman it is possible to relate psychodynamic tendencies to specific hormone functions of the ovaries:

(a) Heterosexual tendency is correlated with estrogen activity; and

(b) passive receptive and narcissistic attitude is correlated with progesterone activity.

(5) Whenever the metabolic gradient correlated with the specific gonadal hormones changes its direction or slope, the psychological material shows a change in the direction of the instinctual drive.

(6) This method affords an approach to the study of parallel and interrelated physiological and psychological processes.

NOTES

1. Originally published in *Psychosomatic Medicine,* I, no. 2 (April 1939), 245–270. (Revised for this volume.) This work was in part supported by a grant from the Rockefeller Foundation to the Brush Foundation, Cleveland, Ohio.

Dr. Rubenstein was associated with the Institute for Psychoanalysis, Chicago, Illinois, for this research project and the Laboratory of Anatomy and Associated Foundations, Western Reserve University, and is a Fellow of the Rockefeller Foundation.

The authors are delighted to express their thanks to Drs. E. Falstein, R. Furest, J. Kasanin, P. Kramer, M. MacDonald, and A. Meyer who psychoanalyzed some of the patients and whose carefully recorded material we have used. We are grateful to Dr. Lucia E. Tower who instructed these patients in the technique of preparing the vaginal smears, and to Dr. Thomas M. French and Dr. Leon J. Saul for their helpful interest in the general problem and in the preparation of this paper. We are particularly grateful to Dr. Franz Alexander for his enthusiastic support and interest in the present investigation.

2. Seward, G. H., "The Female Sex Rhythm," *Psychological Bulletin,* XXXI (1934), 153–192.

3. Rubenstein, B. B., "Estimation of Ovarian Activity by the Consecutive Day Study of Basal Body Temperature and Basal Metabolic Rate," *Endocrinology,* XXII (1938), 41–44; "The Relation of Cyclic Changes in Human Vaginal Smears to Body Temperatures and Basal Metabolic Rates," *American J. Physiology,* CXIX (1937), 635–641; "The Fertile Period of Women," *J. Contraception,* II (1937), 171–173.

4. Ibid.

5. Papanicolaou, G. N., "The Sexual Cycle in the Human Female as Revealed by Vaginal Smears," *Am. J. Anatomy,* LII (1933), 519–616.

6. Mortimer, H., Wright, H. P., and Collip, J. B., "The Effect of the Administration of Estrogenic Hormones in the Nasal Mucosa of the Monkey," *Canadian Med. Assn. J.,* XXXV (1936), 506–615.

7. Allen, E., *Sex and Internal Secretions* (Baltimore, Williams & Wilkins, 1932); Hisaw, F. L., Greep, R. O., and Fevold, H. L., "The Effects of Oestrin-progestin Combinations on the Endometrium, Vagina and Sexual Skin of Monkeys," *Am. J. Anatomy,* LXI (1937), 483–504.

8. Evans, H. M., and Swezy, O., "Ovogenesis and the Normal Follicular Cycle in Adult Mammalia," *Mem. Univ. California,* IX (1931), 119–185; Myers, H. I., Young, W. C., and Dempsey, E. W., "Graafian Follicle Development throughout the Reproductive Cycle in the Guinea Pig, with Special Reference to Changes during Oestrus," *Anatomy Record,* LXV (1936), 381–395; Papanicolaou, G. N., "The Sexual Cycle in the Human Female as Revealed by Vaginal Smears"; Mortimer, H., et al., "The Effect of the Administration of Estrogenic Hormones in the Nasal Mucosa of the Monkey"; Pratt, J. P., "The Human Corpus Luteum," *Archives of Pathology,* XIX (1935), 380–425, 545–562.

9. Hisaw, F. L., et al., "The Effects of Oestrin-progestin Combinations on the Endometrium, Vagina, and Sexual Skin of Monkeys."

10. Rubenstein, B. B., "Estimation of Ovarian Activity by the Consecutive Day Study of Basal Body Temperature and Basal Metabolic Rate"; "The Fertile Period of Women."

11. Zuck, T. T., "The Relation of Basal Body Temperature to Fertility and Sterility in Women," *Am. J. Obstetrics & Gynecology,* XXXVI (1938), 998–1004.

12. Rubenstein, B. B., "The Relation of Cyclic Changes in Human Vaginal Smears to Body Temperatures and Basal Metabolic Rates."

13. Burr, H. S., Hill, R. T., and Allen, E., "Detection of Ovulation in the Intact Rabbit," *Proceedings Soc. Experimental Biology and Medicine,* XXXIII (1935), 109–111; Rock, J., Reboul, J., and Snodgrass, J. M., "Electrical Changes Associated with Human Ovulation," *Am. J. Obstetrics & Gynecology,* XXXVI (1938), 733–746.

14. Zuck, T. T., "The Relation of Basal Body Temperature to Fertility and Sterility in Women."

15. Rubenstein, B. B., "Estimation of Ovarian Activity by the Consecutive Day Study of Basal Body Temperature and Basal Metabolic Rate"; "The Fertile Period of Women"; Sherwood, T. C., "The Relation of Estrogenic Substances to Thyroid Function and Respiratory Metabolism," *Am. J. Physiology,* CXXIV (1938), 114–116.

16. A comparative evaluation of the daily findings by both methods, which offered practically complete correspondence, will be published later.

17. Thomas M. French in his recent dream studies emphasizes that the manifest content of the dream is an "index of the quantitative balance between repressed and repressing forces" ("Reality Testing in Dreams," *Psychoanalytic Quart.,* VI [1937], 62–77) and in another paper, "Reality and the Unconscious," he explains, ". . . I am using the chronological order of appearance of the manifest dream elements in order to trace the shifts of emphasis that bring into focus one after another during the acting of dreams different parts of the latent dream thoughts. These shifts of emphasis I regard as quantitative indicators of the balance between conflicting tendencies just as conscious thoughts and actions during waking life are indicators of the quantitative balance between the motives that activate them" (*Psychoanalytic Quart.,* VI [1937], 48n).

18. Transference is the repetition of emotional experiences which during the analytic procedure becomes manifest in relation to the analyst or to the analytic situation.

19. Freud, S., "Three Essays of the Theory of Sexuality" (1905), *Std. Ed.,* VII, 135–243.

20. Freud, S., "The Ego and the Id" (1923), *Std. Ed.,* XIX, 12–66.

21. Children have their own concepts as to how children are conceived and they very often cling to these fantasies, even after they have full enlightenment as to the natural processes. Freud refers to these fantastic concepts of the children as infantile sexual theories. One of the most widespread conceptions is that children are conceived by eating something such as potatoes, beans, fish, etc.

THE CORRELATIONS BETWEEN OVARIAN ACTIVITY AND PSYCHODYNAMIC PROCESSES: THE MENSTRUAL PHASE[1]

In the first part of this communication[2] we presented evidence indicating that the emotional manifestations of the sexual drives are correlative to gonadal hormone production. This has already been recognized in birds and lower mammals.[3] Inasmuch as human instinctual drives are overtly expressed only in specific situations, it was necessary to infer their presence by study of dreams and fantasies, of free associations, and of all other types of psychological material. Analysis of psychoanalytic records provided a method of inference of the minute changes in the instinctual drives. Day-by-day study of vaginal smears and basal body temperature was the method of determining levels of ovarian function and ovulation time. The endocrine and psychoanalytic records were independently organized, evaluated, and then compared. Thus correlations in the psychological and physiological processes on each day of the cycle were found.

The conclusions of Part I of this paper were: *First,* (a) *whenever heterosexual drive, either as desire or as defense against it, appeared in the psychoanalytic material, estrone was produced in quantities sufficient to be recognized in the vaginal smear.* (b) *Whenever the erotization of the female body markedly dominated the psychoanalytic material, progesterone activity was found in the vaginal smear.* Progesterone production was further correlated with a passive receptive, instinctual tendency which might be expressed on the genital level as a wish for impregnation, as contrasted to the desire for coitus, or on the pregenital level as a tendency toward being generally receptive and dependent.

Second: the psychic apparatus recorded incipient production of these hormones with extreme sensitivity. The change in direction of the instinctual tendencies from the active, object-directed psychic energy to the passive, inwardly-directed instinctual tendencies represented a qualitative change in the cycle. This qualitative change produces the psychological cycle with the same regularity as progesterone, the antagonist of estrone, produces the hormonal cycle.

Third: an abrupt decrease in heterosexual tension along with an influx of passive libido tendencies—narcissistic erotization—characterized ovulation as determined by the vaginal smear–basal body temperature technique.

In our report on the ovulative phase of the menstrual cycle, we centered our attention on ovulation. We described the hormonal changes of this phase.

Our present report concerning the premenstrual-menstrual phase of the cycle centers about the hormonal factors which precipitate the menstrual flow. Unlike the preovulative-ovulative phase of the cycle which was characterized by intense and growing gonadal activity, the present report deals with the phase of diminishing and low gonad function. The premenstrual phase is characteristically the phase of regressing corpus luteum function and, consequently, of diminishing progesterone production. Estrone production during the premenstrual phase is variable. At first it decreases along with the progesterone since both hormones are produced in lessening amounts by the regressing corpus luteum. Later, estrone production may increase if new follicles begin to develop. In general, estrone production fluctuates irregularly but at a low level, since proliferation of the vaginal mucosa is rarely sufficiently stimulated to result in complete cornification of the superficial layers (the cells of which are seen in the vaginal smears). It is worthwhile reiterating that no direct measurements of either estrone or progesterone have been made on any of these patients whose cycles are presented in this paper. Changes in level of production are inferred from the changes in the basal body temperatures and the vaginal smears. At no time is an absolute measure of estrone or progesterone production presented. Indeed, such an estimate is impractical for reasons which have been presented in some detail in Part I of this publication.

The variability of the premenstrual phase, of course, had been predicted on the basis of clinical knowledge, and it had been known that the onset of flow could be delayed by many circumstances such as fear of pregnancy (especially in unmarried women), a long journey, change of climate, or the shock of a death. The onset of flow may also be delayed by hormonal change—by use of either male hormone or progesterone. Conversely, menstruation may be precipitated by an equal variety of emotional shocks, by physical injuries to the uterus or ovaries, or by the withdrawal of hormone medication from women who have been receiving it. The older literature is replete with theories concerning the mechanism of onset of menstruation. The literature is well summarized by Allen et al.[4] Inasmuch as in most women a corpus luteum is formed after ovulation, the progesterone deprivation theory for menstruation probably comes closest to the mark.[5] For experimental purposes it is, of course, possible to simplify the hormone situation. In castrated women the injection of progressively increasing doses of estrone followed by the injection of estrone-progesterone combinations yield a typical uterine development. Upon cessation of treatment, menstrual flow occurs.[6] It has, of course, been recognized that the menstrual flow may be precipitated or suppressed, at least for a time, in both acute and chronic emotional states. The hypothetical mechanism of the precipitation or suppression is probably through hypothalamic autonomic centers. This suggests that menstruation involves neural as well as endocrine mechanisms.[7]

The premenstrual phase is characterized by an unmasking of estrone activity and the development of new follicles which may or may not mature. The unmasking of estrone implies a regression in progesterone production, i.e. in corpus luteum activity.

Usually the peak of progesterone production occurs two to ten days before the onset of flow. After the peak, there is a more or less rapid regression in corpus luteum function which is reflected in the vaginal smears by a reduction in desquamation, the appearance of degenerated cells and cell debris, and the reappearance of leukocytes, bacteria, and mucus. About the same time, a new follicle or crop of follicles, destined not to mature, ordinarily begins its development. As the progesterone production of the regressing corpus luteum diminishes nearly to the vanishing point, the estrone produced by the newly developing follicle is revealed. Its effects are recognizable by (1) a decline in basal body temperature and (2) the reappearance of cornifying and cornified cells in the vaginal smears. Usually these follicles regress, others appear and regress, and none even approaches mature development in the premenstrual phase. The smears, therefore, show the occasional scattered appearance of cornified cells, cell debris, and vaginal secretions. The basal body temperatures fluctuate irregularly but usually on a declining curve. The period is characterized by variably shifting and generally low hormone production.

The onset of flow, heralded by the appearance of increasing numbers of red blood cells and leukocytes, might therefore be called a hormone withdrawal symptom. The onset of flow itself does not necessarily occur at a characteristic estrone level even in successive cycles of the same woman. It does occur after progesterone production is nearly extinguished. There may still be traces of progesterone activity at the time of onset of flow. During the period of flow, new follicles may develop. Luteinization of immature follicles may also occur. Thus the only endocrine characteristic associated with the premenstrual-menstrual phase of the cycle is a diminishing progesterone level.

We have observed a few cycles in which the premenstrual phase maintained progesterone production. In these cycles the temperatures remained high and the vaginal smears showed marked desquamation and aggregation of cells and abundant secretion throughout the period. The menstrual flow was not heralded by any microscopically observable signs. This type of menstrual flow is comparable to the type observed in experimental animals from whom progesterone is suddenly withdrawn. Another type of premenstrual development is the following: upon regression of the corpus luteum a follicle begins to mature and goes on developing without regression. There is an increasing estrone production during this phase of the cycle and no progesterone. In these cycles the premenstrual phase cannot be distinguished from the early preovulative phase. These patients usually have dysmenorrhea.

The type of menstruation which is purely estrone-deprivation bleeding is uncommon in adult women, but common in adolescents. We have one patient with infantile genitalia who has not ovulated during the period of observation. She has no corpus luteum phase during her cycle; her cycle is irregular and her bleeding scanty. This is probably estrone-deprivation menstruation.

In this report we shall attempt to present the correlations between various premenstrual-menstrual hormonal states and the corresponding psychodynamics.

Our present knowledge permits us to recognize the qualitative changes in gonadal hormone production by interpretation of the psychoanalytic material. We correlated the specific hormonal functions of the ovary with specific phases of the sexual drive: estrone production with heterosexual drive, progesterone production with passive receptive, instinctual tendencies. We have also stated that during the ovulative phase there is a semiquantitative relation between the level of hormone production and the dynamic intensity of its psychic concomitants. We are well aware of the difficulties in attempting quantitative evaluation of psychological material. The factors and motives determining the psychic reactions of an individual to her hormones are so complex that even an approximately quantitative evaluation is impossible without a knowledge of personality structure through which the psychodynamic state is evaluated and its changes estimated day by day.

Despite the restrictions imposed by methodologic inadequacy we were prompted to make quantitative estimates of the intensity of the instinctual drives on the basis of their emotional manifestations. Remembering the approximate character of these estimates, we submit some of the technique utilized in the quantitative evaluation. The most successful method of quantitative estimation is the "measuring" of the defense reaction employed to combat the instinctual drive. Thus it is easier to make quantitative comparisons in neurotic women whose inhibited and dammed-up instinctual drives call for strong defense reactions. For example, we presented the ovulative phase of G.S., December 10–26, 1937 (pp. 151–152, Part I, this vol.) and January 15–30, 1938 (pp. 155–156, Part I, this vol.) in which the "noisy" masculine protest and gradually increasing aggression permit a semiquantitative evaluation of the growing heterosexual tension. Anxiety, as the other main reaction against heterosexual drive, also permits estimation of the intensity of the affect. (See R.E., November 13–14, pp. 142–144, Table II.) It is more difficult to evaluate the positive manifestations of heterosexual drive. In some cases heterosexual fantasies flourish. The corresponding hormone level is sometimes quite high, sometimes low. We often find that fantasies on the pregenital level correspond with low hormone production. In other cases, heterosexual desire is expressed with great apprehension which would indicate great hormonal tension, but closer investigation shows that the physiological need is not great; the apprehension expresses the psychological need of the infantile, demanding ego to secure immediate gratification.

The change in personality and in psychodynamics which is the goal of psychoanalytic treatment is an important source of error in our evaluation. The patient whose estrone reaction was an aggressive defense and hateful protest may later react to the same hormone level with less psychic tension. She may yield to fantasies not permitted before, or she may find real gratification which changes her psychological reactions.

The instinctual desires of normal adult women are more readily gratified. Therefore, they depend little on dreams and fantasies. The ovulative phase in such women is psychologically not so obvious as in our case material of neurotic women.

The estimation of emotional intensity is, however, a macroscopic method. There is another evidence of quantitative change in hormone production which we term microscopic. This is the estimation of libido level. It seems that psychoanalytic material on the genital level in dreams, as well as conscious genital desire, capability for orgasm, etc., shows a higher correspondence with hormone production than does psychoanalytic material on the pregenital level. This microscopic differentiation is important for the estimation of hormone fluctuation in those phases in which the estrone level is lower and the instinctual drive is less clearly manifested in the conscious emotional state.

This aspect of evaluation is also important for estimation of progesterone activity. During the luteal phase, the emotional tension is usually not so great as during the preovulative phase. Increasing progesterone manifests itself in the growing clarity of the emotional attitude toward impregnation, pregnancy, and child. The receptive instinctual tendencies expressed on the genital level, either as wish for impregnation and pregnancy or as defense against it, still reflect a rather high progesterone function. Simultaneously there is an increasing preoccupation with the emotional relationship with child or mother. If the personality development involves an intense conflict concerning the mother and great ambivalence toward her pregnancies, then progesterone function may be estimated by the intensity with which this conflict appears in the psychoanalytic material. This pregnancy material expresses conflict on the genital level. When progesterone production does not develop to such a degree, we may miss pregnancy material. The passive, oral-dependent, pregenital-receptive material of adult women corresponds to a lower level of progesterone activity. During the premenstrual and menstrual phase we observed regression to the anal level in the psychoanalytic material which could be related to regression in progesterone production. Progesterone regression, which necessarily precedes the onset of menstrual flow, is correlated with eliminative tendencies. These may appear in the psychoanalytic material as anal or urinary regression (soiling tendency); often the eliminating tendencies remain on the genital level as birth, abortion, or castration fantasies.

In the premenstrual-menstrual phase of the cycle, quantitative estimation of the instinctual drives is prone to error because hormone levels are low and the instinctual tendencies which the hormones control are not clearly manifested in the psychological material. But utilizing the knowledge gained by our analysis of the much clearer pre-ovulative-ovulative phases of the cycle, we were able to interpret the analytic material in relation to the fluctuations of the ovarian hormones and predict the vaginal smear interpretation. Qualitative determination of estrone and progesterone activity could invariably be correlated with the psychodynamic material. We could also recognize the regression of the hormone function.

There were no discrepancies in our correlations between hormone production and instinctual drives when the hormone levels were high. In the late premenstrual phase, despite low hormone levels, the emotional state can nevertheless be tense and acute, as if hormone levels were high. The emotional state before the onset of menstrual flow is influenced by various factors. Its complexity and acuteness cannot always be explained on the basis of the related hormonal state.

Sociological factors are extremely important in the adaptation to the biological task of women. The interplay of biological, sociological, and psychological factors as they manifest themselves in the psychology of menstruation is not within the scope of this paper.

DATA AND DISCUSSION

The material of this paper was selected from a total of 125 cycles of fifteen patients. The selection, as before, was guided by the necessity for brevity and clarity of the psychological material.

We recognize the necessity for knowledge of the individual and her psychodynamic structure for the evaluation of her psychoanalytic records. But in this presentation we must omit any extensive description of the individual cases. We also omit publication of association material which would distract attention from the instinctual tendencies expressed in the dreams and direct attention to the actual problems of the patient, knowledge of which is unnecessary for an understanding of our general thesis. We selected those data in which the underlying instinctual tendencies are expressed at a manifest level in the dreams. When this was impossible, we presented only the interpretation of the dreams or other pertinent psychological data. The interpretations which appear in the psychoanalytic records and the hormone predictions made on the basis of the dreams are presented and compared with the independently evaluated vaginal smear–basal body temperature records.

First Premenstrual Evidence. Progesterone dominance develops after ovulation has occurred, but persists only a few days unless pregnancy intervenes. After the peak of corpus luteum function, regression begins and the production of progesterone diminishes. Many new follicles begin their development. Ordinarily none of these follicles mature. However, estrone is produced in small quantities. The first evidence of premenstrual change is the consequence of this unmasking of estrone. This is seen in the smears as minimal cornification after a period during which cornification was absent. In the basal temperatures the estrone influx produces a gradual decline. The psychological material reflects the change in hormone status by the appearance of heterosexual tendencies. In Part I of this paper we published some examples of this early premenstrual change (V.M., 12/8/37 and V.M., 5/25/38, pp. 166–167, Part I, this vol.) where the heterosexual tendency was clear enough to be recognized. The same patient, V.M., in the cycle 10/25 to 11/18, on 11/9 had the following dream:

> "I was rollerskating down a highway, I wanted to be sure of myself. I went very fast. People became small, the road became rough. I was insecure. I went between different people. The road went under a ledge. We were examining it to see if it was safe enough. Some female person was with me. We went into a little building like a depot. A young man was waiting for me. I had a disagreement with him because I refused to go to his home. It was engineered for us to be together. I was in love with him. I went to his bedroom. I saw his mother. She was Italian. I was wondering how I would get along with her."

In this dream we see the wish to free herself from her home and become independent. The wish for independence conflicted with the fear of being abandoned to her own sexual wishes. The world is full of sexual dangers and so a protective woman appeared in the dream. Only under the guard of this "female person" did she permit herself to express the sexual temptation. But the heterosexual wish also threatened her independence. The mother figure reappeared, now not as protecting her from danger, but interfering with her sexual wishes. The need for sheltered dependency was expressed by ambivalence toward the mother. The mother was at once the protective and the prohibitive person. The heterosexual wish was strong enough to appear in the dream as an illusion of love and sexual desire, but on the whole in this

dream the conflict with the mother was more important; it overcame
the sexual wish. The dream ended with her wondering how she would
get along with the mother. The tendencies ascribed to progesterone
activity appeared stronger than the heterosexual desire. Therefore, the
prediction was: mainly progesterone but slight estrone tendencies, very
early premenstrual.

The vaginal smear 11/9/37 showed few degenerated cells, aggregation, and an occasional cornified cell—very early premenstrual.

Another patient, P.O., had a very long lutein phase from 4/27
until 5/2. During this time her oral dependent attitude was acted out
by overeating. The mother conflict and wish to identify with the baby
brother were central in the psychoanalytic material; her oral demanding
and receptive attitude toward the analyst (female) showed the same
material in transference. The following dream on 5/3 introduced the
premenstrual phase.

> "I was in a hotel lobby, great many people, many of them I
> knew. I was concerned because I was running short of funds,
> but I thought I could borrow. Some sort of conversation.
> There was a woman there. I worked with her years ago. I
> kept thinking whether or not I should go to her and talk,
> finally I did. Then we were in a crowded train; I had difficul-
> ties because I had a lot of luggage. It was like Germany.
> Soldiers got into the train. A soldier sat beside me. He had a
> dog which took a great deal of the room. A porter took away
> my luggage."

The first part of the dream showed the continuation of the demanding and dependent attitude. But the crowded train, the closeness
of the soldier, and the symbolic meaning of the dog (penis) showed
the first appearance of the heterosexual tendency.

The vaginal smear 5/3/38 showed first appearance of cornified
cells, but still moderate aggregation—premenstrual.

Both examples show the instinctual tendencies characteristic of
progesterone function. The heterosexual tendency appears beside the
progesterone material, but not all first premenstrual evidence has this
character. There are cycles in which the lutein phase had not been very
well developed, others in which the progesterone function diminished
before the heterosexual tendency became obvious again in the psychoanalytic material. There are still other cycles in which the reaction to
the slightest heterosexual tendency was so strong an emotional defense
that it overshadowed the progesterone tendencies of the material. For
example, patient R.E. had the following dream on 12/1/37.

> ". . . One thing that does stand out is that the man doing
> the shooting had a gun in his hand and was in the basement.

I don't know whether I was brave or what it was, but I was on the outside; I leaned over and put my hand in through the window and his long fingernails scratched my hand on the back near the thumb; there was blood coming out. It was a long scratch. His fingernails seemed to be so sharp that I seemed to feel it in my dream. This man was a thief and a murderer and he had a gun in his hand. Then there were a bunch of police and people running around. Then all of a sudden the lights went out and it was pitch dark."

This dream reflected mainly heterosexual tendencies. The desire for heterosexual attack and the fear of pain connected with it were so clearly expressed in the dream that we might have predicted a high degree of estrone function. It was clearly premenstrual, but the estrone function was low. Quantitative comparison of the libido tendencies could not be made successfully.

The vaginal smear 12/1/37 showed further degeneration of cells, more mucus and debris, and an occasional cornified cell—early premenstrual.

The following dream of another patient, F.F., is similar. On 11/9/38 she dreamed:

"I went up a long flight of dark stairs to an apartment where I was married to a colored man and had a little girl who was white. I went there to talk to him about something, perhaps about telling people that he and I were married, must have been for some time because the little girl was three or four years old. Some argument with a fat, colored woman or someone else. I phoned the police and when the police came, he was not there. He had slit my throat and I lay in a sack and he had thrown me downstairs in someone's living room or apartment, and then I yelled with the slit throat, croaking out to the police as he went out that he had killed me. He ran out into a field, police after him and I thought, even though I was dead, he would be punished and I would haunt him."

This was her first premenstrual evidence. A slight influx of estrone production manifested itself in a dream which showed that most masochistic expectations connected with heterosexual gratification. The closer knowledge of this patient who was twenty-eight years old, unmarried, and sexually infantile revealed that she repeated her infantile concept of sexuality which she acquired by experiences when she was three to four years old, like the little girl in the dream. The emotional intensity of the nightmare from which she awoke with a headache can easily mislead us to assume that intense heterosexual libido caused the anxiety, but this was not the case. Her emotional reaction to the heterosexual tendency was extremely strong. She reacted with repetition of her infantile trauma and anxiety to even slight heterosexual tension.

The vaginal smear 11/9/38 showed leukocytic invasion and abundant mucus, along with the reappearance of many cornified cells (10%) —first premenstrual evidence.

These examples suffice to demonstrate that the reappearance of estrone is immediately reflected in the psychological material. The change in direction of the psychodynamic tendencies after a well-developed lutein phase is as clearly marked as the change during the preovulative phase, when the first signs of progesterone function reversed the direction of the psychic tendencies. In the incipient premenstrual phase, we can rely with equal certainty on the qualitative change in the psychodynamic material. We never miss the reappearance of the instinctual trend, which is new to the specific phase of the cycle. But, as our examples show, quantitative evaluation of these instinctual trends depends on many factors, chiefly on the individual's personality development and its consequence, the structure of the personality.

The Premenstrual Phase. After the easily identified reappearance of heterosexual material corresponding to new estrone activity, the premenstrual phase is characterized by variably shifting, but generally low, hormone production. The normally decreasing progesterone activity and the low but variable estrone production cause a similar fluctuation in the psychoanalytic material. Where we found heterosexual and active object libido, we predicted the existence of estrone function. The dependent, passive, libidinous tendencies, the wish for impregnation and pregnancy, and the active and passive feeding tendencies we related to progesterone. It is worth noting that when, as is common in this phase of the cycle, hormone production is not so great as in the preovulative phase, the psychoanalytic material usually appears less charged with energy. The conflicts are not so sharply defined. The records leave the impression that the patient had a freer choice of material and of its elaboration. For example, in cases where the mother conflict is central, it will be worked through in this phase, even though the progesterone function diminished, because the intensity of the estrone does not force the patient's thoughts and wishes in another direction. In other cases, when the patient's fear of the heterosexual tendencies was great, e.g., R.E., 12/1 (p. 180), and F.F., 11/9 (p. 181), slight estrone production caused very intense defense reactions; it forced the patient to elaborate her heterosexual conflict, to abandon or suppress the problems corresponding to the lutein phase. Thus our observations show that when hormone production is low, the problems and conflicts of the individual cover the underlying psychodynamic tendencies.

We have selected cycles to demonstrate the varieties of premenstrual hormone states. We propose to show that a detailed analysis of the recorded psychoanalytic material enabled us to recognize the various premenstrual types. Analysis of the conscious emotional state, as expressed in attitudes and symptoms, did not permit such a diagnosis. G.S.'s premenstrual phase from 11/6 to 11/14/37 was introduced by a dream which revealed defensive negativistic tendencies toward her child. The vaginal smear 11/6/37 showed regression in aggregation, earliest evidence of cornification. Since the heterosexual references in the dream are vague, there were no psychological signs of the premenstrual estrone output. On 11/7, however, she reported a fragment of a dream of the night before:

"I found myself on what appeared to be the ground floor, out in the open, exposed to the view of the numerous people present. Dr. X was on the ground with me. He was fondling my breasts and touching my sides with his hands. I responded to him with a strong sex urge but warned him that I would tell you everything and would report to you what he did. He appeared gay, free and relaxed and, while nodding approvingly at what I said, paid little attention to it, but kept on doing what he had before and talking really to the various people.

"I then went in a hallway. At the top of the stairs I saw two women whom I knew. They had evidently sought protection from danger but weren't then greatly alarmed. Suddenly, my sister K., my husband, R. and her husband appeared. R., with real emotion but with some exaggeration in her presentation, said, 'Do you know what has happened to us?' I had rushed forth joyously to greet my husband, but became stricken with fear as I listened to R. I knew my husband would not have left Carl (her child) behind him unless something had happened to him. I called out in a frenzy of fear, 'Carl!' "

The strong heterosexual urge needs no further interpretation. The ambivalent attitude toward the child and the appearance of the two sisters—homosexual element and the need for protection—represent the progesterone material.

The vaginal smear 11/7 showed there was still considerable aggregation indicating progesterone activity. The smear is definitely premenstrual. The amount of cornification is increased by comparison with that of the previous day.

The dream on 11/8 showed further increase of sexual urge and during the analytic hour she gave associations referring to her pregnancy: "I had a need to kill myself when I was pregnant," indicating increasing aggression toward her pregnancy and herself. We have cited very similar material for this patient's preovulative tension. The latter part of the premenstrual period started out with this aggressively colored dream.

The vaginal smear 11/8 was essentially like that on 11/7.

On 11/9 she felt very apprehensive, had accelerated breathing and fear of insanity.

> "I was in a nightgown. My oldest sister K. came in. I was angry that she came in so late. I knew that she had been with a man, having a good time. I realized I was jealous. I wanted to have the same. A little boy came in; something about a legal book."

Prediction: increasing estrone but some progesterone still present.

The vaginal smear 11/9 was clearly premenstrual, showing increasing cornification. On 11/10 there was no analytic material and the vaginal smear was clearly premenstrual, showing increasing cornification. On 11/11 she dreamed:

> "You [woman analyst] were in a car driving away with a man. I told you, 'Something is wrong with my son's sex organ.' You said, 'Oi veh!' I thought, 'You are just a sentimental Jewish woman.' "

The association material during the analytic hour that may be interpreted as a wish to bite off the penis of her son, showed oral incorporative tendency, aggression toward the penis. After the hour she developed abdominal cramps and diarrhea.

The vaginal smear 11/11 was premenstrual, with many blood cells.

On 11/12 she had diarrhea. She was resentful toward the analyst; this increased to conscious hatred and aggression. She identified herself with children who are badly treated and need to be protected.

The vaginal smear 11/12 showed practically no lutein activity. It showed red blood cells, leukocytes, marked cornification, and mucus output.

On 11/13 she showed increased aggression and tenseness. She was extremely resentful because she is not loved. She had necrophage fantasies, directed against (son's) penis.

The vaginal smear 11/13 showed increased cornification.

On 11/14, the dream content showed a longing for home, a regressive tendency of longing for mother's womb. During the analytic hour, she showed fear and defense against passive dependent tendencies, and diminished emotional tension.[8]

The vaginal smear 11/14 was late premenstrual, with increased secretion, degeneration, and low hormonal level. Menstrual flow started on November 14.

It was characteristic of this premenstrual state that the progesterone function was maintained until 11/12–11/13, although there was an increasing estrone production. Then progesterone disappeared while the estrone remained quite high. On 11/13–11/14 the hormone production diminished just before the flow started.

The aggressively charged emotional state had already evolved in the early premenstrual phase, and it became intensified during the last two to three premenstrual days. The conflict was clearly in the transference as a defense against dependence and fear of her own aggression. The premenstrual phase is "eliminative," and here we can see this tendency expressed on the anal and genital level.

The following cycle, 12/10 to 1/8, of the same patient, G.S., is very instructive. We have already described the psychoanalytic material of the preovulative-ovulative and luteal phase from 12/14 to 12/26 (p. 151, Part I, this vol.). The first premenstrual evidence occurred on 12/26. In the vaginal smear there was evidence of varying progesterone function with slight estrone production. This lasted until 1/3 but was accompanied by an increasing emotional tension. She felt "hypersexual." Neither fantasy nor coitus brought her relief. She described her condition on 1/3:

> "I had a great desire to avoid people. I felt inadequate. I did not have any itching until I came here. During most of the time (Christmas vacation) I was depressed. I wanted to come here. Yesterday I thought I did not care to see you. I had a lot of gas in me, terrific pressure. I disliked the idea of coming here. I became conscious of my weight; my body is enormous. This is always connected with distention of my abdomen.
>
> "Last night I dreamt that I weighed 200 pounds. This woman was in an insane asylum. She could come and go at will. Everybody laughed at her and had a good time at her expense. Somebody talked about syphilis. She assumed everybody gave her syphilis. But the woman at the desk told her she gave syphilis to everybody. All men died."

This dream showed her fear of being insane and expressed her guilt and fear. It showed self-consciousness which is the negative aspect of her narcissism, so freely expressed in the postovulative phase of the same cycle. It showed her fear of punishment because of her sexuality and her revenge against men. On this basis, the prediction was made: estrone and progesterone material.

The vaginal smear 1/3 showed more normal cells, minimal aggregation, and traces of cornification.

On 1/4 a skin rash developed. She felt slowed down, dull. It was difficult for her to breathe. She dreamed:

> "You [female analyst] were coming toward me very smilingly. You had a tray in your hand, food on it. You said, 'Here is something to eat.' "

The dream showed the oral need and her dependence on the analyst. At the end of the hour the patient had a weeping spell and headache. The dream material (psychosomatic symptoms) corresponded to progesterone.

The vaginal smear 1/4 showed more aggregation, 25% cornification. Late premenstrual.

On 1/5 there was no analytic hour.

The vaginal smear 1/5 showed more debris but also cornification (50%).

On 1/6 she was depressed but relieved by crying. During the analytic hour she repeated a dream, dreamed on 12/24 (and interpreted as a characteristic womb dream in the postovulative phase, p. 163, Part I, this vol.). She now associated her own birth with this dream. "I was dead when I was born. The doctor put me in hot water. This is what my mother told me."

The birth material was associated with her own experience of labor. She said that today she had an impulse to steal. Prediction: regressive progesterone.

The vaginal smear 1/6 showed more secretion, still 50% cornification.

On 1/7 she reported that after the last analytic hour she felt alert. The analytic material of this hour is presented in some detail. She began by complaining about a loose stool just before the session started. She said:

> "My father forced me to take castor oil. I bit his finger. Once when I was pregnant I took castor oil with orange juice. Since then orange juice has often tasted like castor oil. This morning my orange juice produced the same sensation. Then I had the loose bowel movement. I thought, 'to move my bowels.' "

Then the patient repeated her experience of labor.

> "Terrific pain. I thought, 'How is it possible for people to let you suffer like that? I'll throw myself out of the win-

dow.' I was desperate. I was afraid I would have a bowel movement; the bearing down pains caused the feeling. I found it terrible; I did not want to do it. [Analyst moved in the chair.] Are you moving? I am afraid. I don't know what you will do to me. I dreamt about an old woman; she drew a big knife; I ran away."

The vaginal smear 1/7 showed increased cornification (60%) and slight aggregation.

In this material, highly charged with emotions, we can easily recognize the fear of being destroyed. In the dream it was expressed by the fear of being castrated by a woman and by the vivid recollection of labor pains and loose bowel movements. The birth material related to progesterone, the passive castration dream to estrone effect. Thus, the psychological concomitants of both hormones were present, i.e., the birth material and the anal material were unusually charged with emotion. There was a fear of annihilation connected with this feeling of being abandoned to pain. The bowel movement and labor caused expulsion of all the body contents. The instinctual tendency to discharge was strong enough to cause anxiety comparable to the anxiety which accompanied her preovulative aggression. The eliminative tendency is typical of the late premenstrual phase and is evidence of progesterone regression. In this case, the tendency to discharge was expressed on both the genital and anal level. The strong self-destructive tendency is evidence of emotional tension connected with impending menstruation. This can be compared with the preovulative phase in which the same conflicting tendencies were found, except that the aggression was turned toward herself. The premenstrual emotional tension is created by high estrone production, along with minimal progesterone production, just as in the preovulative phase. The menstrual flow started on 1/8, suddenly, like an abortion: "I had a pressure, I had to move my bowels." The flow was immediately very excessive.

The next cycle of the same patient, 1/8 to 2/4, had a quite different premenstrual phase. We have described the ovulative phase of this cycle, G.S. 1/18 to 2/4. The premenstrual change occurred on 1/29 when she had the following dream:

"I was dreaming of going in my sister's house. There appeared to be some joke attached to it. When I awoke I thought in rapid succession of the two jolly young men whom I had liked in the woods."

This dream showed incipient estrone activity. The conscious emotions and psychoanalytic material still showed hostility toward mother and siblings. Thus the prediction was made: progesterone material and incipient estrone, premenstrual evidence.

The vaginal smear 1/29 showed mostly normal cells, few cornified cells. Premenstrual.[9]

On 1/30 she felt hostile, depressed, and disliked. She felt enormous. The dream showed ambivalence toward her son.

The vaginal smear 1/30 showed mostly normal cells, few folded, few cornified. Very early premenstrual.

On 1/31 she dreamed:

> "My sister K was leaving town to meet a married man. I was concerned because I heard that the wife of this man had hired detectives. I went to her; I found her in bed in an enormous room. It reminded me of a barn where something sexual happened in my childhood. Suddenly there appeared a group of people who have their meetings there. We called the registry of the hotel about this intrusion but they said it was all right, and we had to accept this situation. Then it was on the street. I observed men, trying to find out which was the detective. Then K was going to Detroit to get married."

The association material for this dream was abundant. The main factors in the dream are: (1) fear of the mother who will punish her for her sex life; (2) the heterosexual tendencies; and (3) her defense against the men intruding is, however, not as aggressive as usual. The fear of being observed and the need to observe are connected with self-defense and fear of punishment. The analytic hour showed various regressions. She told of soiling herself, about the odor of her mother's body.

> "I am thinking about the periodic changes which my body undergoes. My breasts enlarged, I look enormous; I prefer black at such times. All the sensations of my body are so disgusting, so ugly."

Before the hour she showed a regressive tendency and self-consciousness about her body which was related to anal material. Prediction: regressive progesterone and not too high estrone.

The vaginal smear 1/31 showed more cells with pyknotic nuclei. Slight increase in cornification. No aggregation.

On 2/1 she looked stubborn and depressed. The main topics of the analytic hour were: defense against her need to be dependent and the problem of toilet-training her child and herself. She was depressed, with great infantile dependency and identification with the baby. On the basis of the anal material which we considered regressive, decreasing hormone production was predicted.

The vaginal smear 2/1 was essentially the same as on 1/31 with no folding, very little cornification. There was a low hormone level, which characterized this cycle until the onset of the flow.

On 2/2 she felt better. Nevertheless, her relationship and emotional reaction to her sister's child were upsetting. "I was afraid to carry the baby, though I felt very tender toward it." This yearning for the child is a typical progesterone reaction, which is usual in the premenstrual phase.

The vaginal smear 2/2 showed more debris and a low hormone level.

On 2/3 she feels like crying, is tearful. She feels she ought to be punished for something. She starts by talking about her spite reactions and temper tantrums toward her father and mother, and is glad that she feels sorry, that she punished herself. The weeping spell lasted long after the analytic hour. Analytic material is infantile; she feels deep, vague grief. Prediction: premenstrual depression, low hormone level.

The vaginal smear 2/3 showed more normal cells, an occasional cornified cell, and was diagnosed as low hormone level.

On 2/4 she said, "I wept yesterday for a very long time. It poured. I felt it rather difficult to breathe. I felt guilty and insincere. I dreamed:

> "I was in my sister R's house. She had a Negro housekeeper who had syphilis. She was not in an infectious state, but she took care of the baby. I had the feeling she should have told it to R. I have to tell it to R. I see her go to the toilet."

In the dream her identification with the Negro housekeeper is obvious. Syphilis is punishment for sexual guilt; her sexual guilt made it impossible to have an undisturbed relationship with the baby. The yearning for the baby continued in this dream, and she complained that her breasts hurt. The further analytic material of the hour brought out her infantile conception of childbirth. The same concept appeared in the previous cycle, in the material on 1/7, but highly charged with emotions. Childbirth = defecation; both represent annihilation. Now, however, instead of fear of childbirth, there is yearning for a child, deep regret that she never will have a child again. There is a feeling of loss. But childbirth itself is like a bowel movement, losing something. However, there is no fear, no associated feeling of self-destruction. Prediction: low hormone level. Late premenstrual.

The vaginal smear 2/4 showed more normal cells, low hormone level.

After the hour the menstrual flow started suddenly. This was a premenstrual phase with progressively diminishing hormone production.

We have presented three premenstrual phases of the same patient, each differing from the others. In the first, progesterone production diminished and estrone increased; in the second, estrone increased while progesterone was maintained; in the third, both hormones progressively diminished. Related to the hormone levels, the conscious emotional state was tense, aggressive, and extraverted in the first; fearful, desperate, and self-destructive in the second; lacking aggression, dependent, and sad in the third. Such a variety of premenstrual moods is not unusual in a single individual.

Table I summarizes the premenstrual phase of patient R.E. which shows low hormone production during the early and also during the late premenstrual phase. On pages 180–182 of the first part of this paper we presented another cycle of the same patient where the premenstrual phase was characterized by increasing estrone production. The flow started at the 90% cornification level.

TABLE I

CYCLE: JULY 1–AUGUST 4

CASE R.E.

Date	Psychoanalytic Material	Prediction	Physiological Findings
July 25	Dream: (1) Prostitution fantasy, (2) Fear of sex attack, (3) Very depressed, womb fantasy.	Estrone and progesterone function. Premenstrual.	Regressive progesterone. Still 75% cornification.
July 26	Fear and wish of being attacked sexually. She is obsessed by the idea of penis.	Estrone tension. Premenstrual.	Diminishing progesterone. Minimal cornification. Premenstrual.
July 27	Conflict with mother on two counts: (a) mother interferes with her heterosexual desire, (b) mother deprives her of her pregnancy.	Progesterone increased. No estrone.	Regressed estrone. Premenstrual. Low hormone level.
July 28	Herpes labialis. Dream: Identification with brother. The masculine identification may protect her against heterosexual attack. Fear and wish of attack.	Estrone. Diminished progesterone.	25% cornification. Slight folding and aggregation.

CASE R.E.—*Continued*

Date	Psychoanalytic Material	Prediction	Physiological Findings
July 29	Dream: (1) Masochistic concept of female sexuality: to be woman means bleeding and death. (2) Brother-incest. Identification with brother on masochistic basis.	Estrone increased. Premenstrual.	Increased cornification. Occasional red blood cells. More secretion.
July 30	Nervous, more fear.		Same.
July 31	No analytic material.		Same.
August 1	Dream: preparation for menstruation. Passive, withdrawing, depressed.	Regressive hormone.	Extreme regression. More debris.
August 2	Feels better. Dream: (1) Mother is protection. (2) Father is also protection. (3) Pregnancy = anal birth dream. Fear of pain.	Low hormone level. Progesterone regressed.	Extreme regression.
August 3	Depression. She talks about her fears. The anxiety is not acute. Vague desire to overcome the fear of pain.	Psychoanalytic material does not show hormone characteristics. Menstrual.	Occasional red blood cells. 25% cornification.
August 4	Cheerful: She talks about the fear of heterosexual and homosexual desire. Primal scene material. Identification with mother.	Low hormone level.	Menstrual. 25% cornification.

We now present in succession the premenstrual phases of three cycles of patient V.M. which not only confirm the correlation between hormone production and psychodynamic tendencies, but suggest also the possibility that psychic factors affect gonadal function. In her cycle

1/12–2/8 the first premenstrual evidence occurred on 1/31 when her emotional state was "startling." She was sexually very demanding. The association material showed mother conflict, demands upon mother. The oral demands were aggresively expressed. Premenstrual evidence.

The vaginal smear 1/31 showed more aggregation and secretion, an occasional red blood cell, and minimal cornification. Early premenstrual.

On 2/1 she was anxious and apprehensive, cried and raved about her mother, and was jealous of her siblings. The association material showed hatred and guilt toward the mother, fear that mother might take away her child just as she wanted to have mother's child for herself. This was progesterone content; but the great aggressive tension indicated that both hormones were present.

The vaginal smear 2/1 showed marked desquamation and aggregation with increasing cornification. Clearly premenstrual.

On 2/2 she dreamed:

> "Social gathering, apartment. I heard that a murder took place. There were several people in the hall with me. A suspicious looking man was looking back and I thought that he was a suspect. He was running away. I went downstairs and he was with somebody else. It seemed he also killed a woman and I was afraid. He embraced me. I found it was L."

In this dream the masochistic sexual concept found its solution in her normal heterosexual wish. She was not angry on that day. The estrone-correlated heterosexual tendency seemed free from any conflicting lutein tendency. Prediction: increased estrone, no progesterone.

The vaginal smear 2/2 showed mostly normal cells, no aggregates.

On 2/3 she was again angry because her demands were not satisfied. She reported the following dream:

> "Mother and father and I are in a place, like a barn. I have a pail with dirt in it. I want to wash it out. I looked at my mother. She objected and showed it. I put it in the stream and I saw the water becoming very dirty, like sewage from the barn. I wondered how this dirty water could wash out the pail, but it did. My brother brought in the cows. Mother showed me family heirlooms, lovely things. I began to feel sex feelings. A studio couch was wide open. As I got into it, I felt another girl there. I was face down and she had her face up. I felt both genitals. It seemed definitely so."

Her associations were "I had the male sex feelings, sex fantasies and experiences."

While the bisexual content of the second part of the dream is clear, it is important to observe the regressive character of the first part of the dream, namely, vaginal—dirty pail—sewage—urine—masculine sexual excretion. Masculine material, fertilizer—sewage. The anal and urethral regression in the dream indicated regressive progesterone function, bisexual tendency. Increasing sex tension indicated increasing estrone.

The vaginal smear 2/3 showed extreme secretion (masturbation or coitus?) with much cell debris. Late premenstrual.

On 2/4 she reported she had intercourse, but was still very tense, irritable, and critical. She talked about male genitals and her fantasies. Increased heterosexual tension.

The vaginal smear 2/4 was like that of 2/3, but with few sperm.

On 2/5 and 2/6 there were no analytic sessions.

The vaginal smears 2/5 and 2/6 showed slightly increasing cornification.

On 2/7 she reported that her heterosexual need was great during the weekend. She had had satisfactory coitus. She felt herself attractive to men and was very proud of it. The increased heterosexual need had had a satisfactory discharge which made her happy, increased her self-esteem. The emotional state was similar to the estrone-related emotions of the preovulative phase.

The vaginal smear 2/7 showed markedly increased cornification (60%).

On 2/8 the patient talked dramatically, giving the impression that she wanted to expose herself to everybody near and far who could hear her. There was great elation and narcissistic satisfaction in her behavior as well as in the content of the material. Prediction: like an ovulative phase, high estrone level.

The vaginal smear 2/8 showed complete cornification but beginning of menstrual flow.

She did not notice the flow at all. It is possible that the high estrone production was responsible for the unusually scanty flow at that time. But it is surprising that a patient taking her vaginal smear daily and accustomed to observing herself closely (she used to report the "spotting" before and after the flow) did not notice the bleeding at all. She was absolutely convinced that she had missed the menstrual period and, during the following four weeks, she was worried about the possibility of pregnancy. Why was she unaware of the spotting? Obviously, there was great emotional readiness to suppress the menstrual flow. This wish might be responsible for the rather scanty flow. The satisfactory coitus on 2/7 and her happiness and narcissistic behavior on 2/8 offer other explanations: (1) she was so satisfied with her sexual life that she did not want to interrupt it by menstrual flow; (2) she did not want to be reminded of being a woman, castrated, bleeding; (3) unconsciously she wanted and expected to become pregnant from the physically and emotionally satisfactory coitus. The records were not adequate to select one or another of these alternatives, until the records of the next month were available, which showed her preoccupation with pregnancy and pointed to the pregnancy wish as being the most likely factor in the patient's partial suppression of the flow.

The vaginal smears 2/8 and 2/9 showed complete (100%) cornification, abundant red blood cells, much secretion, obviously menstrual. Unfortunately, the patient did not prepare smears on 2/10 and 11.

The vaginal smear 2/12 was typically postmenstrual and consisted chiefly of normal cells.

The following cycle, beginning with the unnoticed flow, was from 2/8 to 3/7. She first noticed flow only on 3/8. It was essentially a normal cycle. Ovulation took place on 2/18 and was followed by a clear lutein phase from 2/19 to 2/25 when the first premenstrual change (cornification) appeared in the vaginal smear. (There were no analytic sessions.) From 2/25 to 2/28 there was a period of low, variable, hormone production as is frequent in the premenstrual phase. The analytic material was dominated by progesterone. On 3/1 the late premenstrual period started with increasing heterosexual tension. There was no regression of lutein activity in the psychoanalytic material.

On 3/1, the dream expressed the wish to be feminine, the wish to be given gifts. She wanted to begin again with her marriage, more romantically, with narcissistic gratification. She dreamed:

> "J. [husband] said, 'We should elope and get married.'
> I decided we should get married the second time the right
> way. We decided to arrange a big wedding. We had a lot of
> people. I saw a balcony that could be decorated prettily."

The associations were more demanding, expressed her dissatisfaction. Her breasts ached. She expected and was worried about pregnancy. Prediction: heterosexual wish is estrone material; demanding, receptive, and narcissistic attitude is progesterone material.

The vaginal smear 3/1 showed more aggregation and debris, few cornified cells and red blood cells. Premenstrual.

On 3/2 she reported:

> "I feel terrible. I lost some sleep on account of a dream:
> I was on the couch in the analytic room. I became angry and
> I left. It was a delightful feeling. You [male analyst] called
> me back. You would not let me go.
> "I saw a girl dying in bed, in her hand a rose tree, a
> religious figure, symbol of death of the Savior. I wanted one
> of the roses and I wondered if anyone would see if I picked

it. I heard nuns talking and then I saw I had two flowers in my hand. I was going downhill to the basement. I was afraid something was going to injure me. I found a little hole in a small board. I was angry with you and I was never going to allow anybody to treat me like this."

The wish to be loved—narcissistic, flirtatious, feminine attitude—is expressed in the first part of the dream. In the second part of the dream the dying girl symbolizes the dying virgin from whom she wishes to get the symbol of virginity. She recreates the fear of being hurt by sexuality. There is defense against passive, feminine wishes which she enjoyed. Prediction: heterosexual wish but narcissistic defense. Still progesterone and estrone activity.

The vaginal smear 3/2 showed increased cornification and less aggregation.

On 3/3 her dream showed guilty feelings because she was not a virgin any more. The vagina is not clean, impregnation fear. Associations showed the wish to be a feminine, "real woman," not a masculine woman. This indicates the persistence of progesterone and estrone.

The vaginal smear 3/3 was essentially like that of 3/2, with slightly more debris, lower hormone level.

On 3/4 the patient is ambivalent and dependent on the mother, afraid lest she take away her child. This fear that mother begrudges her the child repeats itself in her premenstrual material. This time it may have been activated by the fear or expectation of her supposed pregnancy. No heterosexual material.

The vaginal smear 3/4 showed more secretion; much less cornification.

On 3/5 and 3/6 there were no psychoanalytic sessions.

On 3/7 she decided to carry out the pregnancy if she is pregnant. She is anxious about a pregnancy test, demanding, and irritable.

The vaginal smear 3/7 showed abundant secretion, but low hormone level. Menstrual smear.

The patient recognized the menstrual flow on 3/8 and had normal flow until 3/11.

It is interesting to compare this premenstrual material, where the patient did not expect the menstruation but thought she was pregnant, with the premenstrual period of the following cycle of the same patient. (The cycle from 3/8 to 4/5 is a normal ovulative cycle; ovulation was on 3/20.)

On 3/23 the first premenstrual change appeared with highly dynamic analytic material, then a lutein phase developed and on 3/31 the "late premenstrual" phase evolved.

On 4/1 the patient was depressed. "There is nothing in my life to be happy about," she cried, "My son likes his father better than me."

She accused her husband of seducing and alienating her son away from her. The analytic material showed only the mother-child conflict. Progesterone.

The vaginal smear 4/1 showed abundant debris, an occasional red blood cell. There was low hormone level, but progesterone dominance.

On 4/2 and 4/3 there was no psychoanalytic material. During the weekend she was more relaxed and willing to admit that the idea that her husband separated her from her child was pure imagination. No vaginal smears.

On 4/4 she felt tense. She thought she was pregnant. She dreamed:

> "I was in Germany in great trouble, trying to get away
> from Hitler, trying to seek protection from Goering."

Her associations were that she had read a story, "A woman left Germany because she was pregnant by a Jew." This dream, although it seemed to have heterosexual content, expressed mainly the wish and fear of pregnancy and the dependent attitude of a pregnant woman. Increased tension, increased estrone output. Pregnancy wish, lutein material.

The vaginal smear 4/4 showed more secretion and aggregation, more cornification.

On 4/5 she dreamed:

> "Mary, my high school chum, and I were sitting in an
> office. I saw across a worker in another building getting ready
> to jump off to commit suicide. Then I began to feel that other
> people should see it too. I told Mary to look, when Lena
> jumped. I went downstairs. She was saved, as the place from
> which she jumped was not so high."

Her associations were,

> "Mary is the name of my little sister. My mother threat-
> ened to commit suicide; it frightened me, yet I wished it. It
> would have been a relief. I could not express my love for
> her, only my hatred. I told my husband that if I should die,
> he should tell my mother how I loved her."

The dream expressed ambivalence toward sister and mother and symbolically, the fear of childbirth. The awareness of her genitals was so strong that the patient felt she was "bursting." The increased eliminative tendency indicated slight progesterone regression.

The vaginal smear 4/5 showed marked desquamation of normal and aggregated cells, few cornified. Progesterone dominance.

On 4/6 she dreamed:

"I seemed to be in the clinic, prenatal. I saw a little girl of five or six coming out of a taxi, pregnant. I tried to help her. She was carrying the baby very low. I asked her if she had a tummy ache. I was concerned if she was in labor. They took her to examine her."

After this dream the menstrual flow started. The associations to the dream expressed a strong wish for pregnancy, "I want to be a woman," and regret that she was menstruating. The onset of the menstrual flow was sudden, with cramps, discharge of clots, like an abortion. We see in this case that although this patient consciously avoided pregnancy, the unconscious pregnancy wish influenced the psychological material.

The vaginal smear 4/6 was the same as that of 4/5 except that there was some blood.

We have presented three premenstrual periods with the following characteristics: the premenstrual phase in the first cycle showed decreasing progesterone and increasing estrone, ending at a high estrone level like a preovulative phase; the woman felt satisfied and narcissistic. The next premenstrual phase showed increasing estrone and maintenance of progesterone. We know that the psychological content was influenced by the fear and expectation of pregnancy. In the third cycle there was low estrone production and maintained progesterone, though there was no justified fear of pregnancy. This is evidence for the closeness of the correlation, but naturally sheds no light on the problem of primacy of gonad or psyche.

The first evidence of impending menstruation is a marked regression in progesterone production which in the psychoanalytic material is represented by eliminative tendencies. These may be expressed on the genital or pregenital level. On the pregenital level they may take the form of urethral or anal soiling and need for discharge. For example, patient R.R. dreamed on 1/19/39:

"My mother and I were washing dirty clothes together. I was not mad at her. I was wondering how she would get the dirty water out of the tub."

In this dream the regression has urinary symbolism and is indicative of regressive progesterone level.

The vaginal smear 1/19 showed much more degeneration, mucus, and debris. Very low hormone level.

Similarly in the cycle 12/10–1/8 of patient G.S., the dream on 1/6–1/7 concerned bowel movement, clearly an example of anal discharge.

On the genital level, the eliminating tendencies may be expressed in dreams or fantasies concerning childbirth, bleeding, loss, abortion, or castration—for example, G.S. on 1/7/38, when these tendencies were expressed on both the genital and anal levels with feelings of self-destruction and V.M. on 4/6/38, when the tendency was expressed as parturition. As an example of the depressed feeling of loss, G.S. dreamed on 11/13:

"I was in a depressed or melancholy state; my baby was dead. Perhaps there was some talk about reconstructing the child."

And on 11/14:

"All day I had the feeling that I had suffered a loss, that I don't have a child."

She recalled during the analytic hour the circumstances and her emotional reaction to her first menstruation when she was twelve years old. She was very tearful. Menstrual flow started the following night, 11/14.

The vaginal smear 11/14 showed abundant secretion of mucus and leukocytes, aggregation, and an occasional cornified cell. Low estrone.

As an example of menstruation representing castration or death, we present the following dream of G.S. on 10/21:

"I observed a body lying in the street. It seemed to be writhing convulsively in a sort of agony. Then there were two bodies, lying side by side. Then one of the bodies was headless. The head had dropped off. There was a hideous red gash, a bloody gash, around the torso where the neck had been. Then neither body had a head. I felt I had to help. Someone had to help. The girl or woman was in agony and kept repeating, 'It's all so hopeless.' I went to her. Suddenly the girl was standing on the sidewalk. She was smiling happily. Her head was on her body again and she appeared to be more cheerful, as though she didn't fear that it would be detached again. She asked for some crème de Cracow, mispronouncing the last word. I said, 'You mean crème de cocoa,' and was willing to give it to her."

The vaginal smear 10/21/38 showed low hormone level, premenstrual.

This dream was as highly charged as if there were a high hormone level. The patient, describing this dream, talked in a hoarse voice. During the last two days she had been nauseated and had difficulties with her voice. "I thought you were choking me." As associations to the dream she repeated in rapid, emotional speech the conflict with her mother after her brother was born; her associations were concentrated on male genitals. The whole material was highly charged emotionally. Analysis of this dream shows the fears connected with menstruation which is feared as mutilation, as destruction of her body. It also shows that the hopelessness is not profound, for if a helpful person (good mother) were to give her attention, love, and food (creme = milk) then life would not be hopeless; it would not be necessary to feel that bleeding, menstruation, or childbirth were annihilation.

Castration fear usually appears in the late premenstrual material as a reaction to loss and discharge, particularly when some estrone production is present. The eliminative tendencies appeared highly charged with psychic energy in the late premenstrual material whenever progesterone and estrone production which had been maintained suddenly regressed during the premenstrual phase.

The emotional reactions during the last premenstrual days are more acute than in any other phase of the cycle. Generally, only this part of the cycle had previously been recognized as the cyclically recurring neurosis of women. Freud wrote an interesting reference to the importance of periodicity in women in an early article on "Types of Neurotic Nosogenesis."

> "As is well known, such rather sudden intensifications in libido are regularly connected with puberty and the menopause. The dissatisfied and dammed-up libido may now open up the path to regression and excite the same conflicts as in the case of absolute frustration."[10]

That is, during the premenstrual phase of every cycle, women may repeat the neurotic constellation which they experienced at puberty as a preparation for or reaction to the menstrual flow.

Since Freud wrote his first articles relating neurotic reactions to physiological changes, there has been a prolific psychoanalytic literature about the dynamics and emotional effects of menstruation. The main publications are reviewed in a small monograph by Mary Chadwick.[11]

It is not within the scope of this paper to discuss the psychology of menstruation. Our objective is to demonstrate how the gonad function is reflected in the emotional state of women during this crucial phase of the cycle. The great variety of our material during the premenstrual phase shows "dammed-up," highly charged libidinous or aggressive material such as Freud described, not only when there is a high hormone production, but even when hormone production is low. Thus we conclude that the premenstrual phase is characterized by a psychodynamic and psychosomatic response, more complex than would be expected on the basis of hormone quantities alone. Sociological, developmental, and constitutional factors may all be involved. Many women, who do not show marked or neurotic reactions corresponding to their gonad function during other phases of the cycle, show psychological reactions during the premenstrual phase.

Restlessness, irritability, and oversensitiveness to all kinds of stimuli are generally accepted as quasi-normal during the premenstrual-menstrual day. Fatigue, tearfulness, emotional withdrawal with more or less severe depression, and a feeling of regret and inferiority frequently characterize the premenstrual depression. In some cycles the eliminative tendencies are highly charged with aggression to which the reaction is anxiety. Fear of what will happen to one's body often suffices to describe the emotional condition preceding the menstrual flow. Fear of pain, fear of mutilation, and fear of birth are expressed in the psychological material with a great individual variety of defenses.

The tense, fearful psychosomatic state usually relaxes when flow starts. An observation not widely accepted, but true for our group of cases at least, is that adult women accept the menstrual flow, once it starts, with emotional relief. Fear, apprehension, and rebellion may have dominated the premenstrual phase; when the flow is established anxiety, apprehension, and rebellion cease. Emotional relaxation corresponds to the sudden decrease in hormone production that ushers in the flow. Failure to find relaxation corresponds to continued production of estrone at a high level.

The correlations between emotional state and hormone production during the period of flow show the same shifting, variable quality that seemed typical for the premenstrual phase. Womb and nursing fantasies and the wish to care for a baby are commonly expressed, particularly in the dreams of the second and third menstrual days. Occasionally the entire period of flow is one of depression and a feeling of loss. At other times, the period is one of elation related to preovulative development. It then takes on the characteristics which we described in detail in Part I of this publication. To present the psychoanalytic and smear material in detail for the period of flow would prove nothing new about the correlations but would involve extensive repetition. Therefore we present in tabular form several premenstrual-menstrual phases. It should be noted that the period of menstrual flow is included.

We have presented the different types of premenstrual-menstrual phase. They demonstrate (1) that careful analysis of the recorded psychoanalytic material permits us to recognize the psychological effects of the gonad hormones, estrone and progesterone, despite their daily (shifting) changes and although they may be produced in but small quantities during this phase of the cycle; (2) that emotional reactions in the premenstrual phase may be more intense, more acute than in other phases of the cycle. Thus quantitative estimate of the emotional material does not always parallel the psychodynamic correlation with hormone production.

TABLE II

CYCLE: DECEMBER 28–JANUARY 20, 1939

CASE: R.R.

Date	Psychoanalytic Material	Prediction	Physiological Findings
Jan. 10	Dream: Incestuous wish. Unhappy, depressed. Cannot work.	Low estrone.	Still marked aggregation and folding. Slightly less lutein.
Jan. 11	She feels depressed, incapable, irritable. Dream: Urethral regression, sadomasochistic tendency.	Regression in level of progesterone.	Regressive luteal smear, degeneration of cells.
Jan. 12	Resistance. No sexual desire. Anal regression.	Regressive progesterone.	Degeneration.
Jan. 13	No analytic material.		Desquamation, degeneration. Low hormone content.
Jan. 14	Depressed, sleepless, critical. Dream: (1) Incorporative penis wish. Aggression toward pregnancy. (2) Incest. Primal scene. Oedipus complex: loves the father and is afraid of the mother.	Lutein regressive. Estrone increased.	No smear.

TABLE II

CASE R.R.—*Continued*

Date	Psychoanalytic Material	Prediction	Physiological Findings
Jan. 15	No analytic material.		Type 5, 6—early premenstrual.
Jan. 16			Type 6, 7—late premenstrual.
Jan. 17	Angry, tense, narcissistic defense against heterosexuality. Narcissism destroys libidinous wishes.	Low estrone.	Minimal cornification.
Jan. 18	Friendly, less tension. Amiable mood. Dream: Identification with mother: to be woman means to be dirty: tendency to discharge. Dirty urine identical with content of vagina—blood or child.	Late premenstrual. Regressive progesterone.	More cornification. Premenstrual. More secretion.
Jan. 19	Amiable mood. She has more relaxed and friendly relationship to men than usual.	Low estrone.	Regression to low hormone.
Jan. 20	Feels well, gay. Menstrual flow started without pains.	Low hormone.	Menstrual, still low hormone.
Jan. 21	Dream: Demands on father, not in sexual sense, but for security. Dream has anal regressive content.	Low hormone.	Low hormone level.
Jan. 22	Dream: Demands on father. But here the sexual symbolism displays the unconscious sexual demands.	Starting estrone.	Low hormone level.
Jan. 23	Dream: Aggressive domineering toward sister. Masculine identification.	Increasing estrone.	More secretion. Little cornification, much pyknosis.

CASE R.R.—*Continued*

Date	Psychoanalytic Material	Prediction	Physiological Findings
Jan. 24	Self-assertive. Feels all right.	More estrone.	Still occasional red blood cells. Bacterial invasion. 75% cornification.

TABLE III

CYCLE: OCTOBER 21–NOVEMBER 18

CASE X.

Date	Psychoanalytic Material	Prediction	Physiological Findings
Nov. 7	Wants to stay in bed. Withdrawing. Dream: oral and homosexual dream content, very depressed dream.	Progesterone function.	Luteal phase.
Nov. 8	Need for oral gratification. Identification with mother with the feeling of inferiority. Wish for masculine identification.	Progesterone. Starting estrone.	Luteal phase regressive.
Nov. 9	Dream forgotten. Talks about her lack of interests. Tearful.	Regression in hormone level.	Minimal cornification. Premenstrual.
Nov. 10	Outgoing, talkative, sudden change. Dream: Birth dream. Father is the protective helpful person. Vagina is dirty: dream shows greater emotional tension.	Estrone. Late lutein. Premenstrual.	Minimal cornification.
Nov. 11	Talking in a vague way about heterosexuality. She never has the courage. Compulsive candy eating.	Progesterone and low estrone level.	Minimal cornification. More aggregates.
Nov. 12	No analytic material.		Predominantly luteal.

TABLE III

CASE X.—*Continued*

Date	Psychoanalytic Material	Prediction	Physiological Findings
Nov. 13	Sleepless. Competitive. Hostile. Quarrel with sisters. Oral envy. Compulsive candy eating.	Progesterone —estrone (?)	Predominantly luteal. Low hormone.
Nov. 14	Hostile, depreciative toward men. Castration wish. Depression, with great tenseness. Compulsive candy eating.	Estrone and progesterone. Clearly premenstrual.	Minimal cornification. Clearly premenstrual.
Nov. 15	Vague heterosexual fantasies. Curiosity about masculine genitals. The heterosexual material less charged with energy than on previous day. Still compulsive candy eating.	Estrone plus regressive progesterone.	Regressive in hormone.
Nov. 16	She awoke crying in angry rage from a dream. Dream: (1) Siblings rivalry. (2) Dependent wish to stay with the mother expressed by womb symbolism. Still compulsive candy eating.	Mainly progesterone. Estrone(?)	Same.
Nov. 17	All day on 16th depressed. Disoriented. In doubt about everything. Today weary, passive —dependent, need for reassurance. Afraid to start anything.	Regressive hormone.	25% cornification. Occasional red blood cells. Debris, late premenstrual.
Nov. 18	Menstrual flow started 17th.		Menstrual, low hormone.
Nov. 19	No analytic material.		Low hormone.
Nov. 20	No analytic material.		No smear.
Nov. 21	Dissatisfied, demanding, no erotic feelings.	Low hormone.	30% cornification.

TABLE IV

This cycle shows a sudden increase of estrone
just before the menstrual flow started.
CYCLE: NOVEMBER 18–DECEMBER 17

CASE X.

Date	Psychoanalytic Material	Prediction	Physiological Findings
Dec. 9	Dream: (1) Infantile sex fantasies. (2) Fear of being attacked. (3) Intercourse = murder. (4) Masochistic concept of female sexuality. Oral and womb symbolism.	Progesterone and estrone. Premenstrual.	Extreme output of secretion. Minimal aggregation. 5% cornification. Earliest premenstrual.
Dec. 10	Dream: (1) Wish to withdraw and be protected at home. (2) Fear of being attacked. (3) Sister protects her. The conflict is the same, as on the previous day, but vague, less emotional charge.	Regressive estrone. Progesterone dominance.	Marked degeneration of aggregated cells. Low hormone level.
Dec. 11	No analytic material.		Same—slight increase in progesterone output.
Dec. 12	No analytic material.		Same.
Dec. 13	She feels sorry for herself. She is full of doubt.	Regressive hormone.	Same.
Dec. 14	The same mood. No analytic material which would permit diagnosis.	Low hormone level.	Same.
Dec. 15	Sudden change. Masturbation on previous evening. Fantasies about abortion. Fear of abortion. Fear of being castrated. Detailed fantasies about suffering by labor, abortion. Masochistic fantasies in which rectum and vagina are identified as in the birth theories of children.	Regressive progesterone on eliminative level. Low estrone.	Reappearance of cornified cells. Estrone increasing. Still some residual progesterone production.

TABLE IV

CASE X.—*Continued*

Date	Psychoanalytic Material	Prediction	Physiological Findings
Dec. 16	Completely superficial material. Unimportant details.	Regressive compared to previous.	Again debris—marked regression in hormone production.
Dec. 17	Highly charged dynamic dream: (1) Mother-womb protects her against sex wishes. (2) Very intense heterosexual wish. There is not only fear of attack, but also very aggressive fight with man.	High estrone level. Low progesterone.	Cornification 50%; rest of smear consists of debris. Marked increase in estrone production.
Dec. 18	No analytic hour.		Menstrual flow. 75% cornification. No progesterone.
Dec. 19	Very superficial. Amiable mood. Menstrual flow profuse. Clots. Cramps.	On analytic material hormone diagnosis not possible.	Menstrual flow. 90% cornification.
Dec. 20	Still menstruating. Amiable mood. Sexual curiosity.		Cornification practically complete. Minimal aggregation.

SUMMARY

We have presented and discussed a selection of premenstrual-menstrual phases of 125 cycles of fifteen patients. Careful study of vaginal smears and basal body temperatures and of psychoanalytic records confirm the correlations inferred in Part I of this publication.

(1) The presence of estrone (cornification in the vaginal smears) corresponds to the presence of active heterosexual libido.

(2) The presence of progesterone (desquamation, aggregation, folding, and secretion in the vaginal smears) corresponds to a passive, receptive instinctual tendency.

Since the premenstrual-menstrual phase of the cycle is one of low hormone production, certain other characteristics appeared, as summarized in Table V which is self-explanatory in the light of the material presented.

TABLE V

Phase of Cycle	Hormone State	Psychological State
Early premenstrual	Minimal estrone. Dominant progesterone.	Incipient recurrence of heterosexual tendency. Mostly impregnation fantasies.
Premenstrual	Diminishing progesterone. Variable but low estrone.	Mixed oral-incorporative and heterosexual fantasies. Generally quiescent phase.
Late premenstrual	Sudden extinction of progesterone.	Eliminative tendencies
		on genital level —childbirth. —bleeding. —abortion, castration.
		on pregenital level —anal or urethral discharge. —vomiting.
		Emotional tension or depression out of proportion to hormone production.
Menstrual	Low hormone.	Emotional relaxation.

Estrone regression —
— Reduction in emotional tension
— Heterosexual tendency on infantile level
— Regression to pregenital level

Progesterone regression
— Eliminative tendencies
  1. Gential level
  2. Pregenital level
— Emotional depression

In addition to confirming the correlations, we have described and discussed the psychological concomitants of regression in hormone production. The data also suggests the possibility that psychological factors influenced the gonad function. In this phase of the cycle, this may account for the occasional maintenance of progesterone production.

During the late premenstrual-menstrual phase of the cycle, emotional reactions are more intense and complex than can be explained on the basis of the accompanying hormone production. After the menstrual flow is established, there is an emotional relaxation which again corresponds to the low hormone production characteristic for this period.

CONCLUSIONS

1. The simultaneous use of day-by-day study of vaginal smears and basal body temperatures and of the analysis of the recorded psychoanalytic material provided clear correlations between the physiological and psychological processes.

2. The investigation confirms the probability that in the adult woman the manifestations of instinctual drives are related to specific hormone functions of the ovaries.

3. The premenstrual-menstrual phase of the sexual cycle is one of diminishing progesterone and low, but variable, estrone production. The metabolic gradient is generally downward.

4. Corresponding with the hormone levels, the instinctual tendencies are on the genital level when hormone production is relatively high; on the pregenital level when hormone production is very low.

5. Upon extinction of progesterone, eliminative tendencies appear in the psychological material. This is most common in the late premenstrual period.

6. There is a pseudo-quantitative correlation between hormone production and emotional tension.

NOTES

1. Originally published in *Psychosomatic Med.,* I, no. 4 (1939), 461–485. (Revised for this volume.)

2. Benedek, T., and Rubenstein, B. B., "The Correlations between Ovarian Activity and Psychodynamic Processes: I. The Ovulative Phase," *Psychosom. Med.,* I (1939), 245–270. This volume, pp. 137–171.

3. Stone, C. P., "Sex Drive," in *Sex and Internal Secretions* (Baltimore, Williams and Wilkins, 1939), pp. 1213–1262.

4. Allen, E., Hisaw, F. L., and Gardner, W. V., "The Endocrine Functions of the Ovaries," in *Sex and Internal Secretions* (Baltimore, Williams and Wilkins, 1939), pp. 520–540.

5. Engle, E. T., Smith, P. E., and Shelesnyak, M. C., "The Role of Estrin and Progestin in Experimental Menstruation," *Am. J. Obstetrics & Gynecology,* XXIX (1935), 787; Hisaw, F. L., "The Physiology of Menstruation in Macacus Rhesus Monkeys," *Am. J. Obstetrics & Gynecology,* XX (1935), 638; Zuckerman, S., "Further Observations on Endocrine Interaction in the Menstrual Cycle," *J. Physiology,* LXXXIX (1937), 49.

6. Hisaw, F. L., Greep, R. O., and Fevold, H. I., "The Effect of Estrone-Progesterone Combinations on the Endometrium, Vagina and Sexual Skin of Monkeys," *Am. J. Anatomy,* LXI (1937), 483–504; Zuckerman, S., "Further Observations on Endocrine Interaction in the Menstrual Cycle."

7. Hohlweg, W., "Das Mechanismus d. Wirkung von Gonadotropen Substancens a. d. Ovar d. infantilen Ratte," *Klin. Wchnschr.,* XV (1936), 1832; Hohlweg, W., and Junkman, K., "Die Hormonal nervose Regulierung

d. Funktions d. Hypophysenvorderlappens," *Klin. Wchnschr.,* XI (1932), 321.

8. The distinction between the psychological content corresponding to progesterone production and to regression in the hormone production needs further elaboration. Here we refer only to the fact that "dependency" is characteristic of an infantile emotional and libidinal state; thus in adults it corresponds to a regression.

9. In the tabular condensation of the cycle published in the monograph (pp. 259–260) the premenstrual change is indicated to have occurred one day earlier, on 1/28. This probably was the result of a greater sensitivity of the investigator to incipient changes in the smear.

10. Freud, S., "Types of Onset of Neuroses" (1912), *Std. Ed.,* XII, 231–238.

11. Chadwick, M., *The Psychological Effects of Menstruation* (New York, Nervous and Mental Disease Publ. Co., 1932).

DISCUSSION

As I undertake a discussion of an investigation almost forty years after it was first published, I wish to speak first of its methodology. The aim of the research required that every interpretation should reveal the particular condition of the sexual drive. The consistent comparison of that condition with the hormonal state of the cycle led to conclusions that opened new avenues for investigation of some fundamental theories of psychoanalysis.

As the circle of conclusions drawn from this investigation widened, I became more aware of the responsibility of the investigators for the dependability of their methods. Therefore, in preparation for this publication, I asked Dr. Rubenstein whether he would now consider the vaginal smear technique as useful in investigating those problems to which we set ourselves originally. In response to this question, he contributed the following statement concerning the current evaluation of changes in the vaginal epithelium under the influence of the ovarian hormones:

Since 1940 there have been many descriptions of the cytology of the human vaginal epithelia. Some of these were well summarized in *The Cytology of the Human Vagina* by I. L. C. De Allende and O. Orias.[1] The cytology, it is agreed, varies in response to estrogen and progesterone of the normal menstrual cycle. The changes in the vaginal epithelium at menopause or after surgical castration and its restoration by estrogens are fairly well documented. From studies of the cytological changes in response to estrogen administration and its withdrawal, rough quantitation of estrogen-induced

effects is possible. Estrogen effects may be simulated by responses to other stimuli to the growth of the vaginal epithelium, e.g., coitus, infection. The possibility of such simulated
responses must be carefully evaluated and controlled for each
subject if the study is to be valid.

It is also agreed that only an estrogen-primed vaginal
epithelium will respond to progesterone. Attempts at quantitation are even riskier than the original assessment of estro-
gen-stimulated responses. I concur, therefore, that no single
vaginal smear can be evaluated as a hormone assay. However, if a series of consecutive smears from a single subject is
evaluated, comparisons may be made among the smears by
ascertaining the degree of cornification and karyopyknosis,
folding and clumping of cells seen in the vaginal smear. From
such comparisons, levels of estrogen and progesterone activity
may be inferred with the rough accuracy required in this report.

Further support for such evaluation is provided by the
study of vaginal smears of women taking contraceptive pills.
In those women who use the sequential type of contraceptive
pills, estrogenic smears are seen during that part of the artificial cycle in which only estrogen-containing pills are taken.
These smears show some increasing cornification and karyopyknosis corresponding to some cumulative effects from the
estrogen intake. When at the end of the cycle the combined
estrogen-progesterone tablets are taken, there is an almost
immediate shift of the vaginal cytology to that characteristic
of the postovulative phase in a normal ovulative cycle, viz.,
clumping and folding of cells. During the time when medication is finally interrupted, smears usually characteristic of the
premenstrual to menstrual phase of a normal cycle are seen.
Thus the contraceptive pills may also stimulate an apparent
flow and ebb of ovarian hormone effect such as characterize
a normal menstrual cycle. In this event, however, hormonal
evaluation is a direct consequence of the hormone intake.
[Boris B. Rubenstein, M.D., 1969]

The question may arise, How does this statement by Rubenstein
relate to his original evaluation of the vaginal smears? Would the
differences necessitate modifications in our findings? Hardly. The influence of estrogen, whether it is the woman's own or whether it is administered, is well documented; the cytologic changes that occur during the
ovulative and postovulative (progesterone) phase, as well as during
the premenstrual phase, are basically the same as was described in the
monograph. Rubenstein developed a scale of eight cell types by investi-

gating a series of cycles of the same individuals. This scale is not in clinical or investigative use now. Our "qualitative" predictions regarding the appearance of an incipient hormone phase, as well as our "quantitative evaluation" of the progress or decline which follows, were based on independent evaluation of the cytologic and psychoanalytic material.

Rubenstein obliged me by adding a paragraph on the effects of the "pill" upon the vaginal smear, a question always asked whenever the sexual cycle is discussed. As far as the effect of the pill upon the emotional cycle is concerned, my observations indicate that the cycle flattens out; there is no marked preovulative tension or postovulative relaxation; premenstrual symptoms are mitigated or disappear, although premenstrual-menstrual depressions appear more frequently than one would expect.

In the evaluation of the psychoanalytic material, even early in our investigation, we went beyond predicting the time of ovulation. As long as we did not have our working hypothesis formulated, our perception of the emotional fluctuations was our guide in selecting the relevant data. After the relevance of those data was confirmed by the diagnoses of the vaginal smears and body temperatures, we could proceed more goal-directedly toward establishing the psychodynamic correlations with the phases of the gonad cycle.

Nevertheless, we were aware that the material, psychoanalytic as well as histologic, was far from complete. We were aware that both methods (the vaginal smear technique and psychoanalysis) were open to discussion as instruments of biologic research. In spite of their limitations, however, the two methods offered a unique opportunity to compare and correlate results. These comparisons, during the 152 cycles that constituted the material of the monograph, are presented in Table 1.[2]

As I survey this material again after many years, it strikes me that it was a "first" in many respects. Psychosomatic interactions are usually investigated to explain pathological conditions. In this instance a normal physiologic process, the gonadal hormone cycle, was observed in neurotic individuals with a specific method. At variance with other psychoanalytic investigations, the personality problem was not the subject matter of the investigation. The personality organization was the background against which to measure the oscillations of emotions and their psychodynamic motivations. In the preliminary reports, no adequate attempt could be made to consider structural differences in the personality organization of the subject. In the monograph, six of the fifteen cases were presented in detail in order to indicate the probability of mutual influences between the personality structure and the gonadal cycle. Those investigations were few; too many variables were involved to allow for any generalization.

The aim of this discussion is not to further elaborate on the sexual

TABLE I

General survey of the case material. This table presents the number of cycles of each patient studied, the length of cycle, the frequency of ovulative as compared with anovulative cycles, the number of cycles for which material was insufficient for characterization as either ovulative or anovulative, and finally the length of the interval from ovulation to the next menstruation (O–M Interval). It should be noted that while ovulation occurred characteristically in the mid-interval between menstrual periods and that while the average time is 14.5 days before the next menstrual flow, the range of variation is extremely wide: 4–26 days.

PATIENT	NO. OF CYCLES	LENGTH OF CYCLE Mean	LENGTH OF CYCLE Range	OVULATION +	OVULATION −	NO DIAGNOSTIC MATERIAL IN OVULATIVE PHASE	O–M INTERVAL Mean	O–M INTERVAL Range
I*	25	27.7	21–37	21†	5	0	15.0	8–24
II	12	26.6	23–30	8	2	2	14.4	9–19
III	8	24.6	18–31	3	2	3	15.1	13–21
IV	7	26.0	24–28	2	2	3	15.2	12–17
V	4	28.3	28–29	2	1	1	14.5	13–15
VI*	4	26.5	21–32	1	1	1	—	—
VII	13	31.2	28–35	4	8	1	16.2	12–21
VIII	20	23.3	17–28	5	9	6	14.2	11–18
IX	21	26.4	23–29	11	4	6	13.6	7–20
X**	7	36.6 50.4	23–52 29–89	1	6	2	14.3	12–16
XI	8	30.2	28–35	2	4	2	15.8	13–17
XII	10	27.3	17–31	3	6	1	16.2	7–26
XIII	8	29.8	23–38	2	5	1	9.2	4–21
XIV	1	31.0	—	1	—	—	—	—
XV	4	28.0	27–29	—	4	—	17.0	—

* The 15th cycle of patient I was incomplete and therefore omitted. Pregnancy occurred in the 4th cycle of patient VI and therefore this cycle was omitted.
† Ovulation occurred twice in one cycle.
** While this patient had only 7 cycles, 2 of them were really double, 52 and 89 days respectively. Each double cycle had two preovulative and postovulative phases, thus accounting for the 9 crucial phases reported.

cycle and its individual variations, but to point out the theoretical conclusions drawn from the consistent application of the reductive technique of interpretation. For this purpose, some aspects of the interpretive
technique are repeated. The investigation had two parallel foci: the
diagnosis of the gonadal hormone state and the corresponding emotional
state. The great variety of motivations of the emotions had to be reduced to one or two manifestations of the sexual drive. Drives are
object-directed. Their "impetus" can be felt as an affect. Thus, in this
investigation the object relationships and the developmental levels that
they represented had to be separated from the affects and emotions
which accompanied them. Obviously such separation is artificial and
should be undertaken only for the sake of investigation.

The perceptive investigator learns quickly the characteristic manner of an individual's affective reactions and their motivations. The
human vocabulary is rich in verbal and nonverbal expressions; both
"semantics" have individual shadings and connotations derived from
past and current experience. The tone of voice, the pressure of the flow
of verbalization, as well as the choice of words reveal the particular
emotional state and help to differentiate the acute significance of one or
more factors among the multiple motivations. These are the impressions,
passing swiftly in the live analytic situation, on which we base the tim-
ing and phrasing of our interventions. Fixated in the recorded material,
these imponderables convey the intensity of feelings, the depth or shal-
lowness of affects available for closer scrutiny and even for comparative,
quasi-quantitative evaluation.

The weight of this discussion centers on the analysis of affects, but
object relationships offer the motivations and the targets of current
affect, just as object relationships are instrumental in developing the
patterns of affective reactions. Object relationships are the axis of the
personality development. Throughout the genetic history of the individual, traces of object relationships are preserved in their psychic
representations, and images of objects are transferred to new objects
with variations depending on age, maturity, and significance of the
relationship. The relationships may belong to the past. If they are current during the period of the psychoanalytic treatment, they are outside
the analytic situation.

Nevertheless, one object relationship is alive and yet not real in
the analytic situation; this is the transference to the psychoanalyst. The
function (and the meaning) of that relationship is that it represents
and/or repeats past relationships. In discussing the transference process,
or the dynamics of the transference, one rarely refers to its manifestations. Here "transference phenomena" refer to distinct psychic events
(be they a gesture, a slip of the tongue, a symptom, or an affect) which
represent the repetition of past experiences in projections to the psychoanalyst. In an analysis of the recorded psychoanalytic material they

reveal, besides biographical and characterological data, emotions which, in this investigation, were evaluated in reference to the hormonal state of the sexual cycle. The investigator is not a transference object of the patient. Being outside the transference situation, he can evaluate the transference-countertransference reactions and their affective content objectively. To express this investigative procedure in terms of meta-psychology, we conclude that the object relationship aspect of the investigation dealt with genetic factors; the analysis of the affects and emotions dealt with the dynamic-economic factors that had to be evaluated in order to arrive at a correlation with the gonadal hormone state.

The fluctuations of emotions in this context demonstrate that every affect has a function in the psychoeconomic constellation in which it occurs. Affects generally are indices of a disequilibrium in the psycho-economic balance. But there are also affects and emotions which accompany the recovery of the psychic equilibrium. To appreciate the psychoeconomic function of affects—not from the phenomenological viewpoint but from that of psychic economy—the affective experience must be analyzed. In analyzing the affect itself, first its instinctual origin and "developmental line"[3] have to be traced in order to appreciate the role of the affect in the total personality, usually recognizable as a character trend. The cognizance of these factors enables us to appraise the significance of external stimulation from the current internal psychobiologic stimulation and/or from the general psychologic predisposition to a particular affective reaction. The second task in analyzing affects (which, however, more often presents itself as first) is the ego's response to the affect. From the ego's side, affects are intrapsychic stimulations which the ego perceives from many aspects, since it is the ego's function to integrate the psychic processes stirred up by dynamic forces such as drives and affects, thus to reestablish psychic equilibrium. This is not a simple process. It includes an unconscious perception of the meaning of the affect to which the ego may respond with a variety of psychic mechanisms. This may be a defense against the affect—such as repression—or it may be a denial which will activate another affect—such as fear or shame. The ego's reverberation to a simple affect may become what Glover terms "affect cluster."[4] This may lead to behavioral manifestations and further elaborations by psychic processes. In this investigation, the complexity of ego-affect interactions had to be considered only for the purpose of peeling off the many layers of superstructure to get down to the dynamics of the affect itself. Affects are psychic structures originating in (or motivated by) instinctual impulses, and accordingly have objects, aims, and impetus.

I am certain that all psychoanalytic investigators who have dealt with the theory of affects have considered the close affinity between drives and affects. The methodology of this investigation led to the

clarification of the biologic significance of this affinity. It was essential
to this study to reduce the manifestations of emotional fluctuations to
their core affects. The inquiry was turned from the concept of sexual
drive to its components, the *psychodynamic tendencies*. Searching for
the manifestations of the sexual drive in the daily fluctuations of emotions, it was impossible not to analyze the affects, whether they were
directly related to sexuality, consciously or unconsciously, or not at all.
Envy, for example, is an affect that plays a role in the personality organization of most people, since sibling rivalry is a manifestation of this
affect. Growing up with envy and struggling against it, some become
ashamed of being envious; others become generous in denying it or in
overcompensating for it. But everyone will recognize it as a tendency to
own, to incorporate, to devour. There are days when patients feel helpless against a "voracious appetite." In any case, the affect of envy is
the manifestation of the psychodynamic tendency to receive, to incorporate. The anxious worry of the miserly person who wants to hold on to
what he owns is the expression of a receptive tendency that cannot be
verbally expressed as colorfully as envy and greed can be. Is this verbal
paucity a manifestation of niggardliness or of the shame of its anal
origin? In classical terminology the former would have been described
as manifestation of oral libido, the latter of anal libido on the basis of
the assumption that libido originates in erotogenic zones of the body.
But the consistent analysis of affects almost inadvertently led to Alexander's vector concept.[5]

Alexander's hypothesis is that emotions deprived of their ideational
content are expressions of one or more fundamental directions that
characterize biologic processes. The vector qualities of intaking, retaining, and eliminating represent directions which can be attributed to
physiologic processes as well as to psychic manifestations of drives. This
concept characterizes the developmental phases, not in terms of erotogenic zones, but by the directions of the psychodynamic tendencies corresponding with the function of the dominant zones at various levels of
development. They are not difficult to diagnose. The dreams presented
in the preliminary reports show that such psychodynamic tendencies are
often represented in the manifest dream content, especially during the
low hormonal states of the cycle, expressing the parallel regression in
the hormonal and the emotional cycle. In contrast, the "genital tendency" of the sexual drive corresponds to the high hormone production
of the ovulative phase. Since the vectors, i.e., the psychodynamic tendencies, are simpler constructs than the sexual drive, they can be
applied to the analysis of any affect or any shift in emotional excitation.
By analyzing affects and reducing them to basic motivations, we can
discern the changing levels of integration and regression of the sexual
drive.

The cyclic variation of the integration of the drive, the relaxation which follows ovulation, and the tension states and transient depression which characterize the premenstrual phase are experienced often as mood changes. What are moods? Webster defines mood in general as "the sum of those mental dispositions which give the dominant emotional character or cast of mind."[6] Other definitions refer to the transient character of moods originating in and/or connected with emotions. Moods are derived from affects; they are not directly motivated by psychodynamic tendencies. In contradistinction to affects, moods are not related to specific content or object but ". . . find expression in specific qualities attached to all feelings, thoughts and actions; they may indeed be called a barometer of the ego state."[7] Paraphrasing another definition by Jacobson, mood is a modification of a generalized discharge.[8] Moods can be stimulated from without and from within. The investigation of the sexual cycle demonstrates that hormonal processes stimulate characteristic mood changes. We may add that moods are psychic processes one step removed from the neuroendocrinologic motivational systems which we investigated by utilizing the manifestations of changing moods.

The observation of Gottschalk et al.[9] indicates the "introversion of libido" referable to ovulation. Their study, which concentrated on the variations of basic affects—anxiety and hostility—showed variations from cycle to cycle. The findings of Rudolf H. Moos et al., whose study was based on measurement of levels in mood changes throughout complete cycles,[10] are generally consistent with our cycle research. The variables measured in their study changed cyclically, related to the menstrual cycle. These investigations show that the neuroendocrinologic influence is recognizable in such general manifestations as mood changes which transiently pervade the ego state.

This investigation did not set out to solve the enigma of woman. However, it does contribute one factor toward that goal—the discovery of the biologic source of the indwelling quality of the female psyche in her procreative function, in the effect of the hormone of the corpus luteum. There are more basic imprints of her gender function on her psyche than psychophysiologic investigation reveals. As an example, I cite here an experiment carried out by Erik Erikson long before he understood its meaning. In a paper reflecting on the meaning of womanhood, he reports his early observations as "a clinical worker in whose mind a few observations linger for a long time."[11] These observations were collected on 150 boys and 150 girls in an experiment; the task of these adolescents was to construct movie scenes from play material on a large table. The scenes were photographed in progress and at completion for further study. The memorable impression of this investigation was the great difference between boys and girls in the use of space. The boys' constructions moved forward toward the edge of the table, spreading over the surface of the available space, sometimes rising to shaky heights. In contrast, the girls employed "inner space" and depth when possible. Erikson used this observation in 1969 to discuss the significance of "inner space" in the development of the female. From infancy on, her procreative function permeates all aspects of her personality.

As the sexual drive, in correspondence with the ovarian hormones, goes through phasic changes in its aim and integration, the psychoanalytic material reveals the psychologic traces of the corresponding developmental phase of the libido. Thus psychoanalytic investigation of the personality structure reveals the conflicts and the solutions, the drawbacks and the sublimations of her especially female indwelling quality.

It took years of psychoanalytic practice, during which I lived with what I had learned from the cycle research, to arrive at other levels of conceptualization and to be able to formulate what I had gleaned from my patients and from their psychosexual cycles. Instead of listing the "discoveries" which originated in the cycle research, I shall refer to them in the later chapters.

The investigation of the sexual cycle demonstrated the integration and regression of the sexual drive during the cycle as a normal accompaniment of the hormonal processes. However, the most important contribution of this project to psychoanalytic theory is knowledge about the organization of the sexual drive in women, the phasic separation of the object-directed tendency of the drive in the procreative physiology. This offers further understanding of the interrelationship between the preprocreative and the procreative aspect of sexuality. (See "On the Organization of the Reproductive Drive," Chapter 16.)

Menstruation and pregnancy are the most conspicuous manifestations of the sexual physiology of women. Both physiologic events and many of their psychologic manifestations can be explained by the hormonal and psychologic processes revealed in the investigation of the sexual cycle. However, neither menstruation nor pregnancy is a part of the sexual cycle; therefore they are mentioned only tangentially in the discussion of the sexual cycle. In order to round out this presentation, a brief discussion of these psychophysiologic processes is added. This is based on the presentation in my article, "Sexual Functions in Women" (1959).[12]

Menstruation. Menarche—the first menstruation—may occur at any time from the beginning of puberty through adolescence. The onset of menstruation takes the central place among all events of the girl's puberty. As if menarche were a puberty rite cast upon women by nature itself, it is expected that it will be accompanied by intense emotional reactions. However, the anticipation of menstruation as well as conscious response to it are influenced by cultural factors. In our present civilization, education and hygiene prepare the girl for the menarche in a sympathetic way. This seems not only to diminish the manifest rebellion against menstruation but even to make the girl expect it with eagerness. Yet the bleeding and the discomfort may stir up latent anxiety. It was one of the early psychoanalytic observations that women connect menstruation with the idea of mutilation. Even mature women may dream about bloody acts which they commit or which are committed upon them about the time of menstruation. This type of anxiety dream indicates that menstruation represents injury to the woman. But whether the injury necessarily means castration in the sense of penis envy remains to be investigated in each case. Menstruation forecasts the pain of defloration and of even more significant injuries connected with childbearing. It enforces the awareness of the uterus through varying degrees of pain and discomfort. At the same time, it activates the process of integration of the latent partial identifications with the mother toward the future task of childbearing. Fliess[13] formulated this theory by calling attention to the womb (Gebär-mutter) as a symbol of the mother. When menstruation stimulates the awareness of the uterus as an integral part of the body, "mother enters the body."[14] The next step in the girl's development is to accept "mother = womb" as a part of the self, and with it to accept herself as a future mother and motherhood as a goal of her femininity. The maturation toward the female reproductive goal depends on the previous developmental identifications with the mother. If these are not charged with hostility, the girl is able to accept her heterosexual desire without anxiety and motherhood as a desired goal. This, in turn, determines the girl's reaction to menstruation. If the feminine sexual function is desired, the girl accepts menstruation without undue protest. In contrast, if the phallic (bisexual) fixation dominates the psychosexual development, the hostility toward the mother continues as a protest against menstruation and also against other aspects of femininity.

The onset of menstruation used to be taken as a sign of sexual maturity. It is now accepted that menstruation begins in most girls before their ovaries are capable of producing mature ova, and that ovulation may take place before the uterus is mature enough to support normal gestation. This brings about a period of adolescent sterility.[15]

Knowing the adolescent's struggle to achieve psychosexual maturity in our society, one is inclined to assume that the processes which lead to superego development, i.e., to the incorporation of parental and cultural inhibitions, necessarily mean a delay of the physiologic maturation of the reproductive functions. Yet the correlation is not a simple one. While arrest of physiologic maturation may occur on the basis of inhibiting emotional factors, one cannot make the generalization that the stronger the prohibitions and the related anxiety and guilt, the longer will sexual maturation be delayed. In this regard, constitutional, genetic, and intrauterine influences may determine the effectiveness of the emotional factors. If all variations were to be arranged in a continuous series, at one end would be those cases in which the stability of the physiologic processes is such that normal reproductive maturation is not influenced by emotions, and at the other end would be those in which emotional factors can permanently arrest maturation. The great majority of women fall between these extremes; they present an innumerable variety of results of developmental interactions of organic and psychic factors as they influence psychosexual functions. Correct psychosomatic diagnosis tends to evaluate the proportionate relation and interaction of organic and psychologic factors in each symptom. This general principle of psychosomatic pathology is pointed out here in connection with menstruation, since we look upon menstruation as a cornerstone of female development, a focal point where physiologic and psychologic factors meet and reveal whether the adaptation to the sexual function will succeed or fail.[16]

Pregnancy. When conception occurs, the cyclic function of the ovaries is interrupted and is not reestablished with regularity until after lactation is finished. Because of the uninterrupted and enhanced function of the corpus luteum, the psychology of pregnancy is best understood as an immense intensification of the progesterone phase. The heightened hormonal and general metabolic processes, which are necessary to maintain the normal growth of the fetus, augment the vital energies of the mother. It is a manifestation of the symbiosis (the reciprocal interaction between mother and fetus) that the pregnant woman's body abounds in libidinous feelings. While some women enjoy this narcissistic state in vegetative calmness, others, especially in the second trimester of pregnancy, find outlet for their physical well-being by enlarging their activities. As the metabolic and emotional processes of pregnancy replenish the primary narcissism[17] of the woman, this becomes the wellspring of her motherliness. It increases her pleasure in bearing her child, stimulates her hopeful fantasies, and diminishes her anxieties. While the mother feels her growing capacity to love and to care for the child, she actually experiences a general improvement in her emotional state. Many neurotic women who have suffered from severe anxiety are free from it during pregnancy; others, despite the discomforts of nausea or morning sickness, feel emotionally stable and have the "best time" during pregnancy. Thus, healthy women demonstrate during pregnancy, as during the high hormone phase of the cycle, an increased integrative capacity of the ego.

Though pregnancy is biologically normal, it is still an exceptional condition which tests the physiologic and psychologic reserves of women. There are many attitudes, realistic fears, and neurotic anxieties which disturb the woman's desire for pregnancy. Some of these may be motivated by realistic situations. Bad marriages, economic worries, or conception out of wedlock may cause the pregnancy to be unwanted and the infant to be rejected before it is born. Usually, even such pregnancies have a more or less normal course. Only if the psychosexual organization is laden with conflicts toward motherhood do actual conditions stir up the deeper conflicts and disturb the psychophysiologic balance of pregnancy.

Since the complex steps toward maturity, motherhood and motherliness begin in the mother's own oral phase of development, it is easy to describe the psychodynamic process of normal and pathologic pregnancy in terms of the oral-dependent phase. Passive-dependent needs revived, the pregnant woman thrives on the solicitude of her environment. If her needs are unfulfilled, the frustration of her oral-dependent wishes may motivate well-known symptoms such as perverse appetite, nausea, or morning sickness. These symptoms seem to diminish in frequency and intensity under cultural influence. The changing relationship between the sexes brings about a change in the conscious attitude of women toward pregnancy. The subjective symptoms of pregnancy are minimal in women who, becoming pregnant by mutual consent, can count on their husband's care and loving participation in their great experience. Mood swings, however, occur in every pregnancy, especially during the first trimester, in which the endocrinologic and metabolic adjustment may cause fatigue, sleepiness, headaches, vertigo, and even vomiting. These symptoms are usually alleviated as the pregnancy progresses. During the last months the increasing bodily discomfort, disturbances of sleep, and fears connected with parturition interfere with the contented mood of pregnancy.

Self-centered and dominated by receptive-retentive tendencies, the pregnant woman is in a vulnerable ego state. The physiologic increase in receptive-retentive needs and the libidinal regression bring about a regression of the ego. In evaluating the psychodynamic significance of this regression, one should consider that the integrative task of pregnancy and motherhood—biologically, psychologically and realistically —is much greater than the woman has ever faced before. In some cases the adaptive task appears greater with the first child, when the woman experiences something completely new. The physiologic and emotional maturation of the first pregnancy makes motherhood generally easier with the second and third child. Yet it may happen that women, fatigued by the never-ceasing labor of motherhood, experience pathogenic regression during later pregnancies.

Normally, the biologic regression of pregnancy and lactation serves as a source of growth and development. The same processes, however, harbor dangers for those who cannot withstand the regressive processes inherent in the reproductive function. External circumstances, such as a lack of love from or for the husband, may stir up the deep-seated conflicts of motherhood. In such cases any change inherent in pregnancy may become a source of irritation and may cause frustration instead of gratification. The frustrated, hostile, pregnant woman becomes anxious, since she feels her inability to satisfy her child. The hostility toward the child and the rejection of the pregnancy go hand in hand with the hostility toward the self, the rejection of the self. Anorexia, toxic vomiting, and consequent severe metabolic disturbance, such as eclampsia, may express the woman's destructive tendencies.

It is a well-established concept of psychoanalysis that regression to the oral phase of development is the psychodynamic condition of depression. Since such regression is inherent in pregnancy and lactation— even in the progesterone phase of the cycle—depressions of varying severity and psychosomatic conditions of oral structure are the basic manifestations of the psychopathology of the female propagative function. The further elaboration of this primary tendency to pathology depends on the total personality of the woman. If the hostility is concentrated on the embryo, women have fantasies of harboring a "monster," a gnawing animal, a cancerous growth. This gives rise to panic and hypochondriasis. The aggressive impulses toward the embryo may be experienced as inadequacy in taking care of the child. Phobic reactions, even suicidal impulses, may represent defenses against the hostility toward the contents of the womb.

The contents of the womb has many meanings in the unconscious emotional life of the woman. Freud assumed that the frustration caused by the lack of a penis is the central motivating factor in the development of woman; he concluded that woman's wish for the child is motivated by the tendency to retain the penis (in the sense of the oedipus complex, the penis of the father). According to this, the male child represents the fulfillment of the originally repressed wish.[18] Freud's hypothesis, inaccurate from the point of view of biology, demonstrates the motivating power of infantile fantasies in many instances. There are many common infantile fantasies which have significance in the development of the personality. During pregnancy the individually significant fantasy may become recathected and may influence the emotional course of pregnancy. (Such an influence may be beneficial or may be anxiety-producing.)

The fetus is a part of the mother's body. What aspects of the body image does the fetus represent? It may be the missing penis in some cases; in others it is the admired beauty or the envied pregnancy of the woman's own mother; most frequently the fetus is the token of the loved self. Normally, the fetus is cathected with narcissistic libido.[19] This, however, does not always mean pleasurable emotional sensations. There are many ambivalent, hostile manifestations of the feelings concentrated upon the self. Thus, the fetus can represent the "bad, aggressive, devouring self," engendering fear of having a "monster." Many women identify the fetus with feces and relive during the pregnancy the ambivalent feelings and mysteries of the infantile sexual fantasy of the anal child. There are many cases in which the anal or other regressive fantasies do not interfere with the pleasure of pregnancy. The mother's object relationship to the unborn child becomes ambivalent or strongly hostile when the fantasy which is projected onto the fetus is highly charged with ambivalence. The fetus, then, becomes the representation of a hated and/or feared person, and motherhood becomes an overwhelming menace.[20]

The anxiety and depression caused by such motivations may remain on the level of neurosis. In many instances, depending on the predisposition of the personality, the anxiety may activate a true psychosis with hallucinations, paranoid defenses, and schizophrenic reactions endangering the woman and the fetus.[21, 22]

Our investigation revealed that there is an instinctual core in the tendency to receive the male and conceive; this motivates the wish for pregnancy and the desire for motherhood. The investigation revealed also that there is inherent danger in this instinctual organization, in the physiology of the fulfillment of the instinctual wish. The fear of being a woman has its roots in the procreative physiology of woman. It is, indeed, an existential anxiety which is normally overcome by libido, by the energy to love. This energy has to be fanned and fostered from infancy on so that the girl may develop into a woman who can be a mother without that primary anxiety which is behind the psychopathology of the sexual function of women.

NOTES

1. De Allende, I. L. C., and Orias, O., *The Cytology of the Human Vagina,* translated by G. W. Corner (New York, Hoeber, 1950).

2. Benedek, T., and Rubenstein, B. B., *The Sexual Cycle in Women, Psychosomatic Medicine Monographs,* III, nos. 1 and 2 (Washington, D.C., National Research Council, 1942), 24.

3. Freud, A., *Normality and Pathology in Childhood* (New York, International Universities Press, 1965).

4. Glover, E., "The Psychoanalysis of Affects," *Int. J. Psycho-Anal.,* XX (1939), 299–307.

5. Alexander, F., "The Logic of Emotions and Its Dynamic Background," *Int. J. Psycho-Anal.,* XVI (1935), 399–413.

6. Merriam-Webster, *New International Dictionary,* Second Edition (1941).

7. Jacobson, E., "Normal and Pathological Moods," *The Psychoanalytic Study of the Child,* vol. XII (1957), p. 75.

8. Ibid., p. 76.

9. Gottschalk, L. A., Kaplan, S. M., Gleser, G. C., and Winget, C. M., "Variations in Magnitude of Emotion: A Method Applied to Anxiety and Hostility during Phases of the Menstrual Cycle," *Psychosomatic Med.,* XXIV (1962), 300–311.

10. Moos, R. H., Koppel, B. S., Melges, F. T., Jalom, I. D., Lunde, D. L., Clayton, R. B., and Hamburg, D. A., "Fluctuations in Symptoms and Moods during the Menstrual Cycle," *J. Psychosomatic Research*, XIII (1963), 37–44.

11. Erikson, E., "Inner and Outer Space; Reflections on Womanhood," *Daedulus* (1969), 588.

12. Benedek, T., "Sexual Functions in Women," in *American Handbook of Psychiatry* (New York, Basic Books, Inc., 1959), pp. 727–748.

13. Fliess, R., *Erogeneity and Libido; Addenda to the Theory of the Psychosexual Development of the Human* (New York, International Universities Press, 1957).

14. Ibid., 216.

15. Pratt, J. P., "Sex Functions in Man," in Allen, E., et al., *Sex and Internal Secretions* (Baltimore, Williams & Watkins, 1939), pp. 1263–1334.

16. Benedek, T., "Sexual Functions in Women," pp. 730–731.

17. Primary narcissism is the libidinal state resulting from a positive metabolic balance, with its attendant "surplus energy." (Alexander, F., "Psychoanalysis Revised," *Psychoanalytic Quart.*, IX [1940], 1–36.)

18. Gerard, M. W., "Genesis of Psychosomatic Symptoms in Infancy; the Influence of Infantile Traumata on Symptom Choice," in Deutsch, F., ed., *The Psychosomatic Concepts in Psychoanalysis* (New York, International Universities Press, 1953), pp. 82–95.

19. Freud, S., "On Narcissism; An Introduction" (1914), *Std. Ed.*, XIV, 67–102.

20. Deutsch, H., *The Psychology of Women: A Psychoanalytic Interpretation*, 2 vols. (New York, Grune & Stratton, 1944–1945).

21. Dunbar, H. F., *Emotions and Bodily Changes; A Survey of Literature on Psychosomatic Interrelationships*, 4th edition, (New York, Columbia, 1954), 1919–1953.

22. Benedek, T., "Sexual Functions in Women," 738–740.

7. The Emotional Structure of the Family

INTRODUCTION[1]

The paper (chapter 5 in this book), "Adaptation to Reality in Early Infancy," which discusses the influence of mothering upon the evolution of psychic structures in infants, reveals the psychologic route of my interest to the psychology of relationships. My involvement in the "objective research" on the sexual cycle of women may give the impression that it interrupted the previous absorbing interest. Actually, it fed back into it. The microscopic evaluation of psychobiologic processes sharpened my perception of the influence of current situations upon the psychodynamic aspects of interpersonal relationships in the family.

Soon after the monograph reached the publisher, war and preparation for going to war became the undertone of psychiatric consultations and psychoanalytic treatment sessions. The emotional condition prevalent at that time could be subsumed under the heading "separation anxiety." Wartime separation, with its insecurity for families and its constant danger of loss, stirred up even the best defended genetic sources of anxiety. It was omnipresent, lurking everywhere, in young men for one reason, in women of all ages for other reasons. Sometimes the anxiety appeared to be the appropriate affective reaction to actual danger; often it was exaggerated or disguised and fused with characteristic or symptomatic defenses. Everyone, civilians and soldiers alike, had to adjust to external pressures, sometimes to drastic changes. At the beginning of the war, we civilian psychiatrists observed with admiration how the soldiers coped with their tasks, how they learned from their experiences and matured through them.

One of the disconcerting effects of wartime separation was that members of the same family were exposed to extremely different circumstances. One brother might be at home feeling secure, functioning in his chosen vocation, whereas another might be in the armed forces, having to adjust to new situations and to impending danger. Even more significant for the psychology of the family was the influence of wartime separation upon married couples. In general, we could observe that members of the same family changed in differing ways and at vastly different rates. It seemed that family members were growing apart.[2]

As the war went on and we became used to the manifest and disguised reactions to separation, our concern turned to the returning soldier, to the problems of his adaptation to civilian life. This was a general problem; it affected every individual in the national community. Its urgency was recognized by the government and there was cooperation at all levels. More hidden was the problem of the adjustment of families whose own soldier returned, but not as exactly the same person.

The result of my preoccupation with these problems was my "war book," *Insight and Personality Adjustment; A Study of the Psychological Effects of War.*[3] Written when the end of the war was not yet foreseen, it was finished when, in the glow of victory, we were stunned by the abruptness with which a new epoch broke upon mankind and threw the shadow of an uneasy peace over all of us. This book presented an investigation of familial relationships which came to light through the families' reactions to wartime separations.

The term "family dynamics" had not yet been coined, but it was recognized by R. Nanda Anschen when she asked me to write a chapter for the book, *The Family: Its Function and Its Destiny.* This chapter, "The Emotional Structure of the Family," presents in condensed form what I learned about the family through wartime separation.

The first chapter in my book, *Insight and Personality Adjustment,* has the heading "The Development to Love." It is a discursive presentation of the psychoanalytic theory of personality development from infancy to maturity and parenthood. This chapter, "The Emotional Structure of the Family," contains the essence of that book. The book and also this chapter were written for a large, nonpsychoanalytically trained public. This, however, was not the main reason for my exclusive emphasis on libido, the integrating psychic energy. It will be noted that I did not mention its antagonist, aggression, the energy that causes ambivalence and complications in the development to love. At that time sociologists and journalists were speculating about the consequences of our changing mores; many felt that the family was threatened by deterioration. This made me feel it was important to concentrate on libido and to emphasize the psychobiologic factors that serve the cohesiveness of the family. The family, as the innumerable anthropologic variations of this timeworn institution show, is adaptable; it can be shaken to its foundations but it cannot be destroyed, since it is in nature's order.

Ten years later when Dr. Anschen asked me if I wished to make revisions for the second edition of *The Family: Its Function and Its Destiny,* she complimented me by saying, "Your chapter was written not for today or yesterday but for time everlasting." For that edition I inserted a few paragraphs on the cultural processes that affect adolescence and the relationship between the sexes. Another decade has passed since then. When I reread these previous publications, I still feel a proprietary pleasure in having written them, but it is mixed with a deep discomfort. With the rumbling of war again in the background, my discussion of love, marriage, and adolescence appears romantic, outdated by the neoromanticism of the present-day adolescents who feel that the future will be different.

It is the task of serious investigators to sort out what is "everlasting" in the family, and why, for only with this understanding can we hope to influence the process of change in the direction of development and positive good.

NOTES

1. First published in *The Family: Its Function and Its Destiny,* Ruth Nanda Anschen, ed. (New York, Harper Brothers, 1949; rev. ed., 1959), pp. 202–225.
2. "Growing apart" does not designate the same psychologic process as we understand today by the term "alienation."
3. Benedek, T., *Insight and Personality Adjustment; A Study of the Psychological Effects of War* (New York, Ronald Press Co., 1946; out of print after second printing).

THE EMOTIONAL STRUCTURE OF
THE FAMILY*

In a period of human history when a growing individualism appears to threaten the family, to shake its well-established hierarchy, and to weaken its functional effectiveness, it appears promising to look upon the family as an organism and to investigate its physiology. For the biological fact of the long-lasting dependence of the human child is the root from which grew, in complex interaction between society and the individual, the family as an institution of many tasks.

For a long time—in fact, until the last decade of the nineteenth century—science did not dare to scrutinize the ways and means by which the family functions. Sanctioned by religion and tradition, the family, the carrier and transmitter of the culture, could not but be idealized,

* Reprinted from *The Family, Its Function and Destiny.* Copyright 1949 by Harper & Bros. and reprinted with the permission of the publishers.

each of its members fulfilling a role entrusted to him by the ideology of the cultural patterns. Since love is the categorical imperative of our culture, love was taken to be the emotion which regulates the interpersonal relations within the family.

The emotional structure of the idealized patriarchal family appeared to be set and static: its main representant, the father-husband, was assumed to be strong and active, providing for his wife and children not only the means of livelihood but also love and protection as the means for emotional security; the mother-wife, connected with her husband in a lasting marriage, was assumed to accept this as the prerequisite for her happiness, which in turn enabled her to love her children with tender, unwavering motherliness. Since there are basic biological needs which regulate the relationship between the sexes as well as woman's natural tendency toward motherhood and motherliness, it was easy to maintain that all children were wanted, loved, and cared for and that the children, raised in a spirit of respect toward an authoritative father (who might delegate his authority to the mother), accepted the authority in devotion and gratefulness until they grew up to be parents themselves and acted in their turn the same way toward their children.

Yet the Greek tragedies, conceived at the dawn of individualism and hewn out of the everlasting material of human emotion, demonstrated to an audience which already knew of the pang of conscience that love is not absolute, that even the parent's love of the child and the child's love for the parent are endangered by wishes and desires of other intentions, by conflicting tendencies. From the time of the Greek tragedies until our modern scientific era it remained for the artists—for Shakespeare, Dostoievsky, and others—to grasp intuitively and express indelibly the emotional struggle of the individual for individuality.

It was an intellectual revolution when Freud and his followers began to study methodically the boiling cauldron of emotions underneath the static-appearing, smooth ideological surface of the patriarchal Victorian family. These investigations led to our present understanding of the psychodynamic processes which motivate the emotional maturation of the individual and also the interpersonal relationships as they unfold in our culture, not only within the family but also from generation to generation. For Freud disclosed the process through which the individual becomes the carrier of our cultural inheritance and relives "the traces which the biological and historical fate of mankind left behind in the Id."[1]

It is regrettable that space permits us here only a most concise presentation of the evolution of the emotional patterns from early in-

1. Sigmund Freud: "Das Ich und das Es," in *Gesammelte Schriften,* Volume VI (Vienna: Internationales Psychoanalytischer Verlag, 1923), pp. 351–405.

fancy until they become established in the course of the individual development as an inner psychic organization which Freud called the *superego,* the function of which we experience as conscience.

In the beginning there is only the instinct of self-preservation. The total energy of the newborn child is in its service; hunger is the sensation which expresses the need for the material out of which his body is built, and the infant's crying represents the mobilized self-assertion to achieve satisfaction of his need. He will cry until gratification arrives or until he has exhausted his motoric energy. If his hunger is satisfied in such a way that the infant does not have to use up all his energies, there is a positive balance in his energy household; he has a surplus for physical and mental growth. Out of this surplus the infant gains the first pleasurable sensations of his own body as well as the first positive orientation toward the external world: a confident relationship to the mother, who is soon recognized as a source of gratification. It depends primarily on the mother—on her emotional satisfaction in being a mother and her readiness to nurse, to take care of the baby, and to supply him not only with his physical needs but also with the pleasurable sensation of love—whether satisfaction and security or frustration and fear will dominate the emotional life of the child. The mother's attitude also will determine whether the infant, sheltered by the security of his confidence in the mother, will learn from her easily or whether every step will be acquired with mobilization of fear and hostility.

Although the infant very early becomes aware that in his orbit there are other individuals besides the mother (he recognizes his father and also his siblings and responds to them), generally speaking we may state that the mother is the first teacher of the child. Through her he learns to respond to other persons; with her help he learns to talk, to walk, and to master his sphincters. Thus the mother is the one who at first impresses upon the child the cultural pattern; for infant training reflects, in the mother's behavior, the hygienic and ideological requirements of a civilization. Thus in our times mothers begin to train the ego of the child early. Almost from the beginning the infant has to learn to be "independent," to be self-assertive, and even to "make up his mind." These individualistic requirements mobilize, especially if the infant has not enough resource in love and security, much fear and overcompensative self-assertion: hostility. It does not take long for the child to begin to know what are the actions for which the mother will like him and those which will increase the expressions of her love—thus enhancing his security—and he also will soon realize what are the actions which bring about punishment, that is, a reduction of love and thus a reduction of his basic security. This mobilizes the child's fear, which in itself may again increase his need for self-assertion. Every nursery in our society produces frank and often brutal examples of this vicious circle between the two aspects of self-preservation: the need for love, and the need for self-assertion.

In the great variety of solutions which the infant learns to find in order to reconcile the struggle for security, one may early observe definite differences in the behavior of the sexes. Although an undisturbed confidence in the mother is important for the normal development of infants of both sexes, the emotional security which results from it affects boys and girls differently. It gives the boy permission for self-assertion and a sense of courage. Thus he may free himself from his dependence on the mother in order to start a development in which identification with the father becomes the leading motive. The girl's development takes a different course. A sense of security gives her the first and most effective impulse for identification with the mother. Thus through manifold identifications with the parent of the same sex the child reaches the *oedipal phase* of his development. He is then about three to five years old. This is the age when the child's identification with the parent of the same sex has evolved strongly enough to motivate his erotically colored demands toward the parent of the other sex.

This, however, creates the crucial conflict. The boy, whose erotic desire toward his mother has made him a competitor of his father, feels threatened by his father's revenge: castration. His fear impels the repression of his sexual desire toward his mother. In the girl the conflict has the opposite direction. The girl, who becomes a competitor of her mother, feels threatened by the realization of her feminine wishes and represses them in order not to be threatened by the loss of her mother's love. In both sexes the fear of punishment forces the child to repress the oedipal tendency and to introject the prohibition of the parent. From this time on the child will know, by the strength of the internalized fear of the parent, what is right and what is wrong: he has a conscience. Thus, as a result of love and fear and competitive self-assertion, is raised the inner-psychic institution which is the cornerstone of the emotional structure of the individual and of the family in our culture.[2] For, whatever were the original causes of sexual prohibition at the origins of our social structures, they are relived within every normal family of our civilization. This is—or until recent decades used to be— characterized by the inhibition and negation of sexuality.

It cannot be the task of the present chapter to describe the psychological processes of growing up from the oedipal age level through the period of sexual latency, during which the psychodynamic tendencies which constituted the oedipus complex become absorbed in the total personality. Nor can we afford to discuss the process of maturation during the period of adolescence, when, with the developing hormonal

2. Sigmund Freud, *The Ego and the Id* (London: Hogarth Press, 1927).

function, heterosexuality becomes an emotional reality and physiological necessity.

In primitive societies where puberty rites are celebrated, society takes charge of, and responsibility for, the individual's sexual activity. The adolescents in such societies do not need to overcome so many internal obstacles as exist in our society, where the individual himself is responsible and has to deal with his emerging sexual urge more or less by himself.

At puberty the unfolding sexuality is confronted with restrictions and prohibitions, as well as with permissions and gratifications, incorporated in the emotional structure of the personality since childhood. Hence the confusion and insecurity, the longing and suspense, the shyness and the rebellion, all so characteristic of adolescence. In these attitudes the struggle which once was fought between the parents and the child becomes manifest again. The repression had to succeed; now the emotional struggle of the adolescent has the task of diminishing the power of the original sexual prohibition. Yet this does not mean alone a permission for physiological satisfaction of the sexual need. The struggle is for a higher goal, for the capacity to form a lasting relationship with an individual of the other sex.

There is good reason to discuss here the psychodynamics of love, for our culture tends to make it the sole basis of marriage.

Heterosexual love is an attraction between a man and a woman who have reached a specific level of their individual maturation, for the completion of which they need each other. To elaborate this definition we have to go back to the adolescent. Well known is the melancholia, the introverted depressive mood, of the adolescent. This mood expresses the conflict between his ego ideal and the realization of the awakening sexual need, which is regarded as "sin," unacceptable to the ego ideal. Love is an emotion which resolves this conflict. Through it sexuality becomes acceptable and the ego, liberated from a state of suspense, feels elated. This does not necessarily occur only in adolescence or with the first love. Everybody who feels the loneliness of unsatisfied sexual tension experiences the same sort of abject mood which keeps the person preoccupied with the desire for love and compels him to seek a mate and companion. If the individual has the emotional maturity which our culture conveyed to him and requires him to carry on, he has to find the solution with the help and in the framework of his conscience. This accounts for much delay and suspense. For both man and woman that wating period means an experiencing of doubts which in itself elevates the emotion of love and raises the beloved person to the level of an ideal.

Love means the surrendering of what one calls one's personality, and it makes the beloved person the measure of all measures. *Romantic love,*[3] that is, the acute phase of love, is self-effacing. Being loved by one's ego ideal means that one surrenders one's own personality—even if temporarily—to another individual. In our society, where men and women are not only mates but also individuals, this appears to be a great risk. Afraid of being hurt by love, many women guard themselves against men who could become their masters in love; in the same way, men may avoid women whom they fear because they may become emotionally dependent upon them. If such intense, acute love is allowed to develop, however, the man or the woman becomes dependent for emotional gratification upon one person exclusively. The aim of sexual passion is to transcend the boundaries of the individuality through unification with the beloved. The need for this is gratified by the sexual act, but it encompasses more than the need for physiological satisfaction—it achieves gratification within the total personality of each of the lovers. Fearful as either of them might have been before the union, after love is satisfied the ego feels relieved of its insecurity. Each partner feels: I became like you because you, whom I admired, loved me. Each becomes a better and worthier person. Each comes closer to his ego ideal through love. No wonder that an emotional experience of such force appears to be transcendental. It projects itself into the future with optimism; it promises to endure in marriage.

So long as society concentrated its ethics and customs on securing stability for the marriage, there was little need to investigate the dynamics of love itself. Even psychoanalysis studied love rather as a force than as an experience. It investigated its function in the development of the personality; it assumed tacitly that, if an individual achieved the capacity to love, the marriage would last and satisfy the individual's needs. If complications arose—if, for example, psychoneurotic disturbances developed—one investigated the individual and found the causes of the maladjustment.

But love, like any force, is not static; nor can interpersonal relationships, even if regulated by the purest of love, be static.

Up to this point we have discussed the effect of love as an emotional expectation of and a sexual satisfaction for the ego, and we have found that satisfaction in love enhances the ego. Strengthened by the satisfaction of being loved, the individual becomes more independent of the demands of the love partner. For a period, the length of which is determined by the personality of each of the lovers, the pair may say like Juliet, "The more I give the more I have—for both are infinite." Yet after a while one or the other, or both, may begin to feel envious of the other who receives so much. The envy, hostility, and rebellion against surrender to another person becomes manifest repeatedly in

3. Theodore Reik, *A Psychologist Looks at Love* (New York: Farrar and Rinehart, Inc., 1944).

quarrels between the partners. Nevertheless, if the hostility is not so great that it interrupts the relationship it becomes an important factor in its further development. The guilt resulting from the quarrel creates anew a mood of contrite dependence which can be undone only by passionate love. If the identification between the lovers progresses as it does in marriage (where common interests associated with their social and economic position also further the identification), the original intensity of the suspense, the original passion, will not be achieved again. This does not indicate a devaluation of the sexual partner; rather it expresses the emotional reality, the balance of the dynamic interrelation between husband and wife. The originally deprived ego of the lover dependent for gratification, having received reassurance from being loved, does not again feel insecure. The fulfillment of love has changed the basis of the relationship. It has grown from an exchange of ego ideals to the relationship of individuals who share the same reality; the oneness may be expressed in common ambitions and desires. Yet, if the suspense which initiated passion cannot be continued, the mutual sexual excitability decreases. Lovers know this instinctively and therefore often consciously seek to arouse a limited degree of hostile tension—such a degree as does not interfere with the process of enriching the identification but renders new stimulus to it.

Through the desexualization of the projected ego ideal (the lover) the love relationship reaches its next phase. To arrive at it usually requires the complex intimacy of marriage. The wife who becomes a mother and the husband who becomes a father slowly undergo a metamorphosis in their relationship to each other; as though both of them were identifying themselves with the child whom they love, they begin to represent for each other the parent as well. Husband and wife often address each other as their children address them—call each other "father" and "mother" or "mommy" and "daddy"—or in the more modern type of marriage they let the children call them by their first name (as if in that way they could avoid becoming the parents).

But all this is more than imitation. It expresses a psychological reality, namely, that the marital partners (as if they were parents for each other) become, as once the parents did, a critical forum, a measure for each other's personality. And, as the individual's development has proved, it is easier to live with a conscience which developed on the basis of gratitude, love, and respect than with one which developed out of fear and punishment. So the love of the husband and wife, though partially desexualized, is not lost in the process of the change. Even if this development only rarely is smooth and the husband or the wife may resent it or rebel against it from time to time, yet, if they stay together as they were forced to do before the era of divorces, they eventually accept this new phase of their common development. The identification between husband and wife, whether it is expressed in cultural or economic aspirations, in their children, or in the thousand details of everyday living, will hold the marriage together even after erotic passion recedes. For this is the emotional dialectic of marriage; each of the partners, stimulated by the other, undergoes a process of maturation which leads to a further integration of his personality. Thus, even if the acuteness of passion recedes, there remains enough of its glow to enrich the relationship with mutual respect, tenderness, and gratitude. Indeed, they who achieve such maturation within their marriage have much for which to be grateful. They represent the rare examples of happy marriage.

In order to discuss the emotional structure of the family we have delineated the individual's development from infancy through adolescence and through the process of maturation—the adaptation of personalities—in the symbiosis of marriage. This is an abstraction of dynamic interaction between personalities; yet one may question its validity, or rather its relationship to erotic, romantic love. There is no doubt that marriage—this ambivalent, struggling, passionate, and confident interpersonal relationship—requires from the marital partners that they give up to one another, and to their children, some of the aspirations of their individualistic personalities in order to achieve a common goal, a combined individuation: *the family*. This process, however, appears to have succeeded better in societies where marriages function by tradition, with neglect of the individual's preference for the marital partner, than in our society where, on the basis of the ethical principles of individualism, we expect that "free will" and "free choice" will not only support the marriage but enhance its happiness as well. One may also object that such psychobiological interaction between marital partners as has been described assumes such an equality between man and woman as may exist in the passion of love though never afforded to husband and wife by society. And now, when that equality becomes the prerogative of some classes, it often does not lead to a demonstration of lasting identification between husband and wife.

Yet marriage between equal partners is the ideal of a democratic, individualistic society. It represents the goal of a development which began in the nineteenth century and progressed by leaps and bounds during the socio-economic changes of two world wars. Thus our cultural aspiration is that marriage shall function by and for the sake of love, that is, not only and not primarily for reproduction but also for the pursuit of happiness, for the heightened individual maturation of each of the partners. To help each other in this process is the mutual obligation. Yet marriages burdened with such individualistic expectations often do not endure. Interaction between two individuals involves a compromise and a sacrifice for which many of the younger generation are not ready.

It is certainly impossible to account for all the factors which may interfere with the harmonious adaptation of the marital partners. Although love is praised so highly, many marriages even in present times are motivated rather by external and internal circumstances other than love. Women as well as men may easily mistake for love their willingness to marry a person who is able to satisfy their social ambitions. Very often not the obvious factors of convenience are responsible for such marriages but rather certain deeply rooted emotional factors, such as a fear of love, an unwillingness to wait, a hope that marriage will diminish emotional insecurity.

And, after the marriage has fulfilled this task, the woman—more often than the man—may realize with distress that she has abandoned the opportunity for a great love. We can often observe in the panic of a young woman the valiant struggle against falling in love when it is no longer permitted. For women, much more often than men, still struggle against polygamous tendencies.

Whatever the psychological foundations of a marriage may have been, there are too many stimuli in our highly differentiated life which may cause conflicts by provoking different responses in the marital partners. The fulfillment of love—as has been pointed out—leaves the partners free and confident to pursue enhanced ego aspirations. In fortunate cases this will be mainly the result of a mutual interchange; in other cases it takes separate directions. The marital partners may go too far, and too much alone, leaving the other one behind. Or it may be that hostility or unforgiving competitive ambition destroys the basis of identification between the partners. To repeat: There are almost as many variations and discrepancies between the characters of husband and wife as there are marriages. Some of these cause little discontent, others indicate incompatibilities which may appear irreparable, especially if divorce is accepted as an easy way out.

What is often referred to as adjustment in the marriage is a part of the process of adaptation which occurs unconsciously through the passage of love. Another part of the adjustment is achieved by conscious attempts to reach a solution by compromise.

The traditional marriage of the patriarchal family emphasized the realistic aims of the marriage. It gave this adjustment a one-sided direction. By blocking divorce, it forced compromises until adjustment —sometimes dearly paid for with individual unhappiness and neurotic disturbances—finally was achieved. The domineering role of the patriarchal husband and the apparently dependent role of his wife expressed the emotional structure of the core of the traditional family. In the modern marriage the balance between husband and wife has shifted. Each of the marital partners represents the double aspiration of our transitional culture. The role of the husband is not free from the responsibilities and illusions of the patriarchal husband-father. Although he is expected to perform his functions to satisfy that ideology, he also is expected to recognize the equality and in some respects also the independence of his wife. The wife, though she cannot free herself from her psychosexual desire for a strong man as a husband, in other areas of her personality requires from him as well as from herself the acceptance and obligation of her drive for independence. Thus the modern marriage —in each of its partners—manifests the conflict between the passing patriarchal and the present individualistic society. This conflict lies deeper than the purely sociological plane; it is rooted in the psychosexual (emotional) needs of both of the sexes. No wonder that adjustment is often difficult. We speak about "working out the marriage," so aware are we of the problems involved and of the amount of good will necessary to solve them.

The axis of the emotional structure of the modern family is this conflict-laden interpersonal relationship between husband and wife. To them is entrusted the biological and sociological task of producing and raising the next generation. And we may emphasize the word "entrust," because it now has more meaning than it ever had, since parenthood itself has become a matter of individual decision.

Birth control, used extensively as it becomes a custom in our civilization, is like a large-scale experiment; its effects can now be evaluated. No doubt it can be recognized as one of the most effective factors in the emancipation of women and also in the economic regulation of family life. Here, however, we wish to emphasize that contraception has exposed the psychobiological factors which motivate parenthood to scientific observation.

Since paternity depends on one act, and since its biological function is achieved with the sexual intercourse which leads to impregnation, we have rarely stopped to analyze the psychodynamic factors involved in fatherhood. Our age of planned parenthood, however, affords many opportunities for observing and analyzing the awakening of a man's propagative instinct, his compelling desire to become a father and to survive in his child. Women, overburdened by childbearing and the ensuing responsibilities, have often complained; pregnancy and motherhood have appeared to them as a function without pleasure, forced upon women by nature and used by men as means for enslaving women. Yet careful investigation of the sexual cycle in women has revealed the psychobiological tendencies which in monthly periodicity express the genuine quality of female sexuality, namely, the tendency toward bearing children.

It would be alluring to describe the interplay between the male and female psychobiological tendencies, since we have to emphasize that, when having children is a matter of choice, knowledge of the motivations for parenthood has a more than theoretical significance. For not only do these compel husband and wife to have children as a natural course of events, but they also enter into the many emotional conflicts which arise when husband and wife avoid and delay having children. Yet the psychobiological tendencies of both remain unconscious. Closer to the conscious awareness of the parent are the psychic elaborations of these tendencies: the wishes and desires, the images, illusions, and expectations which each one projects—the father his and the mother hers—onto the child.

Earlier, in discussing the passage of love—the process of identification between husband and wife—we only cursorily mentioned parenthood, through which the identification is achieved biologically. Now we may say more about the exchange of ego ideals between the lovermates. Before the period of contraception the possibility of impregnation was inherent in every sexual act. People rarely took time to indulge in fantasy about their offspring before pregnancy occurred, or even after that. They took the facts of life more as facts—inevitable—than it is necessary to take them nowadays. Now in marriages we often observe the contented and pleasurable period when husband and wife decide that to give each other the most and to manifest their oneness they should have a child. Frequently today we hear the phrase, used either by a wife or by a husband, "When we were pregnant"—so conscious have they become of their identification in the process of reproduction. The husband in our present day seems to participate in the placid, self-centered contentment of the wife, the characteristic mood of pregnancy; he tries to share her expectations and expresses much consideration toward her physical inconvenience. These attitudes of the husband enhance the gratification of pregnancy and diminish its discomforts. Thus we observe that symptoms like "morning sickness" have decreased in frequency.

The exchange of fantasies about the child between husband and wife, the desire to satisfy each other's emotional needs in and through the child, has further significance for the child; it determines to a high degree the parents' relationship to him and often carries in itself the core of the conflict which the parents may develop with the child. There are many aspects of their expectations, all of them determined by the personality development of each of the parents. One of them, the sex of the expected child, so often stands in the foreground and there is so much wish and fear connected with it that we may take it as an example of the numerous problems which may arise.

There are many motivations for the almost universal preference for a male child. Among these, society's higher evaluation of the male sex, although it is always kept in the foreground, appears actually to be only secondary and a result of the biological motivation of parenthood in the male. This primarily is intended for the continuation of the self and can therefore be satisfied directly only by a child of the father's sex. It is of no avail even to try to deny the father's overflowing gratification if his newborn child is a son, or to attempt to minimize the emotional adjustment which is necessary if it is a daughter. Thus the woman's desire to give birth to a son may be motivated by her desire to produce what society wants most and so probably to fulfill her unconscious desire for masculinity. But it is also in keeping with her love for her husband to wish to reproduce him, or to produce what he values the most.

These motivations, however, do not cause the desire for a son to be an exclusive one. For, however intense the desire for a son may be, there is dormant in every woman a tendency to wish to continue the self, to reproduce herself in her daughter. Identification with her daughter, the projection of her own aspirations to her, appears to a womanly mother normal and without conflict. The wish to have a son, however, may become dominant in a woman if her own masculine aspirations are pathologically intensive, or—generally speaking—if the developmental conflict with her own mother remains unresolved. Then she remains apprehensive that the struggle which she once had with her own mother will repeat itself in her daughter's relationship to her. If a woman's developmental conflicts with her mother, or with motherhood altogether, are resolved, she will be ready and able to accept her child with love, regardless of its sex. Yet the woman's wish to have a daughter may also become exclusive and neurotically motivated. In some women a repressed hostility toward the male sex may cause a dread of the outbreak of her conflicts had she a son, and she therefore maintains an uncompromising desire for a daughter.

Although a sex preference for the expected child is in normal cases a sort of fantasy-play between the parents and is easily adjusted to reality after the child is born, in neurotic cases an apprehension about the sex of the infant may expose severe disturbances in the parent. In a neurotic woman a fear of her inability to love the child engenders feelings of guilt even during pregnancy. It may cause anxiety and depression or either of these. It may also threaten the woman with a total bankruptcy of her personality when she realizes her lack of love and motherliness toward her child. The father has an easier task in disguising his ambivalent attitude toward the expected or newborn child. He does not necessarily feel threatened and guilty when he is unable to develop the positive participation described above. Nature as well as society permits him to develop his fatherliness slowly in direct relationship to the growing child.

It is not our intention here to describe the evolution of motherliness and fatherliness. We merely wish to point out that these complex attitudes, rooted in the personality development of each of the parents, are nurtured by the dynamism of their interpersonal relationship and that when they unfold toward the child they create an intrinsic psychodynamic unit to which we refer as *the triangle*—father-mother-child. In this triangle the child, much before he can be aware of or responsible for it, even before he is born, plays a dynamic part:

> *Weil, wo wir zwei sind, du wir beide bist,*
> "Because, where we are two, you are both of us."[4]

For, in the child, the mother and also the father unconsciously relive a specific part of their individual personalities as well as their relationship to each other. Fortunate is the child whose emotional security may grow undisturbed, nurtured by the reservoir of love on the part of his parents for each other and toward him.

The first such triangle in the family, the relationship between the parents and the first child, exists undisturbed—based only on the interplay of this intrinsic relationship of the three—as long as the child is an only child. The balance is disturbed and changed by each following child or, for that matter by any other emotional experience of either parent which is strong enough to break through the exclusiveness of this primary unit. Such a relationship—the triangle—develops between the parents and each of their children separately and with varying emotional content. Since each of the parents will project different expectations onto the child, each may experience different variations of his own personality problems with each new child. It is not rare that the second and third child have more fortunate constellations than has the first one, since the parents have matured through the previous experience. In some families each of the later children is expected to complete what previously has remained unfulfilled in the parent. In other families, the child born later may find emotionally closed doors; the parents' life already having been fulfilled, there remains but little emotional need for the latecomer to satisfy. Thus it happens that the psychological environment of the first child is different from that of the second, or from that of each of the following children. Though each forms a distinct triangle in itself, each triangle unit is dynamically influenced by the other units within the family. The steady interaction between these various psychodynamic contingencies determines the personality development of each of the siblings.

The family certainly is a closely knit organism thriving on a delicate balance of its emotional currents. However complex a description of these forces and their effects on the Gestalt of the family may sound, the configuration of its several triangles is so deeply ingrained in all of us that it needs but little training to invoke in everyone very definite associations in relation to any mention of an individual's place within any family. Every case history begins by revealing that the patient is the Nth

4. Anton Wildgans, *Im Anschaun Meines Kindes* (1913).

among X children, for only few details are then necessary to tell a great deal about the emotional constellation of the person within his family.

Yet the psychodynamic trends which hold the balance of the emotional system of the family are unconscious or normally become so. This is a keenly sensitive balance which must continually be reestablished in adjustment to everyday events. There are always happenings, both pleasant and unpleasant; there are always tensions and reliefs, worries and joys, which either may come and go or may leave lasting traces and indelible memories. The balance of the family changes decisively when one or several of its members separate from it. Children grow up and leave the family for school, for work, for marriage. The continuity of the relationships is disrupted if one of the family dies. Either event requires new adjustments on the part of those who remain. Almost similarly traumatic is the separation necessitated by military service during wartime, since this contains the threats of dangers inherent in war. Such a separation disturbs the existing balance, mobilizes the psychological trends, and exposes the original conflicts which have already receded into the background through the usual adjustments of living. Thus wartime separations have afforded a good opportunity for studying the emotional dynamics of family life.[5]

We have already described the family as an organism and have pointed out that the physiology of that organism changes with the changing trends of our civilization. The main issues in this are: (1) the emancipation of women, which alters the relationship between husband and wife; and (2) birth control, which makes parenthood an individual responsibility. Indeed, we may conclude that a family so balanced with equal privileges and responsibilities for the two parents appears to be best ordained to transmit to the children the requirements of a higher individuation, which is at least one of the goals, if not the main one, in our culture.

Thus we might end our discussion here, were it not that too many observations of our present family life call to our attention the fact that what we have defined here is an *ideal* and that the reality is far from it; that the modifications and shifts in our present-day family often appear rather as pathology than as the course of normal development. It is certain that the task of the family is much more complex if it is to fulfill the developmental goal of an individualistic modern society than it was in the patriarchal family, since the latter aimed to transmit through simpler, well-established patterns a more homogeneous and almost repetitious developmental goal.

To restate the function of the family at present: it must afford the conditions which enable each of its members to pursue and attain the

5. Therese Benedek, M.D., *Insight and Personality Adjustment* (New York: Ronald Press, 1946).

best integration of his individuality and at the same time in his own marriage to gain and retain his capacity to adjust himself to the requirements of family life. For the family has a double function: it is conservative and conserving, since it secures the attainments of the past; it is progressive and progressing, since it transmits the new cultural gains. The clash between these two directions can best be studied in the conflicts of the individual within his family.

In the beginning of this presentation we set forth that the establishment of the superego in the course of the individual development furnishes the intrapsychic instrument by which the family achieves its cultural function. Later, in describing this as a crucial factor in the psychic growth of the child, our discussion was based on the emotional balance of the traditional family. We presented an abstract description of psychodynamic processes in which we did not consider actual relationships between the child and the parent. Now we shall be more realistic and consider this process as determined not only by the natural evolution of the child's growth but also by the parents' *actual behavior*. For it does not help us in understanding the problems of the individual today if we continue to generalize and to believe that what a child experiences and builds up in himself as an image of his parents is, as postulated above: a mother, the main and only source of pleasurable gratification; a father, strong, infallible, and a threatening representant of the moral code. In the minds of children today the lines of their imagery of their parents are not so sharply defined, and this for good reason.

The equality between husband and wife, together with their equal responsibility for and their similar enjoyment in their children, colors the parents' behavior toward the newborn child. The young American husband who helps his wife in the many chores of child care—who gets up in the night to walk the baby, who establishes the routine of giving the "early" or the "night bottle" himself, and so on—unknowingly begins the process by which it will become difficult if not impossible for him later to perform the patriarchal role of the father. He becomes in the child's mind a part of the mother image. In the same way, the mother who relinquishes the privilege and the liability of being the only person who cares for the infant unwittingly interrupts the symbiosis between herself and her child, and this may have many implications for her own emotional life as well as for that of her child.

In another context we have referred to the emotional insecurities mothers may have toward their children. Often, since they have had the privilege of wanting children, mothers have needed to reassure themselves that they really *did want them enough*. That such a sense of insecurity may arise even if the child was very much desired may easily be understood. A wanted, well-cared-for, healthy pregnancy is a deep gratification in a woman's life, for to its calm, self-centered mood is added the permission of self-indulgence and even more the indulgence of the husband and others. After the child is born a great part of these dependent gratifications are interrupted. Since the confining task of child care appears too difficult for many young women, they employ their husbands' and also others' help and in so doing become more and more insecure and feel increasingly guilty toward the child. They never know whether they have done enough for him. This insecurity may become extremely painful if the infant shows the slightest difficulty in his development. Every disturbance, every sickness of the child, represents both an increased demand and a reproach and also mobilizes the fear of self-reproach. Thus the woman becomes more and more dependent on her husband, her mother, her sister, or even her mother-in-law, not only for help but also for reassurance. If in addition she has to become dependent for help on a person whose love for herself she cannot trust, the fear of being criticized increases her emotional tension. Afraid of her conflicts, many a young mother soon seeks diversion in activities outside of the home. Social and professional ambitions or the necessity and possibility of increasing the family earnings may lure the woman from her tasks of child care. Since work is an easily justifiable escape, mothers may relieve their guilt toward the child through it. And work often is the advisable therapy, since it is better to make the mother able to love her child on a part-time basis than to have her become depressed and altogether unable to love. Thus it often occurs that young mothers become active in various spheres of life and grow in several capacities of their ego; but their psychosexual maturation, the growth of motherliness, remains suspended and full of conflicts. Often they are anxious to have a second or third child in order to repeat the pleasurable experience of pregnancy and, just as much, "to do better" with the new child. For she, the so-called modern mother, is also desirous of experiencing motherhood in its simple, sensuous gratifications through which she can vicariously enjoy with the child the satisfactions which she affords to him. She wants, too, to experience motherhood as a continuation of her self, of her personality, and to relive what was her past, her hopes, and her expectations in the future of her child.

What is it in our society which, instead of securing the emotional process of motherhood—and fatherhood as well, for that matter—complicates and threatens it? One factor, and we believe it is the main one, lies in the dynamics of human emotions. Choosing parenthood, for whatever conscious and unconscious purposes, endows the parents with a responsibility toward the child which they feel with a deep sense of bondage. Much as this responsibility may be enjoyed, it is also feared, since our superego, our conscience, understands how to make the most of it—how to use, and even in some respects how to abuse, this sense of responsibility. So far as infants and small children are concerned, the mothers are primarily responsible.

In a society in which hygiene is a demigod, and knowledge—psychological, educational, and the like—counts almost as much, mothers are anxious to raise their children perfectly. Perfection, although it is not an intellectual goal in motherliness, is measured by intellectual means. When there is no security and stability in one's self—and what young woman can achieve it early and without struggle when the requirements are so high?—a steady intellectualization undermines motherliness. It causes the mother to measure and to compare herself and her child, to envy others and depreciate her own, or to become proud and more than necessarily indulgent. Such and innumerable other attitudes of the parents convey to the child their emotional insecurity. This may enhance the child's feelings of self-importance too early; being the center of the family is a gratification but also a danger for the child. Playing with the parents, which should yield merely a pleasurable stimulation, may make excessive demands on the child if applied too soon or too strictly, and the child may become confused and afraid unless he can comply easily. Overstimulation, a steady play and display for love and attention, is one reaction of the child, and this is culturally more acceptable than some of his other reactions. For great is the frustration of the parents if an infant with a need for greater emotional stability begins early to rebel against the demands of an environment which he, for some reason or other, cannot fulfill. This may lead to various complications in child care—such as eating difficulties, relapses and involvements in toilet training, stubbornness, sullenness, and over-assertiveness—which may all try the mother's skill and patience.

Whatever these manifestations may be, the little and the big worries in the care of small children are looked upon by the mother as the manifestations of her own weakness, as a failure of her own personality. However contrite she may be, she cannot help but convey to the child a sense of her disappointment in him. In fortunate cases—if the evolution of other identifications and the course of intellectual growth are favorable—the child may respond positively even to the conflict-pervaded stimulation; every good turn may then relieve the tension. In less favorable situations, the disappointed mother often mobilizes in the father reactions similar to her own, though fathers usually are more apt to "wait and see" before they accept disappointments in the child. The mother—probably with justification—assumes that this more positive attitude of the father is caused by the fact that he is less actively occupied and preoccupied with the child and that he "does not know" or "does not care." Thus there may develop a period during which, on account of the child—and, they usually believe, for his sake—the emotional tension between the parents grows disagreeable and unfavorable for the child. This increases the insecurity of the child not only toward one but toward both parents. Thus the psychodynamic triangle functions as a vicious neurotic circle, resulting in a more or less severe developmental disturbance. One often speaks about the "child being rejected" if, in the course of such emotional events, either parent, or both, becomes so conflictfully involved that the hostile tension finally outweighs the love, the hope, and the willingness to give, even if the parents started out with all of these.

Naturally this ultimate, unfortunate outcome is avoided except in pathological situations. We have to admit, however, that some ambivalence enters into all parent-child relationships—and this not only in our modern families, for it plays a role in traditional families as well. Then, too, all parents—traditional as well as modern—live in the illusion that their child will grow by and through the best that they can do for him and will by this means fulfill their own ideals, that which is the best in them. Parents who have children who are responsive and responding, easy to love, and rewarding to give to, may praise themselves as fortunate. But there are also less fortunate parents, whose children, to the painful surprise of the parents, display what they did not know or recognize in themselves—children who took over from their parents what was repressed deep in their unconscious or expressed only in the complex ways of their more or less neurotic personalities. This is what the young parents fear; they feel exposed in the child and by the child. If the child exposes their faults instead of their virtues, the parents, in the process of defending themselves against what they feel to be obvious accusations, become desperate, hateful, or even delinquent. For there are children who bring out the worst in the parents. Thus again we may quote the Austrian poet, Anton Wildgans, who expressed precisely the problem that some modern parents fear. He says, addressing his newborn son: "Our judge you may become—you are he already."[6] And, in spite of this fear, all modern parents strive toward that goal; for it represents the ultimate expression of responsibility for the child—the acceptance of his individuality. He, the child, having taken over from his parents their biological and cultural inheritance, becomes their equal as an individual.

We have followed some aspects of that intricate interplay between the parents' individualities and their instinctive desire for their own completion in the child; we have described some of the cultural complications of those strivings. These and many other aspirations are transmitted to the child through the manifold interactions between him and his parents. We may conclude then, that when the child, in the process of his emotional development, passes the oedipal phase and integrates the images of his parents within himself, those images are inevitably complex. All sorts of terms and directions which we use to define psycho-

6. Anton Wildgans, *op. cit.*

logical attitudes—such as "active—passive," "masculine—feminine," "prohibitive—permissive," and so forth—can be attributed to either of the parent figures.

On the level of the psychic experiences of the small child this conclusion probably is not much different from that of Freud, who by observations of individuals who were raised in a patriarchal society, came to the conclusion that the superego carries the cultural demands from generation to generation, in simple but categorical terms. Yet doubtless there exists a great difference in the educational attitudes of the patriarchal parents and those of the individualistic parents. The former were emotionally more independent of their children, less worried about them, and less afraid of them than the latter are or can be. This attitude is strongly expressed in connection with children in the latency period and in early adolescence. In the patriarchal family the educational influence received impetus from the authority of the father and from the stable values of the family and of society; it was as if it were simple and safe to know for what one educated one's children. Thus it was easier for the father to maintain his demands and for the mother to transmit her desires.

It is different in the modern family. The reasons for the insecurity of the modern family will be pointed out elsewhere in this volume; here we are dealing only with the emotional factors. We have indicated the dynamic processes which have changed the interpersonal relations between husband and wife and have caused the authority of the father not to remain unchallenged. We do not expect him to appear authoritative; we would criticize him as an overbearing tyrant were he assertive of his authority. We expect him to regard his wife's authority as equal to his own and to accept the opinion and freedom of decision of his growing children as the leading motive of their educational process. Should he not succeed in balancing the family on that basis, we criticize him for his lack of strength, his lack of masculinity, and we easily fall into the error of calling him passive when he is not domineering. The personality of the father seems weaker now that it is not supported by tradition; actually at present it must be more elastic, more adaptable, and therefore stronger than it was in earlier periods, since he has to hold out without the traditional support and often under attack—for he may be exposed to the open competition of his wife and even to the criticism of his children.

The same is true in a different way of the modern wife-mother. Though she has gained more freedom as an individual she also has suffered unfortunate losses. She is no longer protected by the security of a lasting marriage. The challenges of freedom often create conflicts with the desires of motherhood. Insecure as to whether marriage and motherhood should be her only satisfactions or whether she may strive for independence and work, afraid that she will not be able to reconcile both strivings, she may become confused in her aims and may easily convey her own indecision to her children. She may confuse them with incoherent demands, with conflicting permissions, and with contradictory prohibitions. Thus the children at an early age have to learn to make their own choice. Actually, the parents' goal is achieved if the children become able to make independent decisions and are free from conflict with themselves and with society. Nevertheless, the urgent demand of many mothers, "Make up your mind," often fails. In many instances it comes too soon—even in the nursery—and then it represents to the child a threat rather than a freedom. Growing children often sense a mother's weakness rather than her strength in her impatience to make them independent, they may abuse such weakness, or they may become protective of their mother. While they struggle their way through to their own decision they often meet their parents again, for the parents themselves may "grow up" with their children in a common emotional maturation of free individuals. For, ideally, we like to conceive of family life among adults as such a free exchange between mature people. Indeed, the educational goal of the modern individualistic family is an ambitious, exacting stimulus for human development.

The emotional structure of the family, then, expresses dynamically the function of the family. The study of the interaction of the emotional processes within the family reveals the ways in which the family affords the conditions through which the human personality can gradually emerge from its state of infantile, diffuse dependency to that of a self-determinative, adult individual possessing conscience, as required by our culture. Yet it is necessary to expose the vicissitudes of these processes and to reveal those dangers inherent in the same dynamism which may cause its failure.

In every phase of the cultural process there have undoubtedly been many who did not reach the desired goal of self-development and many who have paid for it dearly. Indeed, the psychoanalytic study of individuals and the large-scale comparison of the prevalent emotional disturbances in any period reveal not only the process of attainment of the cultural goal but also its typical failures. As an illustration of this statement the typical emotional disturbances of the patriarchal family (in Western civilization, from the second half of the nineteenth century well into the post–First World War period) were hysteria and compulsion neurosis. Hysteria is recognized as being the result of a highly prohibited and repressed sexual desire as it was incorporated in woman's conscience during the Victorian era. Compulsion neurosis is a condition caused by the strictness of a punitive superego; it develops when rebellion and hostility toward authority have to be repressed early and under the threat of great fear. The incorporated prohibition and anxiety return in painful doubts and complex ceremonies which should make it impossible for the individual to become guilty again. By now it will be apparent to everyone who reads our exposition of the family structure that these forms of emotional disturbance are caused by and correlated with the authoritative organization of the patriarchal family.

The prevalent emotional disturbance of our own era is what we call character disturbances and depression. Understanding the ambiguities of modern family life, we cannot but expect that its insecurities may often perforate the fabrics of the personality makeup of the present generation. What Dr. Adelaide M. Johnson termed "superego lacunae" describes this very phenomenon.[7] Too many children incorporate the doubts and conflicts of their parents in such a way that, in specific areas of their personalities, they do not learn to distinguish right from wrong. Instead of overcoming the conflict within themselves, some of these children remain fixated to those conflicts and feel inwardly compelled to repeat them, to "act them out." Thus we learn to recognize various character deformations. For society, however high the degree of individuation it permits, at the same time also requires that the individual conform. No wonder there are clashes between the attempts of individualism and the requirements of society. Many people internalize those conflicts and fight an intrapsychic struggle. Depression is one manifestation of that fight; it is a punishment doled out to the self, even before it could become guilty in action.

This chapter, though it is of necessity a brief survey of the gamut of pathological manifestations, may suffice to indicate that the interaction between society and the family determines the forms of emotional pathology. Yet, if pathology is so intricately interwoven with the organismic function of the family, is it to be feared that pathology may finally overcome its natural bounds and destroy the family completely? Of course there are, and there always were, such incidents; life proceeds by and through eradicating what is rotten and decayed. Nevertheless, through understanding the laws of its functioning, we should be able to be more optimistic and to assume that our knowledge may help not only to cure but also to avoid much of the pathology.

Individual psychotherapy may help to relieve complications within the family and to cure the evil already wrought. More important than cure, however, is prevention. Our understanding of the family as an organismic whole may open many avenues of preventive psychiatry. But we should term that complex interaction between the social, economic, and cultural forces of our society—which only all together can insure the security necessary for the family—not psychiatry but, rather, philosophy.

7. *Sanctions for Superego Lacunae in Adolescents,* in process of publication.

DISCUSSION

Because of their concentration on the study of intrapsychic processes, psychoanalysts were slow to conceptualize the dynamics of interpersonal relationships within the family. These relationships were subjects of observation, of course, since every psychoanalytic case history evaluates the parents' role in the intrapsychic structure of the child; the function of any "significant object" in a patient's life is assessed in regard to the personality organization and the pathology of the patient.

Freud's masterful abstraction, the conceptualization of internalized controls as superego, is a monument of deduction from his many-faceted observations. He perceived and assessed parent and child in interaction, influencing each other's behavior. But in the conceptualization of psychologic phenomena, the child, i.e., the patient, was his focus. The parent as an adult was assumed to be "normal" until proved otherwise. As a normal adult, he was not supposed to be influenced in his psychic structure by interfamilial occurrences. The emotional stability of the parent and his unquestionable love for his children were sanctioned beliefs of the culture.

Every individual functions within the boundaries of his culture; even a genius is culture bound. Freud and his early followers, individuals of the nineteenth century and individualistic in that sense, took the stable family organization for granted; correspondingly, they assumed that the psychologic distance between parents and children was natural law and therefore the parents' authority over their children would forever be the same. When Freud in "The Ego and the Id"[1] formulated the function of the superego as being the carrier of cultural inheritance from generation to generation, he conceptualized in terms of mental structure the world view (*Weltanschauung*) of the patriarchal culture.

Flugel was the first psychoanalyst to describe the interpersonal structure of the family on the basis of the psychoanalytic theory of personality development.[2] Accordingly, the center of his investigation was the oedipus complex as it functioned unconsciously in parents and set the goal of development for each child.[3] The cultural function of this family was achieved through the superego, modeled on the introjected image of the father. In spite of the restrictions of that concept, so richly documented by the cultural milieu in which Flugel was reared and worked, he assumed that the development of the child required corresponding readjustment in the parents' attitude and behavior at every stage. Writing soon after World War I, he recognized the mutuality of intrafamilial developmental processes decades before anyone spoke of "family dynamics."

It would require extensive study to outline the evolution of psychoanalytic theory from 1921 to 1949, from the appearance of Flugel's book to the date of the paper reproduced here. Some of the salient points of the complex process demonstrate the time lag in the formation of psychoanalytic theory and they show the vast amount of observational data necessary to make a shift in our theories and turn our attention in new directions.

The new era of psychoanalysis was inaugurated by "The Ego and the Id" in 1923.[4] It took some years until the structural model of the mind became an integrated part of the working knowledge of psychoanalysts. Until then, psychoanalysts observed the variations in libidinal conflicts and studied their representations and derivatives in the frame of the topographic model of the mind. It is difficult to imagine this now, but it was the almost perceptible scaffolding of the structural model that enabled psychoanalysts to conceive of the "total personality" and analyze the processes occurring between its components—ego, id, and superego.

Years later the psychoanalytic theory of ego development shifted from the classical libido theory to find its roots in object relationships. The origin of this goes back to Freud's "Narcissism, an Introduction" (1914)[5] and "Mourning and Melancholia" (1917).[6] In the former, Freud described the reciprocal interaction between libidinal objects; in the latter, the process by which internalized objects, de-libinized, become part of the self-system. The metapsychology of the processes of introjection and identification was formulated by Freud—the first as a process by which the instinctual drive achieves gratification through its object; the second as an intrapsychic process which leads to sublimation and structure formation.

To illustrate this it is well to cite the oral phase of development since this traditional term, covering many aspects, is the best example of the linkage of our concepts. For the newborn the object of gratification is nourishment, the milk itself. As the perceptual system of the infant matures, the "object" expands from hunger-satisfying nourishment and includes the breast; with further maturation, the "object of gratification" becomes the need-gratifying mother. The root of this early object relationship is biologic, i.e., instinctual. Introjections and identifications represent continuation of biologic theory. They are the unconscious contributors to all significant object relationships beyond infancy, throughout life. Functioning as silent partners in interpersonal and intrapsychic processes, introjections and identifications are usually conceptualized to explain psychologic changes in the dependent recipient —the child but not the parent, the patient but not the therapist.

There are many aspects of psychoanalytic psychology; the object relationship leads from instinctual drives to interpersonal relationships.

Anna Freud's fundamental study[7] of the ego's defenses offers a systematic approach to processes between id and ego. With new theories, the scope of psychoanalytic investigations broadened. Yet, as Heinz Hartmann wrote, "Recent developments in psychoanalysis have not changed its salient characteristics, namely, its biologic orientation, its genetic, dynamic, economic and topographic points of view and the explanatory nature of its concepts."[8] With this statement Hartmann introduced a new aspect to the biologic orientation of psychoanalysis; he integrated ego psychology with problems of adaptation.

Adaptation to what and in what manner? Such questions have formed the basis of research projects for biologists and ethologists for many decades. Freud in "Inhibitions, Symptoms and Anxiety" (1926)[9] described in terms of metapsychology the process by which a symptom, first perceived as ego-alien, becomes internalized, a psychic structure, with the result that the individual becomes adapted to it. Not only symptoms and object losses are internalized in this matter, but events of external reality also; they become psychologically meaningful if the individual has to adapt himself to them. Thus Hartmann's essay introduced reality into psychoanalytic ego psychology, not only as an ego function such as reality testing, but also as a fact that motivates an adaptational process. This leads either to adaptation or, if the task is too great, to maladaptation. In any case, reality has to be dealt with. Hartmann's essay conceptualized much of the daily experiences of psychoanalysts and offered a unifying concept under which to classify observations of interpersonal and group processes which were usually considered as bordering on psychoanalysis proper, yet were outside of psychoanalytic theory.

The significance of the adaptational point of view for psychoanalytic theory and its application to psychoanalytic therapy lies in the fact that adaptations are psychologic consequences of interpersonal processes. It may be that the continuity of adaptational processes between parents and children and between husbands and wives caused psychoanalysts to neglect the mutuality of those processes and attracted attention only if one or both partners had failed, causing unexpected, even pathologic reactions.

It was not until 1950 that Erikson succeeded in bringing the general attention of psychoanalysts to the viewpoint that a "neurosis is psycho- *and* somatic," that an event is "psycho- *and* social, interpersonal."[10] He elaborated social reality as a factor in personality development. Studying the roots of the ego in social organization, he arrived at the conclusion that *identity* is a goal of psychic organization which, if attained, maintains the self-concept of the individual within his multiple social roles, in his sociologic reality. In 1954 Erikson defined identity in transactional terms. He says, "The young individual learns to be most himself when he means most to others, those others who mean most to him."[11] This recalls Freud's description of the intrapsychic processes of lovers in their dependence on one another.[12]

Recent years have given ample opportunity to Erikson and many others to study various aspects of identity as clinical problems. We observed its diffusion, its crises, and sometimes its emergence from crises. Indeed, we have lived to see "identity crisis" as a mass phenomenon.

It was not only Erikson's conceptualization of the term "identity" or his revealing anthropologic and historical demonstrations that made the term such a useful catchword; the sociohistorical processes of the era presented situations that could best be diagnosed as identity problems, whether they referred to individuals, to families, or to sociologic entities. Indeed, in the ten years from 1950 to 1960, the dynamic thinking of psychoanalysis permeated sociology and anthropology; and psychoanalysis itself became more truly dynamic by expanding its investigation to include interpersonal processes.

Until the end of World War II, the traditional family of the nineteenth century was characterized by the high value vested in the identity of the family. The individual's sense of identity, his prestige, and his ambitions were subordinated to the goals of the family, to the image that the family as a whole conveyed to its members. The status of the family, the esteem in which the family was held, represented an axis of identification; it was also a collective channel for the narcissism of its individual members. My discussion (1949) of the emotional structure of the family did not mention "family narcissism" as a psychodynamic factor in the cohesiveness of the traditional family. In the patriarchal family structure it appeared inescapable that as the individual received his moral strength, his social and ethical values from his family, he invested his own achievements, his social and moral standing in the family as a whole and in its members, according to the nature of their relationship. The growing individualism that seems now to threaten the cohesiveness of the family led to the identity crises of the next generation. The historical and socioeconomic factors which motivate such seemingly paradoxical effects are well known. Here we have to ask, how did the family contribute to it?

As in any other area of research, problems stimulate investigation; the fear of impending crisis necessitated a better understanding of the family as a functional unit. It was understandable that after World War II, a flood of research reports, books, and papers concerning the family were published by sociologists, anthropologists, psychologists, and psychiatrists. The wartime disruptions of families focused my attention on frequent, and usually adjustable, disturbances in the emotional balance of families. Almost ten years after the publication of my paper on the family, the first comprehensive study of family dynamics by a psychoanalyst was published. Its title, *The Psychodynamics of Family Life,*[13] shows its divergence from the customary psychoanalytic viewpoint by presenting the family as a psychodynamic unit. Ackerman announced in the title of his book that he was dealing with the family as a living entity. This cannot be done without generalization. Ackerman achieved his aim by using the dynamic and economic concepts of psychoanalysis to explain the function of the family in establishing its identity and maintaining its stability by continually adjusting and readjusting its emotional balance—its interpersonal homeostasis. These are the subterranean processes of adaptation that enable the family to fulfill its obvious surface function, ". . . to insure physical survival and build the essential humanness of man."[14]

Did my psychoanalytic study of the family twenty years ago suggest any of those psychodynamic processes that have since become flagrant and have brought about the contemporary generation gap which seems to be undermining the structure of the family? Yes, it did, although vaguely. Did psychoanalytic insight detect roots of "the crisis about being" that might undermine the structure of the family and, with it, the organization of the personality?

Shifts in the relationship between the sexes are pointed out in this paper and the broad spectrum of sociologic factors in the emancipation of women has been briefly discussed to show that the trend of our culture indicates a progressive alteration of the father's role in the family. This brought about structural changes in the personality organization of individuals reared by parents who themselves doubted the "rights of parents" to believe that they knew what was best for their children. The doubt and insecurity of an emotionally insecure parental generation brought about crises in superego development. Reciprocal influences between family and culture do not show up during one generation. As the genetic approach to personality development is necessary for the understanding of interpersonal processes within the family, so is the appreciation of the interactions between at least three generations necessary to discern the ways by which cultural change penetrates the family.

The poet whom I quoted in the foregoing paper, the father who visualizes in his newborn child the future judge of his essential self, was an exception at that time, before the First World War. But that feeling reverberated in those who became fathers after they returned from that war and faced, with disappointment in themselves and in their parents, the conditions that led to the Second World War. During that period psychoanalysts observed a change in personality structures that became obvious in the frequency of certain psychiatric symptoms. The typical emotional disturbances of that generation were hysteria and compulsion neurosis, the results of a childrearing system that aimed at repression of instinctual tendencies, both libidinous and aggressive. This system built into the child's psyche a strong intrapsychic control system, an integrated superego. At the time I wrote the paper, the superego which earlier had received its strength from the "castrating" patriarchal father had already been influenced by a more liberal parental attitude. Parents who had reared their children between the two world wars aimed at bringing them to a higher level of individualism and a greater sense of responsibility; they were less interested in the repression of instinctual tendencies than in their children's awareness of their conflicts on account of them. Thus the two prevalent diagnostic categories became depression and character neuroses in the generation of their children. Depressive reactions developed in those individuals whose parents, in spite of their liberal attitude, conveyed to their children a high ego ideal. The various manifestations of narcissistic neurosis form a link between depressions and character neuroses. In direct opposition to depressive individuals are those persons who are described as "acting out" characters. Their pathology, rooted in the "superego lacunae,"[15] i.e., in a deficiency of an intrapsychic control system, was brought about by the emotional insecurity of the parent toward the child.

When Erikson formulated the concept of ego identity (1950)[16] I doubt if he assumed that "identity problem" would become a widespread diagnostic category. Why does this generation have such difficulty in achieving a personality integration that assures "identity"? It would sound flamboyant to answer this question with one sentence: they have too many choices. For even if we consider identity just in the sense of Erikson's original definition, a developmental attainment that maintains the individual's self-concept in his social (and sociologic) reality, then young people today have more choices and fewer conditions that limit their opportunities and compel them to adaptation. Yet this answer refers only to external reality and neglects the weakness of the ego. This weakness lies not only in the actuality of the variety of choices, but even more in the idea ingrained from childhood that the choices represent not possibilities, but rights. The root of identity problems may go deeper into the origins of primary relationships. Since the roles of father and mother in childrearing are not as strictly separated as they used to be, the early introjects and identifications of the child are not as distinct as they were in past generations. The giving, tender mother soon becomes the disciplinarian, while the father, who is often a substitute for the mother, has become a somewhat distant but dependable friend. With this generalization I am still describing a fortunate, healthy emotional balance in the father-mother-child triangle. But this picture indicates some of the factors that diminish the father's role as superego builder. Now the father, being distant from that traditional task—at least by one generation—and satisfied with himself in his permissive and tolerant attitude toward the child, does not realize that he offers choices to his child instead of setting limits. To this we might add that fathers and mothers very often offer different choices.

What we subsume under the general but ambivalent term, "parental permissiveness," has by now a developmental history, at least through two generations. The developing individualism has given parenthood a more difficult task of childrearing than parents ever had before; ". . . to raise children in a democratic society by individualistic parents in order to achieve their individuality and by this become assets to society . . ."[17] is a task complicated by the fact that parents, imbued with the virtues of their "disciplined and tolerant conscience,"[18] are often less sure of how to convey their values to their children than were the authoritarian parents. Dissent and deviation of their adolescent children caught parents unawares. Convinced of their intention to do their best to promote their children's development, parents were shocked and often resentful. This, of course, widened the gap. Caught between their existential anxiety of an insecure world which they try to repress and their need for support which they wish to deny, they often act out their helplessness in dangerous aggressivity. This again causes a deeper sense of helplessness in the parental generation. So it goes, the transactional process from generation to generation.

The identity of parents lies in their biosocial function of parenthood. There has been no evaluation of the significance of this problem. Repercussions in the parents' personalities to their dissenting adolescent children often present psychiatric problems for which help is sought by parents for themselves and/or for their children. This is a general problem for which preventive measures must be found. Not only do the young have to be educated, but parents have to learn how to adapt to their children. Indeed, the cohesiveness of the family seems to be threatened by the generation which is yet too young to be responsible parents.

We have neglected one aspect of the parent-child relationship that tends to enhance the cohesiveness of the family, especially in our urban industrial population: the pride of the child who can do a valued service for the family. We do not mean exploitation of children. Being needed, however, gives a spurt to identification with parents and other adults. While it affords ego gratification to the child, it ties him to the family, who appreciate his contribution as achievement. Parents in an affluent society, so gratified by their ability to provide amply, rarely offer to adolescents this kind of gratification in a realistic, honest way.

We might conclude that the outlook is pessimistic for a culture dedicated to individualism as a basic right of man. No doubt, the technological civilization spiraling upwards without considering spiritual needs and values or two wars and their aftermath has brought disappointment and mistrust in the adult generation. But does this of necessity prove that a nonauthoritarian but tolerant and understanding childrearing system is doomed to failure? Is the real and only meaning of the current cultural revolution the negation of the permissive childrearing system? There are signs that forecast the opposite. The education that has pervaded this generation with the sense of their individuality has conveyed with it a sense of responsibility, at least in a few who may become future leaders. Keen observers of the social scene perceive indications that as adults begin to take the social criticism of the young seriously, the destructiveness that originates in helplessness diminishes, and cooperation becomes possible. The culture which is evolving out of the clash between two generations may become viable if parents of the next generation incorporate the constructive aspects of their own experience in the structure of their own families and thus convey them to the next generation.

NOTES

1. Freud, S., "The Ego and the Id" (1923), *Std. Ed.*, XIX, 13–66.

2. Flugel, J. C., *The Psychoanalytic Study of the Family* (London, Hogarth Press, 1921).

3. Anthony, E. J., and Benedek, T., eds., *Parenthood, Its Psychology and Psychopathology* (Boston, Little, Brown and Co., 1970).

4. Freud, S., "The Ego and the Id" (1923) *Std. Ed.*, XIX, 13–66.

5. ———, "Narcissism, An Introduction" (1914), *Std. Ed.*, XIV, 67–102.

6. ———, "Mourning and Melancholia" (1917), *Std. Ed.*, XIV, 243–258.

7. Freud, A., *The Ego and the Mechanisms of Defense* (1936), (New York, International Universities Press, 1946).

8. Hartmann, H., *Ego Psychology and the Problem of Adaptation* (1939) (New York, International Universities Press, 1958), p. 5.

9. Freud, S., "Inhibitions, Symptoms and Anxiety" (1926), *Std. Ed.*, XX, 87–156.

10. Erikson, E. H., *Childhood and Society* (New York, W. W. Norton, 1950), p. 19.

11. ———, "Identity and Totality: Psychoanalytic Observations on the Problems of Youth," *Human Development Bulletin* (Chicago, University of Chicago Press, 1954), p. 51.

12. Freud, S., "Narcissism, An Introduction."

13. Ackerman, N., *The Psychodynamics of Family Life. Diagnosis and Treatment of Family Relationships* (New York, Basic Books, 1958).

14. Ibid., p. 18.

15. Johnson, A., "Sanctions for Superego Lacunae in Adolescents," in *Searchlights on Delinquency*, ed. K. Eissler (New York, International Universities Press, 1949), pp. 225–254.

16. Erikson, E. H., *Childhood and Society.*

17. Benedek, T., "The Family as a Psychologic Field," in *Parenthood, Its Psychology and Psychopathology* (Boston, Little, Brown and Co., 1970), p. 134.

18. Erikson, E. H., *Young Man Luther* (New York, W. W. Norton, 1958), p. 263.

8. The Psychosomatic Implications
of the Primary Unit: Mother-Child

INTRODUCTION

The year 1949 appears to have been a productive time for me. In that year two papers, "The Emotional Structure of the Family" and "The Psychosomatic Implications of the Primary Unit," were published. In the introduction to the former, I described the "developmental lines" that enabled me to write that essay. Now in the introduction to the following paper, I note that this study seems to be a direct continuation of an earlier paper, "Adaptation to Reality in Early Infancy" (Chapter 5), although it was never planned as such. Not only its content but also its methodology followed that article. In connection with "Adaptation to Reality in Early Infancy" I described observations, distant in time and differing in significance, to show how they led to the formulation of hypotheses; with time and experience the insights slowly matured and gained the strength to become a paper. The cycle research (Chapter 6) came about differently; it was planned; its investigative method had to be established and adhered to. Such planned research was an exception in the life of psychoanalysts of my generation. It was also a singular event in my life. The following paper was not a result of planned research; it was the yield of what I had learned in years of experience in clinical investigations.

For the analyst with an overcrowded schedule of training analyses, teaching, and private practice, how much time and leisure remain for the integration of experience that impels one to write? Prodding helps. When Dr. George Mohr was the program chairman of the oncoming annual meeting (1949) of the American Orthopsychiatric Association he asked me imploringly, "Would you—surely, you could—present something new and of great interest about women at this meeting?" He even added, "The meeting will be held in Chicago so it will not take much of your time." My reply was, "I will think about it and let you know." I did not need to think about it very long; a few days later I gave him the title. It came to my mind like an insight, ready with its explanation which did not even appear new to me. From the time I began to analyze women's emotions in response to the ovulative and postovulative phases of the sexual cycle, I had struggled to put into words the unconscious communication between a would-be mother and the not-yet-existent infant, as expressed in dreams and fantasies and in the behavior of sexually mature, ovulating women. The word "symbiosis" came to mind and I suddenly knew that this was the key to motherhood, to motherliness. In a few evenings I wrote the paper.

The term *symbiosis* had never been used in psychoanalysis. The word originates in the Greek *symbion* (living together) and refers to "dissimilar organisms living together in more or less intimate association or even in close union," according to Webster's Dictionary. When I described the mother-child relationship during early infancy in "Adaptation to Reality in Early Infancy," I did not use the term symbiosis.[1] At that time I did not think of the mother-child interaction as beginning with conception. I recoiled from the idea of the embryo as a parasite on the mother, although he is manifestly taking from the mother. Does he also give to the mother? I had seen many women looking rejuvenated during pregnancy. The unconscious psychosomatic communication was in my mind and it needed elucidation.

At that time the literature contained references illustrating the psychobiologic responses of infants to their mothers' emotional state.[2] These observations confirmed my assumptions based on the psychodynamic processes of the ovulative phase.

The concept of symbiosis as discussed in the following paper is derived from the psychobiologic processes that maintain pregnancy and motivate its characteristic emotional state; the same psychobiologic processes regulate the communications between mother and newborn, evolving as the "emotional symbiosis" of infancy.

NOTES

1. I referred to the "mother-child unity" in the same sense as Alice Balint did in her paper, "Die Entwicklung der Liebesfähigkeit und der Realitätssin" (Budapest, Lelekelemzesi Tanulmanyok, 1933).

2. See footnote 1 of paper.

THE PSYCHOSOMATIC IMPLICATIONS OF THE PRIMARY UNIT: MOTHER-CHILD[1]

In the recent literature, several observations have been published demonstrating that the child, by some not clearly defined psychic process, incorporates the emotional attitudes of the mother, embodies her anxiety, and develops symptoms which the mother used to have or might have had.[2] The motivations which play a role in the presenting symptom of the child also exist in the mother and can be elicited by analysis. The dynamics of such preconscious or unconscious communication between mother and child may be clarified by a better understanding of the psychobiological factors which motivate motherhood and motherliness.

This discussion deals with the *psychodynamics of the symbiosis* which exists during pregnancy, is interrupted at birth, but remains a functioning force, directing and motivating the mental and somatic interaction between mother and child.

As long as gratification of the emotional need for motherhood was fulfilled without interference by human controls, one rarely had opportunity to study the primary psychobiological factors in childbearing. The behavior manifestations which are usually accessible to psychoanalysis reveal that the woman's identification with her mother motivates her attitude toward motherhood and determines her behavior toward her children. While such psychoanalytic observations elucidate how emotionally determined attitudes may be carried over from generation to generation, they do not answer the question whether there is a genuine, primary psychological need (instinct, in Freud's sense) which directs the woman's desire for conception and motherhood and motivates her motherliness.

The study of the sexual cycle in women (5)—a detailed analysis of the emotional processes as they unfold in correlation with the hormonal cycle of the ovaries—has thrown new light upon the female psychosexual organization.

1. Presented at the 1949 Annual Meeting of The American Orthopsychiatric Association and reprinted from *The American Journal of Orthopsychiatry*, Vol. XIX, no. 4 (October, 1949).
2. Beata Rank (1) and her collaborators observed such psychic transmission of conflict constellations to children who became feeding problems. Betty Joseph (2) has shown the same in infants of five to seven months who developed biting symptoms and anxiety. Margaret Fries (3) investigated the interaction between mother and infant during the lying-in period, and Dr. René Spitz (4) demonstrated the infant's reactions to the mother's depression.

A complete discussion of the sexual cycle is beyond the scope of this presentation. In order to elucidate the psychology of motherhood, however, I shall discuss one phase of the cycle, the postovulative, progestin phase. After ovulation, the wall of the ruptured follicle, from which the ovum has escaped, undergoes a process of luteinization and produces a hormone called lutein or progestin. The function of this hormone is to prepare the mucous membrane of the uterus to receive the impregnated ovum and to help to maintain pregnancy if conception occurs. If conception does not occur, the progestin production declines after four to six days, the uterine mucosa breaks down, and the uterus is prepared for menstruation. The emotional state which develops in correlation with the progestin phase can be compared with the "quiet period" in lower mammals. The psychic apparatus seems to register the somatic preparation for the pregnancy by a change of emotional attitude: the woman's interest shifts from extraverted activities to her body and its welfare. Expressed in psychodynamic terms: the libido is withdrawn from external, heterosexual objects, becomes concentrated upon the self. This is the phase of the cycle during which the woman's desire for pregnancy, or her defense against it, dominates the psychoanalytic material. At the same time, or some days later in the cycle, the analytic material may show preoccupation with care of the child.[3] However, as if mother and child were identical or interchangeable, the tendencies toward child care may be expressed at one time *actively,* as a wish to nurse, to feed, to take care of the baby; and at other times the same woman may express the same tendencies *passively,* as a desire to be fed, to be taken care of.

Helene Deutsch (6) found that a *deep-rooted passivity* and a *specific tendency toward introversion* are characteristic qualities of the female psyche. Our study of the sexual cycle reveals that these propensities of female psychology are repeated in cyclic intervals, in correspondence with the specifically female gonad hormone, *progestin,* during the postovulative phase of the ovarian cycle. On the basis of such observations, we assume that the emotional manifestations of the specific passive-receptive and narcissistic-retentive tendencies represent the psychodynamic correlates of the biological need for motherhood.

The *psychology of pregnancy* is easily understood in the light of the psychodynamic processes which accompany the progestin phase of the cycle. Just as the monthly repetition of the physiological processes represents a somatic preparation for pregnancy, so the corresponding monthly repetition of the emotional attitudes represents a preparation for that introversion of psychic energies which motivates the emotional attitudes of the pregnant woman.

3. We could not determine whether this occurs in correlation with progestin alone or in correlation with *prolactin* production in these women who are neither pregnant nor lactating.

The interaction between mother and child—*the symbiosis*—begins after conception. The enhanced hormonal and general metabolic processes which are necessary to maintain normal pregnancy produce an increase of vital energies. The pregnant woman in her placid vegetative calmness enjoys her pregnant body, which is like a reservoir replenished with libidinous feelings. While such feelings enhance the mother's well-being, they also become the source of her motherliness: they increase her pleasure in bearing the child and her patience in regard to some of the discomforts of her pregnancy. Primary narcissism—the result of surplus energy (7) produced by active metabolic balance—is the reservoir which supplies with libido the various emotional tasks of living. As the hormonal processes of pregnancy replenish the primary narcissism of the woman, this becomes the source of her motherliness. The general behavior and the emotional state during pregnancy may appear "regressive" if we compare them with the usual level of ego integration of the same woman; yet the condition which appears regressive on the ego level represents a growth of the integrative span of the personality on the biological level. While the mother feels her growing capacity to love and to take care of the child, she actually experiences a general improvement in her emotional balance. We have observed that many neurotic women, who suffered severe anxiety states before, have become free from anxiety during pregnancy. Others become free from depression and from desperate mood changes. Many women, despite the discomforts of nausea or morning sickness, feel emotionally stable and have the "best time" during pregnancy. This does not mean we are forgetting that some women become severely panic-stricken and/or depressed during pregnancy. (Usually, this happens in the latter part of pregnancy or after delivery.) If the woman's developmental disturbance is such that her ego is unable to master the productive task of childbearing, a dissociation of the functions (physiological and mental) may occur during the pregnancy. In this paper, however, we are discussing the emotional course of the normal pregnancy, which enriches the somatic and psychic energies of the woman to a degree that she becomes able to master emotional conflicts which were disturbing to her at other times. The force which maintains pregnancy is responsible for the characteristic attitude of withdrawal which sometimes becomes intensified to such a degree that nothing else, no other reality, counts for the pregnant woman, and she lives as in a daze.[4]

Another aspect of the psychology of pregnancy is expressed by an increase in the *receptive tendencies*. This is a manifestation of the biological process of growth which it serves. The voraciousness and the

4. This is the reason that some women, even if they have to hide the pregnancy—for example, unmarried mothers—do not realize the actual difficulties they have to face, but forget about them until the delivery creates a different emotional situation.

bizarre appetite of the pregnant woman are well known. "She eats for two" expresses permission, especially when gratification of such needs is not limited by medical control. The pregnant woman thrives on the sympathy and solicitude of her environment. If, however, her passive receptive needs are unfulfilled, if her husband or her family are not adequately attentive, the sense of frustration may set in action a regressive process which may increase her receptive needs to an exaggerated degree. The resulting anger may destroy the primary narcissistic state of pregnancy, and thus it may interfere with the development of motherliness.

The difference between primary and secondary narcissism in the development of motherliness can easily be seen when we contrast the vital libidinal energy (produced by the metabolic processes maintaining the pregnancy) and the secondary ego gratifications which the pregnant woman may expect in connection with her pregnancy and her child. The need for ego gratification may change the fantasies of the mother from the unqualified desire for a child to definite wishes and ambitions which she hopes and intends to fulfill through the child. Thus the child becomes a means for gratification of individually determined goals, even before it is born. A mother may worry during the pregnancy lest her child will not be all that is desired, i.e., a son for one reason or a daughter for another. Many other conflicts, arising from the secondary narcissistic goals of the personality, may disturb the development of genuine motherliness.[5]

The important role that hormonal stimulation plays in development and performance of motherliness has been well studied in animals. In the human one is inclined to overlook the role of hormonal stimulation, since motherliness, an idealized attitude of highest value, is considered as the fulfillment of ethical aspects of the personality rather than of "animalistic" biological functions. Yet motherliness is a function of a specific—biological and psychic—maturation; its completion, as many observations prove, is only rarely reached at and about the birth of the first child.

While *the trauma of birth*—the interruption of the fetal symbiosis —in recent years has been studied often from the point of view of the infant, its significance for the mother has been relatively neglected. I do not refer here to the massive obstetrical traumata and the resulting

5. There are other factors in the psychology of pregnancy which may interfere with the development of motherliness, such as the fear of death at childbirth, exaggerated fear of labor pains, etc. These are, however, symptoms motivated by developmental conflicts of the woman and are, therefore, secondary. Here the discussion is limited to those aspects of the psychology of motherhood which are related directly to the hormonal processes. However, the hormonal processes may be influenced by environmental factors which motivate the psychosexual development *in toto,* such as the girl's identification with the mother (5).

pathology. I rather want to point out that when the newborn leaves the womb and has to become active in securing the basic needs for living, the mother's organism has to become reorganized also. In some sense, this may be considered as a trauma for the mother. The hormonal and metabolic changes which induce parturition, the labor pains, and the excitement of delivery, even without intensive use of narcotics, interrupt the continuity of the mother-child unity. After delivery, when the organism as a whole is preparing for the next function of motherhood —*lactation*—mothers, especially primiparas, may experience an "emotional lag." For the nine months of the pregnancy, they were preparing to love the baby. After delivery, they may be surprised by a *lack of feeling* for the child.[6] Usually love for the newborn wells up in the mother as she first hears the cry of her baby. The sensation of love reassures the mother about the continuity of her oneness with the child and she may relax and wait serenely to receive her child on her breast. It is different if the mother, instead of love, feels a sense of loss and emptiness; if she has the feeling of a distance between herself and the infant; views the baby as an outsider, an object; and she asks herself with estrangement, "Is this what I had in me?" Mothers having such a disquieting experience usually muster all their self-control to suppress this feeling and try to summon their previous fantasies to establish an emotional relationship with the infant. Such mothers, disappointed in themselves by the lack of love, feel guilty, become anxious; and with this the insecurity toward the child begins.[7]

The further development of the mother-child relationship depends on the total personality of the mother; she may develop a depression and withdraw from the child; she may turn against the child who exposed her failure in loving and reject it completely; or she may overcompensate the fear of not being able to love and may become overindulgent and protective. This early postpartum *emotional lag* is a critical period during which the husband's relationship to his wife, his readiness for gratifying his wife's dependent needs, is of great importance. The postpartum woman, for many reasons, including physiological motivations, has a regressive tendency, and therefore has a great desire to be mothered. Through the love which she passively receives, she may be able to overcome the depression and give love to her child.

6. This occurs more often if delivery was performed under complete anesthesia, so that the mother has no memory of the experience.
7. Whether the postpartum metabolic processes have such a generally depressing effect on the mother that she is unable to feel love, and consequently becomes afraid of the tasks of motherhood, or whether the lack of motherly emotions is the result of the immaturity of those psychic and somatic processes which result in motherliness, deserves further study and probably needs to be established in each case.

Whether the mother, through the feeling of love, is able to maintain the sense of unity with her child, or whether she has to miss this most significant gratification, the organism of the mother is not ready to give up the symbiosis after parturition. The need for its continuation exists in the mother, whose hormonal household is preparing to continue the symbiosis by *lactation*.

The psychosomatic correlations during normal lactation have not been studied closely because lactation is a contented period in the woman's life. The hormonal function—related to *prolactin* production —which stimulates milk secretion, usually suppresses the gonad function and induces an emotional attitude which is similar to that of the progestin phase of the cycle. As is now known, during the monthly preparation for pregnancy, the intention toward motherliness is expressed by active and passive receptive tendencies. During lactation, both the active and passive receptive tendencies gain in intensity; they become the axis around which the activities of motherliness center. The woman's desire to nurse the baby, to be close to it bodily, represents the continuation of the original symbiosis, not only for the infant, but for the mother as well. While the infant incorporates the breast, the mother feels united with the baby. The identification with the baby permits the mother to "regress," to repeat and satisfy her own passive, dependent, receptive needs. The emotional experiences of lactation, while they permit a process of identification between mother and child, afford a slow, step-by-step integration of normal motherliness.

What have our present methods of child care done with the woman's ability and readiness to nurse the baby? It would lead us away from the primarily psychosomatic frame of this presentation if I went into a discussion of the sociological and anthropological factors which, in our culture, interfere with the continuation of the symbiosis between mother and infant during lactation. The result of the suppression of the natural process of motherliness is, however, very serious. Possibly the baby's "formula" can improve on nature as far as chemistry is concerned; possibly it can regulate the metabolic needs of the infant better than breast feeding does; but it cannot develop motherliness through the bottle, even if the mother is permitted to hold her baby in her arms while she feeds him, as present-day nursing care encourages.

One example of incipient disturbance of motherliness I observed recently: this young woman was very anxious to have a second baby and was very happy when she became pregnant. Her moodiness, which often led to suicidal ideas, disappeared and she felt serene during the pregnancy. While the delivery of the first baby in a military hospital during the war had been a frightening experience, this fear was now overcome since everything could be arranged according to her wishes. She had a normal delivery with anesthesia only at the end. To the great surprise of the nurses, she wanted her baby rooming-in with her. She felt happy and contented, watching her infant and nursing him, concentrating on him completely. Then she developed a slight infection and the baby was taken away from her. When she went home, a nurse took over the care of the baby. As the nurse watched her feeding the baby, she felt her milk being dissipated. The nurse was eager to give the baby the bottle. The mother became uncomfortable and depressed. Although she felt that she was losing what she wanted so much, her friends began to tell her that it was time for her to go out, to enjoy her freedom while she had the nurse. She became moody. "I spend time fantasying about being sick and in the hospital again," she confessed. She complained that she was superfluous to the baby, yet she did not dare to send the nurse away and take full responsibility, for she was not certain that she could enjoy at home the same concentration upon the infant as she had felt in the hospital. "That would be unfair to the older child," she protested, and it would also seem silly to some of her friends. Thus, five weeks after delivery—in old times, she would still be "in confinement" —she was in the psychiatrist's office complaining about two things: (a) that she loved the baby in the hospital, but now did not know how to love him; and (b) that the baby, who was so quiet and gained weight so well, had become fussy, was crying a great deal, and had even vomited once or twice, and this frightened her.

No single example can completely illustrate the point which I want to make: namely, that not only the infant has the need for the mother's readiness to nurse, to take care of him; not the baby alone thrives on the closeness of the mother, by her warmth and tenderness; but the mother also has an instinctual need to fulfill the physiological and emotional preparedness for her motherliness. If this process of the mother's development is suppressed, the enforced changes in the hormonal function may disturb that psychosomatic balance which is the source of motherliness. The vulnerability of the integration of motherliness can be explained by a summary of the psychosomatic processes of the puerperium[8] and lactation.

1. When one compares the psychosexual integration of the personality during the puerperium with that of the "highest" integration of the personality, the lactating or puerperal mother appears *regressed* to an oral level.

2. While this psychosexual state accounts for the (unconscious) communication—identification between mother and infant—it also accounts for the depressive reactions of the mother.[9] Thus the mother

---

8. Puerperium is the period from termination of labor to the completion of the involution of the uterus—usually six weeks.
9. That the intensification of the oral receptive tendencies represents the psychodynamic conditions for the development of depression is a well-established concept of psychoanalysis.

becomes oversensitive in regard to her capacity for fulfilling the function of motherhood.

Every indication of her failure increases the mother's sense of inferiority and creates anxious tension and depression. Just as the suppression of lactation interferes with the development of motherliness, so failure of motherliness, originating in other sources of the personality, may interfere with lactation. In old times, one used to say that the emotional disturbance of the mother "goes on the milk," and it was assumed that the emotional disturbance influenced not only the quantity, but also the quality of the milk, so that the baby received milk which was "difficult to digest" and caused colic and other suffering. For many years, one shrugged scientific shoulders over such "superstition." Today, we accept it as fact, although we admit that we do not know the pathways by which the emotional tensions of the mother are transmitted to the infant.

In an earlier paper, I examined the interaction between mother and infant in regard to the development of the adaptive capacity of the infant's ego (8). It is pertinent to summarize here the main conclusions of that study.

According to our hypothesis, the symbiosis between mother and child continues on a different scale during the neonatal period. The sleeping infant is in a condition closely resembling that of intrauterine life. The arising physiological needs disturb the sleep, and then the course of gratification is as follows: crying—gratification—sleep. This process evolves, as far as the newborn is concerned, *within the self,* without realization of the external environment. The mother's genuine motherliness, her desire and ability to supply the infant with the sensations of "protectedness," reduce the frequency of disturbing stimuli and diminish the intensity and length of the crying fits. Through the rhythmic repetition of the gratification of his physiological needs, the infant develops to the perception that the source of the need (hunger, pain, discomfort) is *within,* and the source of gratification is *outside* the self.

By the same routinely returning process of gratifications, the infant acquires a *sense of confidence* that the mother will gratify his needs. It is difficult to describe the phenomenology of this early emotional state, although mothers will recognize its manifestations—in the baby's way of turning his head, following with his eyes, ceasing to cry for a short while when the mother is near, etc. This indicates that confidence plays an important role in the economy of the psychic apparatus during infancy: it preserves the mother-child unity; it helps to decrease the intensity of the outer stimuli and thus averts anxiety. Lack of confidence stimulates tension which may grow into discomfort and anxiety. This emotional shelter—confidence—and the positive, dependent relationship to the mother which is its consequence, facilitates learning in the normal infant. The ego, strengthened by the libidinal relationship to the mother on the one hand and by the absence of anxiety on the other, develops an adequate capacity to perceive the objects of the outer world; such an ego is able to accept new and unexpected situations (always in a degree which corresponds to the developmental level of the child) and masters them by trust in the mother.[10]

Quite different from this ego structure is the ego of those infants whose development was not guided by the confident relationship to the mother. *Hospitalism* (10) is a severe state of inhibition which develops in infants raised in institutions, where routine substitutes for love. Without the loving stimulation of one individual, children with such dependent needs do not turn to any person with confidence. Such children do not watch the person, but rather the bottle, or some other phase of the routine. It was observed that such children refused the bottle when it was offered from the side of the bed other than the one they were used to. Such children adapt to the routine gratification of their needs with conditioned reflexes.

Conditioned reflexes represent a significant part of primary learning in normal children also. Yet there is an important difference between the learning of the healthy infant and that of the infant developing various degrees of hospitalism. Conditioning is an adaptive mechanism, which serves as protection against anxiety. Anxiety has several sources. One of them is the body itself, which generates pain by the sensation of unsatisfied physiologic needs; the other source of anxiety is the danger in which the weak ego finds itself when alone and isolated. Infants raised by loveless routine are exposed to anxiety-producing situations more often than those whose needs are met with loving care. The ego, beset by anxiety too often, and for too long a time, remains fixated to the level of primitive conditioning. Such reflex adaptation saves the child from further increase of tension, and the child remains calm as long as every step of the routine is followed without a change. Every new situation, even a slight change in the routine, will, however, be experienced as a danger; the child responds with anxiety, i.e., with crying. If the environmental situation cannot be improved, the inhibition increases; the child, in order to avoid anxiety, finally refuses to respond and does not accept any new situation. If only the bare physiologic needs of a child are supplied, he may grow up to become a deeply inhibited person. For such an individual, every new situation will

10. The concept of *confidence* can be compared with the concept of *hope* (9). French shows how "hope" facilitates the mental processes necessary for achieving a goal. We believe that *hope* develops as a mental habit on the basis of *confidence*. Through confidence in the forthcoming passive gratifications and in the forthcoming help and support in attempts at active mastery, the ego develops to a stage in which it is able to project the expectations for gratification in the future. Hope, like confidence, diminishes the sense of frustration and already in early childhood enables the individual to *wait* for gratification without a sudden increase in the psychic tension.

reactivate a part of that anxiety which he experienced as an infant. The individual who did not learn to love during the first year of life will be threatened whenever he shall develop a new object relationship.

I have presented two extremes. In the one environment, the processes of growth appear to be ideally regulated by the infant's own needs, the mother responding to them in a way which all but repeats the symbiosis, permitting the infant to develop to independence at his own pace. In the other environment, the symbiosis was interrupted, the nursing care did not supply enough gratification to enable the infant to develop emotional—interpersonalized and intrapsychic—defenses against anxiety. These extremes illustrate that the ego's capacity to learn to master the object world goes hand in hand with the development of object-libidinal relationship. The ego structure developing through the buffer of confidence has a greater span and flexibility in adaptation to reality. In contrast, if the psychic economy is not relieved by a sense of security in the relationship with the mother, but has to concentrate upon mastering and avoiding anxiety, it will produce an ego structure fixated to rigidly conditioned adaptation. Such ego structure may break down at any time when a new adaptive task emerges.

The interaction between mother and infant, however, can be studied in even more detail in the large majority of instances ranging between these extremes.

The activity pattern of the newborn depends upon the irritability of his nervous system, on the one hand, and upon the degree of protection against the disturbing stimuli on the other. In the light of our discussion, we may say that the infant born with a nervous system of greater sensitivity would need a longer, better-functioning substitute for the intrauterine symbiosis.[11] However, experience shows that the mothers of the "nervous" babies are usually less able to provide their infants with an environment of fewer stimulations. The mature, normal newborn calms down under the influence of normal nursing care to this rhythm: need—crying—gratification—sleep. It takes usually four weeks, i.e., the neonatal period, to advance in physiological adjustment to a degree which assures smoother vegetative functioning.

It is observed that a large proportion of babies, instead of becoming "happier" at about the age of four weeks, show a new type of crying. Gesell and Ilg (11) state: "The baby shows a tendency to cry prior to sleep." This "wakefulness crying" tends to occur in the afternoon and the evening. It loses its prominence at about ten or twelve weeks.

11. First-born infants, on account of lesser maturation, or on account of greater birth trauma, represent a more difficult task to a mother who has also less maturity in handling the child. Thus, the first-born infant's activity pattern is more fitful; it takes longer for him to quiet down than for subsequent children of the same parent. This statement must be checked, however, in regard to the many factors which may influence mother and child.

What is the cause of this irritability? In the light of our assumption that the mother as well as the baby has a need for continuation of the symbiosis, we may speculate on the significance of the baby's increased demand on the mother at a time when she begins to turn away from the baby and becomes more active in the other areas of her existence. Do infants then demand more intensely the reestablishment of the symbiosis? Or do they respond to the increased tenseness of the mother? Be that as it may, the infant has no means other than his crying fit for discharging tension. It is fortunate that the infant has no memory of the amount of discomfort and pain which his crying fit would indicate. The unreadiness of his nervous system, the lack of internal barriers (*Reiz-Schutz*), accounts for the spreading of the tension which may increase to a veritable "storm of excitation" and may invade the viscera (12). It will depend on the degree of maturity of the vegetative nervous system and the gastrointestinal tract whether such excitation becomes bound to definite parts of the gastrointestinal system and its functioning. Thus, symptoms like pyloric spasm, as well as colic, can be explained as steps in the mastery of the general excitation of the nervous system. Generally, the intensity and frequency of such disturbances during the first three months measure the pace of interaction between mother and child.

Melanie Klein (13) assumes that infants, struggling with a breast which does not feed or which overflows, infants suffering from pain of hunger, colic, or other bodily discomfort, acquire the concepts of "good" and "bad" within themselves. Even if we do not follow Klein's complex psychologic elaborations, we may accept, on the basis of observation, that anxiety and pain (any sort of discomfort may cause anxiety in the infant) increase the urge to reestablish security by being close to the mother. The crying, grasping infant bites the nipple with force and suckles with greed; the sick infant, too, gasping with opening and closing of the mouth, wants to incorporate the mother, to reestablish the symbiosis which once supplied all needs without pain. If such intensification of the incorporative needs leads to gratification, the interaction between mother and child improves. If, however, the mother does not succeed in pacifying the infant, his physiological tension increases and the need for incorporation becomes more and more charged with motor energy. We speak of "hostile incorporation" although the psychic representation of hostility can hardly exist so early. But its model is formed. The *hostile incorporation* augments the internal tension of the infant; at the same time, it alienates the helpless mother who feels rejected by her child. Thus while a vicious circle develops between mother and infant, another vicious circle within the infant becomes intensified. The infant, after his attempts at incorporation which have failed to satisfy his needs, is helpless and exhausted. Rado and Fenichel (14) pointed out that the first regulator of self-esteem (*Selbstgefühl*) is the satisfaction acquired by all the processes connected with feeding;

they assume that the early disappointments, anxiety, helplessness, which some infants experience in connection with feeding and digestion, may cause a sense of helplessness, of inferiority, of worthlessness; as if "badness" were existing within the self.

It is beyond the scope of this paper to elaborate how the primary self-esteem becomes the basis of ego development. Secure and stable, it is the core of a strong adaptable ego; helpless and insecure, it gives rise to a rigid ego structure which, under the strain of adaptive tasks arising later in life, may regress to the basic insecurity of early childhood. The regressive processes may then bring to the fore psychosomatic conditions which were determined by the developmental processes of infancy.

SUMMARY

The psychosomatic (hormonal) aspects of motherliness were discussed to demonstrate the mother's biological need for continuation of symbiosis in the puerperium and during the child's infancy. This instinctual tendency toward motherliness corresponds to the helplessness of the newborn; it is gratified by sundry intimate functions of motherhood which supply both mother and infant with the gratification of their dependent needs. Motherliness, developing through sublimation of instinctual impulses, enlarges the span of the mother's personality; it encompasses her child.

The physiologic and mental apparatus of the infant represents a system which communicates broadly and fluently with the system of the mother—with all aspects of the mother's personality: with her id, her ego, and her superego. Through the processes of identification with the mother, the infant develops from the undifferentiated state of the newborn to an individual with structuralized mental apparatus which is in control of psychic and somatic processes.[12]

NOTES

1. Rank, Beata, Marian C. Putnam, and Gregory Rochlin. *The Significance of the "Emotional Climate" in Early Feeding Difficulties.* Psychosomatic Med., 10: 279–283, 1948.

2. Joseph, Betty. *A Technical Problem in the Treatment of the Infant Patient.* Internat. J. Psa., 29: 58–59, 1948.

12. It would be a mistake to conclude that breast feeding holds the answer to all problems and that by itself it assures a conflictless evolution of the child-mother relationship. Long-term observations are necessary to evaluate the significance of breast feeding and the variations in its techniques for specific developmental conflicts.

3. Fries, Margaret E. *Psychosomatic Relationships Between Mother and Infant.* Psychosomatic Med., 6: 159–162, 1944.

4. Spitz, René A. "Anaclitic Depression: An Inquiry into the Genesis of Psychiatric Conditions in Early Childhood." In *The Psychoanalytic Study of the Child,* Vol. II, pp. 313–342. Internat. Univ. Press, New York, 1947.

5. Benedek, Therese, and Boris B. Rubenstein. *The Sexual Cycle in Women: The Relation Between Ovarian Function and Psychodynamic Processes.* Psychosomatic Med. Monogs., Vol. III, Nos. 1 and 2. National Research Council, Washington, D.C., 1942.

6. Deutsch, Helene. *The Psychology of Women: A Psychoanalytic Interpretation,* Vols. I and II. Grune & Stratton, New York, 1944, 1945.

7. Alexander, Franz. *Psychoanalysis Revised.* Psa. Quart., 9: 1, 1940.

8. Benedek, Therese. *Adaptation to Reality in Early Infancy.* Ibid., 7: 200–215, 1938.

9. French, Thomas M. *The Integration of Social Behavior.* Ibid., 14: 159–165, 1945.

10. Spitz, René A. "Hospitalism: An Inquiry into the Genesis of Psychiatric Conditions in Early Childhood." In *The Psychoanalytic Study of the Child,* Vol. I, 1945, pp. 113–117.

———. "Hospitalism: A Follow-up Report." Ibid., Vol. II, 1947, pp. 53–74.

11. Gesell, Arnold, and Frances M. Ilg. *Infant and Child in the Culture of Today.* Harper, New York, 1943.

12. Peiper, Albrecht. *Die Krampfbereitschaft des Saüglings.* Jahrbuch fuer Kinderheilkunde, 125: 194, 1929.

13. Klein, Melanie. *The Psycho-Analysis of Children.* Norton, New York, 1932.

14. Rado, Sandor. *The Psychical Effects of Intoxification: Attempt at a Psychoanalytical Theory of Drug-Addiction.* Internat. J. Psa., 9:301–317, 1928.

Fenichel, Otto. *Fruehe Entwicklungsstadien des Ichs.* Imago, 23: 243–269, 1937.

DISCUSSION

The discussion of this brief clinical paper requires further elaboration of the concepts implied in its material because of their general significance for psychoanalytic theory. One of these concepts is "primary narcissism," which has never been clarified; the other is "regression," presented here for the first time as a factor in the processes of growth and development.

Since this paper was published, the concept of "emotional symbiosis" as an unconscious, nonverbal communication between mother and child has often been described and extensively investigated in the normal course of infancy and its various psychobiologic deviations. Generally, it was related to Freud's concept of "primary narcissism"

(1914).[1] My conceptualization of symbiosis, however, is based on a concept of primary narcissism which differs from the various definitions formulated by Freud. It is derived from the psychodynamic processes accompanying ovulation and pregnancy. The emotional state of the postpartum period is the consequence and continuation of the psychology of pregnancy.

It may appear irrelevant to this discussion to mention the reluctance of psychoanalysts to consider physiologic processes as motivating factors in problems under psychoanalytic investigation.[2] Because of this attitude basic assumptions and theories of psychoanalysis may come into disregard, others may remain uninvestigated, untested, forgotten, thus hampering the development of our science.[3] One of those unclarified concepts is Freud's concept of primary narcissism. James Strachey in Appendix B to "The Ego and the Id" surveyed Freud's definitions under the title "The Great Reservoir of Libido."[4] Not all the statements cited will be repeated here, but enough to point out what appears (to me) the probable source of the obscurity.

In the third edition of "Three Essays," Freud said: "Narcissistic or ego libido seems to be the great reservoir from which the object-cathexes are sent out and into which they are withdrawn once more; the narcissistic libidinal cathexis of the ego is the original state of things. . . ."[5] In the paper "On Narcissism, an Introduction" (1914) he wrote, "Thus we form the idea of there being an original libidinal cathexis of the ego, from which some is later given off to objects, but which fundamentally persists and is related to the object-cathexis. . . ."[6] In "Beyond the Pleasure Principle" (1920) Freud said, "Psychoanalysis . . . came to the conclusion that the ego is the true and original reservoir of libido, and that it is only from that reservoir that libido is extended on to objects."[7]

In "The Ego and the Id" (1923) comes the change: "At the very beginning all the libido is accumulated in the id while the ego is still in process of formation or still feeble. . . . The narcissism of the ego is thus a secondary one which has been withdrawn from objects."[8] In his encyclopedia article (1923) he also states, "Now that we have distinguished between the ego and the id, we must recognize the id as the great reservoir of libido. . . ."[9] This position appears consistent with Freud's theory, according to which libido is psychic energy originating in instinctual drives which, being on the border between the organic and the psychic, primarily belong to the id. Yet in his "Autobiographical Study" (1925) Freud again said, "All through the subject's life his ego remains the great reservoir of his libido, from which object-cathexes are sent out and into which the libido can stream back again from the objects."[10]

After all these quotations it can be easily understood that the statement in the "Outline of Psycho-Analysis" (1940) appeared clarifying and misleading at the same time. There Freud stated, "All that we know about it [libido] relates to the ego, in which at first the whole available quota of libido is stored up. We call this state absolute, *primary narcissism*. It lasts till the ego begins to cathect the ideas of objects with libido to transform narcissistic libido into object-libido."[11] Since we assumed that for the newborn his need and the need-gratifying mother are not yet differentiated, I assumed that the above definition of primary narcissism meant that the mother-child unit represents the "great reservoir of libido," of primary narcissism. I am now certain that Freud did not mean that; yet his oft-repeated metaphor of libido, "just as the pseudopodia of an amoeba . . ." reaches out and cathects the object, seemed to confirm that unity. The ". . . facility with which it [libido] passes from one object to another"[12] certainly characterizes the communication between mother and newborn. This idea favored my wish that there be agreement between Freud's concept of primary narcissism and mine. Since the infant by himself cannot be "the great reservoir of libido" it must then be the mother-child unit from which the infant will become differentiated through the growth process when the mother becomes an object outside the self of the child.

Investigation of the sexual cycle made me aware of the qualitative and comparatively "quantitative" changes in the libidinal states of women; the abundance of libidinous feelings during normal pregnancy and in the healthy, lactating woman made me cognizant of what Alexander termed "surplus energy." On this basis Freud's concept of the "great reservoir of libido," i.e., primary narcissism that maintains pregnancy and postpartum symbiosis, appeared not in need of further elaboration.

In his last definition of primary narcissism (quoted above) Freud did not speak of ego libido and object libido since these belong to the same integrating psychic energy, libido. He considered primary narcissism the amount of available libido. This was a new way of putting it. To me it implied that libido is not a given quantity but changes with growth and in response to need. At the time I was struggling with the conceptualization of my observations on pregnant and lactating women, Freud's statement echoed the feeling-tone of "mother-infant symbiosis."

I cannot attempt to reconcile the inconsistencies in Freud's definitions. Indeed, the term "primary narcissism" as descriptive of the undifferentiated phase of infancy is unsatisfactory for many reasons. Jacobson arrives at the conclusion that one may be compelled "to dispose of the concept of . . . primary narcissism."[13] I would agree so long as authors understand as primary narcissism the libido localized in the not yet differentiated psychic system of the newborn.

My concept of primary narcissism is derived from the observable physical and mental states of well-being which accompany biologic growth, such as ovulation, and from the emotional states of healthy pregnant and lactating women. According to this, primary narcissism refers to free, not yet object-bound libido which, produced by physiologic processes, supplies with energy the psychologic process of growth and adaptation. Even if the function of primary narcissism were in the self-service of the organism and in this sense "narcissistic" (as Freud's definition indicates in his paper "On Narcissism"), it becomes necessarily object-related, since the "object-mother" is a part of the instinctual system of the infant.

This concept of primary narcissism is an extension of the first instinct theory of Freud. It defines libido as a quantitatively variable force that has a somatic source from which it streams to the mental apparatus, and *in this process it is transformed to become psychic energy*. This addition is implied by Freud; it appears necessary, however, to make it explicit since the somatic origin of psychic energy is often overlooked. It is Franz Alexander's concept of surplus energy that might reconcile the difference which besets various aspects of psychoanalytic theory concerning "primary instinctual energy" and "purely psychic energy."[14]

Alexander saw in Freud's instinct theories a direct avenue to the understanding of growth, not only from birth to sexual maturity, but beyond this, ". . . as growth overstepping the limits of the individual, in reproduction (in the propagative function)."[15] His "vector concept" was an attempt to provide a broad conceptual basis for his psychosomatic investigations. Although it did not include problems of the reproductive functions, the vector concept led to his hypothesis of "surplus energy."[16] This concept for Alexander was what I referred to earlier as an "experiential concept." Positive metabolic balance is a condition of growth; it produces vital energy that directs the extraversion of libido to objects in healthy infants, energizes the play of children and the work of adults; it motivates sexuality and the reproductive function and also the sublime creative processes that man is capable of. Alexander's surplus energy refers to and, in some respects, explains the source of that "quantitatively variable force" that can be considered primary narcissism so long as it is not applied in its object-directed manifestations. The difference between Freud's concept of primary narcissism and Alexander's of surplus energy is that the former is a potential localized within the infant, while the latter refers to ongoing physiologic processes and their psychic accompaniments.

Investigation of the monthly repetition of the ovulative cycle and the psychobiology of pregnancy and lactation gives evidence of the surplus energy, the unbound libido, defined by the term primary narcissism. The fount of this energy is in the mother. Primary narcissism in the infant can be understood only as complete inward-directedness, the absolute receptivity of the newborn. Yet the reciprocal processes between mother and infant soon show signs of object-directedness in the infant. In the mother the surplus energy maintains the libidinous state of lactation which transcends the mother's body and encompasses her infant. The infant, suckling on the breast, stimulates the mother's libido; the manifestation of the infant's well-being motivates libidinal responses in the mother. Thus the emotional symbiosis is refueled in the mother by the thriving infant; in time the infant perceives the gratification provided by the mother as coming from outside his own body. Thus symbiosis evolves to a reciprocal object-relationship between mother and child.

Not independent from problems of primary narcissism and the procreative psychology of women is the problem of regression. The old concept of psychoanalysis is placed in another relief by the investigation of the psychophysiology of the procreative function. The concept of regression refers to the unconscious process by which a higher level of psychic integration reverts to a lower level of integration, to an earlier phase of development. The term regression usually refers to the incipient phase of a pathologic process. Kris's observations of the creative process led him to the discovery that regression induces creative processes, and he made the formulation that such regressions are "in the service of the ego."[17] His extensive exploration of the creative process is topically far from psychobiologic investigations, yet it shows on the psychologic level what occurs also in the biologic processes of growth.

Usually we evaluate psychosexual maturity on the basis of the integration of genital sexuality with the object-relatedness of the individual. The highest level of genital integration in women occurs at the peak of the hormonal cycle, at the time of ovulation. Yet a "deep-rooted passivity" and a specific tendency toward introversion accompany that physiologic state. Here we have an example of the most intense hormonal stimulation activating a psychodynamic process which appears regressive if considered (as is customary) from the viewpoint of ego-object relationship; the libido is narcissistic, self-centered. Ovulation, the preparation for conception, is truly in the service of the species. During the postovulative phase of the cycle, the woman's receptive needs are increasing. From the point of view of the developmental history of the individual, these tendencies relate to the oral phase; thus, from the point of view of the id, they are regressive needs; yet the ego and id respond to them with preparation for the heavy tasks of motherhood. Normally, the ego is highly integrated during this phase of the cycle.

It has taken a long time for psychoanalysts to generalize from the psychosomatic processes to psychoanalytic theory and conclude from observation of the psychic concomitants of physiologic growth that regression is part and parcel of physiologic growth.

Being aware of the regression in both physiologic and psychologic growth processes, I followed with deep satisfaction Anna Freud's publications in the years 1963–1965 in which she discussed regression as a principle of mental development. She states, "It is only the recognition of both movements, progressive and regressive ones and the interactions between them, that leads to a satisfactory explanation of the happening on the developmental lines."[18] This is even more true of the processes of the procreative function. For the crossing of the lines occurs not only between progression and regression, but also between the ego and the id. Regression takes place only in the service of the ego, but one might say the ego is in the service of the id when the id is serving the survival of the species.

NOTES

1. Freud, S., "On Narcissism, An Introduction" (1914), *Std. Ed.*, XIV, 69–102.
2. In the therapeutic analysis of psychosomatic cases those factors might be considered, but they are rarely integrated into the whole of psychoanalytic theory.
3. In his major works on instinct theory, "Three Essays on the Theory of Sexuality" (1905) and "Beyond the Pleasure Principle" (1920), Freud explicitly expressed his hope that biology would give the answers to riddles that psychoanalysis had not solved.
4. Strachey, J., "Appendix B, The Ego and the Id, The Great Reservoir of Libido," *Std. Ed.*, XIX, 63–66.
5. Freud, S., "Three Essays on the Theory of Sexuality" (1905), *Std. Ed.*, VII, 218.
6. Freud, S., "On Narcissism, An Introduction" (1914), *Std. Ed.*, XIV, 75.
7. Freud, S., "Beyond the Pleasure Principle" (1920), *Std. Ed.*, XVIII, 51.
8. Freud, S., "The Ego and the Id" (1923), *Std. Ed.*, XIX, 46.
9. Freud, S., "Two Encyclopedia Articles" (1923), *Std. Ed.*, XVIII, 257.
10. Freud, S., "Autobiographical Study" (1925), *Std. Ed.*, XX, 56.
11. Freud, S., "An Outline of Psychoanalysis" (1940), *Std. Ed.*, XXIII, 150.
12. Ibid., p. 151.
13. Jacobson, E., "The Self and the Object World" (1954), *Psychoanalytic Study of the Child,* IX, 83.
14. Rosenblatt, A. D., and Thickstun, J. T., "A Study of the Concept of Psychic Energy" (1970), *Int. J. Psycho-Anal.,* LI, 265–278.
15. Alexander, F., "Psychoanalysis Revised," *Psychoanalytic Quart.,* IX (1940), 1–36. Reprinted in *The Scope of Psychoanalysis* (New York, Basic Books, 1961).
16. Alexander, F., *Fundamentals of Psychoanalysis* (New York, W. W. Norton, 1948).
17. Kris, E., "The Psychology of Caricature" (1935), in *Psycho-*

analytic Explorations in Art (New York, International Universities Press, 1952), pp. 173–188.

18. Freud, A., "Regression as a Principle in Mental Development," *Bul. Menninger Clinic,* XXVII (1963), 127. This paper is preliminary to her extensive study, *Normality and Pathology in Childhood* (New York, International Universities Press, 1965).

9. Psychobiological Aspects
of Mothering

INTRODUCTION

The following paper represents, not in chronological order but in content, a continuation of the study of the "emotional symbiosis" (1949). When I was asked to participate in a panel discussion which dealt with the "Disturbances of Mothering," I wished to emphasize mothering as an innate, biologically preordered process and thus to give a broader basis for orientation regarding its disturbances. The effects of cultural factors upon genuine motherliness and mothering behavior have to be evaluated with regard to specific clinical problems such as psychosomatic infertility and other conditions.

PSYCHOBIOLOGICAL ASPECTS
OF MOTHERING[1]

Mothering—the suckling, feeding, succoring of the young—is a complex behavior pattern; its motivation is innate and regulated by hormones. The pattern of maternal behavior is rigidly set and is characteristic of the species throughout the animal kingdom. When we observe the female taking care of her young, we assume by empathy that there is a strong instinctual force which makes the female behave in a "motherly" way. She is patient and attentive; she seems to be tender, vigilant and discerning; she is also active and pugnaciously aggressive if necessity arises. All these attitudes which appear as results of a "higher knowledge" are consequences and manifestations of the end phase of the reproductive cycle. When this phase is over, the female will let her young go and will get ready for the next series of her reproductive functions. In the human female, the physiologic processes

276

which regulate maternal behavior are disguised by the complex super-structure of cultural patterns which make for variations in overt and covert individual attitudes; indeed, they often interfere with and destroy what nature has carefully prepared to secure the survival of the species. Yet the psychodynamic processes of motherliness and its pathology can best be understood in terms of the psychophysiologic integration of the personality.

Growth, neurophysiologic maturation, and psychosexual development are intrinsically interwoven processes. The propagative function is but a specific phase of growth in the individual organism. Thus pregnancy and motherhood represent a phase of organic growth and of psychosexual development inherent in the female constitution. The master gland, the anterior lobe of the pituitary, secretes the hormones which regulate metabolism and growth as well as the propagative function, lactation and maternal behavior.

In reference to the human female, I begin with a general statement on which I wish to elaborate: *the psychodynamic tendencies which motivate maternal behavior—the wish to feed, to succor the infant—originate in the alimentary (symbiotic) relationship with the mother which she as an infant has experienced with her own mother.*

We are all but a link in the chain of generations. This truism, besides all the problems which are implied, poses the question of where to begin the discussion of the psychodynamic development of motherliness —with the child or with the mother?

In a previous publication[2] I referred to the dynamic interaction between mother and child as a symbiotic unit. *The term symbiosis signifies a continual reciprocal interaction between mother and child.* The psychodynamic process of this two-way communication is oral, or alimentary, for both the child and the mother.

The term "alimentation" here comprises all aspects of succoring. From the child's point of view, we refer to them as his "dependent needs." The psychologic processes which evolve on account of the child's dependent relationship to the mother have been well studied. In the mother, the term indicates two basic phenomena of motherhood. One implies the active, giving, succoring tendency with which the mother responds to her child and satisfies his needs; the other comprises the physiologic and emotional manifestations of the enhanced "alimentary"—i.e., passive-receptive and retentive—tendencies of the mother. In her actions of motherliness, each woman's personality expresses the integration of these originally opposing tendencies. The integration of motherliness is the result of learning and physiologic maturation.

In the early phase of development, the physiologic and psychologic aspects of living can hardly be differentiated. *Alimentation* is the central function of that period which, while it supplies the energy for physical growth, leads to the differentiation between the feeding organism (the child) and the food-supplying mother. What psychoanalysis terms the *oral phase of development* signifies the psychic representations of the gratification and frustration connected with alimentation. They also include the sensations, pleasurable or painful, which originate in the functions of the growing organism. These processes are the same in infants of either sex; boys and girls begin their development as individuals through identification with the mother. Soon, however, the femaleness of the little girl will be obvious in her behavior. Besides her flirtatious interest in the other sex, her play with dolls reveals the "little mother." Usually we assume that the identification with the mother motivates her behavior. Boys, however, on the basis of identification with the mother, do not show the same skill with dolls; they do not fantasy about pregnancy in the same way. The little girl's actions, facial expressions, and her inventiveness often express a coordination of motherly attitudes which appear more motherly than the child experienced with her mother, or, as some of my observations show, than the same girl is able to experience when she becomes a mother herself. Thus it seems that the play with dolls is not just imitation; nor is it just identification with the mother. It is more than these; it expresses a need which originates in a primary, instinctual anlage which directs the child's fantasies toward a future goal of maturation in motherliness. The play with dolls is given up usually before the ovarian function becomes active at puberty, taking over the physiologic regulation of the emotional preparation for motherhood.

The psychobiologic symbiosis of pregnancy and lactation has been discussed. (See Chapter 8, this volume.) In order to elucidate the basic emotional attitude of motherhood in relation to the practical tasks of mothering, I differentiate the terms, *mothering* and *motherliness*. "Mothering" refers to the many active and practical attitudes necessary to take care of the offspring and guide its maturation and primary learning; "motherliness" is the characteristic quality of woman's personality which supplies the emotional energy for maintaining the tasks of mothering. Motherliness is the result of sublimation achieved through the cyclic repetition of the preparation for motherhood as well as through the metabolic and emotional upheavals involved in the experience of motherhood. But motherliness is not a function of childbearing alone. There are mothers of many children who do not seem "motherly," and there are childless women who, unperturbed by the physiologic and emotional stresses of motherhood, demonstrate exquisite motherliness.

The complex maturational process toward motherliness can also be expressed as a change of the instinctual tendency of giving and taking from a passive to an active direction. In the communication between infant (subject) and mother (environment), the infant is passive. His dominant tendency is *to be fed,* to receive. During maturation the need to be fed changes to an active tendency, *the need to feed.* It is an oscillating process in which the dominant tendency changes from passive to active. While the girl is growing up and her ego is learning the techniques and attitudes of giving, her ego ideal becomes the representation of the aspiration to feed, to be a mother, a good mother, probably even a "perfect mother." (The ego ideal of the adult man, although to a lesser degree on a biological level and to a greater degree on a sociological level, includes the aspiration to be a father, a provider.)

In each phase of motherhood, or even in each act of mothering, we might differentiate two levels of motivation as well as of action. One is dominated by the emotional manifestations of passive receptive tendencies; they accompany the processes through which the metabolic and emotional energy is stored to be used for the sake of the child. The other, more accessible to consciousness, activates the loving, giving, succoring activities of mothering. In simple societies, the biological and the ego aspirations of the woman are easily integrated in her ego ideal. Our culture, however, conveys to the woman the active, extraverted, in some sense "masculine" ego ideal of our civilization. This is in conflict with the passive tendencies inherent in the propagative function. Indeed, the modern woman in her ego ideal has to integrate these opposing goals of her personality. The dominant factor in the ego ideal is the one which, rooted in biological functions and developed through identification with the mother, approaches its fulfillment through motherhood. Our population statistics show that opportunity for work and career has not diminished but rather increased the urge for fulfillment in motherhood. But the personality organization of the modern woman, through integrating masculine aspirations and value systems, acquires a strict superego. Consequently, women may respond with guilt reactions to the biological regression of motherhood. Many women cannot permit themselves to be passive; they repress their dependent needs and overcompensate for them, sometimes to exhaustion. Thus they deplete the source of their motherliness. After the child is born and mothering becomes a continual task, these women suffer from guilt reactions if they sense any deviation from the required standards of motherliness. As if the superego were standing guard over her capacity to be a mother, such a woman responds with anxiety and with frustration to any diminished ability to give, to live up to her biological need for motherhood and to be motherly.

I want to repeat and emphasize that the psychodynamic processes which interfere with the undisturbed evolution of motherhood originate in two continually interacting sources, namely, in biology and in culture.

Cultural factors affect and complicate the biological processes of motherhood in two major ways: (1) by changing the aims and aspirations of women, thus changing the interpersonal relationship between husband and wife; and (2) by changing the patterns of child care and thus influencing the interpersonal relationship between mother and child.

The dynamic processes of motherhood reflect the metabolic and emotional challenge which this biological function represents and at the same time they explain its inherent psychological dangers. As stated before, the physiological processes of the lutein phase of the cycle, of pregnancy and of lactation find their psychodynamic expression in the increased manifestations of the receptive tendencies. Indeed, it is easy to describe the psychological attitudes which accompany women's procreative function in terms of the oral-dependent, "alimentary" phase of development. For the healthy woman the introversion and the biological regression of the lutein phase, pregnancy and lactation, serve as a well to replenish her energies. The same processes, however, represent a danger to those who, for whatever reasons, have not reached that level of ego integration which is necessary to withstand the regressive processes of the reproductive functions.

It is a well-established concept of psychoanalysis that regression to the oral-receptive (alimentary) phase of development is the psychodynamic constellation of depression. The psychopathology of the lutein phase as well as of pregnancy and the postpartum period can be characterized as depressive emotional states of varying intensity and of different symptomatic reactions. The introversion of libido results in a sense of loss and emptiness, in an emotional withdrawal from the child. If the attempts to reestablish the continuity of the sensation of oneness with the child seem to fail, the mother becomes a victim of a regressive tailspin. The onrushing metabolic processes activate a regression of the ego. This recharges the deepest emotional conflicts; instead of reactivating the pleasurable sensations of growth as experienced in infancy and in adolescence, it mobilizes the anxieties and pains of the oral-dependent phase and with it the conflicts of mother identification. The fear of inability to mother her child is expressed in the mother's "rejection" of the child. And even if the withdrawal is not severe, the insecurity and helplessness of the mother convey to her child the conflicts which she once incorporated in her relationship to her own mother. Thus the psychodynamic processes which make possible the evolution of motherliness are the same as those which may bring about the depressive emotional reactions in the mother and subsequently, through the mother's behavior, in the child as well.[3]

The banal statement that we are all but a link in the chain of generations becomes more meaningful as we learn to evaluate the consequences of the symbiosis between mother and child.

NOTES

1. Originally presented at the 1955 Annual Meeting of the American Orthopsychiatric Association in a session "Disturbances of Mothering: Causal Factors and Problems of Therapy." Published in *The American Journal of Orthopsychiatry*, XXVI, no. 2 (1956), 272–278. Revised for this volume.

2. Benedek, T., "The Psychosomatic Implications of the Primary Unit: Mother-Child," *Am. J. Orthopsychiatry*, XIX (1949), 642–654. (Chapter 8, this volume.)

3. Benedek, T., "Toward the Biology of the Depressive Constellation," *J. Am. Psychoanalytic Assn.*, IV (1956), 389–427. (Chapter 14, in this volume.)

DISCUSSION

To enliven the discussion, I return to the meeting in which my presentation was followed by a stimulating paper of Dr. Herbert G. Birch, an ethologist, who spoke of the maturation of mothering behavior in animals. Since maturation is necessary and depends on environmental factors such as the mother animal's behavior toward her offspring, he contradicted the assumption that the motivation of the complex behavior pattern of mothering is "innate." My emphasis on this small difference would be quibbling if Dr. Birch's presentation had not illustrated the basic uniformity of maturational patterns of mothering behavior throughout the evolutionary scale of mammals. He presented beautiful material to show that "Animal mothering involves an ordered sequence of events which admirably promotes under normal conditions the appearance and healthy development of offspring."[1] Whether ethologists experiment on rats or on monkeys, it has been demonstrated by many investigators that mothering behavior, the care of the offspring, is the result of a maturational process, the potential for which is invested in the newborn through the manipulation of the mother animal from the time of parturition through the period of lactation, i.e., through the period of the dependence of the litter. Indeed, maternal behavior is not innate, does not spring forth as a whole, but it is the consequence of those ordered events which constitute an inherent characteristic of the species. Dr. Birch went further and gave examples to illustrate the assumption that ". . . in mammalian organisms the relation of the mother to her offspring may well be an extension of her acquired relation to herself."[2] His discussion indicates that mother animals not only repeat actively the mothering behavior that they experienced passively, but they also transfer to their offspring the pleasurable experiences that they practice on their own body, such as licking and grooming, which belong to the ordered events of the maturational process toward motherhood.

To emphasize the contrast between human and animal mothering, we must keep in mind how few of those ordered events are prerequisites for the normal course of the reproductive cycle in animals. The biologic processes of the maturation of mothering in the human female are analogous to those of other animals, but they are not so distinctly definable since the maturation processes toward motherhood in the child

282 PSYCHOANALYTIC INVESTIGATIONS

as well as the mothering behavior in the adult admit many variations. In human beings, instinctual needs and their gratifications may change according to motivations and substitutions of the "object," i.e., the means of gratification.[3] They prepare not only the physiologic maturation of the female child but also her psychologic development toward motherhood and motherliness.

This development is lengthy; beginning with the emotional symbiosis between the infant girl and her mother, it progresses after puberty by monthly repetitions of the hormonal cycle until it is completed in motherhood, actually through the mothering of her own child. Although this complicated developmental process has many pitfalls, the topic of this discussion is not the genetic course of development but the conflict between id and ego tendencies activated by the physiology of the reproductive function itself. Since an intensification of receptive-retentive tendencies is the psychodynamic substratum of this process of many phases, the biologically normal regression is in conflict with those tendencies of the personality which oppose the regression. We know many manifest reasons for a girl's fear of becoming a woman.[4] We know many conscious reasons and unconscious motivations which bring about realistic and/or psychologic defenses that may suppress the wish for conception or complicate the course of pregnancy and may turn motherhood and mothering into a terrifying experience.

In the discussion of the paper on symbiosis, I mentioned only the positive aspects of the biologic regression which, by enhancing the receptive and retentive needs of the mother, supplies the surplus energy for her motherliness. The reproductive processes themselves may mobilize regression which, reviving (recathecting) fixated developmental conflicts, bring about a pathogenic regression. The two kinds of regression are dynamically related. The biologic regression exerts stress upon the psychoeconomic balance of the woman; the disequilibrium causes further regression which reactivates developmental conflicts, causing psychosomatic symptoms. Many of these symptoms, such as sleeplessness, undue fatigue, and exhaustion, disappear when the mother is relieved of the burdens of child care. The evolving object relationship with the developing infant helps to reestablish the emotional balance of the mother. Only if severe anxiety necessitates a continuing defensive struggle of the ego against the normally gratifying tasks of mothering does the mother-child relationship turn into a pathogenic interaction.

NOTES

1. Birch, H. G., "Sources of Order in the Maternal Behavior of Animals," *J. Am. Orthopsych. Assn.,* XXVI, no. 2 (1956), 279.

2. Ibid., p. 283. I cannot omit mentioning the sense of gratification that psychoanalysts feel when they find analogies in animal behavior of processes

they conceptualize on the basis of psychoanalytic theory. On the other hand, ethologists are often surprised to find that what they elicited through experiments on lowly creatures such as rats is not completely alien to us and can be discovered by psychoanalytic investigation. Such surprises have been diminishing during the last ten to fifteen years because of the respect that investigators feel for each other's fields.

3. See Chapter 15, this volume, "On the Organization of the Reproductive Drive."

4. Rheingold, J. C., *The Fear of Being a Woman* (New York, Grune & Stratton, 1964).

10. Problems of Infertility

INTRODUCTION

Infertility was a puzzling problem long before medicine became interested in it. There were many instances in which infertile women seemed to become fertile miraculously. Just as there is a legendary literature on this subject, there are also clinical reports testifying that women not infrequently became pregnant after they had made medical appointments to be treated for their infertility, before the treatment actually began.[1] I have had two such cases among my relatively small number of patients. Taking the large number of cases cited in the literature, the frequency of such chance occurrences justifies the assumption that many infertile women look for medical help when their fear of becoming mothers has already lifted, or that women need but little reassurance to overcome their fear.

It is not our task to review the extensive literature on the subject of infertility. There are only a few definitely known reasons for "absolute infertility," but reasons for relative infertility are manifold. What are the causes that hinder ovulation or bring about tubal spasms which interfere with conception? It is generally assumed that, besides delayed physiologic maturation that might change with time and sexual experience, emotional factors are responsible for psychophysiologic infertility. It is assumed that emotional factors may play a role in infertility even when some organic pathology is present.[2] Knowing the complex maturational processes of the female reproductive function and the many interpersonal events that may influence it, it is surprising that functional infertility is rather rare and often only a transient symptom.

Investigating the factors which bring about such organismic protection of the self, we first have to take into account the constitutionally given differences in the fertility rates of women. It would be extremely difficult if not impossible to establish a complementary series of fertility rates from one extreme to the other. The variables are too many. They vary in the same individual under the influence of interpersonal factors such as the sexual potency and/or the reproductive potential of the mate. Omitting some well defined variables, one might construct an abstract series: at one end would be the absolutely fertile woman who conceives each time she is exposed; on the other end the "absolutely infertile" woman who, on the basis of constitutional and developmental factors, is unable to conceive, although no hormonal or organic pathology can be diagnosed. There is also the woman whose fertility potential is so low that any kind of emotional disturbance may inhibit conception or effect interruption of the pregnancy. Yet clinical experience shows that at any point inside these extremes, normal pregnancies occur and happy motherhood may result.

The second general category of the causative factors of psychophysiologic infertility lies in the developmental history of the woman and the third in the cultural influences that interact with the former factors in the personality organization of the woman. The first paper of this chapter emphasizes this last point.

The second paper is a clinical investigation undertaken to evaluate intrapsychic and interpersonal factors which might play a role in fertility. It is known that artificial insemination in animals results in pregnancy in 99 percent of single inseminations. In women, pregnancy by artificial insemination occurs on the average after three to twenty inseminations. Such defense against becoming pregnant after the woman has agreed to the procedure is noteworthy and requires investigation. We assumed that psychoanalytic investigation of women who were undergoing repeated artificial inseminations might reveal specific emotional factors which play a role in conception. The subjects of the investigation were women who, in spite of having normal ovulative hormonal cycles, had never conceived during many years of marriage; the husbands' sperm were inadequate. The investigation revealed a variety of intrapsychic and interpersonal factors which showed that infertility might be a "conjugal symptom."

About the time this paper was published, Westoff and Kiser expressed probably the same idea on the basis of similar observations. They said, "The woman's ability to conceive would depend on the psychosomatic balances both within and between the would-be parents. . . ."[3] This, of course, is a changeable balance and might diminish the fertility in women who are predisposed to infertility on the basis of anxiety and as a result of their developmental and marital conflicts.

NOTES

1. Buxton, C. L., and Southam, A. L., *Human Infertility* (New York, Hoeber, 1958) cited from Rheingold, J., *The Fear of Being a Woman* (New York, Grune & Stratton, 1964), p. 581.

2. Morris, T. A., and Sturgis, S. A., "Practical Aspects of Psychosomatic Sterility," *Clin. Obstetrics & Gynec.,* II (1959), 900.

3. Westoff, C. F., and Kiser, C. V., "Social and Psychological Factors Affecting Fertility. 21. An Empirical Re-Examination and Intercorrelation of Selected Hypothesis Factors," *Milbank Mem. Fund Quart.,* XXXI (1953), 421.

INFERTILITY AS A PSYCHOSOMATIC DEFENSE[1]
(1952)

In discussing pathologic processes we still like, in general, to distinguish between symptoms which originate in organic pathology and those in which an "emotional" or "psychic" pathogenic factor can be detected. Thus we adhere to a dichotomy which at the same time we intend to overcome. In a broader frame of reference any symptom represents specific manifestations of the adaptive processes. Since internal stresses can be reduced and/or exacerbation of stresses alleviated through symptom formation, any symptom may be considered an attempt to safeguard the organic-psychic equilibrium.

In this paper I wish to discuss this concept as it applies to *functional sterility,* namely, infertility which is considered here as a *somatic defense against the stresses of pregnancy and motherhood.*

It is "the way of the body," as the anthropologist Margaret Mead put it, "to grow, to learn and fulfill its biological purpose in procreation."[2] Although the infant's relationship to the mother is biologically determined, anthropologic studies point out the different ways in which unconscious, nonverbal communications are conveyed from mothers to children. When we accept the concept that such biologically determined identification with the mother is the source of later motherliness in the daughter, we have to admit the role which cultural patterns play in this process. Such identification evolves in natural simplicity in societies where daughters are exposed to the many pregnancies of their mothers, where they can watch mothers nursing, probably year after year, and thus grow up participating in motherly activities day after day. How different it is in our civilization where, even if daughters are exposed to the pregnancies of the mother, the experience is an unusual one, handled with great care and much intellectualization, where the daughter is more aware of the mother's wish to retain her figure than of a natural acceptance of her biologic role, as for example, her pleasure in breast feeding.

In general, cultural factors affect and complicate the biologic processes of motherhood in two ways: (1) by changing the aims and aspirations of women, thus also changing the interpersonal relationship between husband and wife, and (2) by changing the patterns of child care, thus changing the interpersonal relationship between mother and child.

This paper would become a book if I were to attempt to illustrate the psychologic processes by which cultural influences become incorporated in behavioral patterns of individuals. One can easily recall the many articles which describe types of women. We speak of "modern woman" as distinct from "Victorian woman," of the "American woman" as distinct from the "Chinese" or the "European woman." The types represent differences not only in many aspects of behavior but also in psychologic changes which become manifest in the attitudes toward childbearing.

The "type" is the result of a shift in the personality structure of large numbers of individuals, a shift which occurs through the psychosexual development. This shift implies a change in the relative significance of that aspect of the personality which represents cultural values (in psychoanalysis this is usually termed the ego-superego system) and that which represents biologic necessity. In other words, women incorporating the value system of a modern society may develop personalities with rigid ego defenses against their biologic needs. The conflicts which arise from this can be observed clinically, not only in the office of the psychiatrist, but also in the office of the gynecologist and even of the endocrinologist. An example of the special problems of infertility are women who, after having used contraceptives for many years in order "to have time" to achieve all that they want to achieve, are disappointed in their early or middle thirties when they have difficulty in becoming pregnant. The psychoanalytic observation of such women during their self-imposed infertility often reveals pent-up emotions directed toward motherhood and motherliness which receded unfulfilled with each menstruation.

It is the physiologic characteristic of woman that her propagative function requires an increase in the metabolic processes. These necessarily go hand in hand with an increase in *receptive tendencies,* the psychologic representation of the need for energy to supply growth. This indicates that the lutein phase of the cycle brings about a psychodynamic process resulting in emotional attitudes which can be considered regressive compared with the emotional attitudes of the same woman during the estrogen phase. It is to be emphasized that the change from the follicular to the lutein phase, and the lutein phase itself, do not necessarily indicate an emotional disturbance. On the manifest level of behavior, the woman's personality functions in continuity. It is the unconscious, the id, which reveals in the material for analysis the differences in the biologic impulses transmitted by the hormonal regulation. Many factors, originating in the development as well as in the current aspirations of a woman, account for the "noisy" reactions to the course of the ovarian cycle.

In our civilization, in which the active, extraverted, in a sense "masculine" aspects of personality represent the educational goal of women, the passive tendencies inherent in the propagative function may be experienced as a source of conflict, an opponent of the ego ideal. Thus many women struggle against the biologic need for motherhood and respond to its psychodynamic manifestations with defenses. From the psychiatric point of view, such defenses can be recognized both in character trends and in symptoms. Psychoanalytic investigations usually reveal their genetic roots in the developmental processes of infancy.

Infancy is the period during which the physiologic processes of growth are not yet differentiated or are least differentiated from the psychic processes, when the surfaces of physiologic and psychologic interactions are broadest, when, since barriers and isolations are not yet developed, these interactions occur at a quicker pace than they do later, in the more mature stages of organization. This warns us against considering infancy as a period of bliss and satisfaction and reminds us of its discomforts and pains. These might originate in the unreadiness of the vegetative system itself or they may be caused by deprivations imposed by the environment, primarily the mother. The vicious circle created by any one or a multitude of these factors may seriously impede satisfactory development during infancy. They may leave memory traces (organic and psychic) which may be revived by the maturational processes of puberty and, if not outgrown, become activated by pregnancy and the task of motherhood.

Ovulation, with the ensuing function of the corpus luteum, is that impulse to growth which mobilizes the "regressive" psychodynamic processes and then produces *surplus energy*. This is a source of emotional manifestation which represents a task for developmental integration. In cases of uncomplicated development, the intensification of the receptive tendencies recharges the psychodynamic manifestation of growth and revives its narcissistic pleasures as well as the positive gratifications of the dependent relationship to the mother. While this represents an adaptive task, it is mastered unconsciously without conflict, leading to the development of motherliness. In other cases the same, primarily normal, physiologic process recharges, through the intensification of the receptive tendencies, not only the pleasure but also in varying measure the pains, anxieties, and conflicts connected with the alimentation of the early dependent phase and the resulting conflicts with the mother. In these cases, the primarily physiologic regression activates conflicts which lead secondarily to pathologic manifestations; regression represents only another, albeit more severe, adaptive task. Even though many women succeed in resolving these conflicts during the maturational process, others bear the core of a danger within, to be reinforced if conception occurs or later on—during pregnancy or after parturition in the relationship to the child.

The psychodynamic processes of pregnancy and lactation reflect the positive aspect of the metabolic and emotional challenge which motherhood represents; at the same time they explain its dangers. The enhanced hormonal and metabolic processes which are necessary to maintain pregnancy as well as lactation find their psychodynamic expression in the increased manifestations of the receptive tendencies. They result in a positive metabolic balance which produces surplus energy. In her vegetative calmness the pregnant as well as the lactating mother enjoys her body, which abounds in libidinous feelings. This enhances her well-being and paves the way for her motherliness. Her dependent needs revived, she thrives on the solicitude of her environment. Indeed, it is easy to describe the psychologic attitude of pregnancy and lactation in terms of the oral-dependent phase of development. Her psychic energies having become self-centered, the emotional state of the pregnant and lactating woman appears regressed in comparison with the usual level of ego integration of the same woman. Yet, on biologic levels, this state represents growth and a new developmental phase in the woman's personality. For many women the biologic gratifications of pregnancy and lactation remain a continual temptation. In simple societies, women can give in to this urge naturally and without awareness, while in our civilization many women feel compelled to control the desire for motherhood and thus cause complications of its functions.

While for the healthy woman the introversion and seeming regression which accompany pregnancy and lactation serve as a well for replenishing her energies, the same processes represent a danger for those who, for whatever reasons, have not reached that level of psychosexual integration which is necessary for the evolution of the reproductive functions. The metabolic and psychic processes inherent in pregnancy, instead of reactivating the pleasurable sensations of growth as experienced in infancy and adolescence, mobilize the anxieties and pains of the oral-dependent phase and with it all the conflicts of mother identification. Thus, the onrushing metabolic processes of pregnancy recharge the deepest conflicts with such intense emotions that they overwhelm the ego and render it helpless in the face of the most significant task of the woman's life.

Infertility, if not caused by organic pathology, can be considered a *defense* against the dangers inherent in the procreative function. The term "defense" is defined as an unconscious function of the ego to protect the self—the total personality—against the dangers originating within the organism, in this case, the physiologic processes of the procreative functions. The psychic apparatus registers the responses to the physiologic processes continuously. Responding to the hormonal stimulation, the woman perceives her inner, psychic reactions to the task of motherhood. Through its monthly repetition she may, step by step, overcome her anxieties and absorb its conflicts. This is what happens in the course of normal maturation. Such a process involves the ego's function. It also prepares the woman for the great integrative task to be mastered when she experiences the passive tendencies and active functions connected with motherhood. It is different in those women who, perceiving the stimulations of the progesterone phase, are stirred by anxiety and recoil from this task. They respond to the preparation for pregnancy with an inner psychic realization of a danger which they are unable to face. Thus they "build up" their defenses. The psychic process by which this is achieved is *repression*.

Repression is the function of a relatively strong ego which has the capacity to maintain the repression, i.e., to keep the repressed from becoming conscious. Thus, after the conflicts regarding childbearing are repressed, the woman, free from anxiety, may even assert that she has an *unambivalent wish for motherhood*.

I do not believe that it is necessary to answer the question: Why do not all women respond in this "easy way" if they are afraid of childbearing? Why do some need to succumb to mental and physical illness? The choice is not free. In investigating the psychologic factors in any organic event, we arrive at a point where we shift the responsibility for a specific organic response to a primary, constitutional susceptibility to that symptom. Yet we do not do this hurriedly!

In comparing the woman who becomes infertile with the woman who becomes ill, we may wager a general answer: infertile women have a stronger ego than those who, overcome by anxiety, often have not been able to repress the conflict. There is a constitutional difference in ego strength for the mastery of conflicts by repression. This may sound like psychologic finesse rather than an explanation, but it is more than that.

Another discussion, that of the cultural influence upon motherliness, has been included in this paper in order to show that the ego of the modern woman is trained to have aspirations which are, or may be, in conflict with the propagative functions. It has been pointed out that such influences may modify the gonadal hormone production. This implies that either one or both aspects of the ovarian cycle may be affected. If the developmental conflict is such that it interferes with the heterosexual manifestation of the personality, the estrogen phase of the cycle may be impaired or even suppressed, inhibiting ovulation. If the mother-conflict is prevalent and the development toward motherhood is also inhibited, the progesterone phase of the cycle will appear as the starting point of a vicious circle in the gonadal and emotional processes. In a study of the processes leading to infertility in an individual, the conflicts, as revealed by the developmental history or even by the current dream and fantasy material, are not specific enough for evaluation of the pathogenesis and prognosis of the symptoms. For several reasons, the same developmental conflicts not only motivate a great variety of symptoms, but frustrations may cause regression which mobilizes a variation in the intensity of the same developmental conflicts.

As long as contraceptive practices did not interfere with the "facts of life," women more or less patiently or anxiously waited for conception. Now that exposure to conception has become a matter of decision, women, probably afraid that their contraceptive practices have caused irreparable harm, soon become anxious and seek help. If help is not forthcoming, the sense of guilt and frustration may mobilize the developmental conflicts related to childbearing. Thus women who come to the gynecologist or the psychiatrist for help because of infertility are usually in a depression. The severity of this depression and its genetic significance for the infertility, as well as its prognostic significance for the development of motherliness in the same woman during a future pregnancy, are not easily evaluated.

The therapy of infertility carries with it responsibility for the future development of the patient as well as the child. It is fortunate that more often than not the cure lies outside of medical practice, in maturation by experience. Such maturation may be stimulated, even relatively late in life, with improvement of the emotional adjustment and heterosexual practices between husband and wife. Adoption often brings about a "miracle"; the woman, having overcome her anxieties regarding a child by practical experience, may become fertile.

In treating the infertile woman and in dealing with her anxiety, frustration, and rage, we should not forget that the psychologic outcome of pregnancy can rarely be predicted, that women have a better chance to achieve completion of their physical and emotional maturation through motherhood than they have if motherhood is denied to them.

SUMMARY

All phases of the procreative function—the lutein phase of the sexual cycle, pregnancy, and lactation—represent stimulation toward growth. This biologic goal is achieved through intensification of the receptive and retentive tendencies. Accordingly, what appears as regression from the ego's point of view is an emotional manifestation accompanying the growth process. Yet, in each instance, it presents an adaptive task to the personality. Normally, the monthly repetition of these processes leads to maturation of the procreative functions and to the development of motherliness. If, however, physiologic regression mobilizes such severe infantile conflicts that they interfere with normal development, the unresolved conflicts present a psychic danger which may be reactivated during any phase of the procreative function.

The psychic perception of these processes indicates to the woman, in monthly repetition, the danger to which motherhood would expose her. She may then, step by step, build up psychic defenses against it. In susceptible individuals, this may lead to infertility. The interaction between the hormonal processes and the ego's defenses against conception is not a static equilibrium. Under the influence of a variety of experiences, functional sterility might prove to be a transitory, curable condition.

NOTES

1. Presented at the Eighth Annual Meeting of the American Society for the Study of Sterility, Chicago, Illinois, June 7, 1952. Published in *Fertility and Sterility,* III, no. 6 (1952), 527–537. (Revised for this publication.)

2. Mead, M., *Male and Female* (New York, William Morrow & Co., 1949).

SOME EMOTIONAL FACTORS IN INFERTILITY

With George C. Ham, M.D., Fred P. Robbins, M.D., and Boris B. Rubenstein, M.D.*

Functional sterility as a diagnosis refers to the somatic effects of psychodynamic factors resulting in a more or less persistent inhibition of the propagative function in individuals whose functional capacity for sexual intercourse is adequate. (5) Psychoanalytical studies of women often reveal data in regard to childbearing. Psychoanalytical studies of men, however, hardly touch on the problem of fertility, as if it were tacitly assumed that man's fertility, belonging to the realm of organic physiology, lies outside of the territory of psychological investigation. Even in this project, in which at the onset was assumed that the subjects

* From the Institute for Psychoanalysis, Chicago, Illinois.

Presented at the Annual Meeting of the American Psychosomatic Society, March 29, 1952, Chicago, Illinois.

We wish to express our gratitude to Helen V. McLean, M.D., for her encouraging interest in this project, for her participation in some of the discussions and dispositions about the subjects of this study. We also are indebted to Samuel D. Lipton, M.D., who made some of the case records available and participated in our discussions.

of our investigation were fertile women whose husbands were sterile, we did not plan an investigation of the emotional motivations of the infertility of these men. Our aim was to investigate the emotional factors which inhibit conception by artificial insemination at the time of ovulation in women whose wish for pregnancy and motherhood appears obvious. We hoped in this way to secure more concrete data about emotional factors which might inhibit or facilitate conception.

It is known that artificial insemination is a successful procedure in animals, resulting in pregnancy in more than 99 percent of single inseminations. The successful impregnation of women by artificial insemination, however, occurs only after three to twenty inseminations, or in from 4 percent to 30 percent of the attempts; the average number of such procedures before pregnancy is eight. These data include only those instances of artificial inseminations which were attempted during the presumptive fertile periods as determined by basal body temperatures, vaginal smears, changes in the cervical mucus, and in hormone excretion. Artificial insemination is not attempted until after three months of observation of the patient to determine whether or not she ovulates and develops a secretory endometrium premenstrually. It has been observed that following artificial insemination the first few times, women who had previously ovulated regularly failed to ovulate for varying lengths of time. To the psychoanalyst, it cannot be surprising that artificial insemination, a mechanized, "unnatural" technique, as a substitute for an action of intimacy and highly emotional gratification, is a traumatizing procedure; that it naturally leads to the inhibition of its own aim.

This study is limited to six cases; all of them were in treatment by one of the investigators* for varying lengths of time for the purpose of achieving pregnancy by artificial insemination. After several unsuccessful attempts, psychotherapy was recommended. There was no further selection of the cases in regard to indication and suitability for psychotherapy; no preliminary diagnostic studies were made. We expected to study relatively healthy women who would reveal easily the emotional factors which motivated them to submit to artificial insemination, and made them infertile at the same time. Altogether, we had the opportunity to analyze the recorded psychoanalytical material in correlation with the artificial insemination in twelve instances. In this study, as in many others in which the project requires carrying on psychoanalysis parallel with continued medical procedures, we encountered a methodological difficulty—that of keeping these patients in analysis. When the problem centers around motherhood as in this investigation, it is understandable that the woman prefers to select a procedure which, by its very method, demonstrates her willingness to be a self-sacrificing

* Boris B. Rubenstein, M.D.

mother, rather than to choose a therapy the technique of which questions her motivations and reveals her conflicts about motherhood. In conducting most of these cases, the psychoanalyst was willing to accept the attitude of the patient toward childbearing. Although we recognized that, in several cases, the wish for the child was a symptom rather than the manifestation of a normal biological tendency, we would not have felt justified in destroying the patient's illusion. Usually this was not in our hands. Each patient sought her own solution. The course and outcome of these cases therefore vary. Although they do not permit definite generalization, they are nevertheless instructive.

CASE NO. 1

The patient, a twenty-four-year-old woman, had been married four years. Her husband's sperm count was found to be low: 1.8 million, motility 15 percent. Artificial insemination with the husband's concentrated semen had been unsuccessful in eight attempts when psychotherapy was recommended. The patient accepted this with the rationalization that it might help her to relax during the artificial insemination. During psychotherapy, she had one artificial insemination. She interrupted psychotherapy after three weeks because she found it even more difficult than the artificial insemination.

The patient was a timid, childish-looking individual; she considered her marriage successful except that she had become increasingly depressed because her marriage was infertile. She was not aware of any conflicts. She accepted the mutual interdependence between her and her mother as "natural," although her mother was not eager for her to have a child because it would interfere with the relationship between them. In the first dream which she reported, she expressed her dependence on her mother.

> Dream:
> "I am excited and happy because Mother came to Chicago to visit me." (*Association:* "She was supposed to come in the fall, but she came in the spring.")

On the afternoon following the artificial insemination, she took a nap and dreamed about a relative who often asked her why she had not had a child.

> Dream:
> "In this dream this relative was telling me something about my father. I was saying, 'No, no.' I was crying, 'It cannot be true.' " (*Association:* "It's in connection with Dr. R. [artificial insemination]. It could not be that I am pregnant.")

The manifest level of the dream and her associations refer to her father. From this, one may infer that her protestation against having a child by the unnatural means of artificial insemination is equated, in her unconscious, with the repressed but now mobilized oedipal wish of having a child by her father.

This was the last session of her psychotherapy as well as her treatment by Dr. R. The two therapeutic situations together mobilized a conflict which threatened her to such a degree that she became unwilling to continue with artificial insemination. Under the influence of the impact which the therapy had on his wife, the husband consented to adoption. While they were waiting for the adoption proceedings, the husband underwent hormone therapy. By the time the adoption proceedings were completed, she had already conceived, normally, by her husband. Her pregnancy was uneventful.

CASE NO. 2

This patient is a highly intelligent, emotionally disturbed woman. At the age of thirty-eight, she married a passive, dependent man in his late forties. It was found that he had azoospermia. Artificial insemination with donor semen was begun in the third year of their marriage. She had ten artificial inseminations before psychotherapy and one during psychotherapy.

The patient had an extremely deprived childhood; however, she had been able to achieve an independent profession and be the "provider" for her inadequate husband. The psychotherapeutic interviews revealed that this was an "exhausted personality"; that, her ego strength declining, she was driven to regressive behavior. In spite of her sublimated motherliness, in this case the wish for pregnancy was used as a rationalization for substitute erotic gratification by means of artificial insemination as well as through psychotherapy. She was eager to exchange one form of therapy for the other; after the one artificial insemination during psychotherapy, she admitted that she was glad that she did not conceive. Further material and her preoccupation with the therapy indicated that her ego defenses might crumble rapidly and that a paranoid psychosis might follow. She was advised, therefore, to discontinue both therapies.

CASE NO. 3

The patient was a twenty-nine-year-old woman, married seven and a half years. She tried to become pregnant in the normal way for six years. Her husband, who had had his sperm count determined before marriage and was certain of his fertility and potency, was surprised to find on examination that he could be responsible for their infertility. His sperm count was 4.8 million with 60 percent motility.

The patient had four artificial inseminations with her husband's concentrated semen before psychotherapy began. During the necessary manipulations his potency diminished and he became resentful. Consequently the patient felt that the artificial insemination was endangering her marriage. She was in psychotherapy for a period of only four months in two separate phases. During each of these periods, she had one artificial insemination; after she interrupted psychotherapy, she had eight more inseminations by the last of which she conceived and aborted in the sixth week of pregnancy. After the abortion, she had one more insemination, after which she did not ovulate for several months. She remained in treatment with Dr. R. until she and her husband left Chicago.

The patient is the youngest of nine children and the last of her mother's fifteen pregnancies, six of which were lost by death or abortion. She stated bitterly, "Mother probably would have liked to lose more." Anxiety-laden dependence on the mother seemed to dominate her life and her symptoms. This patient, shy and inhibited, had never lived away from some member of her family, even after her marriage. She and her husband lived in her mother's small apartment; the mother did the cooking while the patient acted as a permanent "sitter" for her sister's children. Although she believed that it was her obligation to live with her mother in order to take care of her, actually she lived with her in childlike subservience. Her husband was apparently infantile enough to permit himself to be caught in the web of the interdependence between mother and daughter. The patient often expressed a sense of responsibility and guilt that she had caused her husband's sexual impotence and infertility and the "loss of his ego." Thus, in spite of his low sperm count and her normal ovulatory cycle, she considered herself responsible for his sterility.

During psychotherapy she had two inseminations. In the preovulative phase before the first of these inseminations she was anxious; she expressed her feeling that pregnancy is dangerous. In the analytical session which immediately followed the insemination, she stated in regard to the painfulness of both situations, "This is going to the fire from the frying pan." In the next session she reported happily that her temperature remained high: "Everything seems all right." She smiled as if in fantasy; then, in the course of her free associations, she discussed the negative attitudes which her mother as well as her in-laws might have against her child. She began the next session happily, "Everything revolves around the possibility that I may be pregnant. From this moment on, I don't feel sorry for myself." But as she continued with her associations, she said, "My child may be called a bastard." She was "torn between" her wish to be pregnant, "even this way," or to adopt a child, or to give up "beating my head against a stone wall."

Several months later, after the second insemination during therapy, she had a nightmare which she was able to describe only after she "reassured" herself by saying, "I don't believe in premonitions."

> *Dream:*
> "I got my period; it flowed black as coal; I called my husband and said to him, 'This is the end.' I knew I had cancer. My husband said, 'Go see the doctor.' I said, 'There is no one to help—it is too far gone.' "

She awoke with anxiety. "This dream was enough," she stated, "I would like to give up going to Dr. R. and just try not to think of getting pregnant."

She could not, however, abide by her own recommendation. It seemed that the artificial insemination as well as the idea of pregnancy became an obsessive preoccupation instead of sincerely goal-directed behavior. Soon after she had given up the psychotherapy, she continued with the artificial insemination, which succeeded in impregnating her in the eighth of these attempts. Her behavior during her short period of pregnancy was motivated by hypochrondriasis and superstitious anxieties. When, after so many attempts she really did conceive, she could not believe that it was true. She took her basal temperature twice daily; if it fell one or two tenths of a degree she called the doctor in a tense, anxious mood to ask what she should do to avoid abortion. At the same time she did not permit a pregnandiol test of the urine; she kept herself in constant suspense, being afraid "to find out more about the pregnancy." She had many nightmares about miscarriages, dead babies; she had a dream in which she and her baby were suffocating. Two hours after she began to bleed she passed a large clot which contained the fetus. When she was told this, she became quite euphoric; her rationalization of this mood change was that she had been relieved of her fear that she was definitely sterile and that she can now hope for more pregnancies.

The psychotherapy of this patient was too short to allow an evaluation of the role which the hostile dependence on her mother played in her anxiety regarding pregnancy. Her hypochondriasis, which centered around the fear of having cancer of the uterus, was expressed toward her mother who had so many pregnancies and still might be harmed by the effects of childbearing; this worry was closely related to her anxious expectation that she might be harmed, "eaten up" by pregnancy. This fear and her anxiety that she might be the cause of the death of someone, indicate that her conflicts in regard to childbearing are similar to the conflicts of those women who develop postpartum depressions.

CASE NO. 4

The patient, a thirty-year-old woman, had been married for seven years when she began artificial insemination after trying for four years to become pregnant in the normal way. The husband's sperm count was 6.9 million, showing 25 percent motility. Artificial insemination with the husband's concentrated semen was performed seven times before psychotherapy was advised. During the psychoanalysis, she had two more inseminations. At the time of the treatment, the husband appeared to be an externally overcorrect, compulsive personality who accepted artificial insemination as a "face-saving" device, but did not seem to be interested in having children.

This patient, too, was an unusually timid individual. Her history, however, revealed tomboyishness and overcompensative "masculine protest" attitudes. Her mother was a worrisome, overprotective person, not anxious for the patient to have a child. The mother's dependence on the patient was quite obvious; even more so was the patient's wish to use this as a rationalization of her denial of her own dependency. The psychoanalytical material revealed the patient's exhibitionistic tendencies as well as her preoccupation with heterosexual fantasies. These appear to be like the fantasies of a young adolescent; sexuality is forbidden, therefore she does not actively participate in it; she is the victim of it.

Analysis of the record indicates that this patient projected onto the analyst the role of the mother and this made it impossible for her to talk about artificial insemination, which represented an important sexual experience to her. She was afraid of the analysis because it might bring out whether or not she really wanted a baby, whether she loved her husband, etc. She developed symptoms such as dizziness and phobic reactions, which increased as the transference neurosis became more complex. The analyst (male), first representing the prohibitive mother, later became the heterosexual object as well. Her analysis was concentrated on the fear and denial of being sexually stimulated. This seemed to be characteristic material of the estrogen phase of her cycles. During the ovulative and progesterone phases of the cycle, the fears and complaints about artificial insemination as well as the fear that a child would interfere too much with her own ambitions prevailed in the material. The following dream, which occurred the night after Dr. R. diagnosed an anovulatory cycle, illustrates this point.

Dream:
"I was in a dramatic production. I had a song I was supposed to sing. I was supposed to memorize it; I never actually performed. I had to do the dishes after each performance. Everyone else went home. Finally I objected. Suddenly I had two babies at home. I could not get anyone to take care of them

so I could go to the performance. Finally I got a Negro man as sitter but I was too late to perform. I was annoyed and hurt because my mother was so uncooperative."

The dream shows the conflict between her exhibitionistic tendencies and childbearing; between her dependence on her mother and the obligations of her own motherhood. It also reveals the inferiority feelings, Cinderella attitudes, which she attributed to feminine sexuality; she is the one "who has to wash dishes," who has the depressing aftereffects of her sexual desire.

At this time she was preoccupied with the idea of giving up artificial insemination and of adopting a child. However, she was only half-hearted about it since "adoption as well as pregnancy would stop the analysis." At the time of the last insemination, her preovulative dreams revealed the wish to "run away" from sexuality as well as from the conflict of having a child by adoption. If the forthcoming insemination should fail, she was determined to choose the analysis rather than adoption. It did fail. She reported immediately afterwards her negativistic attitude before and during the procedure, her wish to "shake it off." The next day she reported great fatigue, increasing somatic and phobic symptoms. During the remaining part of this sexual cycle, she was increasingly depressed, irritable, and quarrelsome. In this mood, all plans for parenthood were abandoned and she settled down to work out her emotional problems in psychoanalysis.

CASE NO. 5

The patient, a thirty-four-year-old, active, attractive woman, began artificial insemination in the eighth year of her marriage. Her husband was a successful, outgoing, businessman. During the first two years of their marriage, the patient did not attempt to become pregnant because the husband's job involved much moving around. In the third year the patient felt homesick and depressed; she felt that she could overcome her depression if she had a child. For her each menstrual period was associated with acute disappointment and depression. The husband's sperm was tested repeatedly; at the time artificial insemination was advised, his sperm count was 3.1 million with 85 percent motility. The patient underwent eight inseminations before psychotherapy was recommended; during therapy she had two and later four more inseminations. After psychotherapy was interrupted, her husband underwent hormone therapy.

This patient was the third of four siblings; she smiled dreamily when asked about her mother, who was a self-sacrificing, long-suffering woman. The father was hard-working, impatient with the children, but he saw to it that they received an education. They were a poor but closely knit family. The patient was particularly close to her older sister.

She described herself as a tomboy. At her first menstruation she cried from anxiety. After the first scanty flow, she did not menstruate again until she was fourteen years old. She did not date much; she was afraid of men. She met her husband when she was twenty-four and married him when she was twenty-six years old. She was frigid and at the beginning she felt frightened by intercourse.

Although her behavior was that of an active, sensitive, headstrong woman, the "masculine protest" of this patient barely covered her masochistic and dependent character structure. She could recall no memory of her father until she was seven years of age. Since then, in spite of her appreciation of him, she remembers him as a crude person whose lack of understanding of her mother's needs made her feel that she should protect her mother against him.

Such an outcome of her early heterosexual (oedipal) development is in accordance with her fear of men in her adolescence, as well as with her deep reluctance to make such a final commitment as is represented by having children. Indeed, as she once imagined that her mother needed her protection, so she now was in need of her mother's protection. All patients in this series demonstrated an exaggerated interdependence between mother and daughter; this patient seemed to differ in that she did not seem to be afraid of her mother, did not complain about her, and admitted a greater dependence on her mother than the mother showed towards her. This patient suffered from psychosomatic symptoms. Besides dizziness and phobic reactions in crowded places, she complained of headaches and nausea; she had allergic reactions. These symptoms appeared around the time of her ovulation as well as in the premenstrual phase of her cycle. The following dreams occurred in the preovulative phase.

Dream:
(a) "I went home; my mother was standing in the garden. She was so happy to see me. She kissed me and kissed me."
(b) "Railroad station—my husband came out; it was pouring rain. I went back to get an umbrella."

Dream (a) illustrates the patient's wish to return to her mother and be loved by her; dream (b) expresses her wish to be protected from her husband = from sexuality = from insemination.

On the morning when the patient found that her temperature had dropped and knew that she should go to the hospital for artificial insemination, she fell asleep again and had the following dream:

Dream:
"My mother called me long distance. She asked me if I called the hospital and whether they said that it was all right to go."

The patient wondered about the mystic significance of dreaming about her mother twice in a row. To us it means that she needed the mother's encouragement to follow the procedure. Artificial insemination was performed at 10:30 A.M. that day. Soon after the insemination, a pimple suddenly appeared on her nose. She also had a "heartache" which she felt all afternoon. The following night she dreamed.

Dream:
"I was knitting, but I wasn't. There was something I was doing over and over again. I was getting tired. I was in an apartment looking out of the window. There was a stage on the street. Lots of people looking. . . ."

The dream indicated her discouraged mood about doing what she did not want to do—artificial insemination—and being exposed in doing it.

Since her temperature had fallen, she knew that she was not pregnant. Her next dream expressed depression and the regression of her sexual feelings. She had cramps, the sensation of menstruation. The "premenstrual depression" actually lasted from the time of the insemination until menstruation began. During this time her dreams revealed a sense of deprivation and identification with her deprived mother. During the whole period of menstrual flow, she was dizzy, faint, and anxious.

Before the next artificial insemination, she complained about a slight discharge and pain in the ovaries which she related to oncoming ovulation. Her dream that night was vague: she was looking for her childhood home. This dream, like the one before the previous insemination, expressed the wish to return to her mother, instead of becoming a mother. Another dream revealed her great reluctance to have intercourse, to receive the semen which she expected would be ruined rather than fertile. The preovulative tension motivated an increased feeling of hunger. "I just cannot eat enough," she stated. The night before the artificial insemination, she had the following dream.

Dream:
"I walked into a large building, all hallways and stairs. They were not well lighted. Kept walking around and got to the basement; it was a bakery shop. There were a lot of counters with pastries of all kinds. I could not make up my mind which I wanted. There were two cakes. I picked one. . . ."

This dream indicated her preoccupation with the forthcoming artificial insemination = the basement = the sexual organ = the bakery shop producing sweets = children.

The next analytical session followed immediately after the insemination. She complained of severe cramps which disappeared during the session. Later the patient developed herpes on the perineum. Her dreams revealed the wish to escape sexuality, "to leave it to men" and to return to mother and have only receptive dependent needs, which the mother would satisfy. In another dream she expressed the fear that her receptive wishes were insatiable and that this insatiability was interfering with pregnancy. Some days later, when she could have been certain that she had not conceived, her dream expressed the fear that pregnancy changes the body. In the next session, she reported a dream in which she realized that her body was "empty" and that it would not change; in an attempt to accept her sterility, she rationalized that her husband would not like her body if she were pregnant; thus she gave up motherhood for sexuality.

After this cycle, the patient used the excuse of a business trip to interrupt the analytical treatment to which she did not return. The analysis of the sexual cycle outlines her conflicts in regard to both aspects of female sexuality: heterosexuality and motherhood. The realization of these conflicts might have caused her to continue only with the artificial insemination. After four unsuccessful attempts her husband took the responsibility of being treated.

CASE NO. 6

The patient was a thirty-six-year-old woman, married in 1942. She became pregnant in the first year of her marriage but had a miscarriage in the sixth week. Since then she had not been able to conceive again. Examination of the husband's semen revealed a sperm count of 11.4 million with 25 percent motility. Artificial insemination with the husband's concentrated semen was recommended. The patient had two inseminations before and three during psychotherapy. She was also on thyroid medication, taking three and three-quarters grains per day. During the psychotherapy this couple decided to discontinue artificial insemination and to adopt a baby. Four months after this decision, the patient became pregnant normally by her husband; she delivered at full term. She is now well advanced in her second pregnancy.

This patient, unlike the others, pursued the therapy with unusual vigor and concentration. Upon reading the record of this psychoanalysis, it was surprising that the material dealt, almost without deviation, with the conflict with her mother. Although the presenting problem of this patient was her frustrated wish for pregnancy, she rarely mentioned any aspect of her sex life; her dreams and manifest emotions, preoccupied with one problem only, did not reveal either the heterosexual or the progestation phase of the cycle, until the last cycles before pregnancy. One may say there was almost no libido expressed in her analytical material, which showed a conscientious working-through of the painful, central problem of her life.

A summary of the course of the analysis will best reveal the intensity of the interpersonal conflicts and their resolution as related to the change in the fertility of this couple.

The patient began treatment with an attempt to describe her mother with the words "a holy terror," and a great part of the analysis was taken up in illustrating these words. Her mother always acted as if her daughter, her only child, were a piece of property. On one hand, she depreciated the patient, was critical of her, sided with others against her. On the other hand, she took the shortcomings of the patient as a personal humiliation since she had unlimited ambitions for her daughter, that is, for herself, to be satisfied by her daughter. The patient recognized both aspects of the mother's behavior and while she hated her mother for her punitive attitude, she hated herself for not being able to fulfill the mother's ideal for her. Her analysis started with an "unhappy dream" which expressed the wish to return to her mother's home. While the patient made conscious efforts to liberate herself, she also recognized her dependence on her mother.

All her life she expected her father to be her ally in this struggle. Yet she also knew that her father—under the domination of his wife—was not a free agent in his emotions. The patient's relationship to her father as well as to her husband was motivated by the mother's attitude: in the process of appeasing her mother, she learned to depreciate her father and as a consequence she depreciated her husband in spite of all the love and gratitude she professed to feel.

This material was shortly interrupted by the statement that she had an insemination after which for a couple of days she felt nauseated. After she was certain that she was not pregnant, she dreamed:

Dream:
"The baby should be delivered by parcel post," i.e., by adoption.

During the same cycle—as her premenstrual depression increased—she analyzed her own feelings as parallel to her mother's depression: "One cannot satisfy Mother because she wants to be unhappy." "I expect failure in anything that I start." There was no sense of her even thinking of adoption since "I should not inflict myself upon a child." In this period of her analysis, the patient had a dream.

Dream:
"My husband and I were handcuffed and driven away to be executed."

In her associations to this dream, she related the tragic incident of her childhood. When she was three years old, her mother gave birth to a boy who died eleven days after delivery. Shortly after this, her mother suffered a spine injury in an accident which the patient witnessed. She remembered that her mother was frequently hospitalized. It was her emotional conviction that she had always been deeply involved in her mother's unhappiness; that her sense of obligation was such that she was unable to extricate herself.

Her sad mood was not interrupted even at the time of the next artificial insemination. After she found out that she had not conceived, she wanted to stop the analysis. Her depressive reasoning was: even if analysis were successful, it would not mean success for her, since an "increased joy of living" would only be a new source of unhappiness. She had to live like her mother, unhappy and complaining, causing unhappiness to others by her complaints.

During the next four weeks' period (until the next artificial insemination) the patient worked through important aspects of her problem; she realized her mother's great need for her and also that she felt inadequate and guilty because she was unable to satisfy this need. She considered this need of the mother "insane," in her adult life as well as in her childhood. To this she related her sudden, anxious tension when her mother entered the room where she had played as a child. As if she had to protect herself against an unknown danger, she had to shy away from her mother. In connection with her mother's need for her, she realized that her own wish for a child originated in the need to fill a lack in her personality, to sustain herself. After this insight she developed a "tragic sympathy" for her mother; "I am busy tearing myself in two between my mother and my husband, like a mother tears herself in two between her husband and her child."

This material led up to the last artificial insemination. Her response to this was fear of having a child: "I would smother it with love." This feeling of a dangerous love for the child—the repetition of her mother's smothering need for her—was soon transferred back to her parents. Her regressive need for her mother was expressed in her crying spells, in her sense of being lost and lonesome (premenstrual depression after the last artificial insemination). At the same time this increased dependent love for her parents activated her guilt toward her husband. Once again she realized that her need for her mother resulted in identification with her and this brought with it the depreciation of her husband.

During this phase of depression, a significant incident occurred. Her father had come to town and in a discussion of these problems with him, as well as in a business transaction with him, the patient recognized that her father and mother represent a solid front against her, that she had no "friend and ally" in her father. Her disappointment and anger interrupted her depressive mood. She turned to the analyst as well as to her husband for help. It was not too many days after this that her husband consented to her wish to adopt a baby. The patient was very happy about this and eagerly took the necessary steps for adoption. Yet at the same time she pleaded with the analyst to interfere with the plan. The patient realized that only by having her own child could she resolve the bondage to her mother.

As her fantasies and expectations regarding an adopted baby took more definite form, her wish to be reconciled with her parents became more acute. "I shall die of loneliness if they don't participate." The fear that "Mother may resent my child, the guilt about having a child (when Mother's child died) keeps me from getting pregnant."

Parallel with all these emotional events, her husband's business venture began to promise success; he felt more secure and settled. In spite of the adoption plans, they talked a great deal about their own child. The patient said with love and pride that her husband loved *her* and wanted *her* baby, etc. In the following session the patient discussed with obvious narcissism what having a child meant to her: "I need a child. If I can't cling to the source, I shall become a source." In spite of the theatrical expression, this represents the wish for fulfillment in motherhood. Yet, or probably because of this, the patient became depressed again.

About this time, her parents returned to town; her mother wholeheartedly supported the plan for adoption. This activated an almost hectic desire to reach a decision between the plan for adoption and the attempt to achieve her own pregnancy. Probably this motivated her increasing the thyroid medication to almost twice the dose (seven grains). This indicated also that the patient really did not believe that her husband was sterile. In her dreams and in her conscious fantasies, she expressed the wish "to give him what he wants."

Her menstruation was delayed in this cycle; she hoped that she was pregnant. Her dream expressed the idea: "Since Mother is always with me wherever I am, I could become pregnant more easily if my parents, especially my mother, would accept my husband." The day after she was told that the Aschheim-Zondek test was positive, she began to menstruate. Whether or not this was an early abortion is uncertain. She was very disappointed; she felt frustrated, angry, and depressed. Yet the analytical material during the following cycle was the first which clearly revealed cyclical change. Her dream in the estrogen phase was like the dream of a young girl. The interpretation of this dream can be summarized: "Sexuality is dangerous, degrading; Mother will protect me from it; my sexual organs are 'dirty,' 'broken'; only when Mother will accept them can I relax and function as a woman." Yet in the same period she had a headache after every conversation with her mother. As the analytical material showed, during such conversations, she had to suppress many conflicting feelings: one was the fear of disloyalty toward her husband, the other the anger because she still wanted to appease her mother and escape the guilt because she could not love her.

With this she gained new insight into one of the significant motivations of her fears about having a child: "A child, instead of loving its mother, may wish her dead." Her death wish toward her mother seemed to be motivated by the sense of fear and guilt connected with the birth and death of her baby brother. The result of these feelings was her idea that her mother did not want her to have a child (as she once did not want her mother's child to live). With all these depressive moods, her next menstruation, the last before her conception, was approaching. After this it seemed that she experienced a great release of sexual feelings; she decided to enjoy life. Yet she was afraid that just saying it might interfere with it. In the same way, when menstruation did not begin, she hardly dared to fantasy; she fantasied about her husband— what a good father he would be—as if protecting her pregnancy from her "smothering" love.

When she returned to analysis after summer vacation, she was in her third month of pregnancy. There were three more months of analysis before the treatment was interrupted. Her dreams during this time revealed her fears—that she might suffer, be harmed by the pregnancy, and that her child, being born alive, might die, as her mother's child did. But these occasional anxiety dreams did not amount to pathology; she had no acute anxiety attacks. Her pregnancy and parturition were normal.

A summary of the factors which might have played a role in changing the fertility of this couple can be given as follows. The *wife,* (1) after she had worked through her guilt toward and her fear of the mother, achieved a reconciliation with her mother; (2) since she felt accepted by her mother as a woman and as a potential (adoptive) mother, her own fear of being a hostile-incorporative mother (as her mother had been) diminished. (3) Her libido production changed. Instead of a depressed, listless woman whose response to her husband was characterized by depreciation, frigidity, and consequent guilt, she became able to respond to him with love.

The *husband's* willingness to assume the responsibilities of fatherhood by consenting to adoption can be considered as a reaction (1) to the change in the emotional attitude of his wife and her parents toward him; and (2) to a greater success in his business, which afforded him greater security and more ego gratification.

DISCUSSION

In investigating the psychogenic factors in any organic event, a primary susceptibility to a specific organic response is taken for granted. Such susceptibility usually represents a variant of the modification of constitutional factors through experience. Psychoanalytic studies usually attempt to determine the experiences which, during and in connection with the psychosexual development, modify the individual's responses to stimuli and thereby may account for deviations in physiological processes.

Today we know enough about the psychosexual maturation of women to recognize in each case the emotional factors which modify attitudes toward heterosexuality and motherhood. Regardless of which aspect of her sexual function is primarily disturbed, the interaction between the two phases of the propagative function—as influenced by hormonal regulation and by life experience—may lead to infertility. (1) Our knowledge about man's sexuality is more limited. The developmental factors which may influence and modify his heterosexual attitudes and his sexual potency have been well studied, but almost nothing is known about the emotional factors involved in man's fertility. Although the husbands of our cases were not studied, one can infer from the clinical course of these cases that the interpersonal relationship affected the fertility of both marital partners. This indicates that infertility may be considered as a conjugal phenomenon.

ADOPTION

The period of infertility of the six couples reported varied between three to eight years up to the time when artificial insemination was initiated. The husband's sperm was used in five cases; a donor's sperm was applied in one case. These women, consciously eager to have children and frustrated by the husband's sterility, submitted to artificial insemination in order to have an "own child," which they preferred to adoption. The husbands agreed to artificial insemination more readily than to adoption. Whether this was due to the emotional significance which his own child has for the father, or because adoption would reveal his inadequacy, has not been shown in these cases. The women, however, were consciously motivated by the idea that artificial insemination, if successful, would protect the husband from exposing his inadequacy. When several attempts at artificial insemination had failed, each of these women began to consider herself sterile. As the patient's sense of inadequacy grew, she professed that she would be satisfied with an adopted baby. Usually the husband held out against the adoption.

It often happens that adoption, or even the idea of adoption, improves the woman's ability to conceive. (7) In cases in which artificial insemination is not used, we assume that the plan for adoption, or the experience with an adopted child, relaxes the tension which, originating in the sense of inadequacy, interferes with the processes of conception. We also assume that the woman's anxiety regarding motherhood diminishes through the experience of her motherliness, through her ability to love and care for a child. We do not know whether the experiences of fatherhood have a similar effect upon the husband's fertility. No doubt, in an unstable and conflictful marriage, the decision for adoption may reassure the partners in regard to the stability of their marriage.

THE ROLE OF THE HUSBAND

In evaluating our six cases, we may say that the plan for adoption could be considered as a measure of the sincerity of the wish for a child in both or either of the marital partners. In Case 1, the husband consented to adoption as well as to hormone treatment; now they have two children. In Cases 2 and 5, adoption was not considered. In Cases 3 and 4, the idea of adoption recurred whenever the therapy appeared disappointing; adoption was used as a means of resistance in the analysis, but it was not actually pursued. In Case 6, the adoption plan, like everything else that this woman decided, was undertaken with precise purposefulness. In this case more detailed information leads to further evaluation of the ways by which a plan for adoption may influence fertility.

The course of the psychoanalytical treatment of this last case illustrates that the psychoanalytical working-through of this conflict had a favorable influence upon the interpersonal relationship between wife and husband. The first important sign of this improvement was the husband's consent to adoption. For this woman the consent of her husband, and even more, that of her parents, meant a reassurance of her worth as a potential mother. The plan for adoption permitted this patient to give up artificial insemination without giving up the hope of motherhood. For the husband, giving up the artificial insemination meant relief from the manipulations involved in the procedure. Case 3 complained about the effects which the sexual manipulations necessary for artificial insemination had upon her husband's potency and even his fertility. This relief might have influenced his potency and thereby have influenced the sexual gratification of his wife in a positive manner.

Since the patient became pregnant four months after the artificial insemination was discontinued, we feel justified in assuming that the improvement of the emotional relationship between the husband and wife directly affected the husband's fertility. That this was not a fortuitous occurrence is indicated by the fact that without any further medical treatment, his wife is now well advanced in her second pregnancy.

The conscious interference with a natural process even in the manipulation necessary for investigation of the semen might have an influence upon the quality of the semen; even more so if this procedure were continued for many months in an individual whose semen production is vulnerable. (6) If one considers the great variety of fantasies (especially homosexual fantasies) that may enter in a sexual act in which attention is directed toward a third person (who quasi completes the act) one can expect that not only sexual relations but also the quality of semen may improve after these procedures are given up.

That the procedure of artificial insemination affected the woman's capacity for conception was the starting point of our investigation. That the procedures connected with it may influence unfavorably the husband's potency and fertility and by this may perpetuate a vicious circle is an assumption based on incidental findings. It is supported by the positive influence which the psychotherapy of the wife had upon the husband's fertility in Case 6. This observation, although singular, calls our attention to the possibility that continual emotional tension (as well as the relief from it) may affect the subtle interaction which regulates fertility, if the marital partners, for any reason, are susceptible to this type of reaction.

ARTIFICIAL INSEMINATION

The next point of this discussion is to evaluate the meaning of the emotional responses of our patients to artificial insemination and to examine some of the contraindications in our observations. In this study we are not concerned with the physiological processes by which an emotional factor—such as fear of conceiving by an unnatural method—might bring about the failure of conception by artificial insemination. We want to point out that such anxiety played a role, at least, in five of the six cases and most directly in Case 1, the youngest of these women. When she realized that the artificial insemination brought with it a confusion of her feelings which might disturb the equanimity of her pregnancy, she discontinued the artificial insemination. The psychoanalytical material of Cases 3, 4, and 5 expressed not only the resistance to the procedure itself but also the conflict in regard to having a child "that way." This feeling might have been even stronger in Case 6, but the record of her analysis does not provide evidence of this. Yet these women continued the procedure for many months or even for years. While the ambivalent attitude toward the procedure is conscious, dreams and free associations during the ovulative period, before and after insemination, express fear of pregnancy and fear of the child. Thus one may assume that the unconscious motivation for their persistence is the wish to deny the emotional conflicts in regard to childbearing. This is confirmed by the great resistance to the psychoanalytical therapy which might expose those conflicts and also by the fact that in the analysis the husband's sterility is barely mentioned. The failure to conceive by artificial insemination is accepted as the manifestation of their own infertility and this becomes the focus of the analytical process.

In this study as in other psychoanalytical studies, dreams are considered the objective material of investigation. We used the dreams primarily to illustrate the patient's preconscious attitude toward conception in the specific situation of artificial insemination. The analysis of the dreams was based on the assumption that the preparation for and reaction to the artificial insemination provided the impulse for the dream during the ovulative-postovulative phases. In interpreting the dreams in terms of this impulse, we arrived at the conflicting tendencies between the patient's actual cooperation with the procedure and her ambivalence toward its success. From further interpretation of the genetic and structural elements of the dreams, one might infer the conflicting tendencies regarding motherhood in each of these individuals. In this respect, the psychoanalytical material of these women reveals similar, almost identical conflicts. Whether the woman is shy and apparently passive as in Cases 1, 3, and 4, or active, ambitious, and aggressive as in Cases 2, 5, and 6, they all manifest an unusually intense dependence on the mother; they complain—although not with the same intensity—of frustration and deprivation at the hands of the mother; they are afraid of motherhood, afraid of pregnancy which may cause harm to the body, and also afraid of the child as if it were an enemy. (3, 4) The passive dependency on the mother is well illustrated in Cases 1 and 5, and the mutual, incorporative dependence between mother and daughter is illustrated in Cases 3 and 4, and even more so in Case 6.

The progesterone phase of the sexual cycle represents the somatic and psychic preparation for pregnancy. (1) While it enhances the metabolic processes, the psychic apparatus registers the increase in the receptive tendencies and elaborates the various aspects of the dependent needs. Thus a biologically useful "adaptive regression" characterizes the emotional aspects of the progesterone phase. This finds expression in the repetition of the developmental relationship to the mother. In general, the psychoanalytical material during the progesterone phase expresses the trials and errors as well as the gratifications of the identification with the mother; it reveals the anxieties and satisfactions of the dependence on the mother as well as the fears and hopes of outgrowing her and becoming a mother. Thus, it reveals the development to motherhood.

Since this is universal, the question arises whether the material which is repeated with varying intensity in each sexual cycle had any significance for the psychogenesis of the diminished fertility of our cases. No doubt, these women, during the period of investigation, lived in anxious suspense, awaiting the fulfillment of their wish for motherhood. The frustration which the woman experienced when she did not become pregnant in the natural way increased her wish for the child and, at the same time, it activated her anxieties and conflicts related to motherhood. Since these emotions originate in the developmental relationship to the mother, the thwarted wish for motherhood propels the related conflicts into the foreground. In other words, the frustration activates a regressive process through which the wish for pregnancy becomes an urge which dominates the psychic economy. The more these women wish to become mothers, the more dependent they appear.* Whether

---

* It is necessary to differentiate "dependence" as a character trait from the "receptive-dependent tendency" which motivates dreams and fantasies as well as variations in behavior during the progesterone phase. This occurs in women under normal conditions during the progesterone phase.

the dependence, expressed in the preovulative phase, is passive, positively related to a loving mother as in Case 1 or 5, or appears charged with the hostility of a frustrated incorporation as in Case 6, the tension of the conflict grows with the frustration. These women try to fight against this regressive process by submitting to artificial insemination. When the miracle does not happen, the frustration becomes even stronger. Then the woman feels responsible for the sterility and therefore her wish for the child becomes more and more compelling until, as in Case 3, it becomes an isolated obsession rather than a libidinal wish.†
The libido is tied down and exhausted by the faulty economy of the vicious circle.

This means that there is very little libido left over for the heterosexual aspects of marital life. While the woman obsessively wants to become a mother, she becomes more and more frigid toward her husband. Indeed, the estrogen phases of the sexual cycles of these women (Cases 3, 4, and 6) are hardly noticeable; the preovulative phase is then characterized by a negativistic concentration upon the artificial insemination or upon the intense wish for impregnation; the libidinal emotions which should facilitate this event are absorbed by the frustration.

Does this mean that the presenting conflict with its high emotional charge is not the cause but the effect of the frustrated wish to have a child? (8) The answer to this question is not simple. Since the husband's infertility might account for the original frustration of childbearing, these women actually are not suitable subjects for the investigation of the psychogenesis of infertility. Yet we do not know whether the choice of the husband was not an indication of the fear of childbearing. Some of these women knowingly chose infertile men for husbands (Cases 1 and 2). In other cases (Cases 3 and 6) we assume that the husband's infertility was but a result of a long frustration of his virility in the marriage.

Our assumption is that the current psychoeconomy of these women, the intensity of their presenting conflicts, is the result of the frustration. Whether or not the same conflict also has genetic significance for the infertility of these women must be evaluated in reference to the total personality and life experience of each of them. The psychoanalytical material of our cases is not sufficient for such an evaluation and the comparison of our cases cautions us against generalizations. For exam-

† It is not within the scope of this paper to evaluate the "meaning" of what having a child had for these women. Pregnancy and motherhood represent a stimulation for developmental integration in the mother's personality. (1, 7) While, under normal conditions, these processes occur unconsciously, these desperately longing women expect—as their analytical material indicates—that having a child would undo the harm which the long frustration has wrought in their personality. Thus they assign consciously an "integrative task" to motherhood which is apt to fail since it is charged by the emotions which originate in the frustration itself.

ple, on the basis of the intensity of the hostile, destructive interdependence with the mother, Case 6 would be the most "emotionally sterile" of them all, but she became a mother. Case 5, whose passive dependence on her mother appears much less "pathogenic," did not consider adoption in the event that she did not become pregnant. Her desire to become a mother is much less compelling. What we know about the psychosexual development to motherhood (3) and about the psychology of the progesterone phase indicates the necessity for differentiation between the psychodynamic motivation of the current emotional state and the role which the same psychodynamic tendencies (the same conflicts) might play in the psychogenesis of a symptom and/or in the inhibition of a function. It is evident that the same or even more severe conflicts in regard to childbearing exist without affecting the fertility of women or causing sterility in men.

Fertility is a labile quality. It differs not only according to the individual, but also it changes in the same individual depending upon maturation as well as upon sexual potency and compatibility of the partners. In our cases of "transitory infertility," it seems that the frustrating experiences caused by the husbands' infertility reactivated the developmental conflicts in regard to motherhood.

The psychic economy of infertility creates a vicious circle between the marital partners. The influence of the husband's infertility upon his wife's propagative and emotional household is evident. Some of the ways of this interaction have been demonstrated in these cases. It is more difficult to prove what some of our cases indicate, that the frigidity of the wife affects the propagative function of the husband similarly. Thus infertility might be the result of the emotional interaction between the marital partners. This again indicates that the transitory infertility which is the subject of this study should not be considered a circumscribed psychosomatic symptom, but rather an inhibition, an arrested phase of the developmental process.

SUMMARY

Six women, whose husbands' sperm was inadequate, underwent artificial insemination and did not conceive in spite of several attempts. One of the women became pregnant after the couple planned for adoption and the husband had treatment with testosterone; another husband was able to impregnate his wife normally, after the psychoanalytical therapy of his wife resolved her conflict with her mother and thus affected an improvement of the relationship between the marital partners. This case and some observations in the other cases led to the conclusion that the "transitory infertility," as observed in these cases, is a conjugal phenomenon.

The artificial insemination itself, instead of relieving the mutual infertility in these cases, rather increased it.

The effect of frustration in the reactivation of the developmental conflicts with the mother is discussed; it is emphasized that these conflicts, although they motivate the current mood, cannot be unqualifiedly identified as the psychogenic factors responsible for infertility.

REFERENCES

1. Benedek, Therese, and Rubenstein, B. B. "The sexual cycle in women." In Benedek, Therese: *Psychosexual Functions in Women.* New York, Ronald Press, 1952, pp. 3–325.

2. Benedek, Therese. "Some psychophysiological problems of motherhood." In Benedek, Therese: *Psychosexual Functions in Women.* New York, Ronald Press, 1952, pp. 407–418.

3. Deutsch, Helene. *The Psychology of Women: A Psychoanalytic Interpretation.* New York, Grune & Stratton, 1944, 1945. Vols. I and II.

4. Jacobson, Edith. A case of sterility. *Psychoanalyt. Quart.* 15:330, 1946.

5. Kelley, K. Sterility in the female with special reference to psychic factors. *Psychosom. Med.* 4:211, 1942.

6. MacLeod, J. The male factor in fertility and infertility. *Fertil. & Steril.* 1:347, 1950.

7. Orr, D. W. Pregnancy following the decision to adopt. *Psychosom. Med.* 3:411, 1951.

8. Rubenstein, B. B. An emotional factor in infertility. *Fertil. & Steril.* 2:80, 1951.

DISCUSSION

Infertility is a pathophysiologic reaction that, by inhibiting conception, protects the woman from anxiety that might overwhelm her during any phase of her reproductive function. This is, however, a post hoc psychodynamic formulation, arrived at by psychiatric and psychoanalytic investigation of infertile women. Most infertile women do not attribute their condition to fear of childbearing. Indeed, if they are married, if their actual and emotional situation does not act against it, they consciously clamor for pregnancy. This efficient organismic protection (not to use the term ego defense) is undermined by the continual influence of intrapsychic factors. Foremost among them is the instinctual drive that maintains a genuine wish for survival in one's own child and the woman's ego ideal of becoming and being a mother. Besides intrapsychic motivations, there are interpersonal factors such as the husband's wish for parenthood, intrafamilial relationships, and social pressures which keep the infertile woman preoccupied with her shortcomings and compel her to wish "with all her heart" for that which comes so easily to most women.

Obviously, this brings about envy, an increasing sense of frustration, and anger. While such an emotional state makes the woman's wish for pregnancy appear almost unbearable, it also mobilizes unconscious developmental conflicts. Women in that condition need help, seek it, and are exceedingly analyzable. Whether they are curable, i.e., made fertile, cannot be predicted. Indeed, the interaction between organismic, psychologic, and environmental factors is so complex that the actual relation between the fertility potential and the personality organization of a woman in a specific time of her life cannot (even approximately) be determined.

Since these two papers were published, psychosomatic infertility has been studied by many investigators. In general, they have confirmed the assumption that the psychogenic course of the mother-daughter relationship is an essential factor in development toward motherhood. But the concepts that explain developmental processes do not clarify the pathogenesis of this uniquely specific symptom. Summarizing Helene Deutsch's attitude[1] regarding infertility, Seward says, ". . . The immaturity may appear either directly, as oral dependence displaced from mother to husband, or defensively, as aggressive denial of femininity and the pursuit of masculine career strivings." The author continues, "Gynecological observations have lent weight to the theory that ambivalent dependence on their own mothers has made these women reluctant to adopt the mother-role themselves in spite of their expressed desire for children."[2]

The work of Seward and her associates led to negative results. These investigators hoped that a battery of psychological tests would reveal characteristic differences between the "feminine identity" of infertile women and that of multiparas. Actually, the tests indicated a more positive attitude toward childbearing in infertile women than in the control group of mothers. This finding, however, confirms psychoanalytic observations which suggest that women frustrated in their instinctual wish for motherhood often clamor for pregnancy. Yet this does not exclude the possibility that the same women might avoid conception or would suffer severe anxiety if they conceived. Psychoanalysts are always prepared for the multiple possibilities of solutions of a problem posed to the ego by the unconscious. This also explains why psychoanalysis, which in individual cases can clarify convincingly the interacting factors, so far has failed to give an answer of more general relevance to the problem of infertility. We hope that investigations of this psychosomatic problem in the frame of the general theory of psychoanalysis will clarify the significance of the interacting factors. The nature of this publication does not allow a detailed discussion of the theoretical issues involved, but I hope that by raising some pertinent questions, further investigations will be encouraged.

The first question for the clinician is, Into which nosologic category does psychogenic infertility fit?[3] Freud would agree with the definition of infertility as an inhibition since it "represents a relinquishment of a function because its exercise would produce anxiety." He added, "Many women are openly afraid of sexual function."[4] Freud, however, related inhibitions to restrictions of ego functions, which fertility is certainly not. Whether it is caused by suppression of ovulation or by tubal spasms, infertility is the result of an inhibition of a physiologic process. It is a psychosomatic symptom. Accordingly, neither the characteristics of conversion of libido (or aggression) nor primary ideational content can be attributed to it.[5] Psychogenic infertility is not a conversion symptom, although it occurs rather frequently in women whom we would consider "hysterical" regarding their personality organization, behavior, etc. At the same time, we emphasized, as the investigation of Seward et al. also indicated, that psychogenic infertility does not fit any category of neuroses; it can appear in individuals of all varieties of personality organization, independent of or in interaction with other psychiatric problems. Hence I repeat, infertility is an inhibition resulting from chronic stress.

In spite of all this, it should not be forgotten that developmental conflicts participate in bringing about and in maintaining intrapsychic stress. The infantile mother-daughter conflict is not the only source of the fear of childbearing. A strongly cathected oedipal fixation which motivates the little girl's wish to be pregnant with her father's child may aggravate the fear of pregnancy. The psychotic regression of anorexia nervosa patients begins at adolescence with such vehement repression of sexuality that it destroys its hormonal tributaries before other serious symptoms develop. In these cases the infertility is a consequence of starvation, but the starvation is brought about by the interaction of the developmental conflicts which, in other instances, bring about infertility without such serious mental symptoms or, in many more cases, do not interfere with fertility at all.

The next question concerns the nature of stress. Intrapsychic stress originates in intrapsychic conflicts and is maintained by a hierarchy of their interactions. Does the chronology, the sequence of developmental conflicts, account for the significance of a particular conflict in a given pathology? This question can be answered with an unconditional "yes" only in one respect: it is a biologic fact that the younger an organism is, the greater the harm caused by any noxious agent. Expressing this in terms of human psychology, the younger the infant, the less developed is his psychic apparatus which would afford defenses in order to diminish the effects of the trauma or the anxiety. Considering infertility as a psychosomatic defense against the dangers of pregnancy, parturition, and motherhood, infertility is a condition which (convincingly) fits into the "flight" pattern of reactions to anxiety.

A fundamental characteristic of this primarily self-preserving affect is that it may overwhelm the ego and so render the ego unable to perform its defensive, protective function. Early in his career, Freud speculated about the mechanisms that would restrain anxiety. In the "Project" written in 1895, he discussed a mechanism by which the ego restricts the painful experience of anxiety and ". . . restricted in quantity acts as a signal to the ego to set normal defense in operation."[6] The differentiation between signal anxiety and acute anxiety is important for this discussion of disturbances of the reproductive function. Although acute anxiety might overwhelm pregnant women or women in parturition, infertility, whether purely psychogenic or effected through organic pathology, is brought about by chronic stress. This may be discovered in the analysis of dreams and can be characterized as signal anxiety.

The role of anxiety in the frame of Freud's instinct theory is discussed in the first chapter of this volume (p. 29–49). Here we must refer to the biochemical affinity of the two primary affects, anxiety and anger (Chapter 1, p. 51–70, and Chapter 2), since they have direct relevance to the problem of infertility. When two instinctual drives are in fusion, they neutralize each other and thus supply energy for the physiologic and psychologic function of the organism. Under stress, defusion of these basic instinctual energies takes place, causing a disequilibrium that is perceived as affect. This very general formulation has to suffice here to indicate that the gamut of external and internal stresses as well as a whole range of possible affective responses are implied. It is further implied that the ego's function in dealing with the "defused" instinctual energies strives for a constructive, i.e., life-preserving, solution. The clinical significance of the dual instinct theory lies in the concept of fusion of libido with aggression.

Psychoanalytic theory offers an explanation of the universal fear of being a woman which is expressed in mythology, in folklore, in any form of creative art, as well as in individual psychology and its pathologic manifestation.[7] Not only the psychology of woman is permeated by signal anxiety pertaining to her reproductive function, but the psychology of the male may be motivated by it also. This fear is the manifestation of bisexuality in individuals of both sexes.

The discussion of the problem of infertility from the viewpoint of the second instinct theory serves the aim of focusing the attention on the biologic processes involved in childbearing. The physiologic processes so directly responsible for the survival of the species put the primary psychic energy, i.e., libido and aggression, under such stress that defusion results and sets free aggression which mobilizes massive anxiety. The woman has this at stake in becoming a mother. It appears that evolutionary biology could not do better than to make the female able to deliver her offspring, though in pain and anxiety.[8] In spite of everything, children are born. Whether by choice or by "nature's order," evolutionary biology has endowed woman with psychic equipment to love her child as much as or more than she loves herself. Mother love that overcomes anxiety and often the instinct of self-preservation itself is a manifestation of a fusion of the primary instinctual drives, but not necessarily of their mutual neutralization.

Fusion implies the possibility of defusion. The often used but rarely defined term "ambivalence" refers, in its psychodynamic meaning, to the potentiality of defusion of psychic energies. The aggression of the loving mother might become free under the stress of frustration and thus activate anxiety. The anxiety warns the mother of the danger to herself; the activated aggression warns her of the danger she might represent to her child. She controls her anger, represses her impulses, in order to protect the child from her anger and herself from remorse; her love for the child emerges again. Originating in the lability of the fusion of instinctual drives, ambivalence may be a characteristic emotional state of the woman after parturition.[9]

Rheingold begins his large-scale elaboration of "The Fear of Being a Woman"[10] with the discussion of parental cruelty, illustrating the general significance of basic ambivalence which endangers the infant. In our concept of reciprocity, it would endanger the parent also. The repression of aggressive impulses maintains a continual "signal anxiety" that adds to the intrapsychic stress of the mother and influences the transactional processes between mother and child during and after the symbiotic phase. While the girl-child's object relationships evolve and her individuation proceeds, her interactions with her mother reflect the traces of the mother's fearful experience of her anxiety over childbearing. They become implanted in the daughter as anticipation, as signal anxiety, in respect to all phases of childbearing. The hypothesis developed in Rubenstein's paper[11] could be modified. The daughter's fear of childbearing might be the result of the reciprocal and mutually ambivalent identifications between daughter and mother.

Having discussed the dynamic factors which might interfere with fertility, we have to admit that it seems impossible to clarify the genetic factors beyond this general statement. The function of ambivalence in the mother-child relationship from infancy on is discussed in the paper "Toward the Biology of the Depressive Constellation" (Chapter 13, this volume). Developing further the hypothesis presented there, we could assume that the nuclear conflict, i.e., the depressive core, originating in the contrasting, primary instinctual forces carries the high cathexis of those energies.

The ambivalence that originates in the conflict of the reproductive function itself forecasts a gloomy picture since it seems to put the roots of mother love in the soil of the primary processes of the symbiotic relationship, into the mother-child unit alone. We have said, however, that in this phase the emotional balance of the mother is under great stress and this promotes defusion of instinctual energies exposing her to feelings of hostility and anxiety. The infant's not yet organized psychic apparatus, responding only to his own needs and frustration, is exposed to throes and pangs of his own not yet neutralized aggressive energy.

To brighten this picture, we should recall the innate, albeit individually different, potentials of the organism such as the potential to grow and develop. According to our theory, this implies the neutralization of the contrasting instinctual forces which provide the organism with neutralized energy for its physiologic and psychic functioning. Primary for normal development is "integrative capacity." By this is meant an innate ability, usually attributed to the ego, to organize the constant flow of "input" from organic and psychic sources and to organize it in such a way that, in spite of the steady oscillations and variations in the infant, positive, libidinal, integrative energy will prevail and direct the living toward loving.

Having discussed the theoretical implications of infertility as psychosomatic defense, we shall turn to the clinical investigation of some emotional factors of infertility. The only general conclusion was mentioned in the Introduction: the emotional attitude of the would-be parents toward parenthood has to be investigated. The obstacle is that an ad hoc evaluation of their attitudes toward parenthood at the time both are willing to undertake a series of psychiatric interviews rarely reveals the intrapsychic history of the problem as it affected each of the marital partners during the years of childless marriage.

The husbands of the women who were the subjects of the investigation had undergone the necessary examination to establish the state of their sterility; accordingly, either artificial insemination with the condensed semen of the husband or with a donor's semen was recommended. The husband's desire to be a father was not evaluated; it seemed sufficient that he was willing if his wife became pregnant. The question arises, why are women so recalcitrant to artificial insemination? Is the "transitory infertility" motivated by the artificiality of the situation, or by an unconscious loyalty to the husband, or is it an adaptation to the husband's sterility? Two observations indicate the problems which may be relevant to answering these questions.

Not only during the study of these cases, but in many others, the wives showed an unusual willingness to protect the husband's secret and not to offend his self-esteem by revealing his deficiency. As long as the wife does not want a divorce, she will protect the husband's narcissism by not even urging him to seek medical help. (The exception seems to be sterility caused by epididymitis as a consequence of mumps.) It seems that this undue discretion may have motivation in the wife's own fears of childbearing and motherhood. Our Case 3 held herself responsible for her husband's sterility, and this is probably not an unusual occurrence. The fear of hostility toward the unborn child was responsible for the infertility of the couple. It seems that the wife's neurosis caused the husband's aspermia. The opposite happens probably more often. During several years of childless marriage, the unconscious fear of pregnancy and motherhood exerts influence as chronic stress and this becomes more affective, leading to infertility even if the wife had been able to conceive years before, in the beginning of the marriage when husband and wife were younger. It seems that more could be learned from emotional factors in conjugal infertility through psychoanalytic investigation of both husband and wife.

The nature of life and living renders psychic conflict inevitable and therefore multiplies enormously the number and variety of circumstances which increase organismic and psychologic stress. The investigation of such a basic problem of life as inadequacy of fertility raises painful, individual problems, whether it concerns infertility of women or sterility in men. The instinctual wish to survive in one's own children is so all pervasive that the idea of conflicting tendencies being involved in parenthood is repressed, guarded by guilt and shame from becoming conscious. The problem of psychogenic sterility in men is not raised, as if it could not be investigated. The motivations of psychogenic infertility are varied and many. As psychoanalytic investigation probes deeper, the differing weight of various developmental factors in individual cases becomes more and more obvious. When an investigator generalizes, he knows that his hypothesis covers only a definite group and that individuals within the group will require qualifications of the hypothesis.

When I wrote that structural changes of the ego caused by cultural influences might modify the fertility of women, I did not consider that hypothesis valid for all women in the same culture, not even for all infertile women of the same culture, or for all "career-striving" women. The population statistics of recent years show that work alone rarely interferes with fertility. On the other hand, work and career-striving may postpone the time when a married couple will consider themselves prepared for parenthood. It may happen that after many years of contraception, it may be too late; the woman may be infertile. Analysis of such cases might reveal that the motivation for postponing parenthood was just rationalization—the external circumstances served to protect the woman from recognizing her fear of pregnancy and motherhood. This is the basic motivation of the fear of being a woman.

Engel organized the somatic consequences of psychologic stress into two main groups. One of them constitutes the "flight-fight pattern," the other the "withdrawal-conservation pattern."[12] The latter group is activated by the extreme need for conservation of energy. In discussing the infertility of anorexia nervosa patients, it was pointed out that primary regression and withdrawal causes a condition which fits the flight pattern; it is the starvation-deprivation which leads to the later phase of the "withdrawal-conservation" pattern necessary for self-preservation. The "flight-fight" pattern of defense functions at a high cost of energy discharge, but not in psychosomatic infertility. Massive anxiety is warded off; flight-fight defenses require but minimal discharge of defensive energy, originally aggression. This permits the normal function of libidinal, integrative energies and their sublimations by protecting the personality from the anticipated danger of childbearing.

NOTES

1. Deutsch, H., "Motherhood," in *The Psychology of Women*, vol. II (New York, Grune & Stratton, 1945).

2. Seward, G. H., Wagern, P. S., Heinrich, J. F., Bloch, S. K., and Myerhoff, H. L., "The Question of Psychophysiologic Infertility: Some Negative Answers," *Psychosomatic Med.*, XXVII, no. 6 (1965), 533; Rubenstein, B. B., "An Emotional Factor in Infertility; A Psychosomatic Approach," *Fertility & Sterility*, II (1951), 80. This was an independent psychoanalytic investigation conducted by Rubenstein about the same time that our investigation on the problems of artificial insemination was in progress.

3. "Psychosomatic symptom" is a nonspecific term. The more we know about the interactions of psychodynamic and physiologic processes, the more will various conditions be designated under this heading.

4. Freud, S., "Inhibitions, Symptoms and Anxiety" (1926), *Std. Ed.*, XX, 88.

5. Alexander, F., *Psychosomatic Medicine* (New York, W. W. Norton, 1950).

6. Freud, S., Editor's Introduction to "Inhibitions, Symptoms and Anxiety," *Std. Ed.*, XX, 83.

7. Rheingold, J., *The Fear of Being a Woman* (New York, Grune & Stratton, 1964).

8. If young mothers in our urban civilization were to read this, they might answer, "No, we can have anesthesia if we want it but we say proudly we won't need it; we can have natural childbirth." "Natural childbirth" is not that way. But it seems that we can train mothers to overcome their anticipation of anxiety in the confidence that help will be available. Besides this, the hormonal state of pregnancy normally diminishes anxiety.

Indeed, the pain and anxiety of childbearing is the basic difference between male and female, between man and woman. The reproductive function of the male is not a danger, not a threat to life in a biologic sense. The individual and cultural consequences of this difference are secondary gains and losses that have happened to the female of our species during its history.

9. "The term ambivalence is often used to express the fact that attitudes of love and hate are simultaneously directed toward the same object." (Hartmann, H., Kris, E., and Loewenstein, R. M., "Notes on the Theory of Aggression," in *The Psychoanalytic Study of the Child*, Vol. III–IV (1949), p. 32.

10. Rheingold, J., *The Fear of Being a Woman.* Bibliography, note 7.

11. Rubenstein, B. B., "An Emotional Factor in Infertility; A Psychosomatic Approach."

12. Engel, G. L., *Psychological Development in Health and Disease* (Philadelphia, Saunders Co., 1962), p. 291.

11. Climacterium:
A Developmental Phase

INTRODUCTION

"Climacterium is a developmental phase." This concept came to me as an insight one bright, sunny morning in 1947, when I was starting out to conduct a seminar. It became a conviction as I surveyed the American scene of World War II and its aftermath. Women of all ages were working productively in industry and in the professions in various capacities. Many of them were of climacteric age or beyond. I was thinking of those who had always worked and therefore took work for granted and of those who had never worked before. They went to work in what I felt was a womanly manner; they did it because they were needed. They complained little and accomplished a great deal, some of them holding several jobs. I had to wonder, what were the psychologic processes that made such a release of constructive energy possible at this stage of life? In spite of my enthusiasm, when I presented this paper to the Chicago Psychoanalytic Society (1948), I qualified my thesis and defined normal climacterium as a progressive psychologic adaptation to a regressive biologic process.

This concept may appear sentimental compared with the attitude of many other investigators of climacteric women. The difference reflects old and new value judgments, culturally motivated concepts that confounded the physiologic issues and with them the psychology of women. Helene Deutsch describes an infantile personality when she states that a woman is mortified because she has to give up everything that she received at puberty, or she may have been thinking of the narcissistic woman when she said that "Mastering the psychologic reactions to the organic decline is one of the most difficult tasks of a woman's life."[1] The idea that women are mortified by the approaching climacterium is still prevalent in the literature. Szalita considers it "the threshold of senescence"; it is "invariably perceived as trauma." She describes it as

322

involution accompanied by despair and regret, followed by hopelessness and helplessness.[2]

Even if one considers that women bemoan the decline of sexual power or reproductive capacity with the onset of climacterium, it is obvious that women's attitude toward climacterium has changed at least as much as modern girls' attitude toward menstruation. The same cultural factors which seem to lead toward the equalization of the sexes have naturally diminished the girl's fear of the male sex and also her fear of menstruation. It may appear paradoxical but it is logical that as girls learn to accept the "feminine role," so mature women learn to give it up when the time arrives, without that sense of loss of identity that appeared threatening to many women not long ago.

What was responsible for that haunting fear of aging mixed with relief from the burdens of childbearing? Are Chinese women, who become a power in the family after their sons have married, also afraid of menopause? Do they connect with that age a loss of their own value, or do they take their position as a compensation for what they have lost, i.e., the power of sexual attractiveness and of bearing children? If so, why did Western man never get the idea of such a realistic compensation, why did he remain satisfied with the idealization of motherhood? Historians and anthropologists might provide us with data and so broaden the base of our conclusions. As psychoanalysts we must stay with our model of the genetic history of the individual. In it we find reflection of the culture which influenced the events that modified the individual's response to psychobiologic facts.

NOTES

1. Deutsch, H., *The Psychology of Women*, vol. II (New York, Grune & Stratton, 1945), p. 456.

2. Szalita, A., "Climacterium," in *The American Handbook of Psychiatry*, vol. III, ed. S. Arieti (New York, Basic Books, 1966), pp. 66–67. Szalita discusses male and female climacterium, but neither the syndrome of the fifty-year-old man nor of the climacteric woman justifies her general description.

CLIMACTERIUM: A DEVELOPMENTAL PHASE*

I wish to begin with a defense of the term "climacterium" which has made its way into medical dictionaries only very recently. The word was

* Read before the Chicago Psychoanalytic Society, February, 1948, and reprinted from *Psychoanalytic Quarterly*, XIX (1950), 1–27.

probably so neglected because of its hybrid, incorrect formation. It is derived from the word "climacter" which means the "round (or the bout) of the ladder"; thus, "climacteric" refers to something or somebody being around the top of the ladder and starting on the way down. Hence the popular term "change of life" is a meaningful translation of the medically often used, if linguistically haphazard, climacterium. It designates a particular period in life characterized by the termination of the reproductive period in women and is usually associated with the gradual cessation of the menstrual function—the menopause. Although the terms menopause and climacterium often are used as if they were interchangeable, the former should be reserved for one aspect of that period, the cessation of the menstrual flow, while climacteric or climacterium encompasses the more general bodily and emotional processes which usually coincide with menopause or follow it, and which are not necessarily causally related to it. However characteristic of the climacterium these manifestations may be, they are dependent upon the previous history of the individual; they are motivated by trends which, woven into the personality of the mature woman, may be reactivated by the internal changes associated with that period.

The concept of climacterium as a developmental phase can hardly be defended from the biological point of view. The growth of the individual in the climacterium was finished several decades, a full generation ago, when the physiological maturation channelized the "overflow of surplus energy" (1) to nourish the propagative function. Now this source is exhausted. The climacterium indicates that the ovaries have ceased to produce mature ova, that the cyclical production of the two ovarian hormones (estrogens and progestins) has ended, and therefore menstruation, which generally for about thirty to thirty-five years appeared regularly, now abates, indicating the end of the childbearing period. Helene Deutsch (2) summarized the hormonal changes of the menopause: "With the cessation of ovarian activity the remainder of the endocrine system is deranged in functioning." However exaggerated this may sound, the fact remains that at the climacterium the developing hypo-ovarianism indicates hormonal imbalance which may be accompanied by various systemic disturbances. The most generally known of these are manifestations of an increased instability of the sympathetic nervous system. Restlessness and insomnia, vasomotor instability, palpitation, and hot flushes are the most common, immediate symptoms of menopause. Other physiological signs of aging develop more slowly: the fat distribution changes, the breasts may atrophy, and in some individuals some growth of hair appears where before there was none. Aging is an involutional process which hardly can be called "development" from the biological point of view.

The psychodynamic point of view, however, is different. Development is a process in which the internal physiological changes and the psychological processes stimulated by them are integrated (or responded to) in a way which enables the individual to master further, and anew, environmental stimulations. While adaptation also includes regressive phenomena, development (as the term is used here) means progressive adaptation.

Do the observations justify the assumption that normal climacterium represents a progressive psychological adaptation to a regressive biological process? No doubt, adaptation is necessary. There is no other period in life—except puberty—when internal changes of the organism put the individual's capacity to master those changes to such a test; and while puberty may be difficult for many girls, even greater is the number of women who at the time of their climacteric show signs of stress, strain, and emotional disturbances of variable severity. Studies (*3*) of the medical and psychiatric aspects of the climacterium are confusing. In surveys of large groups of women it has been shown that eighty-five percent pass through climacterium without interrupting their daily routine; and of the remaining fifteen percent it could not be established that the menopause was the sole cause of the complaints. In a recent study Greenhill (*4*) questioned the advisability of using the term "climacteric syndrome." There are several recent psychiatric studies which speculate about the nature and cause of the reactive depression as the characteristic psychiatric picture of the climacteric woman. But to what are those women reacting?

Human development is determined by the past—as the past lives in the parents; in reference to women, specifically, the past resides in the mother whose personality is continued in the daughter. For it is well known that the intricate processes of identification with the mother during the preœdipal phase and the struggles with her during and after the œdipal period determine the girl's reactions to the pleasures and pains of that complex developmental task to which we usually refer as "the acceptance of the feminine role." Its first testing ground is puberty. The climacterium cannot be discussed without referring to some aspects of puberty, especially to the reactions to the first menstrual flow—the menarche.

Menstruation is one of the conspicuous manifestations of the physiological differences between the sexes. It signalizes the existence of an organ of which the girl previously was unaware and indicates its future functions of pregnancy and childbirth. It is no wonder that menstruation, often painful and always bloody, was surrounded in all cultures with a sort of mystic fear. Folklore as well as medical knowledge connected the ebb and flow of emotions in woman with the phenomenon of menstruation. Since Mary Chadwick (*5*) published a psychoanalytic interpretation of customs related to menstruation, several other significant anthropological investigations have dealt with society's response to and its defense against the menstruating woman (*6*). These studies show that society, probably indicating man's society, is, or used to be, deeply afraid of the menstruating woman. This fear, expressed in the great variety of taboos and customs, necessarily influenced the girl's reaction to menstruation. She learned from her mother indirectly and by observation that she would be excluded from society, that she would be regarded as dangerous. As a result of such expectations we all assume it to be quite normal that the girl responds to her menstruation with rebellion. In our culture women and men alike are so accustomed to referring to menstruation as "the curse" that we can ask with some amazement why we readily accept the idea that women should be desperate when the pains and inconveniences of menstruation disappear from their lives.

Although the aging woman does not appear to be a promising subject for anthropological studies, there are observations indicating that in several primitive societies the woman gains status and enjoys greater freedom in social functions after she passes her menopause (7). Beyond the sociological setting, folklore and fairy tales reveal the emotional attitudes toward the aging woman. There exists a large fairy-tale literature about the kind, discerning, loving, and undemanding grandmother; she is very often the one who undoes the harm of the world and the harm done by the parents, especially by the mother. (This aspect of fairy tales deserves special consideration.) Even more extensive is the folklore about the vicious, "bad," old woman. The various activities of witches in many cultures and centuries reflect the fear which men, and women too, harbor regarding the old woman who has lost her charms, her capacity to love, and who, because of this loss, or (psychodynamically speaking) as a result of it, becomes hostile and irrationally dangerous. One fought against her during the Middle Ages with unreasonable, bigoted vigor. The stories about witches and witch hunts and the documented processes against them represent the struggle against the woman who became dangerous because she became sexless. Does this relate to the climacteric woman? To her rage and relentless anger because she has lost her ways and means of sexual gratification? Folklore knows better. It depicts the witch either as a young, narcissistic woman who does not desire the man and therefore is unconquerable by him; or as a very old woman who either never had children, or hated them and therefore was completely disappointed and frustrated by them. Thus folklore accounts in a broad way, but very clearly, for those aspects in women's personality and fate which finally lead in some women to the picture of the aggressive and/or anxious—and in any case, unloving and self-centered—old woman. The model of that fairy tale is the old woman as she had become after a long period of involution, and does not symbolize woman at the age of the "change of life."

It is well known that sexual excitability, desire for sexual gratification, and the capacity to achieve it do not cease immediately with the menopause; women who were not frigid before may keep their orgastic potentialities for a long time. There are also some women whose orgastic capacities, as if released from fear, definitely increase for a period during the climacterium. There is little of the mystic fear and the tendency to isolate the climacteric woman in the way menstruating women are customarily isolated in some cultures (7). On the contrary, women who are about to lose their propagative powers and sexual attractiveness gain power and prestige in many cultures. It would be interesting to know more about the emotional and psychosomatic reactions of women to menopause in societies like the Chinese where the woman becomes a real power within the family only after her son is married. The "change of life"—we may assume—is not as threatening to them as it is to women in our society in which youth is at a premium. Probably this prompted Helene Deutsch (2) to state: "The woman [in the climacterium] is mortified because she has to give up everything that she received in puberty." This, of course, could be true only if woman received a gift of sexual maturity at puberty in one parcel and kept it as a stable asset until—just as traumatically as it came into her life—it disappeared.

Much of the exaggerated fear of menopause appears to be culturally determined. It is an expression of the expectation—in woman and in man alike—that the abating sexual function will be experienced as an irreparable blow to the ego. These observations do not, however, sufficiently take into account the changes which occurred in our own civilization during the last decades. In Western civilization, not only the attitude toward the climacteric woman, but the climacteric woman herself, seems to have changed in many respects. The responsibility for this lies with the cultural process known as "the emancipation of women." The interaction of cultural and biological factors could be directly demonstrated in the evolution of the psychosexual personality of women in our times (8).

The woman's life, more markedly than the man's, is divided into periods which are defined by the reproductive functions. There are many signs of physiologic maturation before the first menstruation. Recent investigations have shown that the onset of menstruation does not indicate complete functional maturity (9); from the menarche to full physiologic capacity for childbearing several years may pass. These years of complex interaction between physiologic and emotional events of maturation represent *adolescence;* the length of this period, as well as its manifestations, show great individual variations. It should not be forgotten that female psychosexual development is more complex than that of the male, since woman has to adapt to sexuality not only as a pleasurable function but also has to adapt to its pain. Pain is an integrative part of the psychosexual experience of woman. This may be exaggerated by secondary masochism or may be erotized by the normal feminine libidinal processes. Which of these will be the fate of a girl is determined by many factors. The most significant is her mother's personality—her mother's emotional and sociological orientation to her own feminine functions. Through identification, this determines the girl's attitude toward herself as a woman; it motivates her reactions to menstruation, her acceptance of or her rebellion against the painfulness of the female sexual functions. Emancipation and mental and physical hygiene no doubt minimize the trauma of menstruation. Yet the psychosexual integration of menstruation in the total personality is a complex process of maturation which is usually not finished during adolescence. Psychosexual development receives new impetus when the sexual function reaches its completion by impregnation, pregnancy, and childbirth.

From menarche to menopause, in cyclic intervals, the woman prepares for conception, failure of which results in the menstrual flow. From one menstruation to another, with an average interval of twenty-eight days, the female sexual cycle revolves.

The sexual cycle in women represents a complete correlation between the preconscious manifestations of emotions and the hormonal function of the ovaries (10). The busy life of a woman may cover up what is happening to her physiologically. However rarely and however little she may permit herself to express her emotional needs, dreams, and fantasies, the subtle changes in the tempo of her daily living reveal a close and unbroken response to the physiological stimuli originated by the ovarian hormones. These hormones, and this should be clearly understood, do not create the personality or its characteristics, but do stimulate and bring to the fore the specific emotional needs which participate in creating specific emotional tensions. The woman responds to the estrogens—to the follicle-ripening hormones—with an increased tendency for extroverted activity; her heterosexual desire increases parallel with it and usually reaches its height about the time of ovulation. After this the woman is under the influence of the progestins, the hormones which prepare the uterus for nidation. This stimulation turns the woman's emotional interest toward herself, pregnancy, and children. If pregnancy does not occur, the hormonal production declines, the uterine mucosa breaks down and menstruation follows. The study of the premenstrual phase of the cycle, i.e., of the emotional events which accompany the physiological decline of hormone production, gives us a clue to the physiology and pathology of climacterium.

Freud recognized in his early observations that during the days approaching menstruation, the woman repeats the neurotic constellation which she established at puberty (11). This concept has its validity today although closer scrutiny of the hormonal and emotional processes qualifies its psychodynamic meaning.

In every cycle the woman's feeling of love, her capacity to love—sexually as well as in a more sublimated sense—increases with the rise of the sexual hormone level. It is our conclusion that, normally, the woman reaches the highest level of her psychosexual integration at the height of her hormonal cycle. This integration, in emotion and behavior, changes as the woman responds to the inner perception of the hormonal decline. Corresponding with Freud's original assumption of a "premenstrual neurosis" most psychoanalysts assume that women respond to the conscious expectation of menstruation as if it were a repetition of the trauma of the first menstruation. In this way they explain that women, during the days preceding menstruation, often become restless, anxious, and irritable. Sensitiveness to being hurt, fearfulness, crankiness, and fatigue often alternate with tense, impatient, hostile moods which should indicate the woman's fear and resentment of the "fact of castration" which—it is assumed—menstrual flow represents to her. This interpretation seems to be justified since the accompanying dreams and fantasies often reveal the young woman's anxious preoccupation with her body. Dreams often express the fear of bleeding, rebellion against femininity, hatred toward men, the wish to attack and hurt men, the fear of harm to her own body, or fear of being killed. Such reactions may be accompanied by sexual desire which has an urgent character, as if the woman, fearful of frustration, would demand gratification with the expression of hostility rather than love. Other women, or the same woman in other premenstrual phases, may lack sexual desires; they are depressed and feel depreciated; a sense of loss, or a fear of losing something, may best describe their emotional state. Dreams then usually contain the symbols of anal-eliminative, soiling tendencies. During the premenstrual phase the woman appears and acts less composed, less mature; she is more dependent and demanding than she was at the height of the same sexual cycle. Thus, observation of behavior indicates a regression, however temporary this may be. A study of the psychoanalytic material reveals that in correlation with the premenstrual hormonal decline, the libido (psychosexual energy) regresses from what is called the "level of genital integration" to a more primitive, anal-sadistic, or to a passive-dependent level.

If such regression may occur in every sexual cycle with the decline of hormone production, what should the woman expect when there is a permanent decline of hormonal production? Such monthly experiences would justify every pessimistic expectation in regard to the menopause and on a physiologic basis would challenge the concept of climacterium as a developmental phase.

The persistence of premenstrual symptoms, their severity and character, have a prognostic significance for the climacterium. Yet fortunately, this itself belongs in the realm of pathology. Although one or the other of these symptoms may occur in every woman normally, the premenstrual symptoms decrease with the progress of psychosexual maturation. While dreams may still reveal signs of psychodynamic regression, the adult woman and mother, especially if she is not frustrated sexually, has usually little or only negligible signs of her premenstrual phase. There is a developmental absorption of those conflicts which are responsible for the premenstrual tension. (Here I mean by "conflict" not only the psychological, but also the hormonal aspect of the functional disturbance.) Physiological maturation, as well as emotional development, is favorably influenced if the propagative function evolves completely—if the woman has children.

There are women to whom life denies this fulfillment. Early disturbances of psychosexual development may be responsible for a personality which, in itself frustrated, impedes the woman's interpersonal relationships in such a way as to enforce external frustrations. A woman has to have a personality which permits her to be passive, to be loved and cared for, so that she may give in to her physiological needs with pleasure, without protest, and thus may enjoy pregnancy and motherhood. If her personality does not permit her to respond to her physiological needs, she will struggle against them within herself during every sexual cycle. These are the women who suffer from the symptom complex of premenstrual tension or premenstrual depression to such a degree that the condition may become an expression of serious emotional disturbance.

This is the case of a young, married woman of twenty-five, tall, slender, boyish in build, but feminine and sensitive in facial expression. She came for treatment for what she described as "negativistic behavior." Her withdrawal from social and professional life had started soon after she married about four years previously. She had suffered from dysmenorrhea from the time she entered college and began to have more or less serious flirtations. Three to ten days before every menstruation, she was sick; she felt heavy and swollen, she had cramps, was depressed and irritable; a sense of hopelessness and emptiness alternated with an anger which she described as "wrath without adrenalin." She felt rage without energy for expressing it. She had diarrhea, colic, nausea with her menstrual pain. Throughout her analysis she appeared to be sterile. During the time of the premenstrual depression and even at times when she was free from depression, she was self-centered. She lived in fantasy, and did not dare to take any responsibility except taking meticulous care of her little household for fear that she could not live up to her own ideal. This was her rationalization for not wanting a child.

The patient was the second of two daughters. Her developmental history revealed that she suffered from the distant, reserved, undemonstrative attitude of her otherwise conscientious parents, especially from the coldness of her mother. As a preschool child she speculated whether she was adopted. Her mother's answer to this question was, "As far as I can remember, I bore you." This answer the patient always consciously connected with her feeling that "nothing is certain in this world." Probably such frustrations drove her into temper tantrums so severe that her father once said, "Take that child away before I kill her." Yet her need for affection turned her toward her father, who offered more tenderness than her mother. Her œdipal struggle ended with a strong masculine identification. In her fantasies she often was a boy. She and her sister fancied themselves brothers rather than sisters. Her fantasies showed that her feminine libidinal needs were in conflict with her masculine identification; yet her overcompensatory masculine drive was not too intense. After she gave up her temper tantrums in childhood, she became rather retiring and shy. Her mother prepared her for menstruation in a purely intellectual way, telling her also about the changes she would experience in the "change of life." Thus she behaved very "reasonably" when she started to menstruate at the age of thirteen. Her menses came irregularly, at six to eight week intervals. She did not have severe pains until she was about seventeen years of age. On the purely physiological side we may speculate that this was because her ovaries were functioning inadequately. Viewing it psychologically we may say that sexuality was not an actual problem in her life until she felt threatened by her awakening needs and rebelled against her feminine role. This is the usual explanation of dysmenorrhea. Now we must add that this "rebellion" was the emotional manifestation of an organic dysfunction: retarded development, puerile organs, insufficient hormone production went hand in hand with this patient's "psychosexual inhibition." She received hormone treatment for two and a half years during which the intervals between menses became shorter, but the dysmenorrhea did not improve. (It seems that intensifying the estrogen stimulation at a time when she was still struggling against her feminine desires was not an etiologically sound therapy.) Her marriage intensified the conflict. Depression, agitation, sensitivity, and quarrelsomeness increased; she was sterile.

Vaginal smears revealed that the patient's hormonal production was insufficient in comparison with women of her age. Although her psychoanalytic material had shown that she responded emotionally even to a slight degree of estrogen or progesterone production—the content of her dreams and fantasies changed characteristically with either of the hormone groups—her feeling in either case was frustration. Her own words often expressed clearly that she felt the deficiency in herself as a lack, a want, an emptiness which, she explained, "took part of her" so that the remaining part was unable to produce a feeling of satisfaction, either in herself, by herself, or by her husband. Instead of responding sexually she was "seeking that part of herself which she needed in order to be whole, satisfied, and satisfiable." The anger accompanying such a sense of frustration was turned toward herself when she felt helpless, inferior, withdrawn; when it increased so that she could not hold it any longer, she projected the reasons of her unhappiness and discharged her anger against others, particularly against her husband. We may say the patient responded to the inefficient hormone production with emotions revealing a perception of being frustrated internally by processes, within her organism, beyond her control. The sense of futility, as well as the effort to discharge the emotional tension, necessarily created conflicts with her environment, in this case, with her husband. Thus the internal frustrations, the emotional manifestations of the lack of hormones, and the external frustrations (real or secondary, created by her own behavior) entered into an emotional vicious circle which explained her wrath as well as her depression. That the patient suffered from this most intensely during the very long, low hormone level period before menses is easily understandable. For then, not only is the hormone level lower than usual, but the vegetative nervous system at this time appears to respond to the lack of hormonal stimulation with a greater sensitivity. In the premenstrual phase the ego seems weaker, the psychic apparatus less capable of fulfilling its tasks of mastering stimulation and frustrations, whether produced without or within the individual.

This case demonstrates that the psychosexual development—arrested, involved, or complicated—may lead to an inhibition of the hormone production which was perceived by this sensitive and introspective woman as an "internal frustration."

In psychoanalysis the term frustration indicates that a drive is thwarted in attaining its goal. Thus, frustration may be the result of external prohibitions, or of the internal prohibitions of the superego which debars the instinctual need from gratification. It is assumed that the perception of being frustrated is dependent upon the dammed-up libido, i.e., the psychosexual energy of the thwarted impulses. Here, however, we use the term *internal frustration* to refer to the patient's description of her feelings which reveals a perception of her inability to feel gratified. Although in this case we assume that this was the result of the development of her personality, this was not our concern in the study of the patient's hormonal cycles. In correlating the inefficient ovarian production with her sense of frustration, we assume that the latter expresses a lack of libidinous emotions rather than the reaction to or expression of "dammed-up libido." This distinction is significant for the psychodynamics of climacterium. For the sense of internal frustration—as the patient described it—not only explains many symptoms of premenstrual tension and depression, but it is also in the center of the emotional experience of the climacterium.

Much of the confusion about the climacterium originates in the lack of understanding of the physiology and psychology of the sexual cycle. "The Sexual Cycle in Women" (*10*) describes the fluctuations of emotional manifestations in correlation with the hormonal cycle. Although it contains only a sketchy and incomplete demonstration of immensely complex events, it permits a rough differentiation between two kinds of emotional tensions: one is created by, or can be correlated with high gonadal hormone production; the other represents the manifestation of the lack of libidinization, and it seems to be created by a lack of desire, a sense of internal frustration which coincides usually with low hormonal phases of the sexual cycle. We know that the former, libidinal tension, expresses itself in sexual wish, desire, or need, while the latter manifests itself with anger and other regressive phenomena.

Keeping in mind what we know about the sexual cycle, many observations about climacterium fall in line. The emotional tension originating in the conflicts of feminine development may return when the hormonal function, which formerly neutralized (or libidinized) the tension during the years of sexual maturity, declines and its integrative effects dissipate. This may explain why many psychological aspects of climacterium seem to represent a repetition of puberty, especially the puberal reaction to menstruation. The rebellion of puberty appears to be repeated when the internal frustration of the declining hormonal function activates aggressive, hostile, and regressive behavior. Hormone therapy is considered to be the method of choice. Yet the complex psychodynamic motivations which lead to the symptoms—whether they be "premenstrual" or actually "climacteric"—may account for the failures of hormone therapy. While hormones usually alleviate the vasovegetative symptoms, they do not resolve the emotional conflicts without adequate psychotherapy. It requires a thorough understanding of the patient's personality to discover the emotional problem to which the woman responds when she suffers from a reactive depression. It is the consensus that the psychiatric symptoms around the time of climacterium can be classified as reactive depression.

Many women present a period of anxious overactivity instead of, or before the development of depression. Women who could not develop enough emotional security, who feel that they did not achieve the goal of femininity, may be seized by fear of aging, or fear of losing their sexual attractiveness. These women appear driven, inwardly urged to start life again. Such women, more than others, will overreact to the outward, superficial signs of the climacterium. Like a young girl who is afraid of blushing because it reveals sexual emotions, the climacteric woman may be afraid that the hot flushes expose her secret. Fortunately, estrogenic hormones control the hot flushes completely and also diminish the other signs of physiological instability. Another manifestation of sexual decline in the climacteric is the tendency to indulge in eating. Nowadays women feel that they have to fight this tendency; thus they often enforce an external frustration at a time when they have to adjust slowly to the internal upset of their equilibrium.

In accordance with our observations on the premenstrual phase, we may assume that such narcissistic, more or less regressive, preoccupation is one of the manifestations of declining hormonal production which diminishes the ego's capacity to love. However, at a time when there is an increased tendency to regression, the woman has to meet the tasks of her life situation and they may be very complex and demanding just at this period. Not to mention marital discord which may occur on account of the changing pace (sexual and otherwise) between husband and wife, there may be many events upsetting the emotional balance of the family. Daughters grow away and begin their own sexual lives; sons bring home their wives. Many similar situations may activate tensions in the woman which she has difficulty in mastering. As long as she is able to relate her difficulties to actual situations and responds to them in the manner and degree she did during her adult life, she is safe. In many instances, however, the external conflict activates responses in her which she cannot reconcile with her accustomed behavior or with her ego ideal. Then her self is hurt. Her ego-alien emotional responses threaten her. "This cannot happen to me," is an often heard defense of the climacteric person. Which aspect of the decline will mobilize in the woman the disappointment in herself depends on the total personality. Any disappointment in the self engenders feelings of inferiority and self-accusations which may finally lead to severe depression.

The following two cases illustrate the psychodynamics of severe climacteric depression. One patient was a successful professional woman, compulsive in her personality makeup, rigid, and ambitious. She was unmarried and had never had sexual relations with men, although she was appreciated and respected as a friend and a clever companion. In her early forties, her relationship to one of her professional woman friends became intimate and sexual. She felt some guilt about this but was satisfied for many years. Then the early vasomotor disturbances of the approaching menopause forced her to take a vacation, after which she went to work with relentless vigor. Slowly she began to feel that her friend did not appreciate her work, that she was being taken advantage of. She became very "nervous," insecure, and sleepless. She took another vacation—her need for it explained by her menopause. But while she was away from her work she became panicky. Suddenly she felt that everything was wrong with the friendship and the work which had seduced her into this relationship. Yet she hoped she could get hold of herself by mustering all her will power, collecting all her ego strength. "This can't happen to me," she repeated to herself, and while she fought against it, she became more and more aware of the failings of her ego defenses. She became desperate because her ability to do what she wanted and had found to be right had vanished. Her ego strength submerged in panic, she developed a psychotic episode.

On the basis of conclusions drawn from the premenstrual symptoms, namely, that the lack of hormone diminishes the ego's integrative strength, we can assume that as this woman's hormonal function declined, her ego (like that of some women in their premenstrual phase) lost the power to integrate all the demands of her daily life. Since she did not produce enough libido to meet those demands, she felt frustrated. She projected the reasons of her internal frustrations and began to respond with great sensitivity to an environment which before had been completely compatible and satisfactory. This oversensitive reaction brought about the patient's critical attitude toward her friend and thus her great disappointment. Clinically one would say that this woman, in her menopause, developed a reactive depression because of a grave disappointment which she experienced due to a homosexual relationship. Psychodynamically, we assume that the hormonal decline and all the psychophysiological changes which it implies, mobilized a regression of the ego's integrative capacity. This regression brought to the fore various previously compensated aspects of her personality, such as oversensitiveness, narcissistic reactions, etc. Evaluation of all factors raises doubt as to whether one should consider such a depressive, psychotic reaction as a simple reactive depression.

Another case ended with suicide. This woman, who had many advantages of money and education, was dissatisfied all her life. She was married, had children, had a profession, yet her narcissistic character neurosis interfered with every area of her life. Time after time she went from a blissful satisfaction with her own artistic understanding into a state of desperation, since she felt she could not share her own feelings with anyone else. Neither her husband, nor her children, could ever live up to her expectations. About the time of her menopause, the periods of depression became longer and increasingly severe, while menstruation still occasionally occurred. Her depression represented a rebellion against aging; it progressed to a fatal termination because of her narcissistic character neurosis. Her emotional gratification resulted from intellectual and esthetic pleasures, yet her sublimations did not represent a balanced growth of the total personality. They went parallel with an adolescent expectation of purely platonic, idealized relationships with men—a sort of fulfillment of her bisexual tendencies—which should elevate her above the disappointments and dejection of female sexuality. She was unable to achieve happiness in interpersonal relationships. No matter how enthusiastically she began them, she soon reverted to herself, to her past, to her idealized experiences. The present never measured up to the past; she never measured up to her ego ideal. When aging destroyed the hopes for the realization of her ego ideal, the flexibility of her ego was already exhausted by the great internal strain of many previous attempts and, with the beginning of old age, the hope for narcissistic gratification became more remote than ever. As if she had overdrawn her account for substitute gratification, when the internal frustration became unbearable, she committed suicide. Her rationalization was that she wanted to free her children from her inadequate personality. Thus she won a final (narcissistic-aggressive) victory: she did not need to go through the deterioration of aging.

These examples demonstrate that the symptoms of psychiatric disturbances of the climacterium are determined by lifelong, individually characteristic methods of mastery of psychic tension. The analysis of the factors involved in the mastery of frustration—as it can be studied in the sexual cycle—may serve as indication for the psychic reaction to be expected about the time of the menopause. In the two examples cited, the psychic adaptation failed during and after the climacterium. If adaptation to frustration occurs always, or usually, at a cost of an increase in the narcissistic defenses of the ego, we may expect that the narcissistic armor will break when it becomes overtaxed by the internal and external frustrations of the climacterium. Yet it seems that in the cyclical repetition of the gonadal function the woman has a method of practicing her adaptive capacities. The repetitiveness of the sexual cycle prepares the woman not only for the tasks of motherhood but, through the mastery of the emotional fluctuations corresponding to hormonal decline and menstruation, for the physiologic cessation of gonadal stimulation at the climacterium.

Psychoanalysis as a genetic theory of personality recognizes the marked influx of sexual energy as the crucial impetus to development. Our question is whether it is justified to characterize the more or less chronic but well-defined cessation of the reproductive function also as a "developmental phase." Its hazards and the factors which may be responsible for its pathology have been discussed. It has also been shown that the pathology which becomes manifest or dangerously aggravated in climacterium existed previously. The climacterium adds only one factor: it diminishes that part of the integrative strength of the personality which is dependent upon stimulation by gonadal hormones.

Every developmental phase has its pitfalls. The psychoanalytic theory of neurosis and of personality development represents but an evaluation of the fate of the œdipal phase. In our culture, the greater part of the libidinal influx which affects the œdipal phase has to be repressed in order that the personality may develop normally. The mastery of the œdipal complex—as Freud assumes—is a process of desexualization which is responsible for establishing human personality with its internalized psychic faculty, the superego. The sexualized eros needs to be freed from its genital-libidinal qualities to act as an integrative force. We know that at puberty the influx of sexual energy attacks the already achieved integrity of the personality; thus a period of developmental struggle follows, after which mature sexuality—socially permissible and gratifying function—becomes a fundamental part of a complex adult life.

Psychoanalysis has tried to formulate in various ways the psychodynamic meaning of mature "adult" love. We assume that it is a combination of genital-propagative tendencies with "goal-inhibited," "postambivalent," i.e., tender, protective empathic qualities of heterosexual feelings. Helene Deutsch (2), in her extensive study, has taken great care to explain the specific manifestations of feminine love and its sublimations—intuition and motherliness. Her concepts of a deeply rooted passivity and a specific tendency to introversion, as specific qualities of female psychology, were confirmed by our studies of the sexual cycle in women. Our investigation revealed that the "deeply rooted passivity" and the "tendency to introversion" are repeated in cyclic intervals in correlation with progesterone production; and we conclude that these characteristics of the emotional life of woman represent the psychodynamic manifestations of the female propagative tendency, the woman's biological need for pregnancy and motherhood. The emotional manifestations of the passive-receptive tendency may appear regressive (or rather "recessive") in comparison with the active, extroverted heterosexual behavior. Yet its monthly repetition can be considered as preparation for the withdrawal and introversion of psychic energies which motivate the moods and emotional attitudes during pregnancy. The concentrated libidinal charge of the body—a result of the physiological processes maintaining the pregnancy—enhances the woman's willingness for and pleasure in bearing the child; her pregnant body, like a reservoir replenished with libidinal feelings, becomes the source of motherliness. Motherliness, complex and emotionally charged, is not independent from hormonal functioning. As it unfolds with its many functions and shades of feelings, it serves not only the infant, but also the mother; it affords her pleasures originating in infantile erotic as well as in highly sublimated gratifications. The emotional interaction between mother and child, while it establishes the child's identification with the mother, maintains and furthers the mother's identification with the child; for the mother's psychosexual life encompasses her child, all her children. Psychoanalytic studies reveal that with her daughter more directly than with her son—but with each child in a somewhat different manner—the mother repeats those emotional attitudes which originally determined her own psychosexual development. Thus, with each child the mother takes the chance and has the hope of reliving and overcoming the conflicts in her own personality. Identification with the child may be the pitfall of motherliness as well as its bliss. Many mothers do not outgrow early, infantile-possessive identifications with the child, and various pathological distortions of motherliness ensue. Yet normally the mother progresses with her child, especially if she lets the child develop; she regains her own emotional independence as she permits her child to become independent of her. Motherhood, indeed, plays a significant role in the development of woman. Physiologically, it completes maturation; psychologically, it channelizes the primarily introverted, narcissistic tendencies into many psychic qualities designated "feminine," such as responsiveness, empathy, sympathy, and the desire to do, to care for others, etc. Thus, from motherliness it is only one step to many forms of feminine achievement since these, or many of them, represent the extension and expansion of motherliness.

The accomplishments of the reproductive period—and this means not only the propagative function, but also the total developmental achievement of the personality, its lasting sublimations, its capacity for love—will sustain the personality when the cyclically returning hormonal stimulation abates and the woman faces the "change of life." This change in the normal course of events does not occur as a sudden upheaval which breaks the established code of the personality, but evolves as a slow process of maturation. As the desexualization of the emotional needs proceeds, the balanced personality finds new aims for the psychic energy.[1]

This statement recalls the œdipal phase and invites comparison. In the œdipal phase, repression of the sexual impulses leads to superego formation and socialization of the child; in the climacterium, the cessation of biological growth affects further intrapersonal integration— a transmutation of growth—and releases new impetus for socialization and learning.

Many of the interpersonal attitudes of the woman change. She does not love with youthful ardor, but much of her ambivalence, jealousy, and insecurity have been overcome. Thus her love becomes more tolerant and shows those "postambivalent" qualities which Abraham (12) expected from maturation at a younger age. This attitude evolves unconsciously and effortlessly toward grandchildren; identifica-

---

1. In the discussion of this paper, it was called to my attention that it may be confusing to the reader that we speak about the effects of the gonadal hormones as *stimulation* for development, and that then we state that the cessation of the gonadal activity serves again as a sort of stimulation for developmental achievements.

From puberty to menopause, the sexual cycle represents the individually characteristic struggle between the sexual drives and the ego. The mastery of the resulting conflict-tension is in the service of the propagative functions, from the biological point of view. Psychodynamically, the same processes achieve a greater integrative capacity within the personality. Thus when the approaching menopause diminishes the fluctuations of the sexual drive, the ego is flexible enough to use the energies released from previous tasks for new integrations. (We used the terms maturation and development as do Hartmann, Kris, and Loewenstein in their paper "Comments on the Formation of Psychic Structure," in *The Psychoanalytic Study of the Child*, vol. II, New York, International Universities Press, 1947.)

tion with her pregnant daughter or daughter-in-law permits the aging woman to be a mother again—even if one step removed. It is well known that a woman's love toward her grandchildren is free from the conflicts of a mother toward her own children.

Closer to awareness, because they require more deliberate effort, are the middle-aged woman's intentions toward greater socialization. As if her superego would become stricter, she demands more from herself now than she did before; her ambitions may be reserved for her household or for accomplishments for the sake of her family, but almost as often it happens that her activities expand to include new and larger fields of interest. A greater social conscientiousness, and often an avid desire to learn, stimulates women to various, even if sometimes incongruous, activities for which—as they usually rationalize—they "did not have time" before.

Is it just a problem of time, of unaccustomed leisure, that women, freed from the tensions and fluctuations of sexuality, released from fears of and desires for childbearing, finished with the time-consuming duties of child care, suddenly feel an influx of extroverted energy? Probably one will be inclined to answer that women, emancipated from childbearing, throw themselves with great eagerness into a competitive, communal life or even into professions and business in order to act out a "masculine protest," so long stagnant behind the duties of their feminine role." It may be! Yet our case studies have shown that those women whose personalities have been exhausted by narcissistic defenses and masculine protest do not show such a postclimacteric development; rather, they become sick. The women described here are not those whose activities, even if goodwilled, become destructive because they are charged with aggression. Fortunately, there is a larger number of those who, while they learned to accept frustrations and substitute gratifications in earlier life, become able to open up new areas of satisfaction for themselves after the climacterium. It is as if these women, reassured that their main job is done, may draw on the emotional capital invested in that achievement so that they overcome feelings of inferiority and insecurity which inhibited them before. No doubt the emancipation from sexual competition and from the fear of sexual rejection often releases talents and qualities unsuspected before. What may appear as the overconfidence of the dilettante may be growth for the individual. Measured on another scale, these attempts may be insignificant; their primary purport may be the individual's psychological gain: they enable a woman to rise above regressive phenomena which make the climacterium such a critical period for others. Yet the uncountable attempts add up to an important contribution to the creative and social life of the nation.

Harvey O'Higgins (*13*), in an excellent book, *The American Mind in Action,* deals with these problems in discussing the role of women in

American society. With fine psychological understanding, he describes the various types of American woman. He gives greatest importance to the Puritan woman who used to be and still is the "home and mother type." To her he ascribes the emotional and ideological education of the nation. The effectiveness and influence of the American mother does not spread merely through the channels of home living and the raising of children. Much of the work was done, and is being done, through the almost inexhaustible idealism and educational ambition of women, outside the family, in communal and cultural activities; and much of it is accomplished after they reach and pass the climacterium. All this would not be possible if women did not, and could not, meet the climacterium as a developmental phase.

Our discussion has dealt so far only with woman, in spite of the fact that one uses the term "male climacterium" to refer to phenomena attending the decrease of normal sexual function in the male. It is not our intention to present a study of the male climacteric here. Yet it seems opportune to mention that the male climacterium necessarily differs from that of the female since there are fundamental differences in the biological functions of both sexes, and also in the cultural and sociological attitudes in regard to them.

In the female, the two psychodynamic tendencies of the propagative functions—the need for heterosexual gratification and the need for reproduction—are separated, while they are fulfilled by one act of the sexual function of the male. In the male, the sexual desire tending toward genital gratification reaches consciousness with a sense of active urgency while the need for reproduction does not need to become conscious at all. Although there is evidence indicating that the human male also has a primary instinctual need for parenthood which he may express in the desire for offspring, yet the cultural and sociological significance of fatherhood usually overshadows the instinctual need. Accordingly, in the male, there is no cyclically returning recession and reintegration of the gonadal and emotional pattern comparable with the female sexual cycle. Thus the psychosexual maturation of the male does not prepare him either for parenthood or for the cessation of the gonad function by a similar repetition of the adaptive processes by which the woman is prepared. In women, the menopause indicates the cessation of the reproductive function in an unmistakable manner, even if a capacity for sexual gratification remains. In men, the termination of the reproductive function is not expected as long as orgastic potency remains. Actually, both the sexual urge and the reproductive capacity may be rekindled even if they appear to be extinguished. Thus, men have not to meet the hazards and benefits of a "change of life," circumscribed in time and in its manifestations. Aging is a slow, insidious process in men which they may fear and deny, and against which they are not protected by an adequate emotional preparation.

In the patriarchal society, the social significance of the aging man was beyond doubt. Whatever the oscillations of his psychosexual potency were, he did not need to feel threatened since his importance as head of his family was not impaired and his social prestige was growing rather than declining. Our society, however, puts little premium on aging. The decline of sexual potency becomes a double threat if marriages are insecure. In a competitive society, the necessity to prove himself never ceases for a man. Men in our society, less protected by tradition than they were before (and less than women are protected even today), try to compensate for their insecurity with increased self-reliance and with unceasing competitive productivity. And while these efforts sap his energy, he prepares for his old age only in terms of a "retirement plan." This is his illusion of security, qualified by the idea of having time to play. But play—even if he could succeed with his preparations for it in time—does not give enough gratification for an ego which is used to getting its satisfaction by hard-gained and well-fought-for attainments. As long as the retirement age is far away, one can think of it with relish; when it approaches, the first signs of diminishing potency—sexual and otherwise—bring about a serious narcissistic conflict. The psychosomatic and psychiatric aspects of geriatrics deal with a great variety of attempts toward the mastery of the conflicts of the aging man.

Various aspects of biological and social life converge to make aging a task less difficult for women than for men. Probably this is the key to the secret that women, after they reach the end of their reproductive period, have a longer life expectancy than men in the corresponding age group. After the woman succeeds in mastering the adaptive task of her climacterium, she can plan an active life which promises much ego gratification. She can reap the harvest of her previous work, for she may feel loved and important in a family which now grows as a part of her, but without pain and effort; besides, whatever she produces with her sublimated endeavors is looked upon by herself, as well as by others, as a surplus. This surplus gratification—while it cannot propagate growth directly—sustains emotional satisfaction and helps to balance the regressive phenomena of the oncoming exhaustion of vital energies in senescence.

SUMMARY

The climacterium is characterized as a period of intrapersonal reorganization in women. Parallel with the declining hormone production, menopause is that aspect of aging which proceeds with the desexualization of the emotional needs; this in turn releases psychic energies for sublimation and further integration of the personality.

Anthropological data concerning menstruation and menopause are cited to indicate that cultural patterns determine to a high degree the anticipation of and the reactions to a physiological experience of the individual. In our culture, the climacterium is anticipated with exaggerated fear. The psychiatric symptoms which often accompany the menopause are, however, not related in simple causality to the physiology of that event; they are rather motivated by the psychosexual history of the individual.

Study of the sexual cycle affords the clue to the psychopathology of the climacterium. The sexual cycle represents the correlation between the hormonal function of the ovaries and the conscious and preconscious manifestations of emotions. The highest level of psychosexual integration corresponds to the peak of the hormone production; parallel with the premenstrual hormone decline a regression takes place. The manifestations of this regression represent the premenstrual neurosis.

An instance of premenstrual depression is cited to illustrate that disturbed psychosexual development may lead to inhibition of the gonadal function, and that inadequate production of hormones may be perceived as a lack of libidinous emotions causing a sense of frustration from within. The individually characteristic methods of mastery of psychic tensions—as they may be studied in the sexual cycle—serve as indications of the psychic reactions to be expected about the time of menopause. Two cases of severe climacteric depression are presented to demonstrate that the failures of adaptation to the internal frustration of the menopause were determined by the already previously exhausted and rigid adaptive mechanisms of those individuals.

In the female, the two psychodynamic tendencies of the propagative functions—the need for heterosexual gratification and the need for reproduction—are separated; cyclical repetition of these two trends of the sexual drive prepares the woman for the complex physiological and emotional processes of her reproductive function. Motherhood is a further step in the integration of the personality. Physiologically, it completes sexual maturation; psychologically, it channelizes and sublimates the specifically feminine trends of the sexual drive. The accomplishment of the reproductive period, and its lasting sublimations, sustain the personality during the climacterium so that after the woman has succeeded in mastering the adaptive task of her climacterium, she can plan an active life which promises ego satisfaction.

REFERENCES

1. Alexander, Franz: *Psychoanalysis Revised*. Psychoanalytic Quarterly, IX, 1940, p. 1.

2. Deutsch, Helene: *The Psychology of Women*. Volumes I and II. New York: Grune and Stratton, 1944 and 1945.

3. Pratt, J. P.: Sex Functions in Men. In: *Sex and Internal Secretions.* Edited by E. Allen. Baltimore: The Williams and Wilkins Company, 1939, p. 1263.

4. Greenhill, M. H.: *A Psychosomatic Evaluation of the Psychiatric and Endocrinological Factors in the Menopause.* Southern Med. J., XXXIX, 1946, p. 786.

5. Chadwick, Mary: *Woman's Periodicity.* London: Noel Douglas, 1933.

————: *The Psychological Effects of Menstruation.* New York: Nervous and Mental Disease Publishing Company, 1932.

6. Mead, Margaret: *From the South Seas.* New York: William Morrow and Company, 1939.

7. Simmons, L. W.: *The Role of the Aged in Primitive Society.* New Haven: Yale University Press, 1945.

8. Benedek, Therese: *Insight and Personality Adjustment.* New York: The Ronald Press Company, 1946.

9. Montagu, M. F. A.: *Adolescent Sterility.* Springfield: Charles C. Thomas, 1946.

10. Benedek, Therese and Rubenstein, Boris B.: *The Sexual Cycle in Women. The Relation between Ovarian Function and Psychodynamic Processes.* Psychosomatic Monographs III, Nos. 1 and 2, 1942. (I. The Ovulative Phase. II. The Menstrual Phase. In: Psychosomatic Medicine, I, 1939, pp. 245 and 461.)

11. Freud: *Female Sexuality.* Int. J. Psa., XIII, 1932, p. 281.

————: *Predisposition to Obsessional Neurosis.* Coll. Papers, II.

12. Abraham, Karl: The First Pregenital Stage of Libido. In: *Selected Papers.* London: The Hogarth Press, 1927, p. 248.

13. O'Higgins, H. and Reede, E. H.: *The American Mind in Action.* New York: Harper and Brothers, 1924.

DISCUSSION

This paper gives the impression that it set out to clarify too many problems—the hormonal influences on developmental processes, personality factors that modify and outlast the influence of gonadal hormones, cultural changes that affect the relationship between the sexes. The complex interactions and feedback cycles between the processes which influence women's attitude toward their sexual functions begin in childhood, often become manifest at puberty, and continue through the childbearing period and menopause. Indeed, the problems involved would require monographic presentation. At the time the paper was written, neither the psychoanalytic material nor the cultural changes appeared convincing enough to encourage such an undertaking. Now the cultural changes and their effects upon women are so obvious that just a reminder of them can serve as basis for discussion of the psychophysiologic reactions to menopause and for sorting out the individually significant factors that motivate the psychopathology occurring characteristically at that age.

This discussion will be limited to normal menopause and will not deal with variations that occur if, either early in life or during the child-bearing age, menopause followed extirpation of the ovaries.

Since the somatic reactions to menopause are due ". . . rather to a lack of balance of hormones than to simple deprivation,"[1] the meno-pausal phase is of individually different duration and its end often cannot be clearly defined. (Not infrequently the menstrual bleeding con-tinues for several years after ovulation has ceased.) But the climac-terium is not a "critical phase" as pregnancy is.[2] More often than not, it passes without causing undue somatic and/or psychologic symptoms.[3]

I use the term developmental absorption to refer to the adapta-tional processes necessitated by the cyclical changes in ovarian hormone production and menstruation, and later by stress as of pregnancy and motherhood, which gradually lead to diminishing tension and eventually to resolution of the conflicts originating or connected with the pro-creative physiology. These processes prepare the woman for menopause. Thus, this event does not have the impact that one used to and is still inclined to attribute to it. (Recent comparisons with the "male climac-teric" put women at an advantage.)

The physiologic patterns of adaptation to menopause are uni-versal. Cultural factors, however, influence not only women's anticipa-tion but also the conception of scientists concerning the psychology of the climacterium. The "dangerous age" which meant an increased (and often uncontrollable) sexual excitability of climacteric women was so persuasive an assumption that Freud wrote, "As is well known, such rather sudden intensifications in libido are regularly connected with puberty and the menopause with the reaching of a certain age in women; in many people they may in addition manifest themselves in periodici-ties as yet unrecognized."[4] His assumption that the sexual excitability of the climacteric is comparable with that of puberty is outdated, but he analyzed with perspicacity the contemporary cultural scene. In post-Victorian Vienna the behavior of women in their "dangerous age" was described, even defined by the slogan, *Torschluss-panick,* which means, the panic of the closing door. This witty catchword, recognizable by every Viennese, referred to the typical scene of rushing to reach the opera house before the doors closed for the beginning of the perfor-mance. Freud explained the dynamics of the behavior succinctly; the anxious rushing is caused by the fear of the impending frustration.[5]

The frustration of climacteric women may still come from the outer world, but this in itself is not the cause of the pathology of climacterium. The pathology is motivated by the sense of "internal frustration," caused by perception of the inability to feel gratified. Depression is the affective disorder inherent in the psychophysiology of the female pro-creative function. Each of its phases—ovulation, pregnancy, and lactation—requires an increase in metabolic energy, thereby intensifying the receptive needs, thus leading to oral regression and under certain conditions to depression. Yet the depression which is correlated with a high hormonal phase is phenomenologically different from the depression that occurs during the low hormone phases of the cycle (corresponding with the premenstrual phase and the beginning of menstruation). The climacteric depression is patterned on the premenstrual depression, which often forecasts the course of the climacterium; it indicates the individual's tolerance of the sense of frustration caused by hormonal withdrawal. To conceptualize this syndrome in terms of the instinct theory, as long as libido is sufficient to keep the instinctual energies in fusion, depression does not occur. In the climacterium, with the decline of gonadal hormones as during the premenstrual phase, there is a deficiency of integrating energy. When aggressive energy is set free, the angry woman hates her unsatisfiable self. Against this self-destructive hatred, projection is her defense; the angry, agitated woman seems to hate everyone else. Since external reality during the same period may set several integrative tasks for the woman which she cannot meet adequately, her frustration is increased by her sense of inadequacy. Narcissistic as well as hormonal reasons may account for her disappointment, self-hatred, and the ensuing depression.

In the paper progressive adaptational processes of normal climacterium are emphasized. The cases presented demonstrate severe "climacteric depression" not caused by the involutional process itself. The first demonstrates in a young woman the type of personality structure characteristic of low hormone levels; the other two cases show that the hormonal deficiency triggered the depression for which narcissistic character structure predisposed them; it made them unable to adapt to aging.

The psychopathology of these patients is similar to the structure and dynamics of the syndrome often referred to as "male climacterium." This syndrome was only briefly mentioned in the publication for two reasons. One was that medical attention was just beginning to turn to the "syndrome of the fifty-year-old man"; the other, that men really do not have climacterium comparable on physiologic grounds with the menopause of women. Not because of the diagnostic label, but because of the frequency and seriousness of psychosomatic conditions which befall middle-aged men, a comparison between male and female climacterium seems justified.

There is general agreement that ". . . for men, there is no evidence of a menopausal state secondary to diminished secretory action of the sexual glands consequent of aging."[6] It is questionable whether the slow, prolonged, gradual decline of sexual desire parallels the regressive changes in hormonal balance, yet the term "male climacterium" has persisted; even the term "andropause" was coined to parallel the term menopause.

Gregorio Marañon wrote (1929), "For myself I boldly assert the existence of the critical age in the male"[7] and he defined it: "the climacterium or the critical age is, then, a necessary phenomenon in the evolution [sic] of every human being who reaches old age, be it man or woman."[8] (I believe the author meant "involution.") Everyone would agree with this; argument will ensue about the difference between the "critical age" and "old age." In any case, the extension of the "critical age" into senescence would wipe out the contours of that period which is considered critical for men in the current civilization.

After World War II, attention was focused on the "young, middle-aged men" who suffered from a great variety of psychosomatic symptoms—duodenal ulcers and high blood pressure being the most common—leading all too often to disease of the coronary arteries and so to early death.[9]

It is revealing that men so affected are usually the high-powered, hard-driving achievers who at that age level often do not show signs of declining sexual power, or if they suspect that this is occurring, they find ways of rationalizing their symptoms or overcompensating for them. If one considers the "syndrome of the fifty-year-old man" as characteristic of middle-aged men, it then appears to be a cultural phenomenon, a side effect of our technologic civilization.

This seems a far-fetched generalization since the effect of civilization upon the individual will be modified in large measure by his psychologic makeup and not by impersonal civilization. This is taken for granted. To explain the effects of a competitive civilization upon the individual, the function of work in the psychic structure of men should be discussed, however briefly.

Work is a psychic organizer; it functions as such in the awakening psychic system from infancy on. Parents recognize the "activity-lust" (pleasure in activity) in the three- to six-months-old infant; they proudly recognize the glow of satisfaction on the face of the one- to two-year-old toddler when he has reached the spoon or the toy that he wanted. The psychology of this is that the child's ego registers the satisfaction of having achieved a self-set goal. The affective experience of achievement becomes incorporated in the self-image as the "achieving self." Self-esteem originates in such minute experiences, leading to a self-concept, e.g., "I am a good, lovable, capable, achieving self." The ego thus becomes cathected with "secondary narcissism." But the self-concept is not a stable structure in one's psychic apparatus. Through the same processes by which it is established, it is also measured. Play is not the opposite of work. From infancy on, play is the way of learning skills, of mastering techniques by which a goal can be achieved. Through its own achievements the self establishes its own measuring rod, the ego ideal. The superego is the taskmaster; it confronts the individual with a sense of responsibility that the achievement of his task implies. When the superego enters, play becomes work.

One has only to know the age and occupation to have a clear idea of what a certain person expects of himself and what is expected of him. The unlimited variations of such expectations can be formulated in terms of the interplay between superego and ego ideal. A characteristic quality of work is that it must be done;[10] the superego demands it. The ego ideal sets the goal of attainment. If the goal is achieved, the superego and the ego ideal are in harmony. Psychic energy expended in work attains harmonious gratification by satisfying the superego; thus the ego feels closer to the ego ideal.

The motivations for work, even in the most complex civilization, can be reduced to two basic roots. One is grounded in biology, in the instinct for survival which includes survival in one's children. The other is the urge to achieve beyond the immediate need for the sake of security, to achieve "surplus." Probably it is not incorrect to assume that secondary narcissism, so charming in the child and so exhausting in the middle-aged man, originates in the need for surplus achievement. Work achievement and what one can buy with it, e.g., status and money, is not for the working, achieving self alone; it turns into giving; it must provide for the family. One kind of man does not begrudge the giving because the giving was the sole or main goal of achieving. Another man, consciously or unconsciously, cannot give, cannot give himself, for he has become identified with the work itself. The first man derives his emotional gratification from object relationships; the other invests his available libido (psychic energy) in his work. If the goal is achieved, the feeling of satisfaction charges the ego with secondary narcissism.

Normally, the two areas of gratification—the interpersonal, object-directed and the self-directed—complement each other. From childhood on, achievements, in whatever form they occur, become absorbed in the personality organization and thus enlarge its span. Fortunate is the man whose primary object relationships supply emotional gratifications and keep in balance the spending of energy necessary to sustain the intrapsychic and interpersonal processes of his work, his ambitions, and his relationships with others in his work situation. Otherwise, the expenditure of energy necessary to provide the success he desires becomes a steady drain upon his emotional resources, leaving little libido for primary emotional gratification.

Work in itself is not what causes chronic attrition of primary libido. Produced abundantly in childhood, adolescence, and early adulthood, it diminishes slowly with middle age and old age. The attainments of adulthood, the growing family and success in work, normally afford enough gratification to expand a man's personality and potential capacities in age-adequate adaptations so long as his goals are within his capacity. However, if the drive for power and success, be it financial or otherwise, is relentless, the psychic sources may become exhausted, even if the goal is achieved. Since such driving can maintain the narcissistic cathexis of the ego only at the cost of primary libido, it exhausts the adaptive capacity, rendering the organism susceptible to illness. Protracted stress burdens the susceptible organ or organ system with the tension caused by the conflict. Often only an added factor, be it disappointment, pleasure, or sudden excitement, is needed to throw off the tenuous balance and expose a lurking illness. Our hard-driving, competitive society, offering many choices and chances, requires more adaptive capacity from men on their way to success than many are able to sustain.

Man's self-esteem is derived not only from his work achievement but also from his sexual potency. These two sources of gratification are complementary. One functional capacity may be used to overcompensate for the other. In young men or in a happy marriage, the intrapsychic result of such processes is usually positive; in middle age or later, it may be the opposite. Whatever fires the work ambition of the middle-aged man, intensified work with its various pressures may channelize his psychic energy to a degree which adversely affects his sexual potency. On the other hand, emotional reaction to sexual failure may activate a depressive reaction and impede the work capacity secondarily.

How about women? Do not these structures—i.e., self-esteem, ego ideal, and superego—play the same role in the personality organization of women? How do these factors influence the course of climacterium? Self-esteem, ego ideal, and superego are the mainstays of women's personality as they are of men's. They develop in women through the same psychologic processes for the same intrapsychic functions. But the work goal of women has a biologic basis in the procreative function of motherhood. Women's work has always been and still is largely a derivative of the biologic function of caring for children, cooking, sewing, and managing the household. There are relatively few women whose work and accomplishment are remote from that home base, even those who often combine the biologic goal of motherhood with activity in the competitive world of men. Since the main accomplishment of women is to become and to be a mother, since this is an inalienable attribute of the gender, women can enjoy attainments of the ego without the stress that burdens men in our competitive society.

SUMMARY

The course of the sexual decline of middle age is different in the sexes according to their reproductive physiology. (1) In women climacterium indicates the cessation of procreative function; in men this can be rekindled, even after it has been arrested for many years. (2) Woman's menopause is accompanied by manifest hormonal imbalance.

The decline of testicular function occurs slowly in old age. (3) The male climacterium is caused mainly by the multiple psychic and psychosomatic effects of man's struggle in a competitive society.

At present, it seems as if women were winning the struggle between the sexes. Since childbearing no longer harbors many dangers and menopause does not herald the end of womanhood, the expectancy of a longer life seems to have made it easier for women to accept and overcome the physiologic reactions to menopause. The period of adaptation to aging is entered with the optimistic expectation of a new beginning. This is the difference between the middle age of women and men. Men are not prepared by their procreative biology to become old. They would wish to become old in the wisdom and mellowness of their forefathers and be cherished as they once were, yet they often find themselves in the clutches of a "critical age."

NOTES

1. Hoskins, R. G., *Endocrinology. The Glands and Their Functions* (New York, W. W. Norton & Co., 1950), p. 296.

2. Benedek, T., "Psychobiology of Pregnancy" in *Parenthood: Its Psychology and Psychopathology,* ed. E. J. Anthony and T. Benedek (Boston, Little, Brown & Co., 1970), p. 137.

3. It was not unusual to diagnose every symptom in women over thirty-five—from simple headache to incipient neurologic conditions, from sleeplessness to divorce—as fear of the oncoming climacterium.

4. Freud, S., "Types of Neurotic Nosogenesis" (1912), *Collected Papers,* vol. II, 1924 (London, Hogarth Press, 1946), 119.

5. This theme was often used by great novelists and dramatists of the nineteenth century—Balzac, Flaubert, Tolstoy, Ibsen, etc. Today the problem is not challenging since women are not so helpless in respect to their emotional needs.

6. Noyes, A. P., and Kolb, L. W., "Psychophysiological Autonomic and Visceral Disorders," in *Modern Clinical Psychiatry* (Philadelphia & London, W. B. Saunders Co., 1958), p. 472.

7. Marañon, G., *The Climacteric* (St. Louis, C. B. Mosby Co., 1929); reprinted in *Men; the Variety and Meaning of the Sexual Experience,* ed. A. M. Krich (New York, Dell Publishing Co., 1954), p. 244.

8. Ibid., p. 245.

9. During the First World War the most frequent diagnosis of psychiatric illness was "war neurosis." A reaction to traumatic experiences, it was considered mainly as a conversion hysteria. During the Second World War the most common diagnosis was psychosomatic condition, depression and other affective disorders, or psychotic reaction. It is probable that the syndrome of the fifty-year-old man is a consequence of the stresses connected with that war and the events subsequent to it.

10. Lantos, B., "Metapsychological Considerations of the Concept of Work," *Int. J. Psycho-Anal.,* XXXIII (1952), 439–444.

12. An Approach to the Study of the Diabetic

INTRODUCTION

This paper was planned as a preliminary report on the investigation of psychosomatic processes in diabetes mellitus undertaken in the Chicago Institute for Psychoanalysis in 1947. The paper outlines the method of the investigation which was based on the study of the recorded psychoanalytic material of the patients parallel with the course of their metabolic derangement as expressed in their insulin need and other metabolic reactions to the "free diet."

I. Arthur Mirsky was the consultant for the clinical and laboratory aspect of the research. I was the supervisor of the psychoanalyses conducted by several analysts. In regular biweekly seminars the cases were discussed. Several diabetic adolescents were studied in this project; anamnestic interviews with their mothers revealed useful information; occasional consultations were rewarding from the point of view of the therapeutic process and the management of the diabetes.

After almost five years of investigative efforts the project had to be interrupted in 1952 since several members of the group, because of a change in their professional situation, could not continue. The analytic investigation of the voluminous psychoanalytic and clinical records appeared to be a gargantuan task, presenting problems which could not have been fruitfully dealt with without close collaboration with Arthur Mirsky and the other psychoanalysts on the project.

AN APPROACH TO THE STUDY
OF THE DIABETIC[1]
(1948)

We have designed this project to permit (1) observation of the correlations existing between emotional and metabolic reactions; (2) detection of behavioral responses which reflect the perception of metabolic dysfunction and physiologic changes; (3) investigation of the presence or absence of some "basic biologic pattern" or "instinctual constellation" which primarily burdens the organism in such a way that the arising conflict tension finally breaks the chain of the normal metabolic process and leads to the disease. Only when such "instinctual constellations" become accessible to psychoanalysis will we be able to estimate the role of environmental influence in inducing diabetes. This design indicates that we were prepared by our previous investigation of the sexual cycle to assume that physiologic changes might result in predictable emotional reactions motivated by specific psychodynamic processes.

Unlike the study of a specific physiologic cycle—the sexual cycle —the psychoanalytic investigation of diabetes involves the study of the psychologic concomitants of a derangement of the homeostasis. While the derangement of the homeostasis may reflect itself in a variety of clinical symptoms (in varying degrees of hyperglycemia, glycosuria, increased fat and protein catabolism, loss of body weight, etc.), the psychologic concomitants to such symptoms—the significance of drives and their emotional elaborations and their participation in these physiologic processes—appear not easily accessible to our technique of investigation.

Subjects were selected who were not only accessible to psychoanalytic treatment, but also willing and capable of cooperation in the collection of physiologic data. As may be anticipated, initial observations are being made on a much larger group than will be subject to our extensive investigation. At the present time, we have under study six male and three female cases, from eight to twenty-seven years of age. Two of these subjects have now been studied for about one year each.

In order to reduce to a minimum as many of the variables as possible, the clinical care of all the subjects was standardized. Before the onset of psychoanalytic therapy, the physiologic status of each subject was established. After emphasizing the need for a minimal diet in order to prevent insulin hypoglycemia, the patients were advised that they could eat whatever they wished in addition. However, they were instructed to record their daily diet and body weight. They were taught methods for collecting their urine; female subjects were asked to record their basal body temperature on arising in the morning in order to provide an index for the ovulatory phase, etc. The course of the metabolic disturbance is determined by means of the dietary intake, the insulin requirement, the body weight, the acetonuria, and the glycosuria. We intend to study not only the emotional factors related to glycosuria, but also the interrelationship between the psychologic material and as many metabolic factors as are subject to measurement.

It is known to clinicians that the severity of the metabolic disturbance in diabetes can be aggravated by anxiety arising from sexual conflict and/or from the frustration of aggressive impulses. In addition, it has been demonstrated by Daniels[2] and by Meyer, Bollmeier, and Alexander[3] that conflicts which are specific for the individual may produce an increase in glycosuria; that a diminution in the tension of the conflict may result in a decrease in glycosuria, and the resolution of the conflict may actually improve the metabolic derangement. Yet these observations do not prove conclusively the interaction of psychologic and metabolic factors in the basic diabetic disturbance. In the presence of a disturbance in the regulation of carbohydrate metabolism, a mechanism exists which the organism can utilize as the "path of least resistance." Thus glycosuria resulting from an increase in the rate of the breakdown of the liver glycogen may be regarded as an *unconsciously functioning emergency response* of the diabetic. To evaluate its significance as an expression of the interaction of emotional and metabolic factors, we have to consider glycosuria along with other symptoms and behavior responses, and relate it to other measurements of the metabolic picture.

The diagnosis of diabetes affects the patient as a trauma. If the individual is a young child, the anxiety of the parents in regard to his diabetes is soon transferred to the patient. Our observations suggest that the trauma caused by the discovery of diabetes is deeper and more stirring than the anxiety induced by other chronic diseases. Some of the patients react as if all guilt related to oral gratification were mobilized, as if they somehow caused the disease themselves, and they become fearful that the responsibility for the course of the disease rests with them. The mothers of our diabetic children responded to the disease in a defensive manner. Each mother behaved as if the diabetes of the child proved that the mother did not feed or love the child properly and consequently she appeared eager to show that the relationship between herself and her child was perfect. To diminish her sense of guilt, the mother becomes overzealous about the diet, while the child soon becomes aware that food, which is regarded as poison, may be used as a weapon in his relationship to the environment. Thus begins a sado-masochistic interdependence between mother and child, which in itself may interfere with the child's further emotional development. The reaction is basically the same even in the chronologically adult diabetic patient. Food, which is representative of mother, of security, of life itself, becomes dangerous for the diabetic. When every gram of food is magnified in value, the patient may develop a *conscious habit* of dealing with every external and internal situation, with pleasure as well as with frustration, in terms of food, in terms of his diabetes. Thus we may observe various types of character reactions in patients with diabetes: (1) those who react with extreme compulsiveness in regard to diet; their ego being strong, they are able to ward off anxiety by self-restriction, and (2) those who respond with overeating, with spiteful, provocative, and even with delinquent attitudes in regard to diet; these are the individuals whose ego is weak; they cannot stand frustration; they neglect their diet, not only for the sake of primary pleasure, but also for secondary gain.

In such a manner, a triangular struggle is created by the preoccupation with food which is regarded as dangerous, with the glucose content of the urine which is used as an indicator of the disease, and with the insulin which mediates between the two. The patient plays these three factors of his disease against each other. Thus he develops an emergency regulation of his own which he can use *consciously* as a battlefield for all of his emotions, whatever their motivations may be. The awareness of a decreasing blood sugar level, the anxious tension caused by it, becomes a means for discharging all sorts of anxiety. Insulin becomes the tool for mastering anxiety, a source of gratification, a symbol of power. No wonder that it often acts as if it were a habit-forming drug. Although we differentiate between the "unconscious emergency function" and the "secondary" conscious use and abuse of the diabetic reaction formation, the boundary between the two aspects of the metabolic adjustment does not remain sharp. The secondary processes of the diabetes become an integrating part of the personality, so that we may speak of a "superstructure" of the diabetic individual.

The adaptation to the chronic condition of the diabetes patient is a process which may create a regressive vicious circle, thus increasing the severity of the metabolic and psychiatric symptomatology. However, there are diabetics who show little of the regressive superstructure. Discussing the individual differences in the adaptation to diabetes we reach another level of our investigation. The capacity for adaptation is one of the basic biologic attributes of the individual; its psychologic manifestations can probably be best measured by the integrative capacity of the ego. Generally, as we have already indicated, the weaker the ego, the greater is the part which the superstructure will play; the stronger the ego, the larger is its integrative span, and the more will the individual be able to adapt to the disease without the creation of a secondary vicious circle between the emotional and metabolic processes.

In regard to the study of these basic psychologic processes in diabetes, the *free diet* has a primary significance. Our preliminary studies suggest that not only the total caloric intake but also the kind of food which the patient selects, as well as other dietary habits, have psychologic significance. Were we to force our patients to a rigid diet, such data would not become apparent. On the other hand, permitting the patient to select his food freely and checking the entries in his diary and his psychoanalytic record against each other give us significant information. The first and almost general reaction to the recommendation of a free diet is the mobilization of *anxiety*. The restrictiveness of the diet, the attempts to adhere to it, and the intensity of guilt felt by the patient when he breaks away from it all become a part of his emotional life; the dietary restrictions become his way of creating and resolving psychic tensions. When they are taken away, the patient feels unprotected, endangered. Only after the patient has developed confidence in the therapist can he accept the new freedom. After he begins to live with his dietary freedom he realizes that with his "diabetic defenses" shaken, he must make a new adaptation to his disease. Whenever this appears difficult, such as when the patient has a conflict or develops a "negative transference" reaction, the longing for the old restrictive regimen recurs. Thus while the strict dietary regime seems to make of diet a weapon between the patient and his environment, or a weapon between him and his conscience, the unrestricted diet becomes an important battlefield of the transference in the analysis. So long as the analyst himself adheres to the concept that a rigid diet is essential, he represents to the patient the same level of reality as does the remainder of the patient's environment. In such circumstances, the therapist becomes a defender of the existing inadequate adaptation and this prevents the repetition of deeper instinctual phenomena in the transference. Thus its only effectiveness is in the analysis of those defenses which develop against the frustrating and threatening aspects of the disease and not in the reintegrations which permit new adaptations.

NOTES

1. Originally presented at the Annual Meeting of the American Psychosomatic Society, Atlantic City, May 2, 1948; published in *Psychosomatic Medicine,* X, no. 5 (September–October, 1948). Revised for this volume.

2. Daniels, G. E., "Analysis of a Case of Neurosis with Diabetes Mellitus," *Psychoanalytic Quart.,* V (1936), 513–539; "Emotional and Instinctual Factors in Diabetes Mellitus," *Am. J. Psychiatry,* XCIII (1936), 711–724.

3. Meyer, A., Bollmeier, L. M., and Alexander, F., "Correlation between Emotions and Carbohydrate Metabolisms in Two Cases of Diabetes Mellitus," *Psychosomatic Med.,* VII (1945), 335–341.

DISCUSSION

Emotional factors that complicate the management of diabetes are reactions to the precarious metabolic balance of diabetics. In our investigation we differentiated two levels of emergency reactions, the basic "flight or fight" reaction and the secondary emergency reaction, caused by the ever-oscillating course of adaptation to the illness.

Since Cannon's investigation (1914)[1] it has been confirmed by many investigators that the disturbance of carbohydrate metabolism is the result of a complex chain of interacting processes. Of the many links of that chain (and their feedback circuits) it should be mentioned that increased secretion of epinephrine is involved in that chain at more than one point. Epinephrine, the hormone produced in reaction to frustration, mobilizes fear and anger, i.e., the flight or fight reaction. The pathologic processes leading to diabetes mellitus qualify this illness as a manifestation of organic flight reaction, a defense against anxiety, against the fear of frustration and probably against the fear of starvation. In reporting what we observed in our patients and in their families regarding the disease, we emphasized that the diagnosis itself is a threat and responded to as trauma. The adaptation to the illness, and even more the adaptation to the necessity of balancing the metabolic derangement with continuous watchfulness of diet, insulin intake, etc., cause a chain of stresses which influence the basic metabolic process. Although they are measurable by the metabolic derangement that accompanies them, these stresses are secondary to the disease process. Their oscillations depend on the nature of the illness and, beyond this, on the personality of the diabetic individual.[2]

Two aspects of the research project intrigued me from the beginning. One was psychosomatic, the correlation of psychodynamic factors (constellations) with endocrinological processes; the other was clearly psychoanalytic, the investigation of the developmental factors in the pathogenesis of diabetes mellitus. Diabetes is a disease of alimentation. Caused by innate, genic factors, it raises the question, where does the stress begin? Does the course of the emotional symbiosis play a part in the evolution of the disease from an innate disposition? The opportunity to investigate mother-child interactions in relation to diabetes in adults and children contributed much to my knowledge of the dynamics of anxiety and aggression in the disturbances of motherliness. Pathogenic factors conveyed by disturbances of motherliness have been discussed in innumerable contexts since David M. Levy first published his investigation, "Maternal Overprotection."[3] The psychoanalytic investigation of several cases of the same organic and related psychic pathology carried the impact which led to the formulation of the concept of "depressive constellation." (See Chapter 13, page 356.)

NOTES

1. Cannon, W. B., "The Interrelation of Emotions as Suggested by Recent Physiological Researches," *Am. J. Psychology*, XXV (1914), 256–282.
2. Mirsky, I. A., "Emotional Factors in the Patient with Diabetes Mellitus," *Bul. Menninger Clinic*, XII (1948), 187–194; Hinkle, L. E., Jr., and Wolf, S., *JAMA* (Feb. 16, 1952), pp. 513–520.
3. Levy, D. M., *Maternal Overprotection* (New York, Columbia University Press, 1943).

13. Toward the Biology of the Depressive Constellation

INTRODUCTION

One year after the diabetes research was interrupted, I presented the concept of "depressive constellation" to the Chicago Psychoanalytic Society (1953). The discussants, Dr. Roy R. Grinker, Sr. and Dr. Helen V. McLean, were impressed by the (circular) "feedback" processes presented in the paper. At that time the term was not yet applied by psychoanalysts, but my discussants were more at home with it than I. Grinker said, "Her work leads to clarification of psychoanalytic theory and hence feeds back to the psychosomatic field, rather than being a direct contribution to the understanding of the psychogenesis of specific diseases."[1] Helen McLean was more specific in her reference to the research that led to the first presentation of this concept. It was planned at that time as a preliminary report on a monographic presentation of a research project on diabetes mellitus. Referring to the feedback between the various aspects of my investigations, Helen McLean commented, "Starting with an investigation of the possible psychogenecity in diabetes mellitus, a feedback mechanism operated. The fundamental problem of the mother-child relationship demanded clarification."[2] With this she referred to my earlier publications and indicated that the concept of depressive constellation matured slowly.

It was easy to formulate the concept of "confidence" as an intrapsychic precipitate of positive libidinal processes of the symbiotic phase of the mother-child relationship. However, it was necessary to evaluate the role of ambivalence in individual cases of any age, for it took the impact of the transactional processes of ambivalent relationships between mothers and their children, as revealed by diabetic patients, to impress upon me the universal meaning of these processes beyond their role in the pathogenesis of disease entities.

356

NOTES

1. Grinker, Roy R., Sr., Discussion of Benedek, T., "Toward the Biology of the Depressive Constellation," Chicago Psychoanalytic Society, February 24, 1953. Unpublished.
2. McLean, H. V., ibid.

TOWARD THE BIOLOGY OF THE DEPRESSIVE CONSTELLATION[1]

In "Instincts and Their Vicissitudes" (1915) Freud[2] came to the conclusion that "instincts are subordinate to the three polarities which govern mental life as a whole" and stated these three antitheses as "subject-object," "active-passive," and "pleasure-pain." In the same paper he discussed the anaclitic origin of libido and on this basis proposed that ego instincts and libidinal instincts are not antagonists *ab origine*. In 1917 he published "Mourning and Melancholia"[3] in which he demonstrated explicitly that a process which is necessary for survival—alimentation—leads to that organization of the mental apparatus which is responsible not only for the pleasure of the mind but also for its anguish.

The earlier studies of depression were concerned mainly with conflicts between the individual's superego and the psychic representations of his experiences during the oral phase of development. More recent studies seek to explain the tendency toward depressive reactions by groping backward into the earliest phases of life in which the maturation of sensory, vegetative, and regulative processes includes the first processes of mentation. Indeed, these studies indicate that the "fixation" which predisposes to psychosomatic disease is closely related to the psychodynamic factors predisposing to depression.[4]

The aim of this paper is to demonstrate the universal nature of a depressive constellation. This concept defies understanding so long as one investigates the problem only from the viewpoint of the child's anaclitic relationship to the mother. On the contrary, *the origin of the depressive constellation lies in the psychobiology of the female procreative function, in motherhood and motherliness itself.* Therefore, the depressive constellation as well as its significance for the individual can best be understood in terms of reciprocal interactions between mother and child (symbiosis). This symbiosis in turn determines the psychic processes in the offspring which, repeated from mother to child, constitute a psychodynamic link in the chain of generations.

To avoid repetition and yet not lose our focus on the basic conflict that leads to the "human condition," I emphasize again the dilemma built into the physiology of the female reproductive function. The increasing receptive-retentive tendencies necessary to maintain pregnancy create a severe physiologic and psychologic stress that may bring defusion of neutralized psychic energy, permitting aggressive energy to become free and thus mobilize anxiety and guilt. That childbearing normally occurs without such untoward experience is due to the maturational process maintained by the monthly repetition of the hormonal cycle. The corresponding psychologic process reveals the potential ambivalence embedded in the woman's development toward motherhood.

The study of hormonal correlations and psychodynamic processes in motherhood demonstrates that in each stage of procreative growth— the lutein phase of the cycle, pregnancy, and lactation—we can differentiate two levels of motivation and action.[5] One is dominated by the emotional manifestation of receptive-retentive tendencies, which are an integral part of the process through which metabolic and emotional energy is stored to be used for the sake of the child. The other tendencies, more accessible to consciousness, mobilize the active, giving, succoring attitudes of motherliness. This duality of function involves the metabolic and emotional challenge which procreative processes represent for women and at the same time explains its inherent dangers. It is a well-established concept of psychoanalysis[6] that regression to the oral receptive phase of development is the psychodynamic constellation of depression, and we found that each phase of procreative growth necessarily brings about such regression. While for the healthy woman the introversion of her psychic energies and the biological regression implicit in this process constitute sources of well-being and maturation, these same processes hold dangers for those women who, for whatever reasons, cannot withstand the stress of this normal regression essential to the physiology of motherhood.

It is the burden of this discussion to confront and compare the mother and her infant as two individuals in a symbiotic unit.

Birth, the trauma of separation, has been studied almost exclusively from the standpoint of the newborn. Here we shall point out some of its emotional significance for the mother. The hormonal and metabolic changes which induce parturition, labor pains, and the excitement of delivery interrupt the emotional continuity of the mother-child unity and leave the mother's physiologic and emotional household in a state of derangement. Fortunate is the mother whose love for her child wells up as she hears the first cry of her baby. Many mothers, however, especially primiparas, experience an "emotional lag" after delivery. Mothers having such a disquieting experience usually try to muster self-control to suppress the feeling of disappointment in themselves and in the child, whom they then view as a stranger. Indeed, this is a trauma which mobilizes the mother's guilt and fear and renders her insecure toward the child. Yet, normally, repeated physical contact with the newborn, especially the sensations of nursing, helps the mother to re-establish the emotional relationship to her child, and by this to regain her emotional security and serenity.

When the newborn leaves the womb and must become active in securing the basic needs for living, his physiology changes. But this does not mean that there is yet an awareness of the separation. Closer study of newborn infants has revealed that their condition resembles that of intrauterine life.[7] While this does not imply absolute bliss, as we used to assume, it does seem to indicate that the mental apparatus of the new-born is not yet developed to the degree that he is aware of separation. Indeed, if the rising physiological needs disturb sleep, the course of gratification evolves, as far as the newborn is concerned, within the self, without realization of an external environment. Thus hunger, the need for food, is probably the first indicator of being separated. Hunger is also the stimulus to overcome the separation. Satiation and the subsequent resumption of sleep, or of the sleeplike condition, indicate that the separation has been overcome. It takes several weeks of postnatal development until, through the rhythmic repetition of need and its grati-fication, the infant develops the perception that the source of his need (hunger, pain, discomfort) is *within* and the source of gratification is *outside* the self, i.e., separation in the psychological sense begins to exist for the infant. Yet the infant is an individual, if only to his mother. Mothers know, even with the first child, that this baby grasps the nipple and sucks stronger, that the other one is lazy, etc.

The inborn self-action patterns of the newborn can best be studied in his response to need, in the crying fit, and in his sucking behavior. Sucking on the mother's breast is an action occurring in two phases: (1) reaching for the object and getting it in the mouth and (2) sucking. During sucking the child clenches his fists and increases his grasp. Grop-ing and grasping are subsidiary to sucking. They are phylogenetic rem-nants of the function of maintaining posture and tonic orientation of the body. Groping, grasping, and sucking express the urge to come in con-tact with the succoring object. These actions are nuclei of the ego and while they involve in the motor apparatus and appear to express aggres-sion, self-preservation—not destruction—is their aim.

There are great differences in the feeding behavior of newborns, determined in part by the inborn activity pattern of the infant and also by the mother's ability to nurse. The "angrily" crying, strong infant, turning toward the breast with tonic, almost spastic attention, grabs with his hands and clasps his mouth around the nipple with a tight grasp. Not only the lips but often the gums close tightly over the nipple, sometimes causing excruciating pain in the loose, succulent tissues of the aureola. If the nipple is well developed and the breast is free flow-ing, the sucking infant loosens his grasp and both mother and infant relax in the pleasurable sensations of the mutual rhythmic experience. If the nipple is too small or inverted and escapes the baby's grasp, or if the breast does not flow, the experience is frustrating not only to the infant but also to the mother, and is often physically very painful for her. Similarly, painful feeding experiences occur for the mother if the infant is apathetic and does not suck well. The "lazy" infant drops the nipple or licks at it until it may become macerated, painful, and even infected. The emotional responses of mothers to such experiences become by necessity disturbing to the smooth course of symbiotic events. The mother's fear of being hurt may result in an instinctive withdrawal of the breast; this again increases the frequency of fitful crying of the infant.[8] The mother's defensive withdrawal from the symbiotic relationship stirs up her fear of not being able to give, and this in turn increases her need to receive. To whom does the mother turn with her receptive needs, with her wish for care and love? Naturally, to her husband, her mother, and other members of her immediate environment who are the sources of her physical and emotional security. But on a deeper level of her personality, her unconscious emotional needs are turned toward her infant for satisfaction. From the time of conception the offspring has stimulated the receptive-retentive tendencies of the mother, and after parturition the newborn remains the object of these instinctual needs. These drives constitute the psychodynamic source of the symbiotic need of the mother for her child as well as the motivation of the communication between them.

The oral dependent needs of the child as well as the psychologic processes which evolve on account of them are well studied. The mother's receptive needs toward the child, however, are not easily recognized in their normal manifestations. Normally, the infant, by the very fact of his existence, represents the most significant fulfillment of the mother's receptive tendency. With her baby the mother feels "whole," "complete"; but not without him. (Many young mothers feel "emptiness," have a slight depression, or feel compelled to eat when they leave the child for even a short time. The fantasy elaborations of the separation trauma of the mother are often expressed as "eating up" or "putting back" the child, even in women who do not undergo severe regression. In pathologic instances harming the child, especially starving him, may be the expression of the same, but more aggressively charged, underlying wish. These tendencies are prevalent in mothers who have diabetes or who develop diabetes later in life.)[9]

The increased charge of incorporative fantasies indicates that during pregnancy and in the postpartum period the mother may respond to the increased demands on her with an increased wish to receive. These are exaggerated manifestations of the very emotions which originate in the biological regressions inherent in motherhood. The affect hunger of the mother, her need for love and affection, her wish to reunite with her baby and to overprotect and overpossess him disturb the smooth course of symbiotic events. Although these are pathologic exaggerations of the normal process, such manifestations bring our thesis even more sharply into focus: that *the postpartum symbiosis is oral, alimentary, for both infant and mother.*

The "undifferentiated state"[10] is the early neonatal period in which ego is equated with perception of physiologic need and with the reflex apparatus mobilized toward gratification of need. The satiated neonate gradually drops the nipple and falls into a sleeplike state. One aspect of neonatal growth is the organization of sleep[11] and the phasic change between sleep and wakeful states. As the infant matures, manifestations of attention and expectation can be observed. Although data reported by various authors differ in regard to the sequence of such events and the time of their appearance, we can consider these phenomena as signs of "outward directedness" of the child. These are manifestations of the incipient awareness of a differentiation between inward-self and outward-external world (environment). With each nursing and feeding, one part of this external world, the mother, becomes part of the self again. Introjection of the mother and the tendency to retain her, as if to enjoy the pleasurable, satisfying part of the self, is obvious quite early in the behavior of the infant. For example, the satiated infant continues to play with his lips and fingers at the breast, or the half-sleeping infant starts when the mother moves to put him down and tries to grasp the breast again. Step by step as physiologic maturation evolves, the biologic unity between infant and mother gives place to psychologic communication between them.[12]

When the stored energy produced by the metabolic processes is sufficient to sustain longer or shorter waking states, this energy also supplies the infant with pleasure. Primary narcissism is the term for the energy which maintains this state of contentment. Yet the two- or three-month-old infant, who can stay awake and listen to his own cooing sounds, also smiles at the mother his first recognizing and wanting smile. That is, when surplus energy is sufficient to maintain a wakeful state, it is then projected to reestablish a communication on a psychologic level, a unity between mother and child.

Introjection, incorporation, and identification are terms which symbolize unconscious processes by which memory traces are stored and object relations are assimilated and organized. In the earliest stage of the neonatal period, memory traces relate mainly to alimentation. Through the repetition of this experience, tactile, olfactory, auditory, and visual perceptions also leave memory traces of sensations connected with feeding. All this adds up to a memory of a pleasant, feeding mother. The same mother can also be connected with unpleasant memory traces and can become the introject of pain—for example, painful, unpleasant, "bad mother"—when she is unable to alleviate the infant's hunger or his colicky pain.

The balance between introjection-projection which an infant can sustain is, of course, very labile. If an expectation is not fulfilled—for example, if the smile is not rewarded by being picked up or cooed to or fed—a crying fit may follow. Although the crying fit might finally bring about the desired satisfaction, this need not be considered a sign of infantile omnipotence. Describing the dynamics of such a crying fit, not caused by a commanding physiologic need such as hunger or pain, but by the thwarting of an attempt at emotional (psychologic) communication and satisfaction, is probably a hazardous speculation. I feel quite safe, however, in stating that we can see in it the prototype of regression. As an example, take the fleeting moment when the child catches sight of his mother. In his cognitive field the mother evokes memory traces of pleasant, gratifying experiences; these in turn mobilize an urgency for their continuation. This is conveyed by a mimical expression of hope and pleasure and is communicated to the mother through a smile. If satisfaction does not follow, the ego (i.e., the function which maintains goal-directed behavior and attention) regresses, the integrative field disappears. The infant (three to six months and older), now being in the throes of a "storm of excitation," has regressed to his earlier "undifferentiated" state of existence. Watching the infant's smile turn into a crying fit of frustration, we might say that the libido which sustained the ego is consumed by frustration and dissipated, causing the ego to regress. With the dissociation of libidinous affects, the aggressive affects take over and mobilize the undirected "storm of excitation."

Each crying fit of the infant is a task (or a test) for the physical and emotional readiness of the mother to succor her child. Fortunate are those infants whose mothers can summon the right response to the child's needs from the instinctual reservoir of motherliness. Just as fortunate are those mothers, for they act securely, without the doubt and strain of the intellectually learned approach. In any instance, it is a most rewarding experience to watch an infant calming down—falling asleep if sick or exhausted, or "reestablishing his ego" if he is well and older and if the traces of object relationship with the mother are already functioning. Then the baby smiles at the mother as if recognizing her as the source of satisfaction; he smiles as if continuing the object relationship where it was left off. Such an interruption of communication is a natural, everyday event and is not necessarily traumatic. Even if it were, the trauma heals quickly as long as the balance of the infinite number of communications is positive; this applies to both infant and mother.

Confidence is used as a term to designate an emotional state of the infant which has developed through multiple repetitions of the gratifying experiences of symbiosis. The concept implies an ego organization in which the effects of the libidinal relationship with the mother through introjection have become a part of the mental organization of the child. This is similar to French's concept of hope.[13] Both confidence and hope are qualities of the ego organization which enable the infant (and the adult as well) to span an unpleasant situation in the present and project the expectation of gratification into the future.

The development of confidence does not depend solely upon the mother's ability and willingness to give, but also upon the child's innate or acquired ability to receive, to suck, to assimilate, and to thrive. If the infant, because of congenital or acquired disability, cannot be satisfied, he remains frustrated and in turn frustrates the mother. The frustration of the mother manifests itself in anger and discouragement, in the fear of her inefficiency, and probably in (more or less) conscious guilt feelings. These attitudes and feelings affect the course of the emotional symbiosis. The balance between the positive (libidinal, gratifying) and the negative (aggressive, frustrating) symbiotic events influences the ego organization of both the child and the mother. In her case, of course, the aspect of the ego organization which is affected is the function of motherhood, namely, the developmental integration of motherliness.

Parallel with the developmental process which leads to confidence in the infant, the mother, through introjecting the gratifying experiences of successful mothering, establishes her self-confidence, her trust in her own motherliness. These are reciprocal ego developments: in the infant, through introjection of good mother = good self, the development of confidence and hope; in the mother, through the introjection of good, thriving infant = good mother = self, the achievement of a new phase in her development. Successful mothering offers the mother libidinal ego gratification by the fulfillment of an ego aspiration of women, namely, to be a good mother and to project her ego gratification into the future, to be fulfilled by the development of her child.

Both the satisfactions and the frustrations of mothering are repeated with each child, depending on the maturity of the mother, her circumstances, and, most of all, on her reaction to each child. Through the repetition of the reciprocal processes of projection and identification, each child seems to activate in the mother a particular aspect of her personality, expressed in her love for the child. Whether the love be unwavering or ambivalent, it becomes deeply interwoven with the personality organization of the mother.

This developmental process is one cycle in the emotional symbiosis, one which is the result of the positive balance of transactional processes—confidence in the child and trust by the mother in her motherliness (and therewith, positive, unambivalent mother love). The course of development is different if the symbiotic relationship between mother and child has not succeeded in creating and maintaining a positive balance.

When the infant is not sustained by the protective relationship to the mother, he responds to external and internal frustrations—as though without emotional shelter—with more frequent and more intense crying fits, which are expressions of increasing need. Hunger or pain involves the motor apparatus (not only the skeletal but also the visceral muscles) in the struggle for survival. Spread of excitation ensues because the undeveloped neuronal inhibitory system does not permit a localization of the homeostatic derangement.

What kind of memory traces do such crying fits leave in the immature, unstructuralized mental apparatus of the infant? How does it happen that the frustration of a "dependent wish" (i.e., frustration of introjection on the psychologic level) is enough to activate the kind of homeostatic derangement which accompanies the hunger cry of the infant? What is the trigger to a regression which, as a response to an emotional frustration, submerges the ego in a spreading aggressive orgy? On a psychologic level we might interpret it as follows: an infant who expresses the need to be smiled at, picked up, talked to, etc., desires to maintain the "emotional symbiosis." Since he cannot maintain the relationship by his own mental processes (fantasy, memory) he responds to the lack of participation from the adult as to a complete interruption of the symbiosis, as if he were abandoned and hungry.

The effect of frustration is opposite to that of hope. Frustration gives rise to the sensation of inability to span an unpleasant situation in the present and to project one's expectation to a gratification in the future. Since the young infant's total reaction does not yet permit distinctions in affective expressions, we cannot know whether it is frustration, anger, and/or anxiety. However, it is not difficult to imagine that a regression which submerges the ego and threatens it with loss of all its faculties would activate panic in an individual mature enough to have even an incipient ego organization. We therefore assume that infants not protected by "confidence" against psychic tensions will be prey to crying fits more often than those infants whose ego integration functions with such a protective barrier. Repeated crying fits establish a vicious circle of great significance to the further organization of the personality. We should also mention those infants whose crying fits do not bring about gratification; they cry until exhausted and then give up crying altogether. Their worried expressions and painful whining indicate a serious disturbance.[14]

The crying fit indicates a need for revival of the neonatal symbiosis. It is up to the mother to make an effort to reestablish the child's ego and, in doing so, she becomes an object of the diffuse, aggressive discharge. In the process of calming down, the infant expresses (projects) the motor excitement (a minimal part of it) onto the mother. This is evident in the intense grasping and the unrhythmic, hasty sucking of the excited infant.[15] It appears that the infant has developed hatred for the object which he needs to establish his ego, his self, again. "At the same time he develops a precursory hatred of the subject that he needs."[16]

In the next step of the process of being satiated or calmed down the aggressive impulses disappear; they are "introjected." As a result of such introjections, we assume, the memory trace of "bad mother = bad self" is established. At this point I want to emphasize once more that when the libidinous state of well-being is replaced by a storm of excitation, the infant is returned to a state in which there is no differentiation between *I* and *not-I,* between the self and the external world. With the disruption of the relationship, the mother is lost as an object. In the process of calming down, the infant reestablishes his ego and resumes communication with the mother. With the memory traces of frustration and the accompanying diffuse aggression, the infant introjects his own aggressive impulses, which then become a part of his psychic organization. Just as there are memory traces of satisfying, good mother and frustrating, bad mother, so are there also memory traces of good (satisfied) self and bad (angry) self. *By this the core of ambivalence is established within.* This is the psychic representation of a momentary frustration of the universal biological need for alimentation (for food and succor).

Growth and development are the results of the continuous change in the symbiotic unit with time.[17] For the newborn, only a simple world of outward and inward direction of his needs exists. Accordingly, the neonate is subject to a diffuse feeling of unpleasure (need) and a similarly diffuse sense of pleasure (lack of need, sleep). From this stage, through continual processes of introjection and projection and through introjection and identification, the objects of symbiosis (self and mother) become integrated into each other's psychic organization. From the child's point of view this development means that he can maintain his ego in relative independence from the mother. The duration of the manifestations of independent ego (without breaking down into crying fits) depends upon the economic relation between the libidinal components and the aggressive components of the ambivalent core. This psychoeconomic equation expresses the tolerance to frustration which can be observed in the infant's ability to wait without regression. Tolerance to frustration shows great individual variations. These may be due to differences in the innate anlage, but an individual's response to a simple frustrating experience may be modified according to the influence which earlier frustrations have had upon his psychic organization. Step by step the child learns to respond to frustration, not with a total regression (which implies the restitution of symbiotic need) but with a partial regression which is manageable by intrapsychic processes alone.

Just as we can detect the intrapsychic processes which occur in the mother corresponding with the thriving of her infant, so can we recognize the emotional processes induced in her by the frustration in her child. The frustrated infant frustrates his mother; by this he induces a regression in the mother which intensifies the aggressive components of her receptive needs. While in the infant such tendency is directed toward the mother = self, in the mother it is directed toward her infant, toward her own mother, and, through identification with both, also toward herself.

The regression stirs up in the mother the preverbal memories of the oral-dependent phase of her own development. If the recathexis of the infantile relationship with her own mother activates in the mother confidence and hope, she will overcome the actual disappointment and frustration, secure in her wish to love the child and to take care of him as she herself was loved and cared for. But if the crying fits of the infant or other signs of his debility stir up not only justified concern but also anxieties which originate in the mother's oral-dependent conflicts, the psychodynamics of the mother's response can best be formulated by stating that both levels of her identification—that with her mother and with her child—turn negative. This means in terms of herself that she becomes the "bad, frustrating mother" of her child as well as the "bad, frustrating infant" of her mother again. In terms of the infant, it means that the "bad, frustrating infant" becomes the irreconcilable "hated self" and at the same time her infant becomes the needed and feared object as her mother once was. Just as she could regain emotional equilibrium as a child by satiation through her mother, her emotional balance can now be reestablished only through "reconciliation," through the thriving of her child. As a child, when she was the receiving part of the symbiotic unit, her frustration led to the incorporation of the ambivalent core of her personality organization, and now, when she is the active, giving part of the symbiosis, her infant's frustration mobilizes ambivalent responses toward him.

The process which we have described in the mother is the result of reactivation of the ambivalent core of her personality. Clinically, this leads to a variety of depressive manifestations which are expressed, so far as the child is concerned, in disturbances of motherliness. Inadequate mothering turns the symbiotic relationship into a vicious circle, which leads to intensification of the hostile-aggressive component of the ambivalent core in the child. We refer to such an organization of the nuclear conflict as *depressive constellation*. This term does not signify the pathogenesis of any particular clinical entity, but indicates a significant variation in the primary psychic organization which, in transaction with all other psychic processes, participates in the further developmental organization of the personality and its adaptive reactions, and represents one of its primary (basic) determinants.

Abraham differentiated two phases within the oral stage of development.[18] The first is the passive-receptive oral phase, which is considered to last until the child is able to reach actively for objects; the second is the active-incorporative oral phase, which is characterized by attempts at mastery through incorporation. Considering the total physiologic and mental growth of the infant, there is justification for such a distinction between an early phase of infancy dominated by the symbiotic needs alone and a later period during which attempts at active mastery are directed outside the mother, toward animate and inanimate objects of the infant's environment. The tendency toward active mastery is not identical, however, with active or aggressive incorporation but is a sign of maturation in which security, lack of anxiety, permits the ego to expand.[19] For this reason, a differentiation between the passive-receptive and the active-incorporative oral phase cannot be based upon an intensification of the aggressive tendency. Actually, intensification of aggressive tendency does not characterize a specific phase of development. The aggressive component, which intensifies the manifestations of receptive tendencies, does not grow in progression with the child's age. It is more likely that the opposite is true.[20] Through the maturational processes the normal infant achieves the integration of confidence and hope, mental attitudes which protect the ego from immediate and total regression in response to frustration. It is through frustration and regression that aggressive energy becomes free (defusion, dissociation) and intensifies the manifestation of receptive tendencies (or any other psychodynamic tendency). The aggressive tendencies, although appearing to be hostile, lead to gratification of the need and in this way enable the infant (the growing individual in general) to store energy. By the latter process aggressive energy is bound and becomes a participant in the process of organization of the psychic apparatus.[21]

It is characteristic of the spiral of human growth that *pari passu* with the loosening of the symbiotic relationship, the growing individual incorporates the mental characteristics of the parents, including their cultural inheritance. Although this process is in itself "oral," i.e., it occurs through introjection, we should realize that not all of this incorporation originates in the anaclitic, dependent needs of the child; its other source is the self-action of the infant. As an early example of this we might take the "primordial dream" of the newborn.[22] The sleeping infant just before awakening often, but not always, "practices" sucking. When sleep is disturbed by hunger, an attempt to preserve sleep seems to take place. The reflex mechanism which was prepared for its function at a time when the umbilical cord supplied all needs without effort sets in and maintains sleep just a little longer. Since the hallucinatory gratification cannot satisfy hunger, the need increases; the infant then awakes crying and the mother satisfies the need.

The meaning of feeding = introjection from the standpoint of maintaining symbiosis was discussed previously. Turning now to some of the steps by which the symbiotic relation is resolved, the newborn from the time of birth seems to behave as if he had two sources of gratification—one which he seeks to mobilize within his body and the other which, in reality, is outside his body. Included in this phenomenon is the precursor of the anticipation of mastery—i.e., a precursor of that intrapsychic process which, combined with other mental attitudes such as confidence or the lack of it, evaluates from within the ability to satisfy a need or to achieve a goal, and at first does so by "trial satisfaction," by fantasy. When the infant becomes able to differentiate between *I* and *not-I* and later is able to make active efforts toward mastery, he appears to have two resources on which he can draw to reestablish his psychic equilibrium. It would lead us too far afield to describe even the most typical trials and errors which accompany the child's attempt at mastery. But the child's disappointment is visible and audible when, for example, he wants to take a spoon from the mother's hand and she opposes his wish, or when the child drops the spoon, or when he struggles with the spoon and food, failing to get his favorite pudding in his mouth. The expression of anger and frustration is immediate. Probably much earlier than we generally assume, children begin to feel anxiety, humiliation, and shame because of failure. Of course, the individual variations are great in this respect. These manifestations of a rudimentary ego ideal are not our concern here. From the standpoint of the emotional symbiosis, however, it is significant that when a child faces frustration or finds himself in a conflictual situation, whether because the obstacle is too great or because his response to it is too highly charged, his need for the mother's protection increases. This response is a temporary and partial regression which revives the dependency of the child.

It is obvious that the younger child has less choice than the older one; the younger the child, the less frustration he is able to bear without immediate recourse to the mother. Yet one can observe that an infant (in the second half-year of life) attempts under certain conditions to hold his own by mobilizing his internal resources to maintain his psychic equilibrium. For example, a small child busy with a toy is startled by something, or drops the toy, or someone takes it away from him, or he is hurt by the toy, or something else hurts him, although not to the degree of real pain. An expression of amazement appears; then his lips turn down and quiver; it looks as though the child were thinking it over. "Is this all right? Do I still feel well?" Then, as if having made a decision, he begins to cry and cries the more intensely the longer it takes to get a response from the mother. The somewhat older or more object-directed child with the same type and intensity of injury, after an evaluation of the situation, might return to his previous activity or to a modified one; for example, the child might lie down and start to suck his thumb. His ego can maintain itself by its own resources.

What is the mother's role in this situation? The response of mothers might be classified into three groups: (1) the oversolicitous mother might jump to the child's aid before the child has made his "own decision" to call for her; (2) the discerning, responsive mother, knowing that no real danger exists, might speak some reassuring words, giving support to the child by indicating her presence; (3) the angry, rejecting mother might scold, "Why do you get into this again?"—in which case the child will cry in response to the anger of the mother. We might state that the mothers of the first and third type actually respond to their own needs, while mothers of the second type respond to the child's needs. In the child's subsequent behavior one could observe whether the mother's response encouraged or discouraged the child's further reliance upon himself and upon the mother's help, or whether the child mobilized defenses against disappointments in her and in himself. In any case, the child and the mother interpret the situation, each in his own way, each within the frame of his own needs. Such minute happenings —affective communications between mother and child—influence the child's adaptive techniques toward the mother and at the same time they mold his self-esteem, his confidence in his own growth. In turn, the developmental reactions of the child affect, exaggerate, or reconcile the mother's emotional response to the child's behavior. Her response is not static; although it is rooted primarily in her own developmental experiences, her attitudes and behavior depend on her specific response to the particular child. Along with related motivating factors, this determines whether a mother is able to mature with the child and permit him to grow, or whether she will inhibit his development.

Study of the transactional processes between mother and child (emotional symbiosis) reveals that not only does the mother's attitude influence the psychic organization of the child, but also that the infant brings about changes in the mother—changes which reach beyond her manifest emotional responses and extend into her psychic organization. This occurs through the same processes of introjection and identification which we consider to be primary processes in the organization of the personality of the child. The parent (the father as well as the mother), through introjection of the object cathexis directed to the child, incorporates the child into his or her personality organization.

The pathology of maternal behavior is the consequence of the regression which is initiated by the normal concomitant of procreative growth, namely, by an increase in receptive tendencies. This regression recharges the ambivalent core of the personality. If this involves the reactivation of preverbal memories of frustration and the "incorporation of the bad mother," the mother's security in her own motherliness is shaken. Under such conditions, "identifying with her mother" means being the "bad mother." Her intention to be a good mother is gnawed by doubt. This brings to the fore the counterpart of the "bad mother," namely, the "bad self = bad infant." The mother lives the symbiosis on two levels: she is the mother, but she also identifies with the child. As the mother, she actually intends and wishes to love her child and to take care of him as she herself wishes to be loved and cared for; her aspiration is to be a better mother than her own mother was, in order to produce a better, happier child. This wish, which has for many years provided food for fantasy, now is out of the realm of fantasy; its fulfillment is a pressing need, but its gratification depends on the infant. If the infant, through crying fits, demonstrates his frustration, the mother's insecurity about her motherliness appears justified. Indeed, it increases her anxiety and impatience. As she experiences through her child that she is not a "better mother" (than her own mother was), the infant comes to represent the "bad infant." This occurs not only on account of the mother's projection of the "bad infant = self," but also because the crying, sick, not thriving infant actually appears to be bad and hostile to his mother. Thus the infant, dependent as he is for everything on the mother, can (unknowingly) wield an immeasurable power. Just as once the mother was the only person who could alleviate frustration and pain, now the infant alone, through his thriving, can alleviate the mother's frustration and anxiety. Normally, the libidinal aspects of mothering, satisfied by an increase of the receptive tendencies, keep a positive psychoeconomic balance, so that instead of perceiving the intensification of her ambivalence, the mother is aware only of the gratifications of motherliness.

Since for the woman procreative growth in all its phases stimulates a reactivation of the alimentary phase, the differences in the organization of the ambivalent core—the depressive constellation—seem to have more significance for the woman than for the man. This is true only insofar as the procreative function and mothering are directly concerned. In all other normal and pathologic transactions the significance of the nuclear conflict and its pathogenic variations—the depressive constellation—is the same for both sexes.

What holds true for both sexes is this: each step of development draws energies necessary for its completion from two sources. One is outside the organism, the other is within. *When higher integration requires a fresh supply of psychic energy, it is produced through the intensification of the receptive-retentive tendencies which were involved in the primary organization of the psychic structure.* Not only do individual and procreative growth increase the need for a greater supply of integrative energy, but also, each time a regression makes aggressive energy free, the resulting disequilibrium in the psychic organization signifies the intensification of a need for libidinal supply, i.e., for integrative energy to reestablish the psychic equilibrium. This (instinctual) need recharges the organized patterns of the oral alimentary (symbiotic) processes. In other words, *regression to the oral-dependent phase might reactivate the depressive constellation in man and woman alike.*

NOTES

1. Originally presented at a meeting of the Chicago Psychoanalytic Society, February 24, 1953. Published in *J. Am. Psychoanalytic Assn.,* IV, no. 3 (July 1956), 389–427.

2. Freud, S., "Instincts and Their Vicissitudes" (1915), *Std. Ed.*, XIV, 117–140.

3. Freud, S., "Mourning and Melancholia" (1917), *Std. Ed.*, XIV, 243–258.

4. Grinker, R. R., Sr., *Psychosomatic Research* (New York, W. W. Norton, 1953).

5. A discussion of the biologic symbiosis of pregnancy and the postnatal symbiosis can be found in "Psychosomatic Implications of the Primary Unit: Mother-Child." This volume, Chapter 8.

6. Abraham, K., "Notes on the Psychoanalytical Investigation and Treatment of Manic-Depressive Insanity and Allied Conditions" (1911), *Selected Papers on Psycho-Analysis* (London, Hogarth Press, 1927), pp. 137–156; Alexander, F., "Psychoanalysis Revised," *Psychoanalytic Quart.*, IX (1940), 1–36.

7. Gesell, A., and Amatruda, C. S., *The Embryology of Behavior* (New York, Harper & Bros., 1945).

8. Being pushed away from the breast before being satiated for reasons which do not originate in the child—for example, in the tempo of his breathing, swallowing—might bring about the primary affect of separation anxiety. In a case of anorexia nervosa which was very severe during infancy and again became severe in young adulthood, the feeding disturbance of both mother and infant could be traced to such occurrences.

9. The emotional fluctuations of the postpartum period naturally do not interrupt the continuity of the personality of the well-integrated mother. A mother does not live only with and through the child as the infant lives through the mother. Mothers have other sources of gratification which play a more or less significant role in the "overcoming" of the psychobiologic processes connected with parturition. In our civilization these gratifications often take over at a time when it is premature for the infant as well as for the mother.

10. Hartmann, H., Kris, E., and Loewenstein, R. M., "Comments on the Formation of Psychic Structure," *The Psychoanalytic Study of the Child*, vol. II (New York, International Universities Press, 1946), pp. 11–38.

11. Gesell, A., and Amatruda, C. S., *The Embryology of Behavior.*

12. The concepts of confidence, primary narcissism, and surplus energy are discussed in this volume in "Adaptation to Reality in Early Infancy" and in "The Psychosomatic Implications of the Primary Unit: Mother-Child."

13. French, T. M., *The Integration of Behavior, Vol. I: Basic Postulates* (Chicago, University of Chicago Press, 1952).

14. Spitz, R. A., and Wolf, K. M., "Anaclitic Depression; An Inquiry into the Genesis of Psychiatric Conditions in Early Childhood, II," *The Psychoanalytic Study of the Child*, vol. II (New York, International Universities Press, 1946), pp. 313–342.

15. It is also apparent in the diffuse hitting and kicking of the older child.

16. Grinker, R. R., Sr., Discussion of this paper, Chicago Psychoanalytic Society, February 24, 1953. Unpublished.

17. Gerard, R. W., "Higher Levels of Integration," *Biol. Symposia*, VIII (1942), 67–87.

18. Abraham, K., "A Short Study of the Development of the Libido,

Viewed in the Light of Mental Disorders," *Selected Papers on Psycho-Analysis* (London, Hogarth Press, 1927), pp. 418–501.

19. Although infants put into their mouths all objects with which they want to get acquainted, these gestures do not express a tendency toward aggressive incorporation. It is "learning with the mouth" which, being a better coordinated and more used organ than the hands or even the eyes, gives the needed information about the object. Seeing, tactile sensations, and investigation with the fingers are integrated later with the "learning by mouth."

20. Naturally, this does not mean that the absolute output of motor energy cannot be greater in an older child or in an adult than in an infant. But the young infant's global excitation—motor storm—represents a greater relative output than is discharged by the more organized aggressive behavior of the older child and of adults.

21. Hartmann, H., Kris, E., and Loewenstein, R. M., "Notes on the Theory of Aggression," *Psychoanalytic Study of the Child,* vols. III and IV (New York, International Universities Press, 1949), pp. 9–36.

22. Freud referred to this phenomenon in "The Interpretation of Dreams," *Std. Ed.,* IV and V, 1953.

DISCUSSION

Psychoanalytic propositions are dynamic and genetic. Can psychoanalysis move toward biology? The title of the paper indicates such intention, but the investigation itself led quickly and necessarily to interpersonal processes, to the evolution of object relationship and its intrapsychic representations and behavioral manifestations, thus away from biology. The psychic representations of such processes are signified by word symbols, such as introjection, identification, etc., which refer to theoretical constructs; these retain traces of their biologic origins. How much of the biologically rooted instincts or drive motivations is contained in those constructs? How "biologic" is a mother's mothering behavior toward the child? What are the origins of those psychologic factors which account for *confidence* and for the *depressive constellation?* The argument leans one-sidedly toward behavior introjected reciprocally as experience between mother and infant. What is missing in this elaboration is consideration of the constitutional element. This is, of course, always implied, but its investigation is considered "off limits" by many psychoanalysts.

Freud felt the necessity of defending himself against the charge of having denied the importance of constitutional factors. In a footnote to "The Dynamics of the Transference" (1912) he wrote:

> Psychoanalysis has talked a lot about the accidental factors in etiology and little about constitutional ones; but that

is only because it was able to contribute something fresh to the former, while, to begin with, it knew no more than was commonly known about the latter. We refuse to posit any contrast in principle between the two sets of etiological factors; on the contrary, we assume that the two sets regularly act jointly in bringing about the observed result. Endowment and Chance determine a man's fate—rarely or never one of these powers alone. The amount of etiological effectiveness to be attributed to each of them can only be arrived at in every individual case separately.[1]

Observation of newborn infants reveals differences in activity and sleep patterns and in the general irritability of the nervous system, which may influence sucking ability and gastric functions.[2] Yet even in the newborn we cannot be certain that the differences are determined by constitutional factors, since intrauterine conditions and the trauma of birth, an external event as far as the newborn is concerned, may exert influence on the constitution.

The discomforts of the newborn, even if manifested in crying fits, cannot be designated as anxiety, but they may indicate a predisposition to anxiety. Phyllis Greenacre in her investigation of "The Predisposition to Anxiety" (1941) differentiates three phases. First, there is the "basic, blind or amorphous anxiety" which manifests itself in an irritable responsiveness to the organism at a reflex level; second is "the anxiety in response to these fresh experiences of danger and frustration, and third, the secondary anxiety" as reaction to later psychological dangers in life.[3] Her discussion, faithful to Freud's proposition in "Inhibitions, Symptoms and Anxiety" (1926),[4] does not include basic instinctual factors which may contribute to the predisposition to anxiety. Yet Freud's second instinct theory, as has been pointed out (Chapter 1, this volume), may serve as the key to the problem of anxiety since it elucidates the dynamic factors in the predisposition.

In the paper "Death Instinct and Anxiety" (1931), I discussed aggression as an affect resulting from the defusion of the contrasting psychic energies and suggested that the predisposition to anxiety depends on the unbound, "free" aggression which may be experienced as danger. Freud defined aggression toward the self as "primary masochism." I concluded that "Freud made a contribution to our knowledge of constitution by the discovery of primary masochism."[5] I tried to exploit only the observable facts in the frame of such primary concepts as introjection and identification.[6] I was satisfied that my observations of the infant-mother relationship demonstrated the reciprocity of the psychologic processes. Concentrating mainly on the interpersonal processes that influence the evolving relationships between parent and child and their intrapsychic consequences, I did not ask, what is the role of constitutional factors in the outcome of the fluctuating balance between the primary constructs, confidence, and the depressive constellation? How do constitutional factors alleviate or aggravate the effects of infantile experience of alimentation? This is, of course, a much investigated territory of psychoanalysis.

The investigation of a psychosomatic-somatopsychic condition, diabetes mellitus, confirmed the permanent influence of the infantile ambivalence which is intrinsic to the nature of instinctual drive, namely, that there is always a time lag between need and its gratification.[7] This, of course, exists for animals also, probably with even greater hazard than for human infants. But only human infants develop object relationships, introject and then project the sense of frustration and gratification along with the memory trace of the object whom the infant holds responsible. Only human infants learn to wait with the awareness of waiting and, with waiting, internalize the confidence that need will be satisfied or the tension that need may not be satisfied. The tension-pain then breaks down the fusion and the crying fit breaks out. The crying fit appears to any observer as anger. The point which must be added to previous discussions is that the constitutional factors, genic in origin, are responsible for the infant's ability to learn to wait. The ability to keep the opposing psychic energies in fusion is probably not the only constitutional factor which enables the infant to integrate the perception of need and its gratification as "confidence"; other factors may also be involved.

In discussing "instinctual processes" we deal with what Freud referred to as the prehistoric past of the individual, with that phase of postnatal existence when psyche and soma, ego and id, are not yet separated. The primary psychic constructs refer to processes initiated by the course of alimentation before the infant's ego is able to differentiate affects. Anxiety, the warden of individual survival, develops several weeks or months later when the maturation of the organism has developed a psychic apparatus able to differentiate between tension states.[8] The predisposition to anxiety is determined by the individual's innate capacity to keep opposing psychic energies in fusion, thus neutralizing aggression. If the tendency to such neutralization remains deficient, the psychic equilibrium is frequently endangered by free aggression; the affective expression of this is anxiety. Both anxiety and aggression act as drives motivating the coordination of defensive behavior.

One of Freud's first discoveries was that emotional illnesses, psychiatric conditions, serve as defenses against repressed but conflicting instinctual tendencies. This included psychic as well as somatic reactions to instinctual conflicts and their manifold interactions. This leads back to the problem of diabetes mellitus. Indeed, we did not set out to solve the riddle of diabetes mellitus, but our observations revealed that the fear experienced by a mother during her childhood may cause that mother to fear herself in her mothering function and, consequently, to fear her child. The transactional spiral of these interactions maintains a chronic stress which burdens the organism in such a way that the arising conflict-tension finally breaks down the chain of the normal metabolic process and leads to the disease.[9]

The specific genic factors which are responsible for diabetes mellitus have been established. We are probably talking about a secondary order of constitutional factors when we assume that the innate propensity of the organism to maintain conflicting instinctual forces is tested in each feeding situation from birth on. In the feeding situation, the "innate" need meets the "environment" and begins to learn its ways and adapt to it. The assumption that the origin of the emotional factors which lead to diabetes is in the depressive constellation is not far from those observations which indicate that diabetes begins about the time of birth, irrespective of the fact that only much later in life does it become apparent clinically. For psychoanalysts, it is not difficult to imagine that the intrapsychic stress, caused by incorporated ambivalence which leads to crying fits and thus to negative interactions with the mother, increases the frequency and intensity of the crying fits which in time indicate not only diffuse tension but also anxiety. It is rather surprising, however, to learn about the parallel processes that occur somatically.

Freud's concept of the fusion and defusion of opposing psychic energies combines with the observation of the psychologic effects of infantile feeding experiences to justify the assumption that these interacting factors constitute a predisposition to anxiety. The concept "depressive constellation," to paraphrase Freud's famous definition of instinct, is a concept on the border between the innate and the environmental, developing at that early phase of postnatal existence when the borders are not yet sharply defined. Confidence and depressive constellation are psychic precipitates of nuclear biologic processes which predispose and determine the ego's capacity for enduring delay. Neither confidence nor depressive constellation are expressed directly as affects. The emotional state correlated with confidence can be equated with a sense of well-being in the infant and the depressive constellation equated with tension and discomfort. Internalized in connection with the organ or organ system which is involved in the frustration, the discomfort may become the source of chronic stress. Indeed, the term "depressive constellation" does not refer primarily to depression as an affective disorder. It signifies the first link in the psychologic processes which participate in the causative chain of psychosomatic illness.

Ambivalence is the psychic representation of the bipolarity of instinctual forces. "Toward the Biology of the Depressive Constellation" deals with the ambivalence intrinsic to the processes of alimentation. In the term "emotional symbiosis" are conceptualized the ongoing processes of the hungry infant being fed, the feeding mother's need to care for the child, and the intrapsychic precipitates of these processes in the child and in the mother. The vector of all this, however, is directed out of the symbiosis toward individuation. Each microstep on this long route involves two poles: need → tension → fulfillment; separation → anxiety → union. It is true that life encompasses ambivalence with all its implications, but ambivalence is not all of life. The processes which maintain life not only repeat but also overcome the obstacles of ambivalence. In this way higher integration is achieved. Each higher integration in the growing individual as well as in the parent occurs through the reactivation and the overcoming of the ambivalent core.

NOTES

1. Freud, S., "The Dynamics of the Transference" (1912), *Std. Ed.,* XII, 99.

2. Benedek, T., "Adaptation to Reality in Infancy," this volume, Chapter 5.

3. Greenacre, P., "The Predisposition to Anxiety" (1941), in *Trauma, Growth and Personality* (New York, W. W. Norton, 1952), p. 55.

4. Freud, S., "Inhibitions, Symptoms and Anxiety" (1926), *Std. Ed.,* XX, 87–156.

5. Chapter 1, this volume.

6. The paper, "Death Instinct and Anxiety," belonged to that period of psychoanalysis in which the lines between the instinct theory and the structural theory were not yet sharply drawn.

7. Kubie, L. S., "Instincts and Homeostasis," *Psychosomatic Med.,* X (1948), 15–30.

8. This seems to be substantiated through all species of animals. The offspring have to mature and "learn" the method of survival and, until that age, the animal parents' instinctually coordinated equipment secures the protection of the offspring.

9. Mirsky, I. A., "Emotional Factors in the Patient with Diabetes Mellitus," *Bul. Menninger Clinic,* XII (1948), 187–194.

14. Parenthood as a
Developmental Phase

INTRODUCTION

The aim of the paper, "Toward the Biology of the Depressive Constellation," was to elaborate the role of the aggressive psychic energy in the formation of psychic representations and intrapsychic conflicts. Since aggression, just as libido, is introjected and organized beginning with the processes of alimentation, we assume that both forms of psychic energy participate in the development of object relationships in each phase. This means that every object relationship is ambivalent, more or less. Accordingly, one could assume that the genetic theory of psychoanalysis is complete only if one considers in each developmental phase the motivational power of both forms of psychic energy.

Regarding early infancy the concept of depressive constellation represents an extension of the psychology of the symbiotic phase which thus includes the function of both forms of psychic energy. Since the study of the symbiotic phase revealed that the psychobiologic processes of pregnancy and motherhood lead to a new level of developmental integration in the mother, it was a challenging task to follow the psychology of parent-child interactions through the oedipal period of the child. Although the following paper necessarily contains some material discussed in connection with the depressive constellation, the theoretical basis of this paper is the classical libido theory.

Development refers to the positive, integrating and integrated aspects of the processes; the negative factors, motivated by aggressive energy, are either assimilated by the ongoing adaptations or, if not, they interfere with development, leaving conflicts and fixation on the way. Since pathologic complications, numerous and frequent as they may be, were not in the scope of this essay, the regression of parental love to its component parts is not discussed.

I feel that the title of this paper needs explanation. A careful

377

reader may ask the question, is parenthood a "phase" in terms of the genetic theory? I would reply no, but I remember clearly that I chose this term in analogy with the genetic theory to emphasize that the developmental processes continue beyond adolescence and are repeated in reversed fashion in the parent. Indeed, parenthood is not just one phase in the psychic evolution of the parent. Prepared for unconsciously from infancy on until it becomes reality, parenthood is a dominant factor in the emotional life of the parent, requiring a continual adaptation from the parent to the child.[1]

The metapsychology of parent-child interaction still needs to be investigated in such a way as to take into account the reciprocal influence in the developmental process of the child and its effect on adaptational changes in the parent. It should not be shaken off with a shrug that would say it is not psychoanalytic since it is not intrapsychic but interpersonal. Life, or living, is interpersonal, although for a long time we have conceptualized only that which we assumed occurred within the psychic system of the individual. In addition to the motivating factors within the individual, we have always considered the activating factors outside him, for only in this way can concepts such as introjection and identification be meaningful.

This generalization is offered here as propitiation for the many repetitions concerning reciprocal interactions and their psychic representations throughout these chapters.

NOTES

1. Benedek, T., "Parenthood During the Life Cycle," in *Parenthood, Its Psychology and Psychopathology,* ed. E. J. Anthony and T. Benedek (Boston, Little, Brown & Co., 1970), pp. 185–206.

PARENTHOOD AS A DEVELOPMENTAL PHASE[1]

A CONTRIBUTION TO THE LIBIDO THEORY

The libido theory implies that the integration of the sexual drive from its pregenital beginnings to its genital primacy is the process by which the organization of the personality takes place. The impact of physio-

1. Presented in condensed form at the Fall Meeting of the American Psychoanalytic Association, New York, December 7, 1958 and reprinted from *The Journal of the American Psychoanalytic Association,* vol. VII, no. 3 (July, 1959).

logical changes at puberty sets in motion the adolescent processes of integration which lead toward maturity. Maturity includes, besides the physiological readiness for procreation, the individual's ability to find gratification for his instinctual needs within the frame of his culturally determined realities. This level of maturity in turn initiates motivation for the next phase of development, which is parenthood.[2] Since it has been assumed that the individual reaches this goal of personality integration during adolescence, the genetic theory does not include the psychodynamic processes of reproduction and parenthood as drive motivations for further development.

The aim of this presentation is to demonstrate that personality development continues beyond adolescence, under the influence of reproductive physiology, and that parenthood utilizes the same primary processes which operate from infancy on in mental growth and development.

I

When birth interrupts intrauterine existence the infant has not yet developed mentally to a degree that he is aware of separation. After breathing is established, hunger is the first indicator of being separated and also the stimulus for overcoming separation. Satiation and the subsequent resumption of sleep or a sleeplike condition means to the child that the separation has been temporarily overcome. It takes several weeks of postnatal development[3] with many repetitions of experiencing need followed by gratification before the infant perceives that the source of his need associated with hunger, pain, and discomfort is *within* and the source of gratification is *outside* the self. It is then that separation in a psychological sense begins to exist for the infant.

Introducing the concept of narcissism, Freud (9) outlined an "undifferentiated phase" of instinctual development in which the subject —needful infant—and the object—need-satisfying mother—together represent the source of energy which becomes stored in the infant. He calls "this state of things absolute primary narcissism" (12). In a previous publication I refer to this "state of primary narcissism" as sym-

2. Erikson's concept of ego identity implies cultural inheritance, maturational development, adult capacities and commitments. He assumes that this "more or less actually attained but forever to-be-revised" sense of reality of the self within social reality is achieved through the adolescent process of self-integration (6).
3. I use the term "development" and not maturation since I refer not to the manifold neuronal, muscular, and other aspects of paced organic growth, but to the intrapsychic processes by which the awareness of separateness evolves, and in continuous interaction with this, the self as a mental structure becomes organized.

biosis, a primary unity of mother and child (2). This is based upon the concept that the physiological and psychodynamic processes of pregnancy and lactation maintain in the mother a drive organization toward motherhood and the activities of motherliness. The object of this drive is the child. The infant's need for the mother is absolute, while the mother's for the infant is relative. Accordingly, the participation of primary drives in the symbiotic state has different "meanings" for mother and child. Yet in the symbiotic processes, the mother is not only a giver, but also a receiver.

As the infant matures and perceives the breast and the mother as outside the self, his ego begins to cathect the objects of his need. With each feeding and with each disappearance of the outward-directed hunger drive, that part of the environment which was instrumental in satisfying the need becomes introjected into the self of the infant. In the feeding process, sensations arise not only from the gratifying object (breast-mother) but also from tactile sensations of the mouth, sensations of sucking, olfactory and kinesthetic sensations of body posture, of stretching and pulling of legs and arms, the agreeable feeling of satiation, and the disturbance of stomach distention. In brief, all the perceptual systems participating in the drive experience form parts of the introject. If the drive is not satisfied, the sense of frustration, the accompanying anger, and the phenomena of the crying fits are also introjected along with the object of the frustrated drive which then becomes the introjected object of anger. The introjected object is merged with the introjected self in the drive experience and thereby object representations and self-representations are established in inseparable connection with each other.

Introjections and identifications are the primary processes by which mental structures develop. They represent the patterns for all later development of the mind. On the basis of processes which Freud studied in "Mourning and Melancholia" (10) he assumed that "the character of the ego is a precipitate of abandoned object-cathexes and that it contains a record of past object choices." More appropriate to our present study is Freud's consideration of "simultaneous object cathexis and identification, in which the alteration in character occurs before the object has been given up" (11). Indeed, the introjection of the "object" of the drive along with the sensations, affects, related to the gratification or to the frustration of the drive, are basic to continuity of interpersonal communication. As the continuity of object relationship is maintained, the memories of object relationship plus drive experience become stored as object representations and self-representations and become the nuclei of organization in the mental apparatus.

"The subject of identification becomes an extension of biological theory. . . . Identifications constitute theoretical bridges between biology and personality and between personalities and social groups"

(Grinker, 14). In this sense, introjection and identification are terms which refer to processes by which memory traces of drive-motivated interpersonal relationships are stored during the entire course of life.

In the earliest stage of the neonatal period the drive experience relates mainly to alimentation. The primary model is simple: need → mother → satiation. All other needs and gratifications, all kinds of perception, tactile, olfactory, auditory, visual sensations, seem to be submerged within the primary model of orality. The repetition of these experiences adds up to a memory of pleasant-feeding-mother equated with pleasant-feeding-self. The same mother in dissimilar feeding situations may also be associated with unpleasant memory traces and become the introject of pain: painful-bad-mother equated with painful-unpleasant-self. The mother's gratification in satisfying her infant's needs as well as her frustration when she is unable to do so affect her emotional life and again reciprocally that of the child. Thus there develops a spiral of interpersonal processes which I refer to as emotional symbiosis. *The term "emotional symbiosis" describes a reciprocal interaction between mother and child which, through the processes of "introjection-identification," creates structural change in each of the participants* (3).[4]

Through each single and interrelated series of identifications not only is an image of the object internalized, but also the mirror image of the object's attitude toward the self. "I am good because she sees me as good and treats me as good; I am bad because she is bad to me and she sees me as bad." These details about the psychology of identifications (18) were implicit in Freud's concept of the development of self-esteem as a precipitate of infantile relations and early "oral" identifications. Yet there are forerunners of "self-esteem."

Studying the adaptations of infants to the realities of the feeding situation in both healthy and hospitalized children, I arrived at the assumption that as the infant introjects the "good mother = good self," he also establishes a mental attitude of confidence (2). The term *confidence* refers to a primary mental construct which develops through multiple repetitions of the experience that need is relieved by gratification and results in a positive emotional balance. As the child learns to know the mother as the need-gratifying person outside the self, he also learns to maintain the mother-child unity on a psychological level. Whether we call this "primary love" (1) or primary object relationship, it enables the infant to project expectations of gratification into the future. Observations show that a four- to six-month-old infant may reveal a

4. Similar reciprocal processes can be attributed to any meaningful (dynamic) interpersonal relationship, i.e., to any such relationship in which exchange of libidinal cathexis takes place. Freud described this process first in connection with the dynamic of romantic love (9) and derived from it his insight into the processes by which the ego contains "a record of past object choices."

confident attitude at the time of feeding, even in a state of moderate hunger. Protected from the sense of frustration by a psychic structure of libidinous origin, the infant has learned, commensurate with his maturational level, to wait.

The mental construct of confidence is integrated not only with the object representation of the "good-feeding-mother" and the self-representation of "good-feeding-fed-self," but also with the precipitate of the affects which accompany the drive experience—satiation, falling asleep, etc.[5] The functions of the primary mental construct of confidence are manifold. It serves as a defense against the sense of frustration, which it delays; it facilitates other relationships beyond the primary object, and it furthers the integration of self-representations within the value system of "self-esteem."

Our assumption is that these processes apply also to the mother. Parallel with the experiences which lead to confidence in the infant, the mother, through introjecting the gratifying experience of successful mothering, establishes self-confidence in her motherliness. The mother's confidence in her motherliness is not just a "reflection" of the child's gratification, a "mirror image" of the smile of her thriving child. The study of the psychodynamic processes of the female reproductive function reveals that the drive organization which motivates motherhood and the activities of mothering maintains dynamic communication between mother and child and leads to changes not only in the infant but in the mother as well. Thus there are reciprocal ego developments. In the infant, through the introjection of good mother = good self, the infant develops confidence. In the mother, through introjection of good-thriving-infant = good-mother-self, the mother achieves a new integration in her personality. As we compare the integrative process of the mother with that of her infant, we can recognize implicit differences in the complex personality of the adult.

On one level, the parallel is simple. Mothering, nursing is motivated by a primary drive, the object of which is the infant. While the infant incorporates the nipple, the mother feels united with the baby. But this identification, pleasurable as it is, is not the main source of the regressive processes of the mother for they are inherent in the female reproductive function. Each phase of motherhood—pregnancy, lacta-

5. The affects originating in the libido of the symbiotic state (primary narcissism) become neutralized in the process of forming the primary ego construct—confidence. This is a gradual process. The behavioral manifestations of confidence, for example, the ability to wait, appear early (in the first three to six months of life). It is tested again and again by transient frustrations and the affects mobilized by them toward the same object, mother-self. Thus the neutralization of drive cathexes necessary to maintain confidence as a part of the ego organization can develop only step by step through a longer period of development.

tion, and also the preparation for these during the progesterone phase of each sexual cycle—is accompanied by a regression to the oral phase of development. The female reproductive functions reactivate the object and self-representations integrated during the oral phase of her development and bring about a repetition of intrapsychic processes which originate in the mother-child relationship during her infancy (4). Thus the mother's object relationship with the child is motivated by psychic energies originating in two levels of her psychosexual organization. One is the primary reproductive drive; the other is a secondary organization, derived from the oral phase of development. The first is expressed by the adult tendency to give, to nurse, and to succor; the other by manifestations of receptive tendencies. This facilitates the mother's identifications with her child.

The oral-dependent needs of the child as well as the psychologic processes which evolve from them have been well studied. The mother's receptive needs from the child, however, are not easily recognized in their healthy manifestations except through psychoanalysis. The analysis of those who cannot stand the physiological and psychological stresses of motherhood reveals that the pathology of pregnancy and postpartum period is brought about by regression to the oral phase. The affect hunger of the mother, her need for love and affection, her wish to reunite with her baby, "to overprotect" and "overpossess" him are pathologic exaggerations of the normal process of mothering. While they disturb the smooth course of symbiotic events, they offer evidence that the postpartum symbiosis is "oral, alimentary for both infant and mother" (3). The mother's ability to receive from her child is strongly affected by the confidence which the mother herself has incorporated into her mental structure while receiving from her own mother. Her "giving," her patience and motherliness are derived from the developmental vicissitudes of primary identifications with her mother. These were fantasies before; now with the actuality of motherhood they are tested in reality.

The child's identification with the mother evolves step by step in accordance with the mother's changing functions in the growing child's personality organization, with her role in the gratification of the child's drive requirements in the various phases of development. This means that the child is not able to identify with the actual experience of the mother. The area of the mother's experience for which the infant has "empathy" are the emotions which affect the infant's security and mobilize anxietylike tensions in him, such as the insecurity of the mother concerning her mothering activities, her anger toward the child, etc. Thus the empathy of the infant with the mother is on the level of primary affects which do not involve organized ego. As the infant does not have the physiologic and psychic organization for motherhood, he cannot envy the mother her breast, or her capacity to nurse (17). The mother, however, having been a child and having introjected the memory traces of being fed, nursed, cared for, in her own mothering experiences relives with her infant the pleasure and pains of infancy. The empathy of the mother for her child originates in the experiences of her early infancy which are reanimated by the emotions of the current experience of her motherhood. Through the gratifying experiences of mothering, sustained by her thriving infant, the mother substantiates the confidence in her motherliness. However complex this intrapsychic process seems, the integrative effect of confidence is the same in the mother as it is in the child. It serves as a defense against the fear of frustration which may occur in every mother's experience and it increases the mother's capacity to love the child. Since through this the mother approaches the realization of one aspiration of her ego ideal— namely, to be a good mother—confidence supports the mother's self-esteem and becomes a source of secondary narcissism and self-assurance. Since motherliness involves the repetition and working through of the primary, oral conflicts with the mother's own mother, the healthy, normal process of mothering allows for resolution of those conflicts, i.e., for intrapsychic "reconciliation" with the mother. Thus motherhood facilitates the psychosexual development toward completion.

Just as the positive balance of the transactional processes leads to confidence in the child and to self-confidence in the mother, so we can recognize the effects of the negative balance of the transactional processes in the mother and in the child. The frustrated infant frustrates his mother; by this he induces a regression in the mother which intensifies the aggressive components of her receptive needs. While in the infant such tendency is directed toward the self = mother, in the mother the aggression is directed toward her infant and toward her own mother, and, through the identification with both, toward herself.

The regression stirs up in the mother the preverbal memories of the oral-dependent phase of her own development. If the recathexis of the infantile relationship with her own mother activates in the mother confidence and hope, she will overcome the actual disappointment and frustration, secure in her wish to love the child and to take care of him as she herself was loved and cared for. But if the crying fits of the infant or signs of his feebleness stir up not only justified concern, but beyond this, anxieties which originate in the mother's oral-dependent conflicts, the psychodynamics of the mother's response "can best be formulated by stating that both levels of her identification, that with her mother and with her child, turn negative. This means in terms of herself that she becomes the 'bad, frustrating mother' of her child, as well as the 'bad, frustrating infant' of her mother again. In terms of the infant it means that the 'bad, frustrating infant' becomes the irreconcilable 'hated self'; and at the same time her infant now becomes, as her mother once was, the needed and feared object. Just as she could regain emotional equilibrium as a child by satiation through her mother,

her emotional balance can now be reestablished only by 'reconciliation' through the thriving of her child. As a child, when the mother was *the receiving part* of the symbiotic unit, her frustration led to the incorporation of the ambivalent core in her personality organization, and now when she is *the active, giving part of the symbiosis,* her infant's frustration mobilizes the 'ambivalent core' of her personality" (3, pp. 405–406). This interferes with those integrative processes which make motherhood a phase of normal development. Clinically, it leads to a variety of depressive manifestations which are expressed, so far as the child is concerned, in disturbances of motherliness. Disturbed mothering turns the symbiotic relationship into a vicious circle. This leads to introjection of objects and self-representations in the child charged with aggressive cathexes. Consequently, the ambivalent core is implanted in the psychic organization of the child.

Confidence and the ambivalent core are primary mental constructs. We assume that one originates in the effects of the positive, the other in the outcome of the negative transactional processes between mother and infant. Each of these primary structures interacts with the other in the further development of the child's personality and concurrently modifies in specific ways the further "emotional symbiosis," i.e., the reciprocal relationship between mother and child.

The conceptualization of the processes resulting in "confidence" and in the "depressive core" also serves as models of the transactional processes between parent and child in the later developmental phases. *I propose that not only corresponding with and as a result of the physiologic symbiosis of pregnancy and the oral phase of development, but in each "critical period" the child revives in the parent his related developmental conflicts. This brings about either pathologic manifestations in the parent, or by resolution of the conflict it achieves a new level of integration in the parent. In turn, the child reaches each "critical period" with a repetition of the transactional processes which lead anew to the integration of the drive experience with the related object and self-representations.*

Before embarking upon material which supports this hypothesis, the father should be considered. Is there also a drive organization which motivates a reciprocal interaction between father and child? Since man's reproductive function depends upon a single act, the motivation of which is experienced as a compelling desire for orgastic discharge, one might ask whether there exists in men a primary biological tendency toward becoming and being a father, protector, and provider. Can one differentiate in man as in woman two goals of the reproductive drive?

In man as in woman, one can differentiate two arcs of the reproductive cycle. While in the female the short arc reflects the cyclical stimulation of the ovarian hormones, in the male the short cycle evolves without recognizable regularity, from one increase of compelling sexual urge to another. With the consummatory act the short cycle of the man's reproductive function is completed. The long arc of the reproductive cycle in man evolves from the time of being conceived as a male to the time when he attains sexual maturity and is able to fulfill his function in procreation. Propagation is a special manifestation of growth. The individual, after having achieved maturity, surpasses the growth of his own body and becomes able to produce a new individual. Under conditions which impede the reproductive function, such as sterility of either of the marital partners or enforced separation during war, man's instinct for survival becomes conscious and accessible to psychoanalytic study. Man's desire to survive, especially in the offspring of his own sex, is also documented by rites and religions, by customs and socioeconomic organization. There need be no doubt that the male reproductive drive has psychic representations of instinctual, biological origin. Yet for the purpose of our present problem, the question is whether we can differentiate in the male a drive organization which, parallel with motherliness, directs the reproductive drive toward fatherliness. My answer is affirmative, based upon the assumption that there are two sources of fatherliness: one, biological bisexuality; and the other, the biological dependency upon the mother.

For the first part of this assumption, zoologists give us support. In the reproductive functions of nonmammalian vertebrates zoologists have found strikingly different patterns of courtship, preparatory activities and—especially surprising to us—marked variations in patterns of caring for the young. Our knowledge of man's bisexuality, however, is extremely limited.

The long-lasting dependence of the human infant is a biological characteristic of the species. This accounts for the significance that the oral-dependent phase has for the personality organization of individuals of both sexes. Each man's earliest security as well as his earliest orientation to his world have been learned through identification with his mother. In the normal course of the development in the male, the early emotional dependence upon and identification with the mother is surpassed by the identifications with the father, directed by the innate maleness of the boy. This results not only in sexual competition with the father but also in identifications with the various roles of the father as protector and provider. These secondary manifestations of maleness are in continual transaction with those psychic representations which were established as a result of the oral-dependent relationship with the mother.

The primary drive organization of the oral phase—the prerequisite and consequence of the metabolic processes which sustain growth, maturation, and lead to the differentiation of the reproductive function —is the origin of parental tendencies, of motherliness and fatherliness. Since in man parental functions do not involve specific physiologic processes, there is no hormonal stimulation which, like the progesterone phase of the woman, would cyclically reactivate the oral phase of development. The drive organization which channels passive-receptive tendencies into the active object-directed behavior of fatherliness reaches its goal through the developmental resolution between male and female identifications, so that the adult male includes in his ego ideal the aspiration to complete his role in procreation by fatherliness.

This culturally influenced drive organization which motivates man's developmental goals toward marriage and fatherhood becomes integrated with the "regressive" tendencies through identification with his wife during her pregnancy. Sharing her fantasies and projecting his own about their yet unborn child, the father revives and relives his identifications with his mother and father in their specific developmental significance.

When Freud (9) states, "That which the fond parent projects ahead of him as his ideal in the child is merely a substitute for the lost narcissism of childhood," he implies that the child represents not only the parent's self as a child but also, or more so, his hope and expectation of self-realization through the child. Parents and children strive toward this goal through the unconscious processes of reciprocal introjections and identifications.

We have discussed the vicissitudes of communication between mother and child in that developmental phase when these processes are closest to their biological origin, during the postpartum period and infancy. But even in this state of emotional symbiosis we do not deal with a dyad only. The emotional attitude of the father in the family triad is significant from conception on. He responds to the receptive-dependent needs of his wife which are increased by her pregnancy, by her anxieties about parturition and the care of the child. Soon after the birth of the child a direct object relationship to the child begins to develop. Independent of hormonal stimulation, the father's relationship to the child is directed more by hope than by drive. Since the infant's perceptive system develops faster than his object relationships to "total objects," the infant soon begins to look, smile, and coo at the father and so reactivates his "motherliness." The father, soothing, comforting the child, playing with him, receives pleasure from the child. Besides the primary, libidinal gratification, he also experiences a secondary narcissistic gratification in the reassurance of his ego ideal that he is a good father.

It is characteristic of the spiral of human development that the representations of the primary object relationship with the mother are in continual transaction with the representations of all later object relationships according to the age and maturity of the child and the significance of the particular object. The first and most important among the secondary object relationships is, of course, the father. In societies where the organization of the family is based on the biological unit, father-mother-child, the interaction between father and child occurs through the processes of introjection and identification, as between mother and child. The father, like the mother, repeats with each child, in a different way, the steps of his own development, and under fortunate circumstances achieves further resolution of his conflicts. The primary source of development through fatherhood is the same as for development through motherhood. It holds true for both sexes that "when higher integration requires a fresh supply of psychic energy, it is produced through the intensification of the receptive-retentive tendencies which were involved in the primary organization of the psychic structure" (3, p. 419).

Whatever the meaning of such "regression" for the father's psychology, the secondary object relationships of infancy with father and also with other persons hold great importance for the development of the child. They diminish the exclusive object interest in the mother and wean the child away from symbiosis. Through the distribution of the gratifications of dependent needs, object relationships are formed which channelize the cathexis of the primary object relationship and its unconscious drive representations.

II

The tendency to internalize outer reality is hereditary, as is the central organization which in man permits a manifold working over of the interacting psychic patterns from their incipient drive-object-self-representations to their integration within the ego organization and the personality. The sequence of these processes is conceptualized around one individual, the child. In this presentation, however, which concentrates upon the parent-and-child interaction, it must be emphasized that internalization and subsequent identification requires more than a parent-child relationship. Originating in the biological pattern—need-satiation—the transactional processes between parent and child show individual variations from their beginning. The self-action pattern of the child motivates his readiness to respond, the choice of response, and its affective meaning; this in turn brings about the integration of responses into patterns which become characteristic for the individual. The parents, on the other hand, meet the child's needs as adult individuals. Their personalities, acting relatively spontaneously, motivate their emotional attitudes and behavior toward the child; they determine the parents' particular interpretations of the child's behavior and their responses to it. This in turn will influence the intrapsychic processes of introjections and identifications in all three of the participants and set the tone of mutual anticipations in the continuum of the transactional processes.

With the loosening of the symbiotic relationship, the ego boundaries of the child evolve and expand. It should be recalled that the
newborn seems to behave as if he had two sources of gratification, one
in reality outside his body and the other from within his body. In the
sucking behavior of the infant one may recognize the precursor of
mastery and antecedents of the impulses which, combined with confidence and/or the ambivalent core, become integrated to enable the
child to evaluate his ability to achieve self-set aims by his own effort.

Spitz (20) describes how the self-action pattern of the *yes* and of
no evolves from its neuromuscular anlage to its semantic expression.
From the viewpoint of the parent, the *yes* of the infant represents a
manifestation of a satisfactory projection of the self-image; it keeps the
child included in the parents' self-system, enhancing love, hope, and
expectations for the future of the child and through this for oneself. The
response is different to the child's consistent *no* or intensively negativistic behavior. The parent's response then depends upon the genuineness of his parental feelings and also upon the role of the original
object whom the child represents. The negativistic behavior of the child
separates him from the self-system of the parent, and this forces the
parent "to see" what he or she does not like within himself or in significant objects of his present or past. If it activates a regressive pattern,
the opposed parent feels compelled to oppose the child. Under the impact of frustration by the child, the parent's ego boundaries weaken so
that the angry parent identifies with the angry child. The healthy, adaptive response to the negativistic behavior of the child strengthens the
ego boundaries of the parent, making him conscious of his role as educator. The culturally assigned role of the parent derives its motivation,
however, not only from its conscious goal, but also from repressed and
remembered significant incidents and conflicts of his developmental experiences. These then motivate the reciprocal interaction between parent
and child.

Jacobson (15) studied the parent-child interaction from the point
of view of the ego organization of the child within each phase of development. She states, "Parental demands and prohibitions can probably become internalized only by joining forces with the child's own
narcissistic, ambitious striving to which they give new direction." But
what determines the parent's ability to wait until the child has matured
sufficiently to join forces with the parent's goals? And what determines
the parent's anxious pressures on the child, watching and urging him to
grow and develop according to expectations?

Pediatricians observe mothers with whom "demand feeding" does
not work because of their eagerness to feed. Pediatricians as well as
psychiatrists know about the anxious ambition with which some parents
concentrate upon the toilet training of the child, and about the permissiveness of others which delays the child's development. Even more

conspicuous are the symptoms which originate in the alternations of both of these extreme attitudes. Recently, the interaction between parent and child has been studied, although primarily with the aim of explaining the pathology of the child.

Adelaide M. Johnson (16) in several publications calls attention to the fact that the child's ego seems to be weakest in those areas which correspond to unresolved conflicts of the mother, father, or significant parent surrogate. This means that the transactional relation between parent and child evolves relatively smoothly until the child reaches the developmental level at which the parent, because of his own developmental conflict, is unable to respond to the child according to the accepted cultural standard and therefore becomes insecure with the child. The child feels the parent's insecurity and interprets it as weakness. This diminishes the child's sense of protectedness, which in turn increases his anxiety. The anxiety motivates the child's regression which serves as a defense against emotional isolation by increasing the demand for the parent's protection. Thus a regressive interaction develops. The child in adapting to the parent's conflictful behavior either does not learn new controls or may give up those which were already established. In order to avoid emotional isolation from the parent, the child introjects the conflict of the parent which threatens his security. In his "regressive adaptation" to the parent's conflictful behavior, the child incorporates a "fixation," thus making certain that he will not become a better person than his parent is.

Johnson's investigations concerning "acting-out" behavior were conducted by "collaborative therapy," i.e., by parallel investigations of the child and the significant parent. Her case material illustrates that the incorporation of the parent's conflicts into the psychic structure of the child occurs beyond the oral phase of development, during the anal, phallic, and oedipal phases. Johnson's investigations seem to offer clinical evidence for Jacobson's metapsychological study of the development of the self-concept through internalization of the object world. Both investigators, however, deal only with the world of the child in which the parent has a central role.

Is there any psychoanalytic evidence which would support the thesis that the child, being the object of the parent's drive, has, psychologically speaking, a similar function in the psychic structure of the parent? Does the child, evoking and maintaining reciprocal intrapsychic processes in the parent, become instrumental in further developmental integration or its failure in the parent? Answers to these questions can be more easily elicited from pathologic than from normal situations. In individual instances when conflicts with children cause undue stress for a parent, or for both parents, we understand its pathogenic significance. Whether it be disappointment in the child's development, anxiety for his well-being, whether it be fear of separation and of illness or real mourning, we understand its meaning by empathy and interpret it in the frame of the developmental history and personality structure of the parent. If we interpret the parent's present plight only in terms of his individual past, we fail to take into account the infinite minute happenings, affective communications which, by keeping the spiral of reciprocal interactions going, actually lead to pathology.

Yet Johnson's investigations reveal that each child in a different way and in a different measure stirs up through his own phasic development the corresponding unconscious developmental conflict of the parent. The parent meets in each child in a particular way the projections of his own conflicts. It is possible that what is more desirable happens more often. Since it does not cause pathology, it does not come to our attention. Parents meet in their children not only the projections of their own conflicts incorporated in the child, but also the promise of their hopes and ambitions. The parent, each in his own way, has to deal with the positive as well as the negative revelations of the self in the child. It is the individually varying degree of confidence in oneself = child and the individually different level of maturity which help the parent not to overemphasize the positive and not to be overwhelmed by the negative aspects of the self as it is exposed through the child. In any case, the parent cannot help but deal with his own conflict unconsciously, while consciously he tries to help the child achieve his developmental goal.

III

Based upon the reciprocal interaction between parent and child during the oral phase, we may generalize that the spiral of transaction between parent and child can be interpreted in each phase on two levels of motivation and in terms of each of the participants. One is determined by the past which motivates current behavior, and the other is the current experience in which the motivational patterns of each of the participants meet. The resulting current experience is introjected and stored as object and self-representations along with the emotional quality which accompanied the drive experience. This introduces a third aspect into the motivational pattern, namely, the anticipation of the emotional course of future experiences. This has paramount influence upon the course of parent-child interactions.

The significance of the child's anticipation of the parent's reaction to his behavior is well known. The child's confident expectation of gratification, his fear of frustration and punishment modifies his sense of security with his parents. Through the day-by-day repetitions of minute

happenings between parents and child, the child learns to trust his anticipation. This, more than massive anxiety, accounts for the autoplastic
and alloplastic adaptive patterns in the ego of the child.

It is expected that it would be different with the parents. The behavior patterns of the parent toward the child are motivated by his long
individual history, through which his identity has been established. It is
generally assumed that his ego organization is such that he is not subject
to changes in his self-representations through drive-determined object
relationship with his child. Indeed, the self-assurance of the parent in
his mature motivations toward his child justifies his authority. His
authority functions, however, not only to protect the child, but also to
insure him against being affected by the child's behavior. It helps the
parent to repress and/or deny his anticipations, fears, and his unconscious feelings toward the child. Thus Freud mentions only the fond
parents' narcissistic expectations projected onto the child. Today it is
difficult to imagine the emotional security of the Victorian parent toward his child, so aware are we of current parents' anxieties. Psychoanalysis often demonstrates that parents become aware of their own
unconscious motivations toward their children by anticipating the
child's behavior and its unconscious motivations. Parents, anticipating
negativistic attitudes in their children, feel insecure, afraid, and angry
even before the child acts, sometimes even more if the child does not
act according to negative anticipation. The prevalence of introjection
in the communication between parent and child invites comparison with
paranoid processes. It seems that parents and children, like paranoids,
achieve what they anticipate with anxiety, and intend to avoid.

Psychoanalysis takes into account the individual variations in the
behavior of the parent toward the child but considers them as exceptions
and the ideal parent the rule. And rightly so. Idealization of the parent
is not just a culturally determined residue of the Victorian era. It originates in the instinct of self-preservation and evolves through reciprocal
communications between parent and child.

Here we shall consider imitation as a manifestation of the reciprocal psychic processes. Imitation is usually investigated only as it concerns the intrapsychic processes of the child. Jacobson states: ". . .
imitation of parental emotional expression influences the child's own
discharge patterns . . . to induce identical affective phenomena" (15,
p. 100). Yet observation of the smiling response makes us ask, who
imitates whom? Weeks before the smiling response develops, the fleeting "stomach smile" of the neonate makes the mother anticipate the
pleasure of her smiling baby, and she cannot help but smile. Since the
affective communications between parent and infant are reciprocal, we
can hope that closer observations, by cinematographic studies, will
allow for a more precise analysis of the interaction and better understanding of the processes which lead to overt imitation by the child.

For this may be secondary, a reaction to the parent's unconscious identification with the child and anticipation of his responses.

As a means of communication, imitation enters into the spiral of emotional transactions and influences the parent-child relationship. The imitating child holds up a mirror image to the parent. Naive and completely intuitive as the child's gestures are, they are also unmistakably true. Thus the parent responding to the mirror image may recognize and even say to the child, "This is your father; this is me in you," or someone else whom the child probably never saw. In this way innate patterns may be enacted in which the parent recognizes himself or persons significant in his or her own past and present. If the child's imitative behavior expresses positive aspects of the parent and positive attitudes between them, it shows that both parent and child are lovable. Thus imitation brings to the fore and by repetition enforces the positive arc of the emotional symbiosis. It can also happen that the parent is shocked by the child's imitative behavior when the child reenacts representations of negative experiences, sometimes with threatening hostility. Imitation of the parent by the child then stimulates, and by repetition may reinforce the negative arc of the emotional symbiosis. It depends upon the maturity of the parent and the genuineness of his love for the child whether such a warning is heeded or whether it leads to rejection of the unloved self = unloved child.

This indicates that imitation is a means of interpersonal communication by externalizing what has been already internalized. Developmentally, imitation is considered the antecedent of true ego identification. Yet it occurs at any age and level of maturity. It is true for animals and man alike that if the ego feels helpless in mastering overwhelming emotions, it reverts to this infantile expression of identification with the aggressor. There are gestures, mimical expressions (5) "designed" to disarm the aggressors, others to threaten them. We can assume that in the imitative behavior of the child a tendency to master one's own emotions and at the same time influence the environment is expressed. Playful as well as hostile imitations represent manifestations of the repetition compulsion, the tendency through which traumatic memories are overcome.

Since the parents', especially the mother's, relationship to the infant is often highly charged with emotions, imitation of the child is used by the parents, often deliberately, and usually unconsciously, as a means of mastering the affects, be they love and admiration for the child's activities, or anger and even despondency because of them. We assume that while parents thus deliberately manipulate the behavior of the child and their current relationship with him, unconsciously they also modify their own intrapsychic processes. The representations of the transacting experience become introjected and influence their anticipations in regard to future events.

The child's playful imitation of the parents' activities constitutes an affective means of learning, coordination, and function. The self-action pattern of the child leans on the parent and uses imitation as the vehicle. This is especially conspicuous in the two- or three-year-old, in the *preoedipal child*. Children of both sexes, beginning to struggle with bowel control, having mastered locomotion, learn to use the parents' tools. Little boys and girls alike learn to sweep, to dust, and to dry dishes with the exact gestures of their mother. A little later, when the girl turns to dolls and the boy to the lawn mower and hammer, the parents delight in the skillfulness of the child and find gratification in such impersonations. For the child, imitation functions in the same way as fantasy; it forecasts (for the child) what he will be able to do, to be sometime in the future. In imitating the parent, the child charges his own actions with the wonderment and admiration which he feels for adults. The gratification from his own actions becomes exaggerated by this.

The secondary narcissistic gratification so achieved is a derivative of the primary narcissism of the child originating in his "action lust," enhanced as it was at an earlier developmental age by the loving acceptance of the parents. Now the child knows that they can do it better than he. This increases the child's self-assurance on one hand and on the other his confidence that the parents are able and willing to protect him, whatever his next step may be. Thus a reciprocal interchange of narcissistic gratifications brings about the child's magic participation in the "magic omnipotence" of the parent.

This constellation of positive communications between parent and child suggests the elaboration of confidence on the developmental level of the preoedipal child. During the oral phase of development the confidence that needs will be satisfied provides intrapsychic protection against fear of frustration. With the loosening of the symbiotic relationship the self-action patterns direct the child's striving toward mastery. Paralleling the growing independence of the child, a more complex introject-identification with the omnipotent parents is needed to afford intrapsychic protection and to maintain the parent-child unity on the psychological level, while it is being severed step by step in reality. While the secondary narcissistic elaboration of confidence is the source of the omnipotent fantasies of the child, it is also the antecedent of the child's idealization of the parents. Thus it prepares for the next level, the oedipal phase of development.

What is the corresponding psychodynamic process in the parent? Since the omnipotent fantasies of the child and the corresponding idealization of the parent represent the positive arc of the transactional pattern, it facilitates the parent's identification with the child for two reasons. One is that the child's fantasies reactivate in the parent the omnipotent fantasies of his own childhood; the other is that the parent, identifying with the current fantasies of the child, accepts the role of omnipotence attributed to him. The normal parent, in spite of his insight into his realistic limitations, embraces the gratifying role of omnipotence. It induces him to identify with his own parent now in reality as he anticipated being able to do in his childhood fantasies. Whatever the real course of events has been between himself and his parents, as long as the fantasies of his child do not become hostile against him, the parent derives from the process of preoedipal identifications the reassurance that he is a good parent and, even more, the hope that he is or can be better than his own parent was.

Under normal circumstances, i.e., if the process of preoedipal identifications is not disrupted too often and by too intense ambivalent interplay, the reciprocal interaction of omnipotent fantasies makes the task of the parent educator easy. This is the process by which the value system of the parent becomes integrated into the precursors of the superego in the child. This becomes very difficult, however, if the parents anticipate that the child's independent activities will expose their mistakes, inferiority, and thus diminish their self-esteem. The spiral of negative transactions can be activated at any time. This hazard increases with the growing self-differentiation of the child. This multiplies the factors which may activate the parent's ambivalent response and interfere with the further course of development.

IV

In this presentation the reciprocal interaction between parent and child has been discussed without differentiating the sex of either the parent or the child. The significance of the child's identification with the parent of his own sex and the role of the parent of the opposite sex in the oedipal phase of development has been established in general. In particular, considering the actual motivations of parent-child interactions, it seems easiest to paraphrase Freud: "Where there are two people interacting, one can always see four" (7). Any current interaction between parent and child is motivated by the parent's past relationship with both of his own parents. When a child reaches his preoedipal phase, his identifications with the parent of his own sex are determined not only by the past history of that relationship but also by the incorporated history of his interactions with the parent of the other sex. (Since the parents' interactions with each other, and especially with their children, are motivated by the total developmental past of each, the simplest family triad, early in the anal phase of development and definitely in the preoedipal phase, is influenced by twelve sources of interacting motivations.)

Since Freud discovered the significance of infantile sexuality, it

is taken for granted that the oedipal phase is a spontaneous manifestation of the innate pattern of the sexual drive. The parents' participation
in its evolution is considered only in exceptional, pathological instances.
The study of the patterns of reciprocal interactions between parent and
child and the resulting shifts in the object and self-representations indicates the role of the ego organization in the development of the oedipal
conflict.

The recent literature on the significance of the oedipus complex
in psychopathology and in normal character structure reveals more and
more convincingly that the processes which were customarily related
to the vicissitudes of the oedipus complex are motivated by experiences
arising in earlier phases of development. It seems that the oedipus complex ". . . has apical importance not so much as the nucleus of the
neuroses but as the nucleus of normal character structure" (Gitelson,
13, p. 354). In this presentation, it is assumed that the oedipus complex evolves as the consequence of the positive balance of the transactional processes between parents and child which, in spite of transient
fluctuations, lead the child from one critical period to the other successfully. In contrast, if the negative emotional balance maintains an
ambivalent course of transactions, this results in failure of the development and of the dissolution of the oedipus complex. This thesis is
significant enough to warrant surveying again the reciprocal patterns of
identifications between parent and child.

As stated, the child's identifications with the parent evolve step by
step in accordance with the drive requirements which the parent satisfies in various phases of the child's development. Accordingly, the parent is at the beginning a "partial object" completely cathected with the
child's drive requirement and introjected by the child with his drive
experience. Corresponding with the growth and maturation of the
child, the parent becomes step by step a "total object" cathected not
only with primary drive requirements of the child, but as a person outside the self, with whom the child forms relationships of different order,
meaning, and value.

There is a corresponding shift in the parent's object relationship
with the child. We have discussed how the fetus and the newborn are
total objects of the mother's drive organization culminating in motherhood and motherliness. The newborn is the total object of the primary
narcissism of the mother. For the father the newborn represents survival and also the hope of self-realization; thus the infant is also a "total
object" of the father's secondary narcissism. As the child with each
progression in his maturation becomes more a person outside the parent, and at least partially independent of the parents' projections, he
becomes the object of the partial drives of the parent. If this involves
only aim-inhibited drive manifestations such as tenderness, empathy,
helpfulness, etc., the emotional interaction is positive and satisfactory

for each participant. If, however, the parent becomes aware of sexual impulses toward the child, his guilt may cause negative transactions even if not acted out. Even more disturbing is the effect when the parent succeeds in denying the nature of his impulses.

Normally the child's idealization of the parent feeds the parent with gratification. The parent cannot help but respond to the child's pregenital strivings with increased object love for the child. There is no need to elaborate upon the father's response to the admiration of his son, or to the flirtation of his four-year-old daughter. Just as obvious is the mother's satisfaction in her daughter's expression of the wish to become like her and/or in the promise of her four-year-old son to marry her because she is the best or most beautiful mother. Innocent as parents and children are in these expressions of their satisfaction with each other, these are the antecedents of the crucial developmental period, the oedipal phase. Since the hormonal and physiologic equipment of the child does not permit the realization of oedipal strivings, the question arises: what accounts for the intensity and significance of the castration fear, the punishment for a sin which cannot be committed?

Not the child but the parent is in possession of the mental and physiological equipment which stimulates sexual impulses and the fear of its consequences. In our culture, the ego ideal and the superego of the parent require complete repression of the parent's incestuous wishes toward the child. It happens more often than our case histories or conceptualizations account for that the analyses of individuals with high superego standards reveal various forms of neurosis resulting from a disturbance of the interaction between parent and child, beginning, for example, when a father becomes aware of a sexual response to his daughter, or when a mother is shocked by her fascination with her son's penis. The emphasis here is on the normal processes. We assume that the gratifying preoedipal relationship between parent and child enhances the object love and stimulates the sexual drive of the parent, the object of which is the child. Normally, i.e., under circumstances which account for successful neutralization of the drive energies involved in the oedipus complex of the parent, his well-integrated superego inhibits sexual impulses directed toward the child before they ever reach consciousness. Yet that does not mean that the child cannot be affected by the aim-inhibited emotions of the parent.

In discussing the oedipal phase, we take, as is customary, the father and son as an example. Why does the father consider him a rival? The father's attitude in this critical period as well as before and after is motivated by his developmental history and by the current interactions with his son. Yet the current interactions with his son are influenced by his own development. The intensity of the castration fear when he was a child, the resulting strictness of his superego are responsible for his severity toward his own impulses and also toward his son.

This brings us back to the question: what makes the fear of punishment so effective for a sin which cannot be committed? The answer to this question can be approached from many aspects. Freud in *Totem and Taboo* (8) traces the answer to the mystical origin of civilization. Today, however, we have sufficient clinical evidence to support the assumption that the aging father by necessity considers the grown son a rival, and therefore begrudges and fears the virility he bequeathes to him. But why should a four- or five-year-old raised in our culture of relatively little violence between parent and child consider himself a feared and therefore threatened rival?[6] The communication between parent and child facilitates the identification between parent and child on the level of fantasied omnipotence. When the father is called upon to restrict his impulses toward his daughter for one reason and toward his son for another, the father's superego conveys to the child the overwhelmingly dangerous significance of the impulses which arise in him. Thus the castration fear of the child corresponds with the incorporated castration fear of the parent, to the strictness of the superego.

Rangell (19, p. 13) states: "The oedipus complex has a continuous and dynamic line of development from its earliest origin through the various phases in the life of man." He describes the exacerbations of the oedipus complex in the parents as responses to the puberty or to the marriage of the younger generation, and also the returning of the repressed when the parent's powers of repression and ego integration decline, as occurs in illness and old age. Whether in classical literature or in case histories, we do not consider these tragic incidents as simple repetitions of the past, using the current love object as a substitute for the original. The adolescent or adult married daughter substituting for the father's own mother, or the son substituting for the mother's father, does not suddenly revive the infantile oedipal complex with pathologic vehemence. A complex intrapsychic structure, which has been built up in the parent through the processes of his participation in the development of his children, undergoes a period of deterioration before it breaks down. The crash serves as evidence that the structure existed.

Here, however, we are dealing with normal processes of development which bring about the oedipal phase in the child and activate a reciprocal developmental pattern in the parent. Our concept emphasizes the "continuous and dynamic line of development" of the oedipus complex: (1) The oedipus complex originates in the dynamics of re-

6. In individual instances this might be independent of immediate cultural influence. Our present culture, however, shows ample evidence of the declining authority of the father which, by diminishing the intensity of the conflict, offers a weaker impetus for the organization of the superego. Consequently, the oedipal impulses and the fear connected with them undergo other vicissitudes in the psychic organization of sons.

ciprocal transactions between parent and child beginning with individual existence. (2) When the child reaches the oedipal phase the parent has participated in its evolution, just as he will be instrumental in its repression and resolution. (3) Since the child is the object of the parent's libido, he activates in the parent a new process of repression and neutralization of the energies participating in the conflict. (4) The conflict in the father, as in the son, is between the id impulse and the intrapsychic repressing forces. In the parent this is integrated in his superego; in the child, only the precursors of the superego and fear of punishment press toward repression. (5) After repression the introjected drive being neutralized permits the object and self-representations to be integrated into the superego system. It is a new level of development for the child. In the parent the dynamic processes of parenthood use the already established organizations of the psychic system. But a new phase in the parent's superego evolves. This encompasses the object representations of the child and self-representations originating in the mature experiences of parenthood. The conflicts which were incorporated in the superego when the parent was a child are "worked over" through the experiences of parenthood; this accounts for a new phase of maturation in the parent. Through the successful relationship of the parent with his child or children, his superego loses some of its strictness; and as it allows for a broader, deeper capacity of experience, it indicates a new step toward the dissolution of its infantile origin. The opposite may also be true. Unsuccessful experience of the parent with unsuccessful children undermines the parent's self-esteem and enhances the strictness of his superego and thus renders it pathogenic for the parent as well as for the child. Incorporated into the psychic system of the parent, the child may mitigate or intensify the strictness of the parent's superego.

Here I recall the Austrian poet Anton Wildgans (21) who in a poem musing about his newborn son says: "Our judge you may become—you are he already." The poet expresses in a few words what modern parents, deprived of the security of parents of less individualistic, more authoritarian cultures, so often feel with more or less anxiety. The child at birth is an enigma. He represents hope and promise for self-realization and at the same time he forewarns that he may expose not one's virtues but one's faults. This threat to the self-esteem of the insecure parent activates the strictness of his superego and intensifies, sometimes to a pathologic degree, his efforts to avert errors, to avoid faults.

Thus parental behavior is directed by the established superego. This directs the psychodynamic processes of the reciprocal communication between parent and child. The intrapsychic processes which result from the interpersonal relationships through the course of the child's development establish the object representations of the child as a part of the psychic structure of the parent. *Considering the transactional process of the oedipal phase and its resolution in the child and in the parent, we venture to say that the object representations of the child become a part of the parent's superego.*

Thus we assume two levels of superego in the parents of growing children, one which is incorporated in the parent's personality through his development from infancy to parenthood. This directs his behavior toward the fulfillment of his ego aspirations, particularly to be a good parent, and by being a good parent to raise a child who by growing up to his own self-realization also fulfills the parent's aspirations. In the process of striving toward this goal, through the continual alternations between success and threatening failures of parenthood, the parent's personality undergoes changes which under normal circumstances seem to justify our assumption that *parenthood activates and maintains a developmental phase.*

BIBLIOGRAPHY

1. Balint, A. Love for the mother and mother-love. *Int. J. Psychoanal.,* 30:251–259, 1949.
2. Benedek, T. The psychosomatic implications of the primary unit: mother-child. *Am. J. Orthopsychiat.,* 19:642–654, 1949. (Republished as Chapter 12, in Benedek, T., *Psychosexual Functions in Women.* New York: Ronald Press, 1952.)
3. Benedek, T. Toward the biology of the depressive constellation. *J. Am. Psychoanalytic Assn.,* 4:389–427, 1956.
4. Benedek, T. The organization of the reproductive drive. Revision of a paper of the same title originally presented at the Twenty-Fifth Anniversary Meeting, Institute for Psychoanalysis, Chicago, November 16, 1957. *Int. J. Psychoanal.* 41:1–15, 1960.
5. Darwin, C. *The Expression of the Emotions in Man and Animals.* London: J. Murray, 1872.
6. Erikson, E. H. The problem of ego identity. *J. Am. Psychoanalytic Assn.,* 4:56–121, 1956.
7. Freud, S. *The Origins of Psychoanalysis; Letters to Wilhelm Fliess, 1887–1902,* ed. Marie Bonaparte, Anna Freud, Ernst Kris. New York: Basic Books, 1954.
8. Freud, S. Totem and taboo (1913). *Standard Edition, 13*:1–161. London: Hogarth Press, 1955.
9. Freud, S. On narcissism: an introduction (1914). *Standard Edition, 14*:73–102. London: Hogarth Press, 1957.
10. Freud, S. Mourning and melancholia (1917). *Standard Edition.* London: Hogarth Press, 1957.
11. Freud, S. *The Ego and the Id* (1923). London: Hogarth Press, 1927, p. 37.
12. Freud, S., *An Outline of Psychoanalysis* (1938). New York: Norton, 1949, p. 23.

13. Gitelson, M. Re-evaluation of the role of the oedipus complex. *Int. J. Psychoanal., 33*:351–354, 1952.

14. Grinker, R. R. On identification. *Int. J. Psychoanal., 38*:379–390, 1957.

15. Jacobson, E. The self and the object world. *The Psychoanalytic Study of the Child, 9*:75–127. New York: International Universities Press, 1954.

16. Johnson, A. M. Factors in the etiology of fixations and symptom choice. *Psychoanal. Quart., 22*:475–496, 1953.

17. Klein, M. *Envy and Gratitude.* London: Tavistock, 1957.

18. Parsons, T., Bales, R. F., et al. *Family, Socialization and Interaction Process.* Chicago: Free Press, 1955.

19. Rangell, L. The role of the parent in the oedipus complex. *Bull. Menninger Clin., 19*:9–15, 1955.

20. Spitz, R. A. *No and Yes; On the Genesis of Human Communication.* New York: International Universities Press, 1957.

21. Wildgans, A. *Im Anschaun meines Kindes.* 1913.

DISCUSSION

This paper ends with a conceptualization of the influence of the child on the parental superego. This much-used term refers here to the structural changes in the psychic apparatus of the parent as a result of the continual, multi-level introjections of positive and negative interactions between parent and child. Can one speak of maturation of the superego? Certainly this could be a topic for an investigation of the psychic apparatus of the parent in transaction with the development of the child. It will suffice here to state that the superego becomes mollified, more conciliatory through the experiences of parenthood. Through parenthood, not only because of its gratifications but even more because of its anxieties and frustrations, people understand more and forgive more. In more scientific language, we may say that the mollification of the superego is expressed by the individual's increasing capacity for empathy. Further study may reveal that the expanding empathic capacity is a result of the transformation of "parental (primary) narcissism" which, through expansion beyond the family, becomes that valuable but rarely investigated attribute, wisdom.[1]

The individual development of parents is the result of many interacting factors. Beyond their natural endowments and psychogenic histories, external circumstances motivate emotional reactions to events and bring about structural changes. Even the growing child becomes "external." Parenthood means change and change requires adaptation. This entails continuous adaptation of the parent to physiologic and psychologic changes within himself, parallel to and in transaction with the child and his changing world. We can differentiate "positive" adaptation from "defensive" and "regressive" adaptations. Positive adaptations facilitate structural changes in the direction of development by diminishing conflict tensions and anxieties. Defensive adaptations aim also at maintaining psychic equilibrium, but achieve it at a cost of defenses which may produce intrapsychic stress; regressive adaptations are complicated because of pathogenic regression in the parent and consequently in the child. While the equilibrium may be maintained on the surface, this process is maladaptive; its negative influence in the spiral of transactional processes may lead to symptom formation which becomes recognizable during psychoanalysis.

To condense the psychologic course of parenthood during the life cycle,[2] it is practical to fit its critical periods in age-graded patterns designed by biology and modified by culture. Pregnancy is a critical phase in the life of woman; its spur to maturation is complicated by its inherent "regressive pull" and by anxieties connected with parturition.[3] Following the separation of parturition, each step in the child's development represents "separation" to the parent. Every parent is prepared for the separation from his child by his own developmental experience. In this perspective, the psychosexual development of the children in one generation is viewed as preparation for the separation of the parents of the next generation from their children.

The first phase of parenthood is, to use Kestenberg's term, "total parenthood."[4] During the whole period of pregenital development including the oedipal phase, the child is usually under the care and psychologic influence of the parents. When the child reaches school age there begins a transitional period which compels the parents to share their exclusive authority and accept the impact of the larger environment, i.e., school, teachers, and peer groups, on the child.

"Latency stands out as a time of *'part-time parenthood'* . . . that prepares . . . for the state of 'childless parenthood'."[5] Going to school is the obvious separation; this is the psychologic separation of the child, who is becoming an individual, often at the cost of internal conflicts and interpersonal struggles with his parents. Whether parents accept and respect the individuation of the child or feel threatened by it, whether their concern is justified because of the child's deviant behavior, or whether they are just disappointed because their own ambition may not be fulfilled by that child, these and many more parental reactions could be listed, both normal and neurotic. A conceptualization would remain inadequate since many variables which influence both parent and child are outside their personalities and their interactions.

Only those transactions between parent and child which are motivated by primary (psychobiologic) needs, as in infancy, can be conceptualized with relative reliability. Communication becomes more complex when it becomes verbal, when the conscious, verbally expressed aim covers up a deeper emotional meaning. We can recognize transactional processes between parent and child when the child's development reaches a level at which he reactivates in the parent conflicts originating in the same developmental phase of the parent. In time, however, these processes become more and more distant from the primary physiologic and emotional processes of parenthood. In the latency period and during adolescence, parents have to learn to respond to the evolving complex personality organization of the maturing individual. The parents' response, whether it is intuitive, or dictated by common sense, or an expression of elaborate educational principles, is the result of many-faceted intrapsychic experiences. With young children, the parent's developmental past is hidden in unconscious processes and is "acted out" toward the child; with latency children and adolescents, parents remember their own behavior and the response of their parents. Emotional responses of conscientious parents to the problems of their older children are often motivated by reaction formation to the actual and psychologic consequences of their own experience. This is more obvious in the observations of psychoanalysts than in the awareness of parents. As concerned as mothers may be about the sexual dangers to which their daughters are exposed, or as worried as fathers may be about the emotional and economic security of their children, they rarely realize that the anxiety is motivated not only by the chronological age of their children but also by their own. Indeed, adolescence is that period during which the thrust of the child's development activates in the parent, beyond memories of his adolescence, the repressed conflicts of the oedipal phase.[6]

Age-graded patterns of parental behavior are motivated by culture. Biologic parenthood, however, does not observe classifications by cultural patterns. In families with several children, when the older ones are in adolescence, there may still be a baby in the home. A parent may be in the early phase of parenthood with one child and in the "middle phase" with another. Nevertheless, parents are "total parents" with each of their children in turn. Parents cling to the incorporated image of their children as separate individuals. They may compare their children and even admit to their own differing feelings for them, but they do not confuse their mental image. It sounds paradoxical, but it appears to be true that parents incorporate into their self-system each of their children, thus identifying with them, but they are usually unaware of their children's identification with each other. Probably this is a means of holding the mental images apart so that the children remain distinct entities. Although continually changing with time, the psychic image of the child remains consistent unless the parent's mental health fails.[7]

The middle phase of parenthood is introduced by the sexual maturity of the child. In the grand design of evolutionary biology, it may coincide with the middle age of the parent, with the climacterium and the decline of the parent's procreative capacity, but not in the actuality of human sexual behavior. Parents of adult children continue their active sexual life, sometimes well into the adolescence of their grandchildren. Nonetheless, the main characteristic of the middle phase of parenthood is the parents' involvement in and preoccupation with the sexual life of their children. One could describe the difference between normal and neurotic behavior of parents in reaction to their children's adolescence by classifying them according to the outcome of their oedipal phase. Parents may rationalize their attitude by the actual behavior of the adolescent, but investigation reveals that repressed developmental conflicts motivate their response to the sexual personality of the grown child.[8]

Every parent in his (or her) narcissistic identification with the children of either sex wants the adolescents and the young marriageable persons to be attractive, happy, and successful. It depends on the parents' "fixation" to the child, maintained under various guises from infancy on, how much their conscious and unconscious motivations will help or hinder the "liberation" of their children. Parents are worried if their daughter is not attractive or, for some reason, not "popular" enough, but they are even more concerned if the daughter is too much attracted to the opposite sex and may be therefore endangered. From the parents' viewpoint, marriage means security for the daughter and relief from their responsibility. In their attitude toward their sons, we recognize traces of the "double standard" which seems to be slowly disappearing in other areas of our culture. Parents generally assume that the "choice" is a male prerogative. The son's emotional and economic security does not depend upon marriage in the same sense and to the same degree as it once did for the daughter. Yet in recent years one frequently observes growing concern in the parents if a son has not married before he reaches the age of thirty. They seem to be concerned about the son's sexual personality. Fathers and mothers want their children to become parents and be happy and fulfilled in their parenthood.

One could write a book—many novels have been written—about the emotional richness and the exhausting complications of the middle age of parenthood. It certainly defies abstractions. We repeat the basic conflict of parenthood: the biologic need to survive in the children's children which is integrated with the instinctual wish to preserve oneself. The marriage of children during the middle phase of parenthood promises the fulfillment of both these needs and unless undesirable circumstances arise, promises to do so without conflict. Probably this implied double promise is the reason that for parents as well as for their children, the marriage vow means the promise to live happily ever after, no matter what actual experiences had taught otherwise.

For parents, the marriage of any one of their children means separation. They cease to be closest of kin by law since the new husband and wife, even if they have known each other for only a few weeks or months, have become the next of kin. This is necessarily so. The law must protect potential parenthood. This fact is so ingrained in our culture that parents rarely experience the child's marriage as separation unless it occurs during war and the son is in the armed services. As the young couple have to adapt to the separation from their parents and must learn to adjust to the new family, so the parents have a double adaptive task. It is not only the separation from their child that may create conflicts, but also the sense of responsibility that remains with the parent, namely, to help their child adjust to marriage and become a member of a new family.

Mothers more often than fathers fail in these tasks. Since mothers are usually more involved with that phase of their married child's life than fathers are, the separation often activates their unconscious identifications. They wish to be involved in every detail of their married children's life. Intrafamilial conflicts which may arise on this basis cannot be elaborated here. They may be conceptualized in terms of the parents' ability to adapt themselves to the separation which the marriage of son or daughter implies. Parents have to objectify their parental relationship to the marriage. This requires insight into their own ambivalence, and understanding of what it means to the young people who, insecure in the new relationship, need the reassurance which only genuine love can give. For parents to solve tactfully their problems with the new married couple is often not easy, but it is a necessary task since any conflict that arises in the parent-child relationship of a young married couple ripples like waves beyond the persons involved and may affect the not yet born grandchildren.

Before the "childless parenthood" of old age arrives, there come the gratifying experiences of grandparenthood.[9] Very little has been written about the psychology of grandparenthood, probably nothing at all by psychoanalysts. The emotional significance of grandparenthood is taken for granted. It is a universal experience, and is often referred to as a "new lease on life" by grandparents themselves and by the new parents, proud of their ability to bestow this status on their parents. Grandparenthood, however, is not bound by chronological age. There are young grandparents, still in the middle phase of their own parenthood, and it is not an unheard of occurrence that a grandmother nurses her grandchild and her own baby at the same time. We have reason to assume that grandparenthood is a different emotional experience for those who become grandparents while in the strength of their own procreative capacity than for those whose first grandchild is born years after they have reached climacterium. Having their own children to care for, young grandparents often do not need a new lease on life, but to older grandparents the grandchild means the reassurance of their survival.

Grandparenthood is a more complex experience for women than for men. The woman whose daughter or daughter-in-law is pregnant identifies with that pregnancy and in many respects relives her own pregnancies with it. The prospective grandmother remembers not only her pregnancies but she recalls also what her own mother told her about childbearing. It is not unusual that the "expectant" grandmother, in her wish to protect her daughter, conveys her anxieties to the pregnant woman. In this anxious overidentification, we see the aging woman's wish to live her daughter's life. Such an attitude often interferes with the actual bliss of grandparenthood.

Grandparenthood is a new lease on life because grandparents—grandmothers more intensely than grandfathers—relive the memories of the early phases of their parenthood in observing the growth and development of their grandchildren. Grandparenthood, however, is parenthood one step removed. Relieved from the actual stresses of motherhood and the responsibilities of fatherhood, grandparents appear to enjoy their grandchildren more than they enjoyed their own children. Since they do not have the responsibility of rearing the child, the love of grandparents is not so burdened by doubts and anxieties as the love of the young parents.

The indulgence of grandparents is proverbial. This does not mean candy and toys, not even the time spent in playing. The genuine love of the grandparents, especially if it is not burdened by interfamilial conflicts, gives the child a sense of security in being loved without always deserving it. While the undemanding love of the grandparents feeds the child's infantile omnipotent fantasies, what does the grandparent receive in return? A loving glance from a happy child, a trusting hand, or an actual appeal for help; whatever it is, it is a message to the grandparent that he or she is needed, wanted, and loved; the grandparents then feel like good parents, accepted gratefully by the child.

Grandchildren, however, grow up and grow away from doting grandparents. As they reach adolescence grandparents are most likely the only "objects" of their "postambivalent" object relationship.[10] The ambivalence of adolescence, the rebellion of youth, is directed toward the parents, who are the objects of their conflicting instinctual drives. Since the relationship with the grandparents was never so highly charged with the energy of conflicting drives, the grandparents become the recipients of the considerate, indulgent behavior of these maturing individuals, who in the fullness of their youth see the weakness in the grandparents even earlier than is justified. But grandparents respond to the manifestations of such protectiveness as balm for whatever wounds old age inflicts upon them.

Old age, if not hastened by illness, arrives slowly and brings with it the adaptational tasks of aging itself. Considering this complex process from the point of view of the elderly parents' relationship with their (by now) middle-aged children, we can only make a vague reference to a state of "nonparenthood" with "nonchildren." It would require a general discussion of the influence of involutionary processes on the elderly parent's self-concept; it would require clinical examples to demonstrate that the old person's self-concept changes in many other areas, but not in the meaning (and status) of his parenthood. The elderly individual can withdraw from many aspects of his mature self, may consider this or that attribute of his personality and achievement as gone, but not parenthood. The cycle completes its course. As once the parent was the need-fulfilling object of the child, now the "adult child" is the need-fulfilling object of the aged parent. Yet the central need of the elderly parent cannot be fulfilled. Clinging to his self-image as a parent, he wants his children to help him (or her) forget he is not what he has been.

A discussion of parenthood as an ongoing process includes not only development but also involution. Its relevance to the process which begins with pregnancy lies in the psychological fact that being a parent remains in the center of a normal parent's self-concept. In old age, removed from his procreative period by two generations, he clings to his adult children and seeks in them the psychic image of what they once were and therefore will always remain, his children. Thus, in the sense of intrapsychic processes, parenthood ends when memory is lost and intrapsychic images fade out.

NOTES

1. Kohut, H., "Forms and Transformations of Narcissism," *J. Am. Psychoanalytic Assn.,* XIV (1966), 243–273.

2. Benedek, T., "Parenthood During the Life Cycle," in *Parenthood, Its Psychology and Psychopathology,* ed. E. J. Anthony and T. Benedek (Boston, Little, Brown & Co., 1970), pp. 185–206.

3. Benedek, T., "The Psychobiology of Pregnancy," in *Parenthood, Its Psychology and Psychopathology,* pp. 137–151.

4. Kestenberg, J. S., "The Effect on Parents of the Child's Transition into and out of Latency," in *Parenthood, Its Psychology and Psychopathology,* pp. 289–306.

5. Ibid., p. 305.

6. Rangell, L., "The Return of the Repressed 'Oedipus,'" in *Parenthood, Its Psychology and Psychopathology,* pp. 325–334.

7. Ibid., p. 334.

8. Anthony, E. J., "The Reactions of Parents to Adolescents and to Their Behavior," in *Parenthood, Its Psychology and Psychopathology,* pp. 307–324.

9. Benedek, T., "Parenthood During the Life Cycle," in *Parenthood, Its Psychology and Psychopathology,* pp. 185–206.

10. Abraham, K., "A Short Study of the Development of the Libido, Viewed in the Light of Mental Disorders" (1924), in his *Selected Papers* (London, Hogarth Press, 1927), pp. 418–501.

15. On the Organization of the Reproductive Drive

INTRODUCTION

This title promises to encompass a much larger field of biology and psychology than was available to me at the time I wrote the paper for the twenty-fifth anniversary of the Chicago Institute for Psychoanalysis, my professional home. At that time, fifteen years after the publication of the monograph on the sexual cycle of women,[1] I was concerned about the lack of reaction from psychoanalysts to the method and yield of that investigation; I found it necessary, therefore, to repeat those findings and integrate them with conclusions drawn from my psychoanalytic experience.

Some readers may find the repetition of the methods and results of the cycle research superfluous and/or even boring. Yet one of the aims of the paper was to demonstrate psychoanalysis as a tool of psychobiologic research. Another, more specific aim, was to call attention to the instinctual, psychodynamic factors in the procreative aspect of sexuality, which had been neglected in psychoanalytic theory. I found that the research on the sexual cycle not only afforded clues to the ontogenic evolution of women's procreative drive, but also that it enabled us to conceive of a psychobiologic link between the sexes by assuming a procreative drive in the male, a manifestation of the instinct for survival in the offspring beyond the need of orgasmic discharge of the sexual drive. The paper aims at substantiating these assumptions and investigates the problem of whether the procreative goal of sexuality has any influence and, if so, what its influence is upon the organization of human personality. This has remained outside of psychoanalytic theory.[2]

In his last comprehensive work, when Freud stated, "It is necessary to distinguish sharply between the concepts of 'sexual' and 'genital,'" and delineated sexual life as including ". . . the function of obtaining pleasure from zones of the body—a function which is subsequently brought into the service of reproduction,"[3] he differentiated pregenital and genital sexuality; he conceived of genital sexuality as the maturational sequence of the phasic pregenital development. Our clinical and theoretical knowledge of personality development—the libido theory and object relationship aspects of ego psychology—originates in and is conceptualized as derivatives of nonprocreative, i.e., pregenital, sexuality. Thus one might say that psychoanalysis studied the biologic and psychologic function of nonprocreative sexuality in the organization of the personality toward procreative (psychosexual) maturity, but did not investigate the function of procreative sexuality as a psychobiologic process.

When Freud struggled with his scientific *Umwelt* for the recognition of pregenital manifestations of sexuality, his observations were taken almost as sacrilege. That which then had to be denied in order to maintain man's illusion of his unique position on the top of the evolutionary ladder has now been proven by scrupulous investigations of several infrahuman and infraprimate species. On the basis of such investigations, one can generalize that procreative sexuality evolves from nonprocreative sexuality in man as in other mammals. The term "pregenital sexuality" refers to manifestations of those innate, autonomous, self-differentiating patterns which evolve in any organism in the process of maturation, leading to procreative sexuality in the species-specific time of maturation.

It was Freud's vision and courage that enabled him to conceive of the mind as receiving its energy at least partially from the source that in time would supply the drive for procreation. It was another stroke of his genius that he recognized in the development of children the sequence of evolutionary processes which are repeated in the maturation of the human embryo. These two generalizations are the foothold of the libido theory in biology. It appears that biology begins to fill the gap between evolution and psychoanalytic hypotheses.

Much laboratory research has led to the generalization that the progressive reduction of hormonal control of sexual behavior is connected with the evolution of the brain, especially of the cortex, and has justified the conclusion that the more completely organized the cortex of an animal species is, the more are members of that species susceptible to the effects of learning and personal experience. This, in turn, may lead to a greater variability of behavior and to increasing frequency in modifications of inherited behavioral patterns. "The relation between hormonal and cortical influence on sexual behavior is reciprocal."[4] The reciprocal interactions between the evolution of the brain and sexuality necessitated an increasingly lengthening period for sexual maturation which, in turn, made sexual behavior independent of hormonal stimulation and thus reduced the significance of estrus.

When did the human species in evolutionary history achieve freedom from estrus? What is estrus? Beach defines estrus as ". . . the physiological condition of a female at the time when she can become pregnant as a result of copulation," and he adds, "Some authors differentiate behavioral from physiological estrus, using the former term to cover all periods in which the female will copulate, even though she may not be susceptible to impregnation."[5] The manifestation of such behavioral estrus, however, indicates that the freedom from estrus as an exact differentiating quality of humans from infrahuman mammals is not borne out by observations. "In lower mammals . . . the female's urge is rigidly tied to reproductive functions by means of chemical control through the ovarian hormones."[6] Infrahuman primates are known to indulge in sexual intercourse under conditions in which such behavior cannot result in fertilization. The dependence of males upon testicular hormones for sexual potency is also less marked in infrahuman primates than in lower mammalian species. Menstruation is not a distinction of human females only, since menstruation occurs in all species of apes and some kinds of monkeys, governed by the regularly alternating secretion of ovarian hormones. These are signs indicating the ways by which the estrus has "disappeared" through the ages. The investigation of the sexual cycle has shown that traces of estrus can be discovered by psychoanalytic investigation. In spite of the fact that women may be accessible to sexual intercourse during any phase of their sexual cycle, the biologic peak of the cycle occurs at ovulation. Sexual behavior, however, has become highly independent of its biologic goal.

Gestation and parturition are physiologic processes; the care of the offspring follows instinctual innate patterns in all species, except homo sapiens. Investigating processes which were formerly recognized as "instinctual behavior," ethologists have learned to differentiate the various factors that activate the "innate" and bring it to completion in function. It is generally accepted that every instinctual pattern from the simplest to the most complex has not only physiologic but also learned components. In the discussion of mothering behavior, I cited a paper presented by Birch who reported on his experiments which illustrated "biological learning." His experiments indicate that mothering behavior, the care of the offspring, is the result of maturational processes, the potential for which is invested in the newborn by the manipulations of the mother animal from the moment of parturition through the period of dependency.[7] The same process or its inhibition has been illustrated in many species, including rhesus monkeys.[8] These observations imply that the instinctual behavior of mothering, although it is under hormonal regulation, has a phasic evolution. Full maturity through gestation and parturition evolves only in those females who, after birth, have experienced body contact through lactation and by being groomed and held by the mother. Similar "passive" instinctual learning seems to be a prerequisite for the full development of mating behavior in animals of both sexes. The term "instinctual learning" implies that the drive organization of the procreative function, the potential for learning as well as the conditions upon which maturation depends, are "innate."[9]

A somewhat higher level of learning has been observed in free-living primates about which Washburn and Hamburg report, "The species easily, almost inevitably learns the essential behavior for survival."[10] This phenomenon begins early to show a sexual differentiation of roles related both to survival and reproduction. Animal parents "teach" their offspring techniques of acquiring food, how and where to find it. Observations demonstrate that the male young, more than the female, learn the techniques of fighting and practice them in games. The maturation of reproductive behavior is anticipated through preening and grooming, provided mainly by the mother animal to the young of both sexes. These authors, studying free-living primates, and Harlow in his experimental studies of rhesus monkeys, have demonstrated that development toward the procreative function begins in the mother-infant relationship. Even more impressive is the demonstration of adaptive patterns in free-living apes and monkeys, showing such humanlike attitudes as the formation of pair bonds and familylike group living, which enhances the safety of the mother and enables her to care for the infant and enables the infant to be cared for as well. It has also been observed that motherly behavior is "practiced" by female young in the social group of primates.[11]

Sketchy as this Introduction is, it has arrived via "freedom from estrus" to the very roots of object relationship in infrahuman species. Freedom from estrus means freedom of sexuality as a drive organization from its procreative goal. Freedom of sexuality, however, refers only to sexual behavior leading to mating and conception. In this respect, the drive organization can change its object and aim, but the drive organization of the procreative function is rigidly set in the physiology of maturation and childbearing. This sharp distinction between sexuality and its biologic goal is the result of freedom from estrus.

Beyond the biologic meaning of the freedom from estrus, we become aware of its cultural significance, if we investigate the psychologic and sociologic changes brought about by women's freedom of choice regarding childbearing. As the population explosion shows, women do not give up their biologic role, except under particularly compelling conditions. This raises questions pertinent to the investigation of the procreative drive organization: is the drive which motivates the wish for pregnancy different from the excitation which may be elicited independent of the time of ovulation, from the hidden estrus of women? Is there an instinct for preservation of the species as Freud assumed and as has seemed almost self-evident since Darwin? How is the instinct-drive organization of the procreative function related to the "sexual instinct"? Answers to these questions might be fruitfully discussed after the presentation of the paper.

NOTES

1. Benedek, T., and Rubenstein, B. B., *The Sexual Cycle in Women* (Washington, D.C., National Research Council, 1942).

2. This is not to say that psychoanalysts did not interpret motivations and/or developmental aberrations that might have caused infertility in women who had a manifest desire for pregnancy or that might stimulate the desire to have children in sterile men. Those interpretations were, however, based on the accepted hypotheses untouched by new developments in the field of psychophysiology of sexuality.

3. Freud, S., "An Outline of Psychoanalysis" (1940), *Std. Ed.*, XXIII, 152.

4. Ford, C. S., and Beach, F. A., *Patterns of Sexual Behavior* (New York, Harper Bros., 1951), p. 273.

5. Ibid.

6. Ibid., p. 203.

7. See Discussion of "Psychobiological Aspects of Mothering" in this volume, Chapter 9; Birch, H. G., "Sources of Order in Maternal Behavior of Animals," *Am. J. Orthopsychiatry*, XXV, no. 2 (1956), 279–284.

8. Harlow, H. F., "Sexual Behavior in the Rhesus Monkey," in *Sex and Behavior*, ed. F. A. Beach (New York, John Wiley & Sons, 1965), pp. 234–265.

9. Much detailed knowledge has been accumulated about the "releaser mechanisms." They constitute the links between the needs of the offspring and the response of the mother. I want to call attention to the fact that the same kind of body contacts which we consider so important for the development of human infants are biologically indispensable for lower species since they have less chance or no chance at all for surviving maternal deprivation.

10. Washburn, S. L., and Hamburg, D. A., "The Study of Primate Research and Implications of Primate Research," in *Primate Behavior,* ed. I. DeVore (New York, Holt, Rinehart & Winston, 1965), p. 5.

11. Ibid.

THE ORGANIZATION OF
THE REPRODUCTIVE DRIVE[1]

Psychoanalysis considers the organization of the reproductive drive a result of ontogenetic development. It develops from the postnatal "un-

1. Revision of a paper of the same title presented at the Twenty-Fifth Anniversary Meeting, Institute for Psychoanalysis, Chicago, November 16, 1957 and reprinted from *The International Journal of Psycho-Analysis,* Vol. XLI, Part 1 (1960).

differentiated phase" in which needful infant and need-gratifying mother are a symbiotic unit. From this state which Freud termed (from the infant's point of view) a "state of absolute primary narcissism" (22) the reproductive drive evolves in continual interaction with those environmental factors which influence the personality development of the individual.[2] When, through phasic thrusts toward maturation (directed by the dominance of the erotogenic zones) integration of "genital primacy" is achieved, we assume that with physiological maturation the individual has also reached a degree of psychosexual maturity.

The term *genital primacy* refers to a drive organization which is consummated in heterosexual coitus reaching its climax in orgasm. This definition includes the heterosexual consummatory action of both sexes, but actually it was based on the model of the male. The reproductive function of the male, under the regulation of one hormonal group, the androgens, is discharged in one act, the aim of which is to deposit semen in the vagina. The female reproductive function cannot fit into this model, since the female sexual function has three phases. Heterosexual intercourse in the female, from the point of view of reproduction, is only a preparatory act. The care of the impregnated ovum during pregnancy and of the offspring after parturition by lactation are two other phases of the female reproductive function. Pregnancy and mothering constitute the completion of psychosexual and reproductive maturity in women. Yet the drive organization which motivates pregnancy and lactation is not "genital" in the same sense as is mating behavior. The investigation of the sexual cycle in women has clarified the phasic course of the female reproductive functions and the psychodynamic processes correlated with them.

When this investigation began about twenty years ago, it was not the author's intention to elucidate theoretical concepts. Biologically, women are accessible to intercourse during any part of the cycle. Experientially, their sexual behavior has multiple cultural and interpersonal motivations. Our task was to determine whether by means of psychoanalysis one could discern signs which are comparable to "heat" in animals, from which one may infer ovulation. For this purpose the state of the ovarian cycle was established by daily vaginal smears and basal body temperature charts. The psychoanalytic records were analyzed specifically in relation to the hormonal cycle. When the independently obtained data were compared, it was found that they coincided

2. Until not too long ago, we considered the plasticity of the innate sexual anlage a special human distinction. The research of Heinroth, Lorenz, Tinbergen, and others, however, has shown that similar plasticity of the innate pattern can be observed in animals, although to a lesser degree. Thus Tinbergen writes: "In all species where the parents take care of the young, the behaviour of the latter may be conditioned by the adults in a number of ways. But an individual may also learn from experiences with other parts of environment" (36).

almost exactly. Both methods were able to establish the significant phases of the ovarian function.[3]

The aim of this presentation is to bring into focus some of the principles that are involved in applying the psychoanalytic method to research in the "source" of sexual drives; to discuss the conclusions which may be drawn from the effectiveness of the predictive method; finally, to indicate how the psychodynamic processes derived from the study of the reproductive drive in women may suggest new approaches to the study of that drive in the male.

I

Bernfeld stated simply but succinctly: "To start off with the observation of facts, to draw from them predictions which are verifiable by other facts, that is the modest endeavor of scientists today" (9).

What then were the observational data transmitted in the material recorded during analytic sessions? Our records were not verbatim. They included, however, the dreams, fantasies, and free associations which reflected the flow of emotions. For the most part they were sufficient to be approached by the usual method of psychoanalytic interpretation.[4] Actually, psychoanalytic data are so manifold that a significant part of every research is to distill from the complexity of material the data pertinent to the problem under investigation.

In general, we consider two kinds of data: the primary data of observation, and secondary data at which we arrive by interpretation. Since each interpretation is based on one or more hypotheses accepted in the theoretical structure of psychoanalysis, psychoanalysts are accustomed to a "practical," "ad hoc" method of investigation,[5] which, however, often takes assumptions for facts. It is necessary to distinguish

3. Physiological research conducted by Boris B. Rubenstein, M.D. (4).
4. When this investigation was in progress, the advantage of psychoanalytic research outside the "live analytic situation" was not yet recognized. Since then the use of records has become the custom and the demand for "complete" records is growing. Therefore it seems necessary to emphasize the advantage of such records, which were not intended to be complete and were in most cases taken by analysts who were not involved, or even interested, in the research. Yet such records contained sufficient relevant data without submerging them in masses of misguiding details.
5. French was the first to investigate systematically whether psychoanalytic interpretations can be validated by psychoanalytic method. Such investigation, in which the various levels of interpretations during the different phases of the analytic process serve as checks on previous interpretations, can be done only on recorded material. Starting from the "focal conflict" of the day, French proceeds to interpret the unconscious factors from which he finally formulates the intricate pattern of behavior which, in each instance, is part and parcel of the total personality (19).

not only the data of observations but also the theories on which our interpretations are based, and these again, from those "secondary data" and/or secondary theories which we derive from interpretations.

What then were the "fundamental facts" we observed? The consistent analysis of the psychoanalytic record revealed to us more than any other experience that the fundamental facts of psychoanalytic observation are affects, emotions, feelings, to which we respond primarily with empathic understanding. "Empathy has to be explicitly recognized as the basic fact of psychoanalytic communication and experience" (Kohut) (29). Since empathy is our fact-finding tool which may be blurred or blinded by the observer's resistances, the insight of the analyst into his own empathic, intuitive understanding is a prerequisite for the purification of the data, whether for the purpose of therapy or research. This is a simpler task in the analysis of the psychoanalytic record than in the immediate experience of the analytic situation. In interpreting the record, the "countertransference" which originates in the "scientific appetence" of the researcher, in his emotional involvement with his hypothesis, in his avidity for proof, may become the source of error. Yet these motivations are closer to consciousness and can be more easily controlled than those unconscious motivations which interfere with the sound evaluation of the experiences in the analytic process.

The events occurring during psychoanalytic sessions cannot be repeated. All events, external, interpersonal, and intrapsychic, can occur only once. (Even though patients report similar dreams repeatedly and use the same symbols frequently, they may have varying significance each time.) But analyzing the record, the investigator can recognize the events which occur repeatedly in the psychoanalytic situation and can account for the factors responsible for the repetition. In our investigation we could count on two facilitating factors. One is that our research project acted as a selector, organizer of the material. Fluctuations in sexual affects and emotions present themselves to the empathic observer as direct experience. The other was that since the physiological processes are cyclic, some kind of repetition could be expected, after the pilot study revealed that the time of ovulation can be predicted from the analysis of the psychoanalytic record. This led some of the critics of our work to assume that, knowing the time of menstruation, the time of ovulation could have been assumed and not needed to be predicted. Taking into consideration the variations in the time of ovulation, "guesses" would not have resulted in such high correlations as we arrived at by analysis of the material, especially of dreams.

Soon after the publication of our preliminary reports, Altmann, Knowles, and Bull investigated the physical and mental aspects of the menstrual cycle in fifty-five cycles of ten "healthy," mature college women (2). While the average for ovulation determined by electrical method was the 11.8th day of the cycle, they found that "even for the same individual there was rarely a repetition of the spacing of ovulation in consecutive cycles, a variation from the fifth to the sixteenth day being no exception." These authors found that ovulation was accompanied by elation and relaxed activity, while the premenstrual phase was characterized by tense activity, irritability, and also by depressed mood.

This investigation is cited here not only because it confirms our findings but because it gives us a welcome opportunity to point out the difference between the clinical method of observation and the psychoanalysis of the recorded material.

Sexual impulses, wishes, desires are, or can be, expressed overtly. Even if hidden in fantasies and dreams, they precipitate moods and feelings which are experienced. Frustration of sexual impulses causing tension, anger, etc., is recognizable by the observed and the observer. The intensity of affects can be "rated" by the empathic response of the observer as Altmann and co-workers did. (Such are also the primary data of psychoanalytic investigation.) Although careful observation succeeds in isolating the superficial motivating factors and arriving at correlations with the particular phases of the ovarian cycle, the task of the psychoanalyst begins beyond this. He tends to discern the psychodynamic processes which are not accessible to experience, which through the processes of physiological maturation and psychological development have become incorporated in the structural and drive organization of the individual. Psychoanalysis discovered the "repressed," those instinctual tendencies which were and remained unconscious or had become so during the developmental processes. We are so accustomed to searching for the repressed sexual tendencies and their vicissitudes that we often forget that we arrive at them from the currently experienceable phenomena of sexuality. Actual wishes, longings, desires, urges, and impulses, their current suspense and frustration and/or release and gratification, mobilize the drive energy which recharges the channels of repressed affects and impulses (and their related mental representations and symbolic elaborations) and thus reanimate the past to become incorporated again as an integral (and modifying) part of the present experience. Applying this concept consistently to the analysis of the psychoanalytic records, we followed the ebb and flow of emotions; we accounted for the individual variations of motivations and expressions as well as for the influences of currently changing life situations. (The psychoanalytic process itself also is a significant part of this.) Thus we drew conclusions about the dominant psychodynamic tendencies which motivated the current emotional attitude and behavior. From this we inferred the gonadal, hormonal stimulation. We assumed that this is what accounts for the woman's *preparedness* for a particular response at a given phase of her cycle.[6]

6. An attempt to present this was made in Chapter 1, Section II (4).

It is not possible to give a complete account of the application of psychoanalytic technique in this research. Here, therefore, only the main propositions will be reviewed.

(i) First, the genetic, structural, and psychoeconomic integration of the personality is established. Such longitudinal analysis goes along as one studies the record, just as in the actual analytic process the analyst's understanding deepens and branches out to encompass what is newly learned. It is assumed that the organization of the personality is a permanent system, even if this is true only in a limited sense.

(ii) Analyzing the day-by-day variations of emotions we interpret the fluctuations of the psychic equilibrium which shifts continually under the influence of internal needs and external demands.

Among the variety of behavioral and psychological manifestations which gave access to such interpretations, dreams proved to be the reliable "objective material" of psychoanalysis. The detailed analysis of dreams was utilized to gauge the qualitative and quantitative shifts in the sexual drive during the dream process. The dependability of the dream interpretation can be explained by the consistency of our search. However complex the dream elaboration might have been, the interpretation had to answer the following questions: What manifestations of the sexual drive can be recognized in the dream? What is the motivational origin of the dreaming ego's conflict in regard to the sexual impulse? What is the process leading to the dream solution? Each dream thought is a step toward the dream solution, often motivated by shifts in the manifestations of the sexual drive. For example, often a forbidden genital tendency is resolved by an acceptable (usually not recognizable) substitute motivated by a pregenital tendency. At other times, dreams build up step by step toward a genital tendency which might provoke anxiety as a defense or might break through accompanied by pleasurable or painful emotions. The "feeling tone" of the dream, the affects and emotions experienced by the dreaming ego, as well as the emotional response of the waking personality to the dream experience, afforded primary data for our investigations.

(iii) In the center of our investigation is the "mental event" (23) of the affective experience. In analyzing the function of the affective experience in a given psychoeconomic constellation we interpret (at least) two levels of data: one is the affect, and the other is the ego's function which in response to the affect integrates the psychic processes through which psychic equilibrium is reestablished. This may result in manifest behavior and/or in further elaboration of psychic processes.

How do we derive from such complex mental processes our secondary data, to be compared with the data from physiological estimates of the gonadal hormone state?

There are massive shifts in the psychoeconomic equilibrium, such as the sense of frustration and anger, reactive to need tension; emotions such as contentment, pleasure, joy, and elation are responses to release and gratification; others like sadness and grief are responses to loss. These phenomena and many others can be considered expressions of the total personality to need and gratification; they express unmistakably psychic pain or pleasure in various coloring and intensity. They are directly accessible to empathy; they can be analyzed from the point of view of the participating ego, but they do not permit further reduction in regard to the motivating instinctual energies (not within the frame of the first instinct theory).[7] In our investigation we interpreted these phenomena of reactive affects in relation to the psychodynamic processes which activated them.

The quality of an affective experience cannot be further defined—we simply feel it. The sexual quality of an experience, even in its distortions and defensive elaborations, is easily recognizable to the observer as well as to the observed. Hostility in all its disguises gives an unmistakable (negative) feeling tone. Love and hate, however, are complex emotions. Each of them, when it appears as a current phenomenon, brings with it a long history of the developmental experiences of the past which, at least partially, can be recognized in the current emotions. Regarding loving and hating, psychoanalysis has established that individual experiences of these emotions, from infancy on, interact with the ego and supply the genetic and structural motivations for the ego's propensity to a particular emotional response. Thus in the analysis of an affective experience, we confront the psychodynamic factors which presently precipitate the affect with the genetic motivations of the response; the latter is considered again from the point of view of the affect and of the ego since affects, in the course of development, become an organized part of the personality. This can be easily illustrated in such complex affects as envy, jealousy, generosity, miserliness, ambition, indolence, etc. The whole gamut of human emotions which originate in an instinctual drive during the development of an individual may become a structuralized part of personality. For example, envy; almost by empathy one knows that envy is such an intensification of the wish to receive and own that it includes hostility toward the person who has what one wants. Envy can be traced back to the infant's lack of security that hunger will be followed by satiation. It is often renewed, for example, by a threat of losing love, by sibling rivalry. The greed and envy of the child is an anxious, tense affect; its immediacy, however, diminishes step by step as envy becomes integrated as a character trend with a specific function in the personality. Generosity, the ability to give freely, originates also in the oral give-and-take of infancy; associated with positive object relationships, its repetition as affective experience in-

7. Psychoanalytic phenomenology attempts to formulate the metapsychology of such phenomena from the point of view of neutralization of psychic energies, i.e., in the frame of the second instinct theory.

dicates a different level of personality (and, relating to our investigation, also hormonal) integration from that of envy. The anxious wish to retain—the affect content of miserliness—is assumed to originate in the anal retentive wishes of childhood. These examples suffice to illustrate that *each complex affect can be analyzed in regard to* (a) *the psychodynamic tendencies which constitute it;* (b) *its genetic motivation; and* (c) *its function in the total personality.*

(iv) In the detailed analysis of psychodynamic processes, Alexander's vector concept proved to be a dependable tool of psychoanalytic research. Alexander's hypothesis states that emotions deprived of their ideational content are expressions of one or more of the fundamental directions that characterize biological processes (1). The vector qualities of "intaking," "retaining," and "eliminating" represent directions related to physiological processes. On their orderly sequence life depends. Through them the energies are produced which supply internal stimulation and maintain the dynamic stability of the organism. Alexander characterized the known developmental phases not in terms of the erotogenic zones, but by the direction of the psychodynamic tendency corresponding to the function of the dominant zone at various levels of development. Thus the oral phase is characterized by receptive, the anal phase by retentive, the urethral (phallic) phase by eliminative tendencies. In the organization of genital sexuality, the three vector qualities —the receptive, retentive, and eliminative tendencies—achieve functional balance. Thus the vector concept permits further breakdown of the sexual drive into its components, each of which can be defined, like the drive itself, by its direction, aim, and object. Since the psychodynamic tendencies are simpler constructs than the sexual drive, they can be applied to the analysis of any affect or to any manifestation of shifts in excitation. By analyzing affects as manifestations of one or more psychodynamic tendencies, we can discern the changing level of the integration of the sexual drive.

Besides this, however, we have to take into account the impetus of the drive, the intensity of the psychodynamic tendency. It is obvious that there are periods when the envious person is not so bothered by envy; when the bountiful appears not to care so much. The quantitative aspects of drives (and psychodynamic tendencies) are communicated to oneself by insight and to the observer by empathic understanding. Observing the daily fluctuations of affective experiences as they are revealed in the psychoanalytic material, we get the impression that the developmental conflicts which we usually refer to the unconscious carry different amounts of psychic energy, cathexis, at different times. Sometimes conflicts are remote from consciousness; at other times they strive for discharge. In sexually mature adults, sexual stimulation is usually expressed in direct desire, impulse, and behavior; while in young individuals or when gratification is impossible, sexual stimulation is usually expressed in the reactivization of the developmental conflicts. The reawakening of the developmental conflict increases psychic tension and at the same time affords a greater variety of expression for the psychic tension. Since every impulse which has a drive toward fulfillment also has the power to call forth the defensive and controlling functions of the ego, the interpretation of the impetus, of the quantitative aspect of the drive, often has to be based on the manifestations of the ego's defenses against the psychodynamic tendency. In interpreting the intensity of the emotion, or of the drive, we equate the psychic tension created by the defense reaction with the impulse which is warded off by the ego's defense. (For example, when the heterosexual impulse is importunate, the ego reacts with anxiety and hostility.) The quantitative factors involved in these processes are more easily accessible to one's empathic evaluation if the sexual tendency is active, object-directed, i.e., during the estrogen and premenstrual phase of the cycle, than during the progesterone phase. Passive receptive needs, the need for withdrawal and concentration on the own body—the concomitants of the postovulative progesterone phase—seldom have a driving quality. So the wish for pregnancy and motherhood and the anxious defenses against these wishes are often symbolic and indirect, which makes empathic, quantitative evaluation difficult. Yet, even in this regard, dream analysis was a dependable guide.

No matter how remarkable, it is well established that the psychic apparatus registers the physiological changes of an organ in dreams. It seems that an organ which has a normal or a pathologic state of tumescence may activate the psychic representation of the organ in sleep even if it does not in the waking state.[8] The female genitals, especially the uterus, go through a period of physiological growth during ovulative and postovulative phases. The increased physiological activity of the organs, although not conscious, is perceptible to the sleeping ego, and the awareness of the womb expresses itself in a symbolic manner. The more intense the feeling tone connected with the symbolism appeared, the safer we felt in estimating a high level of progesterone in the postovulative phase. These are but a few examples of the manifestations of changes in the sexual drive from which we predicted the qualitative and relatively quantitative changes in the gonadal hormones. Although for detailed evaluation of the correlated data we refer to previous publications, a summary of the course of the gonadal cycle and the cor-

8. Freud pointed out (1917) (21) that inflammatory or other pathological organic processes may be perceived unconsciously and that they appear in dreams before the symptoms are sufficiently acute to attract attention. Ferenczi's concept of pathoneuroses (16) deals with the psychodynamic reactions to such perceptions. French (1937) (18) generalized from another viewpoint, stating that there is a physiological excitation perceptible to the dreaming ego in those organs which are symbolically represented in the dream.

responding emotional cycle is necessary here as basis for our further discussion.

II

The gonadal cycle begins, often during menstruation or soon after the flow ceases, with the ripening of the follicle which produces *estrogenic hormones*. Corresponding with this stimulation, an active object-directed, psychodynamic tendency characterizes the sexual drive and brings forth wishes, fantasies, and desires of various intensity and from different levels of maturation. The aim of the unconscious motivating tendency is to bring about contact with the sexual object and achieve gratification through coitus. When progesterone production comes into effect, beginning in the preovulative state, the active, outwardly-directed tendency fuses with a *passive receptive tendency*. Parallel with the peak of the cycle at the time of ovulation the sexual drive reaches its highest level of integration. While the emotional manifestations of this state may vary depending upon the individual's chronological and emotional maturity, and also upon her external situation, analysis reveals that *corresponding with high hormone production an integration of the basic psychodynamic tendencies occurs*. The effect of the fusion of the passive receptive tendency with the dominant heterosexual tendency is recognizable in the emotional manifestation of the ovulative phase, which thus can be characterized as "heat," the peak of the woman's sexual cycle.

Boas (10) doubts this finding and considers it teleological. He found statistically the peak of libido at the postmenstrual phase and this he relates to exogenous, social-psychological factors. Boas seems to confine the term "libido" to the overt manifestations of sexual desire, and does not consider it an integrating psychic energy having complex emotional manifestations which are not always recognizable as sexual in manifest behavior.

After ovulation and relief of preovulative tension, manifestations of the receptive and retentive tendencies dominate the emotional life during the progesterone phase of the cycle. This is a high hormone phase, since both hormones, estrogen and progesterone, are produced. Yet the active heterosexual tendency appears masked, overshadowed by manifestations of passive-receptive and retentive tendencies. The content of the psychological material can be best described as emotional preparation for motherhood. This evolves parallel with the effects of the corpus luteum hormone upon the uterus which prepares for nidation of the impregnated ovum.

If conception does not occur, the corpus luteum, which attains its maximum functional capacity, begins to degenerate about a week after ovulation. With the diminishing progesterone production, which in the late phase of the cycle inhibits estrogen production, the total hormone level declines. Parallel with the low hormone level a regression of the psychosexual integration seems to take place; pregenital manifestations of urethral, anal, and genital eliminative tendencies motivate the psychodynamic trends. This regression and the increased general irritability of the sympathetic nervous system are manifestations of the "moderate degree of ovarian deficiency" of the "premenstrual phase" (26), which is one significant factor in the premenstrual "recurrent neuroses" of women (11). Important as these manifestations may be for the clinician, they are significant for us only in that *parallel with the low hormone production, the sexual drive, which was integrated toward the mature reproductive goal during the high hormone production, is regressed.* Not only is it broken up into its component parts, but each of these tendencies appears to motivate "pregenital" emotional patterns which were characteristic for the individual during her pregenital and prepubertal development.

The end of the sexual cycle is brought about by hormone withdrawal, which ushers in the menstrual flow. Soon after the flow is established, the tense mood relaxes and after a few days the new follicle begins to ripen; the concomitant sexual stimulation suggests the beginning of a new cycle. It appears that the sexual drive repeats its developmental integration with each cycle. The emotional upheaval which accompanies the phasic integration and regression of the sexual drive, however, diminishes with the progress of physiological and emotional maturation. This indicates a developmental adaptation to the physiological and psychological tasks of the reproductive function.

Beneath all the complex and variable superstructure of human personality, one can detect the psychophysiological response to the hormonal stimulation which directs the sexual needs of woman toward her reproductive function. *The term "sexual cycle," which implies the ovarian hormone cycle and its correlated drive organization, designates an innate pattern.*

The term "innate" refers to self-differentiating patterns which come into being during the course of normal development. Since environment always plays a role in development, the term "innate" seems not to do justice to the facts (15). George Engel in his discussion (14) of this paper recommended the term "autonomous." He considers this not only more precise, but also expedient, since the term is established in psychoanalysis to designate certain levels of ego organization and function. The advantage of this term is obvious in reference to the establishment of early self-differentiating patterns, such as sucking, eating, posture, walking, speech, etc. (25). It seems, however, to be confusing in relation to complex functions of adults such as the biological and psychological patterns of human reproduction.

The schematic presentation of the sexual cycle did not indicate the variations of the gonadal cycle; it did not call attention to the significance of the balance between estrogen and progesterone production and the ensuing transactional sequence of the phases of the cycle. This, however, determines the length of the cycle, the time and duration of the menstrual flow, the course of the premenstrual phase, the existence of menstrual symptoms or the lack of them. While these variations of the gonadal cycle exert influence upon emotions, closer analysis of the personality development reveals that the particular gonadal hormone pattern may be the result of psychosexual development (4, ch. ix). Thus when reproductive maturity is attained, not only are the emotional patterns under control of high psychic organizations (superego) but also the physiological patterns are influenced by developmental processes. Neither could be considered "autonomous" (in the sense in which the term is used in psychoanalysis). Yet we feel safe in our assumption that the sexual cycle is an innate, self-differentiating pattern, the evolution of which can be traced through the interacting processes of physiological maturation and psychological development.

The effectiveness of the psychoanalytic, interpretive method in establishing correlations between the gonadal hormones and psychodynamic processes, even through the "irregularities" of individual variations, offers supportive evidence for the psychoanalytic theories upon which the interpretations were based.

Instincts in man subserve adaptive behavior. Freud (20) assumed that the individual, being completely dependent upon the external world in order to survive, regulates his adaptive processes according to the pleasure-pain principle. This fundamental regulator of psychic economy coordinates all functions toward the aim of survival. The instinct of survival is the primary organizer of psychic processes. At a time when the ego is weak and its energies are not yet differentiated in patterned defense mechanisms, if an external danger or internal conflict raises the psychic tension, the adaptation is achieved by a change in instinct. Unconscious are the processes by which primary instincts are repressed and/or change their object, aim, and direction. Psychoanalysis has revealed many examples of such changes in the "partial" instincts, for example, the active, sadistic tendency having turned toward the self changes both its object and direction in masochism.[9] The active tendency to derive pleasure from looking may be turned into the passive tendency to be looked at, etc. Thus what Freud referred to as "vicissitudes of instincts" represents modifications of instincts resulting from specific needs in adaptation. The adaptability of instincts, however, is not unlimited. After having participated in such radical changes, their capacity for further change is reduced and the response pattern of

9. Examples of such changes in the fixed instinctual patterns of animals have been reported by ethologists (33). See note 11.

instincts becomes more or less fixed. The primary pattern resulting from
the adaptive changes of "partial" instincts includes, according to our
present concept, a corresponding organization of the ego. This, in turn,
implies the introject of the object (objects) through whom the primary
instinctual needs were gratified or frustrated. Thus, through primary
adaptive processes the instincts participate in forming patterns of response and discharge; they become primary ego structures; their further
adaptability is limited and also motivated by their genetic history. The
primary ego structures, through continual interaction with each other
in response to the environment, enter further differentiations and syn-
theses which become characteristic for the individual and finally constitute his personality.

Personality, that relatively static system of highest organization of
psychic energies, puts its stamp upon the transient fluctuations of the
psychosexual equilibrium. On the personality, on its genetic and economic organization "depends the ideational content of the affects and
emotions, also the ego's ways and means of dealing with them; even
more specifically on this depends the 'quantity' of libido which is available to fill the channels upon the various phases of gonadal hormone
stimulation" (6). This we recognize as drive. Drive represents that level
of organization of psychic energies which is accessible to experience.
Both the qualitative and the quantitative aspects of the drive can be subjectively distinguished and, in instances, referred to as "somatic source"
of stimulation. The sexual drive is a complex structure. It can be broken
down to its component psychodynamic tendencies. This affords a
method to determine the changes in the direction and aim of the sexual
drive.

The consistent analysis of these three phases of motivational organization demonstrates that (a) the personality represents a system
in which the psychic energies, which participate in developing and maintaining the system, are in continuous interaction with energies supplying
its current functions. (b) The response to the ongoing process of gonadal hormone stimulation—the reproductive drive—is expressed according to the ontogenetically developed patterns of the personality.
(c) Beyond this is the innate, self-differentiating pattern, expressed by
the change in the direction of the sexual drive in correspondence with
the phasic function of the ovaries.

III

Estrogenic hormone is the hormone of preparation. Produced from
childhood on, at the time of prepuberty its function is to stimulate the
growth of secondary sex characteristics and the genital organs and to
maintain the uterus in readiness for the changes that will continue to be
imposed upon it by the corpus luteum after full maturity is achieved

(12). In each sexual cycle the individual's development toward heterosexual maturity is telescoped in the (preconscious) psychodynamic trends of the follicle-ripening phase. Since in the preovulative phase estrogen has already fused with the incipient progesterone, the sexual drive is enhanced and colored by the receptive tendency; the developmental conflicts shift from the heterosexual to those which we find characteristic of the progesterone phase.

Ovulation is a unique physiological event, since it is accompanied by systemic reactions. Of the physiological signs of the systemic reactions, best known are the heightened basal body temperature and the change in bioelectrical potentials of the skin. On the psychological side, a sense of relaxation and well-being seems to flood the woman with libido. A shift of the woman's interest to her own body and its welfare is a characteristic sign of ovulation. In terms of psychodynamics, with each ovulation introversion of the outwardly-directed sexual energy occurs. At the beginning this appears to motivate a narcissistic state and then mobilizes the innate patterns of passive-receptive retentive tendencies which, under the stimulation of progesterone, gain in intensity during the active stage of the corpus luteum. Indeed, the question arises whether that which the psychoanalyst may term a "narcissistic state" can characterize the phase of the cycle when the woman is most accessible to heterosexual intercourse. Yet this is the same in both sexes. The heightened libidinal state is felt as a satisfying state of one's own body. This is the prerequisite in the male for his assurance of vigor and in the woman that she is lovable and may let herself be loved, and also can give of herself and therefore may receive without fear.

It is the physiological characteristic of woman that her reproductive function requires an increase in metabolic processes. This is reflected in the intensification of receptive and retentive tendencies as a response to the need for fuel to supply energy for growth. While this readily explains the psychodynamic processes of pregnancy and lactation, it must make us stop to think regarding the "need for fuel" at the time of ovulation and during the progesterone phase without conception. Indeed, the actual increase in metabolic need must be minimal, and yet the increase of basal body temperature, as well as the psychic responses to ovulation, indicate a vigorous reaction. This signifies that the gonadal hormones have set in motion an innate pattern, the repetition of phylogenetic experience. In the presence of signal stimulation, especially at the beginning of each characteristic phase of the cycle, the central nervous system sets in motion the specific pattern of physiological and emotional responses. Even if they actually are not needed, they afford learning by repetition. While this statement refers to each phase of the cycle, it is ovulation which brings to mind the comparison with the "Innate Releasing Mechanism" (I.R.M.) which the ethologists consider the integrating factor of reproductive behavior in animals. Released automatically when the anatomical structure is ready, ovulation is the signal to which the psychic apparatus responds with a directional change of the drive energy, preparing to supply the psychodynamic correlates for the ensuing "preparation for pregnancy."[10]

Gonadal hormones are not directly responsible for the intensity of the drive nor for the organization of the sexual personality. Sex hormones are facilitating agents which, by changing threshold values, allow specific nervous mechanisms of sexual behavior to be more readily stimulated (3).[11] The hormone stimulation activates, besides the symbol representation of the organ, the psychic representations of its functions.

The symbolic process by which the body image, both as a whole and in its parts, is represented consciously and unconsciously, is subserved by the central nervous system. The gonadal hormones through the central nervous system activate the body image. At the time of ovulation, the whole body image seems to be highly cathected along with the receptive organ, the vagina. But there is evidence that these processes do not depend entirely on hormonal activity and the state of the uterus. Analysis of women who had undergone hysterectomy after full functional maturity indicated that a cyclic representation of the cycle was maintained and they had uterus dreams. The significance of the central organization is even more impressively demonstrated in mature women who have undergone total extirpation. They may show a "reflection" of the ovarian cycle in some cases for several years.

Whether the "organic memory" supplies the stimulation or the wish to be healthy and fertile, it seems as if these processes have some similarity to phantom pain, producing phantom pleasure, wish fulfillment and sometimes pain, pelvic discomfort.

The integration of physiological (bodily) and mental processes can be most clearly observed during the progesterone phase of the cycle. The wish for pregnancy, the fear of it, or the hostile aggressive defense

10. The influence of central nervous stimulation on these processes is indicated in instances when particular sexual experience stimulates ovulation at a time when its physiological readiness cannot be expected, i.e., immediately before or after menstruation.

11. These mechanisms have been well studied by ethologists in regard to mating and parental behavior of animals. Psychoanalysts are especially interested in these experimental studies; they confirm the significance of ontogenic development, even for lower vertebrates. It is of great interest to psychoanalysts that ethologists describe sexual behavior as an interaction between external stimuli (sign stimuli) and the "innate releasing mechanism" (I.R.M.) which functions when "action-specific energy" is accumulated. The process of this accumulation of the species-specific sign stimulus, the species-specific behavior pattern is released and, as Lorenz assumes, the "action-specific energy is consumed." This concept of "discharge of energy," as well as the "displacement behavior" if the need is frustrated, allows for many analogies between psychoanalytic concepts of instincts and their vicissitudes during individual development in humans, and the development of "species-specific behavior pattern" during the evolution of a species in general (31).

against it are characteristic of the psychodynamic material during the progesterone phase of the cycle. Acting through the central nervous mechanisms *progesterone* stimulates two receptor systems. One is obviously the uterus which under the influence of a relatively small amount of progesterone undergoes pregestational proliferation; the other is the "psychic apparatus" which, parallel with the progestational changes of the uterus, appears extremely perceptive to this otherwise dormant organ. While the drive quality of the heterosexual tendency—the estrogenic effect—is easily recognized, the drive quality referable to the progesterone effect is not obvious. Yet the internal physiological processes excite the central intrapsychic representation of the uterus. Archaic symbolic representations of the uterus such as dreams of water and waves, protecting dwelling places and threatening hollows, are characteristic of an unconscious perception of the womb. Fliess (17), without considering the hormonal phase, relates such dreams to the woman's awareness of her womb.

Theories concerning drive discharge phenomena toward the inside of the body corresponding to physiological processes gain support by the phenomena (27) of the progesterone phase. Here we should refer also to the studies of J. Kestenberg (28) which deal with the origin of erotogeneity of the female sexual organs. These studies indicate that when the gonadal hormones set in motion the reproductive physiology, they coordinate already prepared organ sensibilities with prepared drive patterns.

The comparative study of the progesterone phases in several women through a number of cycles reveals the biological learning process under the stimulation of the corpus luteum hormone. Introduced by the introversion of psychic energies at the time of ovulation, the increased receptive and retentive tendencies mobilize the memory traces of the oral-dependent phase of development.

In previous publications (5) I have elaborated upon the reciprocal interactions between mother and infant, in the course of which the infant incorporates into his primary mental structures the memory traces of positive-satisfying and negative-frustrating experiences of the oral-dependent phase of development. When the infant integrates the memory traces of gratified needs with his developing confidence in his mother, he implants the confidence in his well-being, in his thriving, good self. In contrast, with the memory traces of frustrating experiences he introjects the frustrating mother as "bad mother" and himself as crying and frustrated, as "bad self." Thus he inculcates into his psychic structure the core of ambivalence. These primary ego structures, confidence and the core of ambivalence, originating in the rudimentary emotional experiences of early infancy, are significant for the infant of either sex. They determine the child's further relationship with his mother and through it, to a great extent, his personality. A generation later these primary ego structures can be recognized as motivating factors in the parental attitudes of the individual.

Yet, in the biological depth of the organism, the experiences of the oral phase of development are stored for purposes differing as between girls and boys. The innate femaleness of the girl directs her development toward motherhood through step-by-step identification with her mother. The positive psychological balance of the early alimentary phase of development, which accounts for confidence, facilitates a relatively conflict-free process of identification with the mother. The incorporated reaction to frustration (ambivalence), however, complicates the development toward motherhood by charging the representations arising from mother identifications with hostile-dependent and aggressive tendencies. Each woman's development toward motherhood represents an interacting process between these extreme polarities of psychic representations of the biological dependence on the mother. This is reflected in the wish for pregnancy or in the hostile aggressive defenses against it, which characterize the emotions of the progesterone phase, especially in adolescents and in neurotic women.

The processes which, under the stimulation of progesterone, lead to a gradual resolution of the conflicts are unconscious. In the physiologically well defined, repetitive progesterone phase of the cycle are telescoped the oscillations of those processes by which the dominant tendency of childhood—the need to be fed and taken care of—is replaced by the adult woman's physiological and emotional ability to give, to succor, to be a mother. From the point of view of ego development, we may add that not independently of the physiological cycles but in interaction with them the ego matures to incorporate into the ego ideal of the adult woman, as her most significant aspiration, the wish to be a mother.

From the viewpoint of the organization of the reproductive drive, *pregnancy* is associated with an immense intensification of the progesterone phase of the cycle. The enhanced hormonal and general metabolic processes go hand in hand with the emotional manifestations of receptive and retentive tendencies. These account for the "primary narcissistic state" of the mother which is a well-spring of her motherliness.[12] The physiologic and psychologic processes of pregnancy speed up the intrapsychic processes which culminate in motherliness.

The drive organization which represents the psychodynamic correlates of pregnancy does not alone account for the psychology of preg-

12. Many women nowadays, unafraid of the hardship of childbearing, are proudly aware of and give conscious expression to these feelings, even if not with the sensitivity of the poet:
> "Not the land, but her fullness was spread about her
> Walking she felt: one never transcends
> The greatness that she now felt."

(Rilke: *Visitation of Mary*. Translated by E. and R. Fliess) (17).

nancy and motherhood. The object relationships which through the developmental processes became incorporated into the personality explain the specific meaning of the experience of pregnancy for each woman and give the particular coloring to the mother's relationship with each of her children.

The cyclic function of the ovaries brings about the repetition of the developmental conflicts and directs their "working-over" (7) toward reproductive maturity. The special significance of the conflicts and identifications with the mother—relegated mainly to the progesterone phase—has been adequately emphasized. But identifications originating in the heterosexual component of the sexual drive have hardly been mentioned. Freud, considering only one aspect of the sexual drive—the heterosexual tendency—considered pregnancy a fulfillment of the wish to incorporate and retain the penis, especially the penis of the father. In our present way of thinking, Freud's hypothesis implies the motivational significance of one specific introject which originates in the phallic phase of development. This hypothesis, however incomplete, has demonstrated in many instances the motivational power of infantile fantasies. There are many fantasies originating in infantile object relationships. One or the other has greater significance in the development of the personality. During pregnancy the individually significant object relationship may become recathected and influence the course of the pregnancy and also the mother's relationship to her child.

The fetus is a part of the mother's body. What aspect of the body image does the fetus represent? In some cases it may be the missing penis; in others it is the admired beauty, or the envied pregnancy, of the woman's own mother; most frequently the fetus is the token of the loved self. Normally the fetus is cathected with narcissistic libido. This, however, does not always mean pleasurable emotional sensations. There are many ambivalent, hostile manifestations of the feelings concentrated upon the self. Thus, the fetus can represent the "bad, aggressive, devouring self," engendering fear of harboring a "monster." Many women identify the fetus with feces and relive during the pregnancy the ambivalent feelings and mysteries of the infantile sexual fantasy of the "anal child." There are many cases in which the anal or other regressive fantasies interfere with the pleasure of pregnancy. The mother's object relationship to her unborn child becomes ambivalent or strongly hostile when the fantasy which is projected onto the fetus is highly charged with ambivalence. The fetus, then, becomes the representation of a hated and/or feared person, and motherhood becomes an overwhelming menace.[13]

13. The anxiety and depression caused by such motivations may remain on the level of neurosis. In many instances, depending on the predisposition of the personality, the anxiety may activate a true psychosis, with hallucinations, paranoid defenses, and schizophrenic reactions endangering the woman and her fetus (13).

Besides the psychodynamic processes corresponding to the physiology of pregnancy, the ontogenic development of the personality determines what childbearing means to an individual woman. The self- and object-representations projected onto the child during pregnancy determine what each child represents to the mother. This, in turn, will influence her motherliness and her relationship to the child.

When a mother takes the baby to her breast and the infant begins to exercise the sucking reflex, the mother acts in accordance with her mammalian instincts to feed. The infant's need to be fed and the mother's preparedness to feed represent the interacting motivations which maintain mother and child as a symbiotic unit during lactation.

The action of the pituitary hormone upon the integration of mothering behavior has been well studied in animals. In the human female, with the exception of lactation proper, one is inclined to overlook the significance of direct, immediate hormonal stimulation on mothering behavior. This neglect may be explained by the fact that motherliness in human beings is considered a very high ethical value. The development of motherliness in the human being is not a simple response to hormonal stimulation, brought about by pregnancy and the ensuing biological necessity of caring for the young. Motherliness, in mankind, develops through the cyclic repetition of hormonal stimulation which, interacting with other aspects of the personality, reaches functional maturity through a complex process of personality development. Yet there are mothers of many children who do not seem "motherly," and other women who have never had children, unperturbed by the physiological and emotional stresses of motherhood, might demonstrate exquisite motherliness. In spite of the physiological processes which direct the female anlage toward its completion, motherliness is the fruition of an innate quality of the personality.

In each phase of motherhood, or even in each act of mothering, we differentiate two levels of motivation as well as of action. One is dominated by the emotional manifestations of passive receptive tendencies and accompanies the processes through which the metabolic and emotional energy is stored to be used for the sake of the child. The other, more accessible to consciousness, motivates the active, giving, loving attitudes of motherliness. The balance between these two levels of motivation, the "reconciliation" of their intrinsic conflict, accounts for the gratifications of normal motherhood (8).

Our discussion of the reproductive drive of woman has viewed the processes by which the drive, under coordinating hormonal stimulation, integrates in its organization the intrinsically interwoven processes of growth, maturation, and psychosexual development. The evolution of the ovarian cycle forces the emotional processes of adult women into regulated channels and shows how the pattern of the sexual cycle unfolds concomitantly with manifestations of those factors which determine the psychosexual development.

The analysis of the drive organization of motherhood and mother-liness reveals the interaction between two types of cycles which are involved in the reproductive function. One is short; in women it evolves conspicuously from menstruation to menstruation. The other is long; its span is from the beginning of the individual's existence, from being conceived and born as a female, to the time when she conceives, gives birth, and cares for her offspring. The psychodynamic tendencies which motivate maternal behavior originate in the alimentary symbiotic relationship which the mother-individual once experienced with her own mother. When in the course of the next generation she is the mother, her motherliness is motivated by the derivatives of the primary ego structures which she incorporated as an infant. Through her attitudes, she may convey them to her children, whether they become mothers or fathers of the next generation.

The long life cycle is reflected in the progesterone phase of the short cycle. Its monthly repetitions represent the processes by which the oral-receptive and anal-retentive phases, the pregenital-infantile levels of psychosexual organization, become transformed to motivate the genital reproductive maturity of woman. The teleological aim of the drive—to sustain the growth of the offspring—is affected by its ontogenic history. The psychodynamic tendencies which sustained survival and growth of the child by receiving, become organized toward the adult goal, that of giving and thus maintaining the offspring.

IV

At the beginning of this presentation it was pointed out that the male model of the reproductive organization does not explain the female reproductive function. What then does the phasic, female drive organization teach us about man?

Since man's reproductive function depends upon a single act, the motivation of which is experienced as a compelling desire for orgastic discharge, one might ask if there exists in man a primary, biological tendency toward becoming and being a father, a provider. Can we differentiate in man, as in woman, two goals of the reproductive drive?

In man as well as in woman, we can differentiate two arcs of the reproductive cycle. In the male the short cycle evolves without recognizable regularity, from one increase of compelling sexual urge to another.[14] Yet in the psychodynamic tendencies which prepare for and

14. Since the sexual apparatus of man is extremely susceptible to external and internal stimulation, it appears to be more under the influence of psychological mechanisms than under gonadal control—as if the semen, continuously produced and collected in its receptacles, is but waiting for stimulation to be released. A cyclical stimulation referable to the pattern of gonadal hormone function, possibly recognizable on careful examination,

accompany coitus we can find similarities. To highlight this, we may recall the "narcissistic state" of the woman which signalizes the peak of sexual receptiveness about the time of ovulation. The enhanced libidinal state is felt as a satisfying state of one's body. In man, the height of sexual stimulation is accompanied by a libidinal narcissistic tension which involves his whole body. This is prerequisite for his sense of vigor, essential for performing with pleasure his active role in procreation. In contrast to woman's ovulative response, man's intensified libidinal state can be described as an extraverted narcissism channelized in active, object-directed behavior which culminates in penetration and reaches its goal through orgastic discharge. With the consummatory act the male's reproductive function—the short arc—is finished and relaxation follows.

The long arc of the reproductive cycle evolves from the time of being conceived as a male to the time when he attains sexual maturity and is able to fulfill his function in procreation. Propagation is a special manifestation of growth. The individual, after having achieved maturity, surpasses the growth of his own body by producing a new individual. Under conditions which impede the reproductive function, such as sterility of either of the marital partners or enforced separation such as occurs during war, man's instinct for survival becomes conscious and accessible to study. Man's desire to survive, especially in the offspring of his own sex, is documented by rites and religions, by custom and socioeconomic organization. There need be no doubt that the male reproductive drive has psychic representations of instinctual, biological origin.

The question is whether we can differentiate in the male that organization which, paralleling motherliness, directs the reproductive drive toward fatherliness. Is there a biological tendency toward being a protector, a provider, toward raising offspring? I would answer this affirmatively, on the assumption that there are two sources of fatherliness; one is the biological bisexuality and the other is the biological dependency on the mother.

Regarding the first part of this assumption zoologists give us encouragement. In the reproductive functions of nonmammalian vertebrates they have found striking examples of a different distribution of courtship, preparatory activities, and, especially surprising to us, of the

---

seems to be nonexistent. There is an obvious variation of frequency and intensity depending on virility and potency; there is great variation in preparatory actions and their fantasy-stimulated effectiveness. These, however, are determined in men, as in women, by individual development. In humans, individual psychosexual development determines the pattern of preparatory actions of the drive. Cyclic oscillation of the reproductive drive can be more easily recognized in men with marked bisexual anlage.

caring for the young. In many instances the male takes over the care of the deposited ova and/or feeding of the young, as the instinctual organization of the species requires. Even in mammals there are examples of the male's participation in the care of the offspring. Nature seems to be able to reach deep into the bisexual propensities to meet the needs of adaptive processes in a species.

Our knowledge of man's bisexuality is, however, extremely limited. Investigations have been impeded by cultural denial. Thus far, hormone chemistry has helped us but little. Androgenic and estrogenic hormones, even progesterone, are closely related compounds; they occur in both sexes; their function and relation to symptoms are not clarified either by laboratory experiments or in clinical, therapeutic attempts.[15] Yet there seem to be hopeful signs that if reliable laboratory methods can be worked out, careful psychoanalytic studies may help to clarify the functions of "normal bisexuality" in man, just as it helps toward understanding the pathological drive "to be both sexes" (30).

The long-lasting dependence of the human infant is a biological characteristic of the species. This accounts for the significance that the oral-dependent phase of development has for the personality organization of individuals of both sexes. Every man's earliest security as well as his orientation to his world has been learned through identifications with his mother during the oral phase of development. In the normal course of development in the male, the early emotional dependence upon and identification with the mother is surpassed step by step through a developmental identification with the father directed by the innate maleness of the boy. This results not only in sexual competition with the father but also in multiple identifications with the various roles of the father as protector and provider. These secondary manifestations of maleness are in continual transaction with those primary psychic representations which were established as a result of the oral-dependent relationship with the mother.

The primary drive organization of the oral phase, the prerequisite and consequence of the metabolic needs which sustain growth, maturation, and lead to the differentiation of the reproductive function, is the origin of parental tendencies, of motherliness and fatherliness. It should then be emphasized, as is evident, that the primary drive organization of the oral phase has no sex differentiation; it is asexual. Yet its further differentiation toward the ego functions of fatherliness and motherliness

---

15. Animal experiments demonstrate that "infantile experiences" affect the neuromuscular mechanisms mediating sexual behavior in small mammals of both sexes; that hormones influence mating behavior as well as the reproductive potential (34). It is also demonstrated that infantile experiences affect the development of maternal instincts in small mammals (24). Psychobiological concepts elicited by psychoanalysis are becoming integrated with direct animal observations.

can be regarded as bisexual and emphasize that bisexuality means "sexual" only in a very limited area of its manifestations.[16]

Since physiological processes, tissue changes, are not involved in the functions of fatherliness, the drive organization which directs the passive receptive tendencies toward the active tendencies of feeding, protecting, and providing is but diffusely anchored in the bisexual anlage of the male. It reaches its goal by resolution of developmental conflicts—between male and female identifications and drive orientations—so that the adult male includes in his ego ideal his aspiration to complete his role in procreation by fatherliness.

The discussion has centered on the organization of the reproductive drive, to show that it is organized differently in the male and female to serve specific functions in procreation. We have also noted similarities in the psychodynamic trends of the function which has a reciprocal goal, namely, coitus. Another similarity of the drive organization originates in the human infant's experience of his biological dependence. This in its mature phase permits a limited alternation of the roles between the sexes in raising offspring.

The effect of the long-lasting dependence of the human child is that the maturation of the sexual function and the development of the personality are intricately interwoven processes. From the point of view of personality development the goal of maturation is the same in both sexes. Men and women alike reach their psychosexual maturity through the reconciliation of the sexual drive with the superego. This means that man is able to achieve sexual gratification only within the limits of his conscience.

The investigation of the sexual cycle does not contradict this effect of the cultural inheritance of mankind. On the contrary, it demonstrates that when the gonadal hormone triggers off a particular response pattern for each phase of the cycle, not only the drive and its action pattern are activated. The drive also recharges the intrapsychic processes which, through the development of the individual, have become stored in his psychic structure, in his ego and superego. Thus, parallel with the ongoing physiological effect of the hormonal stimulation, the psychic apparatus has to select the adequate response, adequate meaning which satisfies not only the physiological need, but also the internalized standards of the personality. This is true for both sexes. The gonadal hormones mobilize not only the drive but, along

16. Clinical observations of men's responses to their wives' pregnancy and lactation often reveal intensification of the tendencies toward such functions. In two instances the frustration of such emotional needs (because of the innate lack of possibility of fulfillment) was responsible for triggering off diabetes mellitus. The same emotional need often motivates regressions which lead to duodenal ulcer; much more often the regression which floods the mental apparatus with female reproductive tendencies leads to serious mental disturbances.

with it, the factors which inhibit the drive, postpone its gratification, negate its meaning and significance, and organize for its avoidance. It appears that the organizing and controlling functions of the ego and superego through the ontogenetic development of the individual become part and parcel of his physiological response pattern.

This expresses about man what Konrad Lorenz concludes regarding animals. He states, "Behavior patterns are not something which animals do or do not do, or do in different ways, but something which animals of a given species 'have got' exactly in the same manner as they 'have got' claws, or teeth, as a definite morphological structure" (31, pp. 32–33). It is more than an analogy to say that man, through his phylogenetic evolution, "has got" a physiological organization on account of which he "has got" to develop his ego, his consciousness and self-consciousness. Freud once referred to the superego as the most recent phylogenetic acquisition. And so it seems to be. As the superego develops with each individual, it participates in the organization of the sexual drive toward its mature function. It is the distinction of the species that in this process man may disguise the sexual drive, may distort its meaning and function.

BIBLIOGRAPHY

(1) Alexander, Franz (1935). "The Logic of Emotions and Its Dynamic Background." *Int. J. Psycho-Anal.,* **16,** 399–413.

(2) Altmann, M., Knowles, E., and Bull, H. D. (1941). "A Psychosomatic Study of the Sex Cycle in Women." *Psychosom. Med.,* **3,** 199–225.

(3) Beach, F. A. *Hormones and Behavior.* (New York: Hoeber, 1948.)

(4) Benedek, Therese, and Rubenstein, Boris B. (1942). *The Sexual Cycle in Women.* (Washington, D.C., National Research Council.) Republished in: Benedek, Therese. *Psychosexual Functions in Women.* (New York: Ronald Press, 1952.)

(5) Benedek, Therese (1949). "The Psychosomatic Implications of the Primary Unit: Mother-Child." *Amer. J. Orthopsychiat.,* **19,** 642. Republished in *Psychosexual Functions in Women,* op. cit. (4).

(6) ———— (1953). "On the Organization of Psychic Energy: Instincts, Drives and Affects." In: Grinker, Roy R. (ed.), *Mid-Century Psychiatry; An Overview.* (Springfield, Ill., Charles C. Thomas, pp. 60–75.)

(7) ———— (1956). "Toward the Biology of the Depressive Constellation." *J. Amer. Psa. Assn.,* **4,** 389–427.

(8) ———— (1956). "Psychobiological Aspects of Mothering." *Amer. J. Orthopsychiat.,* **26,** 272.

(9) Bernfeld, Siegfried (1941). "The Facts of Observation in Psychoanalysis." *J. Psychol.,* **12,** 289.

(10) Boas, C. van Emde (1955). "Variations of Libido during the Menstrual Cycle." *Int. J. Sexol.,* **8,** 214–219.

(11) Chadwick, Mary (1932). *The Psychological Effects of Menstruation.* (New York: Nervous and Mental Disease Publishing Co.) See also her *Women's Periodicity* (London: Noel Douglas, 1933.)

(12) Corner, George Washington. *The Hormones in Human Reproduction.* Rev. ed. (Princeton, N.J.: Princeton Univ. Press, 1947.)

(13) Dunbar, Helen Flanders. *Emotions and Bodily Changes: A Survey of Literature on Psychosomatic Relationships, 1910–1953.* 4th ed. (New York: Columbia Univ. Press, 1954.)

(14) Engel, George L. (1957). Discussion of original presentation of this paper, Twenty-Fifth Anniversary Meeting, Institute for Psychoanalysis, 16 November, 1957.

(15) Ewer, R. E. (1957). "Ethological Concepts." *Science,* **126,** 599–603, 27 September, 1957.

(16) Ferenczi, Sandor (1916). "Disease or Pathoneuroses." In his *Further Contributions to the Theory and Technique of Psycho-Analysis,* pp. 78–94. (London: Hogarth, 1926.)

(17) Fliess, Robert (1937). *Erogeneity and Libido.* (New York: Int. Univ. Press, 1957.)

(18) French, Thomas M. (1937). "Reality Testing in Dreams." *Psychoanal. Quart.,* **6,** 62–77.

(19) ——— *The Integration of Behavior.* (Chicago: Univ. of Chicago Press, 1951: in progress, to be complete in five volumes.)

(20) Freud, Sigmund (1915). "Instincts and Their Vicissitudes." *Standard Edition,* **14,** 117–140.

(21) ——— (1917). "A Metapsychological Supplement to the Theory of Dreams." *Standard Edition,* **14,** 223–235.

(22) ——— *An Outline of Psychoanalysis,* p. 23. (London: Hogarth, 1940.)

(23) Glover, Edward (1939). "The Psycho-Analysis of Affects." *Int. J. Psycho-Anal.,* **20,** 299–307.

(24) Goy, Robert W., and Young, W. C. (1957). "Somatic Basis of Sexual Behavior Patterns in Guinea Pigs; Factors Involved in the Determination of the Character of the Soma in the Female." *Psychosom. Med.,* **19,** 144–151.

(25) Hartmann, Heinz (1939). *Ego Psychology and the Problem of Adaptation.* (New York: Int. Univ. Press, 1958.)

(26) Hoskins, Roy Graham. *Endocrinology. The Glands and Their Functions.* Rev. and enlarged ed. (New York: Norton, 1950.)

(27) Jacobson, Edith. "The Affects and their Pleasure-Unpleasure Qualities in Relation to the Psychic Discharge Process." In: Loewenstein, Rudolph M. (ed.), *Drives, Affects, Behavior,* pp. 38–66. (New York: Int. Univ. Press, 1953.)

(28) Kestenberg, Judith S. (1956). "Vicissitudes of Female Sexuality." *J. Amer. Psa. Assn.,* **4,** 389.

(29) Kohut, Heinz. "Psychoanalysis and Introspection." Paper read at the Twenty-Fifth Anniversary Meeting, Institute for Psychoanalysis, Chicago, 16 November, 1957. To be published.

(30) Kubie, Lawrence S. "The Need to be Both Sexes (A Study of Virginia Woolf's *Orlando*)." Unpublished paper read to American Psychoanalytic Association.

(31) Lorenz, Konrad Z. *King Solomon's Ring.* (New York: Crowell, 1952.)

(32) —————"Psychologie und Stammesgeschichte." In: Heberer, Gerhard, ed. *Die Evolution der Organismen,* 2nd ed., rev. and enlarged, pp. 131–172. (Stuttgart: Fischer, 1954.)

(33) Menaker, Esther (1956). "A Note on Some Biologic Parallels between Animal Behavior and Moral Masochism." *Psa. Rev., 43,* 31–41.

(34) Seitz, Philip F. D. (1954). "Effects of Infantile Experiences upon Adult Behavior in Animal Subjects. I. Effects of Litter Size during Infancy upon Adult Behavior in the Rat." *Amer. J. Psychiat., 110,* 916.

(35) ————— (1958). "The Maternal Instinct in Animal Subjects." *Psychosom. Med., 20,* 215–226.

(36) Tinbergen, N. *The Study of Instinct,* p. 51. (Oxford: Clarendon Press, 1951.)

DISCUSSION

The "freedom from estrus" signifies that the reproductive goal of sexuality is separable in man from the "preparatory act" which is consummated in copulation. This seems to complicate, if not negate, the long-held hypothesis that in every living organism there is an instinct of self-preservation and an instinct of survival of the species. This is an experientially verified belief; it governs life. Instinct, however, is an elusive concept applicable to so many kinds of phenomena that its specific usefulness is doubted by many scientists. Yet "the concept is still needed."[1] What is instinct? Today we may define instincts as biologic and psychic organizers. This does not say what instinct is, but what instinct does. For Freud, instinct was the somatic source of psychic energy.

The concept of instinct ". . . somewhat obscure but indispensable to us in psychology . . ."[2] served Freud in the formulation of his dualistic concept of psychic processes as the struggle of contrasting energies, the source of which is the body as a whole. This is most clearly expressed in his last biologically conceived instinct theory[3] which focuses on the integrating (developmental) vs. the disintegrating forces characteristic of living systems. His earlier instinct theories were of another order. The first libido theory, contrasting the instinct of self-preservation with the instinct of the preservation of the species, and the second, setting ego instinct vs. sexual instincts, were generalizations which fitted well into German *Naturphilosophie.* Yet Freud quickly took recourse to biology.

Instinct is, as Freud said, "a concept of the frontier between the mental and the somatic."[4] This is a captivating metaphor since it implies both the dynamic and economic aspects of mental functions. It comprises the "dynamics" by referring to instinct as ". . . a constant force of stimulation from within the body," and the economy by defining the nervous system as an apparatus which has the function of getting rid of stimuli, or reducing them to the lowest possible level.[5] This statement expresses succinctly Fechner's "principle of constancy," which had become the basis of metapsychology.[6] Thus instinct as a concept ". . . on the frontier between mental and somatic . . ." was more than a metaphor. It implied also ". . . a measure of the demand made upon the mind for work in consequence of its connection with the body."[7] However, defining instinct according to its source, aim, object, and impetus, Freud actually formulated the concept of drive. He conceived of the mental representations of the processes induced by drives as derivatives of instincts. In the same paper Freud wrote, "I am altogether doubtful whether any decisive pointers for the differentiation and classification of instincts can be arrived at on the basis of working over the psychological material."[8]

The point of this discussion is to show that the psychoanalytic investigation of the sexual cycle revealed the links between the pregenital and genital levels of instinctual organization and thus uncovered the psychodynamic processes fundamental to the procreative function. It should be noted, however, that the investigation of the sexual cycle did not directly stimulate an investigation of the relationship between procreative physiology and the discoveries of the cycle research. It seems that two prerequisites had to be fulfilled: one was a greater distance from my own psychoanalytic concerns with problems of motherhood, etc.; the other was the formulation of a non-Freudian instinct theory which led directly to the somatic roots of psychologic processes.

I feel indebted to Lawrence Kubie for his series of illuminating publications in which he clarified the concept of instinct in biology and its meaning for psychology. His architectonic elaboration of instinct as organizing principle has been helpful in ordering the concepts pertinent to the organization of the procreative drive. This discussion has drawn freely from three of his publications which elaborate the biology of instincts and the mutual influence between instincts and their mental representations.[9]

A systematic presentation of instinct may appear farfetched in this discussion, yet only this can convey in such a short review the basic interrelatedness of "psychic" and "somatic," and the difference between "sexual" and "propagative," and the interrelatedness of them all. There are two groups of instincts: (1) primary, i.e., homeostatic instincts which are in the service of survival of the organism; and (2) secondary, i.e., sexual instincts which are in the service of survival of the species. Needless to say, Freud dealt only with the secondary instincts, or at least that is what he thought.

Kubie generalized from the functions of instincts that instincts are regulatory principles which function automatically, securing the survival of the organism.[10] Cannon refers to the concept of homeostasis when he defines instincts as coordinators of internal regulatory systems which maintain adaptive stabilization.[11] These definitions, as do any others that consider instinct an organizer of systems maintaining homeostasis, imply that the term "instinct" means that there must be interchange between the individual and his environment. Need and its gratification are alternating instinctual manifestations of all living organisms. Thus the term "instinct" refers to open systems.[12]

Since an interval of time between the need and its gratification is unavoidable, the consequences of the time gap are automatic components of instinctual behavior. The first consequence of the time gap is the warning mechanism that signals the forthcoming need before physiologic necessity arises. From a psychologic point of view it is of prime interest that ". . . psychologic processes can occur only where two time lags exist; i.e., the [hardly perceptible] interval between stimulus and response and the interval between synchronized tissue need and its alleviation."[13] This statement refers to the conceptual and structural difference between instinct as organizer and as drive which energizes the mechanisms that lead to alleviation of the need. The more complex the organism, the clearer is the differentiation between the coordinating principle and the anatomy of the physiologic processes which the drive induces. With increasing complexity of the physiologic processes, the time lag between need and its gratification also increases. The growing time lag calls for warning mechanisms of greater complexity. During the evolution of the species, these mechanisms brought about structures capable of symbolic processes which, in turn, influence the instinctual patterns.

It is alluring to imagine that the warning mechanisms stand at the philogenetic beginning of instinctual derivatives leading to the evolution of the mental apparatus. The instincts of homeostatic regulation are primary, vital instincts. They serve the regulation of breathing, water balance, food intake, elimination, and maintenance of tissue substance. This sequence is indicative of the difference in the urgency of the needs which the instinct represents. The sequence thus implies that respiration comes first; the time interval is shortest and no substitute or displacement exists for the substance required. Fluid is also absolutely necessary, but there is a widening temporal separation of intake and output phases which become even broader regarding food intake, elimination, and tissue maintenance. Thirst, a sensation caused by dryness of the mucous membrane of the mouth, cannot be quenched by psychic processes. The warning mechanism cannot be inhibited or reversed regarding respiratory or fluid needs. The possible reactions to frustration or deprivation are limited largely to panic and rage. Warning signals of hunger contractions, however, are almost wholly independent of immediate tissue needs. The warning mechanism can be repressed, inhibited, or exaggerated; thus a wider variety of psychic reactions is possible, bringing about a wider variety of behavior manifestations.

The circle of need → symbolic representation → activity of the instinct plus drive combination can be demonstrated in man even in that vital instinct which is characterized by the greatest immediacy of need, by the shortest time interval between need and gratification, i.e., breathing. We breathe because we need oxygen, but we normally breathe before air hunger arises, before the warning mechanism—anxiety— sounds the alarm. Although instincts represent demands which the body makes upon the mind, breathing illustrates that the mind has developed means by which it can modify instincts, albeit only to a degree. Yogis learn to control their oxygen need and delay breathing. In contrast, the dyspnea of hysterical individuals shows that anxiety may shorten the time lag and, by overbreathing, reverse the rhythm between need and gratification. This indicates that, "Even in the primary instincts . . . the relationships between the underlying biochemical processes and their psychologic representations are neither direct nor simple."[14]

Kubie has called attention to another seemingly neglected fact concerning primary instincts. "When instinctual behavior is viewed as serving the body by effecting the necessary interchange of substances with the outside world, the organ and the function around which all psychological representations focus must be the appropriate aperture."[15] This would have been a good way of conceptualizing the insight that Freud and Abraham must have had when they considered the organ of intake (the mouth) and the organs of elimination (the anus and the urethra) organs of libidinal, instinctual development during infancy. The role of ". . . the animate object [the mother] in the instinctual pattern varies . . ."[16] according to the primary instinctual needs which she supplements as "surrogate ego" for the infant.[17]

Since the symbolic representations of primary instinctual functions center around the apertures of organs that serve primary instincts, this seems to be the key to the mystery of how tensions which originate on the level of psychologic experience (whether conscious or unconscious) are converted into somatic disturbances. Kubie proposed this concept to explain the role of instincts in psychosomatic disorders. The significance of this concept for the genetic theory of psychoanalysis has already been mentioned. This elaboration of the theory of primary instincts gives firmer grounds for the biologic roots of psychoanalytic theory than is generally assumed, even by psychoanalysts today. In turn, psycho-analytic investigations can confirm and extend the heuristic value of Kubie's hypotheses by pointing out the reciprocal influence between primary instincts and psychologic processes.

It is surprising and gratifying to realize that the "apertural hypothesis" puts into the frame and language of biology the same idea that Alexander expressed in his vector concept (1935) and used for thirty years as the basis of his research in psychosomatic medicine.[18] Alexander's hypothesis means that emotions deprived of their ideational content are expressions of one or more fundamental directions that characterize biologic processes. The vector qualities which are expressed in the psychodynamic tendencies of intaking, retaining, and eliminating are psychic representations of instinctual processes and their related apertures. By omitting reference to organs, apertures, or erotogenic zones, Alexander equated primary instinctual patterns with the psychic representations of energy that motivate emotional processes. The two hypotheses complement each other. Both are necessary for the conceptualization of maturation of the secondary (sexual) instincts and their consequence in the organization of the procreative drive.

It has been pointed out that the discussion of the methods and the results of the investigation of the sexual cycle confirmed Alexander's hypothesis. The unconscious motivating factors of psychologic material could be defined precisely only in terms of psychodynamic tendencies. Psychodynamic tendencies represent forces which participate in metabolic processes; regarding the theory of instincts, they represent functions of the primary, homeostatic instincts. This means that when Freud formulated his libido theory on the basis of the sequence of maturational processes which produce libido he dealt with primary, homeostatic instincts and their influence upon the development of the mind.[19]

The gonadal hormone component and the related psychodynamic tendency represent a nucleus of the sexual instinct. Sexual instincts are secondary; their basic differences from primary instincts have been summarized by Kubie. (1) Intake from the outside world seems to play no direct or specific role in the sexual instinct. (2) It is not clear whether deprivation in tissue sense exerts influence in sexual matters. Complete abstinence is wholly compatible with the life of an individual. Therefore, (3) sexual deprivation seems to be significant primarily as a psychologic rather than a physiologic experience. (4) The biochemical substrata of sexual behavior have not been determined for either female or male.[20] Sexual instincts are in the service of procreation; they serve no metabolic needs and therefore involve lengthening intervals between need and gratification. This accounts for a greater complexity of symbolic processes which allow for complex psychic elaborations and distortions. Characteristic of man's sexual instinct is its plasticity.

It is assumed that "sexual energy," its "appetitive strength" and/or the "intensity of its consummatory behavior" (to use the terms of ethologists) are constitutionally given, individual characteristics molded by ontogenic development. Since it is assumed that the regulation of sexual need and activity is central, what role, if any, do hormones play in these processes? Hormones induce changes in the nervous system by affecting those systems that coordinate arousal and mating behavior.

"The courtship and mating activities of many vertebrate species represent one of the most clear-cut and specific types of hormone behavior and relationships," according to Beach.[21] No matter how accurate this statement may be for all species of vertebrates, it does not hold with the same stringency for infrahuman primates. History as well as current anthropologic and cultural changes screen the hormonal effects in man from the physiology of the procreative function; man, however, is the only exception.

Having become independent of the limitations of estrus, from the "obligation" to serve the survival of the species, the factors which promoted that basic, evolutionary fact continued to interact with intra-organismic and environmental conditions and increased the gap between sexual instinct and procreation. Molded by psychologic processes during the long time lag between infancy and sexual maturity, and by the network of instinctual derivatives, the secondary and tertiary elaborations of the instincts seem to break the boundaries of the sexual instinct itself. No instinctual process is governed by the body's biochemistry alone; even respiration becomes the nucleus of a complex psychologic superstructure. Regarding sexual instinct, the process appears reversed: the body's physiologic need is secondary; the activities of sexual behavior seem to be stimulated by psychologic processes. Whether or not they are perceptual—just a visual impression or intrapsychic motivations—it is generally known that the whole gamut of human emotions from love to hate, from tenderness to brutality, from happiness to sorrow, may find release, comfort, and consolation through sexual activity. These characteristics of the sexual instinct hold true for both sexes. In general, they integrate mating, the behavior which may or may not be in the service of procreation. The procreative function, the aim of the sexual instinct, harbors the problem, is it only a physiologic consequence of the sexual act, or has the drive organization of procreative physiology psychic representations? Is parenthood motivated by an instinctual drive?

The phasic nature of the female procreative function revealed the drive organization which is directed toward the procreative goal. The sexual cycle, its hormonal as well as its emotional manifestations, represents preparation for the procreative physiology of women. Our study of the sexual cycle reveals the interrelated phases of the procreative drive organization in women. The psychodynamic tendencies, repeated with each sexual cycle, demonstrate the role of the primary homeostatic instincts in the preparation for mature sexuality. The sexual cycle demonstrates the integration of those tendencies in the receptive and retentive tendencies which accompany ovulation. Originating in manifestations of primary instincts, ovulation and its psychodynamic superstructure indicate that motherhood has an instinctual origin; thus one may speak of "mother instinct" in scientific terms.

But what about men? Is there an instinct for procreation in man?

Man's intuition would respond to such a question with wonderment. How could it be otherwise? Yet it is not just a rhetorical question, raised to emphasize the difference in the organization of the procreative drive between male and female. Although the psychobiologic process which may accompany the maturation of spermatozoa does not appear accessible to investigation, we may assume that the principle is the same, i.e., sexual maturity is rooted in the preprocreative (pregenital) processes of growth and development.

Man's role in the preservation of the species is discharged in one act that does not involve tissue changes beyond the production and deposition of semen. These processes are under hormonal control. Thus the procreative function of the male complies with the definition of instinct, according to which instinctual pattern includes the drive organization and the psychodynamic superstructure of its function. This means that the procreative instinct—the instinct of preservation of the species—is invested in the genic pattern of the chromosome of the sperm cell, just as it is in the ovum of the female. The innate specificity of the procreative function expresses the fundamental difference between the sexes. The psychophysiologic organization of men serves one act, that of insemination; the psychophysiologic organization of women serves the function of pregnancy and motherhood.

This formulation again raises the question whether the procreative instinct has psychic representation expressed in fatherliness. Fatherliness is a mental attitude. On the basis of psychoanalytic investigations, we have proposed that it originates in the psychobiologic processes of the oral phase of development. To this I can only add here a reemphasis on the significance of the pregenital, i.e., preprocreative phase of development in the maturation of procreative sexuality. By this I refer not only to the organization of the personality but to the continual interactions between the underlying biologic forces and environmental influences which make the boy grow up to be a father. Since fatherliness has no known additional physiologic substrata, one could assume that fatherliness is the result of cultural processes only. But there is evidence of the opposite. Civilization did not create fatherliness, but man's instinctual need to survive in his offspring created civilization and cultures. Symbolic representations of man's need for fatherhood are manifest in religions, customs, and cultural and political institutions. We arrive at the conclusion that instincts function beyond the physiologic substrata through symbolic representations in the service of preservation of the species. It appears that the philosophical and common-sense classification of instincts prevails *sub specie aeternitatis:* there are instincts of self-preservation and instincts of preservation of the species.

The psychoanalytic study of the organization of the reproductive drive leads to a unitary concept of sexuality and personality. The correlations between the psychodynamic tendencies with the hormonal component of the instinct and/or the drive show that the physiology of the propagative function is not independent of, but interrelated to, psychosexual development. This conclusion confirms the phasic evolution of personality organization as Freud conceived of it in the libido theory. The investigation demonstrates that the psychodynamic tendencies are not sexual. They originate in the homeostatic instincts. This substantiates the assumption that pregenital libido is not sexual. Originating in the positive metabolic balance of life processes, it is the source of fatherliness as well as motherliness.

NOTES

1. Kubie, L. S., "The Central Representation of the Symbolic Process in Psychosomatic Disorders," *Psychosomatic Med.*, XV (1953), 1–7.

2. Freud, S., "Instincts and Their Vicissitudes" (1915), *Std. Ed.* XIV, 117–140.

3. Freud, S., "Beyond the Pleasure Principle" (1920), *Std. Ed.*, XVIII, 7–64.

4. Freud, S., "Instincts and Their Vicissitudes" (1915), *Std. Ed.*, XIV, 122.

5. Ibid., p. 120.

6. Fechner, G. T., "Ideen zur Schöpfungs und Entwicklungs Geschichte der Organismen" (1873), quoted by Freud, S., "Beyond the Pleasure Principle," *Std. Ed.*, XVIII, 8–9.

7. Freud, S., "Instincts and Their Vicissitudes," p. 124.

8. Ibid.

9. Kubie, L. S., "Instinct and Homeostasis," *Psychosomatic Med.*, X (1948), 15–29; "The Central Representation of the Symbolic Process in Psychosomatic Disorders," *Psychosomatic Med.*, XV (1953), 1–7; "The Influence of Symbolic Processes on the Role of Instincts in Human Behavior," *Psychosomatic Med.*, XVIII (1956), 190–206.

10. Kubie, L. S., "Instinct and Homeostasis," *Psychosomatic Med.*, X (1948), 15–29.

11. Cannon, W. B., *The Wisdom of the Body* (1932), (New York, W. W. Norton, 1963).

12. When Freud theorized about instincts as originating in the body and representing demands on the mind, physiology was not yet advanced to the point of investigation of processes beyond the organism itself.

13. Kubie, L. S., "Instinct and Homeostasis," p. 19.

14. Ibid., p. 21.

15. Kubie, L. S., "The Central Representation of the Symbolic Process in Psychosomatic Disorders," *Psychosomatic Med.*, XV (1953), 3.

16. Kubie, L. S., "Instinct and Homeostasis," p. 28.

17. It is interesting to note that the aperture of breathing, the nose, was not assumed to be an erotogenic zone. Since the time gap is so short and since breathing is regulated instinctually, in the psychologic sense it is automatic. The mother as a supplement to instinctual function is not neces-

sary (except in a crisis). Breathing is not a source of the development of primary object relationship.

18. Alexander, F., "The Logic of Emotions and Its Dynamic Background," *Int. J. Psycho-Anal.,* XVI (1935), 399–413; *Psychosomatic Medicine* (New York, W. W. Norton, 1950).

19. Freud must have been clearly aware of this when he considered libido as integrating energy in "Beyond the Pleasure Principle."

20. Although I assume that the integration of psychodynamic tendencies which accompany ovulation indicates that there is a substratum for being impregnated, it does not necessarily energize the wish or the behavior which could lead to impregnation.

21. Beach, F. A., *Hormones and Behavior* (New York, Hoeber, 1948), p. 270.

16. Discussion of "The Evolution and the Nature of Female Sexuality in Relation to Psychoanalytic Theory" by Mary Jane Sherfey

INTRODUCTION

The following paper, published originally as a discussion of the problems raised by Dr. Sherfey's paper, gives opportunity to enlarge upon the nature of the sexuality of both sexes as it functions in seeming independence of its procreative goal.

What is sexuality? Everyone knows what it is, yet it is rare to find an all-encompassing definition.[1] *Sexuality is a complex manifestation of the sum total of the species-specific processes necessary for the survival of the species.* This definition includes both aspects of behavioral organization which accomplish the survival of the species. It also expresses the fundamental difference between Sherfey's and my own concept of the "nature" of female sexuality. Sherfey considers it to be in the woman's capacity for orgasm; I consider the "nature" of female sexuality to lie in its role in procreation. Orgasm itself is not a necessary requirement for the achievement of its biologic aim.

NOTES

1. *Oxford English Dictionary*. "Sexuality: the quality of being sexual or having sex. According to a strict biological definition sexuality is the characteristic of the male and female elements (genoblasts) and the sex of the individuals in which the reproductive elements arise. A man has sex, a spermatozoa sexuality."

Webster's New International Dictionary by G. & C. Merriam Co., Second Edition (1944). "Sexuality: quality or state of being sexual; possession or exercise of sexual functions, appetites, etc. Sexual dimorphism: biol: the condition of having one of the sexes existing in two forms or varieties."

MARY JANE SHERFEY: "THE EVOLUTION AND NATURE OF FEMALE SEXUALITY IN RELATION TO PSYCHOANALYTIC THEORY"[1]

DISCUSSION[2]

New discoveries in embryology, physiology, and in the most recent branch of the behavioral sciences, ethology, seem to be lifting the veil from the enigma of female sexuality that has puzzled mankind from time immemorial. Freud in his last paper on the subject[3] frankly stated that psychoanalysis has not solved the "riddle of femininity" since "what constitutes masculinity or femininity is an unknown characteristic which anatomy cannot lay hold of."[4] He added, "The explanation must no doubt come from elsewhere, and cannot come till we have learnt how in general the differentiation of living organisms into two sexes came about."[5] Biology has not advanced far enough to give this ultimate answer, yet strides have been made in the direction of understanding the sexual behavior of both sexes. This new knowledge confronts psychoanalysis with the necessity of investigating its own concepts and by developing them further, to participate in capturing the "essence" of femininity, a task which will probably remain in the domain of psychology.

Two recent publications offer psychoanalysts an opportunity to confront their concepts of female sexuality with some of the new discoveries in the field of biology. Masters and Johnson[6] have enlarged our knowledge of the physiology of the human sexual response, and Sherfey brings us highly interesting information regarding the *inductor theory of primary sexual differentiation* developed during the last two decades.[7] Sherfey's paper, as described by the author, "is the initial product of a fairly global approach to the study of man, requiring familiarity with physiology, anatomy, comparative embryology, endocrinology, gynecology, palaeontology, evolutionary biology, population genetics, primatology, and ethology—not to mention anthropology and psychiatry, the central foci upon which the rest converge."[8] Her paper reflects the many-sided orientation of the author and stimulates a review of the psychoanalytic concept of bisexuality in our theory of personality development and adult sexual behavior. My essay will refer first to Sherfey's extrapolations from the theory of primary sexual differentiation, and will then discuss the nature of woman's sexuality in its interrelatedness with and dependence upon the sexuality of man.

The method of direct observation employed by Masters and Johnson in their investigation of the physiology of sexual stimulation and orgasm reveals phenomena which are not accessible to psychoanalysts. Significant as the results of these investigations are for psychoanalysis, it is not impossible that, being presented with little reference to psychoanalytic theory, they might have remained more or less unappreciated without Sherfey's challenging confrontation. Her conclusions concerning the significance of the recent discoveries of embryology, evolutionary biology, and physiology deserve careful examination as to their relevance for psychoanalytic theory.

Sherfey uses the "inductor theory of sexual differentiation" to explain why the classical theory that the embryo is innately bisexual is outdated. On the basis of this she assumes that the role of bisexuality in psychoanalytic theory is also outdated. Actually, evidence offered by research in endocrinology and ethology seems to support what Freud refers to as our having "transferred the notion of bisexuality to mental life."[9] I shall review this evidence as it bears on the nature of female sexuality elaborated in this paper.

Jacques Loeb[10] established at the beginning of this century that genic sex is determined at conception. The discovery that the sexual morphology of embryos of both sexes is primarily female had to wait almost half a century. It was generally assumed by embryologists that structural differentiation stems from an undifferentiated condition. New observations, however, contradict this and demonstrate an initial stage of femaleness, the duration of which differs according to species. In humans it lasts five to six weeks. Then the influence of the sex genes begins to be exerted and brings to the fore the latent maleness of the genetically male embryo. The primordial testes begin to produce androgens which induce the transformation of the until-then female genital anlage into the male growth pattern. After the twelfth week the masculine nature of the reproductive tract is fully established.

Psychoanalysts can learn from this that embryonic development of the female is autonomous, that only the male embryo is required to undergo differentiating transformation of the genital anatomy. If this knowledge had been available to Freud, he would have corrected his views that nature equipped the woman less adequately for her complex reproductive function than it equipped man for his simpler function in the survival of the species. This information would have directed his inquiry, as it has that of Sherfey, toward evolutionary biology and probably he would have come to the conclusion that natural selection, the great constructor, had to find exactly this solution in order to prepare females of all species for their complex double function and thus secure survival of the species.

But does this abolish the significance of "bisexuality" in the theory of the psychosexual development of both sexes?

Much time has passed since Freud transferred Wilhelm Fliess's notion of bisexuality[11] (but not his romantic application of it) to mental life. Since then it has become so integrated into the thinking of psychoanalysts that the concept is applied almost unconsciously. Our concept of bisexuality, however, adds dimensions of psychology and social influences that broaden the understanding of human sexuality. In our language, the term "bisexuality" refers to a specific predisposition to certain psychological reactions to environmental influences which exert control over the development of the personality. Infants of both sexes introject memory traces of responses to both parents. The complex learning during the oral phase of development occurs primarily through identification with the mother in boys and girls alike. The theory of identification has become an integral part of learning theory in general. This implies the basic assumption that children of both sexes have a biological predisposition to develop empathic responsiveness to individuals not only of their own, but also of the opposite sex; without this, communication between the sexes would not be possible. Yet such communication is a prerequisite for establishing a relationship between the sexes, be it "love" (in its most individualistic romantic sense) or "just sex." Observations of ethologists describe some primate behavior that could be considered "empathic,"[13] although empathy is valued as an exclusively human attribute since one assumes that the social behavior of animals is strictly under hormonal control. Yet the knowledge that hormones enter the brain may sooner or later narrow the gap between man and other primates. Thus our present knowledge based on investigations in endocrinology and ethology tends to confirm the psychoanalytic concept of bisexuality as a basic concept of personality theory.

It is beyond the scope of this paper to give a consistent summary of observations which demonstrate that sexual dimorphism is complete only in the area of the reproductive function. For the sake of simplicity and clarity, however, I quote Sherfey: "In their somatic organization, the gonads always retain a greater or lesser amount of the opposite-sex tissue which remains functional throughout life. The amount of androgen-producing tissue developed by the ovaries (and adrenals) and the amount of estrogen-producing tissue retained in the testes (and adrenals) are genetically fixed and species-specific."[14] Thus an abundance of opposite-sex hormones in the fetal stage affects each sex, influencing its development toward the potential for behavioral manifestations characteristic of the opposite sex.

There is the question whether the brain by itself, or because of having been influenced by sex hormones that enter the brain, might have a special propensity in one direction or another.[15] Beach comes to the following conclusion: "The potential contribution of constitutional factors can be regarded as an unresolved issue. It is at least conceivable that there are sex differences in the functional characteristics of the male and female brain, that such differences are manifest at birth, and that they have some effect upon the acquisition of social behavior tendencies including learning the gender role."[16] Endocrinologic evidence seems to confirm Freud's courage in transferring the notion of bisexuality to mental life.[17]

Freud struggled with the problems of female sexuality without reconciling the contradiction which existed between his concepts expressed in his paper, "Some Psychical Consequences of the Anatomical Differences between the Sexes" (1925)[18] and his libido theory.[19]

Within the frame of his first instinct theory Freud[20] defined libido as the psychic representation of sexual energy, "a force that is felt," that is accessible to experience. Implicit in the assumption that libido is a manifestation of energy is the consequent assumption that libido is "active" and therefore attributable to "masculinity" in contrast to "passive," which is equivalent to "femininity." In the second instinct theory, however, libido is not considered a manifestation of sexual energy referable to sexual drive alone, but is defined more broadly as "integrating energy striving for establishing greater unities."[21] In his last paper on the subject of femininity, Freud applied this concept: "Sexual life is dominated by the polarity of masculine-feminine; thus the notion suggests itself of considering the relation of libido to this antithesis . . . But there is only one libido, which serves both the masculine and the feminine sexual functions. To itself we cannot assign any sex."[22]

Freud's emphasis on the nonsexual nature of libido did not help resolve the culturally habituated assumption which is supported by the experience of the sexual act. Considering that the sexual drive aims at gratification, one can maintain that the sexual drive of the man differs from that of the woman since the man's drive is directed actively toward its aim of discharge, while the woman awaits the gratification of her desire which is biologically receptive and therefore assumed to be achieved passively.

Indeed, Freud did not assume that his concept of libido as nondifferentiated psychic energy would undermine the theory that woman's psychosexual maturity is achieved by overcoming a "prehistoric" male anlage which manifests itself in clitoral sexuality and penis envy, which are the "rock-bottom" conflicts in women.[23] Thus it was assumed that the struggle against her bisexuality is the universal biological "destiny" of woman. The conflicts originating in the bisexual tendencies of men were considered exceptional, determined by particular factors in the development of the individual.

It is highly comforting and gratifying for psychoanalysts to find psychoanalytic observations confirmed by physiological research, even to learn that unsatisfactory therapeutic results can be explained by adherence to false theoretical assumptions. The clinical significance of the clarification of sexual physiology cannot be overestimated. But it is just as important to evaluate how far-reaching are the conclusions drawn from it. What does it alter in the theory of human development?

The fact that male morphology evolves from a primarily female embryologic anlage does not say anything about the "nature" of female sexuality, or about the sexual drive of either sex. It appears that Sherfey, like Freud, has been trapped by anatomy. I am not in a position to discuss the evolutional changes in anatomic structures of the female genitalia which, according to Sherfey, "enhanced female sexuality rather than lessening it."[24] The more we know about the complexity of sexuality, the more research is necessary to find the links between those biological processes which are not bound to anatomic structures (such as instincts and drives) and the ways in which they direct and influence the functions of structures. We know that hormones are in the service of the "grand design." But they are responsible neither for the intensity of the drive nor for the orgasmic capacity of the individual. The brain is the relay station and the integrator of instincts, drives, and physiological mechanisms, but as an anatomical structure it does not produce behavior.

A great, unsurpassed scientific feat of Freud was the discovery that the maturation of sexuality from infancy to its reproductive capacity is the axis of the development of the psychosexual personality. The inseparable and interrelated processes of physiological maturation and mental development lead to an integration which enables the individual to find gratification of his sexual drive within the requirements of the culture in which he was reared and/or lives. The idea that "genital primacy" is achieved by overcoming the castration complex was expanded by Abraham.[25] He conceived of it as the necessary developmental goal of "overcoming the fear of the other sex" to achieve the sex-determined role in coitus. This, however, includes more than the maturation of the sexual drive; it implies the intrapsychic controls and integration of value systems which are incorporated in the psychic structures of superego and ego ideal. These developmental processes from infancy through adolescence into adulthood influence the drive itself. While they may modify, complicate, and inhibit it, they give the drive its specific human quality on the basis of which lasting relationships, social organizations, and cultures evolve.

From the point of view of ego ideal and superego development the goal of the adolescent phase of maturation is the same for both sexes. Men and women reach their psychosexual maturity through the reconciliation of sexual drives with the requirements of their superegos. In their ego ideals they have to integrate the responsibilities of the reproductive function with other aspirations of their personalities. However, when we consider the sexual drive in relation to its goal of procreation, the difference between the sexes is biologically determined.

The sexual drive is organized differently in male and female in order to serve the sex-determined reproductive function. From the point of view of evolutionary biology and its manifestations in procreative physiology, this is evident. Yet it was hidden by psychoanalytic theory which, having been derived from observations of neurotic women in the Victorian era and because of lack of basic knowledge, misused the concept of bisexuality and assumed that sexual maturity and genital primacy referred to identical drive organizations. A man's reproductive function requires only one act that is consummated in coitus, climaxing in orgasm. According to the model, the psychosexual maturity of woman was characterized by a genital primacy that, parallel to male orgasm, culminates in vaginal orgasm. According to this idea, vaginal orgasm implies a transfer of clitoral sensation to the vagina, thus eliminating the residual male organ[26] from the experience of a woman. This concept was made a measure of psychosexual maturity and often the goal of psychoanalytic treatment.

Sherfey has given ample evidence of the fact that orgasm is a unified process, that neither clitoral nor vaginal orgasm exists separately; she has also emphasized that the morphology and the physiology of the female genitalia develop to facilitate the reproductive goal—to receive the ejaculate of the male.

The biological aim of receptivity in the sexual act of the female leads not only to the evolution of the anatomic structures but also to the organization of the woman's sexual drive to serve the phasic nature of the female reproductive function. Mating for the female is only a preparatory act. Pregnancy and lactation constitute the completion of the reproductive cycle. But the drive organization which motivates pregnancy and lactation is not "genital" in the same sense as mating behavior. Besides this, the female reproductive function undergoes phasic preparation for impregnation that is repeated at regular intervals in correspondence with the ovarian hormone cycle.

Sherfey's paper does not deal with the female procreative physiology or with its possible influence upon the psychosexual propensities of women. Therefore a lengthy discussion of these problems has been omitted. However, because of its relevance to the problems of the "nature" of female sexuality, I repeat my earlier conclusions: The sexual cycle, i.e., the integration of the hormonal cycle with the organization of the reproductive drive, demonstrates that (1) the nature of female sexuality is not explained by the theory of the primary sexual differentiation nor by the physiology of orgasm, but by that complex organization of a woman's personality which enables her to fulfill her function in the reproduction of the species. (2) The human female is free from the restriction of estrus. Yet her drive organization reveals a peak in her hormone production that has the same biological significance as heat in animals. If impregnation does not occur, the lutein phase of the cycle—similar to the calm period in animals—becomes a calm, introverted period of physiological and emotional preparation for pregnancy. For (3) the specific attributes of femininity originate in that "indwelling quality"[27] of woman's psyche which is the manifestation and result of the central organization of receptive-retentive tendencies of the reproductive drive that becomes the source of motherliness.

Our investigations thus demonstrated that in spite of the complex and variable superstructure of the human personality, in spite of the multi-level interpersonal and intrapsychic motivations of behavior, in the motivational pattern of sexual behavior the correlated hormonal factors can be recognized. It is, however, necessary to qualify this statement. The psychic apparatus registers the change in the quality of gonadal hormones but not their quantitative increase. When the sexual desire is gratified, the psychic elaboration of sexual needs seems to become unnecessary. If sexual gratification recurs frequently, the anticipated gratification keeps the need tension on an even keel. The emotional reactions to frustration are not parallel to the intensity of the need or to the quantity of the hormones, since these also depend on the personality of the woman. This is somehow different during the lutein phase of the cycle; then the physiological change in the uterus, the vasocongestion that prepares the uterus for nidation, is often manifest in symbolic representations of the uterus in dreams. This often makes it possible to quasi-follow the progress of this phase of the cycle, not in an increasing sexual excitation but rather in the symbolic emotional manifestations of motherhood and the symbolic representations of its organ, the uterus. This contradicts Sherfey's concept of sexual drive.

Sherfey describes in the primate female an insatiable sexual excitation "that continues to exist in woman"[28] leading to a state of *"satiation-in-insatiation."*[29] The process which Sherfey describes originates in the vasocongestion in the pelvic organs, which are not completely drained by orgasm. The vasocongestion brings about a vicious circle, especially in multiparas, enhancing the sexual need with each orgasm by increasing the vasocongestion. Its manifestation, however, would not be due to the sexual drive of woman just as the insatiable need resulting from priapism cannot be called sexual drive in men suffering from that condition. Neither "drive" nor libido is produced in the organ of stimulation or in its discharge.

The same may be said about the sex hormones. The gonadal hormones are not the "source" of the drive; they are responsible neither for the intensity of the drive nor for the organization of the personality. "Sex hormones are facilitating agents which by changing threshold values allow specific nervous mechanisms of sexual behavior to be more readily stimulated."[30]

The strength of the drive is a biological attribute of the individual and so is the strength of the ego, the agency which controls the drives and leads them through the organized channels of the personality to their biological aim. The personality, its genetic and economic organization, and its developmental past and internalized control systems determine the ideational content of the affects and emotions and also the ego's ways and means of dealing with them. Consequently, on the organization of the total personality depends the "quantity" of libido which is available to fill the channels in response to sexual stimulation.

Abstract and generalized as these statements are, they will suffice to focus our attention on the fact that not independent of its physiology but interrelated to it, *the human sexual response is an experience of the total personality*. It is even more complex: *human sexual experience is the outcome of a transactional process between two individuals, normally of different sex*.

The success of this process, however natural it appears to be, is burdened by many problems. Much has been written about these, especially since orgasm as an "equal birthright of women" has focused attention on the problematic nature of women's capacity for orgasm. This is the main point of Sherfey's argument based on the discoveries of Masters and Johnson. Accordingly, Sherfey assumes that the process of orgasm, if started, follows the same course to completion in women as in men. Frigidity has been considered either a biological characteristic of the female sex[31] or a derivative of personality development, i.e., a neurotic symptom. In either case it is regarded as independent of the physiology of the sexual response which involves both sexes. One significance of Masters and Johnson's research lies in the fact that it reveals not only the physiological similarities but also the inherent differences in the male and female sexual response patterns.

The four distinct phases through which coitus—or any sexual manipulation—moves toward orgasm have been reviewed in Sherfey's presentation in detail, but without the psychological corollaries that might contribute to or impede the woman's orgasm. The physiological differences create problems which, if not solved by compatible sexual responsiveness, must be compensated for by psychological means for the woman to achieve orgasm.

One of the differences in the sexual response is the tumescent reaction of the clitoris during the excitement phase with its consequent retraction into the clitoral hood (prepuce) which functions like a "miniature vagina" during the plateau phase.[32] If stimulation is reduced, the retracted clitoris descends, i.e., regains its normal size in the buildup of the orgasmic platform at the outer third of the vagina. The clitoris and the lower third of the vagina constitute a functional unit. This "drawing in" of the clitoris, instead of the erectile tension outward, appears like a structural model of our assumption that a specific tendency toward introversion and deep-rooted passivity is characteristic of the female reproductive drive.

The other characteristic of the clitoris is that while its reaction and descent can be repeated several times during an orgasmic process, the stimulation has to be maintained until the orgasmic release is completed, since the woman's orgasmic process is interrupted at any point of the response pattern if stimulation ceases. This is incontestable evidence of the fact that a woman's orgasm is not an autonomous process. In contrast, the male organ, i.e., its manifestation in ejaculation, is autonomous, even reflexive. When through the excitement and plateau phases it reaches the point of full testicular elevation, the sensation of impending ejaculation is unmistakable and also uncontrollable. However emphatic one may be about woman's capacity for orgasm, about the response patterns "which unfold whenever they (women) are sexually aroused . . . with the same regularity of sequential events that has long been known to occur in the sexual cycles of men,"[33] the evolution of the response pattern depends on the male's ability to maintain effective stimulation.

What is "effective stimulation"? Sherfey defines effective stimulation as that to which the woman responds with immediate vasocongestion of all pelvic organs. This answer, however, cannot hold true since the initial physiological response to stimulation does not necessarily lead to orgasm. Indeed, there cannot be a generally valid answer to this question since innumerable physiological and psychological variables influence the course of the physiological response pattern, affecting the experience of women much more than that of men.

In the following I shall try to account for some of the psychological factors which modify women's sexual responsiveness; some psychological factors may facilitate orgasm, others may inhibit it, especially during the lasting relationship of marriage.

Beginning with an unknown physiological and emotional "chemistry" that is experienced as sexual attraction, a flood of libido quickens the sexual response in the man and in the woman. The heightened libidinal state is felt as a satisfying state of one's own body and gives rise to libidinal sensations in the genitals (erection or readiness for it in men and a sensation of moisture in the vagina in women). This sets in motion the "modes of behavior" which maintain reciprocal stimulation until the initial reaction becomes a satiating orgasmic experience. Modes of behavior imply the manifestations of emotions as well as the techniques of love-making; their reciprocal effectiveness depends on the intuitive awareness of the needs of the other. While the physiology of the sexual response is universal, the modes of behavior that bring about orgasm have innumerable variations. From these each man and each woman adopt a few. Motivated by the unconscious representations of their developmental past, these modes are now charged with the current flow of libido and help to arrive at the completion of the mutual experience.

It is well known that lovers in marriage, or outside of it, learn each other's special requirements for stimulation and also the tempo of their physiological changes from the point of initial arousal to the orgasmic experience. When the initial impact of attraction diminishes and formalization of the coital act slowly takes place, the intensity of orgasm diminishes as well. Since the woman's excitement phase, unlike the man's, gets longer rather than shorter through experience with the same partner, the disparity of tempo between the partners increases, leaving the woman unsatiated. This, however, instead of leading to increased sexual desire, as Sherfey on the basis of vasocongestion would assume, more often leads to the woman's losing interest in the sexual act.

Sherfey, on the basis of physiology, assumes that women cannot speed the excitement phase by the use of conscious devices. It is pertinent to the understanding of the orgasmic experience of women to refute this generalization. It is well known that in their autostimulative experiences, women dose the plateau phase and reach orgasm by increased myotonia and by meaningful fantasies. The same happens in intercourse. Women who love their husbands do not flaunt the discrepancy in their sexual tempo but rather help to diminish its effects with the help of their fantasies. Intuitively they know that such adaptation not only aids the husband in maintaining his sexual self-esteem but also assists the wife in preserving a harmonious marriage.

At this point it is worthwhile to include the significance of fantasies in the orgasmic experience of women. Fantasies which play a role preparatory to intercourse and during the excitement phase may vary greatly in the same woman; the "effective fantasy" which is used in the plateau phase to lead to orgasm is usually a typical fantasy, developed from pregenital sexual fantasies often before or during adolescence, which permits elaborative but not basic changes. Although these fantasies have individual variations, masochistic contents with rare sadistic elements prevail to such an extent that their frequency justifies considering them in the light of our present knowledge of sexual physiology. Probably the muscle contractions involved in preorgasmic tension and orgasmic release, which extend beyond the musculature of the pelvic organs to the musculature of the thighs and buttocks, are the physiological substratum of erotogenic masochism. The myotonia that involves the whole body is a component of the physiology of orgasm and it may account for the effectiveness and the persistence of these fantasies. It is in the nature of the "expectant" sexual behavior of women, whose orgasm is physiologically dependent upon the stimulation by their men, that women fantasy more during the coital act than men do.[34]

Masters and Johnson point out some of the psychological factors that influence the sexual behavior of men. They observed the concentration necessary to maintain erection and the emotional significance for men of the ability to maintain erection. Men can lose their erections as a result of any interference, even an insignificant one, coming from external sources, from a gesture of the sexual partner, or from internal sources such as their own fantasies or anxieties. Often the loss of erection may occur before the man becomes aware of what caused the distraction. Masters noticed that his male subjects were more inhibited by preoccupation with their "performance" than were the women.

It is a biological characteristic of man that he be dominant and by achieving orgasm impregnate his mate. It is a cultural achievement that requires men to be concerned also with the sexual gratification of their women. As was pointed out before, it is the integration of the psychosexual personality that, through multiple identifications with both parents and with other "significant objects," fosters in children of both sexes the potential for empathic responsiveness to individuals of the other sex. Only this makes it possible for the sexual response to be completely human; by achieving sexual gratification for himself man also aspires to the gratification of the other, the object of his love. In this statement I have changed the pronoun and refer to the male sex only, since it has been the reasoning of biology that from time immemorial this was considered the man's sexual role. It is probably for the same biological reason that such complete orgasmic experience elevates the man's ego state beyond what is the result of sexual gratification alone. Such experience consolidates a man's sexual identity as it also forges the link of identification with the woman who enabled him to achieve such an experience of his virility.

A similar integration of her sexual identity occurs in the woman as a result of such mutually gratifying orgasmic experience. Yet a woman's sexual identity does not depend on orgasm to the same degree that a man's does. This is a consequence of the difference in the meaning of orgasm in the personality organization of both sexes. While the male response is concentrated on the penis and on supporting its active function, the extragenital body involvement of women is more diffuse. Her sensual experience, stirred by feelings of being lovable and loved, caressed and cherished, overflows to her sexual partner to share his experience with love.[35] But the kind of elated reaction to this achievement which men experience after satisfactory orgasm, women frequently describe after parturition. Then the feeling of a "job well done," having produced a "miracle," flows over the woman's personality and encompasses her child in her psychic self. Such ego growth indicates that woman's sexual identity is invested more in her aspiration to bear children and be a mother than in orgasm.[36]

It is a cultural shift in the relationship between the sexes that has put undue emphasis upon the orgasm of women without an accurate knowledge of its physiology. This has led to one kind of confusion, but "accurate" knowledge of physiology may lead to another kind of confusion if one assumes that her "inordinately high level of . . . a fundamental 'masculinelike' sexual drive"[37] makes the woman responsible for the course of the sexual act. Present knowledge of sexual physiology necessitates the understanding of the coital interaction as a physiological, a psychological, and, in any case, a conjugal process. For this reason I am emphasizing the ego's participation in the sexual experience. This plays a larger role in the sexual behavior of women than in men.

Actually this statement needs no further explanation unless one does not want to neglect the obvious (since it is taken for granted as known). At the same time this seems to be in contradiction to Masters and Johnson's observation that men are more preoccupied with their sexual performance than women are, for obvious reasons. Yet these two statements complement each other. Man's need to prove himself by his sexual power motivates his total investment in the act itself. Woman's ego has a somewhat broader range in the act; she perceives not only herself but also her mate; because of the longer duration of her emotionally passive-receptive attitude, she fantasies and "plans" the next step in their relationship.

This description or many others which one might make about the ego's participation in the sexual experience depend on the developmental integration of the sexual drive and the psychosexual personality. Of course, this encompasses the ego too.[38] Here, however, I wish to point out that the ego in interaction with the drive experiences in each and any phase of its development may build up defenses which make free experience of orgasm impossible.[39] This is true for both sexes, but man's potency is less frequently affected than woman's capacity for orgasm. Women's fertility, however, is rarely affected in comparison with the frequency of frigidity. Biological and psychological factors interact in causing the vulnerability of woman's capacity for orgasm. Her biological receptivity embodied in her genital morphology accounts for the woman's relative dependence for orgasm upon her sexual partner. The dependence often causes sexual fear, shame in revealing herself, reluctance to expose her specific needs to her sexual partner. Although we consider these emotional factors culturally motivated, and thus capable of being eliminated by a change in sexual mores, psychoanalytic as well as ethologic observations hint at basic instinctual roots which are an integral part of the sexual response pattern.[40]

Another type of psychophysiological factor which has been built into the orgasmic process might mobilize defenses against its full evolution. Transient ego regression is a component of the orgasmic capacity in both sexes. Even without or before orgasm, sexual passion may be experienced as a loosening of ego boundaries. This brings about the elation which accompanies the experience of physical and emotional union. Unconscious fear of ego regression may impede the orgasmic capacity of men; this, however, happens more frequently in women. Since her sexual experience is diffuse, this regression often feels to her as a loss of herself. Many women experience this regression in the ego state—a psychological precursor to orgasm—as an intolerable threat. Sometimes this is described as a fear of becoming helpless, of being completely at the mercy of uncontrollable impulses, and of being unable to become oneself again. A significant dynamic factor in such excitement is a threatening dissociation of affects which interferes with the woman's loving union with her mate and brings to the fore aggressive tendencies toward him. Thus the preorgasmic excitement mobilizes the woman's apprehension that her ego ideal, her self-esteem, might collapse. Therefore, the ego's defenses against regression become intensified and may lead to inhibition of the orgasmic experience, no matter what effective stimulation is applied. This is a description of the psychological process which often leads to frigidity in ambitious and passionate women whose intensely libidinal response to premarital foreplay gives promise of a most gratifying sexual life; yet they often do not achieve full orgasm.

This problem has been brought up to indicate that sexual passion is not identical with capacity for orgasm. To endure passion the individual must be able to submit to increasing sexual tension without anxiety; she must be able to accept change in her behavior and in her body without shame. In some women the signal anxiety accompanying incipient sexual excitement—an anxiety that is normally overcome by the rhythmically increasing waves of libidinal tension—may activate ego controls that suppress the orgasmic process. Thus the psychological prerequisite of undisturbed orgasmic capacity in women is an ego organization which enables her to accept her role in coitus. This means, for the sake of brevity, to accept her sexual drive and its manifestations as part of her total personality, and to be able and willing to adjust her sexual responses to the sexual dominance and/or responsiveness of her mate.

To wind up this discussion, its main points should be emphasized again: (1) the present theory of embryonic sexual differentiation does not contradict "bisexuality" as it is implicit in the psychoanalytic theory of personality development. (2) The physiology of the woman's sexual response demonstrates orgasm as an integrated process in which the clitoris and the lower third of the vagina participate in developing the orgasmic plateau, but the orgasm itself physiologically and psychologically involves the total personality. (3) The interlocking physiology of the reproductive function of both sexes is reflected in the drive organization of their respective functions in reproduction and the psychic representation of these functions. These, in turn, modified by cultural and ontogenic factors of individual development, influence the capacity for orgasm and the orgasmic experience itself.

NOTES

1. Sherfey, M. J., "The Evolution and Nature of Female Sexuality in Relation to Psychoanalytic Theory," *J. Am. Psychoanalytic Assn.,* XIV (1966), 28–128.

2. Benedek, T., Discussion of above, *J. Am. Psychoanalytic Assn.,* XVI (1968), 424–448.

3. Freud, S., "Femininity" (1933), *Std. Ed.,* XXII, 112–135.

4. Ibid., p. 114.

5. Ibid., p. 116.

6. Masters, W. H., and Johnson, V. E., *Human Sexual Response* (Boston, Little, Brown & Co., 1966).

7. For an extensive bibliography on this subject, see Sherfey's publication, "The Evolution and Nature of Female Sexuality in Relation to Psychoanalytic Theory."

8. Sherfey, M. J., "The Evolution and Nature of Female Sexuality," p. 30.

9. Freud, S., "Femininity," p. 114.

10. Loeb, J., *The Mechanistic Concept of Life* (1912), ed. D. Fleming (Cambridge, Harvard University Press, 1964).

11. Indeed, Freud's speculation went in this direction; regarding the theories of evolution, he expressed the idea of enlisting Lamarck to support psychoanalytic theories. (*The Letters of Sigmund Freud and Karl Abraham* [New York, Basic Books, 1965], p. 261.)

12. Fliess, W., *Gesammelte Aufsätze zur Periodenlehre.* (Jena, Diederichs, 1925).

13. Mirsky, I. A., Miller, R. E., and Murphy, J. V., "The Communication of Affect in Rhesus Monkeys: I. An Experimental Method," *J. Am. Psychoanalytic Assn.,* VI (1958), 433–441.

14. Sherfey, M. J., "The Evolution and Nature of Female Sexuality," p. 47.

15. Levine, S., and Mullins, R. F., Jr., "Hormonal Differences in Brain Organization in Infant Rats," *Science,* CLII (1966), 1585–1592.

16. Beach, F. A., "Retrospect and Prospect," in *Sex and Behavior,* ed. F. A. Beach (New York, Wiley, 1965), p. 565.

17. To avoid repetition of issues discussed in connection with the organization of the procreative drive I have omitted an elaboration of the role of bisexuality in "instinctual learning," i.e., in the adaptive behavior of animals and its function in the evolution of fatherliness in the male of our species. (See "On The Organization of the Reproductive Drive," Chapter 15).

18. Freud, S., "Some Psychical Consequences of the Anatomical Differences between the Sexes" (1925), *Std. Ed.,* XIX, 248–258.

19. A historical compendium of this struggle is presented in the Editor's Notes to the above paper *Std. Ed.,* VII, 125–243.

20. Freud, S., "Three Essays on the Theory of Sexuality" (1905), *Std. Ed.*, VII, 125–243.

21. Freud, S., "Beyond the Pleasure Principle" (1920), *Std. Ed.*, XVIII, 3–64.

22. Freud, S., "Femininity," *Std. Ed.*, XXII, 131.

23. Both aspects of the theory were questioned early by psychoanalysts. Karen Horney ("The Genesis of Castration Complex in Women," *Int. J. Psycho-Anal.*, V [1924], 50–65) was the first to question the biological root of penis envy. Felix Bohm ("The Femininity Complex in Men," *Int. J. Psycho-Anal.*, XI [1930], 444–469) emphasized the universality of the "Femininity Complex" in men.

24. Sherfey, M. J., "The Evolution and Nature of Female Sexuality," p. 51.

25. Abraham, Karl, "A Short Study of the Development of the Libido Viewed in the Light of Mental Disorders," *Selected Papers on Psychoanalysis* (London, Hogarth, 1927), pp. 418–501.

26. Freud, S., "Femininity," *Std. Ed.*, XXII, 112–135.

27. Simone de Beauvoir in her extensive study *The Second Sex* (New York, Alfred Knopf, 1953) recognizes the "indwelling quality" of the feminine psyche and defines it as "immanence" in contrast to the masculine quality of "transcendence." According to her, immanence is the gratification and escape of the woman, forever excluded from the transcendence of man. Whether she considers immanence a secondary cultural acquisition is not quite clear since her genuine insight into the psychology of woman is overshadowed by the idea that women have been subjugated by men into motherhood since the beginning of time.

28. Sherfey, M. J., "The Evolution and Nature of Female Sexuality," p. 55.

29. Ibid., p. 99.

30. Beach, F. A., *Hormones and Behavior* (New York, Hoeber, 1948).

31. Kinsey, A., et al., *Sexual Behavior in the Human Female* (Philadelphia, Saunders, 1953).

32. Sherfey, M. J., "The Evolution and Nature of Female Sexuality," p. 78.

33. Ibid., p. 59.

34. Nowadays, many women, striving to achieve "psychosexual maturity" just as they struggle to overcome clitoral responsiveness, also try to overcome their "effective fantasy" since they are ashamed of these remnants of early masturbatory practices. They may be disappointed by the disturbance in their coital experience by attempting to avoid and suppress these fantasies. Such patients seem to make better progress in all other therapeutic aims if they come to terms with that characteristic of their sexual personality which they live out only in the privacy of their fantasy.

35. This, of course, like most statements about subjective experiences, should not be taken as an "absolute" rule. Indeed, one often hears from women about their anxious concentration on their genitals in the wish to bring about orgasm. Yet the frustration of such effort very often prompts the woman and also her husband to seek treatment.

36. Helene Deutsch (*Psychoanalyse der weiblichen Sexualfunktionen* [Vienna, Internationaler Psychoanalytischer Verlag, 1925]) assumed that the

female genital act has two phases; the first, the genital act, comes to resolution with the grand discharge of parturition.

37. Sherfey, M. J., "The Evolution and Nature of Female Sexuality," p. 55.

38. Fried, E., *The Ego in Love and Sexuality* (New York, Grune & Stratton, 1960).

39. Benedek, T., "On Orgasm and Frigidity," in Panel: Frigidity in Women, reported by B. E. Moore, *J. Am. Psychoanalytic Assn.,* IX (1961), 571–584.

40. "Courtship" patterns show that a period of suspense that appears as anxious behavior is part of the excitement phase in animals. In a similar stereotyped manner, erotized shame and erotized anxiety in humans might also have primary instinctual roots. Therefore, further psychoanalytic investigations are necessary to establish whether the removal of these attributes from human courtship would add to the orgasmic capacity of women and whether it would facilitate or interfere with psychosexual maturity and the sexual identity of individuals.

ADDENDUM, 1971

The further discussion of Sherfey's investigation prompts the question, what is it that we call "sexual drive" in man? The answer is not simple and probably can never be all-inclusive. Sexual drive can be experienced; as a phenomenon it can be described more easily in men than in women. Freud was satisfied to define the difference in the basic quality which is expressed by the direction of the drive: active in the male and passive in the female. The passive aim, however, might be the cause of the diffuseness of its manifestations.[1] Sherfey, however, equated the female sexual drive with the stimulation which may be brought about by venous congestion of the pelvic organs. To this I took exception. (In the same sense, the male sexual drive could be equated to the pressure on the seminal canals which obviously plays a role in the need for ejaculation.) "Drive" is not a synonym of "need." Drives are consequences of instincts[2] which are organizers of the somatic and mental processes instrumental in achieving the aim of the instinct. The sexual drive is the energizing principle, the motor of the "sexual instinct."[3]

Human sexuality is phasic. The motivational system which activates the sexual drive is independent of its biologic aim, the procreative function. Freud, indeed, paid attention to the sharp demarcation between the two aspects of sexuality. He wrote (1914):

> The individual does actually carry on a twofold existence: one to serve his own purposes and the other as a link in a chain, which he serves against his will, or at least involuntarily. The individual himself regards sexuality as one of his

own ends; whereas from another point of view he is an appendage to his germ plasm, at whose disposal he puts his energies in return for a bonus of pleasure. He is the mortal vehicle of a (possibly) immortal substance. . . ."[4]

Freud knew that the phasic sexuality of man, a consequence of the freedom from estrus in the female, is motivated by a single system; but in accord with other scientists he did not consider that the motivational systems serve different functions according to the sex of the individual.[5]

There is one biologic motivational system for the survival of the species, divided between the sexes. Man and woman may have been aware from time immemorial that the man's urge for intercourse and his powerful orgasm make her pregnant. But he did not know, and his woman did not know either, why intercourse at times led to pregnancy and at other times did not. The time of estrus, the period during which the female animal is desirous of intercourse and can be impregnated, has been observed and used in animal husbandry since the dawn of civilization. Since the human female is always accessible to intercourse, her estrus—the time of her ovulation—is hidden. To this I add a speculative note: religious and other cultural influences which emphasize man's difference from the brute may offer one explanation for man's wish to suppress sexuality. The active, outwardly directed, male sexuality, however, cannot be easily suppressed. In comparison, the manifestations of female sexuality are invisible; it could have been assumed that it did not exist. The male of the species was not responsible for this; it did not happen by his choice. It developed that way because of the physiology of the procreative function of woman.

To learn more about female orgasm, it is not enough to know that the female genital tract permits a phasic evolution of orgasm and to know that such evolution depends, at least partially, on the mate's ability and willingness to maintain stimulation until the orgasmic release is accomplished. More questions could be asked about the relationship of the sexual drive and the propagative function. Freud wondered whether one should attribute a passive aim to the concept of drive, but he found it necessary (1915). Later he formulated the theory that the psychic representation of drive energy, libido, has no sex differentiation (1933). Today we may say that drive as energy structure assumes the direction which accomplishes its function. Thus it can be active and/or passive, not only according to sex, but during any sexual act in either participant. This is experientially so manifest that it covers up the direct reaction to the (biologic) instinctual motivation.

The initial sexual response of woman is the lubrication of the vagina. Is there a psychologic, emotional correlate to this physiologic reaction? The female response to the moisture is an "opening up." This normally refers not only to the gesture but to a sensation which may have the intensity of drive—the desire to embrace, to receive the male, to submit. Whatever sexual tactics and techniques human couples may use to develop, enhance, prolong, and vary their experience, it begins with the man's tendency to take over and the woman's wish to submit.[6] (This discourse is not supposed to be an "ars amandi." What follows after this on the physiologic level is described by Masters and Johnson.[7]) It would be more difficult, if not impossible, to generalize what happens on the intrapsychic and interpersonal levels of human communication between partners. Beyond question, the orgasmic process of women can be interrupted or exaggerated by psychologic processes such as memories, fantasies, etc. Much more data would be necessary to evaluate the influence of more active participation of women in coitus in the conjugal experience. Observations indicate that women, especially young and unmarried women, consider their sexual experience satisfactory if their performance is praised by the partner; women often do not know, or even care, whether or not they had orgasm.[8]

There are many aspects of the psychoanalytic instinct theory that have remained uninvestigated. On the basis of his early investigations, Freud categorized instinct as "ego instinct" and "sexual instinct," the former to serve the aims of the individual, the latter to serve the survival of the species. Later investigations revealed that these instinctual forces are not antagonists. Instinctual forces are involved in the development of the ego.[9] This is not only a human prerogative, although one cannot speak about the ego of animals without qualification.[10] Ethologists, however, for a long time have described a "dominance quality" of apparent strength, even of superiority, as a manifestation of individual differences among the members of a herd. It is usually attributed to the manifestation of the sexual drive. A. H. Maslow studied the role of dominance in infrahuman species and compared it with a "dominance feeling" in man.[11] He assumes that the dominance feeling is a source, if not the source, of self-esteem in men and women alike. He considers it a regulating factor in sexual behavior in men and women as well as in infrahuman primates. That the quality of dominance is not a male attribute only and that its influence extends to nonsexual areas is demonstrated, for example, by the "pecking order" that polices chicken coops.

We assume that the male chimpanzee is not aware of his dominance feeling, of his superiority within the group. But he accepts its consequence, not only in sexual advantages, but in the burdens of leadership. It seems that in the animal the sexual strength, ego strength, and self-esteem are simple correlations of the interacting physiologic systems.

But man is aware. Although it is an organizing principle of the personality, his dominance feeling suffers vicissitudes. Emerging in infancy from the libido reservoir through interactions with primary objects, his dominance feeling forms the labile ego attributes of self-esteem and self-confidence. They feed back to sexual instincts and allow for an unencumbered maturation of the sexual drive and along with it the development of the self-concept which includes sexuality as an integrating part of one's identity. This is the prerequisite and result of human sexual experience in man and woman alike.

Ego instincts and their manifestations as primary narcissism are the reservoir of libido which, with sexual maturation, become channelized into sexual behavior. The sexual drive, although its biologic aim is procreation, fills the experiencing ego with the pleasure of gratification, not only of an instinctual need but also of the achieving self. It is, therefore, worthwhile emphasizing that constitutional factors, beyond the instinctual response patterns, determine sexual attraction between a man and a woman. Neither in the human male nor in the female does the dominance quality have such general effectiveness as observed in infrahuman primates. In man, individual developmental experiences may influence the dominance quality; they also motivate sexual responsiveness between individuals. A particular man and woman may have exclusively strong attraction to each other, but not to anyone else in their social group. This is relevant to the general problem of female orgasm, in the initial vaginal response and the emotional acceptance of it with the desire to submit. Individuals often describe this reaction as a "chemical reaction," thus attributing their response to the physiologic aspect of the drive. It is not infrequent that they therefore suppress such physiologic reactions and build defenses against them.

In the long period from infancy to psychosexual maturity during which the pregenital instincts bear influence upon the ego development, the individual learns to modify his reactions to his sexual drive. The long time gap between desire and fulfillment, the freedom of object choice, etc., create a web of intrapsychic and interpersonal motivations. The psychic representations of motivations originating in instincts thus become connected with many other nonsexual tributaries. One may be justified in asking, do human beings have pure "sexual drive" not molded by other instincts and by pressures of direct environmental and/ or cultural influences? The answer probably is no. Kubie cites a telling illustration of this problem. A male patient who had been sluggish in his sexual behavior and shown little sexual interest in his wife discovered, when he returned after a longer than usual absence, that his wife had had an affair. "Thereupon he erupted into an incessant sexual urgency with intensity of need and erotic feelings which he had never experienced before. What mosaic of rage, anxiety, vanity and unconscious homosexual need made up this pseudoerotic frenzy of genital need which wore the cloak of heterosexuality?" Kubie asked.[12] No doubt, every psychoanalyst can add similar examples that illustrate that the flood of strong affects may act like "sexual instincts."

This is not just a human attribute. Tinklepaugh observed that infrahuman primates, frustrated by being separated from a banana which they desire but cannot reach, spontaneously ejaculate.[13] It would be a teleological explanation that the ejaculation serves a pacifying aim. One would prefer to speculate that the tension breaks down the barrier between discharge channels of affects. It has nothing to do with the sexual drive itself. Every psychoanalyst has an opportunity to investigate with almost every patient the displacements which are adaptive mechanisms in their sexual behavior. My references to the instinctual nature of sexual attraction and to the dominance quality which encompasses the total personality indicate that instincts still exist.

Such primary instinctual qualities of an individual appear to be manifestations of that libido reservoir which Freud termed "primary narcissism." This requires investigation beyond the scope of this discussion to elucidate its relationship to sexuality. In itself, primary narcissism is not sexual, not genital, but it is in communication with sexuality, not only with and through the sexual drive, but through the ego; it enhances the ego's capacity for sensual experience. It is one of the main factors in establishing "identity," which cannot be adequate without sexual identity.

What is identity? "I am I" is a self-evident experience. Identity is an unconscious awareness of one's wholeness delineated as self, distinct from others. It changes with time, yet remains continuous through past, present, and future. Since identity is experientially evident, sexual identity is not raised as a general problem. In spite of our knowledge of the bisexual anlage and the variety of instinctual conflicts originating in it, in spite of our knowledge of neuroses, perversions, and other aberrations of sex, the belief survives that the sense of one's sexual identity is given, as the gender, with the chromosomes. No doubt, biology planned it that way. But masculinity and femininity are attributes which are also motivated by cultural influences. Every individual from early infancy incorporates in his self-concept what he as a person is expected to represent as man or as woman. How much of gender identity is innate and how much of it is learned?[14]

It is true for both sexes that "the concept of identity is based upon the integrity of ego structures which in turn are rooted in the physiological and biological structure of man."[15] The gender identity of the male is obviously manifest in his active role in the sexual act, in his physical strength, and in his freedom from childbearing. It has been easy and natural for a father to assume that his son wants to be a man, but not that his daughter really wants to be and is not just biologically predestined to be a woman. Gender identity is a psychobiologic experience that pervades and influences all psychologic processes. Normally it impedes the ability of men to identify with the feminine gender experience and thus comprehend "in depth" woman's acceptance of and gratification in her procreative function.

Motherhood is a primary psychobiologic function; fatherhood is a secondary one. But the prerequisite of becoming a father is an active sexual drive culminating in orgasm. The first phase of female procreative function may succeed without an emotional need for cohabitation. The female sexual drive is assumed to have a passive aim, but women have sensual pleasure and gratification from sexual intercourse. It has also been shown that they have the physiologic accoutrement for a phasic evolution of orgasm. Does this mean that women's orgasm is like that of men? As a sensual experience it has to be different. The physiology of the orgasmic process does not determine the nature of the sexual experience. Although the sexual drive may qualify the impetus in the active direction in men and in the passive direction in women, the sexual experience depends not only on the drive but also on the experiencing self. Thus we arrive at the interacting circuits between developmental processes and the resultant experiencing self.

NOTES

1. Freud, S., "Instincts and Their Vicissitudes" (1915), *Std. Ed.*, XIV, 117–140.

2. Benedek, T., "On the Organization of the Reproductive Drive" this volume, Chapter 15.

3. Both the sexual drive which motivates behavior and the instinct for preservation of the species are included.

4. Freud, S., "On Narcissism: An Introduction" (1914), *Std. Ed.*, XIV, 78.

5. In 1970 one cannot help being concerned if such a statement will be taken as manifestation of "sexual politics," grist for the mill of "Women's Liberation." It is not meant as such, but the one-sided concept of "penis envy" as a biologic given might have been avoided if one had considered the woman's role in procreation beyond drudgery and/or sacrifice for which she is either admired or abused.

6. Deutsch, H., *Psychoanalyse der weiblichen Sexualfunktionen* (Vienna, Internationaler Psychoanalytischer Verlag, 1925). Not translated.

It is regrettable that the term masochism is so overladen with connotations that are beyond the instinctual that Helene Deutsch's concept of "primary masochism of women" seems to have lost its significance.

7. Masters, W. H., and Johnson, V. E., *Human Sexual Response* (Boston, Little, Brown & Co., 1966).

8. We often tend to forget the importance of narcissism in sexuality. The emotional correlate to the physiologic event (which can occur in reversed sequence) has been mentioned here to focus the attention on the sexual drive and interplay between its active and passive aims.

9. Hartmann, H., "The Mutual Influences in the Development of the

Ego and the Id," *The Psychoanalytic Study of the Child,* VII (1952), 9–30.

10. I assume that not speaking of "ego" in animals is an unwritten, uncoded convention. The perceptual system and the drive organization of responses to perception function like ego, mediating between the organism and its external reality. Thus we assume a rudimentary ego in animals.

11. Maslow, A. H., "The Role of Dominance in the Social and Sexual Behavior of Infrahuman Primates," *J. Genet. Psychol.,* XLVIII (1936), 310–338.

12. Kubie, L. S., "The Influence of Symbolic Processes on the Role of Instincts in Human Behavior," *Psychosomatic Med.,* XVIII (1956), 206.

13. Tinkelpaugh, O. L., "Sex Behavior in Infrahuman Primates as a Substitute Response Following Emotional Disturbance," (abstract), *Psychol. Bul.,* XXIX (1932), 666.

14. Stoller, R. J., "Gender Identity and a Biological Force," *The Psychoanalytic Forum,* II (1962), 318–325.

15. Sarlin, C. M., "Feminine Identity," *J. Am. Psychoanalytic Assn.,* XI (1963), 813.

17. Five Papers on Psychoanalytic Training

INTRODUCTION

The following five papers, written years apart for various occasions, do not aspire to be "discussions in depth" of any aspect of psychoanalytic training. They may reveal, however, the reasons for the slow development of the psychoanalytic training system and the even slower evolution of its educational philosophy. A presentation of the problems may afford a glimpse of the crucial issues which are as essential to psychoanalytic training as conflicts are to human development.

One cannot think of the problems of psychoanalytic training without considering its experiential nature and its origin in the self-analysis of Freud. The vigor, depth, and intensity of that first self-analysis, not revealed to his followers during Freud's lifetime, are reflected in the convictions at which Freud arrived by that experience. Vilma Kovacs formulated this succinctly: "Freud supposed that in stating the theory of analysis he was putting into the hand of all who grasped his principles the key to their unconscious."[1] Her statement refers to that early phase of psychoanalytic training when contact between the neophyte and his older colleagues consisted of "probing through the walls of infantile amnesia following clues from dreams, symptoms and slips of the tongue."[2]

In a review of the history of training analysis, Balint differentiates a first period, which he characterized as "instruction," from the second which he described as "demonstration."[3] These are appropriate distinctions. The first period refers to a purely didactic contact between teacher and student; it served to convey to the student the method and the theory of psychoanalysis on a conceptual basis. In the second phase, the student had undergone a short period of personal analysis which, as Balint put it, was enough to demonstrate to him as a patient how psy-

469

choanalysis works, how repressed memories emerge, how the unconscious meaning of a dream can be experienced, etc.[4]

If one wants to place the overlapping periods of psychoanalytic training within chronological boundaries, one can say that the first period lasted from 1902 to 1912; the second from 1912 to 1922 or 1925. In "On the History of the Psychoanalytic Movement" (1914), Freud set the beginning of psychoanalytic training in the year 1902.[5] By 1910, he was aware that neither the knowledge of the theory nor the associative responses of the analyst (to the patient) were enough to warrant correct psychoanalytic interpretations. He learned about "blind spots" in his self-analysis, observed their effect in discussions with his student colleagues, and related them to "countertransference." In his address to the Second International Psycho-Analytical Congress held in Nuremberg, in 1910, he said:

> We have become aware of the "countertransference," which arises in him as a result of the patient's influence on his unconscious feelings, and we are almost inclined to insist that he shall recognize this countertransference in himself and overcome it. . . . We have noticed that no psycho-analyst goes further than his own complexes and internal resistances permit; and we consequently require that he shall begin his activity with a self-analysis and continually carry it deeper while he is making his observations on his patients. Anyone who fails to produce results in a self-analysis of this kind may at once give up any idea of being able to treat patients by analysis.[6]

In that severely worded recommendation, he referred to self-analysis as he had experienced it and probably as only he was able to experience it. Two years later, he was more emphatic and at the same time less severe by requesting that a physician should begin his analytic training by being analyzed himself.[7] Thus began the period of "demonstration," brief periods of training analysis which were recommended but not codified. In 1918, at the Fifth International Psycho-Analytical Congress in Budapest, Nunberg proposed that every student of analysis have a thorough *therapeutic* analysis.[8] This proposal was the first which officially acknowledged that the removal of "blind spots" has a therapeutic effect; indeed, it is the means of psychoanalytic teaching-learning as well as of therapy. The proposal was accepted as a desideratum and remained a vital goal of the International Psycho-Analytic Association until 1922 when the Seventh International Psycho-Analytic Congress in Berlin established the rule that "only those persons should be authorized to practice psychoanalysis who as well as taking theoretical courses of training had submitted to training analysis conducted by an analyst approved by the Society at that time."[9]

One might well date the third phase of psychoanalytic training and also that of the training analysis with the establishment of the first psychoanalytic institutes and with the codification of training analysis. Balint, however, connects it, and with good reason, with a seemingly less significant event, the publication in 1924 of a small volume by Ferenczi and Rank, *The Development of Psychoanalysis*.[10] The goals of training analysis were not pointed out. Since for many years "demonstration" seemed to be sufficient, training analyses were not even as thoroughgoing as the therapeutic analysis often had to be in order to achieve the goal of the therapy. These authors called attention to the fact that to safeguard psychoanalysis as a science, psychoanalysts had to know more than just how to make correct interpretations; they stressed that "psychoanalysis is essentially an experience involving both the patient and the analyst and therefore is an onerous emotional task for the analyst for which he has to be prepared through his training analysis."[11]

Appreciating the reasons and consequences of the Ferenczi-Rank publication, Balint dates the beginning of the third period of the development of analytic training from 1924. The recommendation stirred up resistance. Although it did not propose anything more than deeper and more thorough analysis for candidates than had been practiced before, the resistance argued, "Don't touch the character."[12] It was obvious that character analysis had to follow. Balint assumes that another, a fourth period, evolved after 1928, when Ferenczi stated explicitly that "training analysis has to be character analysis. . . . The analyst himself must know and be in control over even the most recondite weakness of his own character and this is impossible without a fully completed analysis."[13]

The periods which followed after that, whether called "supertherapy" or "post-training analysis," were the consequences of the problems of the "classical technique of training analysis" which still had not completely integrated Eitingon's simple definition. In addressing the International Training Commission in 1924 he said, "The point in which instructional analysis or didactic analysis differs from therapeutic analysis . . . is not in having a special technique but . . . in having an additional aim that supersedes or goes hand in hand with the therapeutic aim."[14] He did not spell out how to achieve that additional aim through training analysis and/or through supervision which he then recommended. The Scylla and Charybdis of training analysis is the problem: can one teach when one analyzes a patient who is a future analyst? Do we teach or treat?

The question has been asked by many training analysts and argued with much puzzlement and with many qualifications, as if the answer were not implied in the two intrinsically interrelated aspects of the psychoanalytic process. In that first recommendation by Freud in which he advised self-analysis, he saw in this a method for removal of blind spots (i.e., therapy). In the codification of training analysis, the removal of blind spots was considered a method of "instruction." As the complexity of the process designated as "instructional" became better known, the goal of the training analysis shifted again to therapy. As one at first wanted only to teach and not touch the future analyst's character, so later, when training analysis became character analysis, the instructional aim was submerged, as if the therapeutic aim would be influenced or even endangered by "teaching." In reverse, it required that the psychoanalytic supervision should only be teaching; it was considered as "analyzing the supervisee" if the supervisor included in his considerations how the student-analyst's personality influenced his approach and his reactions to the patient. (How, otherwise, can the supervisor make his supervisee appreciate his role in the process of the analysis?)

The discussion returns to the same problem, to the removal of blind spots—to develop the analyst as an instrument to see, not only what he did not see before, but also to learn as the eye moves—not only as a microscope but as a periscope—to see the obstacles which interfered with his seeing, and by overcoming the obstacles, to observe how he learns to see more. All this is implied in the psychoanalytic process. Why was it so difficult to conceptualize psychoanalytic treatment and teaching, learning and therapy as interacting processes? It appears that this was the consequence of the psychoanalyst's attitude, his placing himself outside the psychoanalytic process. This attitude has many motivations; some were rational and necessary, some were and remained unconscious. No doubt, psychoanalysis could not have become the body of knowledge, a science, if its method was not pursued with the necessary rigor (and exclusiveness). This, however, is no excuse for avoiding the investigation of the influence of the psychoanalyst's attitude on the psychoanalytic process.

I am aware that this statement must appear not only as exaggeration but also as negligence of the literature which is concerned with the function of "countertransference" in the analytic process. "Countertransference" was considered the "raison d'être" of supervision and still seems to be its central if not its only subject. It is defined by Freud as ". . . a result of the patient's influence on his [the analyst's] unconscious feelings."[15] Freud considered that the origin of the countertransference was in the patient, but he knew that the analyst had to be analyzed to recognize this in the ongoing process of analyzing. In his paper, "The Elasticity of Psychoanalytic Technique," Ferenczi speaks about a "covert collusion" between the analyst and his candidate;[16] he refers to preconscious communications which direct the transference toward introjecting the idealized analyst.

It is interesting to note that Henry Racker, Michael Balint, and I became concerned about the same problems of transference-countertransference interactions in the psychoanalytic process at about the same time. In 1949 I presented a paper, "Dynamics of the Countertransference," in a panel discussion of the Chicago Psychoanalytic Society; this paper presented a viewpoint so different from the accepted concept that I did not submit it for publication until three years later. (pp. 492–499, this volume.) Racker's first paper on this subject appeared in the same year,[17] and Balint's paper one year later. Since "Dynamics of the Countertransference" is republished in this volume, its content will not be discussed except to point out its differing and rather provocative viewpoint. Certainly it was not unique to discuss the problems of countertransference, but no one went so far as to assume that probably the most important influence in the development of severe transference neurosis was the patient's reaction to the countertransference of his therapist. Such countertransference attitude is not always—as is implied in the definition of countertransference—a reaction to the unconscious conflicts of the patient; it may be the analyst's response to the patient's behavior, or to the patient's current emotional reaction to which the analyst's response is motivated by his own unconscious conflict. (Example given on pp. 497–498.) The spiral of the negative transactions may begin with the analyst and be responsible for the severity of the transference neurosis.

We tell our candidate to respect the patient, but we often fail to make him realize that the patient, a sensitive, perceptive human being, may respond to the analyst as a "real person," with empathy for both his positive and his negative attributes. The patient may see him as if he were outside his office, even when he is invisible behind the couch. The expression of such responses (of the patient) should not be shrugged off as transference neurosis. Instead, the first response of the psychoanalyst to such associations of his patient should be self-analysis: is the patient right? In what respect is he correct and in what regard is he wrong? Did the patient exaggerate, distort, or even deny something and if so, why? Only after he has some empathic understanding of the emotions involved on both sides[18] should the answer be chosen to express or reestablish the therapeutic rapport between analyst and patient. Such an interpretation can rarely be schematic and it usually fails to achieve its aim if one responds in terms of the transference patterns of the patient. For every patient feels the lack of respect in the analyst toward him if his real feelings are overlooked.

It was not a technical innovation that was proposed in that panel discussion in 1949 nor in its publication in 1953. The presentation emphasized what was known by experience, that psychoanalyzing involves the personality of the analyst. Therefore, it requires self-analysis; this is necessary to enable him to carry the burden of his responsibility for the dynamics of the psychoanalytic process, which depends on a workable transference neurosis. This, the analyst's role in the transference, was the focus of my discussion. I assume that Balint had the same problem in mind when he asked regarding training analyses: "Who is the subject and who is the object of the research . . .?" Is the aim of training analysis ". . . that with the help of the analyst the candidate shall find out something about the deeper layers of the human mind, his mind, or is it the analyst who with the help of his candidate wants to find out something about the possibilities and limitations of his own understanding and technique?"[19] The answer is clear; whether student and analyst or patient and therapist, both learn and discover.

The next paper, "Countertransference in the Training Analyst," presented in a panel discussion one year later, focused on the specific problems of countertransference in the training analyst. Today these are usually subsumed under cover of the syncretistic dilemma of the psychoanalytic training system. (The term syncrisis, regarding psychoanalytic education, was not in such general use as it became later, following the thorough survey of psychoanalytic education in the United States by Bertram D. Lewin and Helen Ross.[20]) Acknowledging the influence of the training system as a factor in the intimately personal process of training analysis, I cannot help emphasizing the necessity of each training analyst's awareness of the responsibility which he carries by being a training analyst. Such awareness is not served by putting the responsibility on the training system, but by being conscious of how he himself responds to his functioning as a training analyst. Such stock taking may have motivated the points discussed in the paper in the early fifties when the training system was burdened by postwar demands.

Rereading the paper now, I can see positive and negative aspects in the "patriarchal organization" of the system, which is a consequence of the training analysis. As could be foreseen and was predicted in my paper, the patriarchal organization of the training system has loosened up with the expansion of psychoanalysis and with the improving communication between institutes and graduates. Since training analysis continues as a prerequisite of psychoanalytic education, it affords opportunity for training analysts to work through with each candidate the conflicts intrinsic in father-son relationships and so to develop as training analysts. Such maturation involves a lessening of narcissistic investment in the student; this will improve the training analyst's job as a psychoanalytic educator who will be able to pass objective judgment on his own "product," the future psychoanalyst.

The narcissistic involvement of fathers (or mothers) with their children, be they sons or daughters, has many colorings, all of which influence the training analysis. There are parents who cannot bear to see their children become adults and independent. This attitude may account for the endless training analyses. There are others who want to see the continuation of their life work carried on by their children. Glover analyzed the process by which training analyses have the tendency to build "schools"; he discussed the advantages and disadvantages of this aspect of the training analysis which can hardly be avoided.[21] Here again I recommend self-analysis of the researchers, psychoanalytic discoverers, and teachers. Today we know more about narcissism, the ego's investment in the creative process and its product, but we do not discuss it freely in regard to training analysis or to any other aspect of psychoanalytic training. Yet the well protected narcissism of psychoanalytic educators may be one of the root motives of the syncretistic dilemma of the training system.

The task of the paper dealing with the termination of the training analysis, "A Contribution to the Problem of Termination of Training Analysis,"[22] appears overwhelmingly complex compared with those which discuss the transference process. When and how shall one terminate an interminable process? Assuming that Freud would answer in the sense of his last discussion of that issue, we may say, the preparatory analysis could be terminated if and when the training analyst can assume that the process of ego transformation will go on of its own accord and that he (the candidate) will bring his new insights to bear upon all his subsequent experiences.[23] Freud's view of the interminable process and my experience as training-supervising analyst were the basis of my recommendation that a preparatory analysis may be terminated when its thoroughness is demonstrated not only by the student's awareness of the working of unconscious processes, but also by his having worked through in the transference his prevalent developmental conflict. I assumed that the self-analysis of the candidate, stimulated by his experience in analyzing patients and helped by supervisors, would provide him with new insights to bear upon his subsequent work. I thought that this would shorten the first part of the training analysis by emphasizing its definite goal and referred to it as "preparatory analysis." The implication was, of course, that the training analyst assesses objectively the student's readiness for matriculation and for analyzing, as tested by the supervisor of his first case. This recommendation was not accepted. The general policy of the American Psychoanalytic Association is that the student shall analyze his first one or two cases under supervision while he continues his personal analysis. This system may have its advantages but I was concerned about its disadvantages. Psychoanalysis is a dyadic process; supervised analysis involves a triadic system; it might become a quadratic situation. Its complexity may interfere with the ongoing psychoanalysis of the student and thus influence his work with his patient and also with his supervisor. Thus my proposal implied a greater independence for a novice of psychoanalytic practice.

There was another reason for the suggestion of "preparatory analysis," and it was based on the practice of long, "nonterminated," training analysis. It was well known that sooner or later after the termination of the training analysis, students, either before certification or some time thereafter, returned for a second analysis. Such a second analysis may have been requested by the educational committee or may have been a spontaneous need in the candidate who realized that his difficulties with patients or in his personal life required more psychoanalysis. This second or even third analysis was often regarded by the candidates as a sign of failure, even as a punishment if it was prompted by the educational committee. Much has been written about the advantages of the second analysis, undertaken independently of the training system, and its influence. It is not called "training analysis," but, in reality, it is a process which expands and often achieves the goals of the training, for whatever reason it was undertaken. My proposition divided the training analysis into two parts. The first (preparatory analysis) achieves its goal when the student is ready to begin to psychoanalyze cases under supervision. After a period of freedom from supervision (during which, of course, the student may ask for consultations when he finds it necessary or may present his cases in seminars) but before he gets his third supervised case, he resumes his training analysis—if it is advisable or if he so wishes, with another training analyst. Writing this after so many years, I realize that I still feel that this is or could be a workable modification of the present system.

Whatever the policy may be, the fact remains that psychoanalysis is interminable, but training analyses have to be terminated. The termination of the analysis as well as the analytic process is the function of the training analyst as educator and therapist. These two functions are inescapably intertwined and often catch even the best of training analysts in a web of their "optimistic illusion."[24] Training analysis is a process which stimulates creative learning by removing resistances; it makes free preconscious communication within one's own psychic systems and between the self and the other. While it widens and deepens the person's understanding of himself, it prepares him to understand the other. Since such experiences are so impressive, they encourage the optimistic illusion, the hope in the training analyst as well as in his analysand that if only the personal analysis is carried on long enough, all problems can be resolved and the goal of his personal development will be achieved. This mutually shared belief, the cradle of positive transference and positive countertransference, may be that collusion which leads to introjection of the idealized analyst.

It may be disconcerting that a discussion of the problems of termination arrives back at where we started. We began with the discussion of the training analysis carried out, as Sachs viewed it, under the aegis of optimistic illusion. We define the optimistic illusion as the manifestation of a positive balance, indeed, a state of emotional symbiosis between the training analyst and his student analysand. To this we add, it is the training analyst's task to create a terminable educational experience from the labile equilibrium.

NOTES

1. Kovacs, V., "Training and Control Analysis," *Int. J. Psycho-Anal.,* XVII (1936), 346–354.

2. Fleming, J., "Freud's Concept of Self-Analysis: Its Relevance for Psychoanalytic Training," in *Currents in Psychoanalysis,* ed. Irwin Marcus (International Univ. Press, 1972), pp. 14–45.

3. Balint, M., "Analytic Training and Training Analysis," *Int. J. Psycho-Anal.,* XXXV (1954), 157–162.

4. My description of my personal analysis fits Balint's description. (We had the same analyst.) See Fleming, J., and Benedek, T., *Psychoanalytic Supervision* (New York, Grune & Stratton, 1966), p. 9.

5. Freud, S., "On the History of the Psychoanalytic Movement" (1914), *Std. Ed.,* XIV, 7–66.

6. Freud, S., "Future Prospects of Psychoanalysis" (1910), *Std. Ed.,* XI, 145.

7. Freud, S., "Recommendations to Physicians Practicing Psychoanalysis," *Std. Ed.,* XII, 111–120.

8. Eitingon, M., "Report of the General Meeting of the International Training Commission," *Int. J. Psycho-Anal.,* XVIII (1937), 346–348.

9. Kovacs, V., "Training and Control Analysis," *Int. J. Psycho-Anal.,* XVII (1936), 346–354.

10. Ferenczi, S., and Rank, O., *Die Entwicklungsziele der Psychoanalyse* (Int. Psychoanal. Verlag, 1924). In English, *The Development of Psychoanalysis,* NMD Mono. Series #40 (New York, Nervous and Mental Disease Publ. Co., 1927).

11. Fleming, J., and Benedek, T., *Psychoanalytic Supervision,* p. 11.

12. Balint, M., "Analytic Training and Training Analysis," p. 157.

13. Ferenczi, S., "The Problem of Termination of Analyses," *Int. J. Psycho-Anal.,* XXXV (1954), quoted from Balint, M., "Analytic Training and Training Analysis," p. 158.

14. Eitingon, M., "Preliminary Discussion of the Question of Training Analysis" (1925), An Address to the International Training Commission, *Int. J. Psycho-Anal.,* VII (1926), 132.

15. Freud, S., "Future Prospects of Psychoanalysis" (1910), *Std. Ed.,* XI, 145.

16. Ferenczi, S., "The Elasticity of Psychoanalytic Technique," *Int. Zeitschrift f. Psycho-Analyse,* XIV (1928). English translation in his *Final Contributions to Psycho-Analysis* (London, Hogarth Press, 1955), pp. 87–101.

17. Racker, H., "A Contribution to the Problem of Countertransference," *Int. J. Psycho-Anal.,* XXXIV (1953), 313–324.

18. It is unusual to refer to the psychoanalyst's "empathic understanding of himself." Here the concept implies that the analyst "feels" his response to his patient; the motivation often remains unconscious unless the analyst turns his attention to himself in order to understand the motivation of his feelings, to become aware of how his empathy functions.

19. Balint, M., "Analytic Training and Training Analysis," *Int. J. Psycho-Anal.*, XXXV, 161–162.

20. Lewin, B., and Ross, H., *Psychoanalytic Education in the United States* (New York, W. W. Norton, 1960).

21. Glover, E., "Research Methods in Psychoanalysis," *Int. J. Psycho-Anal.*, XXXIII (1952), 403–409.

22. Benedek, T., "A Contribution to the Problem of Termination of Training Analysis," *J. Am. Psychoanalytic Assn.*, III, no. 4 (1955), 615–629; this volume, pp. 503–515.

23. Freud, S., "Analysis Terminable and Interminable" (1937), *Std. Ed.*, XXIII, 210–253.

24. Sachs, H., "Observations of a Training Analyst," *Psychoanalytic Quart.*, XVI (1947), 157–168.

TRAINING ANALYSIS—
PAST, PRESENT AND FUTURE*

The necessity of personal analysis for those "who want to apply psychoanalytic technique" was expressed by Freud (1910) very early. Yet the evolution of the training analysis as the prerequisite and core of psychoanalytic education has been a slow process. This is not surprising. Psychoanalysis was conceived originally as an instrument of therapy; the personal analysis of the future analyst had the therapeutic goal of removing "blind spots." "[The idea] that one should be analysed for the purpose of learning the method had occurred to none of us . . . ," said Eitingon (1937, p. 351). Since therapy and the preparation for the profession were to be achieved by the same method, the educational value of the psychoanalytic process appeared secondary during the years and decades when Freud and his followers were mainly interested in establishing solid foundations for their newly won knowledge. Gitelson (1964), in his last paper, following a theorem of Thomas Kuhn (1963), points out that the "psychoanalytic movement" was becoming a "normal science" by organizing its training system to prepare for and safeguard the future of psychoanalysis.

This, however, was not easy to achieve; it took several years of struggle marked by crises in the budding psychoanalytic organizations

* Revision of a paper originally presented at the First Three-Institute Conference on Training Analysis, Pittsburgh, 1965.

and by the catastrophe of the Hitler years. To outline it briefly, the "movement" began to organize its training system by the establishment of the Berlin Institute in 1920, followed by the Institute in Vienna in 1921 and by others soon after. This training program consisting of three interacting phases—training analysis, academic curriculum, and supervised analyses—was codified in 1927. The training program was followed in the already established institutes, yet I myself and, I believe, all those who entered the professional field of psychoanalysis in the early and even in the late 1920s, could testify how easy it was. The spreading of psychoanalysis and the appearance of eager students from distant cities make it understandable that initiating new training centers had the characteristics of a "movement." This kind of ambience recurred again and again with local variations until the modern period of "organized psychoanalysis" could evolve.[1]

I am the product of that period of pioneering organization. I mention this not to arouse a desire to imitate the laxity of that period in enforcing its policies, but to convey how during the period, when not only the analysands but also the analysts were more naive than they are now, not only was the organization of psychoanalytic teaching-learning different, but psychoanalytic learning itself was a very different process. What might be enviable is the fact that at that time one learned so much in a relatively short time; one learned more through direct emotional experiences than through intellectualization.

My own analysis took place before the first psychoanalytic institute was established. Short as it was, nevertheless it was a meaningful experience; it carried with it the conviction of knowing something that was unknown and unknowable before. It was a specific experience of oneself against something that was also oneself from which the new awareness, the new knowledge, emerged. Also experienced were the simple prerequisites of the analytic process: listening, observing, and interpreting. I think interpretations were less complex then, more rooted in emotional experience. What I want to emphasize is that the basic experience of the analytic process was more impactful when analysis was young and new than it is now when theoretical knowledge creates anticipations, not only in our psychiatrically trained students, but also in the general public seeking analytic treatment. This is, however, even more true for the analyst than for his patients. Theoretical knowledge as well as the seeming repetition of psychoanalytic constellations dulls our senses to the unique qualities of each psychoanalytic experience. An example from the first decade of my psychoanalytic practice illustrates this.

1. Some of these events can be gleaned from the correspondence between Freud and Abraham (1965) and are mentioned in Fleming and Benedek (1966).

I still recall vividly an analytic hour in which I was convinced that I had just discovered, during that very hour and for the first time, the castration complex in men. I have no notes of that hour but I remember the room vividly, the light; it must have been in the winter of 1923–24. The patient was a tall, lanky man with a pale, Christ-like face, with a Christ-like, reddish brown beard. He suffered from severe migraines, his profession being a Communist organizer at a time when the Nazis were also organizing. He had often been threatened that he would be beaten up at meetings and he had been. Today it would be easy to assume that his need to fight for his convictions at a time when fighting was physically dangerous would create enough tension in this "saint-like," sensitive man to cause his migraines. At that time, however, I patiently and unknowingly waited for the emerging unconscious. I cannot document the details of that session, but I remember him in his ghost-like paleness as he was lying on the couch, his body trembling as he poured out associations: his driven feeling toward his mother, how his fear of his father was so tremendous and how his fear of being punished, literally castrated, affected his life. In that hour it appeared to me that, although I had read and heard all that was known then about the castration complex, until that experience it was not real to me. In that hour it became not only true but a self-discovered truth. Even after the session was over, I thought that the discovery was new and original. After I realized that it was just the same castration complex that Freud had elaborated from many points of view, I clung to the uniqueness of the experience and only later tried to reconstruct what made it so. Yes, it was in the first decade of my analytic experience, but he was not my first male patient. I succeeded then in feeling, almost in seeing, not so much the falling away of his resistances but more—as it happens in a kaleidoscope—the sudden formation of a "Gestalt" put together from pieces of different depths, colors, and shapes, the result of the falling away of *my* resistances.

The memory of that experience, revived again by similar events in psychoanalytic situations, became the experiential core of the conceptualized knowledge learned by studying Freud and the other first generation of psychoanalysts. Today more is known about the significance of preconscious processes in learning (Kubie, 1965), but at the time when learning theories wore their baby shoes, the steps by which unconscious mental content becomes conscious was considered only a part of the analytic process and not a specific form of learning—creative learning.

If I were to answer a question which my generation of analysts anticipates from our younger colleagues, i.e., how did training analysts work in the 1920s or even in the 1930s, I would recall one statement in Eitingon's report to the International Training Commission (Eitingon, 1926). Introducing the necessity for three phases in psychoanalytic training, he said,

I will not here enter any further into the problem of the technique of instructional analysis. There is really no question of an essentially specific technique, for instructional analysis is simply a psychoanalysis, and there is only one psychoanalytic technique, namely, *the correct one.*

And then he continued,

The point in which instructional or didactic analysis differs from therapeutic analysis (I must ask for your indulgence if I am obliged to emphasize trivialities) *is not in having a special technique but, as we say in Berlin, in having an additional aim, which supersedes or goes hand in hand with the therapeutic aim* (Eitingon, 1926, p. 132; my italics).

What Eitingon at that time apologetically considered trivialities expressed in a nutshell the function and purpose of training analysis. Now one might define training analysis as a process aiming at professional development that includes therapy also. Beyond this, it is a situation which affords opportunity for the student to learn from experiencing passively as an analysand what he will practice actively and may experience as a psychoanalyst. But it took several years of such experience before psychoanalysts recognized the specific problems created by the dual goals of training analysis; they have to be solved by the training analysis and by the other methods of learning psychoanalysis.

When Ferenczi and Rank (1925), concerned with the development of psychoanalysis, emphasized the significance of the training analysis, their appeal was only that the training analysis be deeper, more thorough than the therapeutic analysis usually was. By this they meant that the training analysis should go beyond the oedipal phase into the pregenital phase of development. Their recommendation dealt only with an expansion of the clinical goals and not with didactic aspects of the training analysis. By that time, not only Ferenczi and Rank, but also the Berlin and the Vienna schools were convinced that while the analysis of a patient can be satisfactorily concluded if the therapeutic aim is achieved, the analysis of the training candidate has to give him insight into his "total personality" and "work through" analytically—i.e., in the transference—as many factors in the organization of that personality as possible. Thus the period of long, often interminable, or just not terminated training analyses began and it continued without a definition of its specific goals until training analysts became able to look upon themselves, not only as clinicians having at their command a method of achieving therapeutic aims, but also as educators whose psychoanalytic technique had a particular goal that "supersedes the therapeutic aim" but could not be separated from it.

Indeed, the interest in supervision as an intrinsic part of psycho-analytic education but separate from the training analysis was mani-fested about ten years after the codification of the training regulation. In 1935 and 1937 there were two meetings at which members of four Cen-tral European psychoanalytic societies met (Four Countries Conference) for scientific discussion. The training committees of those societies held closed meetings to discuss problems of supervision. In 1925 Helene Deutsch presented a paper on control analysis at the first of these meet-ings in Vienna. At the second meeting Edward Bibring (1937) outlined his concepts of the educational function of the supervisor. The abstracts of that paper reflect his thinking about the training analysis as prepara-tion for clinical work. I could assume that other theoreticians such as Fenichel or Glover had also been thinking about the problems of "teaching" through psychoanalyzing, but no one wrote about it, as if it were a tabooed subject. Imbued with an idealistic optimism about the effectiveness of psychoanalysis and convinced that they had mastered the "correct technique," these theoreticians interpreted Eitingon's two goals for training analysis as those which could be achieved by psycho-analysis. Freud (1937) was the first who tried to counteract this atti-tude.

The "illusional optimism" (Sachs, 1947) about psychoanalysis as a whole interfered with establishing criteria for selection of training analysts. If one were a recognized analyst in the society for five years, it was assumed that one had enough practical experience to become a training and (at the same time) a supervising analyst. This nonselective method was practiced long after the paucity of trained psychoanalysts that had necessitated it.

What did training analysts aim for in the early 1920s? The aim of analysis was to conduct analysis, to maintain the analytic process; even a therapeutic aim was considered secondary, a quasi fringe benefit of analysis. The professional aim was not as alluring as it would be today, and it was not a primary motivation for those who were my training candidates in Leipzig. The motive then for both student and training analyst was to discover and to learn. Had Leipzig (where I functioned as the only training analyst) not been an isolated island at that time, an "unsolvable syncretistic dilemma" would have developed, interfering with the analysis of the future analyst. As it was then, the same individ-uals whom I analyzed five to six mornings of the week also came to my house one evening a week to discuss psychoanalytic literature and learn theory from books. At that time it did not appear difficult to me or to them to change from one role to another. It seemed that I did not speculate about my role as the leader of a study group conflicting with my role as an analyst. Nor did my elders in Berlin. In the evening I was a student with my students; in the analytic session, if something came up in reference to or as a reaction to the interactions in the evenings, it was viewed either in the frame of the reality of the incident or interpreted in the transference.

From 1936 on, in the United States and in close contact and interaction with the faculty and students of the Chicago Institute for Psychoanalysis, the uniqueness of my situation in Leipzig dawned on me. I realized that had I been in Berlin[2] the competitiveness of the students in itself might have made it impossible to carry on my double function relatively successfully for more than ten years. In Chicago in the context of the operations of a large institute, I learned a great deal from other training analysts, especially through indirect communication. I supervised the analyses of their analysands or listened to them in clinical conferences. I came to realize that the "correct technique" to be applied in training analyses had many shadings. As I evaluated voluntarily but mostly intuitively the meaning and effectiveness of the training analysis for candidates, some ideas regarding goals and aims of the training analysis slowly grew upon me. They were far from any generalizable concepts, however. Indeed, the war years with their upheaval and the immediate postwar period with its urgency to expand psychoanalytic training were not opportune times to clarify the goals of training analysis or the methods by which these goals could be obtained by the means of psychoanalytic technique.

The mounting problems of training analysis might have troubled many analysts, the more since they were not alleviated by discussions. Even the principles of training analysis were shrouded in confidentiality. The last paper by Freud (1937) seems to indicate his concern with them. Since he regarded psychoanalysis as an interminable process for a psychoanalyst, he counteracted the idea that one therapeutic analysis would be enough to supply what the job of the analyst required. He recommended that in the training analysis the future analyst should learn to analyze himself since analysis is interminable. Since, however, not all latent conflict can be mobilized in one "analytic situation," he advised renewing the analytic situation in (almost) regular intervals of five years. This, indeed, would afford only limited opportunity for the self-analysis of the analyst. Blind spots, however, may and do occur in interaction with any patient or on any level of analysis, even in any phase of the clinical experience of an analyst. Whether the blind spots are transient or permanent depends to a high degree upon the analyst's capacity for self-analysis. Whether this means searching into the recesses of one's personality or just the evaluation of one's empathy and sympa-

2. I worked in Berlin from 1933 to 1936 also as a training and supervising analyst. At that time, however, under the continual threat by the Hitler regime, the functioning of the Institute was far from normal and my contact with its Educational Committee was peripheral.

thy with the experiences of patients, self-analysis accompanies the process of analyzing and as such is the only clearly formulated goal of the training analysis. In contrast to it, the "interminable analysis with one's training analyst" may act as a crutch.

Hanns Sachs was the first appointed training analyst at the Berlin Institute (1920). Shortly before his death in 1947 he wrote a paper in which he crystallized his experience in two recommendations; the first was:

> [The successful selection of psychoanalytic candidates rests on] defining as clearly as possible the special qualifications, uniquely different from those of any other profession, which give the promise of a good analyst (Sachs, 1947, p. 159).

The second formulated the goal of the training analysis. The purpose of all analysis is to remove resistances obstructing the development of a freely functioning ego.

> *The further objective [of the training analysis] is to make the understanding of the nature, language and the mechanisms of the unconscious sufficiently intimate, profound and intense that it becomes a permanent fixture in the mind and will be fully available when it is needed for sounding the unconscious of future analysands* (p. 165; my italics).

The aim of training analysis is described here with the artistic finesse of a first generation analyst, but neither the criteria implied in the first recommendation nor the method and indices of the second were outlined. Sachs might have felt, according to the habit of first and second generation analysts, that *Sapienti sat.* It is enough to call attention to the end; the means are afforded by the "correct technique."

In the same spirit Sachs made another significant allusion. In referring to the "optimistic illusion" of the candidates in training analysis, he observed that training analysts are inclined to share the student's illusion. Thus he called attention to the influence of the training analyst's emotional investment in his student-patient upon the course of the training analysis.[3] This cautious reference to the countertransference of training analysts shifted the responsibility for it—at least, in part—to the training analysts and, beyond that, to the professional ideal of psychoanalysis that, although it was not explicitly formulated, encompassed the realization of a high level of humanness.

This high goal of psychoanalytic education is also the implicit motivation of the candidate for training analysis; it deserves to be evalu-

3. This problem is discussed from another standpoint by Benedek (1954).

ated in the light of the general assumption that student-patients do not have as strong a motivation for forming therapeutic alliances as do patients suffering from neurotic symptoms. All patients come to analysis with the hope and wish that they will become healthier and happier people. The optimistic illusion of the training candidate, however, implies more than that. He wants to achieve more than freedom from symptoms; he aspires to attain not only professional status but also his ego ideal through psychoanalysis. He therefore idealizes psychoanalysis itself and, of course, his personal analyst along with it. This contributes to the unquestioning therapeutic optimism that did not subside after Freud's sincere and rather pessimistic warning (Freud, 1937). The training analyst's optimistic reliance upon his therapeutic instrument thus became a resistance against investigating its effects upon the course and outcome of the training analysis. It is fortunate if the student's striving toward realization of his professional ego ideal is in harmony with his endowment for the profession. It is the task of the training analyst to guide the student-patient toward such harmony. Whether the sights of the analyst can be raised or have to be lowered in the process, his double function as therapist and educator requires that he be aware in any phase of the student's analysis of how his own ambitions and professional ideals influence the course of the training analysis and the future of the student with it.

It is beyond the scope of this presentation to attempt to explain the time lag between a particular psychoanalytic educator's awareness of a specific educational necessity and the acceptance of it by a majority of training analysts. We should remember that Eitingon's emphasis upon the educational aim of training analysis was not heard, as if it had been drowned out by the noise of rumbling conflicts concerning the organization of psychoanalytic training. Yet the scope of the training analysis widened with the expansion of psychoanalytic knowledge and by the growing experience of individual training analysts. The technique might have, and largely did, remain the "correct one" as Eitingon envisaged it. But we have to face the fact that even the "correct technique" had changed since the time when the "psychoanalytic situation" was devised. In the same "experimental" setting, the evolving psychoanalytic process shifted, especially under the influence of psychoanalytic ego psychology.[4] Yet the significance of expanding psychoanalytic knowledge for the goals and techniques of the training analysis has not yet been investigated systematically.

The literature on training analysis in the last fifteen years differs from the literature of the past, not by elucidating its aims or by formulation of technical refinements or discriminations by which those aims

---

4. One of the shifts was from the "instinctual" to the "structural"; another—which interests us here especially—was from the "reductionistic" to the "experiential."

could be achieved, but rather by a greater awareness of its complications and shortcomings and by an urgency to do something about them.

The first overall sign of that urgency was the American Psychoanalytic Association's enthusiastic support of a survey of psychoanalytic education in the United States. The Survey Directors, Dr. Bertram Lewin and Miss Helen Ross, did what they were asked to do; they made an excellent report (Lewin and Ross, 1960), but they did not make recommendations. There was, however, a noticeable readiness to continue where Hanns Sachs left off. Attempts were made to formulate the specific qualifications which gave promise of a good analyst. The Chicago Training Analysts' Seminar devised its recommendations in 1954 but they have not been published. Probably other institutes have done the same. Holt and Luborsky (1958) at the Menninger Clinic investigated aptitude for general psychiatric work, not considering the specific requirements for practicing psychoanalysts. Joan Fleming's "job analysis" (Fleming, 1961) was the first investigation of what analytic work requires of an analyst from the viewpoint of the interaction between the analyst and his patient during the analytic process. Her recommendations can be expressed in the slogan, "Know what you are selecting for." From this it follows, "Know that you have to train your students for that for which you selected them."

This might have sounded strangely concrete to psychoanalysts who were used to relying on their intuition in forming opinions about applicants for psychoanalytic training, who felt that a cognitive approach would interfere with the specific psychoanalytic attitude and minimize the significance of the "touch with the preconscious." No wonder that only few psychoanalytic educators could have foreseen that the formulation of qualifications for training soon were to be followed by qualifications for the "job" of the training analyst. As the educational goal of the training analysis became more comprehensible as separate from but interrelated with the therapeutic aim of the analytic process, it also became clear that training analysts, besides being experienced, good analysts, needed to be individuals who have an interest in and aptitude for pursuing educational goals.

Indeed, it is right to raise the question, how did training analysts learn what they wanted to convey to their student-patients? I can try to answer this question only for myself. In the 1920s and 1930s training analysis was more an exploration by analytic technique than an analysis. But just because those early experiences were so meaningful, I have often compared how I functioned as a training analyst at the beginning with what I have learned since then. I can say that I learned primarily by my experience as a supervisor to know what would make a better training analyst. Through my work as a supervisor I experienced and practiced functioning in two roles at the same time—as an analyst of the patient and as the teacher of the student; I learned to perceive and diagnose what needed to be developed in the student to be able to function as an independent analyst in the future. After many years of such experience, I became aware that my attitude in training analysis had changed. My diagnostic responsiveness to the student-patient encompassed not only his past and his present but also his future as a psychoanalyst. Since my evaluative function has become an integrated part of myself as an "analytic instrument" (Isakower, 1957) it functions in the psychoanalytic situation in relation to the patient alone. When the time comes to write an evaluative report on the candidate, that function is a different mental activity, distinct from the analytic process. I assume that all psychoanalytic educators function in the same way, whether by intuition, as it used to be, or as a result of a consciously developed attitude as might be expected now.

Now we know more about the aims of the training analysis and about how to prepare the future training analyst who is a clinician for his work as a psychoanalytic educator. The training analyst is entrusted with developing the student's capabilities to function as an instrument of the analytic process. To that aim his diagnostic acumen has to be so well developed that he can perceive and recognize in the manifestations of an analytic process whatever is referable to the student-patient's aptitude for functioning as a future analyst. To function effectively in this role, he must be aware of what he is preparing the student for. Within his therapeutic function the training analyst learns about the student-patient's unconscious, his conflicts and defenses, but beyond this he observes his way of learning about his unconscious (Wallerstein, 1969). He assesses not only the developmental conflicts and the personality of the student, but also his perceptiveness, his communication with his unconscious, his empathy, and his "humanity," as well as his endurance for the empathic understanding of that humanness which continually requires his productive, helpful response. The qualifications could form a long list; it would include the capacity for enduring frustration and tolerating regression, but also an ability to control, quasi "dose" the patient's regressions, etc. This incomplete and haphazardly compiled list will suffice to indicate the sweep of diagnostic activities of the training analyst, a range that is broader than any other clinical analysis would require.

The question arises whether and how training analysts can induce in the present-day student of psychoanalysis that immediacy and directness of experience which is the result of "primary process operations." Since theoretical knowledge, as Freud pointed out in several contexts, is "written on another level of the mind" (Freud, 1912), training analysts have to strive to counteract that knowledge which blinds the perceptiveness of direct experience; they have to keep alive the indelible traces of their psychoanalytic experiences in order to remain empathetically responsive to new impressions, to the experiences of their patients. This safeguards the training analyst against the habit of interpreting in terms of theoretical schemes; at the same time this also affords the method by which he can help the student to develop his self-observation, perceive his signal affects, and so experience his emerging unconscious. What was experienced but often remained implicit in the early days of analysis can now become more definite and explicit since we know more about the ego functions operating in the analytic process. Observations of ego operation, such as the flow of associations, awareness of mood changes and the defenses accompanying them, perception of intrapsychic processes, etc., have more significance than for the usual patient. The training analyst, therefore, keeping in mind the professional aim of his patient, will pay more attention to these processes, will direct his attention to them, so that the student by his self-observation will develop the psychoanalytic equipment and learn to counteract his tendency to "interpret" his patient's psychoanalytic experience in the theoretical scheme of dynamic genetic patterns.

Does the training analyst "teach" in the process of training analysis? No, if by teaching one means exposition of theoretical concepts. He does not teach more in training analyses than with his other patients, i.e., through occasional explanations of his interventions and interpretations. But he teaches, if we understand teaching in the sense in which Isakower applied it to supervision, namely by "clarifying the instrument." For not only does he aim at removing blind spots, but in the process of achieving this aim he develops the student's capacity to "listen with the third ear" (Reik, 1948), to observe his associative processes, his feelings, and to learn to analyze what the patient feels and he understands.

How did he learn it? As long as learning psychoanalysis by being analyzed or even by supervision was considered a diffuse preconscious process, recognizable in its effect on knowing, one could be satisfied with the assumption that the model of learning the method of psychoanalysis was identification. Identification is a psychic representation of the biologic process of internalizing, a condition of learning. The overemphasis on identification in teaching and learning psychoanalysis is, however, rather an impediment to the investigation of those intrapsychic processes that must occur in the mind of the analyst in order to arrive from the primary processes of the psychoanalytic experience to the understanding of its current meaning for the patient and to evolve from them a genetic and dynamic interpretation of that which has taken place. Considering the significance of primary processes in the psychoanalytic method, the study of training analysis and psychoanalytic supervision has much to offer regarding "creative" teaching and learning. More immediate, however, is the importance of such studies for psychoanalytic education itself, since only more knowledge of the processes that are involved in institutionalized education can relieve the burden of the syncretistic dilemma. The syncretistic dilemma as emphasized by Lewin and Ross (1960) is a built-in problem of the psychoanalytic training system that arose from the more vigorous training requirements. Their work, however, instead of relaxing the requirements, called more attention to the conditions of psychoanalytic training.

It is encouraging to observe the vivid interest in the problems of training in psychoanalysis as it grows steadily, not only in surface expansion but also in depth. Having learned the principles of their science, psychoanalytic teachers are facing their problems as educators as if they were more certain of their route. Since the older generations of training analysts are better able to teach, the younger ones are more ready to learn. This was demonstrated by the remarkable experience of the two Three-Institute Conferences on Training Analysis. The first of these conferences sponsored by the Chicago, Pittsburgh, and Topeka psychoanalytic institutes took place on 1–4 April 1965, and was held at the Western Psychiatric Institute and Clinic in Pittsburgh. The report of that conference prepared by Charlotte G. Babcock (1969), the coordinator of the conference, is an impressive document. It was available to all participants before the second conference took place so that they might use that rich documentation of productive discussions between experienced teachers and their colleagues as a springboard for further discussions. The second Three-Institute Conference took place on 10–13 April 1969, and was held at the Menninger Foundation in Topeka. Comparing my experiences I can say that the members of both conferences worked hard from the beginning to the end. There was no fatigue in the groups as a whole; there were always questions asked, answered, and discussed from the point of view of technique, as seen by the teacher or the learner. Those who participated only in the second conference might have missed some of the excitement which we experienced with the first experiment of that kind and its successful outcome. However, those who participated in both conferences had an opportunity to make comparative observations significant enough to substitute for the excitement.

Many of the younger generation of training analysts who participated in the first conference did not attend the second conference; many who were at the second conference were not yet training analysts at the time of the first conference. Thus I had the opportunity to compare the groups of young training analysts, both in the first four years of their experience. It appeared to me that those who were in Topeka were freer in discussion, their questions were more mature, based on more experience and knowledge, than the individuals whom I had observed four years earlier. My conclusion from this was that the preparation for becoming a training analyst was more effective than previously, even if it occurred through the osmosis of the problems of training that seems to be free-floating, at least in these three institutes.

This, of course, is only a personal impression; I did not attempt to gain consensual validation of it. But the satisfaction I gained from it became reinforced as I read in the *Bulletin of the Schweizerische Gesellschaft für Psychoanalyse* the reports from various European institutes. In preparation for the oncoming International Congress in Rome that programmed a pre-Congress meeting on supervision, these institutes (not all of them but a representative number of them) report about their procedures in selecting candidates and their attitude regarding training analyses and supervision. There may be some, especially in Europe or even farther away, who view with disenchantment such institutionalization of the movement, but for those who want to safeguard psychoanalysis in our world of expanded communication this is a challenge and a promise for the future.

I have reviewed the history of training analysis, its changing goals and techniques as reflected through my own experience. My reasons for applying such a self-centered approach in the elaboration of such a fundamental subject are twofold. One is that I was a participant in the evolution of training analysis through more than four decades. I experienced being a training analyst alone and then becoming a part of an organized training system. I experienced the attitudes of students whose only teacher I was and also those who had their psychoanalytic training during the period when the centrally organized training system evoked the mirage of the "syncretistic dilemma." The other reason, which is also the aim of this discussion, is my intention to shift the burden of the dilemma of training analysis from the student to his training analyst, from the effect of the training system upon both the training analyst and his student-patient to the job of the training analyst, to his double function as psychoanalyst and professional educator. To work out this aspect of the training system is the task of the training system. The events of the last decades indicate that there is a growing awareness of the necessity to educate psychoanalysts for their function as educators. The manifold yield of such education justified the optimistic statement that I quote here. Speaking of the termination of the training analysis, I said:

> After the teacher has conveyed the equipment for the voyage to his students, the trip has to be made by each of them alone. Whether they will come back with trivial or great experience, with new discoveries or only with a restatement of the past, in ten or twenty years each of them will know something different from that which their teachers knew and in this sense they will know more (Benedek, 1955, p. 624, footnote 1).

REFERENCES

Babcock, C. G. (ed.) (1969). *Training Analysis; Report of the First Three-Institute Conference on Psychoanalytic Education.* Pittsburgh: Pittsburgh Psychoanalytic Institute.

Benedek, T. (1954). Countertransference in the training analyst. *Bull. Menninger Clin.* **18,** 12–16.

Benedek, T. (1955). A contribution to the problem of termination of training analysis. *J. Am. Psychoanal. Ass.* **3,** 615–629.

Bibring, E. (1937). Second Four-Countries Conference in Budapest. *Int. J. Psycho-Anal.* **18,** 369–372.

Deutsch, H. (1935). Practical training in psychoanalysis: First Four-Countries Conference in Vienna. *Int. J. Psycho-Anal.* **16,** 505–509.

Eitingon, M. (1926). Preliminary Discussion of the Question of Analytic Training, 1925. *Int. J. Psycho-Anal.* **7,** 129–135.

Eitingon, M. (1937). Opening Address by the Chairman of the International Training Commission, 1936. *Int. J. Psycho-Anal.* **18,** 350–358.

Ferenczi, S. & Rank, O. (1925). *The Development of Psychoanalysis; Interrelations between Theory and Practice.* New York and Washington, D.C.: Nervous & Mental Disease Publ. Co.

Fleming, J. (1961). What analytic work requires of an analyst: a job analysis. *J. Am. psychoanal. Ass.* **9,** 719–729.

Fleming, J. & Benedek, T. (1966). *Psychoanalytic Supervision.* New York: Grune & Stratton.

Freud, S. (1910). Address to the Second International Psychoanalytic Congress. *Jb. psychoanal. Forsch.* **2,** 731–732. (Abstract.)

Freud, S. (1912). Recommendations to physicians practising psychoanalysis. *S.E.* **12.**

Freud, S. (1937). Analysis terminable and interminable. *S.E.* **23.**

Freud, S. (1965). *The Letters of Sigmund Freud and Karl Abraham, 1907–1926.* New York: Basic Books.

Gitelson, M. (1964). On the identity crisis in American psychoanalysis. *J. Am. Psychoanal. Ass.* **12,** 451–476.

Holt, R. & Luborsky, L. (1958). *Personality Patterns of Psychiatrists.* New York: Basic Books.

Isakower, O. (1957). Problems of supervision. (Report to the Curriculum Committee of the New York Psychoanalytic Institute; unpublished.)

Kubie, L. (1965). Unsolved problems of scientific education. *Daedalus,* Summer.

Kuhn, T. (1963). *The Structure of Scientific Revolutions.* Chicago: Univ. of Chicago Press.

Lewin, B. & Ross, H. (1960). *Psychoanalytic Education in the United States.* New York: Norton.

Reik, T. (1948). *Listening with the Third Ear.* New York: Farrar Strauss.

Sachs, H. (1947). Observations of a training analyst. *Psychoanal. Q.* **16,** 157–168.

Wallerstein, R. (1969). Comments. In C. G. Babcock (ed.), *Training
Analysis; Report of the First Three-Institute Conference on Psychoanalytic
Education.* Pittsburgh: Pittsburgh Psychoanalytic Institute.

DYNAMICS OF THE
COUNTERTRANSFERENCE*

The concept and the phenomenology of countertransference are dynamically interrelated with the concept and phenomena of the transference.
Since the time Freud defined psychoanalytic process as an interaction between *transference* (i.e., the tendency for the repetition of
instinctual needs) and the *resistance* against it (this tendency), the phenomena of the "transference struggle" (transference neurosis) have
been studied in great detail. The conditions and procedures by means
of which the transference can be kept as an "active motor" of the therapeutic process was enunciated by Freud and discussed frequently by
others. We know that the "transference struggle" can be kept "optimal"
in that it can be increased or decreased in emotional intensity. However,
the fact that the emotions of the therapist can enter actively into this
process or can modify it has received little study or discussion.

This does not mean that the existence of the countertransference
was not recognized in the early phases of psychoanalysis. The fact is
that it was recognized, but was dealt with in a relatively summary
fashion (for which there was some justification).

Toward the general handling of the complexity of the countertransference reactions, the rule was introduced that every individual who
intends to practice psychoanalysis should undergo a thorough psychoanalysis himself. Thereby, the analysand, having become aware of his
own blind spots, should become conscious of his own conflicts and,
consequently, as the therapist, he should become able to see them, to
recognize them in the patients and, having lost his blind spots, be able
to deal with the same conflicts in his patients without being personally
involved, that is, without undue countertransference. This expectation
was not overoptimistic at a time when psychoanalysis consisted mainly
in *seeing,* in *not being blind,* in regard to the unconscious conflicts and
their tendency to be repeated in the phenomena of the transference.

Another general check on the countertransference was the external
arrangement of the psychoanalytic session; the patient lying on the
couch and the analyst sitting invisible behind him and trying to represent
only an impersonal screen. Freud frankly admitted that he used this

* Presented to the Chicago Psychoanalytic Society, March 22, 1949,
Chicago, Illinois. Since this was part of a panel discussion, the literature has
not been reviewed. Reprinted from *Bulletin of the Menninger Clinic,* Vol.
17, No. 6 (November, 1953).

arrangement, inherited from the days of hypnosis, because he did not like "to be stared at"; thus, it served him as a protection in the transference-countertransference duel. Yet this arrangement became one of the mainstays of our therapeutic technique. This could happen only because this "setting" fulfills a specific function; it serves as a protection (defense) for the analyst. The therapist, sitting invisibly behind the patient (except when the patient turns around, which behavior the therapist was permitted to criticize as "resistance"), is surrounded by a screen for his own good. Behind this screen, he can deal with his own emotions; if he is well analyzed and able to objectify his own reactions, he may recognize his countertransference and, consequently, he may suppress his feelings or he may manage them in some manner. He may sample his formalistic and impersonal attitudes, which is his task; for one assumed that such behavior of the therapist permits the patient to develop his transference unimpaired, and as a behavior for which the patient alone is responsible. Thus the therapist may interpret its manifestations and deal with them "objectively." This was the reason that analysts were and still are strictly advised to remain aloof, lest the patient respond in a manner which may confuse the transference and render it unmanageable.

Actually, this attitude of the psychoanalysts helped to refine the "transference-resistance" technique and developed it to a fine tool of research. However, whenever measures were proposd to activate the technique and impose it as a tool of therapy—as was done by Ferenczi, by Wilhelm Reich, and recently by Alexander—the concept of countertransference appeared in the focus of the discussion. As the history of psychoanalysis shows, the discussion of countertransference usually ended in a retreat to defensive positions. The argument to this end used to be that the classical attitude affords the best guaranty that the *personality of the therapist* would not enter the action-field of the therapeutic process. By that, one assumed that as long as the analyst does not reveal himself as a person, does not answer questions regarding his own personality, he remains unknown as if without individuality, that the transference process may unfold and be motivated only by the patient's resistances. The patient—although he is a sensitive, neurotic individual—is not supposed to sense and discern the therapist as a person.

I was aroused from this convenient assumption on a hot summer day, when I was still a very young analyst. The room was darkened against the sun. I was sitting behind the patient, a soft-spoken young woman. During a pause in which there was no noise, no movement, a pause which was not longer than that which I would usually wait for her associations, she began, "Dr. Benedek, should I tell you the dream again? because you did not hear it." She said this calmly, in her soft voice, without aggression. It was the truth. I asked her to tell the dream again, because I had not been listening. But I learned then that a patient *may listen to my silence, too.*

After this experience, the following statement in Freud's paper, "The Dynamic of the Transference," had a different meaning for me. Freud stated: "Experience shows, and a test will always confirm it, that when patients' free associations fail, the obstacle can be removed every time by an assurance that he is now possessed by thoughts which concern the person of the physician." One usually assumes that this statement refers to material concerning the transference reaction. Rarely does one realize that the patient, under the pressure of his emotional needs—needs which may be motivated by the frustration of the transference—may grope for the therapist as a real person, may sense his reactions, and will sometimes almost read his mind.

I am not a sufficiently compulsive observer to have recorded the several experiences which were more striking than the one which I mentioned; they would have demonstrated the emotional dynamics of situations in which the patient surmises the personality of the therapist beyond that which is or shall be accessible for the patient in the therapeutic situation.

You may say, *"This is the transference;* this is the manifestation of the dependent needs of the patient." Yes, the patient, like an infant who needs *to be one with the mother,* in his need for identification with the therapist, bores his way into the preconscious mind of the therapist and often emerges with surprising evidences of empathy—of preconscious awareness of the therapist's personality and even of his problems.

I am not referring here to the exaggerated positive and negative assumptions which are projections originating in the patient's transference needs; nor am I speaking here about information which the patients gather about the analyst before and during therapy. They may use such information provocatively—negatively and positively. Yet such information, whether it is valid or not, has not the same significance to the patient as the assumption, which has the sign of emotional "evidence" because the patient arrived at it intuitively. One may say—the patient arrived at his knowledge the same way as the therapist gains his own insight. In this sense, his knowledge may be the result of a "competitive attitude"; yet this does not diminish either the validity or the emotional significance of such experience, for the so-gained assumptions about the therapist become important for the patient as well as for the therapist during the therapeutic process.

How does the therapist respond to being "recognized" by the patient? I believe the answer to this question is the key to many countertransference situations.

Briefly, let me illustrate with one or two incidents. A patient of mine, a young woman who had one child and much guilt because she felt that this child interfered with her political and professional career, dreamed, in the third week of her analysis, that she was taking care of a neglected and retarded child, while a psychiatrist, who was her friend, was talking to her. Very soon, I could show her that, in this dream, although she exaggerated tremendously the possible neglected state of my children, *she wanted to help me,* because she assumed, and justifiably so, that in reality we had some identical problems. The dream was brusque and depreciating. Yet I felt that it would have been unfair to interpret this as *hostility,* as a "negative transference." The *intention* of the dream was the desire to be "equal" with the analyst. This wish, and its validity, as far as some of its reality aspects were concerned, was discussed sincerely. I am certain that if I had interpreted her dream-thought—to help me in taking care of my children—as a depreciation of myself and a competition with me, the patient would have felt misunderstood and demeaned; she would have become hostile and we would have had a difficult transference neurosis at an early stage of the analysis.

It is the analyst's task to select from the many motivations which determine the manifest dream content the one which gave the significant impulse to the dream. No doubt, the therapist's attitudes toward his patients generally, or toward the one patient specifically, may motivate his selection of the material and his handling of it. Some may even now call this countertransference. The point which I want to make is that the complication in therapy arises usually when the therapist has a blind spot against being recognized and reacted to by the patient as a *real person.* I have seen often that an analysis came to an impasse because the therapist either did not realize that the patient was talking about *him,* or if he realized it, he tended to avoid the issue, or he misunderstood the intention of the patient, because it put the therapist on the defensive.

A young woman, artistically trained, got a glimpse of a drawing which the therapist had made. She commented eagerly and positively. The therapist, however, defensive for some reason, answered coldly, "This [namely, her praise] is just a denial of your competition with men." The girl felt misunderstood and punished. She also felt that a man who misunderstood her intentions to such a degree could not understand her at all. I do not want to indicate that the therapist might not have been right on some deeper level. Yet, what he said was untimely, depreciating toward the patient, and disappointing to her. The patient lost her confidence in the therapist; yet, of course, she did not leave the therapy.

It would be worthwhile to describe step by step how the transference neurosis developed from this point on. However, I shall only sketch the main point of the transference neurosis. The incident with the picture was a normal ego-reaction of the "adult" personality of the patient who wanted to be taken seriously in a field in which she felt competent; beside this, her enthusiasm was also an expression of the desire to be loved by the ideal father. Rejected by him, in the patient's eyes, the father-therapist became "weak," like her real father was. The therapist did not recognize and did not resolve the conflict which originated in the girl's disappointment in him as a protective, father-mother person. He interpreted the hostile, critical attitude of the patient as the manifestation of her unresolved competition with her brothers which—although it was true in some sense—proved to the patient only that the therapist himself was an ambivalent "brother." Thus the patient was quite aware of the countertransference. Yet she was helpless in convincing the therapist. Her helplessness increased her hostility toward the therapist and her aggressive, childlike behavior toward the analyst in turn increased her guilty feelings. Even more, her behavior decreased her self-esteem and her belief that she could really grow through the therapy. Thus the analysis of a relatively simple character neurosis came to an impasse and had to be interrupted when the patient was in a state of severe depression.

Psychoanalysis, with its complex interaction of many motivations, can hardly be compressed and done justice by the selection of one or two factors determining its course. Yet, in studying the development of intense transference neuroses, one comes to the realization that one of the most important motivations in its development is the *patient's reaction to the countertransference attitude of the therapist.*

This statement is—you may say—quite a big one. Its validity should be carefully studied in a great variety of cases; one should study the interaction between transference and countertransference in cases in which the transference process remained optimal, and in those in which various degrees of transference neurosis hindered the therapeutic process.

Here, I shall try only to answer one question or objection: does this phenomenon—the therapist's reaction to the empathy of the patient—fit the definition of countertransference, or does it belong to those "all kinds of feelings which the therapists may have toward their patients"?

We have two definitions of countertransference: one is that countertransference is the therapist's reaction to the transference of the patient. Since "transference" is the repetition of the past, it seems that the empathy of the patient, if it relates to the actual personality of the analyst, is not necessarily a transference phenomenon—not more so than any other manifestation of *Menschenkenntniss.* Yet, as I have shown in these two examples, the analyst's reaction may open widely and almost uncontrollably the door for unconscious transference reactions, depending upon his handling of such occurrence. The countertransference, which then develops, is covered up by the manifestations of the transference neurosis for which, at least partially, the therapist's reactions were responsible.

The other definition is that countertransference is the analyst's projection of an important person of his past into his patient. Our example shows that the motivations which determine the therapist's reaction to the patient's empathy often remain unconscious. As long as the therapist is emotionally free in handling the patient's reactions toward him, whether they be transference reactions, or *actually valid* responses to his personality, the countertransference is kept in check. Yet, sooner or later, the therapist may stamp the patient's attitude, his empathy, his guessing the truth, as "provocative behavior." What does represent "provocation"? Actually, it is the attitude which compels the therapist to give up his position as an *impersonal agent* of the therapy. Then several possibilities which may help or harm the analytic process may occur. One is that the therapist understands the need which provokes the patient's preoccupation with him, and he can channelize this need through interpretations, or through other attitudes which may be profitable for the therapeutic process. The other is that he is really provoked; that is, the therapist becomes afraid of the therapy because the patient's active desire to discern the motivations of the therapist converts the patient to a representative of other persons. The patient becomes—as in the case quoted above—the feared "castrative woman" in the analyst's life, or he may become any person toward whom the therapist once felt helpless. Thus the patient, not only by the actual obligation, but also through the countertransference, becomes a partial representative of the therapist's superego; and then his inhibition in regard to that patient may grow beyond his control. And even if the countertransference does not develop to this degree, it is easily understandable that the therapist's fear of the patient's "insight" into his motivations or his "fear" of the patient's transference reaction will inhibit the therapist's productive imagination. Such inhibition makes it difficult to find the trend which would lead out from the vicious circle which such countertransference creates.

In a very condensed example, I would like to show how the inhibited imagination of the therapist produced in this manner increases the *actual transference* neurosis.

An anxious, schizoid young Jewish man, married and having one child, was treated by a young therapist of another religion and nationality. From the beginning, he projected his fear of antisemitism onto the therapist, who learned to handle the patient's lack of confidence based on this motivation objectively. Yet the therapist was often uneasy with this highly intellectual man, whose desire to be passively dependent on the therapist was often overcompensated by attacks on him (proving that he was not good). Then the patient's wife, afraid of losing her husband, began to clamor for a second child in order to stabilize the marriage. The patient, who was emotionally and economically unable to take on more responsibility, became very depressed. He had a nightmare in which he was lying on the railroad track with his child in his arms. He could not move away when the train came. Although he miraculously was not hit, he awoke with great fear. The therapist did not recognize the significance of the dream, the desperate warning that he would rather kill himself with his child than have another child.

The analysis did not release the guilt which the patient felt toward the child and the anxiety dream was followed by a depression in which the dreams revealed his reproach toward the therapist, who was not helping by pointing out to the patient only the passive homosexual tendencies, his tendency to withdraw and to be taken care of. Finally, the patient had a dream in which he even more clearly than ever identified himself with his hysterical mother. In analyzing the dream, he told the therapist, *"I have to exaggerate my symptoms like my mother did. My mother needed to exaggerate her complaints, lest father did not care; I have to exaggerate in order to make you understand my situation."* No doubt, this brings to the fore the mother-identification of the patient and puts the therapist back into his father position, from whence the therapeutic process may continue.

I brought up this example of the developing *transference neurosis* to elucidate another point, namely: that the phenomena of the countertransference and their effects upon the transference neurosis could be more easily neglected as long as the therapy was mainly concerned with the unfolding of the developmental processes in the transference. In our present-day therapy, however, the ego and its defenses are in the foreground.

As you remember, the analysis of the ego's defenses was consistently employed at first by Wilhelm Reich. His idea, which proved to be correct, was that by attacking the ego's defenses, one may activate the conflict tension against which the characterological defense developed. Such activation of the psychoanalytic technique, however, changed the structure of the relationship between therapist and patient. A therapist who is actively "hammering" on the defenses cannot remain a "screen" at which the patient projects his thoughts and feelings. It is unavoidable then that the patient, deliberately or intuitively, tries to "explain" the analyst's attitudes, his activity, as a manifestation of the therapist's personality. The therapist, dealing with the present ego of the patient, with his actual relations rather than with his past and his fantasies, enters the therapeutic process more directly with his own personality than was his function in previous phases of psychoanalytic technique. While many analysts still perfunctorily repeat at the beginning of the therapy that no important decision should be made during the therapy, it became a part of the therapeutic activity to analyze, and influence many of the actual decisions and life situations of the patient.

Such a function, however, requires—even more than psychoanalysis did heretofore—emotional maturity, psychosexual stability, and personal integrity on the part of the therapist. These concepts, maturity and integrity, have to be more distinctly evaluated in relation to the tasks of the therapist than they are generally for describing ethical and personal attributes. In the analytic situation, they have to be combined with an intellectual honesty which is the result of the therapist's free access to his own unconscious motivations; for he has to be able to understand and check his countertransference reactions through all the vicissitudes of the analytic process.

In conclusion: Psychoanalytic procedure is the unfolding of an interpersonal relationship in which transference and countertransference are utilized to achieve the therapeutic aim. This definition indicates that the therapist's personality is the most important agent of the therapeutic process.

COUNTERTRANSFERENCE IN
THE TRAINING ANALYST*

Training analysis is a therapeutic procedure, the aim of which is—beyond elimination of symptoms—to effect such changes as will make the personality an effective instrument for the professional tasks of psychoanalysis. The *training analyst* is one who is qualified by experience for such a task; that is, he has had enough practice in handling his countertransference reactions to be able to handle them also in the particular complications of a training analysis.

In this short discussion of infinitely complex interpersonal responses, I will omit the discussion of the psychodynamics and the phenomena of countertransference in general, that is, as it may occur in any analysis; as it is rooted in his personality, any training analyst may encounter it in his psychoanalytic response to any of his patients, also, in response to his training cases. I shall discuss only the specific manifestations of countertransference which are motivated by the particular conditions of the training analysis itself.

A profession which necessitates such an extensive and deep-going experience as the training analysis becomes, as a result, an organization in which emotional interpersonal relations are more significant than in any other profession. I assume that the specific countertransference reactions of the training analyst originate at first in the organization of the profession itself.

For, in this organization, the *emotional structure* of the family—its

* Presented in a panel discussion: "Countertransference in the Training Analyst" with Karl Menninger, M.D., Chairman, Sandor Lorand, M.D., and Edith Weigert, M.D., to the American Psychoanalytic Association, April 29, 1950, Detroit, Michigan. Reprinted from *Bulletin of the Menninger Clinic,* Vol. 18, No. 1 (January, 1954).

psychodynamic constellations—is reproduced. This is nothing new. The influence of Freud's personality, not as a great explorer of the human mind, but as a patriarch, has often been discussed. The "rebellion" of the sons, the rivalry of the "brothers" (not to mention the daughters and sisters) has also been evaluated. The patients of each of us regard themselves as siblings, claiming the right to rivalry and ambivalence toward each other. And we all, who are now parental figures, were "siblings," sons or daughters of a training analyst some time ago. We realize the emotional reality, hidden beyond such *façon de parler*. Yet we rarely take cognizance of its significance in our work.

Probably it would be going too far in delineating the dynamics of countertransference in training analysis to discuss the historical development of psychoanalysis. Yet I cannot state my point without referring briefly to the compact closeness in that first group which decided about the necessity of training analysis in 1918. Four years later, Freud published his concept of the dynamics of the organization of the group. That was a living reality at that time in Freud's life and in the lives of the other individualists who formed the psychoanalytic organization. In this group, Freud was the unquestioned leader; the identification with him gave access to membership in the group; the members of the group, while identifying with the leader, were identified among each other. But, at the same time, the members of this group were striving to maintain their own identity by emphasizing their *small* differences. This group, proudly aware of their insight in a new field of knowledge, was a militant minority in a hostile world of medicine and psychology. Hence the intensification of the group narcissism; hence the similarity between this organization and that of the patriarchal family.

In the patriarchal family, the family pride identifies and protects all members of the family against the attacks of external enemies. The role of the individual within the family, however, is defined by the place which he plays in the family constellation and this, in turn, determines in high degree the emotional development of each member. It is the same in the organization of the psychoanalytic family. Through the training analysis, each new member of the group becomes attached to his teacher and when this younger member of the group, some five years later, becomes a training analyst himself, he is, or used to be, in a highly complicated position in the dynamic configuration of the psychoanalytic organization. He has (or used to have) an allegiance to the ideal father, Freud, and he has (or had) a highly ambivalent, emotionally charged relationship to his own training analyst. By becoming a training analyst, he is like a man—like most men—who becomes a father without having resolved his conflicts with his own father. He is compelled by his unconscious to live out in his attitude toward his children those conflicts which he has in regard to his functions and responsibilities as a parent.

You may answer that his own training analysis had to resolve those conflicts. I agree, but I also maintain that there is a difference, even if it is only a quantitative one, between resolving one's childhood conflicts in the transference, and in outgrowing them in real living as a parent. And this is the point where the countertransference of the training analysts plays its tricks. For these specific countertransference phenomena originate in the conflicts which the training analyst has in his function as a parental image. No doubt his parental attitudes are motivated by his childhood experiences, but they are revived by the transference reactions, by the *attachment* formed by his own training analysis and by the strict (patriarchal) organization of the group (probably not as it is now, but as it used to be).

Thus, like fathers who may treat their children in a way which will give the children what the father was deprived of, or will deprive the children because of their own deprivation, training analysts may have an attitude toward the candidate which expresses: "I want you to have a better time in your analysis than I had in mine." (Underneath, this may have the motivation: "I wish you would not become as hostile toward me as I am toward my analyst.") Or, "I want you to have as bad a time of it as I had (then I know and I can control your hostility)."

But even if the training analyst is far removed in time from his own training analysis and has resolved his transference toward his own analyst, he may still with each of the training analysands be put to the task of resolving his own problems in regard to his own parental functions and attitudes. For example, training analysts may be eager to prove that they are good fathers, not competitive with sons and will let them grow up to become full competitors, or they may try to prove that they are good mothers, who allow the sons and daughters to become independent; or that they are not fathers or mothers who would "castrate" their children and, to prove it, they will not attack the defenses of the candidate where it will hurt. Whether the analysand becomes aware of a repressed, unconscious emotion (tendency) in the analyst, or whether in his wish to be recognized as a full-fledged competitor of his training analyst, his fears become exaggerated—in any case his negative transference will soon be expressed. For example, he says, "I know, you never want me to be better than you are; you won't let me be successful," or, "If I become successful, you will use what you know about me against me." Probably it is difficult in every analysis to take the patient's accusations, since the analyst is convinced of his own unquestionably good intentions. But in the training analysis, this becomes often the crux of the countertransference. Why?

Let me return for a moment to the organization of the profession in which every member is eager to maintain his distinction and the training analyst may enhance his position in the group by creating disciples, by becoming the stern father of many. Thus the psychoanalytic procedure which ideally should not have other aims than its own goal, namely, the resolution of the patient's conflicts, becomes a tool for other aims; and this makes the training analyst feel guilty.

On this point, I want to mention what has been currently discussed often as the emulation of the training analyst by his candidate. One may experience a superficial, imitative identification, for a period of time, with any kind of patient. My patients—training cases or others —often tell me that their friends remark that they have now acquired an accent or that they have a habit of beginning their statements with the explanatory "You see," as I do. But they overcome such habits soon. This would have something to do with training only if I were to insist that my candidate should maintain such an attitude as a "technique." The most significant manifestation of the countertransference is the training analyst's unconscious or conscious tendency to *foster the candidate's identification with him, his dependence on him.* For training analysts tend to project themselves unduly in the candidate; they tend to identify themselves—as parents do with their children—with the candidate. One of the most conspicuous manifestations of this identification is the training analyst's overprotective, unobjective attitude toward his training patient. He, the analyst, often takes it as a personal insult if someone is critical of the candidate. The training analysts often act, and often they even behave, as overprotective parents do.

What is the motivation of the "parental overprotection"? The most significant one is the insecurity in regard to the child; the fear of one's inability to handle the child and to treat and educate him to his best advantage. Since one is not certain how to achieve this goal, the parent becomes guilty about his mistakes. The situation in the training analysis is very much the same. The overprotectiveness of the analyst is often the result of the complexity of the goal in the training analysis. The analyst feels as if he had promised too much, as if he had promised that he would make the candidate perfectly happy, perfectly free, and a perfectly good analyst. Since one does not quite know how to achieve this goal, the analyst may feel insecure. At the same time, he is aware of his own tremendous emotional investment in such an analysis. Thus, like an anxious and narcissistic parent, the training analyst feels that his product must be perfect, or at least superior to that of other analysts! His overcompensation grows parallel with the underlying sense of guilt and his guilt toward the candidate is the same as that of parents, who, in a competitive family, want to achieve the greatest prestige through their children.

Since my discussion is based on the assumption that the group organization and the competition of the analysts within the group are responsible for the countertransference reactions, it is justified to ask whether the loosening of the organization would diminish *this* source of error and failure in our work.

There are good indications that this can be expected. For example, in larger institutes, where many training analysts work together, and where, at least within the one institute the standing of the training analyst is secure, his need to produce disciples diminishes. I have also observed that the younger generation of training analysts, themselves trained in large institutes, approach their task with greater objectivity; their reports on their training cases are often more articulate than the reports of their older colleagues. These are good signs!

The psychoanalytic training family has reached that phase of its development where we can afford to express our concern about its procedures and may discuss our mistakes. The countertransference in general has long been neglected in our literature and discussions. The reasons for this, we assume, are obvious. Yet, taking our own defensiveness for granted does not help eliminate the cause of our mistakes. I assume, in general, that unresolved, suppressed, and unrecognized countertransference is the source of irreparable or long and painful transference neurosis and this is true for training analysis too.

Let us hope that the discussion of the problems involved will help to create in the organization of the profession, in its training institutes, as well as in the person-to-person relationship in the training analysis, that optimal condition for transference and learning which is the most beneficial for development.

A CONTRIBUTION TO THE PROBLEM OF TERMINATION OF TRAINING ANALYSIS*

The problems related to the termination of training analysis are determined, just as in any other process nearing its end, by problems related to its beginning and to its course. We cannot hope for clarification of the problems concerning its termination unless we can clarify the function of the personal analysis of the future psychoanalyst in the total psychoanalytic training process.

As long as training in psychoanalysis was acquired in a manner of apprenticeship (1), the interrelation of the three aspects of training —personal analysis, supervised analyses, and theoretical courses—and their effective coordination could not be studied since in each instance the interpersonal relationship between teacher and pupil dominated the

* Reprinted from the *Journal of the American Psychoanalytic Association,* Vol. III, No. 4 (October, 1955).

training. Since Ferenczi (5) stated that training analysis needs to be more thorough than therapeutic analysis, the time required for training analysis, which originally had been of but few months' duration, has become longer and longer. One reason for this is that the goal of the psychoanalytic process has become increasingly complex with the evolution of psychoanalysis as a science and a therapeutic tool. The other reason, however, is rather doubtful because it originates in the expectation that if only the personal analysis is carried on long enough, all problems, which in a given case might interfere with the successful progress of a candidate, could be resolved and the goal of his personal development as well as his training would be achieved. Yet such optimism needs scrutiny beyond the clinical evidence in reference to the various phases of training, since there are indications that the effectiveness of the training analysis might be seriously impeded by the interference of the training process itself.

Balint (1) in a critical study of the psychoanalytic training system calls attention to the dangers of an all too dogmatic and hierarchic training organization. He as well as Glover (9) warns against the possible self-limitation of a scientific training which requires the incorporation of a superego (the training analyst) of such immediate power that creative scientific independence can hardly be maintained.[1] In another panel discussion of this organization (2), I discussed how the countertransference of the training analyst is affected by the group psychology of the training system, and I pointed out that the countertransference of the training analyst may be responsible for the difficult and/or seemingly irresolvable transference neurosis of the training analysand. Such considerations should caution us lest we psychoanalysts too might forget that the training analysis, like any other dynamic process, may become a vicious circle and defeat its own purpose.

In this context I wish to cite Freud's oft-quoted statement regarding training analysis: "It has accomplished its purpose if it imparts to the learner a sincere conviction of the existence of the unconscious, enables him, through the emergence of the repressed material in his own mind, to perceive in himself processes which otherwise he would regard as incredible and gives him a first sample of the technique which has proved to be the only correct method in conducting analysis." And further: "We hope that the processes of Ego transformation will go on of their own accord and that he will bring his new insight to bear upon all his subsequent experience" (8). This Freud wrote, not in an early period of psychoanalytic training, but in 1937 when the Berlin Institute

---

1. In some instances independence may be recovered at the price of rebellion and strife, but in most cases the psychodynamic of the process leads to formations of groups which maintain the scientific structure of psychoanalysis on the basis of tradition rather than on the basis of free investigation.

had already functioned for 17 years and its established model for training had been followed in all other institutes, in a time when character analysis was the usual practice.

Today when all concerned agree that "training analysis" is a character analysis the goal of which is the "working through" of the candidate's conflicts and related characterological defenses, I often wonder about the meaning of Freud's statement. Was his modest formulation of the aim of the training analysis dictated by expediency alone? Freud begins that paragraph by saying, "For practical reasons this [the training analysis] can be only short and incomplete." Or is it, as I prefer to believe, the manifestation of the deeper insight of the master who (at the time when he was thinking of the administration of our psychoanalytic heritage) must have realized the importance of the cohesiveness of a pioneering, scientific group and at the same time have considered the possibility that within the group tensions would develop which might endanger the progress of psychoanalysis? This is just an interpretation apropos of the topic of this panel discussion, the aim of which is the same, i.e., to guide the course of psychoanalytic training between the Scylla of superficial and inadequate personal analysis and the Charybdis of interminable training analysis in order to avoid the introjection of all too rigid, scientific ideals.

In recent years several attempts have been made to differentiate between therapeutic and training analysis and to explain the more advantageous course and prognosis of the former and the difficulties of the latter. Yet the distinction between therapeutic and training analysis is not defined in any other way than by the fact that the latter prepares one for professional training in psychoanalysis. Thus it appears as if the differentiation were but the tacit assumption that one set of individuals, the patients, undergo therapeutic analysis and the other set, future analysts, are subjects of training analysis. There is no explicit consideration given to the fact that the therapeutic and the training analysis have different goals, notwithstanding that they occur in the same individual and are achieved by the same psychoanalytic process.

The goal of therapeutic analysis, in general, is to cure the presenting symptom or symptoms by resolving the conflicts which sustain the symptom. The patient, who for the sake of such a result has experienced a variety of shifts and changes in the dynamic balance of his personality, after the therapeutic goal has been attained, separates himself from the analysis with the hope that his personality organization as acquired through psychoanalysis will have a preventive value in future stress situations. Neither the therapist nor the patient intentionally and repeatedly creates stress situations for the patient to measure his capacity for regaining his mental equilibrium. We are satisfied when, as Freud put it, "A benevolent fate will spare his newly achieved emotional equilibrium from too searching a test."

Not so in the case of a training analysis. Edith Weigert (11) in her paper "Contributions to the Problems of Terminating Psychoanalysis" found moving words to describe the continually repeated stress situations which test the adaptive capacity of the psychoanalyst. Even the experienced analyst feels the emotional drain caused by the "effortless effort" of maintaining an unwavering empathy toward the patient and concurrently analyzing his own responses in order to be certain of his own motivations in interpreting the patient's material. Yet we expect the candidate to be able to bear such strain actively as an analyst and, probably in the next hour, passively as a patient. Besides this we expect him to isolate his emotions sufficiently so that he may learn in an objective manner about his patient and also about himself in the supervisory situation and/or in clinical conferences. Indeed, we can say that training analysis is not therapy in a conventional sense but it is a process, the goal of which is "to effect such changes as will enable the candidate to use his unconscious in a dependable manner in the psychoanalytic treatment of his patient" (2). In other words, the training analysis opens up the personality to the process of interminable analysis, which is the fate as well as the equipment of the psychoanalyst.

The other area of significant difference between therapeutic and training analysis is in the modification of the transference process. Anna Freud (6) points out several factors which she holds responsible for the variations in the transference reactions of the candidate. But she does not discuss the fact that the psychoanalytic training affects, besides the transference reactions of the candidates, the countertransference of the training analyst. The training organization in general and the training analyst as its representative are part and parcel of the reality in which the training takes place. This reality necessarily influences the interpersonal relationship between the training analyst and analysand, and this in turn modifies and interacts with the transference process. I do not believe that we can account for the complexity of this reality by simply placing the blame on the fact that the candidate-patient knows his analyst in reality and therefore cannot use him as an object of his transference.

What do we mean by the patient "knowing" his analyst? There is, of course, the superficial knowledge about the analyst's reputation, about his standing in his professional community, etc. This is available to the therapeutic as well as to the training patient. No patient will shun any possibility or spare any effort in finding out what can be gleaned about the analyst. (The therapeutic patient often has the advantage of choosing his analyst on the basis of what he knows, while the training patient, especially because of the postwar scarcity of training analysts, often cannot do so.) Then there is the other "knowing," the deeper and real one, which evolves through the unconscious communication of the transference processes. This cognition of the patient, although "unobjective," "unrealistic," is the dependable motor of the analytic process. Here is where the therapeutic patient has an advantage over the training analysand. The therapeutic patient has an unobstructed way to project his fantasies, for example, of a "good" or "bad" mother or of an "omnipotent" or "weak," "punitive" or "protective" father, etc., onto his analyst. The unconscious fantasies and projections of the training patient, however, as Anna Freud points out sharply, are often obstructed and complicated on account of the training analyst's significance for the future of "his" candidate-patient.

Against this emotional reality of the candidate we apply an undynamic and, accordingly, ineffectual remedy. We try to exclude the personal analyst from the professional decisions regarding the candidate. Depriving ourselves of the opinion of the person who is in the best position to evaluate at least some of the qualifications of a candidate would not be too great a sacrifice if achievement of its aim were assured; if it would free the candidate from fear and further his analysis. With this policy, I am afraid, we achieve just the opposite; we open the dam to those rationalizations which we wish to exclude from the analysis; we provoke the conflict between the two levels of transference and countertransference interaction in the training analysis. On the level on which the analyst is real, i.e., the patient has real transference, the analyst represents mother, father, or both (or any significanct image of the past); he may be all-protective and all-powerful at one time and all-punitive and restrictive at other times. In any case, he is held responsible for all that happens, good or bad, as once the parents were. Against this most powerful agent of the unconscious shall the analyst maintain that in reality he is powerless? That the patient's expectations are but "transference manifestations" in the real meaning of the word and that this will not be diluted by the professional situation because the training analyst, so far as his candidate-patient is concerned, is outside the professional reality?

One cannot reason with the unconscious just as one cannot escape reality. The unconscious need of the candidate-patient and not his actual need for professional assistance is the motivation which, in spite of the greatest conscious willingness to cooperate with training policies, finally wears down the unrealistic assumption that the training analyst is outside the professional reality of the candidate. The analyst responds to the candidate's fantasies, to his wish to see in his analyst the idealized, all-powerful parent, or to be his most important pupil-child, or the one for whom he will exert the most effort. These and many other motivations are at play when the analyst in a direct or indirect manner finally enters the reality of the training situation of his candidate. He then acts on countertransference motivations. This, of course, complicates matters. The complication, however, originates not in the candidate's realistic relationship with the analyst but rather in the unrealistic training policy, which tends to separate the actual training situation artificially from the emotional reality of the analysis. Although this lengthy argument seems extraneous, it relates directly to our main problem, the termination of the training analysis.

We have shown that the difference in the course of the transference in therapeutic and training analysis can be related to the fact that in therapeutic analysis the transference and countertransference have one source only, that of the dynamic unconscious of the two individuals, patient and analyst. In training analysis, however, transference as well as countertransference has, besides this "real" source, a superficial and, so to speak, artificial but mightily interfering tributary in the professional goal of the candidate and in the professional status of the training analyst. Anna Freud assumes that this interference might be strong enough to render difficult if not impossible the recognition of the transference neurosis as the repetition of the past, since it can be easily rationalized in terms of the emotional dynamics of the "analytic family." This leads to the conclusion that the realities involved in the training process prolong the training analysis. Thus it becomes necessary to define the role of the training analyst in the training process more in accordance with reality. In any circumstance, reality might be disturbing. However, conflicts originating in the reality could be settled directly and immediately on the issues which brought them about. Although they will still interfere with transference, it will be easier to isolate them from the conflicts of that deeper reality of the unconscious which is the field of the analysis. I would expect that skillful handling of reality, freed from countertransference difficulties originating in the training situation, would render the course of the training analysis more effective and less painful. This in turn might help to clarify our assumption that neurotic suffering is a more powerful agent in the analytic process in breaking down the defenses against the unconscious conflict than is the goal of the training analysis. Yet we all agree that the training candidate, "bound to the analysis by the painfulness of the investment" (Anna Freud, 6), does not break up the analysis as the therapeutic patient often does, and this for many reasons. The sadism of the introjected superego, not only as "the analyst" but also as the "analytic process," is only one of the factors which reinforce the persistence of the candidate; another is—and it is high time to mention it—the normal, natural wish and hope to succeed in a chosen profession. I believe that this ambition together with the curiosity of the psychologically talented young scientist are powerful agents of the ego (at least as powerful as neurotic suffering) which, if enlisted in the analytic process, can help to break down the existing balance of defenses, to mobilize the conflicts in transference and so to achieve the goal of the training analysis.

It is time to repeat our question: What is the goal of the training analysis? To answer it again: to prepare the personality of the future psychoanalyst for his professional task. We assume that this usually involves a complex character analysis which might or might not have been undertaken on the basis of therapeutic indication, which may or may not be therapeutically and preventively effective. But we also know that freedom from neurosis and the capacity for psychoanalytic insight regarding oneself and/or regarding others is not a simple one-to-one relationship. The ability to handle transference and resistance phenomena as a tool of psychoanalytic therapy cannot be expressed in terms of mental health alone. The aptitude for the professional task of psychoanalysis and the capacity to resist its professional risks involve intricate, specific functions of the personality which as yet have not been formulated in general psychodynamic terms. Thus it becomes necessary to study separately the two aspects of the candidate's analysis: that which relates primarily to his goal in training and that which involves his personal therapy. I know this sounds as if I were advising that the two faces of a coin be separated. But keeping in mind that it is the same coin and that it has value only as a whole, we can very well attempt such separation on one hand for the benefit of training, and on the other hand for the benefit of therapy. If we identify the therapeutic aims with the goal of training, it may happen that the therapeutic process might delay the training of an otherwise capable psychoanalyst in one instance and in another, the training may delay the cure of an otherwise curable, neurotic individual.

Now that we have so many and such a great variety of applicants for training from whom to choose our candidates, we might think of the candidates as forming a continuous series. At one end of this series is the individual who, although free from clinical symptoms, is of such a rigid personality organization as would make it impossible for him to function effectively as a psychoanalyst. Such an individual would need an endless training analysis while he might feel little need for therapy. At the other end of the series is the individual who, as if born for psychoanalysis, is able to use his personality organization as a tool of psychoanalytic therapy in a correct manner. Such an individual's training analysis might be short while his need for therapy may differ individually. Between these two extremes are our actual candidates; each one of them needs the therapeutic effects of psychoanalysis for the attainment of the goal of the training but in individually varying degrees. Our highly individualized profession demands that the variations required for the best development of the candidate shall be decided for each individual at each of the crossroads of his training.

All psychoanalytic institutes, their educational committees, spend immeasurable time and effort in struggling for the best results. I feel that our results would be better safeguarded if we would take Freud's reservations concerning training analysis more seriously. Instead of an interminable training analysis, Freud recommended the interruption of the analysis after its initial goal has been achieved. Putting the emphasis upon self-analysis which is a constant correlate of analyzing others, he recommended a later, or even periodic resumption of personal analysis as indicated by professional or therapeutic need.

I propose that we formulate Freud's dynamic as well as realistic understanding of the differences between therapeutic and training analysis as a (practical) training policy and consider *training analysis a process of two phases according to indications stemming primarily from the aims of training*. Freud formulated the goal of didactic analysis as preparatory to training, its main object being to convey to the candidate a first-hand experience of his unconscious and ". . . to enable the instructor to form an opinion as to whether or not the candidate should be accepted for further training" (8).[2] According to our present concepts, this first, preparatory phase of training analysis is to be continued until the training analyst is satisfied that the candidate is emotionally ready to conduct psychoanalysis under supervision.[3] Then in contrast to currently accepted training practice the training analysis should be

---

2. All "second generation" and most "third generation" psychoanalysts have been raised according to this concept. Balint (1) assumes that this causes the older generation to feel guilty toward the recent generations since "we were not trained so much." Maybe so! No doubt teachers of psychoanalysis have more to teach today than in those early days when the teacher-pupil relationship would shortly turn into communal experience in discovering the unconscious. Since psychoanalysis has become a body of conveyable knowledge, it is the responsibility of teachers to work out the didactic principles by which psychoanalysis can best be taught. The best method of teaching does not imply the teaching of everything that the teacher knows. In any discipline such didactic attempt would be considered a mistake. Analysts are apt to fall into this error partly because of insecurity in regard to methods and aims of teaching and partially out of overidentification with the student. There is a wish to protect the student from the often painful but exhilarating experience of discovery and therefore psychoanalytic teachers often behave as if experience can be taught. It cannot be taught and probably fortunately so. After the teacher has conveyed the equipment for the voyage to his students, the trip has to be made by each of them alone. Whether they will come back with trivial or great experiences, with new discoveries or only with a restatement of the past, in ten or twenty years each of them will know some things different from that which their teachers knew and in this sense they will know more.

3. The training analyst, in recommending the student for assignment of the first supervised analysis, will include a statement which contains his thinking concerning the interruption of the preparatory analysis. Such a statement, although written in general dynamic terms without revealing personal material, will be a valuable source of data for study of training methods.

interrupted. This would be at or about the time of matriculation, however, before the first supervised analysis has begun. The interruption should occur with the understanding of the candidate that he will resume his personal analysis during the course of his training. More important than policies and regulations to this effect is the outcome of the preparatory analysis; only through this experience can the candidate arrive at the emotional realization that psychoanalysis in itself is interminable and that it is most productive if undertaken for the purpose of resolving conflicts and problems as they arise in life and affect the functional capacity and well-being of the individual.

The function of supervised analytic work in the psychoanalytic training system is the subject of this discussion only as it is related to the termination of the training analysis. The first task of supervised analysis is to enable the teacher as well as the student to test, or better, to feel out, whether or not the goal of the preparatory analysis has been achieved, i.e., to determine if the future analyst is prepared for the use of his unconscious as a therapeutic agent. The other task of supervised analysis is to help the student to recognize in which areas he falls short of his goal. Vilma Kovacs (10) was the first to state that the most significant part of supervision is the handling of the countertransference of the candidate-analyst toward his patient. She stated that the candidate's insight into his countertransference can be successfuly maintained only if the candidate is being analyzed himself while working with his supervised case or cases. Since that time it has become more and more accepted that psychoanalysis under supervision stirs up conflicts, mobilizes transference reactions which help to deepen and to complete the training analysis; it is assumed that the continuation of training analysis during the period of supervised analytic work is necessary to improve psychoanalytic training.[4] We are so accustomed to consider only the advantages of this policy that we do not examine whether it may also have disadvantages for the development of the candidate. Indeed, if the experience of the current analysis of the candidate is, as it should be, in the center of his emotional learning, it tends to interfere not only with the analysis of the supervised case and the supervision itself but also with his learning in theoretical courses; for the conflicts which are in the foreground of his analysis will motivate his countertransference to his patient, his transference to his supervisors and other teachers as well.

Minna Emch in a recent presentation (4) to the Training Analysts' Seminar in Chicago discussed the factors, or better, the psychic repre-

---

4. Blitzsten and Fleming (3) in their paper "What Is Supervisory Analysis?" go even further in emphasizing the function which supervision might have in the total training process since they assume that in some instances the supervision serves to spur on the process of self-analysis in the student.

sentations of individuals who silently, consciously and/or unconsciously, interact in a supervisory situation. To make use of her important contribution for the aim of this discussion it will suffice to mention that in each supervisory session, besides the candidate, his patient and the supervising analyst, there is in the background the training analyst of the candidate to whom he can turn with his problems as they arise; there also exists a relationship between the training and the supervising analyst. There is further the seminar leader who either has in the past or will in the future express his opinion in one way and the candidate another; there again may be the supervisor of another case of the same candidate who is somewhat kinder or with whom the candidate feels more at ease; there are his fellow candidates with whom he may have exchanged notes on his successful or disappointing supervisory experiences. The emotional structure of the "analytic family" is, indeed, intricate. Its multiple interacting relationships, even when functioning at their best, may dilute and diffuse the transference process of the candidate's own analysis by producing endless opportunities for acting out. Thus a training policy should permit time for the integration of the postanalytic personality after a thorough preparatory analysis. Otherwise, the supervised analytic work, instead of helping the learning process, complicates both the learning by practical experience and the training analysis as well. It may prolong the training analysis without warranting its greater effectiveness. Besides this, it is not very promising as a didactic procedure. The candidate who is in analysis during his controls, especially in the beginning of his analytic work, cannot test his self-reliance in analyzing himself (concurrently) with his patients. The supervising analyst has no opportunity to form an opinion as to whether the candidate is able to do so, and unless we know this we have little or no evidence of the progress of the candidate toward this training goal.

You may ask if this proposal to interrupt the preparatory phase of the training analysis means to put aside all the advantages which accrue from working out the countertransference problems by coordinating the supervised analysis with the analysis of the candidate. Definitely not. But we might expect the progress of the candidate to be smoother and therefore faster since the interruption of the preparatory phase would enable him, for a period of time, to analyze some of his supervised cases under conditions which are more similar to the usual psychoanalytic relation between patient and analyst, when his preconscious communication with his patient will not be disturbed by an active psychoanalytic process of his own. The supervisor naturally will remain an agent in the supervised analysis; he will point out the countertransference difficulties of the student-analyst and will observe the way in which he is able to use this knowledge in the analysis of his patient.

There will be instances in which the candidate's progress will be unperturbed by his personality problems; in other instances difficulties may arise which will hasten the resumption of the second phase of the training analysis. This might appear not too different from the current practice since, as we all know, candidates, often on their own initiative or on the advice of the faculty, enter a second or even third phase of personal analysis during the course of their training. By considering the second phase of the training analysis as a general rule and not as an exception the stigma of failure, which is at present attached to the resumption of analysis after the training analysis has been "terminated," will be removed. But more important than this is the fact that the second phase of the training analysis has a definite function in the didactic goals of psychoanalytic training. It has the task of testing the adequacy of self-analysis and gives opportunity to work through the conflicts which were unresolved and/or activated by the supervised analytic work. The second phase of training analysis may be short if its primarily didactic goal is achieved, or may become long, if for whatever reason, it becomes a therapeutic analysis.[5]

I must admit that all that I have done is that I have reduced the problem of termination to that of interruption and, worse than that, I have added a set of new problems, those which are connected with the resumption and with the interruption of the second phase of the training analysis. It seems that I have not only begged the question of the problems related to the termination of training analysis but have complicated them. The same question which relates to termination also holds true for the interruption of the preparatory phase of the training analysis.

Can we formulate criteria by which the training analyst may decide that the preparatory analysis has achieved or is about to achieve its goal?

Since universal dynamic criteria cannot be established, the American Psychoanalytic Association has established formal requirements for safeguarding that the training will be sufficient to prepare the future psychoanalyst for his professional task. These regulations (although born out of expediency and not thought out in dynamic terms) have great value in our attempts to develop the methodology of training in psychoanalysis. In a process of such infinite variables as training in psychoanalysis, the required standards of training represent some equalization of experimental conditions which permits a large-scale study of training in psychoanalysis.

5. Therapeutic analysis, whenever it is undertaken, by increasing the emotional freedom of the analyst benefits his professional skill and maturation. But for the purpose of this presentation therapeutic analysis is consistently differentiated from training analysis.

In discussing the interaction of training analysis and supervised analysis I have pointed out the advantages which the training analysis in two phases offers to training: (1) it renders the preparatory analysis (first phase) more similar to therapeutic analysis by reducing the complications which originate in training policies; (2) it creates a better situation for using the supervised analysis to test the results of the preparatory analysis; and (3) the second phase of the training analysis offers observations by which to check and improve the two most important aspects of psychoanalytic training. Looking upon the proposition as a basis for systematic study in training, immediate observation of the interaction of the various phases of training would enable us to break down the abstract formulations concerning the goal and the termination of training analysis into concrete problems and to collect data related to our objective.

Training in psychoanalysis is comparable to training in other medical specialties in only two of its aspects: supervised psychoanalytic work and theoretical courses. The main prerequisite of psychoanalytic training, however—the training analysis—constitutes a unique exception because there is no specialty in modern medicine or in the sociological sciences which finds it indispensable that its candidates undergo an experience the aim of which is to effect such changes as will make the personality of the candidate an effective instrument of his future professional task. The uniqueness of this requirement, the tremendous investment of emotion and time which it demands (and time is money in more than one sense), implies the measure of responsibility which psychoanalytic institutes have in regard to studying and improving the effectiveness of training analysis. I believe that psychoanalysis has arrived at a phase where this can be done by collecting and analyzing objective data and by deriving from them a well-grounded method of training in psychoanalysis.

BIBLIOGRAPHY

1. Balint, M. On the psycho-analytic training system. *Internat. J. Psychoanal., 29,* 1948.

2. Benedek, T. Countertransference in the training analyst. *Bull. Menninger Clin., 18:*12–17, 1954.

3. Blitzsten, N. L. and Fleming, J. What is supervisory analysis? *Bull. Menninger Clin., 17:*117, 1953.

4. Emch, M. The social context of supervision. *Internat. J. Psychoanal., 36,* 1955.

5. Ferenczi, S. and Rank, O. *The Development of Psychoanalysis.* New York: Nervous and Mental Disease Publishing Co., 1925.

6. Freud, A. Probleme der Lehranalyse. In: *Max Eitingon: In Memoriam*. Jerusalem, Israel Psycho-Analytic Society, 1950.

7. Freud, S. On the history of the psychoanalytic movement (1914). *Collected Papers, 1*. London: Hogarth Press, 1949.

8. Freud, S. Analysis terminable and interminable (1937). *Collected Papers, 5*. London: Hogarth Press, 1950.

9. Glover, E. Research methods in psycho-analysis. *Internat. J. Psychoanal., 33*, 1952.

10. Kovacs, V. Training and control analysis. *Internat. J. Psychoanal., 17*:346, 1936.

11. Weigert, E. Contributions to the problems of terminating psychoanalysis. *Psychoanal. Quart., 21*:465, 1952.

INTRODUCTION

This paper was written many years after those which dealt with particular problems of training analysis. I wrote it under the influence of the investigation which, stimulated by Joan Fleming, became the focus of my interest for many years. Although the collection of the material and the analysis of the tape-recorded and transcribed supervisory sessions were completely separate investigations which revealed our individual differences in approach, the second phase of the research—the study of our way of supervising, our selection of what to "teach," and how to teach it—was a common undertaking which enabled us to formulate many of the intricacies of the supervisory process and to integrate it as a philosophy of psychoanalytic education. In our concept, psychoanalytic education means more than training for a profession; it is a developmental experience.

When I was asked to present a lecture dedicated to the memory of Franz Alexander, I selected this topic. Franz Alexander was a psychoanalytic educator; although a controversial figure, he was an important representative of innovators.[1] The lecture is a condensed representation of the insights at which Joan Fleming and I arrived through our collaboration.[2] In our discussion we learned from each other about psychoanalysis as an experiential and teachable discipline. This is stated here to give credit to Joan Fleming as a psychoanalytic educator. Her share in the ideas and her influence in the wording of the concepts cannot be overestimated.

To avoid repeating what was discussed earlier regarding training analysis and supervision, here only excerpts of the lecture will be presented to outline the three interrelated and overlapping phases of psychoanalytic education, not as policy, but as an experiential learning process.

NOTES

1. Franz Alexander (1891–1964) was the founder and director of the Chicago Institute for Psychoanalysis from 1932 to 1956.
2. Fleming, J., & Benedek, T., *Psychoanalytic Supervision* (New York, Grune & Stratton, 1966).

PSYCHOANALYTIC EDUCATION AS DEVELOPMENTAL EXPERIENCE (1966)

Psychoanalysis is a unique clinical discipline. The mastery of its technique begins with the psychoanalysis of the future analyst by an experienced colleague. The necessity for this unusual teaching method became apparent very early. It was practiced in some measure in every psychoanalytic center. Learning from brief psychoanalytic encounters, learning through psychoanalyzing patients and learning without knowing how and what one learned was the way of the early analysts. Such noncommunicable awareness intensified the need for understanding, for objectification, and generalization which theory could afford. Eitingon (1936) described the ways of learning psychoanalysis in those early times:

> We devoted intensive study to the psychoanalytic writings then available. What we did not dig out of books, we hammered out in discussion; highly animated and exceedingly fruitful discussions they were; they were the germs out of which our present seminars developed.[1]

This shows that theoretical teaching of psychoanalysis was carried on from 1902 when regular meetings took place in Freud's house and ". . . discussions were held according to certain rules."[2] Obviously, theoretical teaching and discussion of clinical cases were the accepted way of psychoanalytic teaching. Of course, since this was the normal, academic method, it never met with the kind of resistance that training analysis did.

Training analysis, "instructional analysis" as Eitingon called it, was recommended by Freud in 1910; practiced on a quasi involuntary basis by members of local societies, it had become the prerequisite for the structured training program by the time psychoanalytic institutes were founded. Well known as these facts are, they are recalled here to emphasize that these loosely organized teaching groups, oriented mainly toward the therapeutic process of psychoanalysis, formed the basis of psychoanalytic institutes. The first institute was organized in Berlin in

1920. It was founded simultaneously with a low-cost ambulatory polyclinic which was to serve as a source of patients suitable for analysis by candidates of the institute. The next was the *Lehrinstitut* of the Vienna Psychoanalytic Society which opened under this name in 1925, attached to an ambulatory clinic which was established in 1922. The English psychoanalysts founded their Institute for Psychoanalysis in 1925, also connected with a clinic. Budapest, Frankfurt and others followed, based on the same model. The pattern of outpatient teaching clinic was broken in 1931 when the New York Psychoanalytic Institute was set up. This, however, had also the usual connection with the psychoanalytic society; the Chicago Institute for Psychoanalysis was the first to be founded independent of the psychoanalytic society (1932), but this institute also had a low-fee consultation service as a pool for cases suitable for training analysis and research.[3]

Psychoanalysts were clinicians whose educational and didactic principles were identified with the theory and technique of psychoanalysis. There were few "educators" among them. Eitingon certainly was one, perhaps the foremost among them. He was soon aware that the experience of a training analysis was not sufficient for developing competent psychoanalysts. In his address to the International Training Commission (1925) he reported on a new course in the Berlin Institute ("An Introduction to Psychoanalytic Theory"), ". . . a course of practical training not limited to any definite period for those who completed their training analysis and were beginning to practice analysis themselves."[4] From this course the third phase of the psychoanalytic program developed.

Imbued with an "optimistic illusion"[5] about the effectiveness of psychoanalysis, Eitingon assumed that those who mastered psychoanalytic technique could apply their knowledge in both phases of clinical teaching, i.e., in training analysis and in supervision. It was ten years after the codification of supervision, in 1935 and 1937, that concerns about the didactic problems of clinical teaching were voiced. In those years two regional conventions were held in Europe. They were the "Four Countries Conferences." In the first, problems of training analysis were discussed; in the second, Edward Bibring outlined his concept of the educational function of the supervisor. About the same time Alexander published a paper, "The Problems of Psychoanalytic Technique" (1935). In introducing the paper he stated that psychoanalytic method is ". . . an indefinite medical art" that cannot be learned from books. "The psychoanalyst must, so to speak, rediscover in his own experience the sense and details of the whole procedure."[6] Evaluating the interrelatedness of the factors in the therapeutic process, Alexander presented the theory of psychoanalytic technique of the time, but not the problems of teaching it. Indeed, he was concerned about how a student of psychoanalysis could recapitulate on the basis of his own experience that for which "a genius needed at least 15 years." Like most of the psycho-analysts of that time, Alexander was too close to the experience of the psychoanalytic process to be able to objectify the teaching-learning problems which the process implied.

Almost thirty years passed after Bibring's discussion of the edu-cational function of supervision before a systematic investigation of supervision as a teaching-learning process was undertaken. This investi-gation revealed the mutual feedback processes between training analysis and supervision. The training analysis can be described as an *on-the-job* learning experience compared to the *in-the-job* learning provided in supervision. Immersed in the analytic process, the student learns some-thing of the analytic method of investigation by applying it to himself. From his experience as a patient, he learns what it means to make an effort to associate freely, to speak out loud against the various resist-ances aroused by inner conflicts and anxieties. As he works in his training analysis to understand his own developmental experiences, he reexperiences them in relation to his analyst. Through the many levels of that recapitulation, he learns to understand his own life history and himself as an active and passive agent in it. What he experiences as a patient introduces him to the tools of analytic work: *introspection, empathy, and interpretation.*

Introspection takes precedence in the training analysis, but the task of a patient in the psychoanalytic process involves more than looking into oneself by oneself alone. It includes communicating to someone else what has been "seen" by introspection. The patient's success in putting his introspected experience into words and saying it out loud in the presence of another person expands the field available for awareness and cognition. As a patient, the student-analyst realizes that psychoanalysis includes interpersonal communication, based on an alliance with an-other person, with his analyst, who also does introspective work.

The second tool, empathic understanding, develops out of vicarious introspection by the analyst a supplementary instrument for the patient's self-observation which becomes a part of the student-analyst's experi-ence. In the beginning phase of training this is usually not integrated cognitively, but through firsthand experience the student learns that an analyst can hear meanings not recognizable to a patient's ears and can empathically translate his understanding into an interpretation which enlarges a patient's area of awareness.

The experience of being understood empathically by his training analyst is fundamental for the development of the student's own ca-pacity for empathy. He learns to listen not only to his analyst's in-terpretations but to himself as well, and to observe his own experience with empathic understanding for the childhood self he once was. Empathy with those parts of himself that belong to the past—that he has outgrown, dislikes, or even rejects—opens the way to the understanding of others.

The concept of the analyst's personality as an instrument of the analysis is not a new one. It was clearly recognized by Freud in 1912 when he described how blind spots in the analyst interfere with his use of himself as an instrument of therapy. But the earliest aims of the training analysis, to demonstrate the analytic method (didactic) and to relieve neurotic conflicts (therapeutic), have been expanded by the professional aim to develop the specific functions of the analyst's apparatus that are "instrumental" in the analytic process.

Although experience, both past and present, plays a part in all learning, the student in the first phase of psychoanalytic training makes his own experiencing a primary object of study. In the analytic "experiment" he is the subject as well as the observer of the nature, language, and mechanisms of the unconscious, and his discoveries constitute basic learning about the psychoanalytic method and its tools—introspection, understanding, interpreting.

The training analysis, viewed as independent of personality problems and therapeutic goals, can be defined as the first stage in acquiring a professional tool, i.e., developing the self as an instrument of the analytic process. With new knowledge gained from clinical work, the educational objective of the training analysis can be formulated in terms of providing an experience which develops the ego functions of introspection, empathy, and interpretation that are essential for work as an analyst.

The experience of the training analysis lays the groundwork for the second phase of the training program; it is the *theoretical curriculum* which refines the instrument further.[7]

In order to focus on the main thesis of this presentation, the experiential nature of learning psychoanalysis, it should be emphasized that each phase of the educational program contributes to the developmental experience of the student in different measure and according to varying approaches. There is no foretelling which experience will have greater or lesser experiential value for a student since this is determined by many factors in the student, in the teacher, and in the material presented.

The chief objective of the second phase is to learn how to articulate the behavioral data of an analysis with explanatory concepts and theories. Individual personal experiences are brought into the analyst's field of cognitive scrutiny where he can find equivalences in more general terms. In this way he correlates an analytic event with his learned concepts of dynamics, economics and genetics of behavior, and so deepens his understanding of the dimensions of a specific phenomenon. Concepts and theories provide the student with a store of new information which gives power to the knowledge acquired by experience. Subjected to secondary processes of thinking and to correlation with a theoretical system, the student's experience in being an analytic patient can be objectified and given more meaning when cognitive understanding of that experience becomes a goal of learning. On the other hand, concepts and theories take on added significance when compared and contrasted with a student's personal experience. Such learning might become conscious, emotionally charged experience without active incentive supplied by classroom teachers or in clinical situations. A sudden recall of an event in his own analysis may occur to a student while he is listening to a lecture and illuminate with new meaning both the analytic event and the ideas being presented by the lecturer. A step in the cognitive organization of experience has taken place; the synthesizing function of the ego has "gone beyond the information" to a new level of integration, and knowledge has been created from experience. Learning at this level can be compared with the therapeutic experience of "working through." Classes in the theory of technique and clinical conferences are probably most directly productive in this sense.

Creative learning occurs through the utilization of preconscious processes.[8] Psychoanalysts, practiced in working with the preconscious processes of their patients, are equipped to utilize the same tool in order to stimulate the scientific development of their students. Much that happens in the training analysis remains preconscious, yet much that is dormant in the preconscious can become accessible to cognitive understanding. It is an old pedagogic technique, inherited from Socrates, which directs the student's attention to a problem (and/or to its solution) by questioning. Joan Fleming introduced this technique—a pedagogic bridge building—into her course on the theory of technique by raising the question, "What did you learn about technique in your analysis and how did you learn it?" Strangely enough, many students are startled by being confronted with this question which never seems to have occurred to them consciously. Moreover, they respond as if the objective examination of their own experience were a forbidden activity, a transgression of the role of "patient" in analysis. This is understandable in view of the fact that many students overcome their resistance to "being a patient" only with great effort. But the resistance to observing that experience, the same as many others, needs to be overcome.

Class discussion stimulated by questions which may touch on noncognitive experiences in the training analysis affords an exercise in on-the-spot self-observation. The student's attention is turned inward, toward himself for a moment. The content of that moment, what was felt and associated, remains unverbalized and outside of the class discussion. Yet it may have conveyed an important facet of the analyst's job: a constant need to tolerate self-examination and to learn from it, vividly experienced in the training analysis and reinforced in classroom and supervision.

This kind of classroom activity does not involve "analyzing" the student by expecting free associations or by making interpretations. It consists more appropriately of a confrontation with an attitude of self-inquiry and a recognition of the value of generalizing from one's own experience. Such an exercise in a classroom situation goes only a short distance on the road toward the skill in self-analysis that belongs to a competent analyst. But it takes the first steps in a direction that continues in *clinical conferences* and supervision.

In the theoretical phase of training, the *clinical conference* provides a variation on the classroom situation comparable to the laboratory in other sciences. Here the correlation of theory and practice is closer to the work of analyzing and the student has an opportunity to practice, in the sense of rehearsing, his diagnostic understanding and his interpretive technique. In the classroom he learns the cognitive language of psychoanalysis, while in the clinical conference he identifies the behavioral cues which he can then categorize as anxiety, resistance, defenses, transference, etc. He follows vicariously the technical maneuvers of the analyst, assesses their therapeutic effectiveness, and makes trial interpretations of his own. This "laboratory" experience has a stimulating effect on the student's self-observation and correlation of his own experiences, past or immediate, with that of the patient being presented, or with that of the student-analyst whose work is under scrutiny. How far each individual goes in investigating his personal reactions in a clinical conference situation cannot be made explicit. Each student must follow his own path in this direction. It is to be hoped, however, that he possesses the attitude and the ability to let his preconscious processing come into consciousness. Many of his responses to the immediate situation will remain on a preconscious level, becoming available for insightful closures as he achieves an integration of learning from all of these different kinds of experiences.

The third phase of the training program is *on-the-job practice of analysis* under supervision; learning by doing continues the experiential testing-out which has been emphasized as the basic component of learning to become an analyst. In the supervisory situation, the student tries out his "analytic instrument" in vivo. With his psychic processes clarified and refined in his training analysis, exercised and strengthened by theoretical learning, the student enters the final step in the sequence of training experiences. He is called upon to carry forward what he has learned as an analyst with a patient, a level of learning that presents its own hierarchy of objectives and teaching techniques. This phase involves learning how to translate intuitive and cognitive understanding back into "experiential" language for communication to the patient. Such a task requires an integration of empathic (affective), cognitive, and executive (decision making) functions into the act of "making an interpretation."

In supervision the two kinds of learning, experiential and cognitive, continue to confront both student and supervisor. Learning in supervision combines experiential testing-out of the tools of introspection, empathy, and tactful interpretation with recognition and coding of "what works" and "what does not work." This level of clinical learning includes increasing awareness of why "this" works and "that" does not. In other words, a good learning experience in supervision goes beyond following rules of thumb or imitating what someone else did or might have done in similar circumstances. It increases the student-analyst's awareness of himself in interaction with his patient. The student travels back and forth across the bridge between his knowledge of how it should be done and what he actually did. The supervisor's function is to help the student in observing his experience and his insight regarding the role of empathy in making choices for his technical action. Between analyzing the patient and himself in an effort to correct his mistakes, the student develops creative skill in his professional work.

Both student and supervisor become involved in "instrumental learning"—how to use what has been learned, how to make the instrument work. Thus the supervisor also becomes learner in discovering via his student not only what makes a psychoanalyst, but also what makes a better training analyst. As the supervisor functions in two roles at the same time as an analyst of the patient and as the teacher of the student, he perceives and continually diagnoses what needs to be developed in the student to enable him to function as an independent psychoanalyst. Psychoanalytic supervision develops in the student the psychoanalyst and in the supervisor the psychoanalytic educator.

It is not new to assert that every psychoanalyst learns with every patient, but it is worth pointing out that he learns differently and learns more as a supervisor. Supervision is a triadic process. As the supervisor listens to the student-analyst's report, he quasi observes the ongoing process between the analyst and his patient. He is outside the psychoanalytic process, but he is "tuned in" to both, to the analyst and to the patient. His trained, sensitized "analytic instrument" evaluates continuously what is "going on" between analyst and patient, and also what is taking place in each of them. His diagnostic acumen functions in two channels: one serves the psychoanalytic process, the other the didactic aim of the learning alliance existing between the student and the supervisor. His intervention is the result of the integration of the information he has received. A preconscious coding of the messages seems to take place, which allows for a rating of urgency among the many possibilities and directs the supervisor's decision in choosing his didactic approach. Such preconscious preparation for a deliberate intervention makes use of the supervisor's empathic understanding of the analyst's sensitivity in the situation of the learner. His didactic approach tends to reconcile the necessity of instruction with the responsiveness of the student. Frequently a nonverbalized blockage (resistance) has to be cleared up before instruction can proceed. Then the teaching by questioning mentioned earlier helps the student to see what he could not see before, even to become aware of why he could not see it before.

All this is better explained and with more documentation in the book *Psychoanalytic Supervision*. This sketch of a paradigm of supervisory teaching is included to indicate the complexity of the analytic instrument of the supervisor.

"The concept of the 'analytic instrument' recommends itself," according to Isakower, "primarily on the grounds of its heuristic value, as a point of reference for clarification of the psychic processes which constitute the foundation of the specific analytic activity."[9] The processes that make the instrument work operate unconsciously, but they can be observed through their effects and can be studied retrospectively. *This retrospective view of the analytic instrument in operation is a major focus of attention in supervision.* The training analysis begins to assemble the tools for functioning as an analyst. The clinical phase of training puts these tools to work and develops their instrumental use, and the process of self-analysis initiated in the training analysis is continued in supervision.

In "Analysis Terminable and Interminable,"[10] Freud referred to the importance of an analyst's capacity to analyze himself when he stated, "We hope and believe that the stimuli received in the learner's own analysis will not cease to act upon him when that analysis ends, that the processes of ego transformation will go on of their own accord and that all further experiences will be made use of in a newly acquired way."[11]

Self-analysis is a learning objective of psychoanalytic supervision, but the term has to be qualified. The self-analysis which the supervisor stimulates in the student does not intend to activate a process of the dimension that Maria Kramer describes in her paper, "On the Continuation of the Analytic Process after Psychoanalysis (A Self-Observation)."[12] The supervisor does not do more than direct the student's attention toward self-observation. He probably can never know the content and/or the effect of the self-observation he stimulates since the aim of his intervention is didactic, not analytic. The supervisor might assess the success of his efforts on the student's progress in his psychoanalytic work.

The first step in stimulating the student's self-analytic function is orienting him to watch for reactions in the patient which are out of contact and when these occur, to look at his own behavior for a possible direct or indirect stimulus. After he has learned this fundamental attitude of self-observation in interaction with his patient, he can comprehend with greater ease the dynamics of the interaction and can turn his attention to his own motivations as well as to the patient's. These are steps on the way to knowing about himself as an analytic instrument and how to function. The next step is to learn to use his instrument in managing interfering counterreactions.

There are many facets of the patient-oriented self-analysis which will be experienced if its usefulness becomes second nature to the psychoanalyst. It should not be forgotten how well that instrument is calibrated during the years of psychoanalytic training; it is a result of "the processes of ego transformation [which] will go on of their own accord,"[13] and will go on through all experience through adjusting "the acquired instrument" to the requirements of the work of psychoanalysts. The instrument itself is a part of the process and therefore changes with time. Thus to the nature of the psychoanalyst belongs his vigilant attitude toward his "instrument in function."

The discussion of the three interacting phases of psychoanalytic education deals with training. The brief discussion of the "supervisor's instrument in function" shall serve as a reminder that the instrument is tested in every analysis on every level of psychoanalytic function. Most of the time the adjustment occurs unconsciously; yet every psychoanalyst, however experienced he may be, often has to ask himself the question, "Why did I respond that way? How would it have gone if . . . ?" There are unlimited ifs. The more experienced the analyst is, the more choices he will be aware of. However, this again should show only that psychoanalytic learning is interminable.

In closing I ask myself, have I succeeded in conveying the experiential quality of psychoanalytic education? To avoid a repetitive summary, I repeat: the self-analysis pervades all aspects of the life of the psychoanalyst. As his life becomes more complex and his functions more demanding, he who became a supervisor realizes how he integrated what he learned, not only from his teachers, but from his patients and from his students.

NOTES

1. Eitingon, M., "Opening Address of the Chairman, General Meeting of the International Training Commission, Fourteenth International Psycho-Analytical Congress, Marienbad, August 2, 1936," *Int. J. Psycho-Anal.*, XVIII (1937), 350.

2. Freud, S., "On the History of the Psychoanalytic Movement" (1914), *Std. Ed.*, XIV, 7–66.

3. Lewin, B., and Ross, H., *Psychoanalytic Education in the United States* (New York, W. W. Norton, 1960), pp. 5–6.

4. Eitingon, M., "Preliminary Discussion of the Question of Analytic Training" (1925), *Int. J. Psycho-Anal.*, VII (1926), 132.

5. Sachs, H., "Observations of a Training Analyst," *Psychoanalytic Quart.,* XVI (1947), 157–168.

6. Alexander, F., "The Problems of Psychoanalytic Technique," *Psychoanalytic Quart.,* IV (1935), 589.

7. The criteria for progression from training analysis to theoretical and clinical learning experiences belong to the problems of training policy. Their formulation, however, is essential if each phase of training is considered in relation to the total educational process.

8. Kubie, L., "Unsolved Problems of Scientific Education," *Daedalus* (Summer 1965).

9. Isakower, O., "Problems of Supervision," Report to the Curriculum Committee of the New York Psychoanalytic Institute (November 1957), unpublished.

10. Freud, S., "Analysis Terminable and Interminable" (1937), *Std. Ed.,* XXIII, 210–253.

11. This quotation was translated by Maria Kramer in her paper, "On the Continuation of the Analytic Process after Psychoanalysis (A Self-Observation)," *Int. J. Psycho-Anal.,* XL (1959), 17.

12. Ibid., pp. 17–26.

13. Ibid., p. 17.

18. Summing Up

Thinking over the variety of problems, personal and scientific, which are contained in this volume, I ask myself, have I succeeded in my original aim? Through my development as psychoanalyst and researcher, have I shown the evolution of any aspect of psychoanalysis as a science?

The beginning of my psychoanalytic career coincides with the establishment of the first psychoanalytic institute in Berlin, that cornerstone which marks the onset of the process through which the "psychoanalytic movement" became a "normal science."[1] The Berlin Institute developed structures and methods by which basic tenets of psychoanalysis could be transmitted and further developed by oncoming generations of scientists. My early papers reflect the struggle of the autodidact who works alone and "uses his mind as his only instrument."[2] The last section of this volume shows my development as a psychoanalytic educator and reveals some of the problems of teaching the seemingly unteachable art of psychoanalysis as a creative process in treatment and in research.

My early papers do not reflect a generation gap but show the concatenation of generations of psychoanalysts. When, as an old member of the "second generation of psychoanalysts," I prepared those early papers for this publication, I realized that I had dealt only with the latest theories and broadest concepts of Freud at a time when my older colleagues hardly considered the explanatory significance of those ideas. Today I find it not only understandable but natural that those whose clinical experience and psychoanalytic learning and teaching were grounded in the first instinct theory declined to use the theory of the death instinct to explain their observations.

Probably I had a primary inclination to search for understanding of the unity of psyche and soma. To me the concepts of Freud's last instinct theory showed the way to the depths of physiology, as is apparent in my early papers. It is not obvious in the investigation of the

526

sexual cycle. This may appear paradoxical in a research which establishes psychodynamic correlations with the cyclical changes of the ovarian hormones. The method of that investigation, as well as the theoretical framework of the interpretation of the recorded material, was grounded in the theory of personality development, i.e., in the libido theory. As long as developmental processes were in the focus of the investigations, the classical libido theory sufficed. Whether the psychosexual functions of women or the transactional processes of mother-child and/or other familial relationships were being studied, developmental processes could be explained on the basis of "integrating energy." Its opponent, aggression, called for attention when the psychic equilibrium was disturbed, and the concept of ambivalence and its function in normal and pathologic processes had to be clarified.

But of what use was the instinct theory when biologists discovered that instincts are not "innate," that their maturation depends on learned patterns of the parent animal's behavior toward the offspring? There are even more reasons to neglect the outmoded concepts of instincts in investigating motivations in human behavior. Indeed, the "Zeitgeist" of psychoanalysis seems to be against further exploration of Freud's instinct theories. It is gratifying to recognize that the investigation of psychosomatic problems confirms Freud's speculations; this raises hope for the fulfillment of his wish that biology may give answers to problems which psychoanalysis cannot reach.

Freud assumed that libido, the integrating energy, has "noisy" manifestations and the death instinct works "silently" by means of the repetition compulsion. At the same time he assumed also that the opposing psychic energies work silently in fusion and defusion in maintaining a balance of normal mental processes and physiologic processes. Study of the psychodynamic components of instinctual (biochemical) processes in the sexual cycle revealed that the psychodynamic tendencies are components of the physiologic processes of maturation as well as of psychosexual development. Thus the investigation which started without any aspiration to contribute to Freud's instinct theory arrived at a unitary concept of sexuality. It showed that the woman's monthly preparation for the procreative function repeats the psychodynamic tendencies which, supporting the metabolic processes of growth, are instrumental in producing what Freud called "pregenital libido."

But what about the death instinct? The hypothesis of fusion and defusion which energizes instinctual processes explains the origin of ambivalence. Aggression, the silently functioning opponent of libido, gains the upper hand in processes which bring about organismic destruction and psychic pathology.

Science has its own cycles. Returning to their origins, these cycles encompass more dimensions than they originally explained. So Freud was tentative when he formulated his theories in terms of opposing instinctual energies. Generations of psychoanalysts have applied these concepts in the study of psychologic and psychosomatic processes. As they describe and explain more phenomena, they arrive at the borders of other disciplines. Freud's outmoded instinct theory can be rediscovered in the diseases which belong to psychosomatic medicine; they explain the transactional processes between the body and the mind, in health and disease, in development and involution.

Freud's concept of the repetition compulsion which is locked into the lawfulness of life and brings about death is not hard to accept when one realizes that molecular biology and modern genetics are grappling with the problems of the origin of organic life and its inborn necessity to die.[3] We psychoanalysts cannot reach that far, but the understanding of psychologic components of physiologic processes, i.e., further study of the intraorganismic function of instinctual processes, forecasts fruition through psychoanalytic research.

NOTES

1. Kuhn, T. S., *The Structure of Scientific Revolutions* (Chicago, University of Chicago Press, 1962).

2. Freud, A., *Difficulties in the Path of Psychoanalysis* (New York, International Universities Press, 1969), p. 19.

3. Monod, J., *Chance and Necessity,* translated by Austryn Weinhouse (New York, Alfred A. Knopf, 1971.)

Index

Abderhalden, E., 30, 35, 36
Abraham, K., 8, 9, 73, 123, 338, 366, 440, 451
Absolute infertility, 284, 285
Ackerman, N., 251
Active-incorporative oral phase of development, 366–368
Adaptation
  to climacterium, 325, 344–345
  diseases of, 52
  infant, 113–114, 126–128, 381–382; *See also* Mother-child relationship
  instincts and, 423–424
  oral fixation and, 73–74, 83, 84
  to parenthood, 401–402
  reflex, 122, 265–266
  regressive, 390, 402
Adolescence
  origins of anorexia nervosa in, 85
  psychosexual development during, 327–328
Adolescent sexuality, restrictions placed on, 230
Adolescents, parental behavior toward, 403–404
Adoption in cases of functional sterility, 291, 307–309
Adult love, psychodynamics of, 337
Affect cluster, 214
Affective behavior, sources of, 44
Affects
  moods and, 216
  psychoeconomic function of, 214
Aggression
  anorexia nervosa and, 86, 88, 89, 111
  anxiety and, 43; *See also* Anxiety
  diabetes and, 352
  homosexuality and, 104–106
  as instinct turned toward self, 80

introjected and organized, 377
morbidity and, 81, 82
oral, 103–104
in oral phase of development, 367
ovulation and, 150–153, 155, 157
premenstrual, 183–184
Aging process, *See also* Old age
  of men, 340–341
  of women
    climacterium and, *See* Climacterium
    folklore and, 326
Alcoholism
  depression and, 71
  oral fixation and, 83
Alexander, Franz, 8, 352
  thought on
    morbidity, 72
    ovarian activity, 131, 215
    psychoanalytic training, 493, 515, 517–518
    reproductive drive, 440, 441
    thyrotoxicosis, 68–69
Alimentation, 277–278
  ambivalence in process of, 375–376
  infant's memory traces connected to, 361–362, 364–365, 384
    See also Feeding of infants
Allen, E., 174
Allende, I. L. C. de, 209
Altmann, M., 415, 416
Ambivalence
  in mother-child relationship, 317–318, 365, 385
  in process of alimentation, 375–376
  in transference, 71
Anal-sadistic phase of development, obsessive ideas originating in, 82
Androgens, 88, 413, 433
Andropause, 345